D1233869

# Forests and Global Change

Forests hold a significant proportion of global biodiversity and terrestrial carbon stocks, and are at the forefront of human-induced global change. The dynamics and distribution of forest vegetation determine the habitat for other organisms, and regulate the delivery of ecosystem services, including carbon storage. Presenting recent research across temperate and tropical ecosystems, this volume synthesises the numerous ways that forests are responding to global change and includes perspectives on:

- the role of forests in the global carbon and energy budgets;
- historical patterns of forest change and diversification;
- contemporary mechanisms of community assembly and implications of underlying drivers of global change;
- the ways in which forests supply ecosystem services that support human lives.

The chapters represent case studies drawn from the authors' expertise, highlighting exciting new research and providing information that will be valuable to academics, students, researchers and practitioners with an interest in this field.

DAVID A. COOMES is a forest ecologist and conservation biologist working with the forest ecology and conservation group at the University of Cambridge. He is Associate Editor of the *Journal of Ecology* and *Biological Reviews* and has authored more than 90 papers, including many from his group's work in New Zealand.

DAVID F. R. P. BURSLEM is a tropical forest ecologist at the University of Aberdeen. He has served as Associate Editor of the *Journal of Ecology*, and is a member of the editorial boards of *Plant Ecology and Diversity* and Ecological Reviews series. He was an editor of the Ecological Reviews volume on *Biotic Interactions in the Tropics* (Cambridge, 2005) and has authored more than 80 papers on the ecology and conservation of tropical forests.

WILLIAM D. SIMONSON is a forest ecologist specialising in Mediterranean systems. He has extensive practical experience, working in the UK and overseas, for governmental as well as non-governmental conservation organisations. As a trained editor, he has worked on a range of scientific and educational publications for Cambridge-based publishers.

**Ecological Reviews**

Ecological Reviews publishes books at the cutting edge of modern ecology, providing a forum for volumes that discuss topics that are focal points of current activity and likely long-term importance to the progress of the field. The series is an invaluable source of ideas and inspiration for ecologists at all levels from graduate students to more-established researchers and professionals. The series has been developed jointly by the British Ecological Society and Cambridge University Press and encompasses the Society's Symposia as appropriate.

*Biotic Interactions in the Tropics: Their Role in the Maintenance of Species Diversity*
Edited by David F. R. P. Burslem, Michelle A. Pinard and Sue E. Hartley

*Biological Diversity and Function in Soils*
Edited by Richard Bardgett, Michael Usher and David Hopkins

*Island Colonization: The Origin and Development of Island Communities*
By Ian Thornton
Edited by Tim New

*Scaling Biodiversity*
Edited by David Storch, Pablo Margnet and James Brown

*Body Size: The Structure and Function of Aquatic Ecosystems*
Edited by Alan G. Hildrew, David G. Raffaelli and Ronni Edmonds-Brown

*Speciation and Patterns of Diversity*
Edited by Roger Butlin, Jon Bridle and Dolph Schluter

*Ecology of Industrial Pollution*
Edited by Lesley C. Batty and Kevin B. Hallberg

*Ecosystem Ecology: A New Synthesis*
Edited by David G. Raffaelli and Christopher L. J. Frid

*Urban Ecology*
Edited by Kevin J. Gaston

*The Ecology of Plant Secondary Metabolites: From Genes to Global Processes*
Edited by Glenn R. Iason, Marcel Dicke and Susan E. Hartley

*Birds and Habitat: Relationships in Changing Landscapes*
Edited by Robert J. Fuller

*Trait-Mediated Indirect Interactions: Ecological and Evolutionary Perspectives*
Edited by Takayuki Ohgushi, Oswald Schmitz and Robert D. Holt

# Forests and Global Change

Edited by

DAVID A. COOMES
*University of Cambridge, UK*

DAVID F. R. P. BURSLEM
*University of Aberdeen, UK*

WILLIAM D. SIMONSON
*University of Cambridge, UK*

CAMBRIDGE
UNIVERSITY PRESS

CAMBRIDGE
UNIVERSITY PRESS

University Printing House, Cambridge CB2 8BS, United Kingdom

Published in the United States of America by Cambridge University Press, New York

Cambridge University Press is part of the University of Cambridge.

It furthers the University's mission by disseminating knowledge in the pursuit of
education, learning, and research at the highest international levels of excellence.

www.cambridge.org
Information on this title: www.cambridge.org/9781107041851

First published 2014

Printed in the United Kingdom by CPI Group Ltd, Croydon CR0 4YY

*A catalogue record for this publication is available from the British Library*

ISBN 978-1-107-04185-1 Hardback
ISBN 978-1-107-61480-2 Paperback

Additional resources for this publication at www.cambridge.org/9781107041851

# Contents

*List of contributors*                                                    *page* ix
*Preface*                                                                      xiii

1   Forests and global change: an overview
    *William D. Simonson, David A. Coomes and David F. R. P. Burslem*          1

    **Part I   Forest dynamics and global change**                           19

2   Forests and the climate system
    *John Grace*                                                             21
3   Global change and Mediterranean forests: current impacts
    and potential responses
    *Fernando Valladares, Raquel Benavides, Sonia G. Rabasa, Juli
    G. Pausas, Susana Paula, William D. Simonson and Mario Díaz*             47
4   Recent changes in tropical forest biomass and dynamics
    *Oliver L. Phillips and Simon L. Lewis*                                  77
5   Disequilibrium and transient dynamics: disentangling
    responses to climate change versus broader anthropogenic
    impacts on temperate forests of eastern North America
    *Charles D. Canham*                                                     109

    **Part II   Species traits and responses to changing resource
                availability**                                              129

6   Floristic shifts versus critical transitions in Amazonian forest
    systems
    *Jérôme Chave*                                                          131
7   Traits, states and rates: understanding coexistence in forests
    *Drew W. Purves and Mark C. Vanderwel*                                  161
8   The functional role of biodiversity in the context of global change
    *Michael Scherer-Lorenzen*                                              195

9   Exploring evolutionarily meaningful vegetation definitions
    in the tropics: a community phylogenetic approach
    *Ary T. Oliveira-Filho, R. Toby Pennington, Jay Rotella
    and Matt Lavin*                                                  239
10  Drought as a driver of tropical tree species regeneration
    dynamics and distribution patterns
    *Liza S. Comita and Bettina M. J. Engelbrecht*                   261
11  Tree performance across gradients of soil resource
    availability
    *Richard K. Kobe, Thomas W. Baribault and Ellen K. Holste*      309

**Part III   Detecting and modelling global change**               341

12  A chemical-evolutionary basis for remote sensing of tropical
    forest diversity
    *Gregory P. Asner*                                              343
13  Forests in a greenhouse atmosphere: predicting the
    unpredictable?
    *Harald Bugmann*                                                359
14  Detecting and projecting changes in forest biomass
    from plot data
    *Helene C. Muller-Landau, Matteo Detto, Ryan. A. Chisholm,
    Stephen P. Hubbell and Richard Condit*                          381
15  Analysis of anthropogenic impacts on forest biodiversity
    as a contribution to empirical theory
    *Adrian C. Newton and Cristian Echeverría*                      417

*Index*                                                             447

*The colour plates are located between pages 160 and 161*

# Contributors

GREGORY P. ASNER
Carnegie Institution for Science, 260
Panama Street, Stanford, California
94305, USA
gpa@stanford.edu

THOMAS W. BARIBAULT
Michigan State University,
Department of Forestry, Graduate
Program in Ecology, Evolutionary
Biology, and Behavior, East Lansing,
Michigan 48824, USA

RAQUEL BENAVIDES
Department of Biogeography and
Global Change, National Museum of
Natural Sciences, Madrid, Spain

HARALD BUGMANN
Forest Ecology, Institute of Terrestrial
Ecosystems, Department of
Environmental Sciences, Swiss
Federal Institute of Technology (ETH)
Zurich, 8092 Zurich, Switzerland
Harald.bugmann@env.ethz.ch

CHARLES D. CANHAM
Cary Institute of Ecosystem
Studies, Box AB, Millbrook,
New York 12545, USA
canhamc@caryinstitute.org

JÉRÔME CHAVE
Laboratoire Evolution et Diversité
Biologique, UMR 5174, CNRS, Université
Paul Sabatier, Bâtiment 4R1, 118 route
de Narbonne, 31062 Toulouse, France
jerome.chave@univ-tlse3.fr

RYAN A. CHISHOLM
Smithsonian Tropical Research
Institute, PO Box 0843–03092, Balboa,
Ancón, Republic of Panamá

LIZA S. COMITA
Department of Evolution, Ecology,
and Organismal Biology, The Ohio
State University, Columbus, OH
43210, USA
Smithsonian Tropical Research
Institute, PO Box 0843–03092, Balboa,
Ancón, Republic of Panamá
comita.2@osu.edu

RICHARD CONDIT
Smithsonian Tropical Research
Institute, PO Box 0843–03092, Balboa,
Ancón, Republic of Panamá

MATTEO DETTO
Smithsonian Tropical Research
Institute, PO Box 0843–03092, Balboa,
Ancón, Republic of Panamá

MARIO DÍAZ
Department of Biogeography and
Global Change, National Museum of
Natural Sciences, Madrid, Spain

CRISTIAN ECHEVERRÍA
Facultad de Ciencias Forestales,
Universidad de Concepción, Casilla
160-C, Concepción, Chile
cristian.echeverria@udec.cl

BETTINA M. J. ENGELBRECHT
Smithsonian Tropical Research
Institute, PO Box 0843–03092, Balboa,
Ancón, Republic of Panamá
Bayreuth Center for Ecology and
Environmental Research, University
of Bayreuth, 95440 Bayreuth,
Germany
bettina.engelbrecht@gmail.com

JOHN GRACE
University of Edinburgh School of
GeoSciences, West Mains Road,
Edinburgh EH9 3JN, UK
jgrace@ed.ac.uk

ELLEN K. HOLSTE
Michigan State University,
Department of Forestry, Graduate
Program in Ecology, Evolutionary
Biology, and Behavior, East Lansing,
Michigan 48824, USA

STEPHEN P. HUBBELL
Smithsonian Tropical Research
Institute, PO Box 0843–03092, Balboa,
Ancón, Republic of Panamá

RICHARD K. KOBE
Michigan State University,
Department of Forestry, Graduate
Program in Ecology, Evolutionary
Biology, and Behavior, East Lansing,
Michigan 48824, USA
kobe@msu.edu

MATT LAVIN
Plant Sciences and Plant Pathology,
Montana State University, Bozeman,
Montana 59717, USA
mlavin@montana.edu

SIMON L. LEWIS
School of Geography, University of
Leeds, Leeds LS2 9JT, UK
School of Geography, University
College London, London WC1E
6BT, UK
S.L.Lewis@leeds.ac.uk

HELENE C. MULLER-LANDAU
Smithsonian Tropical Research
Institute, P.O. Box 0843–03092,
Balboa, Ancón, Republic of Panamá
mullerh@si.edu

ADRIAN C. NEWTON
Centre for Conservation Ecology and
Environmental Science, School of
Applied Sciences, Bournemouth
University, Talbot Campus, Poole,
Dorset BH12 5BB, UK
anewton@bournemouth.ac.uk

ARY T. OLIVEIRA-FILHO
Instituto de Ciências Biológicas,
Universidade Federal de Minas
Gerais, Belo Horizonte, Minas
Gerais, Brazil

SUSANA PAULA
Instituto de Ciencias Ambientales y
Evolutivas, Universidade Austral de

Chile, Independencia 641,
Valdivia, Chile

JULI G. PAUSAS
CIDE, CSIC, Valencia, Spain

R. TOBY PENNINGTON
Tropical Biology Group, Royal Botanic
Garden Edinburgh, 20a Inverleith
Row, Edinburgh EH3 5LR, UK
T.Pennington@rbge.ac.uk

OLIVER L. PHILLIPS
School of Geography, University of
Leeds, Leeds LS2 9JT, UK
o.phillips@leeds.ac.uk

DREW W. PURVES
Computational Ecology and
Environmental Science Group,
Microsoft Research Cambridge, UK
dpurves@microsoft.com

SONIA G. RABASA
Department of Biogeography and
Global Change, National Museum of
Natural Sciences, Madrid, Spain

JAY ROTELLA
Ecology, Montana State University,
Bozeman, Montana 59717, USA

MICHAEL SCHERER-LORENZEN
Faculty of Biology – Geobotany,
University of Freiburg, Germany
michael.scherer@biologie.uni-
freiburg.de

WILLIAM SIMONSON
Forest Ecology and Conservation
Group, Department of Plant Sciences,
University of Cambridge, UK
wds10@cam.ac.uk

FERNANDO VALLADARES
Department of Biogeography and
Global Change, National Museum of
Natural Sciences, Madrid, Spain
valladares@ccma.csic.es

MARK C. VANDERWEL
Computational Ecology and
Environmental Science
Group, Microsoft Research
Cambridge, UK

# Preface

Forests house a significant proportion of global biodiversity and terrestrial carbon, as well as providing livelihoods for millions of people, yet they are changing at an unprecedented rate. They are disappearing rapidly in many parts of the tropics, but are increasing in cover and biomass in many higher-latitude regions. They are responding to industrial pollution and introduced organisms. The dynamics and distribution of forest vegetation are important because they determine the amount of habitat for numerous other organisms, and regulate the delivery of ecosystem services such as carbon storage, and water and soil quality. It is increasingly recognised that forests influence the energy budget of the planet, making an understanding of forest dynamics an essential aspect of climate change modelling.

Despite the importance of forests to biodiversity conservation and the provision of ecosystem services such as erosion control and carbon storage, the community of forest ecologists is strongly differentiated by biome, which constrains conceptual integration at a global scale. In the tropics, there is a concentration of effort and expertise around the networks of large plots co-ordinated by the Center for Tropical Forest Science on the one hand, and the alliance of smaller plots forming the RAINFOR, AfriTRON and GEM networks on the other, with many others working outside these networks. In temperate and boreal forest regions, there are long-term ecological monitoring sites (e.g. the Long-Term Ecological Research Network, LTER) and impressive national inventory systems that were originally established for monitoring timber stocks but increasingly available to ecologists. In this volume we draw together perspectives from across these diverse communities of forest ecologists to attempt a global synthesis of forest responses to global change.

This volume consists of 15 invited contributions, providing a global synthesis of recent scientific developments concerning the interactions of forests with the drivers of global change. Similarly to other volumes in the *Ecological Reviews* series, this one has arisen from plenary talks given at a British Ecological Society Symposium. The meeting, entitled *Forests and Global Change*, was held at the University of Cambridge in 2011, attracting over 300 researchers from at least 30 countries. Chapters are organised into three overarching themes which form subsections of the book: (Part I), forest dynamics and global change; (Part II), species traits and responses to changing resource availability; and (Part III), detecting and modelling global change. Within those themes, there are perspectives on the role of forests in the global carbon and energy budgets; historical patterns of forest change and diversification; contemporary mechanisms of community assembly and implications of underlying drivers of global change; and the multiple ways in which forests supply ecosystem services that support human lives and livelihoods. This volume seeks to target ecologists across the spectrum, from postgraduate students to senior scientists seeking state-of-the-art reviews on specific topics, but it is not an elementary textbook covering all aspects of global change. Rather, our focus is on promising areas of research where new ideas are under development and exciting discoveries are being made.

Technological advances mean that ecologists are better than ever at monitoring how forests are changing, understanding the knock-on consequence of change and making predictions about future responses. The book integrates across different methodologies and biomes to derive a global synthesis based on the following methodologies: statistical analyses of decadal-scale inventory data, ecophysiological approaches, remote sensing and modelling, and historical analyses using phylogenetic information.

*Decadal-scale inventory data*: Traditionally, information on changes in forests has been obtained from permanent plots that sample the local tree flora. In northern temperate regions, distributed networks containing many thousands of plots have established for forestry purposes, and these are now being used to answer ecological questions. Sampling is less systematic in tropical regions; many plots have been established that are 100 × 100 m (1 ha) in size, although often smaller (0.1 ha) plots and occasionally much larger ones (25 and 50 ha) have also been established. These plots may then be integrated into national or regional networks to address questions of importance at these larger spatial scales. The value of census plot data increases with the length of the records available, and there are now robust analyses of forest change based on decadal-scale censuses of multiple plots within regions. Thus it may be possible, for the first time, to derive a truly global picture of forest change based on multi-year time series.

*Ecophysiological approaches*: A network of distributed plots has the potential to capture stand-level data on species composition and dynamics, but understanding the mechanisms of underlying forest–canopy interactions requires instrumentation and manipulative experiments, and measurements over short (diurnal to annual) time scales. Insights into the physiological mechanisms that drive forest responses to changing environments have been obtained from networks of canopy flux towers and experimental sites that now extend across all forest ecosystems. These point-source data provide time series of physiological processes that help to calibrate and interpret the inventory data obtained from plots, but in order to maximise the potential to achieve these aims it is necessary to move across scales using modelling techniques.

*Modelling*: More recently, forest ecologists have begun to use census plot and ecophysiological data to develop and test models that simulate changes on mapped stands. These forest simulators are then applied to topics ranging from theoretical models of tree species coexistence through to scenario-testing for forest management. There is an important synergistic relationship between forest plots and simulation models: plots are required to generate realistic parameters for most types of forest simulation model, while models add value to plot networks by projecting over longer time scales and multiple alternative scenarios. In order to realise the added value of these approaches, it is important for ecologists who hold plot data and those with expertise in modelling to communicate effectively in the same fora.

*Remote sensing*: Remote sensing techniques represent a tool for rapid monitoring of land-use changes over substantial areas, and are likely to increase in importance as the resolution of image analysis improves. Satellite images have a long history for monitoring land-use. For instance, the LANDSAT satellites provide unparalleled evidence of the changes of cover and seasonality of forests. Emerging technologies include the use of LiDAR (light detection and ranging) sensors to provide detailed information about canopy structure, and hyperspectral imagery provides, for the first time, methods to identify the positions of species and functional groups over entire landscapes based on the chemical signatures of individual tree crowns.

*Molecular phylogenies*: Rapid advances in high-throughput sequencing and new bioinformatics tools are allowing ecologists to construct dated community-level phylogenies that permit inference of patterns of diversification in response to historical phases of global change. These data are providing new perspectives into the processes that influence contemporary patterns of plant distribution, and represent an important resource for researchers attempting to forecast the impacts of contemporary global change.

We are indebted to all the authors who contributed chapters, and to everybody who helped make the symposium a memorable success. We are especially grateful to the anonymous reviewers of chapters, the Editorial Board of *Ecological Reviews*, and Cambridge University Press. The future of forests depends on how humans decide to manage them in the decades to come. It is our hope that after reading this volume you will have a greater appreciation of the multiple drivers of forest change, and feel inspired to become involved in conservation of these unique and vulnerable ecosystems.

David Burslem
David Coomes and William Simonson

# CHAPTER ONE

# Forests and global change: an overview

WILLIAM D. SIMONSON, DAVID A. COOMES

*Department of Plant Sciences, University of Cambridge, UK*

and

DAVID F. R. P. BURSLEM

*School of Biological Sciences, University of Aberdeen, UK*

## 1.1 Introduction

Forests provide a range of goods and services upon which humanity depends, from local (e.g. flood prevention) to global (e.g. carbon sequestration). Yet some 13 Mha of forest is lost each year, mostly in the tropics (Canadell & Raupach 2008). Considerable political, media and scientific attention has focused on this forest destruction and fragmentation and its implications for livelihoods, biodiversity and ecosystem services. However, human influences on forests now go beyond deforestation and degradation, to changing the states of atmosphere and climates and altering biogeochemical cycles, which in turn bear heavily on the functioning and composition of forest ecosystems. A range of disciplines are required to chart such change, understand how it works and predict where it is going. They span a broad range of scales from photosynthetic machinery in leaves, to the dynamics of forests across wide regions, to global atmospheric circulation. Integration of these multiple strands and scales of investigation has only recently begun, and this volume makes an important contribution to weaving them together into a more cohesive, albeit still incomplete, picture.

The story is told in three parts, beginning with a collection of perspectives on the global environmental drivers of forest change, the complexity of their interaction and effects, and important feedbacks. The second section concentrates on species-level traits and trade-offs, and how these explain the composition and dynamics of forests in a changing world. Finally, a number of approaches and tools are presented for measuring forest change and forecasting its future direction.

## 1.2 Forest dynamics and global change

Global forest decline has important implications for the atmosphere and climate. Forests are intimately coupled to the atmosphere by both physical

*Forests and Global Change*, ed. David A. Coomes, David F. R. P. Burslem and William D. Simonson.
Published by Cambridge University Press. © British Ecological Society 2014.

and biological processes and feedbacks (Charney, Stone & Quirk 1975). These ecosystems have very different properties in this respect from pastures and croplands, and the widespread conversion of forests to other land-uses is not only contributing directly to climate change, but also compromising the potential for forest-based climate mitigation in the future. In Chapter 2 Grace describes from first principles the fluxes of energy, water, carbon dioxide and other gases between forest canopies, the atmosphere and soil. The importance of albedo in the energy and water balance is highlighted, as is canopy roughness, which helps to explain the difference between forests and vegetation of shorter stature. The predictions derived from parameterising and solving equations for stands are supported by observational data for regions, but at larger scales additional complexities become significant, including the spatial organisation of deforestation activity; cloud formation; phenological change; and teleconnections between different parts of the world (Avissar & Werth 2009). Chapter 2 reviews progress using global circulation model simulations, which predict reduced rainfall and increased temperatures, although only above certain 'tipping points' of deforestation (Walker et al. 2009). Evidence and explanation is also given for forests operating as carbon sinks, even as old-growth systems, although we are warned that a switch in function from sinks to sources is possible as a result of climate warming and drought. The conversion of forests also has important implications for the production of non-$CO_2$ greenhouse gases, as well as aerosols and other chemically important gases. Land-use policy and forest management need to keep pace with our understanding of these systems, and the rapid increase in area of fast-growing tropical plantations (FAO 2011), including oil palm, gives rise to important ethical as well as practical considerations.

In Chapter 3, Valladares et al. explore the ways in which the Mediterranean biome responds to environmental change, showing that we require not only ecophysiological understanding of individual species responses, but also consideration of biotic interactions – both antagonistic and facilitative – and the non-additive interplay of multiple drivers. The mechanisms that confer resilience on vegetation communities in the short term can collapse when threshold situations are reached. Valladares et al. show that differential species responses to abiotic stress may exacerbate negative interactions (e.g. when pathogen life cycles are accelerated by warming) or alleviate them (e.g. when phenological mismatching breaks down the onslaught of a natural enemy). Facilitative effects can also be either enhanced or compromised. For example, the amelioration by shrubs of harsh abiotic conditions for woody seedling establishment is a well-known phenomenon in the Mediterranean, but evidence is mounting that such facilitation may not hold as stress levels increase (Maestre & Cortina 2004). Positive animal–

plant interactions may also be compromised by climate change; the behaviour of animal dispersers of seed and fruit in the face of environmental change, including fragmentation, can be as critical to plant population dynamics as any more direct effect arising from a changing climate.

Shifting land-use is one of the main agents of change in Mediterranean forests, and its implications for biodiversity are significant in a region where the biota has been tightly linked to traditional land-use practices over a very long time (Blondel, Aronson & Bodiou 2010). Forest fragmentation is prevalent, leading to reduction of habitat area, increase in isolation and altered physical environment, with implications for population genetics and species ecology. But it furthermore seriously restricts the survival options for species coping with climate change: these options are either acclimation/adaptation to local conditions, or migration to more favourable areas. Fire suppression and lack of timber management in fragments, for example, can lead to wood accumulation which mediates the long-term effects of climate change on fire regimes. Even a small shift in climate can cause major shifts in flammability (Pausas & Paula 2012). The woodlands of Mediterranean mountains are considered to be particularly vulnerable to changing fire regimes if the regime is afflicted by more severe droughts in the future, as predicted by most global warming models. Changes in fire frequency and intensity are likely to have more profound consequences than the direct effects of drought stress on physiology (Fyllas & Troumbis 2009). The cultural landscapes of the Mediterranean region are a notable example of how a long history of human occupation and land-use shapes forests and other ecosystems.

In the emergent geological epoch of the 'Anthropocene', all of the Earth's ecosystems are affected by human activity. In Chapter 4, Phillips and Lewis document field-based evidence for the world's tropical forests undergoing rapid change as a result of anthropogenic influences on the atmosphere–biosphere system. Such change is more subtle than forest conversion, and can be picked up by persistent, on-the-ground monitoring at fixed locations. Results of diameter at breast height (dbh) measurements in permanent plots across Amazonia (the RAINFOR network), complementing similar networks across Africa (AfriTRON) and Asia (e.g. the Center for Tropical Forest Science, CTFS), are reviewed. Evaluation of change in the plots appears to indicate an increase in biomass carbon, equivalent to 1.3 PgC yr$^{-1}$ in the 1990s when scaled up to the total global old-growth forest area (Lewis *et al.* 2009). These findings have become the subject of much debate and intense scrutiny: it is argued that the statistical noise associated with estimating diameters, heights and wood density is not routinely propagated through biomass-estimation functions, potentially leading to poor estimates of the mean and variance of carbon stocks (see Chapter 14). It is also argued that intense natural disturbances are not picked up by short-term measurements in small plots (the 'slow in, rapid out' argument of Korner 2003 and Coomes *et al.* 2012), which may cast doubt on the magnitude of the tropical forest sink (Chambers *et al.* 2013). Phillips and Lewis use the chapter to lay out the evidence that supports their case. For example, they argue that the plots lack the basic signatures of forests recovering from large disturbances. Instead, they maintain that the trend of biomass gain can be explained in terms of an increase in primary productivity as a result of more available resources such as carbon dioxide (Lewis *et al.* 2004). Other changes to the forests, including increased dynamism (higher rates of mortality and recruitment) and shifts in species or functional group composition (notably an increased prevalence of lianas), are considered to be more consistent with such explanations.

The network of Amazonian plots allows Phillips and Lewis to explore the consequences of a 'natural experiment' – a severe drought that hit the region in 2005. The frequency of droughts in the Amazon seems to be increasing, in line with forecasts made by some global warming models, leading to dire predictions about the fate of the rain forests (Cox *et al.* 2004). These plot-based analyses provide the first glimpses of what might actually happen. Pre- and post-drought plot data suggest that this region lost aboveground biomass of the order of 0.59 Mg ha$^{-1}$ as a result. This represents a loss of between 1.21 and 1.60 PgC for the Basin as a whole (Phillips *et al.* 2009). A switch from being a carbon sink to a carbon source is a scenario for tropical forests that may become more widespread in the future, and the chapter ends by reviewing some of the complexities, related to water shortage, photosynthesis/respiration and composition, relevant to modelling such changes.

In temperate forests, the effects of climate change are even harder to predict because forest composition and function are so strongly driven by anthropogenic disturbance and pollution, and by the legacy of historical management; many factors contribute simultaneously to change, and careful analysis is needed to disentangle them. As Canham explains in Chapter 5, drawing on examples from the northeastern United States, any signal for climate change must be decoupled from contemporaneous effects of a range of additional context-dependent factors such as cycles of land clearance and re-colonisation, herbivore dynamics, changes in fire regimes, logging, introductions of non-native pests, pathogens and plants, and pollution. The tree-specific sensitivity to temperature rise and N deposition (Quinn Thomas *et al.* 2009) illustrates the point. In general, a decline in N deposition of 3 kg ha$^{-1}$ yr$^{-1}$ would largely neutralise the effect of a 3 °C temperature increase, yet the net impact of these two factors will vary in magnitude and even direction for different tree species. He explains how, in principle, individual-based succession models such as SORTIE (Pacala *et al.* 1996) can be parameterised to capture the impacts of these factors on tree demography and make predictions about the future under various realistic scenarios. However, setting realistic initial conditions is critical in such simulations, as successional trajectories depend closely upon them. For this reason it is important to characterise the identity and spatial distribution of trees surviving anthropogenic disturbance events (Papaik & Canham 2006), and this requires spatially explicit data for all species over large areas.

Hence, this section on forest dynamics and global change draws to a close with a key insight: that to understand how a forest responds to global change drivers, it is necessary to understand that overall forest change is the cumulative result of the interacting responses of multiple species and individuals. We need to consider not just the sum of the parts, but the parts themselves: the characteristics, or 'traits', of species.

## 1.3   Species traits and responses to changing resource availability

It is increasingly recognised that characterising the plant functional traits within a forest provides a powerful tool for understanding responses to global change (e.g. Diaz & Cabido 1997; Morin *et al.* 2011). If the traits of individuals vary less within species than they do between species, it becomes possible to describe species traits, and, from species composition of forests, derive predictions about forest functioning and response to change drivers founded on a better understanding of underlying mechanisms.

This is first illustrated for Amazonia by Chave (Chapter 6). This region remains a poorly understood component of the global carbon cycle. It has been predicted that by the end of the twenty-first century, large areas of the Amazonian forest will dry out and convert into open vegetation (the 'Amazonian dieback' scenario; Malhi *et al.* 2009). These predictions result from simulations in which atmospheric global circulation models are coupled with dynamic global vegetation models (DGVMs). Empirical evidence for this scenario remains tenuous, and so it is important to explore some of the key assumptions made by the current generation of DGVMs. One of the key features of these models is that they adopt a coarse description of tropical forest vegetation, with only a few plant functional types (Sitch *et al.* 2003). However, the 'biodiversity insurance hypothesis' predicts that species-poor ecosystems are more susceptible to marked shifts than species-rich ones (Yachi & Loreau 1999). DGVMs, as currently constructed, ignore the interspecific variability characteristic of species-rich ecosystems, as well as phenotypic plasticity and adaptive potential. A finer-grained description of tropical forest vegetation dynamics would allow for a more accurate description of interspecific and inter-individual variability. Chave (Chapter 6) reviews the literature on past environmental shifts in Amazonia and describes the method currently used to delineate functional types for tropical forest trees.

Some aspects of plant physiology that are currently overlooked in the definition of plant functional types are then considered, focusing on the role of stems and branches in conducting fluids towards the leaves while controlling for possible drought stresses. This review emphasises the need for a whole plant perspective, incorporating a greater range of (non-leaf) traits in order to understand the contribution of tropical forest to biogeochemical cycles.

In Chapter 7, Purves and Vanderwel provide a theoretical framework for understanding global change biology that builds on classic models of community dynamics. They point out that coexistence is no longer a paradox from a theoretical perspective: neutral theory demonstrates that it can take many thousands of years for populations of functionally identical species to drift to extinction, while various 'niche' theories show that mono-dominance is avoided so long as traits that affect fitness are influenced by some form of negative feedback (Dislich, Johst & Huth 2010). This rich theoretical background provides a useful resource for understanding global change, they argue. Purves and Vanderwel introduce a traits–states–rates (TSR) framework for helping forest ecologists to understand the coexistence of multiple species in forest communities. Within this framework, a 'trait' is any property of an individual that does not depend on the current state of the community, or that reacts so slightly to the state of the community that it does not affect population dynamics and hence coexistence (Purves & Vanderwel, Chapter 7); 'states' refer to the state variables of a model of a community (e.g. population size and size distribution, soil nutrients, pathogen abundance) and 'rates' refer to the rate of change of each state variable. Traits combine with states to give rates, which in turn leads to new states. The TSR scheme is illustrated by reference to classic Lotka–Volterra modelling, before moving on to more complicated size-structured communities, using a relatively simple but realistic forest model: the 'perfect plasticity approximation' model, PPA (Purves *et al.* 2008; Strigul *et al.* 2008). By parameterising a PPA model using vast forest inventory datasets from the United States, Purves and Vanderwel provide a glimpse of the mechanisms that might, and might not, plausibly promote species coexistence in forested landscapes. With recognition that the traits themselves are not constant, but are affected by environmental change, they show how it is possible to use the TSR approach to explore species composition, forest structure, carbon dynamics and biogeochemistry in the context of global change (Purves & Pacala 2008).

Recent analyses have shown that the consequences of biodiversity loss for ecosystem services are of comparable magnitude to the effects of other global change drivers (Hooper *et al.* 2012). Chapter 8 concentrates on the functional role of biodiversity in forests, and the biological mechanisms behind it, providing a historical perspective before appraising a number of published reviews of the subject of biodiversity and ecosystem functioning (BEF) published since 2005 (Nadrowski, Wirth & Scherer-Lorenzen 2010; Scherer-Lorenzen, Körner & Schulze 2005; Thompson *et al.* 2009). Amongst all possible drivers relating to diversity, the reviewed studies concentrate on tree species richness, and show a predominately positive effect of tree mixes on growth, wood production and other ecosystem processes. Such studies for forests represent a tiny fraction of those for all ecosystems, and indeed pose certain challenges. Silvicultural trials have generally been limited to monoculture versus two-species mixture comparisons, while the applicability of experimental manipulations of forests ('synthetic communities') to real world situations is sometimes questioned (Srivastava & Vellend 2005).

Observational studies and modelling represent complementary approaches to the experiments. The value of national forest inventories for exploring BEF is increasingly recognised, and positive BEF effects have been quantified after accounting for environmental covariates (e.g. Vilà *et al.* 2013). Comparative studies where a similar number of plots per diversity level are deliberately chosen are another form of observational study. The latter are serviced by a growing number of different tools such as forest growth models, process-based succession models, structural equation modelling or mixed-effect models. Although there is still much to understand, the combination of these three different lines of investigation allows some tentative conclusions to be drawn. Whereas individual tree growth, biomass production and diversity of associated organisms are often positively associated with tree species diversity, other ecological functions, such as those related to biogeochemical cycling, seems to be more strongly controlled by site conditions. Perhaps most importantly in the context of species traits, the identity and functional traits of dominant tree species often have strong impacts on ecosystem functions. The functional differences between tree species are the basis for any relationship between biodiversity and ecosystem processes, emphasising the value of trait-based approaches for understanding the biotic control of ecosystem processes.

The evolution and ecology of Brazil's seasonally dry tropical communities, which lie to the south and southeast of the equatorial rain forests, are the focus of Chapter 9. By analyses of a large dataset of woody plants, Oliveira-Filho *et al.* seek to determine whether seasonally dry woodlands (caatinga) and savanna woodlands (cerrado) have distinct phylogenetic structures, and to ascertain which traits and climatic variables are most strongly associated with this structuring. They find that the two floras are phylogenetically distinct, reflecting several million years of divergence and suggesting that these two types of dry-adapted vegetation have different evolutionary histories. The factor that is most strongly associated with the pairwise phylogenetic difference between sites is the leaf trait of deciduousness, which has already been established as shaping plant communities in eastern Brazil (Oliveira-Filho,

Jarenkow & Rodal 2006; Santos *et al.* 2012). This result suggests that phenology is phylogenetically conserved ('phylogenetic niche conservatism'; Donoghue 2008; Crisp *et al.* 2009) and contributes to differential community assembly in this setting. The dry woodlands are critically important for the Amazon region in terms of forecasting which species might thrive there in the drier and more seasonal climates predicted of the future.

As we have already seen (Chapters 6 and 7), functional diversity may play an important role in the resilience of tropical forests to global change. Some climate projections forecast increases and decreases in annual rainfall and length of the dry season for different tropical regions (Hulme & Viner 1998) as well as increases in the frequency of extreme weather events (IPCC 2007), although these predictions are highly uncertain. In the search for predicted responses to increased drought, Comita and Engelbrecht (Chapter 10) review work on the effects of water availability, including experimentally induced drought, on tropical tree regeneration, dynamics and distribution. There are now documented cases of natural drought events causing increased mortality rates of tropical trees and their seedlings (e.g. Condit *et al.* 1995; Potts 2003; Phillips *et al.* 2010), and it is reasonable to propose that changing frequency of drought will result in changes to tree species composition and ecosystem processes.

Comita and Engelbrecht show that there is huge variation among species in their responses to drought, which contributes directly to where seedlings are located within the landscape. Classic studies of the mechanisms of drought resistance differentiate species according to the extent that they avoid or tolerate drought conditions, and search for traits that are associated with these mechanisms. However, the review finds very limited evidence of a consistent role for traits associated with *drought avoidance*, such as deep or extensive root systems, water storage, stomatal responses, cuticular conductance or deciduousness, in promoting differential drought resistance of tropical tree seedlings under field conditions. Instead, mechanisms of *drought tolerance* are decisive in determining differential seedling responses. Thus traits such as turgor loss point, rigidity of cell walls, solute concentrations at full turgor, vulnerability of xylem to cavitation and ability to refill embolised cells seem to be important in determining survival, whereas 'soft traits' often measured by ecologists seem to have little bearing on drought response.

Following considerations of water availability in Chapter 10, Kobe *et al.* (Chapter 11) explore the importance of soil nutrient availability in interpreting and predicting how forests respond to global change. This is because soil resources are major determinants of tree growth and forest productivity, and human activity is changing the availability of key soil-borne resources through atmospheric nitrogen deposition, which accelerates soil acidification and may lead to enhanced leaching losses of phosphorus and nutrient cations.

Nutrient losses may also occur through intensification of tree harvesting, especially when tree bark and leaves are removed, and in response to increases in fire frequency. Kobe *et al.* also show that soil nutrient and water availability are important determinants of the limits to tree species distributions and may influence the response of tree distributions to changing climatic conditions. Pollen records provide evidence that postglacial colonisation of infertile soils in eastern North America by *Pinus contorta* rather than *Abies* or *Picea* species was driven by the edaphic preferences of these taxa rather than the suitability of the climate (Whitlock 1993). Similarly, the physiological response of temperate forest trees to extreme temperature or precipitation is modulated by nutrient supply, leading to declining function under conditions of nutrient imbalance (St.Clair, Sharpe & Lynch 2008). Hence soil resource availability influences the response of forests to facets of global change both directly through responses to atmospheric N deposition, and indirectly through interactions with other abiotic environmental factors.

The scope for these interactions is illustrated by recent research on tree communities in temperate deciduous forests in eastern North America and tropical forests in Costa Rica. One focus has been to understand the balance of nutrient limitation of tree growth and forest productivity by N, P and base cations, as a test of the widespread generalisation of N limitation in temperate forests and P limitation in tropical forests. Contrary to this, Kobe *et al.* conclude that there may be significant limitation of these processes by base cations in both temperate and tropical forests (Baribault, Kobe & Finley 2012; Baribault, Kobe & Rothstein 2010). The identity of the limiting element may vary in response to soil mineralogy, ontogenetic stage, and species or functional group, and different elements may determine contrasting physiological or demographic variables (e.g. wood production, leaf production, seedling growth or reproductive output). The diversity of responses to soil resource availability reflects the multiple mechanisms that trees use to acquire nutrient pools within the soils, which includes translocation of base cations from deep soil horizons to the surface (Dijkstra & Smits 2002), exudation of carbon into the rhizosphere to support the activity of soil organisms (Kobe, Iyer & Walters 2010) and the ubiquitous associations of trees with mycorrhizas. These conclusions support other recent research in temperate and tropical forests based on long-term fertilisation experiments (Kaspari *et al.* 2008; Wright *et al.* 2011) and short-term pot experiments (Burslem, Grubb & Turner 1995; Denslow, Vitousek & Schultz 1987) highlighting an important role for base cations as well as N and P in biogeochemical cycling and identifying contrasts and highly variable within- and between-species responses to nutrient heterogeneity. Understanding these processes within forest ecosystems is important because they will influence the ways in which tree distributions respond to climate change, the management of forest carbon stocks across edaphic gradients and the responses of forests to increased atmospheric N deposition.

## 1.4   Detecting and modelling global change

Throughout this overview of forests and global change, it will have become apparent that building better dynamic models, and servicing them with better empirical data, is critical for understanding current and predicting future trajectories of change. The need to integrate different approaches for more realistic modelling has also been underlined. For example, in Chapter 6 we saw that combining individual-based models with dynamic global vegetation models is necessary to bridge the gap between ecosystem science and community ecology and better understand crucially important future changes to Amazonian forests (Fisher *et al.* 2010). Earlier, in Chapter 3, it was suggested that the coupling of niche envelope models for plants and their animal interactors (e.g. seed dispersers, herbivores) can greatly enhance our understanding of how plant populations will respond to future changes. In this latter case, parallel modelling approaches in which plant models largely ignore animal effects, and animal models only consider plants in terms of vegetation habitat suitability, can underestimate the influence of interactions on the distribution of each species under new climates. Coupled models would be inherently complex because of the scope for high dimensionality, but would help to overcome these limitations.

In this final section, detecting and modelling change comes under greater focus, and from a number of different angles, beginning with an aerial perspective using imaging spectrometers (Chapter 12). One of the key challenges in current forest research is to improve our measurement, mapping and understanding of species diversity and how this is responding to global change. In this chapter Asner describes an innovative approach to this question involving remote sensing of foliar chemical traits. Drawing from pioneering results from the Carnegie Airborne Observatory, he shows how interspecific variation in the hyperspectral signatures of tropical forest species allows for their discrimination in airborne imagery (Asner & Martin 2009). Canopies that appear monotonous green carpets to the naked eye become a kaleidoscope of spectral variation on the basis of leaf chemicals fulfilling the three independent functions of light capture and growth, longevity and defence, and maintenance and metabolism. Crucially, Asner advocates that more variation in the leaf chemistry and spectral reflectance properties is found between species than within species in tropical systems, opening up the possibility of taxon-specific mapping from the air. The power of such an approach for a range of applications is emphasised in the chapter, as are fascinating insights into the ecological and evolutionary significance of the chemical differentiation. Evolution in highly species-rich and productive environments, as found in the tropical rain forests, leads to a high diversity of uncorrelated dimensions of foliar chemical variation (Asner & Martin 2011). This can be explained in terms of a pronounced radiation of species-specific strategies for dealing with herbivores, pathogens and other antagonists (Connell 1970; Janzen 1970), as well as other strategies for capturing light and nutrients (e.g. Coley 1993). As a result, canopy biodiversity maps may help not only in forest biodiversity conservation, but also in developing our understanding of forest function and community assembly.

In Chapter 13 Bugmann reflects on the challenges of forecasting impacts of changes in relation to different spatial and temporal scales. Forests may not be more complex than other ecosystems, but they are characterised by larger-than-normal spatial and temporal scales, with some trees attaining heights of over 100 m and living for thousands of years. Characterising and analysing the long-term dynamics of forests are therefore challenging. For this reason, three sources of evidence are important: observations, experiments and models (picking up a theme raised in Chapter 8). Each has its weaknesses: it is difficult to extrapolate observational conclusions to domains of climate space that lack analogues in the past; it is difficult to scale experimental approaches to long time scales (Bugmann et al. 2000) and complex species-rich communities; and it is impossible to validate the results of long-term predictions. However, in combination they represent the most fruitful way forward.

After asking what we actually do when we, as scientists, assess the future state and fate of forest ecosystems, and urging a more precise use of language in modelling terminology, Chapter 13 goes on to summarise the development of forest succession models, in particular the innovations associated with introducing more physiological reality into the models in the 1990s. 'All models are wrong, some models are useful' was famously stated by Box and Draper (1987). There is no doubt that the usefulness of the current generation of models is increasing, as they make more reliable and refined predictions. For example, whereas the models of the 1980s projected widespread forest dieback as a result of temperature increases and precipitation decreases, only drought-induced mortality is now predicted to become common (Allen et al. 2010), with temperature increase expected only to lead to changes in forest composition (Didion et al. 2011). Among the challenges that need to be tackled by the next generation of models are resolving the debate on whether carbon source or sink limitation is dominating global vegetation processes, and incorporating hitherto neglected processes such as the trade-off between growth rates (early in life) and longevity that is often observed in tree communities.

As we saw in Chapter 4, permanently marked forest plots remain an important tool for quantifying changes in forest carbon stocks, and yet their use continues to inspire controversy and debate because of methodological concerns (Korner 2003; Clark 2007). Muller-Landau *et al.* (Chapter 14) investigate some key issues associated with using data from tropical forest plots to detect and project biomass change, with illustrative analyses of 25 years of data from the 50 ha plot in Barro Colorado Island, Panama (BCI). Sampling errors in biomass change on BCI scale exactly as expected in the absence of spatial and temporal autocorrelation, with variances proportional to $1/(\text{area} \times \text{time})$. Using re-measurement data, it is shown that measurement errors and data cleaning routines can both introduce systematic errors, with data cleaning errors being the more significant of the two for BCI. Recommendations are given that measurement errors should always be quantified, and that any data cleaning should be thoroughly documented and evaluated in terms of its potential to introduce systematic errors. Measurement and analysis methods for trees measured at non-standard heights (e.g. measured well above 1.3 m owing to buttresses or other irregularities) make the largest difference to estimates of biomass change on BCI, where the number of trees measured above 1.5 m has increased over time, causing a downward bias on biomass change. It is recommended that heights of measurement always be recorded, and that new allometric equations for computing biomass be constructed that take these heights into account, incorporating information on taper where possible (Metcalf, Clark & Clark 2009). Finally, a Markov chain modelling approach for projecting biomass change is presented and applied to BCI. This approach is commended for capturing current successional and gap dynamic trajectories to project biomass change in the short to medium term.

In Chapter 15, Newton and Echeverría examine the dynamics of forest loss and fragmentation in dry and humid forests of Latin America in relation to different socio-economic and environmental drivers. This synthesis is based on results obtained from parallel investigations: using time series of satellite remote sensing images to measure forest conversion over large spatial extents, and field surveys supported by statistical and process-based modelling approaches to investigate changes resulting from fire, tree harvesting and livestock browsing. Comparative analysis of different landscapes indicates that results are highly context-specific, limiting the scope for generalisation. However, a number of tentative principles are presented, which are examined in relation to a UK case study characterised by a long history of anthropogenic disturbance: the New Forest National Park on the south coast of England.

The high biodiversity value of the New Forest can be attributed to its high spatial heterogeneity and the intricate mosaic of different habitat types created by its distinctive disturbance regime, principally related to grazing, but also cutting, fire and drainage. Many of the species that now characterise the area are clearly dependent on the maintenance of this anthropogenic disturbance regime for their survival (Newton 2010). The case study illustrates the significance to biodiversity of creating and maintaining a successional mosaic through the localised recovery of vegetation following disturbance. There are parallels with some of the Latin American landscapes that are also characterised by successional mosaics, such as the montane rain forests in southern Mexico. By comparing two very different parts of the world, Newton and Echeverría suggest that the analysis of multiple case studies using common analytical approaches (sensu Shrader-Frechette & McCoy 1994) can help to provide a generally applicable understanding of human impacts on forest biodiversity, and thereby support the development of empirical theory, with practical applications in environmental management. One of their conclusions is that impacts of human disturbance on biodiversity are not always negative. If localised forest recovery is permitted, successional mosaics may develop, maintaining high species richness over the long term.

## 1.5  Concluding thoughts

Forest conservation strategy and practice is struggling to adapt to, and keep pace with, the rapidity and scale of change taking place in the world's forests. This volume emphasises the need to understand the ecology of species in order to understand the consequences of global change for systems. For example, predictions that much of the Amazonian forest will dry out and convert into open vegetation by the end of the twenty-first century come from dynamic global vegetation models that assume all trees have similar responses to drought (i.e. a plant functional types approach). Yet Chapters 6 and 10 provide evidence of the considerable variation in species' responses to water shortage, suggesting that increased drought across Amazonia might lead to shifts in forest composition, as drought-intolerant species die off and tolerant species take over, without a catastrophic transformation of the landscape. The recent discovery that forests in West Africa are gaining biomass despite 20 years of drought, because deciduous drought-tolerant species have grown at the expense of evergreen species, lends further weight to this idea (Fauset *et al.* 2012). Even within the seasonally dry regions of Brazil, species of the caatinga woodlands have different fire responses from those of cerrado savannas (Chapter 9), highlighting the importance of understanding the evolution and ecology of species. Several other chapters report profound differences in the way species respond to environmental change. Predictive models that fail to take biological diversity into consideration are likely to give misleading impressions, because biodiversity has a strong effect on ecosystem functioning, including resilience to change (Chapter 8).

This volume also emphasises that global change incorporates numerous drivers in addition to climatic change. A major source of uncertainty lies in predicting how these multiple drivers will interact in their impacts on forests, and in identifying the drivers that have the greatest impact. For example, the fragments of tropical forests that remain in agricultural landscapes are subject to a multitude of changes, yet anthropogenic fire is one of the greatest threats to the biodiversity in these fragments because few rain forest species are tolerant of fire (Gibson *et al.* 2011). Finally, in parts of the world long occupied by humans, disturbance of natural systems for agriculture creates a patchwork of 'semi-natural' communities which can be beneficial for biodiversity at the landscape scale (Chapter 15). In Latin America, Newton and Echeverría (Chapter 15) conclude that the impacts of global change processes are inherently site-specific and unpredictable.

Ever-improving knowledge of the ecology of plants, global integration of datasets and the application of new technologies mean that current trends in the state of forests are coming into sharper focus and predictions are made with increasing confidence. Yet many uncertainties still remain. This volume has highlighted both the knowledge gains and gaps, and emphasises the need for multidisciplinary approaches, as much within the forest scientific community, as between this community and other stake-holders such as policy-makers, sociologists and global change scientists. Only then can robust assessments of forest change be made at multiple spatial scales, from local to global; and these assessments are critical for securing the continued future of the immense array of goods and services that forests provide to humankind.

## References

Allen, C. D., Macalady, A. K., Chenchouni, H. *et al.* (2010) A global overview of drought and heat-induced tree mortality reveals emerging climate change risks for forests. *Forest Ecology and Management*, **259**, 660–684.

Asner, G. P. & Martin, R. E. (2009) Airborne spectranomics: mapping canopy chemical and taxonomic diversity in tropical forests. *Frontiers in Ecology and the Environment*, **7**, 269–276.

Asner, G. P. & Martin, R. E. (2011) Canopy phylogenetic, chemical and spectral assembly in a lowland Amazonian forest. *The New Phytologist*, **189**, 999–1012.

Avissar, R. & Werth, D. (2009) Global hydroclimatological teleconnections resulting from tropical deforestation. *Journal of Hydrometeorology*, **6**, 134–145.

Baribault, T. W., Kobe, R. K. & Finley, A. O. (2012) Tropical tree growth is correlated with soil phosphorus, potassium, and calcium, though not for legumes. *Ecological Monographs*, **82**, 189–203.

Baribault, T. W., Kobe, R. K. & Rothstein, D. E. (2010) Soil calcium, nitrogen, and water are correlated with aboveground net primary production in northern hardwood forests. *Forest Ecology and Management*, **260**, 723–733.

Blondel, J., Aronson, J. & Bodiou, J.-Y. (2010) *The Mediterranean Region: Biological Diversity in Space and Time*. Oxford: Oxford University Press.

Box, G. E. P. & Draper, N. R. (1987) *Empirical Model-Building and Response Surfaces*. New York: John Wiley & Sons.

Bugmann, H., Lindner, M., Lasch, P. *et al.* (2000) Scaling issues in forest succession modelling. *Climatic Change*, **44**, 265–289.

Burslem, D. F. R. P., Grubb, P. J. & Turner, I. M. (1995) Responses to nutrient addition among tree seedlings of lowland in Singapore tropical rain forest. *Journal of Ecology*, **83**, 113–122.

Canadell, J. G. & Raupach, M. R. (2008) Managing forests for climate change mitigation. *Science*, **320**, 1456–1457.

Chambers, J. Q., Negron-Juarez, R. I., Marra, D. M. *et al.* (2013) The steady-state mosaic of disturbance and succession across an old-growth Central Amazon forest landscape. *Proceedings of the National Academy of Sciences USA*, **110**, 3949–3954.

Charney, J., Stone, P. H. & Quirk, W. J. (1975) Drought in the Sahara: a biogeochemical feedback mechanism. *Science*, **187**, 434–435.

Clark, D. A. (2007) Detecting tropical forests' responses to global climatic and atmospheric change: current challenges and a way forward. *Biotropica*, **39**, 4–19.

Coley, P. D. (1993) Gap size and plant defenses. *Trends in Ecology & Evolution*, **8**, 1–2.

Condit, R., Hubbell, S. P. & Foster, R. B. (1995) Mortality rates of 205 neotropical tree and shrub species and the impact of a severe drought. *Ecological Monographs*, **65**, 419.

Connell, J. H. (1970) On the role of natural enemies in preventing competitive exclusion in some marine animals and in rain forest trees. In *Dynamics of Population* (eds. P. J. Den Boer & G. R. Gradwell), Wageningen: Pudoc.

Coomes, D. A., Holdaway, R. J., Kobe, R. K., Lines, E. R. & Allen, R. B. (2012) A general integrative framework for modelling woody biomass production and carbon sequestration rates in forests. *Journal of Ecology*, **100**, 42–64.

Crisp, M. D., Arroyo, M. T. K., Cook, L. G. *et al.* (2009) Phylogenetic biome conservatism on a global scale. *Nature*, **458**, 754–756.

Cox, P. M., Betts, R. A., Collins, M. *et al.* (2004) Amazonian forest dieback under climate-carbon cycle projections for the 21st century. *Theoretical and Applied Climatology*, **78**, 137–156.

Denslow, J. S., Vitousek, P. M. & Schultz, J. C. (1987) Bioassays of nutrient limitation in a tropical rain forest soil. *Oecologia*, **74**, 370–376.

Diaz, S. & Cabido, M. (1997) Plant functional types and ecosystem function in relation to global change: a multiscale approach. *Journal of Vegetation Science* **8**, 463–474.

Didion, M., Kupferschmid, A. D., Wolf, A. & Bugmann, H. (2011) Ungulate herbivory modifies the effects of climate change on mountain forests. *Climatic Change*, **109**, 647–669.

Dijkstra, F. A. & Smits, M. M. (2002) Tree species effects on calcium cycling: the role of calcium uptake in deep soils. *Ecosystems*, **5**, 385–398.

Dislich, C., Johst, K. & Huth, A. (2010) What enables coexistence in plant communities? Weak versus strong species traits and the role of local processes. *Ecological Modelling*, **221**, 2227–2236.

Donoghue, M. J. (2008) Colloquium paper: a phylogenetic perspective on the distribution of plant diversity. *Proceedings of the National Academy of Sciences USA*, **105** Suppl., 11549–11555.

FAO (Food and Agriculture Organization) (2011) *The State of the World's Forests*. Rome: FAO.

Fauset, S., Baker, T. R., Lewis, S. L. *et al.* (2012) Drought-induced shifts in the floristic and functional composition of tropical forests in Ghana. *Ecology Letters*, **15**, 1120–1129.

Fisher, R., McDowell, N., Purves, D. *et al.* (2010) Assessing uncertainties in a second-generation dynamic vegetation model caused by ecological scale limitations. *The New Phytologist*, **187**, 666–681.

Fyllas, N. M. & Troumbis, A. Y. (2009) Simulating vegetation shifts in north-eastern Mediterranean mountain forests under climatic change scenarios. *Global Ecology and Biogeography*, **18**, 64–77.

Gibson, L., Lee, M. L., Koh, L. P. et al. (2011) Primary forests are irreplaceable for sustaining tropical biodiversity. Nature, **478**, 378–381

Hooper, D. U., Adair, E. C., Cardinale, B. J. et al. (2012) A global synthesis reveals biodiversity loss as a major driver of ecosystem change. Nature, **486**, 105–108.

Hulme, M. & Viner, D. (1998) A climate change scenario for the tropics. Climatic Change, **39**, 145–176.

IPCC (Intergovernmental Panel on Climate Change) (2007) Climate Change 2007: The Physical Science Basis. Summary for Policymakers. Cambridge: Cambridge University Press.

Janzen, D. H. (1970) Herbivores and the number of tree species in tropical forests. American Naturalist, **104**, 501–528.

Kaspari, M., Garcia, M. N., Harms, K. E. et al. (2008) Multiple nutrients limit litterfall and decomposition in a tropical forest. Ecology Letters, **11**, 35–43.

Kobe, R. K., Iyer, M. & Walters, M. B. (2010) Optimal partitioning theory revisited: Nonstructural carbohydrates dominate root mass responses to nitrogen. Ecology, **91**, 166–179.

Korner, C. (2003) Atmospheric science. Slow in, rapid out – carbon flux studies and Kyoto targets. Science, **300**, 1242–1243.

Lewis, S. L., Lopez-Gonzalez, G., Sonké, B. et al. (2009) Increasing carbon storage in intact African tropical forests. Nature, **457**, 1003–1006.

Lewis, S. L., Phillips, O. L., Baker, T. R. et al. (2004) Concerted changes in tropical forest structure and dynamics: evidence from 50 South American long-term plots. Philosophical Transactions of the Royal Society of London. Series B: Biological Sciences, **359**, 421–436.

Maestre, F. T. & Cortina, J. (2004) Do positive interactions increase with abiotic stress? A test from a semi-arid steppe. Proceedings of the Royal Society Series B: Biological Sciences, **271** Suppl, S331–333.

Malhi, Y., Aragão, L.E.O.C., Galbraith, D. et al. (2009) Exploring the likelihood and mechanism of a climate-change-induced dieback of the Amazon rainforest. Proceedings of the National Academy of Sciences USA, **106**, 20610–20615.

Metcalf, C. J. E., Clark, J. S. & Clark, D. A. (2009) Tree growth inference and prediction when the point of measurement changes: Modelling around buttresses in tropical forests. Journal of Tropical Ecology, **25**, 1–12.

Morin, X., Fahse, L., Scherer-Lorenzen, M. & Bugmann, H. (2011). Tree species richness promotes productivity in temperate forests through strong complementarity between species. Ecology Letters, **14**, 1211–1219.

Nadrowski, K., Wirth, C. & Scherer-Lorenzen, M. (2010) Is forest diversity driving ecosystem function and service? Current Opinion in Environmental Sustainability, **2**, 75–79.

Newton, A. C. (2010) Biodiversity in the New Forest. Newbury, Hampshire: Pisces Publications.

Oliveira-Filho, A. T., Jarenkow, J. A. & Rodal, M. J. N. (2006) Floristic relationships of seasonally dry forests of eastern South America based on tree species distribution patterns. In Neotropical Savannas and Seasonally Dry Forests: Plant Biodiversity, Biogeographic Patterns and Conservation (eds. R. T. Pennington, J. A. Ratter & G. P. Lewis), pp. 159–192. Boca Raton, Florida: CRC Press.

Pacala, S. W., Canham, C. D., Saponara, J. et al. (1996) Forest models defined by field measurements: estimation, error analysis and dynamics. Ecological Monographs, **66**, 1.

Papaik, M. J. & Canham, C. D. (2006) Species resistance and community response to wind disturbance regimes in northern temperate forests. Journal of Ecology, **94**, 1011–1026.

Pausas, J. G. & Paula, S. (2012) Fuel shapes the fire–climate relationship: evidence from Mediterranean ecosystems. Global Ecology and Biogeography, **21**, 1074–1082.

Phillips, O. L., Aragão, L. E. O. C., Lewis, S. L. et al. (2009) Drought sensitivity of the Amazon rainforest. Science, **323**, 1344–1347.

Phillips, O. L., Heijden, G. van der, Lewis, S. L., et al. (2010) Drought-mortality relationships for tropical forests. The New Phytologist, **187**, 631–646.

Potts, M. D. (2003) Drought in a Bornean everwet rain forest. *Journal of Ecology*, **91**, 467–474.

Purves, D. & Pacala, S. (2008) Predictive models of forest dynamics. *Science (New York, N.Y.)*, **320**, 1452–1453.

Purves, D. W., Lichstein, J. W., Strigul, N. & Pacala, S. W. (2008) Predicting and understanding forest dynamics using a simple tractable model. *Proceedings of the National Academy of Sciences USA*, **105**, 17018–17022.

Quinn Thomas, R., Canham, C. D., Weathers, K. C. & Goodale, C. L. (2009) Increased tree carbon storage in response to nitrogen deposition in the US. *Nature Geoscience*, **3**, 13–17.

Santos, R. M., Oliveira-Filho, A. T., Eisenlohr, P. V, *et al.* (2012) Identity and relationships of the Arboreal Caatinga among other floristic units of seasonally dry tropical forests (SDTFs) of north-eastern and Central Brazil. *Ecology and Evolution*, **2**, 409–428.

Scherer-Lorenzen, M., Körner, C. & Schulze, E. D. (2005) The functional significance of forest diversity: the starting point. In *Forest Diversity and Function: Temperate and Boreal Systems. Ecological Studies 176* (eds. M. Scherer-Lorenzen, C. Körner & E. D. Schulze), pp. 3–12. Berlin: Springer.

Shrader-Frechette, K. & McCoy, E. D. (1994) Applied ecology and the logic of case studies. *Philosophy of Science*, **61**, 228–249.

Sitch, S., Smith, B., Prentice, I. C. *et al.* (2003) Evaluation of ecosystem dynamics, plant geography and terrestrial carbon cycling in the LPJ dynamic global vegetation model. *Global Change Biology*, **9**, 161–185.

Srivastava, D. S. & Vellend, M. (2005) Biodiversity-ecosystem function research: Is it relevant to conservation? *Annual Review of Ecology, Evolution, and Systematics*, **36**, 267–294.

St.Clair, S. B., Sharpe, W. E. & Lynch, J. P. (2008) Key interactions between nutrient limitation and climatic factors in temperate forests: a synthesis of the sugar maple literature. *Canadian Journal of Forest Research*, **38**, 401–414.

Strigul, N., Pristinski, D., Purves, D., Dushoff, J. & Pacala, S. (2008) Scaling from trees to forests: tractable macroscopic equations for forest dynamics. *Ecological Monographs*, **78**, 523–545.

Thompson, I., Mackey, B., McNulty, S. & Mosseler, A. (2009) *Forest Resilience, Biodiversity, and Climate Change. A Synthesis of the Biodiversity/Resilience/Stability Relationship In Forest Ecosystems. Technical Series no. 43*. Montreal: UNEP Secretariat of the Convention on Biological Diversity.

Vilà, M., Carrillo-Gavilán, A., Vayreda, J., Bugmann, H., Fridman, J. *et al.* (2013) Disentangling biodiversity and climatic determinants of wood production. *PLoS ONE*, **8**, e53530.

Walker, R., Moore, N. J., Arima, E. *et al.* (2009) Protecting the Amazon with protected areas. *Proceedings of the National Academy of Sciences USA*, **106**, 10582–10586.

Whitlock, C. (1993) Postglacial vegetation and climate of Grand Teton and Southern Yellowstone National Parks. *Ecological Monographs*, **63**, 173–198.

Wright, S. J., Yavitt, J. B., Wurzburger, N. *et al.* (2011) Potassium, phosphorus, or nitrogen limit root allocation, tree growth, or litter production in a lowland tropical forest. *Ecology*, **92**, 1616–1625.

Yachi, S. & Loreau, M. (1999) Biodiversity and ecosystem productivity in a fluctuating environment: The insurance hypothesis. *Proceedings of the National Academy of Sciences USA*, **96**, 1463–1468.

# PART I

# Forest dynamics and global change

# CHAPTER TWO

# Forests and the climate system

JOHN GRACE
*University of Edinburgh, UK*

## 2.1 Introduction

The planet was once much more forested. As human populations have grown, the forests have been cleared to make way for crops and livestock. This conversion from forest to agriculture started in Neolithic times (Brown 1997) but accelerated during the European colonisation of North America and other territories. Since the 1970s, it has continued apace in the tropics. The need to produce food is not the only cause of deforestation: humans have always used timber as fuel and as a raw material for construction. They will continue to do so, whilst new threats are likely to emerge: for example, in recent years tropical forests and woodlands have been cleared to make way for biofuel crops and plantations. These changes are causing widespread concern, as they may bring short-term benefits at the expense of the sustained provision of ecosystem goods and services (Foley *et al.* 2007).

Since 1990 the world's forests have shrunk from 28.6% to 27.6% of the land surface, with substantial shrinkage in the tropics and slight expansion in the temperate regions (calculated from FAO 2011). Overall, we expect to see a continuation of this trend as human populations continue to expand and economic development proceeds.

Irrespective of its cause, deforestation represents a profound transformation of the biophysical properties of the land surface, resulting in a step-wise change in energy balance and in the exchange of greenhouse gases and other materials. Charney was one of the first to show that the land surface is so intimately coupled to the atmosphere that it should be considered as part of the climate system (Charney, Stone & Quirk 1975). He recognised that there are important interactions between the vegetation and the atmosphere, and research in the past few decades has revealed how these involve both physical and biological processes and feedbacks.

Here we consider some of the changes and associated feedbacks involving albedo, roughness, evaporation, carbon sequestration, and the fluxes of volatile organic compounds and greenhouse gases.

*Forests and Global Change*, ed. David A. Coomes, David F. R. P. Burslem and William D. Simonson.
Published by Cambridge University Press. © British Ecological Society 2014.

## 2.2  Energy balance considerations

The land surface cover can be partially characterised by the extent to which it reflects solar radiation, known as *albedo*, from the Latin for 'whiteness'. Albedo is a dimensionless quantity, varying from zero (completely black) to 1.0 (perfectly white, reflecting all solar radiation). Although individual leaves of different species vary considerably in their reflectance, the albedo of an entire vegetated surface depends substantially on the structure of the leaf canopy, and to some extent on solar angle (Shuttleworth 1989). For example, Stanhill (1970) made helicopter measurements of albedo and discovered that it is a strong function of vegetation height, being in the region of 0.1 for forest and 0.25 for most short vegetation such as lawns and crops. A full theoretical treatment of albedo was presented by Ross (1975), who demonstrated how albedo depends on several structural features of the canopy as well as the sky conditions. Stanhill (1981) provided a summary explanation of the very low albedo of tall coniferous vegetation. In his words, 'low values of reflectivity are usually found in tall, dense vegetation associations whose foliage forms a system of radiation scattering elements with a high cavity depth to scattering element radius ratio, enhancing internal trapping of scattered radiation – the so-called velvet-pile effect.' But in short crops with larger and nearly horizontal leaves, more photons will be reflected back into space. Albedo is now routinely measured at many sites in the world, showing that Stanhill's early analysis was indeed correct and there is a definite tendency for crops to reflect more solar radiation than forests, and for coniferous and tropical forests to have some of the lowest albedos (Table 2.1).

There have been numerous measurements of albedo stretching over an entire annual cycle (for example see Barlage *et al.* 2005; Betts & Ball 1997; Culf *et al.* 1996). In boreal regions, the difference between albedo of tall and

**Table 2.1** *Albedo of forests and grasslands.*

|  | No snow | With snow cover |
| --- | --- | --- |
| Grass[1] | 0.19 (0.16–0.26) | 0.75 (0.40–0.95) |
| Aspen leafless[1] | 0.12 | 0.21 |
| Aspen with leaves[1] | 0.16 | – |
| Spruce/poplar[1] | 0.08 | 0.11 (0.05–0.20) |
| Tropical rain forest[2] | 0.13 (0.09–0.18) | – |
| Tropical pasture[2] | 0.18 | – |

[1] Data from the BOREAS project in Canada.
[2] Data from the ABRACOS project in Brazil.
Values in parentheses, where given, are the author's estimates of the likely range for that type of ecosystem.

short vegetation is emphasised when there is snow cover (Table 2.1). Coniferous canopies tend to shed their load of snow whereas lawns and short crops retain it for many weeks. The phenomenon can be seen in views from aircraft during the winter where forest often looks black, accentuated against the white snow-covered grassland. In tropical regions, there is a sharp contrast between rain forests and the pastures created by clearing the forest and sowing grass (Table 2.1).

If everything else were the same, we might therefore expect that trees would tend to warm the planet by absorbing more solar radiation. However, the energy balance of the land surface does not depend simply on the albedo. For the total radiation balance, it is important to consider the thermal radiation, referred to as long-wave radiation (in contrast to the so-called short-wave radiation, i.e. solar radiation). The net radiation absorbed, $R_n$, depends on solar radiation $S$, albedo $\alpha$ and the long-wave (thermal) radiation exchange, which we may represent as a downward component $L_d$ and an upward component $L_u$:

$$R_n = (1 - \alpha)S + L_d - L_u \qquad (2.1)$$

The fluxes of long-wave radiation depend, in turn, on the surface temperatures of the canopy and the apparent surface temperature of the sky, according to Stefan's Law:

$$L = \varepsilon \, \sigma \, T^4 \qquad (2.2)$$

where $T$ is the surface temperature in degrees Kelvin, $\varepsilon$ is a physical quantity known as the emissivity, with a value of 0.95–1.0 for natural surfaces, and $\sigma$ is the Stefan–Boltzmann constant, $56.7 \times 10^{-9} \, \mathrm{W \, m^{-2} \, K^{-4}}$. To estimate the down-welling component $L_d$ we need to know the apparent sky temperature, which depends on meteorological conditions such as cloud amount and cloud level. This can be done with a suitable infrared thermometer, although mathematical approximations are sometimes used (Monteith & Unsworth 2008). But generally, researchers simply measure the net radiation with a sensor that views the sky above and the land surface below, and subtract the up-welling from the down-welling radiation to give the net radiation.

The surface temperature of tall canopies is usually within a degree or so of air temperature, whereas the sky temperature is much lower (see Monteith & Unsworth 2008). For short canopies the surface temperature can deviate from air temperature, especially at low wind speed (Grace et al. 1989a) being much warmer than the air in bright sunshine and somewhat colder than the air at night.

Typically, in bright midday conditions, the incoming solar radiation flux $S$ is up to 800 $\mathrm{W \, m^{-2}}$ whilst the net radiation $R_n$ is lower by a few hundreds of $\mathrm{W \, m^{-2}}$ because of the loss of electromagnetic radiation to space as $\alpha S$ and $L_u$.

So far, we have considered only electromagnetic radiation as a component of the energy balance. Now we move to the partition of the absorbed energy between evaporation, convection, conduction and photosynthesis. In this respect forests and crops are rather different.

For the conservation of energy, the net radiation is balanced by fluxes of energy as evaporation $E$, convection $C$, conduction $G$ and photosynthesis $P$, and on short time scales (hours) some energy, $\Delta$, remains stored in the air spaces, biomass and soil:

$$R_n = C + E + G + P + \Delta \tag{2.3}$$

In plants, evaporation can occur directly from wet surfaces (leaves or soil) or indirectly through the stomatal pores on the plant's surface (this process is called transpiration). The rate of evaporation is large in well-watered conditions, but declines to near-zero when the stomata close in drought. When water is evaporated the surroundings are substantially cooled (the latent heat of vaporisation of water at 20 °C is 2452 J g$^{-1}$, and this value does not change very much with temperature). Heat transfer by convection to the air can also be a very important term, and depends on wind speed and roughness (see below). Heat transfer to the soil by convection and conduction can be important in short vegetation on an hour-to-hour basis, but over 24 hours the value is near to zero because gains by day are balanced by losses at night. Photosynthesis, although very important for life on the planet, is a very small part of the energy balance, converting only about 1% of the energy in incoming solar radiation to energy in the chemical bonds of glucose (Monteith & Moss 1977). We may write the energy balance in a simplified form by assuming conduction, photosynthesis and storage to be negligible:

$$R_n = C + E \tag{2.4}$$

The terms $C$ and $E$ may now be defined in terms of a few fundamental variables:

$$C = \frac{\rho c_p (T_s - T_a)}{r_a^{\text{heat}}} \tag{2.5}$$

This tells us that convection, the flow of heat between the vegetated surface and the air, is proportional to the difference in temperature between the canopy surface and the air $T_s - T_a$, and inversely proportional to the aerodynamic resistance which itself is a function of the structure of the vegetation (principally the height). The term $\rho c_p$ is the volumetric heat capacity of air (J m$^{-3}$ K$^{-1}$), made up of the air density ($\rho$) and the specific heat of air at constant pressure $c_p$.

In the case of evaporation, $E$, a somewhat similar equation may be written, in which the numerator (the driving gradient) is the difference in water vapour pressure between the moist air of the leaves and the atmosphere:

$$E = \frac{\lambda \rho c_p (e_s(T_s) - e)}{\gamma (r_s + r_a^{\text{water}})} \qquad (2.6)$$

The quantity $e_s(T_s)$ is the saturated vapour pressure of water in air at temperature $T_s$, which is the leaf temperature, and $e$ is the vapour pressure of water in the atmosphere. The term $e_s(T_s) - e$ is simply an expression of the driving gradient for water to move from inside the leaves to the atmosphere. The term $\lambda \rho c_p$ is the volumetric heat capacity of air multiplied by the latent heat of vaporisation. The term $\gamma$ is known as the psychrometric constant, and $(r_s + r_a^{\text{water}})$ is the total resistance pathway for water to diffuse from inside the leaf through the stomata and through the aerodynamic resistance to the atmosphere.

These equations may be used in various ways to define the surface temperature of the canopy, the rate of evaporation, the heat loss to the atmosphere by convection, and the partitioning of energy between evaporation and convection. The general approach was pioneered by Monteith (1965) and leads to an expression for $E$ which is called the Penman–Monteith equation (Monteith & Unsworth 2008). It can be applied to estimate water use at the scale of leaves as well as the scale of plant canopies. The critical parameters $r_s$ and $r_a$ are required. The former is the total effect of the opening and closing of stomata throughout the canopy, and has sometimes been estimated from a knowledge of the stomatal conductance of leaves (leaf measurements have been technically possible since the 1970s but the main problem is to achieve adequate sampling of the canopy). In the past two decades micrometeorological measurements of fluxes over forests and grasslands have enabled these bulk resistances to be directly estimated for large areas (of order 1 km$^2$), thus overcoming some of the statistical sampling problems (e.g. Grace *et al.* 1995). Here, we show the values of $1/r_s$ for the conductance of rain forest and pasture, obtained at the same time in nearby sites (Figure 2.1).

One of the principal differences between forests and cropland/grassland relates to the aerodynamic roughness of the vegetation surface (the extent to which the surface exerts drag on the airflow). To specify the roughness $z_o$ of any surface in the aerodynamic sense, the height of the roughness elements and their spacing is required (for the relationship see Garratt 1977; Shaw & Pereira 1982), but for plant canopies a useful generalisation is $z_o = 0.1h$ where $h$ is the height of the canopy. This feature was emphasised especially in the early micrometeorological literature (Garratt & Hicks 1973; Geiger 1966) where it was noted that vertical profiles of mean wind speed are gentler over forests than they are over crops, and that forests are rougher than

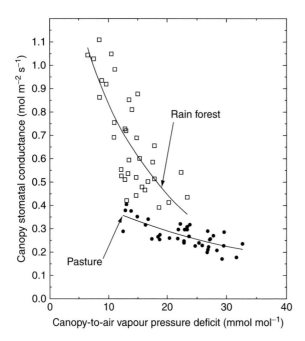

**Figure 2.1** Canopy conductances to water vapour, plotted against the dryness of the air above the canopy. A comparison of two vegetation types, rain forest and pasture, in the same area of Brazil and at the same time in the dry season (Grace *et al.* 1998).

grasslands. The roughness of forests was put to good use in Japan, where a programme of planting 'fog-preventing forests' was established in the 1950s: the rough surface of a forest is effective at absorbing mist particles carried in winds coming from the sea (Hori 1953). Likewise, it has long been known that free water (from rain, dew and mist) on forests will evaporate more rapidly than that on grass canopies (Stewart & Bruin 1985). Environmental scientists discovered that atmospheric pollution is deposited more readily on forest vegetation than on shorter vegetation nearby (Fowler, Cape & Unsworth 1989). Likewise, ecologists have found that short alpine vegetation near the tree line experiences much higher surface temperatures on sunny days than does nearby forested land, simply because it is aerodynamically smoother and heat is convected from dwarf vegetation at a slower rate (Grace *et al.* 1989a). The general phenomenon of vegetation roughness is parameterised by the related variables $z_o$ (roughness length) and $r_a$ (aerodynamic resistance). Forests have high $z_o$ and low $r_a$ when comparison is made with crops under similar meteorological conditions, and may be said to be more 'closely coupled' to the atmosphere (Jarvis & McNaughton 1986). It is beyond the scope of this chapter to develop the underlying theory of resistance analogues; instead the reader is referred to Shuttleworth (1989) and Monteith and Unsworth (2008).

The general behaviour of energy partitioning is illustrated here by the comparison of tropical rain forest and the tropical pasture which has been

**Table 2.2** *Canopy parameters useful in calculating energy partitioning of tropical rain forests and pastures.*

|  | Albedo | Canopy stomatal resistance $r_s$ (s m$^{-1}$) | Canopy aerodynamic resistance $r_a$ (s m$^{-1}$) |
| --- | --- | --- | --- |
| Tropical rain forest | 0.13 | 40 | 28 |
| Tropical pasture | 0.18 | 125 | 40 |

Data from Culf *et al.* (1996), Grace *et al.* (1995).
The resistances quoted refer to the dry season when soil moisture is low.

created to replace the forest in many regions. The calculations apply to the dry season in southwest Brazil. The resistances $r_s$ and $r_a$ have been obtained from several papers from the UK–Brazil collaborative project known as ABRACOS (Gash *et al.* 1996). Equations (2.1), (2.4), (2.5) and (2.6) were combined, using the parameter values from Table 2.2, and a function describing how the stomatal resistance/conductance changes with the leaf to air vapour pressure deficit, based on Figure 2.1, was employed. The energy balance was solved with relative humidity fixed at 80%. The result showed that forest transfers substantially more water to the atmosphere than the pasture does (Figure 2.2). In this case the canopy is dry, and the conductances represent the dry season. In the case of evaporation from a wet canopy the convection term becomes negative, meaning that the canopy surface temperature falls below ambient temperature (the canopy behaves like a wet bulb thermometer). In this case both the forest and the pasture are heat sinks, the forest more so than the pasture.

Although these calculations are simplistic, not allowing for the feedback from the atmosphere to the plant (for example, the stomata will certainly respond to the changes in the heat and water content of the air during the day), and not allowing for successional influences, they nevertheless provide some insight into the effect that the contrasting vegetation has on the atmosphere. Moreover, the result can be compared with some real measurements in the field, where all the terms in the energy balance may be measured using appropriate instrumentation. Here we discuss one example wherein the energy balance of tropical forest and pasture was measured simultaneously in Rondonia, southwest Brazil (Gash & Nobre 1997; Grace *et al.* 1998b). The incoming solar energy was nearly the same for the two sites, but the forest absorbed more energy because of its lower albedo: its net radiation load was 50–100 W m$^{-2}$ higher than that of the grassland (Figure 2.3). However, it dissipated energy more effectively by evapotranspiration, particularly in the middle of the day. The grassland, on the other hand, dissipated more than the forest as sensible heat, thus tending to warm the atmosphere. Essentially the same result was obtained with a larger dataset by Von Randow *et al.* (2004). At the same sites, independent year-round

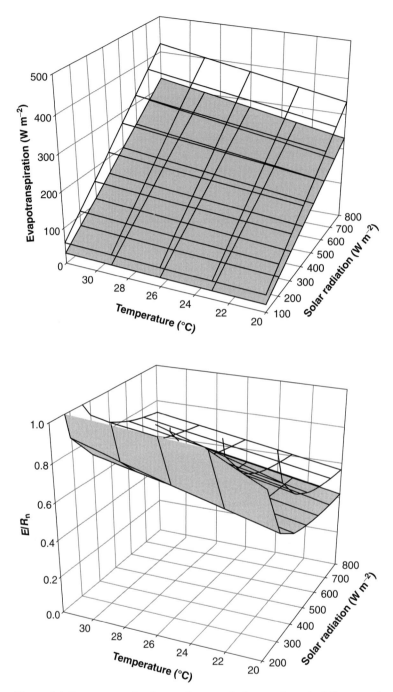

**Figure 2.2** Evapotranspiration and energy balance of tropical forest and pasture plotted against solar radiation and temperature whilst holding relative humidity constant at 80%. The grey surface is the calculation for grassland, and the transparent grid is the solution for forest. The canopy is assumed to be dry, so all the evapotranspiration is, in fact, transpiration. The lower figure shows the fraction of the net radiation $R_n$ which is dissipated by evapotranspiration $E$.

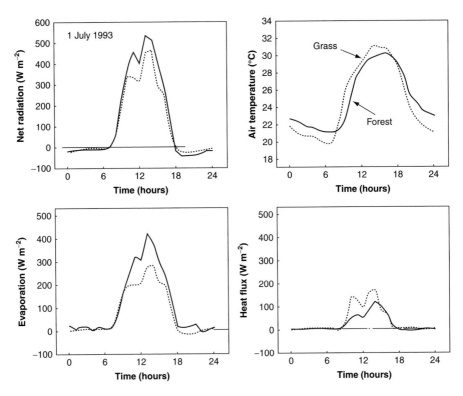

**Figure 2.3** Observational data on net radiation, air temperature, evaporation and heat flux from Rondonia, Brazil. Solid lines are from forest and broken lines from nearby pasture.

measurements of the water stored in the soil using a neutron probe showed that the forest does indeed use more water (Hodnett *et al.* 1996). The result is qualitatively similar to the model calculation.

This forest-to-pasture comparison in the humid tropics probably holds elsewhere, as the essential differences in the biophysical properties occur irrespective of whether the climate is tropical, temperate or boreal. Moreover, forests have a tendency to use more water and continue to use water for longer periods of the year, as a result of their deeper root system and their roughness. We should bear in mind that the dry tropics are important too. Here, land conversion from savanna woodland to pasture is proceeding rapidly, and rather similar changes in the energy balance have been demonstrated (San Jose *et al.* 2008).

## 2.3   The water and energy balance at a larger scale

We have seen how both forest and the grassland exchange water and heat with the atmosphere, and from the example given above, it may be expected that the change in the energy balance brought about by the widespread deforestation seen today in the Amazon (Malhi *et al.* 2008) would impact on the climate over spatial scales of hundreds and thousands of kilometres. The starting hypothesis would be that the planetary boundary layer receives more water when the land is forested, and thus more clouds are formed, producing more rain. Likewise, it may be considered that the grassland transfers more heat to the atmosphere, thus causing buoyancy and general growth of the convective boundary layer. Some approaches to testing this hypothesis have been observational. For example, Salati *et al.* (1979) showed a gradient in the $^{18}O$ content of water from east to west, implying the development of about six cycles of rain, evaporation, condensation and further rain, as the prevailing wind passes from the east coast towards the Andes, conveying water vapour from the Atlantic Ocean inland. Salati and Nobre (1991) supported this argument with a presentation of the mass balance (of water) for the Amazon Basin: $8.1 \times 10^{12} \, m^3$ of water per year enters the region in the air flow, and $5.5 \times 10^{12} \, m^3$ leaves the region as river flow. However, the recorded rainfall is much higher, $13.8 \times 10^{12} \, m^3$. It follows that the rain must be recycled. The rate of recycling will presumably depend on the land cover. When there is an extensive forest cover, the higher evapotranspiration may lead to higher recycling rates. Sparse forest, or pasture, may reduce the recycling rate, causing drought in the regions furthest from the ocean.

It is easy to see that the simple approach of solving the energy balance as outlined above is only a part of the story and certainly not adequate for an understanding of what happens at the larger scales. The cause-and-effect relationships which describe the system as a whole are mapped in Figure 2.4, taken from Strengers *et al.* (2010). We see in this conceptual model that deforestation immediately reduces the roughness, the evapotranspiration rate and the albedo. In the long term it also affects the $CO_2$ concentration of the air, currently contributing about 12% of the total anthropogenic flux of $CO_2$ to the atmosphere (van der Werf *et al.* 2009). For now, we will put aside the $CO_2$ effect, and focus on the more immediate effects of deforestation. The decrease in evaporation is expected to reduce the extent of convective clouds and rainfall, which in turn will reduce the albedo of the region (here, the albedo is defined with respect to the land surface as seen from space rather than the albedo as measured immediately over the land surface). This in turn, changes the incoming shortwave (solar) radiation, which affects the surface temperature and the evaporation rate. The figure captures most of the interactions, but some of them are immediate and others occur on longer time scales. For example, the soil moisture will not change immediately but over periods of weeks and months, giving rise to changes in stomatal conductance and therefore to evapotranspiration. Experimental observations suggest that soil moisture also impacts on the phenology of the plants and

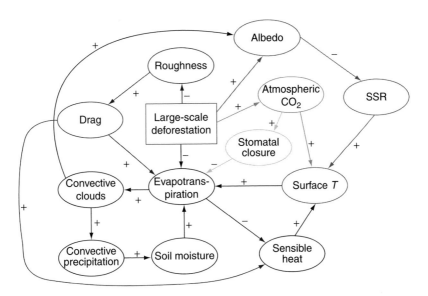

**Figure 2.4** Conceptual model showing interactions of processes in deforestation. Abbreviations: SSR, shortwave incoming radiation; *T*, air temperature. Redrawn from Strengers *et al.* (2010).

therefore affects the albedo (Culf *et al.* 1996). We thus have a complex set of interactions, all of which need to be simulated in any realistic model of deforestation. The models that define the physical conditions of large areas such as the Amazon rain forest do have severe limitations in this respect. The chief limitations are that the spatial (and to some extent temporal) scales over which they operate are relatively coarse. Cloud formation, for example, is a process that takes place on a small scale (tens of metres), and clouds are relatively small objects compared with the spatial resolution of models, which has usually been hundreds of kilometres. Even the patterns of defor-estation have fine grain. In Brazil the patterns are determined by the so-called 'herring-bone' fragmentation pattern set up when primary and secondary roads were made to service the newly created farming regions, for example in the State of Rondonia in southwest Brazil. These patterns are likely to set up atmospheric disturbances because of the edge effects imposed by abrupt changes in roughness and albedo, operating on scales of a few kilometres. Global circulation models do not capture this complexity, although presum-ably they will do so at some time in the future as computers continue to become more powerful. At present, one can approximate small-scale phenom-ena by a 'nested' approach whereby critical regions of the model are dealt with at much higher resolution than the model as a whole.

Nevertheless, global circulation models provide opportunities to carry out deforestation experiments by simply changing the land surface

**Table 2.3** *Amazonian deforestation experiments with large-scale climate models.*

| Authors | Model resolution (lat. × long.) | Change in rainfall (% of control) | Change in temperature (°C) |
|---|---|---|---|
| Shukla *et al.* 1990 | 1.8° × 2.8° | −21 | +2.5 |
| Lean & Warringlow 1989 | 2.5° × 3.75° | −7 | +3 |
| Costa & Foley 2000 | 4.5° × 4.75° | −12 | +1.4 |
| Voldoire & Royer 2004 | 2.8° × 2.8° | −8 | −0.01 |
| Medvigy *et al.* 2011 | 25 km | −2.4 | 0 to +4 |

parameterisation. In Table 2.3 we see the results of many such simulations, of which all but one point to a clear conclusion: total deforestation reduces the rainfall and increases the temperature. In some cases, researchers have attempted to investigate the more realistic scenario of partial deforestation. The result suggests that considerable deforestation is required before a 'tipping-point' is reached at which evaporation, rainfall and temperature are affected (Walker *et al.* 2009). These authors used a well-known high resolution model of the Amazon Basin (RAMS version 4.4) which covered the Amazon at a spatial resolution of 20 km. They used five annual simulations covering the period 1997–2001, and investigated scenarios whereby the Protected Areas became cropland. In the range of deforestation of 10–60% the results were highly variable according to the year, but the 100% deforestation gave nearly the same result for all years, suggesting an 8–19% decrease in precipitation in the dry season and some rather small changes in the duration of the dry season.

One of the most intriguing results from the use of global circulation models is that when deforestation is carried out on a continental scale, the climate of other parts of the world can be affected as a result of perturbations in the normal patterns of atmospheric circulation (Avissar & Werth 2005). The concept, known as 'teleconnections', provokes challenging questions about the environmental services that rain forests provide. For example, Morengo *et al.* (2004) provided evidence to suggest that removal of Amazonian rain forest will reduce the rainfall substantially over agricultural regions of South America (Argentina especially), thus depriving Argentina of export revenues and affecting the price of beef on the international markets. The question then arises, who should pay for the rain-making services that the forest provides? It might be cost-effective for consumer countries to pay Brazil to maintain the existing rainfall patterns. So perhaps the Europeans who buy Argentinian beef should foot the bill. However, there remains considerable uncertainty about the predictions of models, and so it is important to look for additional sources of information, particularly models at a smaller scale of

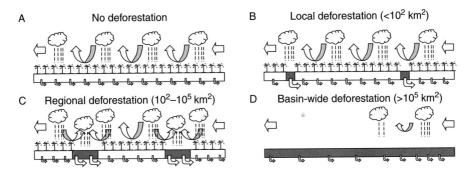

**Figure 2.5** The hydrological impacts of different degrees of deforestation (D'Almeida *et al.* 2007). The horizontal water vapour flux transfers moisture into the region from right to left, and in the pristine state (A) there are cycles of precipitation and evaporation, sustaining rainfall over a wide geographical range. Local deforestation (B) may not affect rainfall but will increase runoff and decrease evaporation. Regional deforestation strengthens convection and increases rainfall (C). Total deforestation causes a severe decline in evapotranspiration (D).

resolution, and satellite data on rainfall over deforested regions. These seem to refute the conclusions coming from global models (Negri *et al.* 2004; Wang *et al.* 2000). They show that at the smaller scale, deforestation may lead to an increase in rainfall. Negri *et al.* (2004) state that the increased surface heating over deforested regions creates a direct thermal circulation which increases the occurrence of shallow cumulus clouds. Analysis of 14 years of data from the Special Sensor Microwave Imager showed an increase in August rainfall in the deforested areas. But these observations do not necessarily disprove the model calculations, as they refer to a particular pattern and extent of partial deforestation, which is associated with multiple inhomogeneities. D'Almeida *et al.* (2007) have attempted to reconcile these observations. According to their scheme (Figure 2.5), a certain degree of patchy deforestation might sometimes accentuate vertical convection, draw in moist air from adjacent forest, and thus stimulate rainfall, whereas complete deforestation will simply cause drying and warming.

## 2.4   Carbon sequestration

All green plants have the capability of absorbing $CO_2$ from the atmosphere by photosynthesis, but herbaceous plants generally die and decompose in a short time period whereas trees endure and accumulate the absorbed carbon for decades and centuries in a chemical form which does not easily decay. Even when trees fall, much of the carbon remains for long periods initially as coarse woody debris, and later as recalcitrant organic matter in the soil. The stocks of carbon as biomass in forests are one or two orders of magnitude larger than in crops. Forests have up to 200 tonnes of carbon per hectare whereas crops seldom exceed 4 tonnes. Determination of the carbon stocks in forests and woodlands is time-consuming, as it involves considerable sampling and reliance on (usually) ill-defined regression equations which relate diameter of a tree to its biomass (IPCC 2000). Older data on carbon stocks, dating from the 1960s, have to some extent been superseded by recent data coming from sites where biomass determinations have been accompanied by direct measurements of carbon dioxide fluxes, using global networks which deploy standardised procedures. There are several hundred stations which report such data, and there have been recent compilations of the results (Luyssaert *et al.* 2007). Flux data from the tropics are still scarce, and in many cases we must rely on calculations based on sample plots.

In forests and woodland, the stocks of carbon as biomass vary between a few tens of tonnes per hectare and 200 tonnes per hectare in the well-developed forests of the temperate and tropical parts of the globe (Table 2.4). Of great significance is the fact that these forests are not merely stocks of carbon. They also are net absorbers of carbon as carbon dioxide, at rates that are useful in terms of absorption of anthropogenic $CO_2$ (Luyssaert *et al.* 2008). The evidence that mature forests (both tropical and temperate) are currently acting as carbon sinks comes from many sources (Grace *et al.* 1995; Lewis *et al.* 2009; Phillips *et al.* 1998). Earlier it was thought that only young forests were carbon sinks (Odum 1969), but using data from a very large number of sites it has been unequivocally shown that mature and old forests continue to act as carbon sinks (Figure 2.6). The reasons proposed to explain this sink effect are various. It is presumed that in a constant climate the forest would reach some steady-state value of biomass, as in Odum's 1969 model. However, now the climate in a broad sense has been changing rapidly, and trees are likely to benefit from both the increase in global $CO_2$ concentrations and also the

**Table 2.4** *Carbon stocks and fluxes.*

|  | Boreal | Temperate evergreen | Temperate deciduous | Tropical humid |
|---|---|---|---|---|
| Latitude (degrees) | $58 \pm 7$ | $44 \pm 8$ | $44 \pm 9$ | 14 |
| Aboveground biomass (tC ha$^{-1}$) | $57 \pm 37$ | $149 \pm 135$ | $108 \pm 56$ | $113 \pm 58$ |
| Belowground biomass (tC ha$^{-1}$) | $14 \pm 8$ | $4.6 \pm 4.6$ | $2.5 \pm 2.6$ | $29 \pm 22$ |
| NEP (tC ha$^{-1}$ yr$^{-1}$) | $1.34 \pm 0.14$ | $4.02 \pm 0.53$ | $3.10 \pm 0.29$ | $4.10 \pm 0.07$ |

Summarised from the database of Luyssaert *et al.* (2007).
Carbon fluxes are given as net ecosystem production, NEP. The numerical values are means with estimated standard deviations.

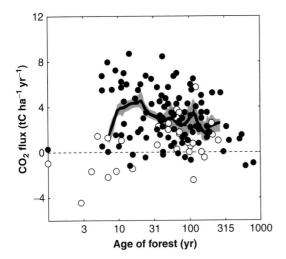

Figure 2.6 The uptake of carbon as $CO_2$ by coniferous (open symbols) and deciduous (closed symbols) forests of different age, based on a global dataset. Positive fluxes mean uptake of carbon dioxide. The thick line through the running mean indicates the trend, and the grey zone is the statistical uncertainty. Based on Luyssaert et al. (2008).

deposition of active forms of nitrogen (although the extent of N-fertilisation is often disputed and is unlikely to be large in the tropics; Magnani et al. 2007; Sutton et al. 2011). In boreal climates and at high elevation, forests also benefit from warming; for example, in many cases the elevational and altitudinal limit of trees has increased in the past 100 years or so (Harsch et al. 2009), meaning that new carbon sinks are being established in areas which hitherto were only weak sinks or neutral.

In the long term, the tendency of respiratory processes to respond more sharply to temperature than photosynthesis does has been thought by some researchers to mean that forests will decline as global warming occurs. When this process is modelled, the predictions of some models are quite striking, suggesting for example that the Amazon forest will undergo dieback as the climate warms and drought becomes more frequent. Moreover, this is a process that will be exacerbated as the atmosphere becomes progressively enriched with the accumulating respiratory $CO_2$, thus contributing to an intensification of the greenhouse effect (Cox et al. 2000). However, not all models agree with this prediction (Friedlingstein & Prentice 2010). Real ecosystems have homeostatic properties which are not always captured by models. For example, biological processes such as photosynthesis and respiration acclimate to changing temperatures. Acclimation is the process whereby the temperature response curve of any physiological process tends to shift as warming occurs. In the soil, acclimation may apply at the ecosystem level, especially in bacterial and fungal populations (Eliasson et al. 2008).

Most ecosystems have survived extremes in the past, and constituent species are, after all, the result of natural selection in a changing environment. Most ecosystems have a degree of resilience, notwithstanding short-term setbacks resulting, for example, from a single drought (Phillips *et al.* 2009). But anthropogenic influences are now being superimposed on climatological impacts. Davidson *et al.* (2012) emphasised the interaction between deforestation, fire and drought, a combination which may result in a profound regional transition in the Amazon basin, leading to a result not unlike that predicted in Cox's model (Cox *et al.* 2000) but for rather different reasons.

There has been a shift in attitudes to the question 'What are forests really for?' Forests and woodlands have traditionally been managed and conserved to provide wood products, but the emphasis is shifting towards management for conservation of species or carbon stocks. To a large extent, these two conservation aims are compatible: both imply maintenance of forest near to a 'wild' state, with little disturbance. In contrast, management for timber production implies frequent disturbance, even when management approaches the ideal of being 'sustainable'. These scenarios are discussed in many recent articles (e.g. Chazdon *et al.* 2008; Morison *et al.* 2012).

The widespread use of tropical plantations to produce timber or biofuels poses interesting research questions and an important ethical dilemma.

### 2.4.1   Fast-growing timber plantations

Such plantations deliver a high yield of timber fairly rapidly, typically in 10 years in the tropics and 50 years in the temperate zone. They may be formed from fast-growing exotic species, often eucalypts, or from domesticated native species, essentially clones which have been selected for fast growth and excellent form. Usually such plantations are established following removal of degraded secondary forest, and in this case the clearing and establishment may lead to carbon losses in the order of 50 tonnes of carbon per hectare. However, the supply of plantation-derived timber provided thenceforth removes the need to exploit old secondary or primary forest, and thus plantations may in the long run be a means of conserving carbon stocks and biodiversity. The global cover of plantations has nearly doubled in the past decade, and they currently make up 6.5% of the world's forest cover (37 million hectares) according to FAO statistics (FAO 2011).

### 2.4.2   Plantations of oil palm

Oil palm plantations in the tropics deliver around 5000 litres of oil per hectare per year, equivalent to about 4.5 tC ha$^{-1}$ (Royal Society 2008) and they currently cover 14.6 million hectares. The oil produced is substituted for fossil fuel in motor car (diesel) engines. Unfortunately, rain forests are often cleared to make way for these plantations, a process that leads to losses of about

100 tC ha$^{-1}$, and so a 'carbon debt' is created. As the plantation grows and yields oil the debt is repaid. However, a recent analysis suggests that production would have to proceed for many years to clear this debt. The payback times can exceed 100 years, according to recent estimates of cases where plantations are established at the expense of rain forests (Achten & Verchot 2011; House *et al.* 2012).

The ethical dilemma presented by these developments is that for the most part the extravagant emissions from people of the developed world are being dealt with by making profound land-use changes in the less-developed world, where carbon emissions per capita are still rather low.

## 2.5   Other processes

There are other contrasts between forests and pastures/crops which may turn out to be highly significant, but which at present are imperfectly understood and not incorporated into most models. Here we touch upon them, and indicate the direction in which they may influence the climate.

### 2.5.1   Non-$CO_2$ greenhouse gases

Nitrous oxide and methane are much more powerful greenhouse gases than carbon dioxide. The global warming potentials of the two gases, i.e. the warming they cause relative to $CO_2$, on a per mass basis and a 100-year time frame, are 298 and 25 respectively.

Nitrous oxide is produced to only a small extent by most natural ecosystems. The processes responsible for $N_2O$ production are microbial, involving the reduction of nitrate or nitrite to nitrogen gas (denitrification), and the conversion of ammonia to nitrite (nitrification). For a full description, the reader is referred to Baggs and Philippot (2010).

When forest is converted to pasture, the soil generally receives a substantial input of nitrogen-rich material in the form of necromass. This pulse of new organic material becomes the substrate for microbial populations, and thus the rate of $N_2O$ emission from the soil is stimulated (Conen & Neftel 2010; Melillo *et al.* 2001). Most tropical pastures do not receive much N-fertiliser, as the cost is prohibitive; Melillo found that after deforestation there was an initial 2-year burst of $N_2O$ but afterwards the rate fell below that of the forest. The highest emissions of all are generally observed in high N-input systems such as temperate-zone agriculture, when ammonium nitrate or manure from livestock is added to the soil as fertiliser. Rates of N-application are often very high, up to 200 kgN ha$^{-1}$ yr$^{-1}$. To estimate $N_2O$ emissions the IPCC methodology assumes (as a 'default', in the absence of any systematic measurements) that 1% of the applied N is converted to $N_2O$ (IPCC 2006), but this may be an under-estimate.

**Table 2.5** *Emissions from four contrasting tropical land-uses, representing increasing intensity of management.*

| Season | Gas | Native woodland | Open woodland savanna | Herbaceous savanna | Cultivated pasture |
|---|---|---|---|---|---|
| Dry season | $N_2O$ | 1.5 | 1.3 | 2.8 | 1.3 |
| | $CH_4$ | −0.15 | −0.35 | 0.3 | −0.06 |
| Wet season | $N_2O$ | 1.2 | 1.6 | 2.5 | 2.5 |
| | $CH_4$ | −0.03 | 0.65 | 0.2 | −0.05 |

Data from the Orinoco region of Venezuela (Castaldi *et al.* 2004).
Units for emissions are geometric means expressed as $mgCH_4\ m^{-2}\ d^{-1}$ for $CH_4$ and $mgN\ m^{-2}\ d^{-1}$ for $N_2O$.

In the tropics, N-emission from biofuel crops has become an important issue (Crutzen *et al.* 2008). The application of nitrogen fertiliser as urea to oil palm results in higher fluxes of $N_2O$, contributing to the high payback time of the greenhouse gas debt, referred to in Section 2.4.

There have been rather few comparative measurements of $N_2O$ emissions in the tropics, where fluxes from different land-uses in the same area have been compared (Castaldi *et al.* 2004; Melillo *et al.* 2001). Castaldi *et al.* (2004) presented a comparison of fluxes from soils in the Orinoco region of Venezuela (Table 2.5).

Methane ($CH_4$) is produced by methanogenic bacteria living in anaerobic conditions. The circumstances in which this occurs are: wetland soils and rice fields; the guts of animals, especially ruminants and termites; and decomposing waste materials in landfill sites and compost heaps. In poorly drained soils, the roots of trees may reach anaerobic regions of the soil, and some of the water drawn into the tree may hold methane in solution; according to Gauci *et al.* (2010) this methane frequently diffuses from the stem to the atmosphere by way of the lenticels. A few years ago it was shown that leaves under aerobic conditions produce methane in the presence of ultraviolet radiation. Global fluxes from this process may be rather small but far more research is needed to establish how these rates may vary between forests, grasslands and crops (for a review see McLeod & Keppler 2010). In addition to these direct sources, biomass burning emits methane as a result of incomplete combustion.

For both $N_2O$ and $CH_4$, the moisture conditions in the soil directly affect the flux (Castaldi *et al.* 2004; von Fischer & Hedin 2007). For example, well-drained forest soils are usually a weak sink for methane because of the bacterial consumption of methane by methanotrophic bacteria (von Fischer & Hedin 2007). As the removal of forest cover affects the hydrology of the landscape, we may suppose that the conversion of forest to pasture and croplands will affect the greenhouse gas balance quite independently of any management action such as the application of fertiliser or manure, as deforestation implies a higher water table and therefore more anaerobic conditions.

Some of the highest rates of methane production are from rice paddies (Conen, Smith & Yagi 2010). As the area of cultivation of rice has been increasing by about 1% per year this has become an important issue. Rates are typically around $200 \ \mathrm{mg \ m^{-2} \ d^{-1}}$, much higher than those found in natural or semi-natural ecosystems in the tropics (Table 2.5), and considerably higher than observations on grazing ruminants in the temperate zone (Dengel *et al.* 2011), or natural wetland ecosystems in Europe (Hendriks *et al.* 2009). The few measurements of methane and nitrous oxide fluxes from forests suggest the rates are very low by comparison to wetlands and agricultural ecosystems (Morison *et al.* 2012; Querino *et al.* 2011; Sakabe *et al.* 2012).

In developed countries the agricultural sector is often a major source of greenhouse gas emissions, producing methane from ruminant livestock and nitrous oxide from the application of nitrogen fertiliser to the soil. In Europe, for example, the biological sink created by forests and plantations is considerable, but it is nullified by the emissions from agriculture (Schulze *et al.* 2009).

### 2.5.2   Other climatically important gases

Plants emit a wide range of volatile organic compounds, known as VOCs, of which isoprene ($C_5H_8$) is quantitatively the most important, sometimes amounting to 1 or 2% of the uptake of $CO_2$ by photosynthesis (Kesselmeier *et al.* 2002; Lerdau & Keller 1997; Pegoraro *et al.* 2006). Isoprene has been extensively studied, as its main sink is the reaction with the hydroxyl radical (OH) to form carbon dioxide; it may thus reduce the concentration of OH and so reduce the extent of the destruction of other organic compounds which are normally oxidised by OH, most notably methane (Pugh *et al.* 2011).

Not all species of plants emit isoprene; in one survey of the Brazilian Amazon it was found that 38% of species are emitters (Harley *et al.* 2004). The provisional ranking of emissions is: broadleaved trees and shrubs > fine-leaved trees > grasses > crops. Guenther *et al.* (2006) describe a model to estimate global emissions of isoprene. We may conclude from this that the conversion of tropical forest to pasture probably reduces the quantity of isoprene emitted to the atmosphere, which in turn has implications for the oxidation of methane.

### 2.5.3   Aerosols

One of the most important discoveries in the past decade has been that forests produce fine particles (aerosols) that may act as cloud condensation nuclei (for a review of the earlier literature see Meir, Cox & Grace 2006). Now it has been shown that this is a widespread phenomenon, and that aerosols are formed over rain forests (Claeys *et al.* 2004), woodland savanna in Africa (Vakkari *et al.* 2011) and coniferous forests in the boreal region (Virkkula *et al.* 2011). There may be more than one route to the formation of these particles. It has been shown that particles result from photo-oxidation of isoprene by the OH radical in the presence of sulphate (King *et al.* 2010). The importance of these particles is that they may form cloud condensation nuclei, and hence encourage clouds and precipitation. A secondary importance is that they scatter solar radiation, thus increasing the ratio of diffuse radiation to global radiation, thereby increasing rates of photosynthesis over wide regions (Mercado *et al.* 2009).

The production of biogenic particles may turn out to be one of the most important interactions between vegetation and the atmosphere. Furthermore, it will possibly be shown that forests and woodlands are more active in this regard than grasslands and crops, as they more often produce terpenes (including isoprene). However, it is at present too early to draw this conclusion; more studies are required.

## 2.6  Conclusions

The energy balance of a forested surface is significantly different from that of grasslands and crops, and so when land conversion occurs there will usually be a change in the water use, and in the water and sensible heat transfer to the atmosphere. The forest-to-pasture conversion will usually produce a significant warming and drying, which on a large scale may propagate to some extent over an entire region and even beyond through teleconnections. However, the quantitative response is hard to predict in the case of a mosaic of land surface types, as rather complex convective processes may occur at boundaries. Forests tend to produce volatile materials which cause cloud condensation nuclei and which may increase the rainfall, but this is still an intense area of research. Forests do store carbon, and even old forests accumulate carbon although with climate warming this may change. Intensive agricultural land is generally a source of greenhouse gases, and the development of climate-friendly agriculture remains an important challenge.

## References

Achten, W. M. J. & Verchot, L. V. (2011) Implications of biodiesel-induced land-use changes for $CO_2$ emissions: case studies in tropical America, Africa, and Southeast Asia. *Ecology and Society*, **16**, 14. doi.org/10.5751/ES-04403−160414

Avissar, R. & Werth, D. (2005) Global hydroclimatological teleconnections resulting from tropical deforestation. *Journal of Hydrometeorology*, **6**, 134−145.

Baggs, E. & Philippot, L. (2010) Microbial terrestrial pathways to nitrous oxide. In

*Nitrous Oxide and Climate Change* (ed. K. Smith), pp. 4–35. London: Earthscan.

Barlage, M., Zeng, X., Wei, H. & Mitchell, K. E. (2005) A global maximum albedo dataset of snow-covered land based on MODIS observations. *Geophysical Research Letters*, **32**, doi:10.1029/2005GL022881.

Betts, A. K. & Ball, J. H. (1997) Albedo over the boreal forest. *Journal of Geophysical Research*, **102**, 28901–28909.

Brown, T. (1997) Clearances and clearings: deforestation in Mesolithic/Neolithic Britain. *Oxford Journal of Archaeology*, **16**, 133–146.

Castaldi, S., de Pascale, R. A., Grace, J. *et al.* (2004) Nitrous oxide and methane fluxes from soils of the Orinoco savanna under different land uses. *Global Change Biology*, **10**, 1947–1960.

Charney, J., Stone, P. H. & Quirk, W. J. (1975) Drought in the Sahara: a biogeochemical feedback mechanism. *Science*, **187**, 434–435.

Chazdon, R. L. (2008) Beyond deforestation: restoring forests and ecosystems services on degraded lands. *Science*, **320**, 1458–1460.

Claeys, M., Graham, B., Vas, G. *et al.* (2004). Formation of secondary organic aerosols through photooxidation of isoprene. *Science*, **303**, 1173–1176.

Conen, F. & Neftel, A. (2010) Nitrous oxide emissions from land-use and land-management options in nitrous oxide and climate change. In *Nitrous Oxide and Climate Change* (ed. K. Smith), pp. 143–161. London: Earthscan.

Conen, F., Smith, K. A. & Yagi, K. (2010) Rice cultivation. In *Methane and Climate Change* (eds. D. Reay, P. Smith & A. Van Amstel), pp. 115–135. London: Earthscan.

Costa, M. H. & Foley, J. A. (2000) Combined effects of deforestation and doubled atmospheric $CO_2$ concentrations on the climate of Amazonia. *Journal of Climate*, **13**, 18–34.

Cox, P. M., Betts, R. A., Jones, C. D. *et al.* (2000) Acceleration of global warming due to carbon-cycle feedbacks in a coupled climate model. *Nature*, **408**, 184–187.

Crutzen, P. J., Mosier, A. R., Smith, K. A. & Winiwarter, W. (2008) $N_2O$ release from agro-biofuel negates global warming reduction by replacing fossil fuels. *Atmospheric Chemistry and Physics*, **8**, 389–395.

Culf, A. D., Esteves, J. L., Marques Filho, A. de O. & de Rocha, H. R. (1996) Radiation, temperature and humidity over forest and pasture in Amazonia. In *Amazonian Deforestation and Climate* (eds. J. H. C. Gash, C. A. Nobre, J. M. Roberts & R. L. Victoria), pp. 175–192. Chichester: Wiley.

D'Almeida, C., Vörösmarty, C. J., Hurtt, G. C. *et al.* (2007). The effects of deforestation on the hydrological cycle in Amazonia: a review on scale and resolution. *International Journal of Climatology*, **27**, 633–647.

Davidson, E. A., de Araujo, A. C., Artaxo, P. *et al.* (2012) The Amazon basin in transition. *Nature*, **481**, 321–328.

Dengel, S., Levy, P. E., Grace, J., Jones, S. K. & Skiba, U. M. (2011) Methane emissions from sheep pasture, measured with an open-path eddy covariance system. *Global Change Biology*, **17**, 3524–3533.

Eliasson, P. E., McMurtrie, R. E., Pepper, D. A. *et al.* (2005) The response of heterotrophic $CO_2$ flux to soil warming. *Global Change Biology*, **11**, 168–181.

FAO (2011) *The State of the World's Forests*. Rome: FAO.

Foley, J. A., Asner, G. P., Costa, M. H. *et al.* (2007) Amazonia revealed: forest degradation and loss of ecosystem goods and services in the Amazon Basin. *Frontiers in Ecology and Environment*, **5**, 25–32.

Fowler, D., Cape, J. N. & Unsworth, M. H. (1989) Deposition of atmospheric pollutants on forests. *Philosophical Transactions of the Royal Society B*, **324**, 247–265.

Friedlingstein, P. & Prentice, I. C. (2010) Carbon-climate feedbacks: a review of model and observation based estimates. *Current Opinion in Environmental Sustainability*, **2**, 251–257.

Garratt, J. R. (1977) Aerodynamic roughness and mean monthly surface stress over Australia. *CSIRO, Division of Atmospheric Physics Technical Paper*, **29**, 1–19.

Garratt, J. R. & Hicks, B. B. (1973) Momentum, heat and water-vapor transfer to and from natural and artificial surfaces. *Quarterly Journal of the Royal Meteorological Society*, **99**, 680–687.

Gash, J. H. C. & Nobre, C. A. (1997) Climatic effects of Amazonian deforestation: some results from ABRACOS. *Bulletin of the American Meteorological Society*, **78**, 823–830.

Gash, J. H. C., Nobre, C. A., Roberts, J. M. & Victoria, R. L. (1996) *Amazonian Deforestation and Climate*. Chicester: Wiley.

Gauci, V., Gowing, D. J. G., Hornibrook, E. R. C. et al. (2010) Woody stem methane emission in mature wetland alder trees. *Atmospheric Environment*, **44**, 2157–2160.

Geiger, R. (1966) *The Climate near the Ground*. Cambridge, MA: Harvard University Press.

Grace, J., Allen, S. & Wilson, C. (1989a) Climate and meristem temperatures of plant communities near the tree-line. *Oecologia*, **79**, 198–204.

Grace, J., Lloyd, J. Miranda, A. C., Miranda, H. & Gash, J.H.C. (1998b) Fluxes of carbon dioxide and water vapour over a C4 pasture in south-western Amazonia (Brazil). *Australian Journal of Plant Physiology*, **25**, 519–530.

Grace, J., Lloyd, J., McIntyre, J. et al. (1995). Fluxes of carbon dioxide and water vapour over an undisturbed tropical rainforest in south-west Amazonia. *Global Change Biology*, **1**, 1–12.

Grace, J., Lloyd, J., Miranda, A. C., Miranda, H. & Gash, J.H.C. (1998b). Fluxes of carbon dioxide and water vapor over a C4 pasture in south-western Amazonia (Brazil). *Australian Journal of Plant Physiology* **25**, 519–530.

Guenther, A., Karl, T., Harley, P. et al. (2006) Estimates of global terrestrial isoprene emissions using MEGAN (Model of Emissions of Gases and Aerosols from Nature). *Atmospheric Chemistry and Physics*, **6**, 3181–3210.

Harley, P., Vasconcellos, P., Vierling, L. et al. (2004) Variation in potential for isoprene emissions among Neotropical forest sites. *Global Change Biology*, **10**, 630–650.

Harsch, M. A., Hulme, P. E., McGlone, M. S., Duncan, R. P. (2009). Are treelines advancing? A global meta-analysis of treeline response to climate warming. *Ecology Letters*, **12**, 1040–1049.

Hendriks, D. M. D., van Huissteden, J. & Dolman, A. J. (2009) Multi-technique assessment of spatial and temporal variability of methane fluxes in a peat meadow. *Agricultural & Forest Meteorology*, **150**, 757–774.

Hodnett, M. G., Tomasella, J., Marques Filho, de O. & Oyama, M. D. (1996) Deep soil water uptake by forests and pasture in central Amazonia: predictions from long-term daily rainfall data using a simple water balance model. In *Amazonian Deforestation and Climate* (eds. J. H. C. Gash, C. A. Nobre, J. M. Roberts & R. L. Victoria), pp. 79–100. Chichester: Wiley.

Hori, T. (1953) *Studies on Fogs in Relation to Fog Preventing Forests*. Sapporo, Japan: Tanne Trading Company.

House, J. I., Bellarby, J., Böttcher, H. et al. (2012) The role of the land biosphere in climate change mitigation. In *Understanding the Earth System* (eds. S. E. Cornell, C. Prentice, J. I. House & C. J. Downy), pp. 202–244. Cambridge: Cambridge University Press.

IPCC (2000) *Land Use, Land-Use Change and Forestry*. Cambridge: Cambridge University Press.

IPCC (2006) $N_2O$ emissions from managed soils and $CO_2$ emissions from lime and urea applications. In *IPCC Guidelines for National Greenhouse Gas Inventories*, Chapter 11. Cambridge: Cambridge University Press.

Jarvis, P. G. & McNaughton, K. G. (1986) Stomatal control of transpiration – scaling up from leaf to region. *Advances in Ecological Research*, **15**, 1–49.

Kesselmeier, J., Ciccioli, P., Kuhn, U. et al. (2002) Volatile organic compound emissions in relation to plant carbon fixation and the terrestrial carbon budget. *Global Biogeochemical Cycles*, **16**, doi:10.1029/2001GB001813.

King, S. M., Rosenoern, T., Shilling, J. E. et al. (2010) Cloud droplet activation of mixed organic-sulfate particles produced by the photo-oxidation of isoprene. *Atmospheric Chemistry and Physics*, **10**, 3953–3964.

Lean. J. & Warringlow, D. A. (1989) Climatic impact of Amazonian deforestation. *Nature*, **342**, 311–413.

Lerdau, M. & Keller, M. (1997) Controls on isoprene emission from trees in a subtropical dry forest. *Plant Cell & Environment*, **20**, 659–578.

Lewis, S. L., Lopez-Gonzalez, G., Sonke, B. et al. (2009) Increasing carbon storage in intact African tropical forests. *Nature*, **457**, 1003–1005.

Luyssaert, S., Inglima, I., Jung, M. et al. (2007) $CO_2$ balance of boreal, temperate, and tropical forests derived from a global database. *Global Change Biology*, **13**, 2509–2537.

Luyssaert, S., Schulze, E. D., Borner, A. et al. (2008) Old-growth forests as global carbon sinks. *Nature*, **455**, 213–215.

Magnani, F., Mencuccini, M., Borghetti, M. et al. (2007) The human footprint in the carbon cycle of temperate and boreal forests. *Nature*, **447**, 848–850.

Malhi, Y., Roberts, J. T., Betts, R. A. et al. (2008) Climate change, deforestation, and the fate of the Amazon. *Science*, **319**, 169–172.

McLeod, A. & Keppler, F. (2010) Vegetation. In *Methane and Climate Change* (eds. D. Reay, P. Smith & A. Van Amstel), pp. 74–96. London: Earthscan.

Medvigy, D., Walko, R. L. & Avissar, R. (2011) Effects of deforestation on spatiotemporal distributions of precipitation in South America. *Journal of Climate*, **24**, 2147–2163.

Meir, P., Cox, P. & Grace, J. (2006) The influence of terrestrial ecosystems on climate. *Trends in Ecology & Evolution*, **21**, 254–260.

Melillo, J. M., Steudler, P. A., Feigl, B. J. et al. (2001) Nitrous oxide emissions from forests and pastures of various ages in the Brazilian Amazon. *Journal of Geophysical Research*, **106**, 34179–34188.

Mercado, L. M., Bellouni, N., Sitch, S. et al. (2009) Impact of changes in diffuse radiation on the global land carbon sink. *Nature*, **458**, 1014–1017.

Monteith, J. L. (1965) Evaporation and environment. In *The State and Movement of Water in Living Organisms, 19th Symposium of the Society for Experimental Biology*, pp. 205–233. Cambridge: Cambridge University Press.

Monteith, J. L. & Moss, C. J. (1977) Climate and the efficiency of crop production in Britain. *Philosophical Transactions of the Royal Society of London B*, **281**, 277–294.

Monteith, J. L. & Unsworth, M. H. (2008) *Principles of Environmental Physics*. Elsevier and Academic Press.

Morengo, W. R., Saulo, C. & Nicolini, M. (2004) Climatology of the low-level jet east of the Andes as derived from the NCEP–NCAR reanalyses: Characteristics and temporal variability. *Journal of Climate*, **17**, 2261–2280.

Morison, J., Matthews, R., Miller, G. et al. (2012) *Understanding the Carbon and Greenhouse Gas Balance of Forests in Britain*. Edinburgh: Forestry Commission.

Negri, A. J., Adler, R. F., Xu, L. & Surratt, J. (2004) The impact of Amazonian deforestation on dry season rainfall. *Journal of Climate*, **17**, 1306–1319.

Odum, E. P. (1969) The strategy of ecosystem development. *Science*, **164**, 262–270.

Pegoraro, E., Rey, A., Abrell, L., Vanharen, J. & Guangui, Lin (2006). Drought effect on isoprene production and consumption in Biosphere 2 tropical forest. *Global Change Biology*, **12**, 456–469.

Phillips, O. L., Aragao, L. E. O. C., Lewis, S. L. et al. (2009) Drought sensitivity of the Amazon rainforest. *Science*, **323**, 1344–1347.

Phillips, O. L., Malhi, Y., Higuchi, N. et al. (1998) Changes in the carbon balance of tropical forests: Evidence from long-term plots. *Science*, **282**, 439–442.

Pugh, T. A. M., MacKenzie, A. R., Langford, B. et al. (2011) The influence of small-scale variations in isoprene concentration on atmospheric chemistry over a tropical forest. *Atmospheric Chemistry and Physics*, **11**, 4121–4134.

Querino, C. A. S., Smeets, C. J. P. P., Vigano, I. et al. (2011) Methane flux, vertical gradient and mixing ratio measurements in a tropical forest. *Atmospheric Chemistry and Physics*, **1**, 7943–7953.

Ross, J. (1975) Radiative transfer in plant communities. In *Vegetation and the Atmosphere Vol. 1* (ed. J. L. Monteith), pp. 16–55. London: Academic Press.

Royal Society (2008) *Sustainable Biofuels: Prospects and Challenges*. London: Royal Society.

Sakabe, A., Hamotani, K., Kosugi, Y. *et al.* (2012) Measurement of methane flux over an evergreen coniferous forest canopy using relaxed eddy accumulation system with tuneable diode laser spectroscopy detection. *Theoretical and Applied Climatology*, **109**, 39–49.

Salati, E. & Nobre, C. A. (1991) Possible climatic impacts of tropical deforestation. *Climatic Change*, **19**, 177–196.

Salati, E., Dall'Olio, A., Matsui, E. & Gat, J. (1979) Recycling of water in the Amazon Basin: An isotopic study. *Water Resources Research*, **15**, 1250–1258.

San Jose, J., Montes, R., Grace, J., Nikonova, N. & Osio, A. (2008) Land-use changes alter radiative energy and water vapor fluxes of a tall-grass Andropogon field and a savanna–woodland continuum in the Orinoco lowlands. *Tree Physiology*, **28**, 425–435.

Schulze, E. D., Luyssaert, S., Ciais, P. *et al.* (2009) Importance of methane and nitrous oxide for Europe's terrestrial greenhouse-gas balance. *Nature Geoscience*, **2**, 842–850.

Shaw, R. H. & Pereira, A. R. (1982) Aerodynamic roughness of a plant canopy: a numerical experiment. *Agricultural Meteorology*, **26**, 51–65.

Shukla, J., Nobre, C. A. & Sellers, P. (1990) Amazonia deforestation and climate change. *Science*, **247**, 1322–1325.

Shuttleworth, W. J. (1989) Micrometeorology of temperate and tropical forest. *Philosophical Transactions of the Royal Society B*, **324**, 299–334.

Stanhill, G. (1970) Some results of helicopter measurements of albedo of different land surfaces. *Solar Energy*, **11**, 59–66.

Stanhill, G. (1981) The size and significance of differences in the radiation balance of plant and plant communities. In *Plants and their Atmospheric Environment* (eds. J. Grace, E. D. Ford, P. G. Jarvis), pp. 57–73. Oxford: Blackwell Scientific Publications.

Stewart, J. B. & de Bruin, H. A. R. (1985) Preliminary study of dependence of surface conductance of Thetford forest on environmental conditions. In *The Forest Atmosphere Interaction* (eds. B. A. Hutchinson & B. B. Hicks), pp. 91–104. Dordrecht: Reidel.

Strengers, B. J., Müller, C., Schaeffer, M. *et al.* (2010) Assessing 20th century climate-vegetation feedbacks of land-use change and natural vegetation dynamics in a fully coupled vegetation-climate model. *International Journal of Climatology*, **30**, 2055–2065.

Sutton, M. A., Howard, C. M. & Erisman, J. W. (2011) *The European Nitrogen Assessment: Sources, Effects and Policy Perspectives*. Cambridge: Cambridge University Press.

Vakkari, A., Laakso, H. & Kulmala, M. *et al.* (2011) New particle formation events in semi-clean South African savannah. *Atmospheric Chemistry and Physics*, **11**, 3333–3346.

Van der Werf, G. R., Morton, D. C., DeFries, R. S. *et al.* (2009) $CO_2$ emissions from forest loss. *Nature Geoscience*, **2**, 737–738.

Virkkula, A., Backman, J, Aalto, P. P. *et al.* (2011) Seasonal cycle, size dependencies, and source analyses of aerosol optical properties at the SMEAR II measurement station in Hyytiälä, Finland. *Atmospheric Chemistry and Physics*, **11**, 4445–4468.

Voldoire, A. & Royer, J. F. (2004) Tropical deforestation and climate variability. *Climate Dynamics*, **22**, 857–874.

von Fischer, J. C. & Hedin, L. O. (2007) Controls on soil methane fluxes: tests of biophysical mechanisms using stable isotopes. *Global Biogeochemical Cycles*, **21**, doi:10.1029/2006GB002687.

von Randow, C., Manzi, A. O., Kruijt, B. *et al.* (2004) Comparative measurements and seasonal variations in energy and carbon exchange over forest and pasture in South West Amazonia. *Theoretical and Applied Climatology*, **78**, 5–26.

Walker, R., Moore, N. J., Arima, E. *et al.*
(2009) Protecting the Amazon with
protected areas. *Proceedings of the
National Academy of Sciences USA*, **106**,
10582–10586.

Wang, J., Bras, R. L. & Eltahir, E. A. B. (2000) The
impact of observed deforestation on the
mesoscale distribution of rainfall and
clouds in Amazonia. *Journal of
Hydrometeorology*, **1**, 267–286.

# CHAPTER THREE

# Global change and Mediterranean forests: current impacts and potential responses

FERNANDO VALLADARES, RAQUEL BENAVIDES,
SONIA G. RABASA, MARIO DÍAZ

*Department of Biogeography and Global Change,
National Museum of Natural Sciences, Madrid*

JULI G. PAUSAS

*CIDE, CSIC, Valencia*

SUSANA PAULA

*Instituto de Ciencias Ambientales y Evolutivas, Universidade Austral de Chile*

and

WILLIAM D. SIMONSON

*Forest Ecology and Conservation Group,
Department of Plant Sciences, University of Cambridge*

## 3.1 Global change exacerbating Mediterranean stresses

Mediterranean forests have always had to cope with challenging environmental conditions that change across different temporal and spatial scales. However, the rapidity of current environmental change, driven by greater-than-ever human influences on natural processes, is unprecedented and has triggered renewed research endeavour into the impacts on Mediterranean ecosystems (Valladares 2008). The climate of Mediterranean areas is expected to become drier and warmer, with decreasing water availability for plants and increasing evapotranspiration (IPCC 2007). This will result in more acute physiological stress, increased importance of species-specific tolerances, plasticity and thresholds, phenological change and recruitment effects (Montserrat-Martín *et al.* 2009; Morin *et al.* 2010; Peñuelas *et al.* 2004). Several studies have demonstrated how the conditions currently experienced by seedlings and saplings are quite different to those when current adults recruited (Lloret & Siscart 1995; Montoya 1995). The anticipated impacts of such changes have led to a renewed interest in classic ecophysiological research into drought stress and tolerance (Wikelskia & Cooke 2006), as well as population-level studies on phenotypic plasticity and the evolution of tolerance in certain key tree species, such as Holm (*Quercus ilex*) and cork oaks (*Q. suber*) (Gimeno *et al.* 2009; Ramírez-Valiente *et al.* 2010).

*Forests and Global Change*, ed. David A. Coomes, David F. R. P. Burslem and William D. Simonson.
Published by Cambridge University Press. © British Ecological Society 2014.

Niche modelling techniques are used to forecast changes to species distributions under future climate scenarios, and the results predict abrupt shifts of dominant tree species in the next decades. Forest diebacks, species migration and displacement, and altitudinal shifts of forest types have already been recorded (Peñuelas & Boada 2003; Allen *et al.* 2010). For example, in northeast Spain *Fagus sylvatica* and *Calluna vulgaris* are being replaced by *Quercus ilex* at high elevations (Peñuelas & Boada 2003).

However, the expected changes do not always match with observations: vegetation stability after extreme climatic events points to a suite of mechanisms – beyond individual physiological stress tolerance – that we are only beginning to understand (Lloret *et al.* 2012). A forest community is characterised by a large number of mutualistic and antagonistic ecological interactions, and the net result of changes to these will determine eventual outcomes of environmental change on forest distribution and dynamics.

In this chapter we review a range of concepts and processes relevant for Mediterranean forests coping with accelerated environmental change. We take the Mediterranean Basin as our focus, but draw in examples and lessons from other Mediterranean climate zones. Rather than concentrating on climate *per se*, we discuss two inter-related drivers of change which are also important in Mediterranean systems: land-use and fire. We then explore the significance of the complex network of biotic interactions for interpreting how forests will respond to global change. We conclude that, whilst in the short term these species interactions will result in significantly less change than could be expected, the simultaneous action of climate, land-use, fire and other global change drivers may lead to threshold situations over which mechanisms underlying this resilience of Mediterranean forests could collapse. Finally, we consider how forest management philosophy and strategy itself needs to adapt to global change, through measures anticipating the most likely impacts to these ecosystems, but also the high degree of uncertainty in how they will play out.

## 3.2   Land-use change
### 3.2.1   Land-use trends in the Mediterranean Basin
Land-use change is one of the most severe drivers of biodiversity loss (Sala *et al.* 2000), and its impact is especially relevant in Mediterranean ecosystems where the richness of the biota has been linked throughout history to traditional land-use practices (Blondel *et al.* 2010). Mediterranean forests have long been subjected to intense exploitation, which is rapidly changing because of urbanisation, industrialisation and pressure from tourism (Valladares 2004). Understanding the response of species to land-use changes has become a major concern in recent ecological research. Some of the most common changes in land-use in the Mediterranean Basin include:

- *Conversion of natural vegetation into cultivated and urban areas.* Native habitat removal to expand agricultural land and pastures has been the most common land-use conversion during the last centuries. In particular, Mediterranean forests have widely disappeared because of exploitation and substitution by agricultural landscapes and, more recently, by urban development around cities and in coastal areas (Blondel *et al.* 2010). These changes in land-use cause irreversible degradation of soil and vegetation, contributing to processes of desertification which will probably worsen because of climate change.
- *Land abandonment.* The abandonment of traditional practices because of socio-economic changes and rural exodus is an ongoing process occurring throughout Europe, and especially in Mediterranean areas with generally low soil nutrient levels. Negative impacts of land abandonment on ecosystems include loss of biodiversity and vulnerable species, altered ecosystem services, and increased size and intensity of wildfires (see Section 3.3 below). Alternatively, land abandonment can lead to an increase in species diversity, favouring the natural regeneration of woodland (Gimeno 2011; Pausas *et al.* 2006; Ramírez & Díaz 2008).
- *Differences in management intensity within the same land-use.* Differences in management intensity have typically not been considered in recent research, because of the lack of knowledge on possible interactions with climate change. For instance, some studies have shown changes in diversity and richness of species due to different management regimes for livestock grazing (Celaya *et al.* 2010; Jauregui *et al.* 2008).

Of all the processes related to land-use changes, habitat fragmentation has been recognised as one of the most significant impacts on biodiversity in Europe (Fahrig 2003). Its relevance for Mediterranean ecosystems is being recognised in a growing number of studies (Gimeno *et al.* 2012a and references therein). We discuss this process in more detail below.

### 3.2.2   Fragmentation, an increasingly important driver in Mediterranean ecosystems

Mediterranean ecosystems have historically suffered from strong human impacts which have led to significant levels of fragmentation. Effects of habitat fragmentation on the populations of forest organisms are widely known. It results in habitats of reduced area, increased isolation and altered physical environment, with important implications for population genetics and species ecology. In small habitat fragments there is an increased influence of genetic drift, homozygosity, accumulation of deleterious mutations and inbreeding within populations (Ellstrand & Elam 1993; Young, Boyle & Brown 1996), processes that reduce the performance of populations. The probability of extinction in small fragments also increases as a consequence of the strengthened effects of stochastic demographic processes on small populations (Lande 1988). Moreover, isolation between fragments favours the increase of genetic differentiation between populations and outbreeding depression, as well as preventing demographic rescue by immigration from individuals coming from adjacent fragments (Templeton 1986; Fischer & Matthies 1997). Evidence of the effects of fragmentation in Mediterranean ecosystems is available for a range of different organisms including birds (e.g. Santos, Tellería & Carbonell 2002), butterflies (e.g. Rabasa, Gutiérrez & Escudero 2007; Stefanescu, Herrando & Páramo 2004) and plants (e.g. García & Chacoff 2007; Jump & Peñuelas 2005). In addition to effects on individual species, habitat fragmentation can also lead to the disruption of biotic interactions such as pollination, seed dispersal and herbivory (see González-Varo, Arroyo & Aparicio 2009; Santos & Tellería 1994). Pollination services may be reduced in small and isolated populations owing to decreased attractiveness and increased distances among fragments (e.g. Cunningham 2000; Duncan *et al.* 2004). Larger fragments attract more predators than smaller ones, but herbivores with limited mobility may have problems in reaching more isolated fragments (Duncan *et al.* 2004; Kéry, Matthies & Fischer 2001). The importance of biotic interactions in the context of global change is explored further in Section 3.4.

The two main options for species coping with climate change (acclimate/adapt or migrate to more favourable areas) are affected by fragmentation. The ability of populations to adapt to changing conditions is decreased because of reduced genetic variation, while dispersal or movement ('range shift') to habitats with optimal conditions is also compromised. Fragmented populations are therefore expected to be more vulnerable to environmental drivers such as climate change than if they were not fragmented (Opdam & Wascher 2004). *Fagus sylvatica* populations in northeast Spain provide an example of a species meeting such challenges (Jump & Peñuelas 2005, 2006; Figure 3.1). In this case, the fragmentation of these forests, which took place several centuries ago, has led to a reduced genetic diversity. The recent rapid climate change can exacerbate the impact of human activities on the dynamics of *F. sylvatica* forests in these fragmented landscapes because of their reduced capacity for adaptation. Habitat fragmentation is also expected to decrease the ability to resist and recover from environmental disturbances such as extreme climatic events, which are expected to increase as a result of climate change (Opdam & Wascher 2004; Travis 2003). Temperature increases are expected to cause shifts to the high-latitude margins of species distributions, but habitat fragmentation could act as a barrier to such colonisation for most species, as has been shown in butterflies (Wilson, Davies & Thomas 2010). It is expected that the combined effects of habitat fragmentation and climate

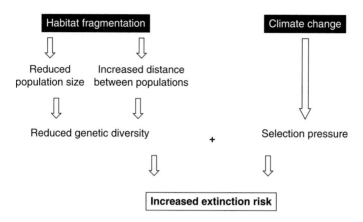

**Figure 3.1** The synergistic interaction of climate change and habitat fragmentation within *Fagus sylvatica* populations leading to a range-wide increase in extinction risk. Conceptual model elaborated from Jump and Peñuelas (2005).

change will be even more pronounced for species that are less mobile (e.g. plants) and at the species' range limits (Opdam & Wascher 2004), which is the case for many of the species in Mediterranean areas. In such cases, species survival will depend on their environmental tolerance. Good colonisers, however, might benefit from climate change and expand their distributions polewards (Hill *et al.* 2001; Warren *et al.* 2001).

Hence, it is clear that the susceptibility of species to climate change is modified by habitat fragmentation, but the way in which individual species respond will depend on many factors, including their dispersal capability, ecological niche, climate sensitivity, life cycles and interactions with other species. Synergy among multiple drivers of change occurs when the net impact of two drivers is significantly higher than the sum of the two operating independently (Sala *et al.* 2000). The interplay between the two important drivers of fragmentation and climate change is not completely understood, and they might generate non-additive effects that cannot be predicted from single-factor studies.

## 3.3 Fire, a characteristic Mediterranean disturbance interacting with global change
### 3.3.1 Mediterranean wildfires and their causes

Wildfires have always been a feature of terrestrial ecosystems; they help explain their biodiversity and distribution (Bond, Woodward & Midgley 2005; Pausas & Keeley 2009). This is especially evident in the Mediterranean Basin, which suffered environmental drying and an increased prevalence of fire in the Quaternary (and probably during the end of the Tertiary; Keeley *et al.* 2012). These fires have shaped Mediterranean plant traits, communities and landscapes (Pausas & Verdú 2005; Verdú & Pausas 2007), and have played a key role in determining this area as a biodiversity hotspot. However, during the past few decades, social, land-use and climatic changes have all influenced fire regimes (Pausas 2004; Pausas & Fernández-Muñoz 2012), sometimes to unsustainable limits, and have generated high social and economic costs (Bowman *et al.* 2009; Viegas 2004).

The main factors determining current fire regimes are debated (Whitlock *et al.* 2010); they result from a complex climate–vegetation relationship, and their role under future climatic conditions is still poorly understood. Both dry conditions (climate) and fuels (vegetation) are needed for fire. Vegetation development depends on plant growth, and so fire activity is tightly related to ecosystem productivity (Bowman *et al.* 2009; Krawchuk & Moritz 2011; Pausas & Bradstock 2007; Pausas & Paula 2012; Pausas & Ribeiro 2013). Drying conditions convert vegetation into available fuel for fire, and this occurs in many regions of the world, although with different frequencies ranging from annual (e.g. savannas; Archibald *et al.* 2010) to centennial (e.g. tropical rain forest; Cochrane 2003) cycles. The fire regime of Mediterranean ecosystems is attributed to their seasonal climate: springtime mild temperatures and abundant rainfall promoting biomass production, followed by summertime warm and dry conditions resulting in severe water deficit (Pausas 2004; Piñol, Terradas & Lloret 1998; Viegas & Viegas 1994). Large fires that occurred in the Mediterranean Basin in the past decade have been related not only to heat waves (Founda & Giannakopoulos 2009; Pereira *et al.* 2005), but also to positive anomalies in the previous wet season that promoted plant growth and fuel build-up (Trigo *et al.* 2006).

### 3.3.2  Fire and climate change

In the past decade, a lot of effort has gone into predicting the potential impacts of climate change on ecosystem dynamics (Sala *et al.* 2000; Thomas *et al.* 2004). Fire is increasingly included in such models, owing to its tight relationship with climate and its relevant role in terrestrial ecosystem functioning (Cramer *et al.* 2001; Scholze *et al.* 2006). Changes in fire activity are expected to occur in most ecosystems worldwide (Flannigan *et al.* 2009; Krawchuk *et al.* 2009; Scholze *et al.* 2006). For a large proportion of the Mediterranean area, a general rise in fire risk is predicted because of an increase in both the length of the fire seasons and the frequency of extreme heatwaves. The strongest changes are expected in mountainous areas (e.g. the Alps, Pyrenees and mountains of the Balkan region; Carvalho *et al.* 2010; Giannakopoulos *et al.* 2009; Moriondo *et al.* 2006). On the other hand, in more arid ecosystems, increasing temperature might reduce productivity and thus fuel amount and continuity, with a consequent reduction of fire activity.

Fire responds to climate, and therefore climate change, in complex ways. It initiates and spreads only when dry and warm weather conditions make

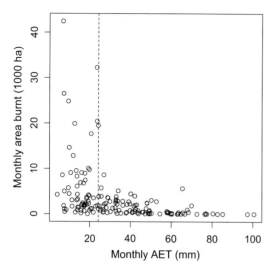

**Figure 3.2** Relationship between monthly actual evapotranspiration (AET) and monthly area burnt for the 1968–2007 period in central Spain. Vertical dashed line indicates the AET threshold from which area burnt increases abruptly. Modified from Pausas and Paula (2012).

vegetation flammable. The fire–climate relationship is not straightforward, however, as the two variables are related in a threshold fashion, with fire probability increasing sharply when certain climatic states are reached (Flannigan & Harrington 1988; Pausas & Paula 2012; Westerling & Bryant 2008; Figure 3.2) and decreasing sharply in dry conditions when a discontinuity threshold in cover is reached (Pausas & Bradstock 2007). Even small changes in climate can therefore cause shifts between non-flammable and flammable conditions. Consequently, future fire regimes may change abruptly, with their impacts on ecosystems possibly overwhelming any direct effects of climate change. For example, vegetation changes in mountainous Mediterranean forests are predicted to relate more to changes in fire regime than to the increased drought due to climate change (Fyllas & Troumbis 2009). Besides, increased fire-induced emissions will have a feedback effect on climate change (Bowman *et al.* 2009), thus amplifying impacts on ecosystems.

### 3.3.3 Fire and land-use

Land-use has an important role in mediating the effect of climate change on fire regimes. When simulations of future fire scenarios take into account how vegetation will track climate change (Cramer *et al.* 2001), predicted changes in fire activity become greater (Krawchuk *et al.* 2009), thus highlighting the key role of fuels. In turn, the build-up of fuels is heavily influenced by land-use change, as confirmed by historical reconstructions of fire occurrence. For instance, global reduction in fire activity during the nineteenth and mid-twentieth centuries is attributed to a decrease in fuel loads due to the expansion of intensive grazing and agriculture, whereas the increased fire activity in the past decades is explained by fuel accumulation resulting from fire suppression policies and land abandonment (Marlon *et al.* 2008; Pausas 2004; Pechony & Shindell 2010).

In the Mediterranean Basin, there was a clear shift in the fire regime in the second half of the twentieth century when fires began to increase in frequency and, especially, in size (Dimitrakopoulos *et al.* 2011; Moreira, Rego & Ferreira 2001; Pausas & Fernández-Muñoz 2012). In another Mediterranean climate region, California, there is no evidence of similar changes in fire regime during the same time period (Keeley & Zedler 2009). The fire regime change detected in the Mediterranean Basin was not gradual but sudden (Figure 3.3), and cannot be explained by the progressive changes in climate observed in this region (Pausas 2004). Instead, changes in fuel conditions need to be considered (Pausas & Fernández-Muñoz 2012), and the turning point seems to be related to a critical threshold in landscape connectivity. As we have seen, one of the main current landscape-scale ecological processes at work in the Mediterranean Basin is the expansion of shrublands and woodlands (Bonet & Pausas 2007). This is driven by the abandonment of agriculture and livestock, and the use of new domestic energy sources (instead of wood). Land abandonment promotes the build-up of large and continuous fuel beds, composed of highly flammable species characteristic of early successional communities (Baeza *et al.* 2011). Concomitant to this land abandonment was the trend of afforesting old fields with conifers and eucalypts and the increasing efforts in fire suppression (Badia *et al.* 2002; Moreira, Rego & Ferreira 2001; Pausas *et al.* 2008). All these factors augmented the biomass and connectivity of landscapes, allowing fires to spread further and thus increase in size. In addition, the increase in human populations and a developing wildland–urban interface led to more frequent fire ignitions (e.g. Keeley, Fotheringham & Morais 1999).

### 3.3.4   Overall impacts of fire on changing Mediterranean ecosystems

Although Mediterranean plant communities show exceptional resilience to recurrent fires, very high fire frequencies reduce their regeneration ability. Fire return intervals shorter than the time period required to recover seed banks (for seeders) and carbohydrate reserves (for resprouters) reduce post-fire recovery (e.g. Lloret, Pausas & Vilà 2003; Moreira *et al.* 2012). In addition, post-fire regeneration in species that neither resprout nor recruit after fire is low when the area burnt is large, given that their recovery relies on colonisation from neighbouring unburned populations (e.g. Ordóñez, Molowny-Horas & Retana 2006). Furthermore, future wildfires are expected to increase in intensity/severity, owing to warmer and drier conditions (Moriondo *et al.* 2006) as well as the higher fuel accumulation resulting from land-use changes. Higher temperatures and/or longer exposure to fire

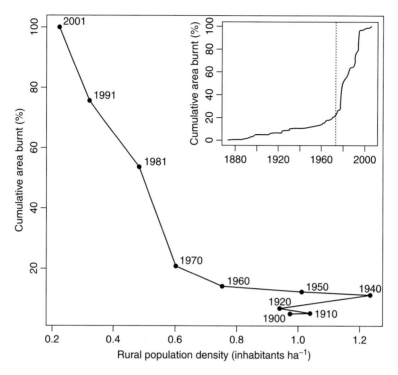

**Figure 3.3** Relationship between the rural population density (inhabitants per ha) and the cumulative area burnt (%) during the twentieth century in the Eastern Iberian Peninsula (from Pausas & Fernández-Muñoz 2012). The inset figure shows the cumulative area burnt (%) for the studied period; vertical dotted line (in 1972/73) indicates an abrupt shift in area burnt coinciding with the rural exodus to the cities.

diminish post-fire regeneration, either by resprouting or seeding (Lloret & López-Soria 1993; Pausas *et al.* 2003; Paula & Pausas 2008). Fuel accumulation can even shift surface fires into more severe crown fires. Such changes are already detected in montane forests, for example threatening the survival of *Pinus nigra*, a species which is able to withstand surface fires but not large and intense crown fires (Fulé *et al.* 2008; Rodrigo, Retana & Picó 2004; Trabaud & Campant 1991).

## 3.4  Biotic interactions
### 3.4.1  Asymmetric responses to abiotic stress and negative species interactions
Species respond in an individualistic fashion to the changing abiotic environment owing to differences in basic life-history traits (e.g. Thuiller *et al.* 2011). However, species are also integrated in complex webs of negative and positive interspecific interactions that are themselves subject to environmental change (Pascual & Dunne 2006). Ecophysiological stress and pathogen attack

may be synergistically affecting overall vulnerability and stability of forest ecosystems, especially for species (including many in the Mediterranean Basin) that are at their distributional limits (Fujimori 2001; Resco de Dios *et al.* 2007). Warmer temperatures can act indirectly on trees by accelerating pathogen life cycles. Some studies have predicted more active attacks of Dutch-elm disease (*Ceratocysits ulmi*) and Hypoxilon canker (*Hypoxylum mediterraneum*) (Tainer & Baker 1996) in southern Europe, and an increasing incidence of Phytophthora root rot (*Phytophthora cinnamomi*) on Spanish *Quercus ilex* and *Q. suber* stands (Tuset & Sánchez 2004).

New interactions between any one species and its antagonists (competitors, herbivores or pests) are expected to arise when the spatial distribution or local performance of the latter is affected by global change, perhaps as a result of the breakdown of climate-driven dispersal barriers (Gilman *et al.* 2010). In one documented case, the processionary moth caterpillar (*Thaumetopoea pityocampa*) expanded its range towards higher elevations in the Sierra Nevada, establishing new contacts with populations of a relict, endemic subspecies of *Pinus sylvestris* (Hódar *et al.* 2003). In general, shifts in distributional range in response to climate change will be fast for small ectothermal organisms with high fecundity and dispersal ability such as most insect pests and pathogens (Helmuth *et al.* 2005), whereas tree responses will be slow owing to low dispersal ability and long generation time, especially for large-seeded species with restricted dispersal in an increasingly fragmented landscape (Jump & Peñuelas 2006).

Many Mediterranean plants are likely to be disadvantaged by asymmetric species responses to abiotic stress and pathogen attack. For example, the capacity of certain Mediterranean tree species to cope with drought is negatively affected by competition with other coexisting species that are less affected, or even benefited, by ongoing climate change (Gimeno *et al.* 2012a, 2012b; Granda *et al.* 2012). In other cases, Mediterranean plants may actually benefit from asymmetric species responses, for example induced by a mismatch between phenologies. This can happen when antagonistic interactions of plants and their natural enemies are broken down. For example, Rabasa, Gutiérrez and Escudero (2009) found that climatic variation between years causes differences in the effect of isolation on the fitness of the Mediterranean shrub *Colutea hispanica*. Contrary to expectations, plant fitness, measured as the production of fruits and viable seeds, increased in isolated patches in years in which a low seed predation coincided with extreme weather conditions (Figure 3.4). The explanation lay in how climatic change affected the temporal and spatial dynamics of the two main seed predators of *C. hispanica* (the lycaenid species *Iolana iolas* and *Lampides boeticus*), which opened a reproductive window for the shrub in isolated patches.

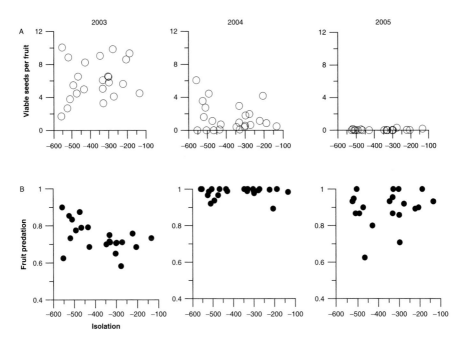

**Figure 3.4** Relationship between the average number of viable seeds per fruit of *Colutea hispanica* (A) and proportion of fruit predation (B) with isolation in three consecutive years with contrasting climate conditions. Isolation index according to Hanski, Kuussaari and Nieminen (1994); less negative values indicate greater isolation. The year 2003 was particularly hot and dry, whereas 2005 was more favourable for plant growth and reproduction. Data elaborated from Rabasa, Gutíerrez and Escudero (2009).

### 3.4.2    Do positive species interactions help reduce global change impacts?

Positive biotic interactions can ameliorate the effects of global change (Brooker 2006; Valladares 2008). In all five Mediterranean regions, facilitation by drought-tolerant plant lineages that evolved during the Holocene has been key for the survival of plant lineages that evolved during the humid Tertiary (Valiente-Banuet *et al.* 2006). However, Brooker (2006) noted that there is less evidence for facilitative plant interactions than for competitive ones in mediating the impacts of environmental change. Indirect interactions and third-party effects on plant–environment interactions can involve threshold situations in which spatial decoupling of the plant and its key positive interactor amplify, rather than ameliorate, changes in abiotic stress (Gilman *et al.* 2010). Facilitation can be transient and it has been shown to be less ubiquitous in Mediterranean ecosystems than previously thought (Granda *et al.* 2012; Valladares *et al.* 2008).

### 3.4.3  The case of plant–plant interactions

Many studies have investigated plant–plant interactions along gradients of environmental severity, supporting the stress-gradient hypothesis (SGH). SGH proposes net positive interactions (facilitation) among plants prevailing in stressful sites, and negative interactions (competition) prevailing under less stressful conditions (Bertness & Callaway 1994). Net positive relationships are frequent in the Mediterranean (Figure 3.5). Facilitation is thus expected to become more and more relevant in Mediterranean ecosystems owing to the nature of the climate change scenarios expected for this region (Christensen *et al.* 2007).

The most frequent case of positive plant–plant interaction studied in Mediterranean areas is the relationship between shrubs (acting as nurse or benefactor) and seedlings of woody species (the *protégé* or beneficiary). Shrubs ameliorate stressful conditions, particularly during summer, reducing irradiance and temperature under their canopies, and consequently attenuating photoinhibition and water stress of seedlings (Castro, Zamora & Hódar 2006; Cuesta *et al.* 2010; Gómez-Aparicio *et al.* 2004; Soliveres *et al.* 2010), as well as providing physical protection against storms or grazing animals (Gómez-Aparicio *et al.* 2004; Smit, den Ouden & Díaz 2008). Similar phenomena have been detected in Mediterranean grasslands, where the scattered trees protect the annual pasture during hard droughts, increasing their growth and yield and delaying their withering (Joffre & Rambal 1993; Cubera & Moreno 2007).

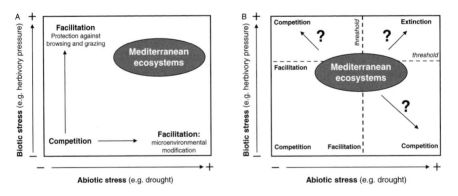

**Figure 3.5** A: plant–plant interactions according to biotic and abiotic stress levels. In Mediterranean areas, both herbivory and drought stress factors co-occur, stimulating facilitation (after Zamora *et al.* 2004, based on Bertness & Callaway 1994). B: positive interactions in severe environments have thresholds after which benefits provided by the benefactor plants do not overcome negative effects. This leads to a change from net facilitative to net competitive interactions, which can lead to extinction under increased levels of both stresses.

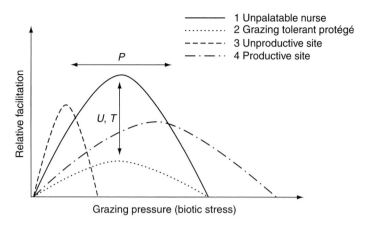

**Figure 3.6** Conceptual model of relative facilitation along gradients of biotic stress (grazing pressure). Competition between nurse and protégé at low grazing levels leads to low relative facilitation. Herbivore damage to nurses at high grazing levels also decreases relative facilitation. Relative facilitation thus peaks at intermediate grazing pressure. The peaks shift horizontally as a function of site productivity ($P$) if the latter determines relative grazing pressure on nurses and protégés, and shift vertically as a function of the unpalatability of nurse plants ($U$) or grazing tolerance of the associated protégés ($T$). Adapted from Smit *et al.* (2007).

The importance and intensity of plant–plant interactions vary temporally and spatially, sometimes in complex ways (Granda *et al.* 2012). As a result, the SGH is not always supported; some studies show a decrease in the intensity of facilitative interactions at the very extreme end of stress gradients. This casts doubts on facilitation being able to help plants to cope with the increased abiotic stress of climate change under Mediterranean conditions (Figure 3.6). Maestre and Cortina (2004) showed that the protection by the tussock grass *Stipa tenacissima* for the seedlings of *Pistacia lentiscus* disappeared under high abiotic stress. Smit *et al.* (2007) similarly demonstrated a bell-shaped relationship between a biotic stress (herbivory) and facilitation in the case of the protection against livestock browsing afforded by thorny shrubs to tree seedlings. In this case the protection became ineffective after a certain threshold livestock density was passed (Figure 3.6). Malkinson and Tielbörger (2010) explained exceptions to the SGH in terms of the non-linear response of plant physiological processes to environmental changes, leading to the asymmetrical change of competition and facilitation along stress gradients, especially when several factors are involved. Together with the multiplicative nature of both facilitation and competition on individual fitness, more complex predictions than those resulting from the original SGH are inevitable (Freckleton, Watkinson & Rees 2009) (Figure 3.6).

### 3.4.4    The case of animal dispersal

Plant–animal interactions may also counteract expected effects of abiotic stress on plant populations under climate change scenarios. Directed dispersal, i.e. the non-random movement of seeds to suitable microsites for plant establishment (Wenny & Levey 1998), may overcome dispersal limitations of dominant, large-seeded forest trees. Recent work has shown how seed dispersal by animals could determine population trends (Montoya *et al.* 2008), recruitment (Pulido & Díaz 2005), regional distribution (Purves *et al.* 2006), community structure (Pausas *et al.* 2006; Svenning & Skov 2007; Zamora *et al.* 2010) and genetic structure and gene flow (Jordano *et al.* 2007) of Mediterranean forest trees facing global change.

Animal responses to fragmentation are usually non-linear, and relationships between presence in patches and patch size are best modelled by sigmoidal/logistic functions including two thresholds: the minimum patch size below which the species is never found, and the patch size above which all patches are occupied (Fahrig 2003). In patches smaller than the minimum threshold for keystone pollinators or dispersers, plant populations will be thus locally decoupled from essential animal interactors, even when this is not predicted by regional-scale models. A further complexity is related to spatial variation in the parameters of incidence functions, with larger minimum sizes for patch occupation towards the borders of distribution areas. This has been shown to be the case for forest birds in Mediterranean regions. Keystone seed dispersers of Eurosiberian affinities, such as jays *Garrulus glandarius* or thrushes *Turdus* spp., show increasing minimum forest sizes towards the southern, warmer borders of their distribution areas, whereas for species of Mediterranean origin such as small *Sylvia* warblers, minimum forest sizes increase northwards (Díaz *et al.* 1998; Santos *et al.* 2006). Local decoupling of plants and seed dispersers due to forest fragmentation will thus be more severe in climate change scenarios for plants depending on birds of northern distribution, such as large-seeded oaks *Quercus* spp. and jays.

Effectiveness of the interaction in patches of intermediate size (i.e. above minimum size but below the fragment size over which all fragments are occupied) will depend on the foraging behaviour of seed dispersers, which is also sensitive to fragmentation (Damschen *et al.* 2008). Differential use of fragments according to size for foraging and resting may lead to a collapse in recruitment in small patches if visitation rates are too low to result in efficient seed dispersal (e.g. Santos & Tellería 1994). Fragment size could also influence the outcome of conditional mutualisms between scatter-hoarding animals and large-seeded plants such as oaks (Forget *et al.* 2005). In this way, scatter-hoarding mice act as keystone acorn dispersers for holm oaks *Quercus ilex* in large forest tracts (Gómez *et al.* 2008) but become a net seed predator hampering oak recruitment in small fragments (Santos & Tellería 1997).

### 3.4.5   The challenge of prediction: modelling plant–animal interactions

Species-specific niche envelope models are currently being developed for both plant and animal species (Thuiller *et al.* 2011). Modelling the effects of global change on the distribution, abundance and foraging behaviour of seed dispersers or herbivores, and coupling these models to predictive models of plant distribution, can significantly improve our understanding of how plant populations will respond to future changes. However, uncoupled, or 'parallel', modelling approaches are still all too common (Figure 3.7). Animal models usually include plant data only through the well-known effects of vegetation-related land-uses on animal distributions (e.g. Vallecillo *et al.* 2009), whereas plant models either ignore animal effects on plants altogether, or include coarse surrogates for them (e.g. dispersal mode; Thuiller *et al.* 2008). This parallel approach may eventually predict new negative interactions

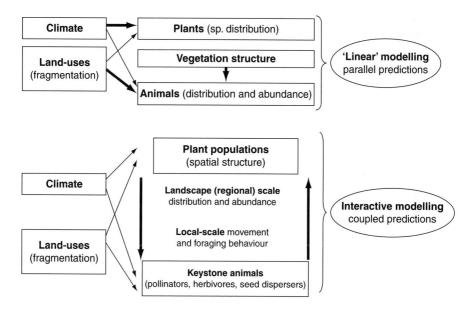

**Figure 3.7** Conceptual modelling approaches to predict plant and animal responses to the two main global change drivers in Mediterranean forests: climate and land-use changes (including forest fragmentation). The upper scheme indicates the current approach, based on parallel niche envelope models for either plant or animal species. Arrow width indicates the relative importance of variables related to drivers in models. The lower scheme outlines basic ideas for developing coupled models for interactive plant–animal systems. Common variables should be used for niche envelope modelling of both animal and plants, as indicated by the arrow width. Sub-models for plants should explicitly include the spatial structure of plant populations, and coupled animal and plant models should consider both regional-scale and local-scale effects.

resulting from new range overlaps, as for instance in the case of the procession-ary moth and Scots pine mentioned earlier. However, this approach fails to estimate the influence of the interaction on the distribution of each species under new climates. Moreover, the spatial decoupling of specialist positive interactions involving plants and their pollinators or seed dispersers will be missed.

Coupled models for interactive plant–animal systems would overcome these limitations. They have four requirements. First, the same variables for measuring climate and land-use changes are needed for niche envelope mod-elling of both animal and plant species. Second, sub-models for plants should explicitly include the spatial structure of plant populations, as this trait is usually key to the modelling of animal distributions under fragmentation and land-use change scenarios (Concepción *et al.* 2008). Third, coupled models should consider both regional-scale effects of plants on the distribution and abundance of keystone animal species (pollinators, herbivores and seed dis-persers) and local-scale effects of plant distributions on the movement and foraging behaviour of these same animals (e.g. Damschen *et al.* 2008). Finally, the consequences of animal behaviour on plant performance should be con-sidered (i.e. dispersal behaviour and seed dispersal effectiveness, or herbivore behaviour and plant reproduction and survival; Schupp *et al.* 2010).

In conclusion, plant–plant and plant–animal interactions can positively influence forest responses to climate change by improving local abiotic and biotic conditions (facilitation) and the ability of large-seeded plants to track environmental changes (directed dispersal). Antagonistic interactions (e.g. herbivory) may also be broken down, leading to net gains for some species. On the negative side of the balance sheet, amelioration of global change impacts is not an inevitable result of existing positive interactions. Non-linear facilitation–competition balances along stress gradients, and the effects of fragmentation on the distribution and behaviour of dispersers, could lead to threshold situations across which positive interactions could vanish or even shift to negative interactions. Mediterranean areas represent an important model system for testing these predictions, owing to their heterogeneity and contrasting levels of fragmentation at a wide range of spatial scales.

## 3.5  Implications for practice

### 3.5.1  Characteristics of Mediterranean forests from a forest management perspective

There are a number of characteristics of Mediterranean forests relevant to management approaches, especially in the context of global change. We have introduced a number of them in the course of our discussion.

- They have a low productivity of wood products and pastures, and – together with the small size of holdings – this leads to low profitability. The Mediterranean climate with summer drought conditions constrains plant growth when temperature is optimum for vegetation development.
- They are highly multifunctional, with a high diversity of non-wood products such as game, cork, honey and mushrooms, as well as a provision of vital ecosystem services such as carbon sequestration and regulation of water resources (Balmford *et al.* 2002; Campos *et al.* 2013; Daily *et al.* 2000).
- They are extremely diverse in species and the interactions between them. Climatic evolution, high interannual variability, topographic diversity and long history of anthropogenic influence have combined to create some of the planet's most significant biodiversity hotspots (Myers *et al.* 2000).

Management of Mediterranean forests has evolved to take account of these particular characteristics, but in the future it needs to adapt to the changes taking place in these systems. The forests are currently subject to rapid socio-economic changes, such as rural depopulation and abandonment of traditional forestry taking place in the European Mediterranean countries since the 1950s (Pausas & Fernández-Muñoz 2012 ). Such changes have serious repercussions in terms of landscape heterogeneity and biodiversity (Atauri & de Lucio 2001). Employment generation, population stabilisation and increasing the profitability of unproductive areas are new challenges relevant to forestry management. At the same time, actively managed forests are an important component of any strategy to preserve heterogeneous landscape mosaics and their biodiversity (Díaz *et al.* 2013). We have also noted how global change drivers will modify species interactions (Lindner *et al.* 1997; Maestre *et al.* 2009; Soliveres *et al.* 2010) and disturbance regimes (Gillett *et al.* 2004; McKenzie *et al.* 2004; Pausas & Fernández-Muñoz 2012 ) in Mediterranean environments. By triggering changes in forest composition and structure, these changes again have important implications for forest management. Moreover, prolonged droughts and heat waves aggravate forest fire risks and subsequent soil erosion (Certini 2005), accelerating the desertification of dry areas. Consequences include a decline in wood production (Bravo *et al.* 2008; Loustau *et al.* 2005), decreased timber values in burned areas, and effects on non-wood products (e.g. mushrooms; Martínez de Aragón *et al.* 2007) and services (e.g. biodiversity and carbon sequestration; Bravo *et al.* 2008).

### 3.5.2   Guiding principles for Mediterranean forest under environmental change

Sustainable Mediterranean forest management and planning is more important than ever in the face of challenges imposed by global change (Lindner

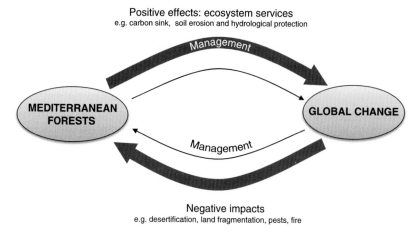

**Figure 3.8** The relationships between global change and forests can be modulated by proper management. The negative impacts of global change on Mediterranean ecosystems, such as desertification, land fragmentation, increased fire or higher impacts of pests, can be reduced by management. Moreover, properly managed forests may help reduce the rate of environmental change, e.g. increasing the carbon sink or protecting soil from erosion and desertification.

2000). Whilst mitigating for such effects, an additional objective of management is to help combat global change itself (Figure 3.8). Mediterranean forest management regimes obviously require tailoring to the specificity of local sites, taking into account main limiting factors (water availability, soil nutrients), species composition and structure, and the products and services required (protection against anomalous fires, carbon sequestration, biodiversity, endangered species). However, some overall guidelines for silvicultural strategies in Mediterranean areas can be suggested to mitigate the effects of global change.

- **Flexible thinning schedules** according to stand age and state. Given uncertainties in how the climate will evolve, high densities of saplings (Aitken 2003), both natural or planted, are recommended to increase the selection opportunities of best-adapted individuals. However, in sites particularly prone to drought, low adult tree densities may be important in maintaining vigour and adaptive ability (Bravo *et al.* 2008), reducing tree competition and favouring good individual mycorrhisation and tree health.
- **Extension of rotations and regeneration cuttings**. Changes in phenology may lead to less than optimal conditions for reproduction and compromise the success of regeneration cuttings and long-term

persistence of stands. Extending the regeneration period, and reinforcing natural recruitment, can mitigate such impacts. Alternatively, the use of shrubs as nurse plants for seedlings can be used in reafforestation protocols.

- **Reduction of tree densities in traditional coppiced forests** (Bravo *et al.* 2008). Over centuries, many stands of principally *Quercus* species were managed to obtain fire wood, favouring forest regeneration from sprouts or root suckers of cut trees. Acorns were also used to feed live-stock. Abandonment of these stands has led to many-stemmed individual trees, reduced growth rates, lack of vigour in seed production and high mortality rates under extreme events. Selecting the most vigorous stems per individual in thinning operations has the potential to improve water availability, carbon sequestration (Tello *et al.* 1994) and recruitment from seedlings.

- **Less intense management** in timber production stands to reduce vul-nerability to disturbances or pest breakouts and to maintain their hydrological protection role. Clear-felling should be replaced by selected cutting of single trees or groups, or else by shelterwood systems with longer rotations, weak thinning and natural regeneration whenever possible.

- **Mixed forests, diversity of stand types and uneven-aged stands** should be favoured as they are more resilient to changing environmental conditions. They provide different products and services to owners, and help mitigate the proliferation of forest fires and pathogen infestations. This should be a priority for forests with specific roles, such as hydrologic or soil protection, biodiversity conservation and landscape enhancement. Selective removal of individuals will favour continuous natural regener-ation, avoiding excessive densities that hinder recruitment and stand rejuvenation and increase vulnerability to pest breakouts or fires.

- **Sustainable strategies for dealing with forest fire** are essential. It is not a reasonable objective to eliminate forest fires from Mediterranean ecosystems, and fire suppression policies can generate more destructive fires in the long term. Mediterranean landscape management should instead be aimed towards a sustainable coexistence with forest fires in terms of both human security and ecological processes/biodiversity (Pausas & Vallejo 2008).

In summary, management of Mediterranean forests should avoid forest sen-escence and high tree densities, and instead favour natural regeneration in mixed and uneven-aged stands. The conservation of biological diversity should be of paramount importance in forest management strategies (CBD,

2001), with measures to preserve the pool of native species, increase genetic variability of trees and reduce habitat fragmentation by creating ecological corridors and restoring degraded lands.

### 3.5.3   Uncertainty, adaptive management and modelling approaches

The uncertainty of global change evolution and the difficulty in predicting the direction and rate of change requires heightened efforts to gather empirical data, develop better knowledge and understanding of ecological processes and mechanisms, and make appropriate management decisions (Zavala *et al.* 2004).

Key to this success are adaptive management approaches (Nyberg 1998; Stephens *et al.* 2010) in which every silvicultural activity is treated as part of a real-world experiment, and systematic learning is developed for future management. Such adaptive approaches are yet to become widely practised in Mediterranean forest management planning. Simulation modelling is another important tool to anticipate species responses. Innovative progress has been made on this front owing to technological and statistical advances, for example in niche-based modelling. Many studies are now benefiting from these to assess future distribution responses to global change (Benito-Garzón *et al.* 2008; Keenan *et al.* 2010). There has been also significant progress in process-based models that incorporate eco-physiological processes from empirical relationships and mechanistic descriptions based on physical laws. Such models include GOTILWA+ (Gracia *et al.* 1999), which has been widely tested in Mediterranean areas. GOTILWA+ is a forest growth model that can assess responses to water availability (Sabaté *et al.* 2002) in changing environmental conditions, because of either climate or management drivers.

In conclusion, silvicultural management of Mediterranean forests should recognise the importance of non-linear, interrelated causes and feedback loops at different hierarchical levels of organisation, spatial and temporal scale (Puettmann *et al.* 2008). Modern ecological understanding of forests as complex adaptive systems must be the new cornerstone (Puettmann *et al.* 2008) of efforts to achieve sustainable management under global change scenarios.

### Acknowledgements

The writing of this chapter was made possible by funding from the International Laboratory of Global Change (LincGlobal), the Spanish Ministry for Innovation and Science (Consolider Montes, CSD2008_00040; VULGLO, CGL2010–22180-C03–03), the Comunidad de Madrid (REMEDINAL2 – CM, S2009/AMB-1783) and the European Union (BACCARA, CE: FP7-226299, 7FP; FUNDIV, CE: FP7-ENV-2010).

# References

Aitken, S. (2003) Adapting forest gene resource management to climate change. *TICtalk*, 14–16.

Allen, C. D., Macalady, A. K., Chenchouni, H. *et al.* (2010). A global overview of drought and heat-induced tree mortality reveals emerging climate change risks for forests. *Forest Ecology and Management*, **259**, 660–684.

Archibald, S., Nickless, A., Govender, N., Scholes, R. J. & Lehsten, V. (2010) Climate and the inter-annual variability of fire in southern Africa: a meta-analysis using long-term field data and satellite-derived burnt area data. *Global Ecology and Biogeography*, **19**, 794–809.

Atauri, J. A. & de Lucio, J. V. (2001) *Modelo de seguimiento ecológico en espacios naturales protegidos. Aplicación a la Reserva Natural de los Galachos de La Alfranca, La Cartuja y el Burgo de Ebro*. Diputación General de Aragón.

Badia, A., Saurí, D., Cerdan, R. & Llurdés, J. C. (2002) Causality and management of forest fires in Mediterranean environments: an example from Catalonia. *Global Environmental Change Part B: Environmental Hazards*, **4**, 23–32.

Baeza, M. J., Santana, V. M., Pausas, J. G. & Vallejo, V. R. (2011) Successional trends in standing dead biomass in Mediterranean basin species. *Journal of Vegetation Science*, **22**, 467–474.

Balmford, A., Bruner, A., Philip Cooper, P. *et al.* (2002) Economic reasons for conserving wild nature. *Science*, **297**, 950–953.

Bertness M. D. & Callaway, R. M. (1994) Positive interactions in communities. *Trends in Ecology & Evolution*, **9**, 191–193.

Benito-Garcón, M., Sánchez de Dios, R. & Sainz Ollero, H. (2008) Effects of climate change on the distribution of Iberian tree species. *Applied Vegetation Science*, **11**, 169–178.

Blondel, J, Aronson, J., Boudiou, J. Y. & Boeuf, G. (2010) *The Mediterranean Basin: Biological Diversity in Space and Time*. Oxford: Oxford University Press.

Bond, W. J., Woodward, F. I. & Midgley, G. F. (2005) The global distribution of ecosystems in a world without fire. *New Phytologist*, **165**, 525–538.

Bonet, A. & Pausas, J. G. (2007) Old field dynamics on the dry side of the Mediterranean Basin: patterns and processes in semiarid SE Spain. In *Old Fields: Dynamics and Restoration of Abandoned Farmland* (eds. V. A. Cramer & R. J. Hobbs), pp. 247–264. Washington: Island Press.

Bowman, D., Balch, J. K., Artaxo, P. *et al.* (2009) Fire in the Earth system. *Science*, **324**, 481–484.

Bravo, F., Bravo-Oviedo, A., Ruiz-Painado, R. & Montero, G. (2008) Selvicultura y cambio climático. *Compendio de Selvicultura* (eds. R. Serrada, G. Montero & J. A. Reque), pp. 981–1004. Madrid: INIA.

Brooker, R. W. (2006) Plant–plant interactions and environmental change. *New Phytologist*, **171**, 271–284.

Campos, P., Huntsinger, L., Oviedo, J. L. *et al.* (eds.) (2013) *Mediterranean Oak Woodland Working Landscapes: Dehesas of Spain and Ranchlands of California*. New York: Springer.

Carvalho, A., Flannigan, M. D., Logan, K. A. *et al.* (2010) The impact of spatial resolution on area burned and fire occurrence projections in Portugal under climate change. *Climatic Change*, **98**, 177–197.

Castro, J., Zamora, R. & Hódar, J. A. (2006) Restoring *Quercus pyrenaica* forests using pioneer shrubs as nurse plants. *Applied Vegetation Science*, **9**, 137–142.

CBD (Convention on Biological Diversity) (2001) *Forest Biological Diversity*, Rep. Mo. UNEP/CBD/SBSTTA/7/7. Montreal: UNEP.

Celaya, R., Jáuregui, B. M., Rosa-García, R. *et al.* (2010) Changes in heathland vegetation under goat grazing: effects of breed and stocking rate. *Applied Vegetation of Science*, **13**, 125–134.

Certini, G. (2005) Effects of fire on properties of forest soils: a review. *Oecologia*, **143**, 1–10.

Christensen, J. H., Hewitson, B., Busuioc, A. *et al.* (2007) Regional climate projections. In

*Climate Change 2007: The Physical Science Basis* (eds. S. Solomon, D. Qin, M. Manning, Z. et al.), pp. 847–943. Cambridge and New York: Cambridge University Press.

Cochrane, M. A. (2003) Fire science for rainforests. *Nature*, **421**, 913–919.

Concepción, E. D., Díaz, M. & Baquero, R. A. (2008) Effects of landscape complexity on the ecological effectiveness of agri-environment schemes. *Landscape Ecology*, **23**, 135–148.

Cramer, W., Bondeau, A., Woodward, F. I. *et al.* (2001) Global response of terrestrial ecosystem structure and function to $CO_2$ and climate change: results from six dynamic global vegetation models. *Global Change Biology*, **7**, 357–373.

Cubera, E. & Moreno, G. (2007) Effects of land use on soil water dynamics in dehesas of Central-Western Spain. *Catena*, **71**, 298–308.

Cuesta, B., Villar-Salvador, P., Puértolas, J., Rey Benayas, J. M. & Michalet, R. (2010) Facilitation of *Quercus ilex* in Mediterranean shrubland is explained by both direct and indirect interactions mediated by herbs. *Journal of Ecology*, **98**, 687–696.

Cunningham, S. A. (2000) Effects of habitat fragmentation on the reproductive ecology of four plant species in Malle Woodland. *Conservation Biology*, **14**, 758–768.

Daily, G. C., Söderqvist, T., Aniyar, S. *et al.* (2000) The value of nature and the nature of value. *Science*, **289**, 395–396.

Damschen, E. I., Brudviga, L. A., Haddadb, N. M. *et al.* (2008) The movement ecology and dynamics of plant communities in fragmented landscapes. *Proceedings of the National Academy of Sciences USA*, **105**, 19078–19083.

Díaz, M., Carbonell, R., Santos, T. & Tellería, J. L. (1998) Breeding bird communities in pine plantations of the Spanish central plateaux: geographic location, fragmentation, and vegetation structure effects. *Journal of Applied Ecology*, **35**, 562–574.

Diaz, M., Tietje, W. & Barret, R. (2013) Effects of management on biological diversity and endangered species. In *Mediterranean Oak Woodland Working Landscapes: Dehesas of Spain and Ranchlands of California* (eds. P. Campos, L. Huntsinger, J. L. Oviedo, M. Diaz, P. Starrs, R. B. Standiford & G. Montero), pp. 213–243. New York: Springer.

Dimitrakopoulos, A. P., Vlahou, M., Anagnostopoulou, C. G. & Mitsopoulos, I. D. (2011) Impact of drought on wildland fires in Greece: implications of climatic change? *Climatic Change*, **109**, 331–347.

Duncan, H. D., Nicotra, A. B., Wood, J. T. & Cunningham, S. A. (2004) Plant isolation reduces outcross pollen receipt in a partially selfcompatible herb. *Journal of Ecology*, **92**, 977–985.

Ellstrand, N. C. & Elam, D. R. (1993) Population genetic consequences of small size: implications for plant conservation. *Annual Review of Ecology, Evolution, and Systematics*, **24**, 217–242.

Fahrig, L. (2003). Effects of habitat fragmentation on biodiversity. *Annual Review of Ecology, Evolution, and Systematics*, **34**, 487–515.

Fischer, M. & Matthies, D. (1997) Mating structure and inbreeding and outbreeding depression in the rare plant *Gentianella germanica* (Gentianaeae). *American Journal of Botany*, **84**, 1685–1692.

Flannigan, M. D. & Harrington, J. B. (1988) A study of the relation of meteorological variables to monthly provincial area burned by wildfire in Canada (1953–80). *Journal of Applied Meteorology*, **27**, 441–452.

Flannigan, M. D., Krawchuk, M. A., de Groot, W. J., Wotton, B. M. & Gowman, L. M. (2009) Implications of changing climate for global wildland fire. *International Journal of Wildland Fire*, **18**, 483–507.

Forget, P. M., Lambert, J. E., Hulme, P. E. & Vander Wall, S. B. (2005) *Seed Fate: Predation, Dispersal and Seedling Establishment*. Wallingford, MA: CAB International.

Founda, D. & Giannakopoulos, C. (2009) The exceptionally hot summer of 2007 in Athens, Greece – A typical summer in the future climate? *Global and Planetary Change*, **67**, 227–236.

Freckleton, R. P., Watkinson, A. R. & Rees, M. (2009) Measuring the importance of competition in plant communities. *Journal of Ecology*, **97**, 379–384.

Fujimori, T. (2001) *Ecological and Silvicultural Strategies for Sustainable Forest Management*. Amsterdam: Elsevier.

Fulé, P. Z., Ribas, M., Gutiérrez, E., Vallejo, R. & Kaye, M. W. (2008) Forest structure and fire history in an old *Pinus nigra* forest, eastern Spain. *Forest Ecology and Management*, **255**, 1234–1242.

Fyllas, N. M. & Troumbis, A. Y. (2009) Simulating vegetation shifts in north-eastern Mediterranean mountain forests under climatic change scenarios. *Global Ecology and Biogeography*, **18**, 64–77.

García, D. & Chacoff, N. P. (2007) Scale-dependent effects of habitat fragmentation on hawthorn pollination, frugivory and seed predation. *Conservation Biology*, **21**, 400–411.

Giannakopoulos, C., Le Sager, P., Bindi, M. *et al.* (2009) Climatic changes and associated impacts in the Mediterranean resulting from a 2 degrees C global warming. *Global and Planetary Change*, **68**, 209–224.

Gillett, N. P., Weaver, A. J., Zwiers, F. W. & Flanningan, M. D. (2004) Detecting the effect of climate change on Canadian forest fires. *Geophysical Research Letters*, **31**, L18211.

Gilman, S. E., Urban, M. C., Tewksbury, J., Gilchrist, G. W. & Holt, R. D. (2010) A framework for community interactions under climate change. *Trends in Ecology & Evolution*, **25**, 325–331.

Gimeno, T. E. (2011) *Ecofisiología, interacciones planta-planta y cambio global en dos árboles del Mediterráneo continental*. Unpublished PhD thesis, Universidad Rey Juan Carlos, Madrid.

Gimeno, T. E., Pias, B., Lemos-Filho, J. P. & Valladares, F. (2009) Plasticity and stress tolerance override local adaptation in the responses of Mediterranean Holm oak seedlings to drought and cold. *Tree Physiology*, **29**, 87–98.

Gimeno, T. E. , Pias, B., Martinez-Fernandez, J., *et al.* (2012a) The decreased competition in expanding versus mature juniper woodlands is counteracted by adverse climatic effects on growth. *European Journal of Forest Research*, **131**, 977–987.

Gimeno, T. E., Camarero, J. J., Granda, E., Pías, B. & Valladares, F. (2012b). Enhanced growth of *Juniperus thurifera* under a warmer climate is explained by a positive carbon gain under cold and drought. *Tree Physiology*, **32**, 326–336.

Gómez, J. M., Puerta-Piñero C. & Schupp, E. W. (2008) Effectiveness of rodents as local seed dispersers of Holm oaks. *Oecologia*, **155**, 529–537.

Gómez-Aparicio, L., Zamora, R., Gómez, J. M. *et al.* (2004) Applying plant facilitation to forest restoration: a meta-analysis of the use of shrubs as nurse plants. *Ecological Applications*, **14**, 1128–1138.

González-Varo, J. P., Arroyo, J. & Aparicio, A. (2009) Effects of fragmentation on pollinator assemblage, pollen limitation and seed production of Mediterranean myrtle (*Myrtus communis*). *Biological Conservation*, **142**, 1058–1065.

Gracia, C. A., Tello, E., Sabaté, S. & Bellot, J. (1999) GOTILWA+: an integrated model of water dynamics and forest growth. In *Ecology of Mediterranean Evergreen Oak Forest: Ecological Studies*, vol. 137 (eds. F. Rodá, J. Retana, C. A. Gracia & J. Bellot), pp. 163–178. Berlin: Springer.

Granda, E., Escudero, A., De La Cruz, M. & Valladares, F. (2012) Juvenile-adult tree associations in a continental Mediterranean ecosystem: no evidence for sustained and general facilitation at increased aridity. *Journal of Vegetation Science*, **23**, 164–175.

Hanski, I., Kuussaari, M. & Nieminen, M. (1994) Metapopulation structure and migration in the butterfly *Melitea cinxia*. *Ecology*, **75**, 747–762.

Helmuth, B., Kingsolver, J. G. & Carrington, E. (2005) Biophysics, physiological ecology, and climate change: Does mechanism matter? *Annual Review of Physiology*, **67**, 177–201.

Hill, J. K., Collingham, Y., Thomas, C. D. *et al.* (2001) Impacts of landscape structure on butterfly range expansion. *Ecology Letters*, **4**, 313–321.

Hódar, J. A., Castro, J. & Zamora, R. (2003) Pine processionary caterpillar *Thaumetopoea pityiocampa* as a new threat for relict Mediterranean Scots pine forests under climatic warming. *Biological Conservation*, **110**, 123–129.

IPCC (2007) *Climate Change 2007: The Physical Science Basis. Contribution of Working Group I to the Fourth Assessment Report of the Intergovernmental Panel on Climate Change* (eds. S. Solomon, D. Qin, M. Manning *et al.*). Cambridge and New York: Cambridge University Press.

Jauregui, B. M., Rosa-Garcia, R., Garcia, U. *et al.* (2008) Effects of stocking density and breed of goats on vegetation and grasshopper occurrence in heathlands. *Agriculture, Ecosystems & Environment*, **123**, 219–224.

Joffre, R. & Rambal, S. (1993) How tree cover influences the water balance of Mediterranean rangelands. *Ecology*, **74**, 570–582.

Jordano, P., García, C., Godoy, J. A. & García-Castaño, J. L. (2007) Differential contribution of frugivores to complex seed dispersal patterns. *Proceedings of the National Academy of Sciences USA*, **104**, 3278–3282.

Jump, A. S. & Peñuelas, J. (2005) Running to stand still: adaptation and the response of plants to rapid climate change. *Ecology Letters*, **8**, 1010–1020.

Jump, A. S. & Peñuelas, J. (2006) Genetic effects of chronic habitat fragmentation in a wind-pollinated tree. *Proceedings of the National Academy of Sciences USA*, **103**, 8096–8100.

Keeley J. E., Bond, W. J., Bradstock, R. A., Pausas, J. G. & Rundel, P. W. (2012). *Fire in Mediterranean Ecosystems: Ecology, Evolution and Management*. Cambridge: Cambridge University Press.

Keeley, J. E. & Zedler, P. H. (2009). Large, high-intensity fire events in southern California shrublands: debunking the fine-grain age patch model. *Ecological Applications*, **19**, 69–94.

Keenan, T., Serra, J. M., Lloret, F., Ninyerola, M. & Sabate, S. (2010) Predicting the future of forests in the Mediterranean under climate change, with niche- and process-based models: $CO_2$ matters! *Global Change Biology*, **17**, 565–579.

Kéry, M., Matthies, D. & Fischer, M. (2001) The effect of plant population size on the interactions between the rare plant *Gentiana cruciata* and its specialized herbivore *Maculinea rebeli*. *Journal of Ecology*, **89**, 418–427.

Krawchuk, M. A. & Moritz, M. (2011) Constraints on global fire activity vary across a resource gradient. *Ecology*, **92**, 121–132.

Krawchuk, M. A., Moritz, M. A., Parisien, M. A., Van Dorn, J. & Hayhoe, K. (2009) Global pyrogeography: the current and future distribution of wildfire. *PloS One*, **4**, e5102.

Lande, R. (1988) Genetics and demography in biological conservation. *Science*, **241**, 1455–1460.

Lindner, M. (2000) Developing adaptive forest management strategies to cope with climate change. *Tree Physiology*, **20**, 299–307.

Lindner, M., Bugmann, H., Lasch, P., Fleichsig, M. & Cramer, W. (1997) Regional impacts of climate change on forests in the state of Brandenburg, Germany. *Agricultural and Forest Meteorology*, **84**, 123–135.

Lloret F., Escudero A., Iriondo, J. M., Martinez-Vilalta, J. & Valladares, F. (2012) Extreme climatic events and vegetation: the role of stabilizing processes. *Global Change Biology*, **18**, 797–805.

Lloret, F. & López-Soria, L. (1993). Resprouting of *Erica multiflora* after experimental fire treatments. *Journal of Vegetation Science*, **4**, 367–374.

Lloret, F., Pausas, J. G. & Vilà, M. (2003) Responses of Mediterranean plant species to different fire frequencies in Garraf Natural Park (Catalonia, Spain): field observations and modelling predictions. *Plant Ecology*, **167**, 223–235.

Lloret, F. & Siscart, D. (1995) Los efectos demográficos de la sequía en poblaciones de encina. *Cuadernos de la Sociedad Española de Ciencias Foresales*, **2**, 77–81.

Loustau, D., Bosc, A., Colin, A. *et al.* (2005) Modeling climate change effects on the potential production of French plains forests at the sub-regional level. *Tree Physiology*, **25**, 813–823.

Maestre, F., Callaway, R. M., Valladares, F. & Lortie, C. J. (2009) Refining the stress-gradient hypothesis for competition and facilitation in plant communities. *Journal of Ecology*, **97**, 199–205.

Maestre, F. T. & Cortina, J. (2004) Do positive interactions increase with abiotic stress? A test from a semi-arid steppe. *Proceedings of the Royal Society of London B* (Supplement) **271**: S331–S333.

Malkinson, D. & Tielbörger, K. (2010) What does the stress-gradient hypothesis predict? Resolving the discrepancies. *Oikos*, **119**, 1546–1552.

Marlon, J. R., Bartlein, P. J., Carcaillet, C. *et al.* (2008) Climate and human influences on global biomass burning over the past two millennia. *Nature Geoscience*, **1**, 697–702.

Martínez de Aragón, J., Bonet, J. A., Fischer, C. R. & Colinas, C. (2007) Productivity of ectomycorrhizal and selected edible saprotrophic fungi in pine forests of the pre-Pyrenees mountains, Spain: predictive equations for forest management of mycological resources. *Forest Ecology and Management*, **252**, 239–256.

McKenzie, D., Gedalof, Z. M., Peterson, D. L. & Mote, P. (2004) Climatic change, wildfire, and conservation. *Conservation Biology*, **18**, 890–902.

Montoya, D., Zavala, M. A., Rodríguez, M. A. & Purves, D. W. (2008) Animal versus wind dispersal and the robustness of tree species to deforestation. *Science*, **320**, 1502–1504.

Montoya, R. (1995) Red de seguimiento de daños en los montes. Daños originados por la sequía en 1994. *Cuadernos de la Sociedad Españolas de Ciencias Forestales*, **2**, 83–97.

Montserrat-Martín, G., Camarero, J. J., Palacios, S. *et al.* (2009) Summer-drought constrains the phenology and growth of two coexisting Mediterranean oaks with contrasting leaf habits: implications for their persistence and reproduction. *Tree-Structure and Function*, **23**, 787–799.

Moreira, F., Rego, F. C. & Ferreira, P. G. (2001) Temporal (1958–1995) pattern of change in a cultural landscape of northwestern Portugal: implications for fire occurrence. *Landscape Ecology*, **16**, 557–567.

Moreira, B., Tormo, J., Pausas, J. G. (2012) To resprout or not to resprout: factors driving intraspecific variability in resprouting. *Oikos*, **121**, 1577–1584.

Morin, X., Roy, J., Sonie, L. & Chuine, I. (2010) Changes in leaf phenology of three European oak species in response to experimental climate change. *New Phytologist*, **186**, 900–910.

Moriondo, M., Good, P., Durao, R. *et al.* (2006) Potential impact of climate change on fire risk in the Mediterranean area. *Climate Research*, **31**, 85–95.

Myers, N., Mittermeier, R. A., Mittermeier, C. G., da Fonseca, G.A.B. & Kent, J. (2000) Biodiversity hotspots for conservation priorities. *Nature*, **403**, 853–858.

Nyberg, J. B. (1998) Statistics and the practice of adaptive management. *Statistical Methods for Adaptive Management Studies* (eds. V. Sit & B. Taylor). Land Management Handbook 42, Victoria, Canada: BC Ministry of Forests.

Opdam, P. & Wascher, D. (2004) Climate change meets habitat fragmentation: linking landscape and biogeographical scale level in research and conservation. *Biological Conservation*, **117**, 285–297.

Ordóñez, J. L., Molowny-Horas, R. & Retana, J. (2006) A model of the recruitment of *Pinus nigra* from unburned edges after large wildfires. *Ecological Modelling*, **197**, 405–417.

Pascual, M. & Dunne, J. A. (eds.) (2006) *Ecological Networks: Linking Structure to Dynamics in Food Webs.* Oxford: Oxford University Press.

Paula, S. & Pausas, J. G. (2008) Burning seeds: germinative response to heat treatments in relation to resprouting ability. *Journal of Ecology*, **96**, 543–552.

Pausas, J. G. (2004) Changes in fire and climate in the eastern Iberian Peninsula (Mediterranean basin). *Climatic Change*, **63**, 337–350.

Pausas, J. G., Bonet, A., Maestre, F. T. & Climent, A. (2006) The role of the perch effect on the nucleation process in Mediterranean semi-arid oldfields. *Acta Oecologica*, **29**, 346–352.

Pausas, J. G. & Bradstock, R. A. (2007) Fire persistence traits of plants along a productivity and disturbance gradient in Mediterranean shrublands of south-east Australia. *Global Ecology and Biogeography*, **16**, 330–340.

Pausas, J. G. & Fernández-Muñoz, S. (2012) Fire regime changes in the Western Mediterranean Basin: from fuel-limited to drought-driven fire regime. *Climatic Change* **110**, 215–226.

Pausas, J. G. & Keeley, J. E. (2009) A burning story: the role of fire in the history of life. *BioScience*, **59**, 593–601.

Pausas, J. G., Llovet, J., Rodrigo, A. & Vallejo, R. (2008) Are wildfires a disaster in the Mediterranean basin? A review. *International Journal of Wildland Fire*, **17**, 713–723.

Pausas, J. G., Ouadah, N., Ferrán, A., Gimeno, T. & Vallejo, R. (2003) Fire severity and seedling establishment in *Pinus halepensis* woodlands, eastern Iberian Peninsula. *Plant Ecology*, **169**, 205–213.

Pausas, J. G. & Paula S. (2012) Fuel shapes the fire–climate relationship: evidence from Mediterranean ecosystems. *Global Ecology and Biogeography*, **21**, 1074–1082.

Pausas, J. G. & Ribeiro, E. (2013) The global fire–productivity relationship. *Global Ecology and Biogeography*, **22**, 728–736.

Pausas, J. G. & Vallejo, R. (2008) Bases ecológicas para convivir con los incendios forestales en la Región Mediterránea – decálogo. *Ecosistemas*, **17**, 128–129.

Pausas, J. G. & Verdú, M. (2005) Plant persistence traits in fire-prone ecosystems of the Mediterranean basin: a phylogenetic approach. *Oikos*, **109**, 196–202.

Pechony, O. & Shindell, D. T. (2010) Driving forces of global wildfires over the past millennium and the forthcoming century. *Proceedings of the National Academy of Sciences USA*, **107**, 19167–19170.

Peñuelas, J. & Boada, M. (2003) A global change-induced biome shift in Montseny mountains (NE Spain). *Global Change Biology*, **9**, 131–140.

Peñuelas, J., Filella, I., Zhang, W. Y., Llorens, L. & Ogaya, R. (2004) Complex spatiotemporal phenological shifts as a response to rainfall changes. *New Phytologist*, **161**, 837–846.

Pereira, M. G., Trigo, R. M., da Camara, C. C., Pereira, J. & Leite, S. M. (2005) Synoptic patterns associated with large summer forest fires in Portugal. *Agricultural and Forest Meteorology*, **129**, 11–25.

Piñol, J., Terradas, J. & Lloret, F. (1998) Climate warming, wildfire hazard, and wildfire occurrence in coastal eastern Spain. *Climatic Change*, **38**, 345–357.

Puettmann, K. J., Coates, K. D. & Messier, C. (2008) *A Critique of Silviculture.* Washington: Island Press.

Pulido, F. J. & Díaz, M. (2005) Regeneration of a Mediterranean oak: a whole-cycle approach. *EcoScience*, **12**, 92–102.

Purves, D. W., Zavala, M. A., Ogle, K., Prieto, F. & Rey, J. M. (2006) Environmental heterogeneity, bird-mediated directed dispersal, and oak woodland dynamics in Mediterranean Spain. *Ecological Monographs*, **77**, 77–97.

Rabasa, S. G., Gutiérrez, D. & Escudero, A. (2007) Metapopulation structure and habitat quality in modelling dispersal in the butterfly *Iolana iolas. Oikos*, **116**, 793–806.

Rabasa, S. G., Gutiérrez, D. & Escudero, A. (2009) Temporal variation in the effects of habitat fragmentation on reproduction of a Mediterranean shrub *Colutea hispanica. Plant Ecology*, **200**, 241–254.

Ramírez, J. A. & Díaz, M. (2008) The role of temporal shrub encroachment for the maintenance of Spanish holm oak *Quercus ilex* dehesas. *Forest Ecology and Management*, **255**, 1976–1983.

Ramírez-Valiente, J. A., Sanchez-Gomez, D., Aranda, I. & Valladares, F. (2010) Phenotypic plasticity versus local adaptation for leaf ecophysiological traits in thirteen contrasting cork oak populations under varying water availabilities. *Tree Physiology*, **30**, 618–627.

Resco de Dios, V., Fischer, C. & Colinas, C. (2007) Climate change effects on Mediterranean forests and preventive measures. *New Forests*, **33**, 29–40.

Rodrigo, A., Retana, J. & Picó, F. X. (2004) Direct regeneration is not the only response of Mediterranean forests to large fires. *Ecology*, **85**, 716–729.

Sabaté, S., Gracia, C. A. & Sánchez, A. (2002) Likely effects of climate change on growth of *Quercus ilex, Pinus pinaster, Pinus sylvestris* and *Fagus sylvatica* forest in the Mediterranean region. *Forest Ecology and Management*, **162**, 23–37.

Sala, O. E., Chapin III, F. S., Armesto, J. J. et al. (2000) Global biodiversity scenarios for the year 2100. *Science*, **287**, 1770–1774.

Santos, T. & Tellería, J. L. (1994) Influence of forest fragmentation on seed consumption and dispersal of Spanish juniper *Juniperus thurifera. Biological Conservation*, **70**,129–134.

Santos, T. & Telleria, J. L. (1997) Vertebrate predation on Holm oak, *Quercus ilex*, acorns in a fragmented habitat: effects on seedling recruitment. *Forest Ecology and Management*, **98**, 181–187.

Santos, T., Telleria, J. L. Diaz, M. & Carbonell, R. (2006) Evaluating the environmental benefits of CAP reforms: can afforestations restore forest bird communities in Mediterranean Spain? *Basic and Applied Ecology*, **7**, 483–495.

Scholze, M., Knorr, W., Arnell, N. W. & Prentice, I. C. (2006) A climate-change risk analysis for world ecosystems. *Proceedings of the National Academy of Sciences USA*, **103**, 13116–13120.

Schupp, E. W., Jordano, P. & Gómez, J. M. (2010) Seed dispersal effectiveness revisited: a conceptual review. *New Phytologists*,**188**, 333–353.

Smit, C., den Ouden, J. & Díaz, M. (2008) Facilitation of Holm oak recruitment by shrubs in Mediterranean open woodlands. *Journal of Vegetation Science*, **19**, 193–200.

Smit, C., Vandenberghe, C., den Ouden, J. & Müller-Schärer, H. (2007) Nurse plants, tree saplings and grazing pressure: changes in facilitation along a biotic environmental gradient. *Oecologia*, **152**, 265–273.

Soliveres, S., DeSoto, L., Maestre, F. T. & Olano, J. M. (2010) Spatio-temporal heterogeneity in abiotic factors modulate multiple ontogenetic shifts between competition and facilitation. *Perspectives in Plant Ecology, Evolution and Systematics*, **12**, 227–234.

Stefanescu, C., Herrando, S. & Páramo, F. (2004) Butterfly species richness in the north-west Mediterranean Basin: the role of natural and human-induced factors. *Journal of Biogeography*, **31**, 905–915.

Stephens, S. L., Millar, C. I. & Collins, B. (2010) Operational approaches to managing forests of the future in Mediterranean regions within a context of changing climates. *Environmental Research Letters*, **5**, 9pp.

Svenning, J. C. & Skov, F. (2007) Could the tree diversity pattern in Europe be generated by postglacial dispersal limitation? *Ecology Letters*, **10**, 453–460.

Tainer, F. H. & Baker, F. A. (1996) *Principles of Forest Pathology*. New York: John Wiley and Sons.

Tello, E., Sabaté, S., Beilot, J. & Gracia, C. (1994) Modelling responses of Mediterranean forest to climate change: the role of canopy in water flux. *Noticiero Biología*, **2**, 55.

Templeton, A. R. (1986) Coadaptation and outbreeding depression. *Conservation Biology: The Science of Scarcity and Diversity* (ed. M. E. Soulé), pp. 105–116. Sunderland, UK: Sinauer.

Thomas, C. D., Cameron, A., Green, R. E. *et al.* (2004) Extinction risk from climate change. *Nature*, **427**, 145–148.

Thuiller, W., Albert, C., Araujo, M. B. *et al.* (2008) Predicting global change impacts on plant species' distributions: Future challenges. *Perspectives in Plant Ecology, Evolution and Systematics*, **9**, 137–152.

Thuiller, W., Lavergne, S., Roquet, C. *et al.* (2011) Consequences of climate change on the tree of life in Europe. *Nature*, **470**, 531–534.

Trabaud, L. & Campant, C. (1991) Difficulté de recolonisation naturelle du pin de Salzmann *Pinus nigra* Arn. spp. Salzmanii (Dunal) Franco après incendie. *Biological Conservation*, **58**, 329–343.

Travis, J. M. J. (2003) Climate change and habitat destruction: a deadly anthropogenic cocktail. *Proceedings of the Royal Society B*, **270**, 467–473.

Trigo, R. M., Pereira, J. M. C., Pereira, M. G. *et al.* (2006) Atmospheric conditions associated with the exceptional fire season of 2003 in Portugal. *International Journal of Climatology*, **26**, 1741–1757.

Tuset, J. J. & Sánchez, G. (eds.) (2004) *La Seca: decaimiento de encinas, alcornoques y otros Quercus en España*. Madrid: MMA Organismo Autónomo de Parques Nacionales Serie Técnica.

Valiente-Banuet, A., Rumebe, A. V., Verdu, M. & Callaway, R. M. (2006) Modern Quaternary plant lineages promote diversity through facilitation of ancient Tertiary lineages. *Proceedings of the National Academy of Sciences USA*, **103**, 16812–16817.

Valladares, F. (ed.) (2004) *Ecología del Bosque Mediterráneo en un mundo cambiante*. Naturaleza y Parques Nacionales. Madrid: Ministerio de Medio Ambiente.

Valladares, F., Zaragoza-Castells, J., Sánchez-Gómez, D. *et al.* (2008) Is shade beneficial for Mediterranean shrubs experiencing periods of extreme drought and late-winter frosts? *Annals of Botany*, **102**, 923–933.

Valladares, F. (2008) A mechanistic view of the capacity of forests to cope with climate change. In *Managing Forest Ecosystems: The Challenge of Climate Change* (eds. F. Bravo, V. L May, R. Jandl & K. von Gadow). Berlin: Springer-Verlag.

Vallecillo, S., Brotons, L. & Thuiller, W. (2009) Dangers of predicting bird species distributions in response to land-cover changes. *Ecological Applications*, **19**, 538–549.

Verdú, M. & Pausas, J. G. (2007) Fire drives phylogenetic clustering in Mediterranean Basin woody plant communities. *Journal of Ecology*, **95**, 1316–1323.

Viegas, D. X. (2004) *Cercados pelo fogo: os incêndios florestais em Portugal em 2003 e os acidentes mortais com eles relacionados*. Coimbra: MinervaCoimbra.

Viegas, D. X. & Viegas, M. T. (1994) A relationship between rainfall and burned area for Portugal. *International Journal of Wildland Fire*, **4**, 11–16.

Warren, M. S., Hill, J. K., Thomas, J. A. *et al.* (2001) Rapid responses of British butterflies to opposing forces of climate and habitat change. *Nature*, **400**, 65–69.

Wenny, D. G. & Levey, D. J. (1998) Directed seed dispersal by bellbirds in a tropical cloud forest. *Proceedings of the National Academy of Sciences USA*, **95**, 6204–6207.

Westerling, A. L. & Bryant, B. P. (2008) Climate change and wildfire in California. *Climatic Change*, **87**, 231–249.

Whitlock, C., Higuera, P. E., McWethy, D. B. & Briles, C. E. (2010) Paleoecological perspectives on fire ecology: Revisiting the fire-regime concept. *The Open Ecology Journal*, **3**, 6–23.

Wikelskia, M. & Cooke, S. J. (2006) Conservation physiology. *Trends in Ecology & Evolution*, **21**, 38–46.

Wilson, R. J., Davies, Z. G. & Thomas, C. D. (2010) Linking habitat use to range expansion rates in fragmented landscapes: a metapopulation approach. *Ecography*, **33**, 73–82.

Young, A., Boyle, T. & Brown, T. (1996) The population genetic consequences of habitat fragmentation for plants. *Trends in Ecology & Evolution*, **11**, 413–418.

Zamora, R., García-Fayos, P. & Gómez, L. (2004) Las interacciones planta–planta y planta–animal en el contexto de la sucesión ecológica. In *Ecología del bosque mediterráneo en un mundo cambiante*. (ed. F. Valladares), pp. 309–334. Madrid: Organismo Autónomo de Parques Nacionales.

Zamora, R., Hódar, J. A., Matías, I. & Mendoza, I. (2010) Positive adjacency effects mediated by seed disperser birds in pine plantations. *Ecological Applications*, **20**, 1053–1060.

Zavala, M. A., Zamora, R., Pulido, F. *et al.* (2004) Nuevas perspectivas en la conservación, restauración y gestión sostenible del bosque mediterráneo. In *Ecología del bosque mediterráneo en un mundo cambiante* (ed. F. Valladares), pp. 509–529. Madrid: Organismo Autónomo de Parques Nacionales.

CHAPTER FOUR

# Recent changes in tropical forest biomass and dynamics

OLIVER L. PHILLIPS and SIMON L. LEWIS

*University of Leeds and University College London*

## 4.1 Introduction

There is a major planet-wide experiment under way. Anthropogenic changes to the atmosphere–biosphere system mean that all ecosystems on Earth are now affected by our activities. While outright deforestation is physically obvious, other subtler processes, such as hunting and surface fires, also affect forests in ways that are less evident to the casual observer (*cf.* Estes *et al.* 2011; Lewis, Malhi & Phillips 2004a; Malhi & Phillips 2004). Similarly, anthropogenic atmospheric change is intensifying. By the end of the century, carbon dioxide concentrations may reach levels unprecedented for at least 20 million years (e.g. Retallack 2001) and climates may move beyond Quaternary envelopes (Meehl *et al.* 2007). Moreover, the rate of change in these basic ecological drivers may be unprecedented in the evolutionary span of most species on Earth today. Additionally, these atmospheric changes are coinciding with the greatest global upheaval in vegetation cover and species' distributions since at least the last mass extinction at ~65 million years ago (Ellis *et al.* 2011). Collectively, the evidence points to conditions with no clear past analogue. We have entered the Anthropocene, a new geological epoch dominated by human action (Crutzen 2002; Steffen *et al.* 2011).

In this chapter we focus on the changes occurring within remaining tropical forests. Most forest vegetation carbon stocks lie within the tropics. Tropical forests store 460 billion tonnes of carbon in their biomass and soil (Pan *et al.* 2011), equivalent to more than half the total atmospheric stock, and annually process 40 billion tonnes (Beer *et al.* 2010). They have other planetary influences via the hydrological cycle, and emit aerosols and trace gases, and they are also characterised by their exceptional variety and diversity of life.

Changes to tropical forests therefore matter for several key reasons. First, the critical role that tropical forests play in the global carbon and hydrological cycles affects the rate and nature of climate change. Second, as tropical forests

*Forests and Global Change*, ed. David A. Coomes, David F. R. P. Burslem and William D. Simonson. Published by Cambridge University Press. © British Ecological Society 2014.

are home to at least half of all Earth's species, changes to these forests have an impact on global biodiversity and the cultures, societies and economies that are bound to this diversity (Groombridge & Jenkins 2003). Finally, as different plant species vary in their ability to store and process carbon, climate and biodiversity changes are linked by feedback mechanisms (e.g. Lewis 2006). The identities of the 'winner' species under environmental changes might enhance, or perhaps mitigate, human-driven climate change.

There is no doubt that remaining forests globally are now changing fast. Analysis of the global carbon cycle shows that after accounting for known atmospheric and oceanic fluxes there is a large, and increasing, carbon sink in the terrestrial biosphere, reaching nearly 3 Gt by the middle part of the last decade (Le Queré *et al.* 2009). Independent analyses of data on atmospheric $CO_2$ concentration to infer sources and sinks of carbon imply carbon uptake over the terrestrial land mass in both tropical and extra-tropical latitudes (Stephens *et al.* 2007). A bottom-up, independent analysis by foresters confirms that forests on every vegetated continent are implicated in this terrestrial sink (Pan *et al.* 2011). This leaves us with a critical question: how should scientists go about documenting and monitoring the changing behaviour of tropical forests?

Of the many approaches and technologies available, it is careful, persistent, on-the-ground monitoring at fixed locations on Earth that can provide reliable long-term evidence of ecosystem behaviour. This is the focus of the current chapter. Most notably, on-the-ground measurements can provide information on subtle changes in species composition, biomass and carbon storage. Assessment of modest, long-term ecological change can be difficult using satellites, as signals often saturate at high biomass (e.g. Mitchard *et al.* 2009), technologies change, and sensors degrade. Yet, permanent sample plot work in the tropics has been very sparse and mostly focused on a few well-known locations, leaving most of the ~10 million square kilometre expanse of the world's richest ecosystems unstudied. This is particularly risky given that no one tropical forest, or small number of studied forests, can be taken as the mean state of all forests. Site-centric ecology is invariably skewed, since peculiar local features – such as fragmentation, unusual soil conditions, cyclones or fires – colour interpretations. In most fields, such as climate change, it would be an obvious folly to infer the presence or absence of global effects from records at a few sites, but in ecological science attempts are still sometimes made to scale results from a few selected locations to draw conclusions about what the behaviour of the whole biome might be.

## 4.2   A networked approach

Evidently, a more robust, synoptic approach is needed. The first attempts at such were inspired by the tropical macroecological approach of Gentry, in

which he used intensive floristic inventories across hundreds of forest locations to reveal the major geographic gradients in diversity and composition
(e.g. Gentry 1988a, b). The first macroecological analyses of tropical forest
dynamics (Phillips & Gentry 1994; Phillips *et al.* 1994, 1998) also made significant claims, but – unlike Gentry's floristic work – lacked complete methodological standardisation. They relied heavily on published data from different
teams worldwide, and had more limited sample sizes. In response, since 2000
and in conjunction with many colleagues, we have focused on developing
standardised, international, long-term networks of permanent plots in
mature forests across Amazonia and Africa. These first draw together the
existing efforts of local botanists and foresters, hitherto often working largely
in isolation. Then, by analysing the gaps in geographical and environmental
space, efforts can be made to extend the site network to fill the gaps, and build
support for long-term, spatially extensive monitoring . The network of
Amazonian-forest researchers, known as RAINFOR (Red Amazónica de
Inventarios Forestales, www.rainfor.org), now represents the long-term ecological monitoring efforts on the ground of 43 institutions worldwide including from all Amazonian countries except Suriname. A parallel initiative in
Africa, AfriTRON (African Tropical Rainforests Observation Network, www.
afritron.org), spans researchers working in 10 countries across the African wet
tropics. Collectively, and with known long-term plots in Asia and elsewhere
(e.g. CTFS network, Chave *et al.* 2008a), there are several hundred long-term
monitoring plots across structurally intact forest. In this chapter our aim is to
synthesise published results from the networks to assess how forests have
generally changed. Our main focus is Amazonia as the network here is most
extensive and mature. Where appropriate, we also discuss results from additional, individual sites where these may shed further light on the processes
involved. Needless to say, an endeavour such as this, realised across two
continents, is only possible with the dedication and perseverance of many
people – botanists, field leaders and assistants – who share the vision of
discovery through widespread, repeated and careful measurement. The contributions of many of these colleagues are acknowledged at the end of the
chapter.

## 4.3  Methodology

For these analyses, we define a monitoring plot as an area of old-growth
forest where all trees ≥10 cm diameter at breast height (dbh, measured at
1.3 m height or above any buttress or other deformity) are tracked individually over time. All trees are marked with a unique number, measured,
mapped and identified. Periodically (generally every 1–5 years) the plot is
revisited, and all surviving trees are re-measured, dead trees are noted, and
trees recruited to 10 cm dbh are uniquely numbered, measured, mapped and

identified. This allows calculation of: (i) the cross-sectional area that tree trunks occupy (basal area), which can be used with allometric equations to estimate tree biomass (Baker *et al.* 2004a; Chave *et al.* 2005; Higuchi *et al.* 1998); (ii) tree growth (the sum of all basal-area increments for surviving and newly recruited stems over a census interval); (iii) the total number of stems present; (iv) stem recruitment (number of stems added to a plot over time); and (v) mortality (either the number or basal area of stems lost from a plot over time). We present results from 50 to 123 plots, depending on selection criteria for different analyses. The 'Amazon' plots span the forests of north-ern South America (Figure 4.1), including Bolivia, Brazil, Colombia, Ecuador, French Guiana, Peru and Venezuela, from the driest to the wettest and the least to the most fertile Amazonian forests. African plots have been moni-tored in Liberia, Ivory Coast, Ghana, Nigeria, Cameroon, Central African Republic, Gabon, Democratic Republic of Congo, Uganda and Tanzania, and span West, Central and East Africa biogeographic regions and from wet (~3000 mm rainfall per year) to dry (those adjacent to the savanna boundary) climates, as well as a range of soil types (Lewis *et al.* 2009a). Most are 1 ha in size and comprise ~400–600 trees of ≥10 cm dbh, but the small-est is 0.25 ha and the largest 10 ha. Many plots have been monitored for more than a decade, although they range in age from 2 to 30 years (mean ~11 years). The earliest plot inventory was in 1968, the latest in 2007. Here we analyse results of censuses completed up to 2007, but for Amazonia we first report results prior to the intense drought of 2005 (Aragao *et al.* 2007) before summarising the impact of the drought. Details of the exact plot locations, inventory and monitoring methods, and issues relating to col-lating and analysing plot data, are omitted from this chapter for reasons of space but are discussed in detail elsewhere (Baker *et al.* 2004a,b; Lewis *et al.* 2004b, 2009a; Lopez-Gonzalez *et al.* 2011; Malhi *et al.* 2002, 2004; Phillips *et al.* 2002a,b, 2004, 2008, 2009). It is important to point out that the samples are not randomly distributed across each rainforest region; historical plot data have been used, where possible, and considerations of access limit where it is practical to monitor forests. Nevertheless, a wide range of environmental space is captured by the whole sample (*cf.* Figure 4.2 for Amazonia).

For Amazonia, diameter-based allometric equations detailed in Baker *et al.* (2004a) are used to scale individual tree measurements to biomass. In brief, we used an equation developed for the Manaus area (Chambers *et al.* 2001a), modified by taking account of the taxon-specific wood density of each tree relative to the mean wood density of trees in the Manaus region. Alternatively, biomass can be estimated by universal, tropical forest equations such as those of Chave *et al.* (2005). The Manaus equation is based on a smaller sample size derived from trees from Amazonia but has the advantage of being local. More allometric equations have been developed by the research community. For

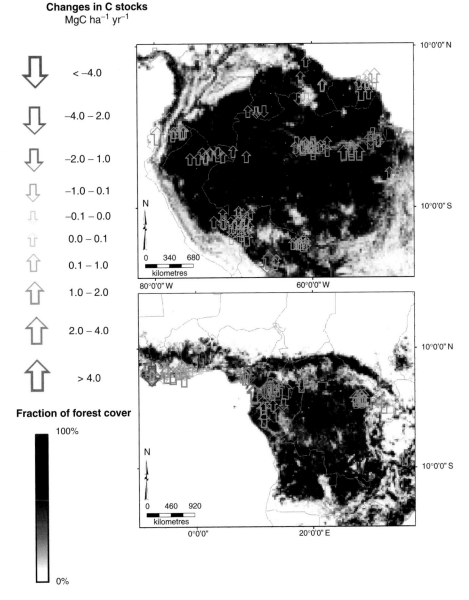

**Figure 4.1** Locations of RAINFOR and AfriTRON network plots used in this study. For each we indicate whether they individually increased in biomass or decreased in biomass over the period monitored (ending prior to the 2005 drought for Amazonia). See plate section for colour version.

simplicity, we do not show results using equations other than Baker *et al.* (2004a) here, but note that while different methods certainly result in systematic differences in biomass estimates (e.g. Chave *et al.* 2003; Feldpausch *et al.* 2012; Peacock *et al.* 2007), the rates of *net* biomass *change* calculated across

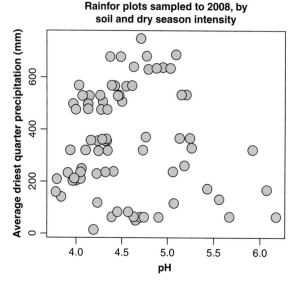

**Figure 4.2** Sampling in environmental space across Amazonia. Most plots sampled are on acid soils in weakly seasonal rain-forest climates, reflecting the dominant conditions of the region, but span a broad environmental range that includes more than two orders of magnitude in soil acidity for example.

Amazonia appear largely insensitive to the equation used (Baker *et al.* 2004a, and unpublished RAINFOR analyses). For Africa, we use the Chave *et al.* (2005) moist forest equation including tree height. We then propagate the uncertainty in both the diameter and height parameters to obtain final biomass estimates (Lewis *et al.* 2009a). We summarise findings from old-growth forests in terms of (i) structural change, (ii) dynamic-process change and (iii) functional and compositional change, over the past two to three decades, including consideration of recent droughts in Amazonia.

## 4.4   Results and discussion

### 4.4.1   Structural change

Among 123 long-term old-growth Amazonian plots with full tree-by-tree data, there was a significant increase in aboveground biomass between the first measurement (late twentieth century, median date 1991) and the last measurement before the 2005 drought (median date 2003). For trees ≥10 cm diameter the increase has been 0.45 (0.33, 0.56) tonnes of carbon per hectare per year (mean, 2.5% and 97.5% confidence limits; Phillips *et al.* 2009). Across all 123 Amazon plots, the aboveground biomass change is approximately normally distributed and shifted to the right of zero (Figure 4.3A). The overall net increase estimated is slightly lower than but statistically indistinguishable from the 0.54 ± 0.29 tC ha$^{-1}$ yr$^{-1}$ estimated by Phillips *et al.* (1998) for the lowland Neotropics using 50 sites up to 1996, and the Baker *et al.* (2004a) estimate of 0.62 ± 0.23 tC ha$^{-1}$ yr$^{-1}$ for 59 core RAINFOR Amazon plots up to 2000. In the larger dataset that is now available, estimates of biomass carbon change always give a positive carbon uptake and are also rather

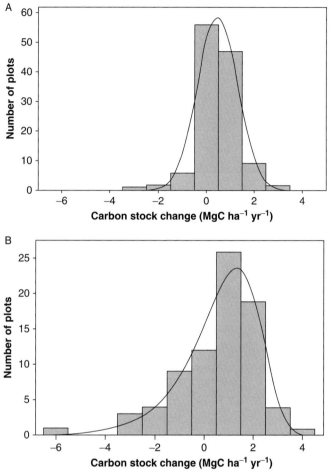

Figure 4.3 Aboveground biomass change (dry weight) of trees greater than 10 cm diameter. (A) Across 123 Amazonian plots, based on initial and final stand-biomass estimates calculated using an allometric equation relating individual tree diameter and wood density to biomass. (B) Across 79 plots from Africa, but including estimated tree height for each stem, in addition to diameter and wood density, to estimate biomass, with uncertainty in the height and diameter measurement both propagated to final biomass change estimates. As would be expected in a random sample of small plots measured for a finite period, some sites show a decline in biomass during that period indicating that at that particular point in space and time tree mortality has exceeded tree growth. However, the mean and median are shifted significantly to the right for both datasets ($P < 0.01$).

insensitive to different weightings based on measurement interval and plot area (supplementary information in Phillips *et al.* 2009). Using the same approach, we recently discovered a comparable phenomenon in African forests. Here, we measured a similar net sink in trees ≥10 cm diameter with a mean of 0.63 (bootstrapped 95% confidence interval, CI, 0.22–0.94) tonnes of carbon per hectare per year ($n = 79$ plots, mean start date 1987 and mean end date 1996; Lewis *et al.* 2009a). The distribution is left-skewed and shifted to the right of zero (Figure 4.3B). Re-sampling shows that obtaining such a sample of increasing biomass from a domain that was not increasing in biomass is highly unlikely ($P < 0.001$; Lewis *et al.* 2009a). African forests have greater biomass per unit area than Amazon forests (202 vs. 154 MgC ha$^{-1}$); once this difference is accounted for, both forest blocks have been gaining net biomass at the same relative rate (0.30% per year for Amazonia, 0.29% per year for Africa).

There are various possible ways by which these plot-based measures can be scaled to tropical forests across Amazonia, South America and Africa. Here, we adopt a relatively simple approach, given the various and not always quantifiable uncertainties, for example in terms of stems smaller than those we measure, belowground (root) biomass carbon, carbon in dead trees and litter, area of each forest type and degree of human disturbance. Thus, we assume that our measurements are representative of the wider forest landscape, and that other biomass and necromass components also increase proportionally, but that soil carbon stocks are static. We estimate the magnitude of the sink in each continent by multiplying the plot-based net carbon gain rate by a series of correction factors to account for biomass of lianas, trees <10 cm diameter, necromass and belowground carbon, and a mid-range estimate of the surviving forest area for year 2000 (Table 4.1). For the 1990s this yields a total estimated South American forest sink of $0.65 \pm 0.17$ PgC yr$^{-1}$ and a corresponding sink in African forests of $0.53 \pm 0.30$ PgC yr$^{-1}$. Meanwhile, $0.14 \pm 0.04$ PgC yr$^{-1}$ in mature undisturbed Asian forests may be assumed if these responded as African and South American forests did (Pan *et al.* 2011). Thus the combined old-growth tropical forest sink in the 1990s is estimated to have been $1.3 \pm 0.35$ PgC yr$^{-1}$, before allowing for any possible net change in soil carbon stock. This is very similar to the figure given by Lewis *et al.* (2009), of 1.3 PgC yr$^{-1}$ (bootstrapped CI, 0.8–1.6) using plots with a mean time interval of 1987–97 and slightly differing methodology (Tropical America, 0.62; Tropical Africa, 0.44; and Tropical Asia 0.25 PgC yr$^{-1}$). In the subsequent decade the American tropical sink declined as a result of the 2005 Amazon drought; we discuss this below.

Clearly these estimates depend on: (i) measurement techniques; (ii) how representative the plots are of forests in South America, and the rest of the tropics; (iii) assumptions about the extent of mature forest remaining; and (iv) the extent to which we have sampled the regional-scale matrix of natural disturbance and recovery. Moreover, they represent average annual estimates for the late twentieth century – forest plots are not measured sufficiently frequently in enough places to estimate biome carbon balance on a year-by-year basis. However, they are consistent with independent evidence from recent inversion-based studies, showing that the tropics are either carbon

**Table 4.1** Estimated annual change in carbon stock ($TgC \; yr^{-1}$) in tropical intact forests by region for the periods of 1990 to 1999, and 2000 to 2007. Table adapted from Pan et al. (2011); see that paper for details of calculations. ND, data are not available.

| | 1990–1999 | | | | | | | | 2000–2007 | | | | | | | |
| | Estimated annual change in C stock ($TgC \; yr^{-1}$) | | | | | Total | | Change per unit area | Estimated annual change in C stock ($TgC \; yr^{-1}$) | | | | | Total | | Change per unit area |
| | | Dead | | | Extracted | | | $MgC \; ha^{-1}$ | | Dead | | | Extracted | | | $MgC \; ha^{-1}$ |
| | Biomass | wood | Litter | Soil | wood | change | Uncertainty | $yr^{-1}$ | Biomass | wood | Litter | Soil | wood | change | Uncertainty | $yr^{-1}$ |
|---|---|---|---|---|---|---|---|---|---|---|---|---|---|---|---|---|
| Asia | 125 | 13 | 2 | ND | 5 | 144 | 38 | 0.88 | 100 | 10 | 1 | ND | 6 | 117 | 30 | 0.90 |
| Africa | 469 | 48 | 7 | ND | 9 | 532 | 302 | 0.94 | 425 | 43 | 6 | ND | 8 | 482 | 274 | 0.94 |
| Americas | 573 | 48 | 9 | ND | 22 | 652 | 166 | 0.77 | 345 | 45 | 5 | ND | 23 | 418 | 386 | 0.53 |
| Total | 1167 | 109 | 17 | ND | 35 | 1328 | 347 | 0.84 | 870 | 98 | 13 | 0 | 36 | 1017 | 474 | 0.71 |

neutral or carbon sink regions, despite widespread deforestation (Denman
et al. 2007, p. 522; Stephens et al. 2007), and the fact that the terrestrial
biosphere as a whole has been acting as a very large net sink for decades
now (e.g. Le Quéré et al. 2009).

The finding of increasing forest biomass over recent decades has proved
remarkably controversial (cf. for example Clark 2002; Lewis, Phillips & Baker
2006, 2009b; Phillips et al. 2002a; Wright 2005), despite the fact that an uptake
of >2 PgC yr$^{-1}$ somewhere on Earth's land surface is evident from independent mass-balance observations of the global carbon cycle. While there is not
space here to review the many early debates, the most persistent area of
controversy can be characterised by the phrase 'slow in, rapid out' (Körner
2003). This argument stresses that forest growth is a slow process while
mortality can potentially be singular in time, thereby causing rapid biomass
loss and sometimes resetting forest stand structure. Consequently, limited
sampling or sampling over short observation periods may tend to miss such
more severe events. Inferences based on such sampling could therefore result
in positively biased estimates of aboveground biomass trends in old-growth
forests when results from plot networks are extrapolated to a large area.
Given the still small number of tropical plots relative to the total biome
area, this concern is understandable. However, we suggest it is unlikely to
be a major source of uncertainty or bias in our calculations for four reasons.

First, large and intense natural disturbances are rare in the lowland tropics,
certainly compared with boreal forests and probably compared with temperate ones too. Thus, even when accounting for Landsat-based measurements
of large disturbances and conservatively using a disturbance frequency/
magnitude model fit that is likely to over-estimate the frequency of large-
magnitude disturbances, it is clear that disturbances capable of removing
100 Mg aboveground biomass (AGB) at the 1 ha scale (i.e. about 1/3 total
standing biomass) have return times of 1000 years or more in Amazonia
(Gloor et al. 2009: Table 4.1). Furthermore, Gloor et al. (2009) used a stochastic
simulator to show for South American forests that any sampling biases resulting from such a disturbance regime, given the sample sizes available in the
RAINFOR network, are too small to explain the gains detected by the plot
network. More recent independent analyses using satellite data from across
the Amazon basin (Espirito-Santo et al. 2010) show that the return time of
stand-initiating scale disturbances in western Amazonia is ~27 000 years,
while in eastern Amazonia it is ~90 000 years. The basin-wide mean,
~39 000 years, is so large that any impacts on our Amazon dataset are negligible, and it explains why we have not sampled a stand-resetting disturbance.
This accords with the first pioneering large-scale analysis, which showed
the rarity of large-scale disturbance events in the Amazon Basin (Nelson
et al. 1994). For Africa, analysis of a single available dataset from large-scale

ground-based surveys of forest gaps, alongside mortality rates in the AfriTRON plots, both showed a similar pattern: the size frequency-distribution of disturbance events contain too few large-scale events to cause the increase in biomass shown in the presented results (Lewis et al. 2009b). This accords with the high biomass and large number of large diameter trees in African forests, which most closely match theoretical 'disturbance-free' forests (Enquist & Niklas 2001), implying that large-scale mortality events are rare. The 'slow-in, rapid-out' debate was magnified by a theoretical paper that unfortunately compared single-year time-step simulations with actual RAINFOR results, which are averaged at intervals of 10 years (Fisher et al. 2008). Furthermore, the size-frequency distribution of disturbance events was also parameterised incorrectly, thus overestimating the frequency of large disturbance events (cf. Lloyd, Gloor & Lewis 2009). These two errors greatly exaggerated the apparent magnitude of the 'slow-in, rapid-out' effect, by more than an order of magnitude.

Second, the RAINFOR network was successfully used to detect the impact of a major disturbance (the 2005 Amazon drought; see below) and to differentiate its dynamic and floristic effects from the background state of long-term biomass accumulation. This biomass decline was in fact dominated by a clearly detectable increase in mortality (Phillips et al. 2009). Thus, if there was a dominating impact of past disturbance events on Amazon forests these would have been detected, as the network is proven to be large enough to detect much more modest disturbance events.

Third, the plot network lacks the basic signatures of forests recovering from large disturbances. Biomass increase is not the only structural change recorded in Amazonian forest plots. Across 91 RAINFOR plots where we tracked populations back to 2002 there has been a small increase in the stand density between the first and last measurements of $0.84 \pm 0.77$ stems per hectare per year, an annual increase of $0.15 \pm 0.13\%$ (Phillips et al. 2004). The same test using a longer-term subset of plots (50 plots from Lewis et al. 2004b) shows a slightly larger increase ($0.18 \pm 0.12\%$ per year). These increases in stand density, while proportionally smaller than the biomass changes, run counter to expectations of declines if the plots were in an advanced state of secondary succession (e.g. Coomes & Allen 2007), as do simultaneous increases in growth rates (see below). In Africa stand density changes have yet to be evaluated, but in both Africa and Amazonia there has been no shift in species composition towards more shade-tolerant taxa that would occur in a domain that was recovering from past disturbance events (e.g. Lewis 2009a; Phillips et al. 2009). In summary, analysis of other structural, dynamic and floristic change in the same plots is not consistent with a widespread disturbance-recovery signature. These results argue against the notion that the generalised biomass increase observed across Amazon and African plots can be explained as a result of a combination of disturbance recovery and small sample sizes.

Lastly, a network of fewer larger plots (Chave *et al.* 2008a), atmospheric $CO_2$ data (Denning *et al.* 2007; Stephens *et al.* 2007) and carbon mass-balance approaches (Le Queré *et al.* 2009) – evidence independent from the plot networks reported here – each imply that there is a carbon sink in tropical forests (summarised in Lewis *et al.* 2009a). Parsimony therefore suggests that the increase in biomass is not the result of a statistical artefact based on forest disturbance episodes that have been poorly sampled.

Nevertheless, our Amazon and African samples are non-randomly distributed. It is possible to test whether this spatial bias might be driving the result by assessing whether we have oversampled unusually heavily in regions that happened to be gaining biomass, and under-sampled those that happened to lose biomass. At smaller scales this is unlikely, since the long-term mean net gain in Amazonia is almost identical whether the sampling unit is taken to be the 'plot' (as here), or a larger unit such as a 'landscape cluster of plots' in both Amazonia and Africa (Phillips *et al.* 2009; Lewis *et al.* 2004b; 2009a). At larger scales, while the networks still leave large expanses of Brazilian Amazonia and the Central Congo Basin unsampled (Figure 4.1), the climate- and soil-environmental space is well covered (Figure 4.2). Greater monitoring efforts in the difficult-to-access regions are of course needed to reduce the uncertainty due to incomplete spatial coverage.

## 4.4.2   Dynamic changes

A complementary way of examining forest change is to look for changes in the processes (growth, recruitment, death): have these forests simply gained mass, or have they become more or less dynamic too? For the Amazon Basin, we have measured the dynamics of forests until 2002 in two ways. First, we examined changes in stem population dynamics, by convention estimating stem turnover between any two censuses as the mean of annual mortality and recruitment rates for the population of trees $\geq 10$ cm diameter (Phillips & Gentry 1994). Second, we examined changes in biomass fluxes of the forest in terms of growth of trees and the biomass lost from mortality events. These stand-level rates of biomass gain and loss should be approximately proportional to the rate at which surviving and recruiting trees gain basal area and the rate at which basal area is lost from the stand through tree death (Phillips *et al.* 1994).

Among 50 old-growth plots across tropical South America with at least three censuses to 2002 (and therefore at least two consecutive monitoring periods that can be compared), we find that *all* of these key ecosystem processes – stem recruitment, mortality and turnover, and biomass growth, loss and turnover – increased significantly (Figure 4.4) between the first and second monitoring periods (Lewis *et al.* 2004b). Thus, over the 1980s and 1990s these forests became, on average, faster-growing and more dynamic,

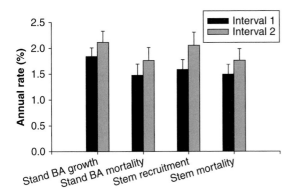

**Figure 4.4** Annualised rates of stand-level basal-area (BA) growth, basal-area mortality, stem recruitment and stem mortality from plots with two consecutive census intervals, each giving the mean from 50 plots with 95% confidence intervals. Paired $t$-tests show that all of the increases are significant. The average mid-year of the first and second censuses was 1989 and 1996, respectively (from Lewis *et al.* 2004b).

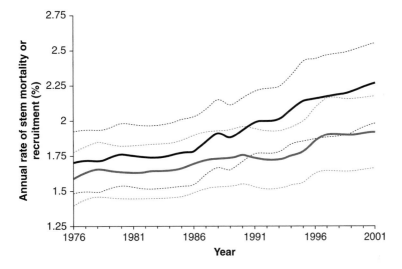

**Figure 4.5** Mean and 95% confidence intervals for stem recruitment and mortality rates against calendar year, for plots arrayed across Amazonia. Rates for each plot were corrected for the effects of differing census-interval lengths, for 'site-switching' (changes through time in the plots being measured) and for 'majestic-forest bias' (potential avoiding of gaps when establishing plots). A detailed justification methodology for these corrections is given in Phillips *et al.* (2004); all trends hold if these corrections are not applied. Black indicates recruitment, grey indicates mortality; solid lines are means, and dots are 95% confidence intervals (from Phillips *et al.* 2004).

as well as bigger. The increases in the rate of the dynamic fluxes (growth, recruitment and mortality) were about an order of magnitude greater than the increases in the structural pools (aboveground biomass and stem density; Lewis *et al.* 2004b).

These and similar results can be demonstrated graphically in a number of ways. In Figure 4.5, we plot the across-site mean values for stem recruitment and mortality as a function of calendar year. The increase is evidently not the short-term result of a year with unusual weather: recruitment rates on average consistently exceeded mortality rates, and mortality appears to have lagged recruitment (Phillips *et al.* 2004; Lewis *et al.* 2004b).

The 50 plots that have two consecutive census intervals can be separated into two groups, one fast-growing and more dynamic (mostly in western Amazonia), and one slow-growing and much less dynamic (mostly in eastern and central Amazonia), which reflects the dominant macroecological gradient across Amazonia (Phillips *et al.* 2004; Quesada *et al.* 2012; ter Steege *et al.* 2006). Both groups showed increased stem recruitment, stem mortality, stand basal-area growth and stand basal-area mortality, with greater absolute increases in rates in the faster-growing and more dynamic sites than in the slower-growing and less dynamic sites (Figure 4.6; Lewis *et al.* 2004b), but similar and statistically indistinguishable *proportional* increases in rates among forest types (Lewis *et al.* 2004b). It should be stressed that these results represent the mean response of all mature forests measured. Within our dataset, there are many individual plots showing different, individual responses, just as within the whole literature there are some reports of individual sites showing

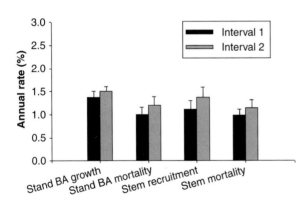

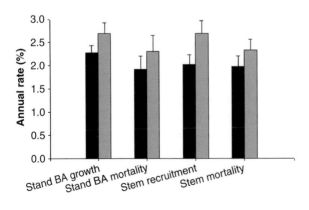

**Figure 4.6** Annualised rates of stand-level basal-area (BA) growth, basal-area mortality, stem recruitment and stem mortality over consecutive census intervals for plots grouped into 'slower growing less-dynamic' (top) and 'faster growing more-dynamic' (bottom) forests. Of the slower-dynamics group, 20 of 24 plots are from eastern and central Amazonia, whereas just two are from western Amazonia. Of the faster-dynamics group, 24 of 26 plots are from western Amazonia, with just one from central Amazonia. The remaining three plots are from Venezuela and outside the Amazon drainage basin. Changes have occurred across the South American continent, and in both slower- and faster-dynamic forests (from Lewis *et al.* 2004b).

similar or different patterns (e.g. Chave *et al.* 2008b; Feeley *et al.* 2007). Nevertheless, when viewed as whole, the permanent plot record from Amazonian and neotropical old-growth forests indicates that increasing growth, recruitment and mortality occurred for at least two decades across different forest types and geographically widespread areas.

The simultaneous recent increases in plot dynamic rates, biomass and stand density raise the question: for how long has this been going on? Only a handful of Amazonian plots were monitored before the 1980s. To go further back in time requires alternative methods: for example annual dating of growth rates of a large sample of individual trees from different species, such as has been done in two locations in non-flooded old-growth forest (Vieira *et al.* 2005), using radiocarbon dating. Although the majority of trees tested did grow faster since 1960 than before 1960, the null hypothesis of no change in growth rate could not be rejected. This technique is complicated by potential ontogenetic variation in growth rates partly related to changing light environments (e.g. Worbes 1999), and could overestimate stand-level growth rates in the past because individual trees with slow and declining growth are more susceptible to mortality (Chao *et al.* 2008) and therefore less likely to survive to the point at which they are dated. Similarly, as trees mature and increasingly allocate resources to flower, fruit, and seed production, ageing cohorts can exhibit slowing growth over time.

An alternative approach has been to analyse multiple dated herbarium samples stretching back to the nineteenth century for $\delta^{13}$C, $^{18}$O and stomatal density to assess possible changes in photosynthesis (and by implication, growth). By this method, results for two species from the Guiana Shield indicated increased photosynthesis over the past century (Bonal *et al.* 2011). A third approach – using tree-rings to project growth of some tree species back in time – suffers from similar biases to the radiocarbon studies, but holds promise if effective techniques are developed to overcome them.

### 4.4.3 Functional composition changes

Changes in the structure and dynamics of tropical forests are likely to be accompanied by changes in species composition and forest function. Phillips *et al.* (2002) studied woody climbers (structural parasites on trees, also called lianas), which typically contribute 10–30% of forest leaf productivity, but are ignored in most monitoring studies. Across the RAINFOR plots of western Amazonia there was a concerted increase in the density, basal area and mean size of lianas (Figure 4.7; Phillips *et al.* 2002b). Over the last two decades of the twentieth century, the density of large lianas relative to trees increased here by 1.7–4.6% per year. This was the first direct evidence that mature tropical forests are changing in terms of their functional composition. A number of subsequent studies suggest that the phenomenon of increasing lianas extends

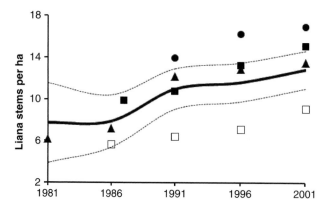

**Figure 4.7** Five-year running means (solid line) with 95% confidence intervals (dashed lines) of liana stem density per hectare (≥10 cm diameter at breast height), with values plotted separately for northern Peru (filled squares), southern Peru (filled triangles), Bolivia (filled circles) and Ecuador (unfilled squares) (adapted from Phillips *et al.* 2002b; see that paper for full details of field and analytical methodology).

across other neotropical forests too (reviewed by Schnitzer & Bongers 2011). There is some limited experimental evidence (Granados & Körner 2002) for growth responses in tropical lianas to elevated atmospheric $CO_2$ concentrations being stronger than those of trees.

Finally, three large-area studies have considered whether there have been consistent changes in tree species composition in non-droughted forests over the past two decades (Chave *et al.* 2008a; Laurance *et al.* 2004; Lewis *et al.* 2009a). In the first, in a large cluster of plots from one Amazon locality, many faster-growing genera of canopy and emergent-stature trees increased in basal area or density, whereas some slower-growing genera of subcanopy or understorey trees declined. Laurance *et al.* (2004) provide evidence of pervasive changes in this locality: growth, mortality and recruitment all increased significantly over two decades (basal area also increased, but not significantly), with faster-growing genera showing larger increases in growth relative to slower-growing genera. Further studies are needed to determine whether comparable shifts in tree communities are occurring throughout Amazonia.

Second, Lewis *et al.* (2009a) reported the relative change in biomass for 916 species from 79 plots across Africa, showing that there was no relationship between the wood density of a species and its change in biomass, relative to the stand. Similarly, there was no relationship between relative change in biomass and mean wood density when 200 common genera rather than species were analysed. Third, Chave *et al.* (2008a) reported functional changes across 10 large forest plots across the tropics, by grouping species into quartiles based on growth rate, wood density, seed size and maximum plant size. On an absolute basis, there were significant increases in biomass of the lowest and highest quartiles of species based on growth rate, no significant change in biomass of the highest and lowest quartiles based on wood density, a significant increase in absolute biomass of the quartile with the smallest seed size, and no changes in biomass of quartiles based on maximum tree size. However, if these shifts are calculated relative to the changes in biomass of the stand, only one result is significant: the largest trees significantly decreased in biomass relative to the stand, whereas the smallest trees showed no relative change. While it is difficult to draw conclusions, results from these three studies suggest that the pervasive increase in forest stand biomass is being caused by concurrent increases in biomass of many species with differing ecological habits.

## 4.5   Recent findings on drought impacts in Amazonia

The results from the Amazon discussed so far reflect forest changes before 2005. In that year the region was struck by a major drought, with the unusual characteristic of being driven by strong warming in the tropical north Atlantic, a feature that appears in projections of climate change from some global circulation models (e.g. Cox et al. 2008). The drought caused substantial economic dislocation by its effect on river transport and resultant fires leading to the disruption of air transport. With the RAINFOR network largely in place and a good forest dynamics baseline established, we had an opportunity to use this 'natural experiment' to assay the sensitivity of the largest tropical forest to an intense, short-term drought, by rapidly recensusing plots across the Basin. Of 55 plots which we monitored through 2005, the mean annual aboveground biomass change was $-0.59$ ($-1.66$, $+0.35$) Mg ha$^{-1}$, and among those plots that were actually droughted the AGB change rate was clearly negative ($-1.62$ ($-3.16$, $-0.54$) Mg ha$^{-1}$). Moreover, across the measured plots the magnitude of the biomass change anomaly was closely correlated to the magnitude of the moisture deficit anomaly experienced in the same period, with most of the difference being driven by increased mortality, implying that it was the unusual moisture deficits that were responsible for the biomass loss by contributing to an enhanced mortality risk.

We estimated the basin-wide impact of the drought on biomass carbon, as compared to the baseline of a net biomass sink in pre-drought measurement period, as between $-1.21$ ($-2.01$, $-0.57$) PgC and $-1.60$ PgC ($-2.63$, $-0.83$) (Table 4.2). The first value is based on simply scaling the per-plot impact by the total area droughted; the second, greater value is based on using remotely sensed rainfall data to model the relationship between biomass change and relative drought intensity. The latter biomass dynamics/climate approach makes use of more of the information on forest response to drought than the simple scaling-up of the mean droughted plot impact, but requires additional assumptions that may introduce error. The consistency of the results from the different analyses indicates a significant regional impact, but much of this might not be 'seen' by the atmosphere until future years. Thus, the main impact is a temporary increase in dead wood production, implying losses to the atmosphere over future years as these dead trees decompose. During the

**Table 4.2** *Estimated 2005 Amazon drought impact, from plot data, using two different approaches. For details of the methodology see online supplementary information published with Phillips et al. (2009).*

**Table 4.2a** *Scaling from the statistical distribution of data for per-hectare plot biomass change (sampling effort-corrected AGB change relative to pre-2005 for each plot), to the whole area of Amazon forest affected in 2005. The method thus applies the mean plot-level biomass impact of the 2005 event (result shown in top line) and scales this by the stated expansion factors, including the simplified assumption of uniform impact across the entire area of Amazon forest suffering drought in 2005.*

|  |  | Mean | 2.5% CI | 97.5% CI |
|---|---|---|---|---|
|  | Mg AGB ha$^{-1}$ yr$^{-1}$ | −2.39 | −1.12 | −3.97 |
|  | Expansion factor |  |  |  |
| Mean 2005 interval length (years) | 1.97 |  |  |  |
| Smaller trees and lianas | 1.099 |  |  |  |
| Droughted forest area (ha) (TRMM data) | $3.31 \times 10^8$ |  |  |  |
| Additional fraction of Amazonia with unreliable TRMM data | 1.031 |  |  |  |
| Sum AGB impact (Mg) |  | $-1.76 \times 10^9$ | $-8.25 \times 10^8$ | $-2.93 \times 10^9$ |
| Belowground | 1.37 | $-6.52 \times 10^8$ | $-3.05 \times 10^8$ | $-1.08 \times 10^9$ |
| Sum biomass impact (Mg) |  | $-2.41 \times 10^9$ | $-1.13 \times 10^9$ | $-4.01 \times 10^9$ |
| **Sum carbon impact (Mg)** | **0.5** | **$-1.21 \times 10^9$** | **$-0.57 \times 10^9$** | **$-2.01 \times 10^9$** |

**Table 4.2b** *Scaling from the plot biomass dynamics vs climate relationship having applied this relationship individually to each TRMM grid cell in the Amazon forest area affected in 2005. The method thus uses the measured plot-level relationship between change in mean annual maximum cumulative water deficit values and change in biomass dynamics, applies this to a spatially explicit pixel-by-pixel measure of the Amazon 2005 climate, to estimate the whole Amazon impact (result in top line) and scales by the stated expansion factors.*

|  |  | Mean | 2.5% CI | 97.5% CI |
|---|---|---|---|---|
|  | Mg AGB | $-1.05 \times 10^9$ | $-5.46 \times 10^8$ | $-1.72 \times 10^9$ |
|  | Expansion factor |  |  |  |
| Mean 2005 interval length (years) | 1.97 |  |  |  |
| Additional proportion of Amazonia with unreliable TRMM data | 1.031 |  |  |  |
| Smaller trees and lianas | 1.099 |  |  |  |
| Sum AGB impact (Mg) |  | $-2.33 \times 10^{-9}$ | $-1.22 \times 10^{-9}$ | $-3.83 \times 10^{-9}$ |
| Belowground (Mg) | 1.37 | $-8.63 \times 10^{-8}$ | $-4.51 \times 10^{-8}$ | $-1.42 \times 10^{-9}$ |
| Sum biomass impact (Mg) |  | $-3.20 \times 10^{-9}$ | $-1.67 \times 10^{-9}$ | $-5.25 \times 10^{-9}$ |
| **Sum carbon impact (Mg)** | **0.5** | **$-1.60 \times 10^{-9}$** | **$-0.83 \times 10^{-8}$** | **$-2.63 \times 10^{-9}$** |

drought year itself the sink may decline (reduction in growth), but not halt (as the new necromass only begins to decompose); the sink could even increase temporarily if potential short-term reductions in soil respiration occur.

Regardless of these details, the total committed carbon impact of the 2005 drought exceeds the annual net C emissions due to land-use change across the neotropics (0.5–0.7 PgC) (Pan *et al.* 2011, Figure 4.1). By combining results from 2005 with published and unpublished information on tropical tree mortality from elsewhere, we have been able to extend the drought–mortality response relationship further. This second analysis (Phillips *et al.* 2010) suggests that across the biome, forest sensitivity to moisture anomalies may be largely predictable, and that even relatively weak drying compared with normal climatology can cause excess deaths once adequate sampling is in place to detect them. However, it should be noted that these are the impacts of short-term intense drought events. Recent analyses of 19 long-term plots from West Africa, which has seen a decades-long drying, saw a net increase in biomass coupled with a strong increase in dry-adapted species over a *c.* 20 year period of monitoring (Fauset *et al.* 2012). A fuller understanding of the impacts of drought will require monitoring of forests through post-drought recovery and repeated droughts (such as in Amazonia in 2010) over the long term.

## 4.6   What is driving the changes?

What could have caused the continent-wide increases in tree growth, recruitment, mortality, stem density and biomass? Many factors could be invoked, but there is only one parsimonious explanation for the pre-2005 pattern. The results appear to show a coherent fingerprint of increasing growth (i.e. increasing net primary productivity (NPP)) across tropical South America, probably caused by a long-term increase in resource availability (Lewis, Malhi & Phillips 2004a; Lewis *et al.* 2004b, 2009a,b). According to this explanation, increasing resource availability increases NPP, which then increases stem growth rates. This accounts for the increase in stand basal-area growth and stem recruitment rates, and the fact that these show the clearest, most highly significant changes (Lewis *et al.* 2004b). Because of increased growth, competition for limiting resources, such as light, water and nutrients, increases. Over time some of the faster-growing, larger trees die, as do some of the 'extra' recruits (the accelerated growth percolates through the system). This accounts for the increased losses from the system: biomass-mortality and stem-mortality rates increase. Thus, the system gains biomass and stems, while the losses lag some years behind, causing an increase in aboveground biomass and stems. Overall, this suite of changes may be qualitatively explained by a long-term increase in a limiting resource.

The changes in composition may also be related to increasing resource availability, as the rise in liana density may be either a direct response to rising resource supply rates, or a response to greater disturbance caused by higher tree-mortality rates. The changing tree composition in central-Amazonian plots (Laurance *et al.* 2004) is also consistent with increasing resource supply rates, as experiments show that faster-growing species are often the most responsive, in absolute terms, to increases in resource levels (Coomes & Grubb 2000). However, it has been proposed by others (e.g. Körner 2004; J. Lloyd pers. comm.) that the greatest proportional response should be in understory seedlings and saplings, which are likely to be close to carbon deficit owing to shading: a small increase in photosynthetic rate here could therefore have a great proportional impact on carbon balance. There is some experimental evidence to support this view (e.g. Aidar *et al.* 2002; Kerstiens 2001).

What environmental changes could increase the growth and productivity of tropical forests? While there have been widespread changes in the physical, chemical and biological environment of tropical trees (Lewis, Malhi & Phillips 2004a), only increasing atmospheric $CO_2$ concentrations (Prentice *et al.* 2001), increasing solar radiation inputs (Wong *et al.* 2006), rising air temperatures and changing precipitation patterns (Trenberth *et al.* 2007) have been documented across most or all of Amazonia over the relevant time period and could be responsible for increased growth and productivity. Additionally, it is conceivable that nutrient inputs have increased: from biomass burning near to once-remote tropical forest plots that are increasingly encroached upon by deforestation (Laurance 2004), and from long-range inputs of Saharan dust to South American (and African) forests, which have increased over recent decades, possibly in response to climate change (Engelstaedter *et al.* 2006).

For only one of these changes, however, do we have clear evidence that the driver has changed over a large enough area *and* that such a change is likely to accelerate forest growth (Lewis, Malhi & Phillips 2004a; Lewis *et al.* 2009b). The increase in atmospheric $CO_2$ is the primary candidate, because of the undisputed long-term increase in $CO_2$ concentrations, the key role of $CO_2$ in photosynthesis, and the demonstrated positive effects of $CO_2$ fertilisation on plant growth rates, including experiments on whole temperate-forest stands (Norby *et al.* 2002; Hamilton *et al.* 2002; Lewis, Malhi & Phillips 2004a; Lewis *et al.* 2009b; Norby & Zak 2011). However, some role for increased insolation (e.g. Nemani *et al.* 2003; Ichii *et al.* 2005), or aerosol-induced increased diffuse fraction of radiation (e.g. Oliveira *et al.* 2007), or nutrient inputs, or rising temperatures increasing soil nutrient mineralisation rates, cannot be ruled out. Elsewhere we have discussed the candidate tropical drivers in more detail (Lewis, Malhi & Phillips 2004a; Lewis *et al.* 2006, 2009b; Malhi & Phillips 2004, 2005). Lastly, given the global nature of the $CO_2$ increase and ubiquitous biochemistry of the plant response involved, we may expect to see the same phenomenon in other biomes. Similarly to the tropics, increases in biomass and/or growth have recently been reported in maritime forests of western

Canada (Hember *et al.* 2012) and across the temperate forests of the northern hemisphere (Luyssaert *et al.* 2008), and indeed on every continent where foresters have measured sufficient sites and land area (Pan *et al.* 2011).

## 4.7 The future: potential susceptibility of Amazonian forests to environmental stress and compositional changes

In summary, long-term observations indicate that Amazonia, the world's largest tract of tropical forest, has shown concerted changes in forest dynamics over recent decades. Such unexpected and rapid alterations – regardless of the cause – were not anticipated by ecologists and raise concerns about other possible surprises that might arise as global changes advance in coming decades. On current evidence, tropical forests are sensitive to changes in incoming resource levels and may show further structural and dynamic changes in the future, as resource levels alter further, temperatures continue to rise and precipitation patterns shift. The implications of such rapid changes for the world's most biodiverse region could be substantial.

### 4.7.1 Carbon sinks to carbon sources?

Old-growth Amazonian forests have evidently helped to slow the rate at which $CO_2$ has accumulated in the atmosphere, thereby acting as a buffer to global climate change. The concentration of atmospheric $CO_2$ has risen recently at an annual rate equivalent to ~4 PgC; this would have been significantly greater without the tropical South American biomass carbon sink of 0.4–0.7 PgC per year (and an African sink of 0.3–0.5 PgC per year). This subsidy from nature could be a relatively short-lived phenomenon. Mature Amazonian forests may either (i) continue to be a *carbon sink* for decades (e.g. Chambers *et al.* 2001b; Cramer *et al.* 2001; Rammig *et al.* 2010), (ii) soon become *neutral* or a small *carbon source* (Cramer *et al.* 2001; Körner 2004; Laurance *et al.* 2004; Lewis *et al.* 2011; Malhi *et al.* 2009; Phillips *et al.* 2002b), or (iii) become a *mega-carbon source* (Cox *et al.* 2000; Cramer *et al.* 2001; Galbraith *et al.* 2010; Rammig *et al.* 2010), with all three responses being reported from a major model-intercomparison project (Friedlingstein *et al.* 2006). For Africa similar scenarios exist: a continued sink, becoming neutral or a small source (Friedlingstein *et al.* 2006), or becoming a large source (Paeth *et al.* 2009). Given that a 0.3% annual increase in Amazonian forest biomass roughly compensates for the entire fossil-fuel emissions of western Europe (or the deforestation in Amazonia), a switch of mature tropical forests from a moderate carbon sink to even a moderate carbon source would impact on global climate and human welfare. The ~0.3% annual increase in carbon storage represents the difference between two much larger values: stand-level growth (averaging ~2%) and mortality (averaging ~1.7%), so a small decrease in growth or a sustained increase in mortality would be enough to shut the sink down. There are several mechanisms by which such a switch could occur, apart from the obvious and immediate threats posed by land-use change and associated disturbances by fragmentation and fire, which we discuss below.

### 4.7.2    Moisture stress

Climate change will alter precipitation patterns. There are critical thresholds of water availability below which tropical forests cannot persist and are replaced by savanna systems. Currently the threshold lies at around 1000–1500 mm rainfall per annum (Salzmann & Hoelzmann 2005; Staver, Archibald & Levin 2011) but this level could increase with rising temperatures which increase evaporation, or this level could decrease if rising atmospheric $CO_2$ concentration decreases transpiration. The outcome of the interplay between these factors is therefore critical to determining transitions between carbon-dense tropical forests and carbon-light savanna systems. The degree to which tropical forests may be ecophysiologically resilient to extreme temperatures, particularly in the context of rising atmospheric $CO_2$ concentration, is a subject of active research, reviewed elsewhere (Lewis *et al.* 2009b; Lloyd & Farquhar 2008), and explored on a biome-wide scale by Zelazowski *et al.* (2011).

The 2005 drought provides direct evidence of the potential for intense dry periods to damage rain-forest vegetation. However, whilst strong events such as the 2005 Amazonian drought are clearly capable of at least temporarily disrupting some of the long-term trends in forest biomass, it remains to be seen whether they are powerful and frequent enough to permanently shift the dominant regime of biomass gains witnessed across old-growth tropical forests wherever they have been extensively monitored. The 1998 El Niño drought was equally strong to 2005 in parts of Amazonia, but its impacts are not distinguishable from the signal of increased biomass and growth over the ~5 year mean interval length available for plots at that time (*cf.* Figure 4.1 in Phillips *et al.* 2009), implying a rapid recovery. We expect therefore that only frequent, multiple droughts would cause the sustained increases in necromass production needed to turn the long-term carbon sink in mature forest into a *sustained* source.

In 2010 a further drought affected the Amazon forest, again dropping some rivers to record lows. If the relationship between water deficit intensity and forest carbon loss that we measured during 2005 also holds for the 2010 drought, then a total impact on old-growth forest biomass carbon in the region of ~2 gigatonnes can be anticipated (Lewis *et al.* 2011). It remains an open question as to how much the forest had recovered from the 2005 drought before the 2010 drought affected the forest plots. Coordinated monitoring with distributed networks of plots is needed to determine whether the recent events represent one-off perturbations for forest carbon stocks from which a full recovery is made within 5 years, or the start of a longer-term climate-induced phase shift in which old-growth Amazonia becomes carbon-neutral or a carbon-source.

### 4.7.3   Photosynthesis/respiration changes

Forests remain a sink as long as carbon uptake associated with photosynthesis exceeds the losses from respiration. Under the simplest scenario of a steady rise in forest productivity over time, it is predicted that forests would remain a carbon sink for decades (e.g. Lloyd & Farquhar 1996). However, the recent increases in productivity, apparently caused by continuously improving conditions for tree growth, cannot continue indefinitely: if $CO_2$ is the cause, trees are likely to become $CO_2$-saturated (i.e. limited by another resource) at some point in the future. More generally, whatever the driver for recently accelerated growth, forest productivity will not increase indefinitely, as other factors such as soil nutrients will limit productivity.

Rising temperatures could also reduce the forest sink, or cause forests to become a source in the future. Warmer temperatures increase the rates of virtually all chemical and biological processes in plants and soils, until temperatures reach inflection-points where enzymes and membranes lose functionality. There is some evidence that the temperatures of leaves at the top of the canopy, on warm days, may be reaching such inflection-points around midday at some locations (Doughty & Goulden 2008; Lewis, Malhi & Phillips 2004a). Canopy-to-air vapour deficits and stomatal feedback effects may also be paramount in any response of tropical forest photosynthesis to future climate change (Lloyd *et al.* 1996). Simulations suggest that the indirect effect of rising temperatures on photosynthesis via stomatal closure is the dominant negative impact on tropical forest growth (Lloyd & Farquhar 2008), which is currently more than offset by increases in photosynthesis from increasing atmospheric $CO_2$. Alternatively, there is evidence that electron transport is the critical step in maximising photosynthesis at a given light level (Haxeltine & Prentice 1996), and the electron transport chain undergoes a reversible point of inflection at a low ~37 °C (Lloyd & Farquhar 2008), thereby reducing photosynthesis at higher temperatures. Additionally, higher air temperature also means higher respiration costs which will also impact on plants' ability to maintain a positive carbon balance in the future. This has been argued to be affecting a forest site in Costa Rica already (Clark & Clark 2010).

Understanding this complex relationship between temperature changes and their impacts on respiration and photosynthesis, plus the impact of rising atmospheric $CO_2$ on tree growth, is critical. The first global circulation model (GCM) to include dynamic vegetation and a carbon cycle that is responsive to these dynamic changes suggested that under the 'business as usual' scenario of emissions, IS92a, atmospheric $CO_2$ concentrations reach >900 ppmv (parts per million by volume) in 2100, compared with ~700 ppmv from previous GCMs (Cox *et al.* 2000, 2004). These concentrations depend on (i) dieback of the eastern Amazonian forests, caused by climate change-induced drought, and (ii) the subsequent release of carbon from soils. The latter process is critically dependent on the assumed response of respiration to temperature, coupled with the simplified representation of soil moisture and soil carbon. A decade on, both Galbraith *et al.* (2010) and Rammig *et al.* (2010) re-analysed the climate and dynamic vegetation models, and found that rising air temperature was an important cause of dieback in most models. However, the dominant temperature-related mechanism differed amongst models with, variously, increases in plant respiration, reduced photosynthesis and increased vapour pressure deficit all resulting in loss of carbon. Yet, $CO_2$ fertilisation had the largest single impact within the models, larger than the negative temperature and negative rainfall reduction impacts. In a recent review of free-air $CO_2$ enrichment ('FACE') experiments, Norby and Zak (2011) conclude that photosynthetic carbon uptake increases in response to $CO_2$ under field conditions, and that the enhancement is sustained over time. But they point out that it remains to be seen whether these growth-related responses also apply to tropical forests. Thus, overall, the uncertainties about (i) how much tropical plants will respond to $CO_2$, (ii) how they will respond to long-term increases in high air temperatures, (iii) how much rainfall may decline by in the dry season, and (iv) how much plants will respond to the decline in rainfall, still preclude robust statements about the timing and magnitude of any slow down or reversal of the tropical forest carbon sink.

To conclude, carbon losses from respiration will almost certainly increase as air temperatures continue to increase. The key question is what form this relationship takes. Carbon gains from photosynthesis cannot rise indefinitely, and will almost certainly be asymptotic. Thus, the sink in old-growth tropical forests will diminish and potentially reverse. The more catastrophic scenarios indicated in some models seem unlikely but cannot be ruled out.

### 4.7.4    Compositional change

Biodiversity change has inevitable consequences for climate change because different plant species vary in their ability to store and process carbon. At the same time, different plant species will benefit and decline as global environmental changes unfold. Yet most models that project the future carbon balance in Amazonia (and future climate-change scenarios) make no allowance for changing forest composition. Representation of composition is challenging, both because of the computational complexities in integrating ecological processes into ecophysiology-driven models, and because the ecological data themselves are sparse. Representing composition better, and its potential for change, is important. Lianas, for example, ignored in all forest models, often contribute little to forest biomass but contribute heavily to productivity (Schnitzer & Bonger 2002), while killing trees (Phillips *et al.* 2005) and preferentially infesting denser-wooded species (Van der Heijden, Healey & Phillips 2008); their recent increase suggests that the tropical carbon sink might shut down sooner than current models suggest. Large changes in tree communities could also lead to net losses of carbon from tropical forests (Körner 2004; Phillips & Gentry 1994). One way this could happen is a shift to faster-growing species, driven by increasing tree mortality rates and frequency of gap formation (Lewis 2006; Phillips & Gentry 1994; Phillips *et al.* 2004). Such fast-growing species generally have lower wood specific gravity, and hence less carbon (West, Brown & Enquist 1999), than shade-tolerant trees. More effort to detect whether such changes are occurring is clearly a priority for future monitoring efforts. The potential scope for such impacts of biodiversity changes on carbon storage is highlighted by Bunker *et al.* (2005), who explored various biodiversity scenarios based on the tree species at Barro Colorado Island: if slower-growing tree taxa are lost from an accelerated, liana-dominated forest, as much as one-third of the carbon storage capacity of the forest could be lost. In Amazonia a small basin-wide annual decrease in mean wood specific gravity would cancel out the carbon sink effect. Currently, the more dynamic forests in the west have ~20% less dense wood than the slower forests of the east (Baker *et al.* 2004b); because these faster western forests also have lower basal area, the differences in terms of biomass carbon stored are significantly greater still (Figure 4.8).

Concerted compositional changes driven by greater resource supply, increased mortality rates and possible increases in the proportion of faster-growing trees that escape lianas, could therefore shut down the carbon sink function of tropical forests earlier than ecophysiological analyses predict. While the initial moves towards individual-based models within GCMs provides the framework within which to evaluate these types of interaction and changing composition (Purves & Pacala 2008), any such analyses will need to be data-driven. Therefore, there are unlikely to be short-cuts to gaining an authoritative understanding of how forest biodiversity and carbon may be changing in the Anthropocene. Repeated, standardised, careful and adequately replicated on-the-ground measurements, coupled with targeted experiments and physiological measurements, will remain key to making significant progress.

## Acknowledgements

The results summarised here depended on contributions from numerous assistants and rural communities in Brazil, Bolivia, Ecuador, French Guiana,

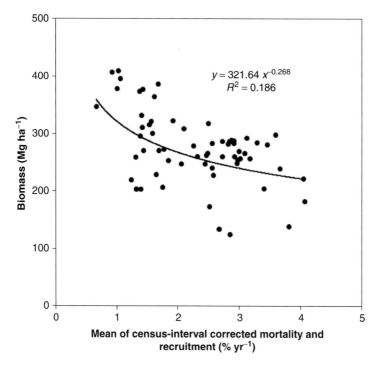

$$y = 321.64\,x^{-0.268}$$
$$R^2 = 0.186$$

**Figure 4.8** Tree biomass as a function of mean stem turnover rates, for 66 lowland forest plots across South America monitored for at least 5 years in the 1980s and 1990s. Note that faster forests, typically in western Amazonia, have lower wood density and much lower biomass.

Peru, and Venezuela (South America), plus Liberia, Ghana, Nigeria, Cameroon and Gabon, and more than 50 grants from funding agencies in Europe and the USA acknowledged in earlier publications. This paper was supported in particular by NERC grants NE/B503384/1 and NE/D01025X/1 (O.P.), a grant to RAINFOR from the Gordon and Betty Moore Foundation, an ERC Advanced Grant (O.P., S. L.: T-FORCES), a Royal Society University Research Fellowship (S.L.), and a NERC New Investigators grant (S.L.). O.P. is a Royal Society Wolfson Research Merit Award holder. We thank M. Alexiades, S. Almeida, E. Alvarez, A. Araujo, L. Arroyo, G. Aymard, T. Baker, D. Bonal, R. Brienen, S. Brown, J. Chave, K.-J. Chao, N. Dávila, C. Diaz, T. Erwin, E. Esparza, T. Feldpausch, A. Gentry, E. Gloor, J. Grace, N. Higuchi, E. Honorio, I. Huamantupa, N. Jaramillo, E. Jiménez, K. Johnson, H. Keeling, T. Killeen, C. Kuebler, S.G. Laurance, W. F. Laurance, J. Lloyd, G. Lopez-Gonzalez, A. Malhado, Y. Malhi, J. Martin, P. Meir, C. Mendoza, A. Monteagudo, H. E. M. Nascimento, D. Navarrete, D. A. Neill, P. Núñez Vargas, S. Patiño, J. Peacock, A. Peña Cruz, M. C. Peñuela, N. C. A. Pitman, A. Prieto, C. A. Quesada, F. Ramirez, H. Ramirez, J. Ricardo, R. Rojas, A. Rudas, L. Salorzano, J. N. M. Silva, M. Silveira, M. Stern,

J. Stropp, H. ter Steege, J. Terborgh, A. Torres Lezama, L. Valenzuela, R. Vásquez Martínez, G. van der Heijden, I. Vieira, E. Vilanova and B. Vinceti (South America), and B. Sonké, K. Affum-Baffoe, L. Ojo, J. Reitsma, L. White, J. Comiskey, M.-N. Djuikouo, C. Ewango, A. Hamilton, T. Hart, A. Hladik, J. Lovett, J.-M. Makana, F. Mbago, H. Ndangalasi, D. Sheil, T. Sunderland, M. D. Swaine, J. Taplin, D. Taylor, S. Thomas, R. Voytere, H. Woell, A. Moungazi, S. Mbadinga, H. Bourobou, L. N. Banak, T. Nzebi, K. Jeffery, K. Ntim, K. Opoku, T. Tafoek, S. Grahame, R. Lowe, L. Banin, K. C. Nguembou, R. Condit, C. Chatelain and L. Poorter for contributing their effort, data and/or discussions including to earlier papers on which this overview is partly based. This chapter also benefited from comments from two anonymous reviewers and guidance from the editors.

## References

Aidar, M. P. M., Martinez, C. A. Costa, A. C. *et al.* (2002) Effect of atmospheric $CO_2$ enrichment on the establishment of seedlings of Jatobá, *Hymenaea courabil* L. (Leguminosae, Caesalpinioideae). *Biota Neotropica* **2**, BN01602012002.

Aragao, L. E. O. C., Malhi, Y., Roman-Cuesta, R. M. *et al.* (2007) Spatial patterns and fire response of recent Amazonian droughts. *Geophysical Research Letters*, **34**.

Baker, T. R., Phillips, O. L., Malhi, Y. *et al.* (2004a) Increasing biomass in Amazonian forest plots. *Philosophical Transactions of the Royal Society, Series B*, **359**, 353–365.

Baker, T. R., Phillips, O. L., Malhi, Y. *et al.* (2004b) Variation in wood density determines spatial patterns in Amazonian forest biomass. *Global Change Biology*, **10**, 545–562.

Beer, C., Reichstein, M., Tomelleri, E. *et al.* (2010) Terrestrial gross carbon dioxide uptake: global distribution and covariation with climate. *Science*, **329**, 834–838.

Bonal, D., Ponton, S., Le Thiec, D. *et al.* (2011) Leaf functional response to increasing atmospheric $CO_2$ concentrations over the last century in two northern Amazonian tree species: a historical delta $^{13}$C and delta $^{18}$O approach using herbarium samples. *Plant, Cell and Environment*, **34**, 1332–1344.

Bunker, D., De Clerck, F., Bradford, J. *et al.* (2005) Carbon sequestration and biodiversity loss in a tropical forest. *Science*, **310**, 1029–1031.

Chambers, J. Q., Santos, J., Ribeiro, R. J. & Higuchi, N. (2001a) Tree damage, allometric relationships, and above-ground net primary production in central Amazon forest. *Forest Ecology and Management*, **152**, 73–84.

Chambers, J. Q., Higuchi, N., Tribuzy, E. S. & Trumbore, S. E. (2001b) Carbon sink for a century. *Nature*, **410**, 429.

Chao, K.-J., Phillips, O. L., Gloor, E. *et al.* (2008) Growth and wood density predicts tree mortality in Amazon forests. *Journal of Ecology*, **96**, 281–292.

Chave, J., Condit, R., Aguilar, S. *et al.* (2004) Error propagation and scaling for tropical forest biomass estimates. *Philosophical Transactions of the Royal Society, Series B*, **359**, 409–420.

Chave, J., Andalo, C., Brown, S. *et al.* (2005) Tree allometry and improved estimation of carbon stocks and balance in tropical forests. *Oecologia*, **145**, 87–99.

Chave, J., Condit, R., Muller-Landau, H. C. *et al.* (2008a) Assessing evidence for a pervasive alteration in tropical tree communities. *PLoS Biology*, **6**, e45.

Chave, J., Olivier, J., Bongers, F. *et al.* (2008b) Above-ground biomass and productivity in a rain forest of eastern South America. *Journal of Tropical Ecology*, **24**, 355–366.

Clark, D. A. (2002) Are tropical forests an important carbon sink? Reanalysis of the long-term plot data. *Ecological Applications*, **12**, 3–7.

Clark, D. B., Clark, D. A. & Oberbauer, S. F. (2010) Annual wood production in a tropical rain forest in NE Costa Rica linked to climatic variation but not to increasing $CO_2$. *Global Change Biology* **16**, 747–759.

Clark, D. A., Piper, S. C., Keeling, C. D. & Clark, D. B. (2003) Tropical rain forest tree growth and atmospheric carbon dynamics linked to interannual temperature variation during 1984–2000. *Proceedings of the National Academy of Sciences USA*, **100**, 5852–5857.

Coomes, D. A. & Allen, R. B. (2007) Mortality and tree-size distributions in natural mixed-age forests. *Journal of Ecology*, **95**, 27–40.

Coomes, D. A. & Grubb, P. J. (2000) Impacts of root competition in forests and woodlands: a theoretical framework and review of experiments. *Ecological Monographs*, **200**, 171–207.

Cox, P. M., Betts, R. A., Collins, M. *et al.* (2004) Amazonian forest dieback under climate-carbon cycle projections for the 21st century. *Theoretical and Applied Climatology*, **78**, 137–156.

Cox, P. M., Betts, R. A., Jones, C. D., Spall, S. A. & Totterdell, I. J. (2000) Acceleration of global warming due to carbon-cycle feedbacks in a coupled climate model. *Nature*, **408**, 184–187.

Cox, P. M., Harris, P. P., Huntingford, C. *et al.* (2008) Increasing risk of Amazonian drought due to decreasing aerosol pollution. *Nature*, **453**, 212–215.

Cramer, W., Bondeau, A., Woodward, F. I. *et al.* (2001) Global response of terrestrial ecosystem structure and function to $CO_2$ and climate change: results from six dynamic global vegetation models. *Global Change Biology*, **7**, 357–373.

Crutzen, P. J. (2002) Geology of mankind. *Nature*, **415**, 23.

Denman, K. L., Brasseur, G., Chidthaisong, A. *et al.* (2007) Couplings between changes in the climate system and biogeochemistry. In *Climate Change 2007: The Physical Science Basis. Contribution of Working Group I to the Fourth Assessment Report of the Intergovernmental Panel on Climate Change* (eds. S. Solomon, D. Qin, M. Manning *et al.*), Cambridge, United Kingdom and New York: Cambridge University Press.

Doughty, C. E. & Goulden, M. L. (2008) Are tropical forests near a high temperature threshold? *Journal of Geophysical Research-Biogeosciences*, **113**, G00B07.

Ellis, E. C. (2011) Anthropogenic transformation of the terrestrial biosphere. *Philosophical Transactions of the Royal Society, Series A*, **369**, 1010–1035.

Engelstaedter, S., Tegen, I. & Washington, R. (2006). North African dust emissions and transport. *Earth-Science Reviews*, **79**, 73–100.

Enquist, B. J. & Niklas, K. J. (2001) Invariant scaling relations across tree-dominated communities. *Nature*, **410**, 655–660.

Espirito-Santo, F. D. B., Keller, M., Braswell, B. *et al.* (2010) Storm intensity and old-growth forest disturbances in the Amazon region. *Geophysical Research Letters*, **37**, L11403.

Estes, J. A., Terborgh, J., Brashares, J. S. *et al.* (2011) Trophic downgrading of Planet Earth. *Science*, **333**, 301–306.

Fauset, S., Baker, T. R, Lewis, S. L. *et al.* (2012) Drought induced shifts in the floristic and functional composition of tropical forests in Ghana. *Ecology Letters*, **15**, 1120–1129.

Feeley, K. J., Wright, S. J., Supardi, M. N. N., Kassim, A. R. & Davies, S. J. (2007) Decelerating growth in tropical forest trees. *Ecology Letters*, **10**, 461–469.

Feldpausch, T. R., Lloyd, J., Lewis, S. L. *et al.* (2012). Tree height integrated into pantropical forest biomass estimates. *Biogeosciences*, **9**, 3381–3403.

Fisher, J. I., Hurtt, G. C., Thomas, R. Q. & Chambers, J. Q. (2008) Clustered disturbances lead to bias in large-scale estimates based on forest sample plots. *Ecology Letters*, **11**, 554–563.

Friedlingstein, P., Cox, P., Betts, R. *et al.* (2006) Climate-carbon cycle feedback analysis: Results from the (CMIP)-M-4 model intercomparison. *Journal of Climate*, **19**, 3337–3353.

Galbraith, D., Levy, P. E., Sitch, S. *et al.* (2010) Multiple mechanisms of Amazonian forest biomass losses in three dynamic global vegetation models under climate change. *New Phytologist*, **187**, 647–665.

Gentry, A. H. (1988a) Tree species richness of upper Amazonian forests. *Proceedings of the National Academy of Sciences USA*, **85**, 156–159.

Gentry, A. H. (1988b) Changes in plant community diversity and floristic composition on environmental and geographical gradients. *Annals of the Missouri Botanical Garden*, **75**, 1–34.

Gloor, M., Phillips, O. L., Lloyd, J. *et al.* (2009) Does the disturbance hypothesis explain the biomass increase in basin-wide Amazon forest plot data? *Global Change Biology*, **15**, 2418–2430.

Granados, J. & Körner, C. (2002) In deep shade, elevated $CO_2$ increases the vigour of tropical climbing plants. *Global Change Biology*, **8**, 1109–1117.

Groombridge, B. & Jenkins, M. D. (2003) *World Atlas of Biodiversity*. University of California Press.

Hamilton, J. G., DeLucia, E. H., George, K. *et al.* (2002) Forest carbon balance under elevated $CO_2$. *Oecologia*, **131**, 250–260.

Haxeltine, A. & Prentice, I. C. (1996) A general model for the light-use efficiency of primary production. *Functional Ecology*, **10**, 551–561.

Hember, R. A., Kurz, W. A., Metsaranta, J. M. *et al.* (2012) Accelerating regrowth of temperate-maritime forests due to environmental change. *Global Change Biology*, **18**, 2026–2040.

Higuchi, N., dos Santos, J., Ribeiro, J. R., Minette, L. & Biot, Y. (1998) Biomassa da parte aérea da floresta tropical úmida de terra firme da Amazônia Brasileira. *Acta Amazonica*, **28**, 153–166.

Ichii, K., Hashimoto, H., Nemani, R. & White, M. (2005) Modeling the interannual variability and trends in gross and net primary productivity of tropical forests from 1982 to 1999. *Global and Planetary Change*, **48**, 274–286.

Kerstiens, G. (2001) Meta-analysis of the interaction between shade-tolerance, light environment and growth response of woody species to elevated $CO_2$. *Acta Oecologica*, **22**, 61–69.

Körner, C. (2003) Slow in, rapid out – carbon flux studies and Kyoto targets. *Science*, **300**, 1242–1243.

Körner, C. (2004) Through enhanced tree dynamics carbon dioxide enrichment may cause tropical forests to lose carbon. *Philosophical Transactions of the Royal Society, Series B*, **359**, 493–498.

Laurance, W. F. (2004) Forest–climate interactions in fragmented tropical landscapes. *Philosophical Transactions of the Royal Society, Series B*, **359**, 345–352.

Laurance, W. F., Oliveira, A. A., Laurance, S. G. *et al.* (2004) Pervasive alteration of tree communities in undisturbed Amazonian forests. *Nature*, **428**, 171–174.

Le Quéré, C., Raupach, M. R., Canadell, J. G. *et al.* (2009) Trends in the sources and sinks of carbon dioxide. *Nature Geoscience*, **2**, 831–836.

Lewis, S. L. (2006) Tropical forests and the changing earth system. *Philosophical Transactions of the Royal Society of London, Series B*, **361**, 195–210.

Lewis, S. L., Brando, P. M., Phillips, O. L., van der Heijden, G. M. F. & Nepstad, D. (2011) The 2010 Amazon drought. *Science*, **331**, 554–555.

Lewis, S. L., Lloyd, J., Sitch, S., Mitchard, E. T. A. & Laurance, W. F. (2009b) Changing ecology of tropical forests: evidence and drivers. *Annual Review of Ecology Evolution and Systematics*, **40**, 529–549.

Lewis, S. L., Lopez-Gonzalez, G. Sonké, B. *et al.* (2009a) Increasing carbon storage in intact

African tropical forests. *Nature*, **477**, 1003–1006.

Lewis, S. L., Malhi, Y. & Phillips, O. L. (2004a) Fingerprinting the impacts of global change on tropical forests. *Philosophical Transactions of the Royal Society, Series B*, **359**, 437–462.

Lewis, S. L., Phillips, O. L. & Baker, T. R. (2006) Impacts of global atmospheric change on tropical forests. *Trends in Ecology & Evolution*, **21**, 173–174.

Lewis, S. L., Phillips, O. L., Baker, T. R. *et al.* (2004b) Concerted changes in tropical forest structure and dynamics: evidence from 50 South American long-term plots. *Philosophical Transactions of the Royal Society, Series B*, **359**, 421–436.

Lloyd, J. & Farquhar, G. D. (1996) The $CO_2$ dependence of photosynthesis, plant growth responses to elevated atmospheric $CO_2$ concentrations and their interaction with plant nutrient status. *Functional Ecology*, **10**, 4–32.

Lloyd, J. & Farquhar, G. D. (2008) Effects of rising temperatures and ($CO_2$) on the physiology of tropical forest trees. *Philosophical Transactions of the Royal Society, Series B*, **363**, 1811–1817.

Lloyd, J., Gloor, M. & Lewis, S. L. (2009) Are the dynamics of tropical forests dominated by large and rare disturbance events? *Ecology Letters*, **12**, E19–21.

Lloyd, J., Grace, J., Miranda, A. C. *et al.* (1995) A simple calibrated model of Amazon rainforest productivity based on leaf biochemical properties. *Plant Cell & Environment*, **18**, 1129–1145.

Lopez-Gonzalez, G., Lewis, S. L., Burkitt, M. & Phillips, O. L. (2011) ForestPlots.net: a web application and research tool to manage and analyse tropical forest plot data. *Journal of Vegetation Science*, **22**, 610–613.

Luyssaert, S., Schulze, E.-D., Börner, A. *et al.* (2008) Old-growth forests as global carbon sinks. *Nature*, **455**, 213–215.

Malhi, Y., Baker, T. R., Phillips, O. L. *et al.* (2004) The above-ground coarse woody productivity of 104 neotropical forest plots. *Global Change Biology*, **10**, 563–591.

Malhi, Y. & Phillips, O. L. (2004) Tropical forests and global atmospheric change: a synthesis. *Philosophical Transactions of the Royal Society, Series B*, **359**, 549–555.

Malhi, Y. & Phillips, O. L. (2005) *Tropical Forests and Global Atmospheric Change*. Oxford University Press.

Malhi, Y., Phillips, O. L., Baker, T. R. *et al.* (2002) An international network to understand the biomass and dynamics of Amazonian forests (RAINFOR). *Journal of Vegetation Science*, **13**, 439–450.

Meehl, G. A., Stocker, T. F. Collins, W. D. *et al.* (2007) Global Climate Projections. In *Climate Change 2007: The Physical Science Basis. Contribution of Working Group I to the Fourth Assessment Report of the Intergovernmental Panel on Climate Change* (eds. S. Solomon, D. Qin, M. Manning *et al.*), Cambridge and New York: Cambridge University Press.

Mitchard, E. T. A., Saatchi, S. S., Woodhouse, I. H. *et al.* (2009) Using satellite radar backscatter to predict above-ground woody biomass: A consistent relationship across four different African landscapes. *Geophysical Research Letters*, **36**, L23401.

Nelson, B. W., Kapos, V., Adams, J. B., Oliveira, W. J. & Braun, O. P. (1994) Forest disturbance by large blowdowns in the Brazilian Amazon. *Ecology*, **75**, 853–858.

Nemani R. R., Keeling, C. D. Hashimoto, H. *et al.* (2003) Climate-driven increases in global terrestrial net primary production from 1982 to 1999. *Science*, **300**, 1560–1563.

Norby, R. J., Hanson, P. J., O'Neill, E. G. *et al.* (2002) Net primary productivity of a $CO_2$-enriched deciduous forest and the implications for carbon storage. *Ecological Applications*, **12**, 1261–1266.

Norby, R. J. & Zak, D. R. (2011) Ecological lessons from free-air $CO_2$ enrichment (FACE) experiments. *Annual Review of Ecology, Evolution and Systematics*, **42**, 181–203.

Oliveira, P. H. F., Artaxo, P., Pires, C. *et al.* (2007) The effects of biomass burning aerosols and clouds on the $CO_2$ flux in Amazonia. *Tellus*, **59**B, 338–349.

Paeth, H., Born, K., Girmes, R., Podzun, R. & Jacob, D. (2009) Regional climate change in tropical and northern Africa due to greenhouse forcing and land use changes. *Journal of Climate*, **22**, 114–132.

Pan, Y., Birdsey, R., Fang, J. *et al.* (2011) A large and persistent carbon sink in the world's forests. *Science*, **333**, 988–993.

Peacock, J., Baker, T., Lewis, S. L. *et al.* (2007) The RAINFOR database: Monitoring forest biomass and dynamics. *Journal of Vegetation Science*, **18**, 535–542.

Phillips, O. L., Aragão, L. E. O. C., Lewis, S. L. *et al.* (2009) Drought sensitivity of the Amazon rainforest. *Science*, **323**, 1344–1347.

Phillips, O. L., Baker, T. R. Arroyo, L. *et al.* (2004) Pattern and process in Amazon tree turnover, 1976–2001. *Philosophical Transactions of the Royal Society, Series B*, **359**, 381–407.

Phillips, O. L. & Gentry, A. H. (1994) Increasing turnover through time in tropical forests. *Science*, **263**, 954–958.

Phillips, O. L., Hall, P. Gentry, A. H., Sawyer, S. A. & Vásquez, R. (1994) Dynamics and species richness of tropical forests. *Proceedings of the National Academy of Sciences USA*, **91**, 2805–2809.

Phillips, O. L., Malhi, Y., Higuchi, N. *et al.* (1998) Changes in the carbon balance of tropical forest: evidence from long-term plots. *Science*, **282**, 439–442.

Phillips, O. L., Malhi, Y., Vinceti, B. *et al.* (2002a) Changes in the biomass of tropical forests: evaluating potential biases. *Ecological Applications*, **12**, 576–587.

Phillips, O. L., Martínez, R. V., Arroyo, L. *et al.* (2002b) Increasing dominance of large lianas in Amazonian forests. *Nature*, **418**, 770–774.

Phillips, O. L., Vásquez Martínez, R., Monteagudo, A., Baker, T. & Núñez, P. (2005) Large lianas as hyperdynamic elements of the tropical forest canopy. *Ecology*, **86**, 1250–1258.

Phillips, O. L., van der Heijden, G., López-González, G. *et al.* (2010) Drought mortality relationships for tropical forests. *New Phytologist*, **187**, 631–646.

Purves, D. & Pacala, S. (2008) Predictive models of forest dynamics. *Science*, **320**, 1452–1453.

Quesada, C. A., Phillips, O. L., Schwarz, M. *et al.* (2012) Basin-wide variations in Amazon forest structure and function are mediated by both soils and climate. *Biogeosciences* **9**, 2203–2246.

Rammig, A., Jupp, T., Thonicke, K. *et al.* (2010) Estimating the risk of Amazonian forest dieback. *New Phytologist*, **187**, 694–706.

Retallack, G. J. (2001) A 300-million-year record of atmospheric carbon dioxide from fossil plant cuticles. *Nature*, **411**, 287–290.

Salzmann, U. & Hoelzmann, P. (2005) The Dahomey Gap: an abrupt climatically induced rain forest fragmentation in West Africa during the late Holocene. *Holocene*, **15**, 190–199.

Schnitzer, S. A. & Bongers, F. (2002) The ecology of lianas and their role in forests. *Trends in Ecology & Evolution*, **17**, 223–230.

Schnitzer, S. A. & Bongers, F. (2011) Increasing liana abundance and biomass in tropical forests: emerging patterns and putative mechanisms. *Ecology Letters*, **14**, 397–406.

ter Steege, H., Pitman, N. C. A., Phillips, O. L. *et al.* (2006) Continental-scale patterns of canopy tree composition and function across Amazonia. *Nature*, **443**, 444–447.

Staver, A. C., Archibald, S. & Levin., S. A. (2011) The global extent and determinants of savanna and forest as alternative states. *Science*, **334**, 230–232.

Steffen, W., Grinevald, J., Crutzen, P. & McNeill, J. (2011) The Anthropocene: conceptual and historical perspectives. *Philosophical Transactions of the Royal Society, Series A*, **369**, 842–867.

Stephens, B. B., Gurney, K. R., Tans, P. P. *et al.* (2007) Weak northern and strong tropical land carbon uptake from vertical profiles of atmospheric $CO_2$. *Science*, **316**, 1732–1735.

108

Trenberth, K. E., Jones, P. D., Ambenje, P. *et al.* (2007) Observations: surface and atmospheric climate change. In *Climate Change 2007: The Physical Science Basis. Contribution of Working Group I to the Fourth Assessment Report of the Intergovernmental Panel on Climate Change* (eds. S. Solomon, D. Qin, M. Manning *et al.*). Cambridge and New York: Cambridge University Press.

Van der Heijden, G., Healey, J. & Phillips, O. L. (2008) Infestation of trees by lianas in a tropical forest in Amazonian Peru. *Journal of Vegetation Science*, **19**, 747–756.

Vieira, S., Trumbore, S., Camargo, P. B. *et al.* (2005) Slow growth rates of Amazonian trees: consequences for carbon cycling. *Proceedings of the National Academy of Sciences USA*, **102**, 18502–18507.

West, G. B., Brown, J. H. & Enquist, B. J. (1999) A general model for the structure and allometry of vascular plant systems. *Nature*, **400**, 664–667.

Wong, T., Wielicki, B. A., Lee, R. B. III *et al.* (2006) Reexamination of the observed decadal variability of the earth radiation budget using altitude-corrected ERBE/ERBS nonscanner WFOV data. *Journal of Climate*, **19**, 4028–4040.

Worbes, M. (1999) Annual growth rings, rainfall-dependent growth and long-term growth patterns of tropical trees from the Caparo Forest Reserve in Venezuela. *Journal of Ecology*, **87**, 391–403.

Wright, S. J. (2005) Tropical forests in a changing environment. *Trends in Ecology & Evolution*, **20**, 553–560.

Zelazowski, P., Malhi, Y., Huntingford, C. Sitch, S. & Fisher, J. B. (2011) Changes in the potential distribution of humid tropical forests on a warmer planet. *Philosophical Transactions of the Royal Society, Series A*, **369**, 137–160.

CHAPTER FIVE

# Disequilibrium and transient dynamics: disentangling responses to climate change versus broader anthropogenic impacts on temperate forests of eastern North America

CHARLES D. CANHAM

*Cary Institute of Ecosystem Studies*

## 5.1 Introduction

Different disciplines within ecology have used a wide range of approaches to predict the impacts of climate change on forest ecosystems. There has been considerable effort by ecosystem scientists to couple vegetation dynamics to atmospheric circulation models, but the spatial scales inherent in those models have required extremely primitive characterisation of population and community dynamics (Sitch *et al.* 2008; Smith *et al.* 2001). Biogeographers have used a variety of approaches to project changes in species distribution under climate change, but those models typically represent steady-state 'potential' responses based on a mapping of current species distributions onto predicted future climates (Jeschke & Strayer 2008; Loehle & LeBlanc 1996). Population and community ecologists have used both contemporary field data and palaeo-ecological methods to understand the consequences of variation in climate for the dynamics of tree species, and have attempted to incorporate those responses into formal models of forest community dynamics (e.g. Bugmann 1996). But it would be fair to say that there is little consensus on the predictive power of any of these approaches.

A challenge faced by all of these approaches has been that climate change is taking place in the context of a broad suite of other anthropogenic impacts on forest ecosystems, ranging from invasive species to air pollution. A number of these clearly have had significant impact on the current distribution and abundance of species, and the functioning of forest ecosystems. In the face of the rapid environmental change of the past century, and given the inherently long time scales of tree population dynamics and forest succession, it seems inescapable that forests are increasingly in disequilibrium, lagging in their responses to both perturbations to species abundances and to changes in

*Forests and Global Change*, ed. David A. Coomes, David F. R. P. Burslem and William D. Simonson.
Published by Cambridge University Press. © British Ecological Society 2014.

the physical and biotic environment. As a corollary, it seems reasonable to expect that the responses of forests to climate change will be conditioned by and interact with transient dynamics already triggered by other aspects of global environmental change. There is also ample evidence that physical and biological legacies of human land-use can persist over time scales from decades to centuries (Foster *et al.* 2003; Katz *et al.* 2010), and that these impacts will also need to be considered in predictions of forest response to future climates.

In this chapter I will review a suite of anthropogenic impacts on temperate forests of the northeastern United States, and ask two basic sets of questions:

(1)   What are the biological and physical legacies and transient dynamics that flow from each of these factors, and how might these legacies and dynamics condition the responses of forests to climate change?

(2)   What are the temporal dynamics of the anthropogenic forcing, and what are the relative time scales of change in the anthropogenic forcing versus community and ecosystem responses? How significant are the time lags in changes in species composition, community structure and ecosystem function in response to fluctuation in the nature and intensity of the anthropogenic impact? In particular, if there are large lags in changes in species abundance in response to these myriad anthropogenic impacts, what effect will this have on the functioning of these ecosystems under climate change?

## 5.2   Ecological setting and theoretical expectations

### 5.2.1   Temperate forests of the northeastern United States

The forests of the northeastern US fall into four broadly defined ecoregions: the spruce–fir (*Picea, Abies*) forests of northern Maine and high elevations along mountains to the south; northern mixed hardwood/conifer forests (*Fagus, Tsuga, Acer, Betula*); oak /hickory (*Quercus, Carya*) forests further south and on drier sites; and pine (*Pinus*) forests that are either dominant on very sandy soils, or present as successional stages following fire within mixed hardwood/ conifer or oak/hickory forests. Fires are the dominant natural disturbance within all but the northern mixed hardwood/conifer forests, where windthrow is typically more common.

While palaeoecologists and vegetation scientists have documented a wide range of climatic and edaphic controls over the broad features of vegetation distribution within the region (Shuman *et al.* 2004), these forests have undergone extensive changes since European settlement (Burgi *et al.* 2000). I will use 'presettlement' conditions as a rough baseline, but note that there is ample evidence of long-term transients in the abundance of dominant tree species prior to European settlement. For example, eastern hemlock (*Tsuga canadensis*), one of the late-successional dominants of the northern hardwood/conifer forests, declined abruptly ~4700 years BP and took over a millennium to recover (Davis 1981). There is still debate about whether the decline was triggered by climate or an insect pest, and what factors were responsible for the slow rate of recovery of regional abundance (Foster *et al.* 2006; Shuman *et al.* 2004), but it is worth noting that transient dynamics of this duration have been predicted in simulations of the impacts of region-wide synchronous mortality of hemlock (Jenkins *et al.* 2000).

Anthropologists are re-evaluating the scope and complexity of Native American impacts on the North American landscape. Ecologists have generally assumed that their primary influence on eastern forests was as a source of ignition for wildfires (Delcourt & Delcourt 1997), and that the abundance of oak/hickory forests was in part a function of the resulting frequent fires (Black *et al.* 2006). Abrams and Nowacki (2008) further suggest that Native Americans may have deliberately managed for and dispersed certain tree species because of the nutritional value of their mast seed crops.

### 5.2.2    Distribution and demography of northeastern US tree species along climate gradients

The primary source of data for both the distribution and demography of tree species along climate gradients in the northeastern US has been the Forest Inventory and Analysis (FIA) network of permanent plots maintained by the US Forest Service. The network consists of randomly distributed plots throughout the US, with a density of roughly one plot per 2430 ha. Species climatic distributions are summarised in online atlases by Thompson *et al.* (1999) and by Prasad *et al.* (2007). A recent analysis of the data by Canham and Thomas (2010) indicates that local frequency (i.e. proportion of plots in which a species is present) varies predictably along gradients of temperature and precipitation, while relative abundance (if present) does not (Figure 5.1). Thus, dominant and subordinate species maintain their approximate relative abundance (if present) throughout their climatic ranges, but become much less frequent within a region outside of the centre of their climatic niche (Canham & Thomas 2010). These results highlight the potential importance of processes that determine species turnover and recruitment on new sites for predicting changes in distribution and abundance of species in response to climate change.

### 5.2.3    Expectations from neighbourhood models of forest dynamics

Models of forest response to climate change tend to fall into three general classes: (a) 'process' models based on ecophysiology and biogeochemistry, usually at the level of biome or plant functional type, rather than species (e.g. Tang & Beckage 2010); (b) largely empirical models that use a variety of

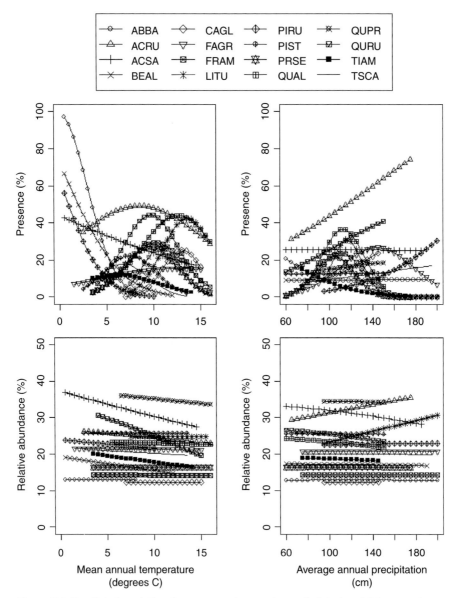

**Figure 5.1** Predicted variation in presence (percentage of plots in which a species occurs, top) and relative abundance (percentage of aboveground biomass, when present) for adult trees of the 16 common tree species in the northeastern US, as a function of mean annual temperature and average annual precipitation. Data from 18 546 plots in the 19 northeastern US states, from the US Forest Service Forest Inventory and Analysis (FIA) network. Redrawn from Canham and Thomas (2010). Species acronyms represent the first two letters of the genus and specific epithet.

statistical methods to relate spatial and temporal variation in climate to variation in forest composition and structure (e.g. Iverson & Prasad 1998); and (c)
models of tree population and community dynamics that incorporate the
effects of climate on the demography of component tree species (e.g.
Bugmann 1996; Gratzer *et al.* 2004). I have argued elsewhere that the mechanisms that underlie many of the spatial and temporal dynamics studied by
ecosystem scientists are best sought at the population and community level
(Canham & Pacala 1994), so my own interests clearly lie in the third class of
models. More specifically, forest ecologists have increasingly viewed the
dynamics of forest ecosystems as the aggregate outcome of interactions
between plants, microbes and animals at the extremely small spatial scales of
local neighbourhoods (Canham & Uriarte 2006; Gomez-Aparicio & Canham
2008a; Gratzer *et al.* 2004).

Individual-based, spatially explicit neighbourhood models such as SORTIE
(Pacala *et al.* 1996) and SORTIE-ND (www.sortie-nd.org) can incorporate a wide
range of neighbourhood interactions, including Janzen–Connell effects on
seedling recruitment (Martin & Canham 2010), neighbourhood competition
(Coates *et al.* 2009), impacts of canopy trees on soil properties and nutrient
availability (Finzi *et al.* 1998; Gomez-Aparicio & Canham 2008a), and allelopathic effects of invasive tree species (Gomez-Aparicio & Canham 2008b). In
effect, the neighbourhood models encapsulate the fine-scale spatial interactions that regulate the demography of component tree species. The spatial
distribution and temporal dynamics of the component species, in turn,
determine spatial variation in a whole host of community and ecosystem
properties (Canham & Uriarte 2006).

There are a number of general features of the population and community
dynamics predicted by these models (Canham & Pacala 1994). In general,
traits related to demography of juveniles (i.e. seed production, seedling establishment, and sapling growth and survival) have the greatest impact on the
successional dynamics of a species (Pacala *et al.* 1996), but traits related to
allometry, growth and survival of adults have the strongest impact on canopy
biomass and productivity, and therefore on ecosystem properties (Grime
1998). Successional dynamics following natural or anthropogenic disturbance
are strongly dependent on the identity and spatial distribution of both the
'survivors' and subsequent colonists (Papaik & Canham 2006). As a result, a
very wide range of successional trajectories in species abundance are possible,
depending on initial conditions. Of particular relevance to debates about
forest response to climate change, analyses with the models suggest that
long-distance dispersal is very ineffective as a process for colonisation of
even moderately disturbed forests (Papaik & Canham 2006), relative to local
input of propagules from individuals that survive a disturbance *in situ*. Finally,
the dynamics of even the shade-tolerant, late successional dominants are

effectively non-equilibrial, since the time transients of the impacts of both initial conditions and cohort age and size structure play out over time scales of centuries to millennia, even in the absence of any change in the environment (Canham & Pacala 1994).

Given that average canopy residence times in temperate forests of the northeastern US are of the order of roughly 100 years (Runkle 1981), and that the shade-tolerant species may spend almost that much time reaching canopy size (Canham 1985), there would appear to be a great deal of potential for time lags and demographic inertia in the responses of species abundance to changes in environment (Kohyama & Shigesada 1995). This potential is amplified by the strong size-dependence of not only growth and survival but also competitive interactions in woody plants (e.g. Canham *et al.* 2006), particularly among juveniles. As a result, while changes in the environment may make seedlings of a given species much less competitive, established saplings and adult trees can continue to dominate a site. There appears to have been very little formal theoretical analysis of this topic in the context of forest response to rapid environmental change (Koons *et al.* 2007).

## 5.3  Human impacts on current and future forests
### 5.3.1  Forest clearing, land abandonment, and regrowth

One of the most pervasive human impacts on northeastern US forests has been the cycle of agricultural land clearing following European settlement, and subsequent abandonment as yields declined and more productive farm-land became available further west (Drummond & Loveland 2010). Roughly two-thirds of the land area of the northeastern US is currently forested, and while there have been no region-wide assessments of the maximum extent of forest clearing following settlement, rates for individual states are as high as 75%. Thus it seems likely that more than half of the current forests have re-established on abandoned agricultural land. There is little evidence that forests are rapidly returning to pre-settlement composition (Fuller *et al.* 1998). One of the most distinctive differences between these post-agricultural forests and forests that were never cleared is in the distribution and abundance of shrubs and herbaceous species (Bellemare *et al.* 2002), a pattern well documented in the ancient woodlands of the United Kingdom (Peterken 1981; Rackham 1980). Recovery of native forest understorey communities is expected to be a very slow process (Flinn & Vellend 2005; Singleton *et al.* 2001), but there has been little evidence that there are impacts of the absence of the native forest understorey on recovery of tree populations.

There are clearly long-term legacies of agricultural land-use history in soils (Baeten *et al.* 2011; Compton *et al.* 1998), although the differences are often subtle (Flinn *et al.* 2005), and direct comparisons of soils of post-agricultural versus never-cleared forests are confounded because farmers made decisions

about what lands to clear and abandon based in part on underlying differences in site quality (Flinn *et al.* 2005; Glitzenstein *et al.* 1990). Nonetheless,
there is ample evidence that even subtle differences in soil chemistry and
soil nutrient availability have significant impacts on juvenile tree growth
and survival (Bigelow & Canham 2002, 2007), and it seems reasonable to
expect that agricultural legacies in forest soils have long-term impacts on
the successional dynamics of post-agricultural forests.

One indirect legacy of land-use history in the region was the near extirpation of an important herbivore, white-tailed deer (*Odocoileus virginianus*), in the
late 1800s. Populations have since recovered to extremely high densities in
some regions owing to a combination of regulation of hunting, extirpation of
predators and the abundance of high-quality habitat (including early successional forests). There is ample evidence that current deer densities can have
significant impacts on both forest structure and composition (Cote *et al.* 2004).
Deer densities are influenced by winter severity and snow depth (Mech *et al.*
1987), so there is potential for impacts of climate change on the distribution
and abundance of this important herbivore (Post & Stenseth 1998).

### 5.3.2   Fire suppression

There is ample evidence that fires were common in presettlement oak/hickory
forests, and it is widely assumed that these fires played an integral role in the
dominance of oaks in those forests (Abrams 1992). It is just as widely assumed
that fire suppression during the past century has played a role in the regional
decline in abundance of some species of oaks, and their replacement by
species that are less tolerant of ground fires and more tolerant of shade
(particularly red maple and sugar maple). Oaks and maples have distinctly
different impacts on soil chemistry and nutrient availability (Finzi *et al.* 1998),
and these differences are of sufficient magnitude to influence juvenile growth
and survival (Bigelow & Canham 2007). There are also potential feedbacks
between changes in canopy composition and risk of fire in these forests – a
process termed mesophication by Nowacki and Abrams (2008). Specifically,
the slow decomposition of oak leaf litter provides abundant fine fuel for
spring ground fires. Maple leaf litter (with higher nitrogen and lower lignin
contents) decomposes much more rapidly, and provides little fuel the next
spring (Mudrick *et al.* 1994). The increased canopy cover from more shade
tolerant species also changes understorey microclimate, and can reduce
the flammability of woody debris (Nowacki & Abrams 2008). As a result,
the need for fire suppression may decline over time. Thus, active fire
suppression over a period of decades may have triggered a process of species
replacement and associated changes in fuel loads, nutrient cycling and
resource availability that would be expected to play out over time scales
of a century or more.

### 5.3.3 Logging

There seems little question that logging has increased the relative abundance of early and mid-successional tree species (Boucher *et al.* 2006), including the most common tree species in the region (red maple, *Acer rubrum*) (Abrams 1998). In contrast, the abundance of the shade-tolerant, late-successional dominant eastern hemlock (*Tsuga canadensis*) in the Catskill Mountains of New York is far lower than in presettlement forests, presumably because of heavy logging of the species for local tanning industries in the mid nineteenth century (McIntosh 1972).

Only a small fraction of forests in the region have escaped some form of logging, but given the region-wide increase in forest cover over the past century (Drummond & Loveland 2010), there appears to be an assumption by ecologists that the impacts of logging are of largely historical interest. As a result of the combination of markets that are now both global and often targeted on only certain species, and technology that allows efficient selective harvest, the use of clearcutting as a silvicultural system has steadily declined in the region in the past 50 years. In fact, there has been a sea-change in both forest land tenure and timber harvesting practices in the region over the past 50 years. Industrial ownership has largely disappeared, with working forests now in either small private landholdings or larger timber tracts owned and managed by investment firms. And while clearcutting is now relatively rare, the overall intensity of harvesting is quite high (Smith *et al.* 2009). The most recent inventory data from the US Forest Service indicate that harvesting is a larger source of adult tree mortality in forests of the northeastern US than all other causes of mortality (natural and anthropogenic) combined, with logging accounting for 58% of adult mortality (on a volume basis) for the 19 northeasternmost states (Virginia and Kentucky north to Wisconsin and Maine).

The newer silvicultural systems using partial harvesting are far less visible to the public, but forest inventory networks document significant regional variation in the intensity of harvest pressure on northeastern US forests, and the often highly selective nature of their impacts on individual species (Figure 5.2). While largely ignored by ecologists, these regional harvest regimes may represent one of the most temporally dynamic and spatially heterogeneous anthropogenic impacts on northeastern forests. Timber markets are highly volatile, and there are economic forces and public policies that can create feedbacks (both stabilising and destabilising) on both overall harvest rates and species removed in a much more dynamic manner than most other agents of tree mortality. For example, public interest in development of renewable energy sources from forest biomass has led to a wide range of economic incentives for investments that will increase demand for forest

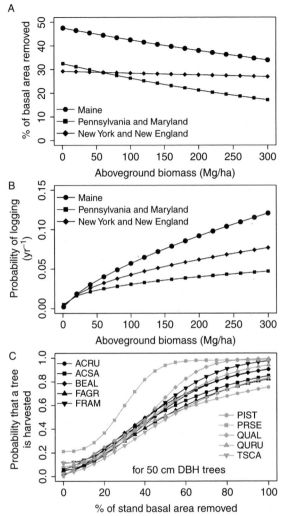

**Figure 5.2** Predicted percentage of stand basal area removed if a stand is harvested (A), and predicted annual probability that a stand is logged (B), as a function of stand aboveground biomass, for different sets of states within the northeastern US. The bottom panel (C) shows the probability that a 50 cm tree is selected for harvest for 10 representative tree species, as a function of total percent of stand basal area removed in a harvest, averaged over the entire northeastern US. All of the functions are from statistical models fit to data on harvest removals from FIA plots and represent harvest activity during the decade from 2001 to 2010. Species acronyms represent the first two letters of the genus and specific epithet.

biomass. Similarly, the threat of spread of an introduced forest pest or pathogen such as the emerald ash borer (*Agrilus planipennis*) may lead to pre-emptive harvesting of host tree species to avoid economic losses. While silvicultural research tends to focus on a relatively small and narrowly defined set of harvest regimes, the inventory data suggest that actual logging practices encompass a much wider range of harvest severity and frequency. Ecologists have a well-developed set of methods and models for the study of natural disturbance regimes that can and should be relevant to the incorporation of the patterns illustrated in Figure 5.2 in our understanding of the effects of logging regimes on forest dynamics.

### 5.3.4   Introductions of pests, pathogens and exotic plant species

Many ecologists would argue that the most significant human impact on northeastern US forests over the past century has been the introduction of a depressingly long list of exotic forest pests and pathogens (Lovett *et al.* 2006). The list includes well-known examples such as the chestnut blight (*Endothia parasitica*), which effectively eliminated adult American chestnuts (*Castanea dentata*) from forests in which it had been a dominant species; Dutch elm disease (*Ophiostoma ulmi*), which has decimated populations of American elm (*Ulmus americana*) in both wetland and upland forests; and beech bark disease, which is causing a widespread decline in American beech (*Fagus grandifolia*), one of the dominants of northern mixed hardwood/conifer forests. More recent threats include the hemlock woolly adelgid (*Adelges tsugae* Annand), which has caused extensive mortality to eastern hemlock (*Tsuga canadensis*); and the emerald ash borer (*Agrilus planipennis* Fairmaire), which is currently spreading rapidly from introductions in midwestern states, and causes high rates of mortality among all of the native species of ash (*Fraxinus*). The Asian long-horned beetle (*Anoplophora glabripennis*) has so far been successfully contained in the few urban sites where it has been discovered, but unlike previous introductions, it has an extremely broad host range – including species of *Acer*, *Betula* and *Populus* – that in aggregate constitute more than a third of tree biomass in eastern US forests.

There is a large and rapidly growing literature on the impacts of these pests and pathogens on host tree species, on the dynamics of the communities within which they are embedded, and on ecosystem function. Lovett *et al.* (2006) provide a conceptual framework for understanding both short and long-term ecosystem impacts as a function of the mode of action, host specificity and virulence of the pest or pathogen, and the importance, uniqueness and community interactions of the host tree species. Like logging, exotic pests and pathogens have the potential to rapidly alter forest composition and structure through high rates of highly species-specific adult tree mortality. It is reasonable to speculate that warming climates could allow northward spread of pests and pathogens to new hosts or currently unoccupied portions of host range. For example, the current northern distributional limit of the hemlock woolly adelgid is well south of the range limit for eastern hemlock, and cold hardiness of the insect is assumed to set this limit (Skinner *et al.* 2003).

There is also a very large and rapidly growing literature on the abundance and impacts of introduced plant species in northeastern US forests (Martin *et al.* 2009). While much of the study of invasive plant species has focused on species with early successional life history traits, there are many species capable of invading shaded forest understoreys (Martin *et al.* 2009). In the northeastern US, common herbaceous invaders include garlic mustard (*Alliaria petiolata*) and Japanese stilt grass (*Microstegium vimineum*), both of which have impacts on soil microbial communities, and in the case of garlic mustard, disrupt associations between mycorrhizae and native tree species (Kourtev *et al.* 2003; Stinson *et al.* 2006). The two most common invasive tree species in the region are tree of heaven (*Ailanthus altissima*) and Norway maple (*Acer platanoides*). Both species have distinctive impacts on nutrient availability and a broad suit of soil ecosystem properties (Gomez-Aparicio & Canham 2008a), and have differential impacts on establishment, survival and growth of seedlings of native tree species (Martin & Canham 2010; Martin *et al.* 2010). Tree of heaven also has allelopathic effects that vary in severity among native tree species (Gomez-Aparicio & Canham 2008b). Despite all of these impacts, simulations predict only relatively slow rates of invasion by either of these exotic tree species (Martin *et al.* 2010).

There have been numerous suggestions that global change (writ broadly, rather than simply climate change) could increase rates of invasion by exotic species (Dukes & Mooney 1999). But beyond this general expectation, there has been little empirical or theoretical exploration of how interactions between invasive species and climate change could impact forest succession in the northeastern US.

### 5.3.5   Air pollution

Much of the early research (1970–1990) on the impact of air pollution on northeastern US forests was focused on acid rain and ozone. The results of an enormous body of research on the effects of both forms of pollution can at best be described as inconclusive. Much of the research was focused on impacts on a few species reported to be in decline (e.g. red spruce, *Picea rubens*; and sugar maple, *Acer saccharum*). Both acid deposition and ozone have a wide range of impacts on tree ecophysiology and/or forest ecosystem processes (Driscoll *et al.* 2001; Jenkins *et al.* 2007). There is conflicting evidence of the effects of acidification on concentrations of base cations, particularly calcium, in forest floors and mineral soils of the northeastern US (Likens *et al.* 1996; Yanai *et al.* 1999). There is ample evidence, however, that variation in status of base cations in the soil can have strong, species-specific impacts on demography of northeastern tree species (Bigelow & Canham 2002, 2007; Kobe 1996). Duchesne and Ouimet (2009) suggested that the recent expansion of beech populations in Quebec (relative to its close competitor sugar maple) is related to depletion of base cations by acid deposition, although this interpretation has been challenged by Messier *et al.* (2011). Nonetheless, quantifying past impacts and predicting future effects of these two forms of air pollution on northeastern forests has proven to be elusive.

The story is much the same with research on $CO_2$ fertilisation effects on northeastern forests. There is ample evidence from chamber studies that northeastern tree species can differ substantially in their growth response to $CO_2$ fertilisation (Bazzaz et al. 1990), and the direct effects under experimental conditions are of sufficient magnitude to have impacts on forest dynamics (Bolker et al. 1995). Studies that have attempted to detect a $CO_2$ fertilisation effect in analyses of long-term tree growth data, however, have had mixed results (Girardin et al. 2011; McMahon et al. 2010). A number of studies have concluded that a variety of feedbacks, including soil nitrogen limitation, will constrain the overall impact of rising atmospheric $CO_2$ on forest growth and dynamics in eastern North America (Norby et al. 2010), but that the overall impact will still be a significant overall increase in net primary productivity (Norby et al. 2005).

A different story has emerged from study of impacts of anthropogenic nitrogen deposition. Nitrogen is widely believed to be the most commonly limiting soil nutrient in northeastern US forests, and decades of field studies and experiments have demonstrated strong species-specific differences in responses to variation in soil N availability. Levels of anthropogenic N deposition in the region are low relative to rates in northern Europe: the area-weighted average total wet plus dry N deposition is approximately ~7 kg ha$^{-1}$ yr$^{-1}$, but with significant regional variation, and hotspots of deposition at high elevations (Weathers et al. 2006). Even at these relatively low levels, there is significant variation in both forest biomass increment and individual tree growth and survival along a deposition gradient (Thomas et al. 2010). The patterns of response are highly species-specific, and vary with the form of mycorrhizal association: all of the endomycorrhizal tree species but only some of the ectomycorrhizal species examined show positive growth responses, and the only species showing declines in survival with increasing N deposition are ectomycorrhizal. Moreover, the growth responses to the ambient variation in N deposition are similar in magnitude to growth responses to the range of annual mean temperature across the region (Thomas et al. 2010).

There have been significant reductions in levels of some of these pollutants over the past 20 years, particularly in $SO_2$ emissions and the resulting acid loading to northeastern ecosystems. Pending federal regulations are expected to lead to further reductions in $SO_2$ and significant reductions in N deposition. Expected rates of change in soil base cation status are much more uncertain. But given the importance of the availability of both nitrogen and base cations for seedling growth and survival in northeastern tree species, it seems reasonable to expect that changes in the balance of N and Ca supply, for example, will have long-term impacts on the competitive balance between tree species. More generally, air pollution has a wide array of impacts on tree ecophysiology and biomass allocation that may ameliorate or exacerbate responses to climate change (McLaughlin & Percy 1999).

## 5.4   Disentangling and detecting responses to climate change in the face of land-use legacies and broader environmental change

Given the diversity of land-use legacies and the rapid pace of human alterations of the biotic and abiotic environment in northeastern US forests over the past century, attempts to isolate the impacts of climate change on these ecosystems would seem to be problematic at best (Pan *et al.* 2009). It is relatively straightforward to quantify the demography of tree species along climate gradients, particularly given the copious data available from forest inventory networks. Such analyses suggest, however, that the magnitude of the impact of predicted climate change on reproduction, growth and survival of tree species is met or exceeded by other anthropogenic changes in the biotic and abiotic environment (Thomas *et al.* 2010). It is also relatively straightforward to incorporate climate impacts on demography of tree species in forest succession models such as SORTIE-ND, under a variety of scenarios of climate change. The models can be parameterised with current forest conditions (again using forest inventory data), and in that sense can integrate the impacts of past land-use and environmental change on current forest composition and structure. Incorporating the breadth of potential interactions between climate change and all of the other anthropogenic impacts on tree demography, however, will be a major challenge.

As an example, consider the interaction between temperature and N deposition. Northeastern tree species differ significantly in their sensitivity to both factors (Thomas *et al.* 2010). In particular, biomass increment of adult trees is either insensitive to or positively correlated with variation in temperature, while adult tree survival shows a more diverse set of responses (Figure 5.3). The tree species show an equally diverse set of responses of growth and survival to N deposition (Thomas *et al.* 2010). Temperatures are expected to rise under climate change, but N deposition levels are equally likely to fall owing to new air pollution control legislation. The net impact of these environmental changes on tree growth will vary from positive to negative, depending on species and the direction and magnitude of change in both temperature and N deposition (Figure 5.4). But in general, a decline in N deposition of 3 kg ha$^{-1}$ yr$^{-1}$ (which seems likely given air pollution regulations currently going into effect) would largely neutralise or even reverse the net impacts on adult tree growth of a 3 degree rise in temperature (Figure 5.4). Thus, failure to incorporate both factors in a model would lead to very different predictions of changes in ecosystem function and dynamics.

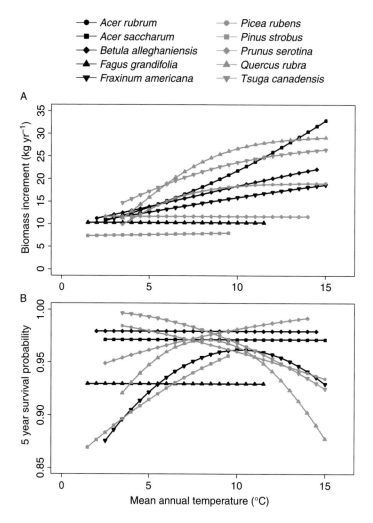

**Figure 5.3** Predicted adult tree annual aboveground biomass increment (kg yr$^{-1}$) (A) and 5 year survival rate (B) for a tree with 500 kg aboveground biomass, as a function of mean annual temperature. Curves are shown for 10 common species in northeastern forests. Figure redrawn from results in Thomas *et al.* (2010).

While the ecophysiological literature has focused primarily on effects of environment on plant growth, differential mortality, particularly in juvenile life history stages, has a disproportionate impact on forest dynamics (Pacala *et al.* 1996). Logging regimes and introduced pests and pathogens represent highly selective agents of adult tree mortality. Paradoxically, it seems possible that both of these forms of biotic disturbance could act to accelerate forest response to climate change by accelerating turnover among canopy trees.

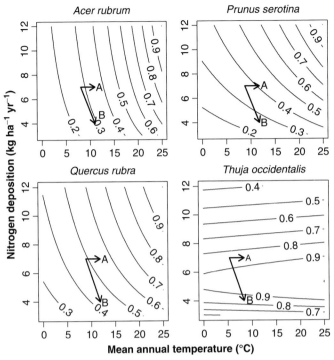

**Figure 5.4** Contour plots of variation in potential growth in aboveground biomass for four species, as a function of mean annual temperature and estimated annual total N deposition, using results from Thomas *et al.* (2010). Contours are relativised to the highest growth rate predicted within the range of the two axes (0–25 °C, and 3–12 kg ha$^{-1}$ yr$^{-1}$ N deposition). Superimposed on the plots are arrows showing expected changes in potential growth under scenarios of either a 3 °C increase in mean annual temperature (A), or that temperature increase combined with a 3 kg ha$^{-1}$ yr$^{-1}$ decline in N deposition rates (B).

Understanding the direct and even indirect effects of changes in the biotic and abiotic environment on demography of component tree species still leaves us far from understanding impacts on composition, structure, and function of communities and ecosystems. Models of forest dynamics are an obvious tool for integrating those impacts, and there is no shortage of models available. They are likely to be our primary tool to address issues of time lags, demographic inertia and resilience in the face of rapid environmental change. The availability of large regional datasets provides a strong empirical foundation for such models. But the complexity of the factors involved in forest response to rapid and myriad environmental changes presents a more profound challenge to the models. The benefits of keeping models simple and the risks inherent in complex models are both well known (Pace 2003). Given that the goal of the models is to understand the nature of community response to anticipated environmental change, model validation will have to come from consensus that they embody the appropriate mechanisms and are based on underlying theory, rather than from direct comparison of model predictions to observed data. But I suggest that we currently have too many potential mechanisms and too little underlying theory of community dynamics in rapidly changing environments to know what degree of model complexity will generate robust predictions.

## References

Abrams, M. D. (1992) Fire and the development of oak forests – in eastern North America, oak distribution reflects a variety of ecological paths and disturbance conditions. *Bioscience*, **42**, 346–353.

Abrams, M. D. (1998) The red maple paradox. *Bioscience*, **48**, 355–364.

Abrams, M. D. & Nowacki, G. J. (2008) Native Americans as active and passive promoters of mast and fruit trees in the eastern USA. *Holocene*, **18**, 1123–1137.

Baeten, L., Verstraeten, G., De Frenne, P. *et al.* (2011) Former land use affects the nitrogen and phosphorus concentrations and biomass of forest herbs. *Plant Ecology* **212**, 901–909.

Bazzaz, F. A., Coleman, J. S. & Morse, S. R. (1990) Growth responses of 7 major co-occurring tree species of the northeastern United States to elevated $CO_2$. *Canadian Journal of Forest Research–Revue Canadienne De Recherche Forestiere*, **20**, 1479–1484.

Bellemare, J., Motzkin, G. & Foster, D. R. (2002) Legacies of the agricultural past in the forested present: an assessment of historical land-use effects on rich mesic forests. *Journal of Biogeography*, **29**, 1401–1420.

Bigelow, S. W. & Canham, C. D. (2002) Community organization of tree species along soil gradients in a north-eastern USA forest. *Journal of Ecology* **90**, 188–200.

Bigelow, S. W. & Canham, C. D. (2007) Nutrient limitation of juvenile trees in a northern hardwood forest: Calcium and nitrate are preeminent. *Forest Ecology and Management* **243**, 310–319.

Black, B. A., Ruffner, C. M. & Abrams, M. D. (2006) Native American influences on the forest composition of the Allegheny Plateau, northwest Pennsylvania. *Canadian Journal of Forest Research–Revue Canadienne De Recherche Forestiere*, **36**, 1266–1275.

Bolker, B. M., Pacala, S. W., Bazzaz, F. A., Canham, C. D. & Levin, S. A. (1995) Species-diversity and ecosystem response to carbon dioxide fertilization: conclusions from a temperate forest model. *Global Change Biology* **1**, 373–381.

Boucher, Y., Arseneault, D. & Sirois, L. (2006) Logging-induced change (1930–2002) of a preindustrial landscape at the northern range limit of northern hardwoods, eastern Canada. *Canadian Journal of Forest Research–Revue Canadienne De Recherche Forestiere*, **36**, 505–517.

Bugmann, H. K. M. (1996) A simplified forest model to study species composition along climate gradients. *Ecology*, **77**, 2055–2074.

Burgi, M., Russell, E. W. B. & Motzkin, G. (2000) Effects of postsettlement human activities on forest composition in the north-eastern United States: a comparative approach. *Journal of Biogeography*, **27**, 1123–1138.

Canham, C. D. (1985) Suppression and release during canopy recruitment in *Acer saccharum*. *Bulletin of the Torrey Botanical Club*, **112**, 134–145.

Canham, C. D. & Pacala, S. W. (1994) Linking tree population dynamics and forest ecosystem processes. In *Linking Species and Ecosystems* (eds. C. G. Jones & J. H. Lawton) pp. 84–93. New York: Chapman and Hall.

Canham, C. D. & Thomas, R. Q. (2010) Frequency, not relative abundance, of temperate tree species varies along climate gradients in eastern North America. *Ecology*, **91**, 3433–3440.

Canham, C. D., Papaik, M. J., Uriarte, M. *et al.* (2006) Neighborhood analyses of canopy tree competition along environmental gradients in New England forests. *Ecological Applications*, **16**, 540–554.

Canham, C. D. & Uriarte, M. (2006) Analysis of neighborhood dynamics of forest ecosystems using likelihood methods and modeling. *Ecological Applications*, **16**, 62–73.

Coates, K. D., Canham, C. D. & LePage, P. T. (2009) Above versus belowground competitive effects and responses of a guild of temperate tree species. *Journal of Ecology*, **97**, 118–130.

Compton, J. E., Boone, R. D., Motzkin, G. & Foster, D. R. (1998) Soil carbon and nitrogen in a pine-oak sand plain in central Massachusetts: Role of vegetation and land-use history. *Oecologia*, **116**, 536–542.

Cote, S. D., Rooney, T. P., Tremblay, J. P., Dussault, C. & Waller, D. M. (2004) Ecological impacts of deer overabundance. *Annual Review of Ecology Evolution and Systematics*, **35**, 113–147.

Davis, M. B. (1981) Outbreaks of forest pathogens in Quaternary history. In *Proceedings of the Fourth International Palynological Conference*. Volume 3 (eds. D. Bharadwaj, Vishnu-Mittre & H. Maheshwari), pp. 216–227. Lucknow, India: Birbal Sahni Institute of Paleobotany.

Delcourt, H. R. & Delcourt, P. A. (1997) Pre-Columbian Native American use of fire on southern Appalachian landscapes. *Conservation Biology*, **11**, 1010–1014.

Driscoll, C. T., Lawrence, G. B., Bulger, A. J. *et al.* (2001) Acidic deposition in the northeastern United States: Sources and inputs, ecosystem effects, and management strategies. *Bioscience*, **51**, 180–198.

Drummond, M. A. & Loveland, T. R. (2010) Land-use pressure and a transition to forest-cover loss in the eastern United States. *Bioscience*, **60**, 286–298.

Duchesne, L. & Ouimet, R. (2009) Present-day expansion of American beech in northeastern hardwood forests: Does soil base status matter? *Canadian Journal of Forest Research–Revue Canadienne De Recherche Forestiere*, **39**, 2273–2282.

Dukes, J. S. & Mooney, H. A. (1999) Does global change increase the success of biological invaders? *Trends in Ecology & Evolution*, **14**, 135–139.

Finzi, A. C., van Breemen, N. & Canham, C. D. (1998) Canopy tree-soil interactions within temperate forests: species effects on carbon and nitrogen. *Ecological Applications*, **8**, 440–446.

Flinn, K. M. & Vellend, M. (2005) Recovery of forest plant communities in post-agricultural landscapes. *Frontiers in Ecology and the Environment*, **3**, 243–250.

Flinn, K. M., Vellend, M. & Marks, P. L. (2005) Environmental causes and consequences of forest clearance and agricultural abandonment in central New York, USA. *Journal of Biogeography*, **32**, 439–452.

Foster, D. R., Oswald, W. W., Faison, E. K., Doughty, E. D. & Hansen, B.C.S. (2006) A climatic driver for abrupt mid-Holocene vegetation dynamics and the hemlock decline in New England. *Ecology*, **87**, 2959–2966.

Foster, D., Swanson, F., Aber, J. *et al.* (2003) The importance of land-use legacies to ecology and conservation. *Bioscience*, **53**, 77–88.

Fuller, T. L., Foster, D. R., McLachlan, T. S. & Drake, N. (1998) Impact of human activity on regional forest composition and dynamics in central New England. *Ecosystems*, **1**, 76–95.

Girardin, M. P., Bernier, P. Y., Raulier, F. *et al.* (2011) Testing for a $CO_2$ fertilization effect on growth of Canadian boreal forests. *Journal of Geophysical Research – Biogeosciences*, **116**.

Glitzenstein, J. S., Canham, C. D., McDonnell, M. J. & Streng, D. R. (1990) Effects of environment and land-use history on upland forests of the Cary Arboretum, Hudson Valley, New York. *Bulletin of the Torrey Botanical Club*, **117**, 106–122.

Gomez-Aparicio, L. & Canham, C. D. (2008a) Neighborhood models of the effects of invasive tree species on ecosystem processes. *Ecological Monographs*, **78**, 69–86.

Gomez-Aparicio, L. & Canham, C. D. (2008b) Neighbourhood analyses of the allelopathic effects of the invasive tree *Ailanthus altissima* in temperate forests. *Journal of Ecology*, **96**, 447–458.

Gratzer, G., Canham, C., Dieckmann, U. *et al.* (2004) Spatio-temporal development of forests – current trends in field studies and models. *Oikos*, **107**, 3–15.

Grime, J. P. (1998) Benefits of plant diversity to ecosystems: immediate, filter and founder effects. *Journal of Ecology*, **86**, 902–910.

Iverson, L. R. & Prasad, A. M. (1998) Predicting abundance of 80 tree species following climate change in the eastern United States. *Ecological Monographs*, **68**, 465–485.

Jenkins, J. C., Canham, C. D. & Barton, P. K. (2000) Predicting long-term forest development following hemlock mortality. In *Proceedings of Symposium on Sustainable Management of Hemlock Ecosystems in Eastern North America* (eds. K. A. McManus, K. S. Shields & D. R. Souto), pp. 62–75. USDA Forest Service General Technical Report NE-267.

Jenkins, J., Roy, K., Driscoll, C. & Buerkett, C. (2007) *Acid Rain in the Adirondacks: An Environmental History*. Ithaca, New York: Cornell University Press.

Jeschke, J. M. & Strayer, D. L. (2008) Usefulness of bioclimatic models for studying climate change and invasive species. In *Year in Ecology and Conservation Biology 2008. Annals of the New York Academy of Sciences* **1134**, pp. 1–24.

Katz, D. S. W., Lovett, G. M., Canham, C. D. & O'Reilly, C. M. (2010) Legacies of land use history diminish over 22 years in a forest in southeastern New York. *Journal of the Torrey Botanical Society*, **137**, 236–251.

Kobe, R. K. (1996) Intraspecific variation in sapling mortality and growth predicts geographic variation in forest composition. *Ecological Monographs*, **66**, 181–201.

Kohyama, T. & Shigesada, N. (1995) A size-distribution-based model of forest dynamics along a latitudinal environmental gradient. *Vegetatio*, **121**, 117–126.

Koons, D. N., Holmes, R. R. & Grand, J. B. (2007) Population inertia and its sensitivity to changes in vital rates and population structure. *Ecology*, **88**, 2857–2867.

Kourtev, P. S., Ehrenfeld, J. G. & Haggblom, M. (2003) Experimental analysis of the effect of exotic and native plant species on the structure and function of soil microbial communities. *Soil Biology & Biochemistry*, **35**, 895–905.

Likens, G. E., Driscoll, C. T. & Buso, D. C. (1996) Long-term effects of acid rain: Response and recovery of a forest ecosystem. *Science*, **272**, 244–246.

Loehle, C. & LeBlanc, D. (1996) Model-based assessments of climate change effects on forests: A critical review. *Ecological Modelling*, **90**, 1–31.

Lovett, G. M., Canham, C. D., Arthur, M. A. Weathers, K. C. & Fitzhugh, R. D. (2006) Forest ecosystem responses to exotic pests and pathogens in eastern North America. *Bioscience*, **56**, 395–405.

Martin, P. H., Canham, C. D. & Marks, P. L. (2009) Why forests appear resistant to exotic plant invasions: intentional introductions, stand dynamics, and the role of shade tolerance. *Frontiers in Ecology and the Environment*, **7**, 142–149.

Martin, P. H. & Canham, C. D. (2010) Dispersal and recruitment limitation in native versus exotic tree species: life-history strategies and Janzen–Connell effects. *Oikos*, **119**, 807–824.

Martin, P. H., Canham, C. D. & Kobe, R. K. (2010) Divergence from the growth-survival trade-off and extreme high growth rates drive patterns of exotic tree invasions in closed-canopy forests. *Journal of Ecology*, **98**, 778–789.

McIntosh, R. P. (1972) Forests of the Catskill Mountains, New York. *Ecological Monographs*, **42**, 143–161.

McLaughlin, S. & Percy, K. (1999) Forest health in North America: Some perspectives on actual and potential roles of climate and air pollution. *Water Air and Soil Pollution*, **116**, 151–197.

McMahon, S. M., Parker, G. G. & Miller, D. R. (2010) Evidence for a recent increase in forest growth. *Proceedings of the National Academy of Sciences USA*, **107**, 3611–3615.

Mech, L. D., McRoberts, R. E., Peterson, R. O. & Page, R. E. (1987) Relationship of deer and moose populations to previous winters snow. *Journal of Animal Ecology*, **56**, 615–627.

Messier, C., Belanger, N., Brisson, J., Lechowicz, M. J. & Gravel, D. (2011) Comment on "Present-day expansion of American beech in northeastern hardwood forests: Does soil base status matter?". *Canadian Journal of Forest Research–Revue Canadienne de Recherche Forestiere*, **41**, 649–653.

Mudrick, D. A., Hoosein, M., Hicks, R. R. & Townsend, E. C. (1994) Decomposition of leaflitter in an appalachian forest – effects of leaf species, aspect, slope position and time. *Forest Ecology and Management*, **68**, 231–250.

Norby, R. J., DeLucia, E. H., Gielen, B. *et al.* (2005) Forest response to elevated $CO_2$ is conserved across a broad range of productivity. *Proceedings of the National Academy of Sciences USA*, **102**, 18052–18056.

Norby, R. J., Warren, J. M., Iversen, C. M., Medlyn, B. E. & McMurtrie, R. E. (2010) $CO_2$ enhancement of forest productivity constrained by limited nitrogen availability. *Proceedings of the National Academy of Sciences USA*, **107**, 19368–19373.

Nowacki, G. J. & Abrams, M. D. (2008) The demise of fire and "Mesophication" of forests in the eastern United States. *Bioscience*, **58**, 123–138.

Pacala, S. W., Canham, C. D., Saponara, J. *et al.* (1996) Forest models defined by field measurements: II. Estimation, error analysis and dynamics. *Ecological Monographs*, **66**, 1–43.

Pace, M. L. (2003) The utility of simple models in ecosystem science. In *Models in Ecosystem Science* (eds. C. D. Canham, J. J. Cole & W. K. Lauenroth), pp. 49–26. Princeton, NJ: Princeton University Press.

Pan, Y. D., Birdsey, R., Hom, J. & McCullough, K. (2009) Separating effects of changes in atmospheric composition, climate and land-use on carbon sequestration of US Mid-Atlantic temperate forests. *Forest Ecology and Management*, **259**, 151–164.

Papaik, M. J. & Canham, C. D. (2006) Species resistance and community response to wind disturbance regimes in northern temperate forests. *Journal of Ecology*, **94**, 1011–1026.

Peterken, G. (1981) *Woodland Conservation and Management*. London: Chapman and Hall.

Post, E. & Stenseth, N. C. (1998) Large-scale climatic fluctuation and population dynamics of moose and white-tailed deer. *Journal of Animal Ecology*, **67**, 537–543.

Prasad, A. M., Iverson, L. R., Matthews, S. & Peters, M. (2007–ongoing) *A Climate Change Atlas for 134 Forest Tree Species of the Eastern United States* [database]. http://www.nrs.fs.fed.us/atlas/tree Delaware, Ohio: Northern Research Station, USDA Forest Service.

Rackham, O. (1980) *Ancient Woodland, Its History, Vegetation and Uses in England*. London: Edward Arnold.

Runkle, J. R. (1981) Gap regeneration in some old-growth forests of the eastern United States. *Ecology*, **62**, 1041–1051.

Shuman, B., Newby, P., Huang, Y. S. & Webb, T. (2004) Evidence for the close climatic control of New England vegetation history. *Ecology*, **85**, 1297–1310.

Singleton, R., Gardescu, S., Marks, P. L. & Geber, M. A. (2001) Forest herb colonization of postagricultural forests in central New York State, USA. *Journal of Ecology*, **89**, 325–338.

Sitch, S., Huntingford, C., Gedney, N. *et al.* (2008) Evaluation of the terrestrial carbon cycle, future plant geography and climate-carbon cycle feedbacks using five Dynamic Global Vegetation Models (DGVMs). *Global Change Biology*, **14**, 2015–2039.

Skinner, M., Parker, B. L., Gouli, S. & Ashikaga, T. (2003) Regional responses of hemlock woolly adelgid (Homoptera: Adelgidae) to low temperatures. *Environmental Entomology*, **32**, 523–528.

Smith, B., Prentice, I. C. & Sykes, M. T. (2001) Representation of vegetation dynamics in the modelling of terrestrial ecosystems: comparing two contrasting approaches within European climate space. *Global Ecology and Biogeography*, **10**, 621–637.

Smith, W. B., Miles, P. D., Perry, C. H. & Pugh, S. A. (2009) *Forest Resources of the United States, 2007*. Gen. Tech. Report WO-78. US Department of Agriculture Forest Service.

Stinson, K. A., Campbell, S. A., Powell, J. R. *et al.* (2006) Invasive plant suppresses the growth of native tree seedlings by disrupting belowground mutualisms. *PLoS Biology*, **4**, 727–731.

Tang, G. P. & Beckage, B. (2010) Projecting the distribution of forests in New England in response to climate change. *Diversity and Distributions*, **16**, 144–158.

Thomas, R. Q., Canham, C. D., Weathers, K. C. & Goodale, C. L. (2010) Increased tree carbon storage in response to nitrogen deposition in the US. *Nature Geoscience*, **3**, 13–17.

Thompson, R. S., Anderson, K. H. & Bartlein, P. J. (1999) *Atlas of Relations Between Climatic Parameters and Distributions of Important Trees and Shrubs in North America*. US Geological Survey Professional Paper 1650 A&B. Online at http://pubs.usgs.gov/pp/p1650-a/

Weathers, K. C., Simkin, S. M., Lovett, G. M. & Lindberg, S. E. (2006) Empirical modeling of atmospheric deposition in mountainous landscapes. *Ecological Applications*, **16**, 1590–1607.

Yanai, R. D., Siccama, T. G., Arthur, M. A., Federer, C. A. & Friedland, A. J. (1999) Accumulation and depletion of base cations in forest floors in the northeastern United States. *Ecology*, **80**, 2774–2787.

# PART II

# Species traits and responses to changing resource availability

# Floristic shifts versus critical transitions in Amazonian forest systems

JÉRÔME CHAVE

*Laboratoire Evolution et Diversité Biologique,*
*CNRS & Université Paul Sabatier*

## 6.1 Introduction

Tropical forests hold close to 250 Pg of carbon, with Latin America contributing half of this (Saatchi *et al.* 2011). Although the rates of deforestation appear to have decreased over the past decade, tropical deforestation still represents the bulk of the *c.* 1.1 PgC yr$^{-1}$ of C emissions due to land-use change (Friedlingstein *et al.* 2010). The direct impact of deforestation and degradation has the potential to be mitigated through a performance-based mechanism such as REDD (Reducing Emissions from Deforestation and Forest Degradation), by monetising carbon held in both managed and unmanaged forests (Agrawal, Nepstad & Chhatre 2011). Additionally, tropical forests contribute to a terrestrial carbon sink (Le Quéré *et al.* 2009), offsetting fossil carbon emissions into the atmosphere through a physiological response of the vegetation (Lewis *et al.* 2009; Lloyd & Farquhar 2008). Thus tropical forests offer critically important ecosystem services by reducing the short-term effect of anthropogenic carbon emissions into the atmosphere.

However, in the face of global climate trends, the resilience of tropical forests has been called into question (Cox *et al.* 2000). South America is sensitive to a number of large-scale climatic anomalies, including the El Niño Southern Oscillation, the Pacific Decadal Oscillation and the North Atlantic Oscillation. All of these contribute to displacing the yearly course of the Inter-Tropical Convergence Zone (ITCZ) and increase the strength of the dry season in some regions (Garreaud *et al.* 2009; Marengo 2004). The 2005 and the 2010 climatic events over Amazonia have exemplified these atmospheric regime shifts, and these may occur more frequently during the twenty-first century. As a result of the increased likelihood of severe droughts, models suggest that Amazonian forests may shift by 2100 to a different biome type akin to a woodland savanna or dry forest (Cox *et al.* 2000, 2004; Huntingford *et al.* 2008; Malhi *et al.* 2009; Poulter *et al.* 2010). Aside from the radical implications for human and wildlife populations inhabiting Amazonia, this new biome type would have far less potential to hold carbon, and such a shift

*Forests and Global Change*, ed. David A. Coomes, David F. R. P. Burslem and William D. Simonson.
Published by Cambridge University Press. © British Ecological Society 2014.

would have important consequences for global life support services. Some of the predictions of this 'Amazon dieback' scenario have been empirically tested (Phillips *et al.* 2009). Theoretical work has also attempted to understand whether a shift showing alternative stable states is a likely outcome. Within a realistic range of precipitation regimes, a stability analysis comparing the current cover of three biome types – forest, savanna and treeless areas – has shown that forest and savanna do appear to behave as alternative stable states, substantiating the claim that climate change may trigger a critical transition from forest to savanna (Hirota *et al.* 2011; Staver, Archibald & Levin 2011). Although this approach needs to be backed by more empirical studies and confirmed by more detailed simulations, it appears to be a universal feature of tropical biome dynamics (Murphy & Bowman 2012). Thus, this body of knowledge collectively suggests that Amazonian forests are functioning today at the verge of a major environmental tipping point.

Support for the Amazon dieback scenario is one of the major findings of a new generation of Earth models where atmospheric global circulation models (GCMs) are synchronously coupled to dynamic global vegetation models (DGVMs). These DGVMs have a long tradition in vegetation modelling (Cramer *et al.* 2004; Krinner *et al.* 2005; Sitch *et al.* 2003), being related to the development of agricultural or forestry management models (Shugart 1984) and to the need to model short-term fluxes between atmosphere and biosphere in atmospheric physics. Here, I discuss two limitations of existing DGVMs that have until now been seldom addressed, but that are especially critical for an accurate modelling of tropical old-growth forests and woody savannas alike.

First, few DGVMs attempt to account for demographic stochasticity, in spite of the importance of these local processes in explaining the dynamics of unmanaged vegetation (Purves & Pacala 2008). One notable exception is the Ecosystem Demography model (ED model; Fisher *et al.* 2010; Moorcroft, Hurtt & Pacala 2001), where demographic stochasticity was taken into account through a spatial averaging procedure inspired from statistical physics (Iwasa, Andreasen & Levin 1987). With increased computer power, an alternative to the ED modelling strategy is to develop individual-based DGVMs for forests, for example Sato, Itoh and Kohyama's (2007) 'SEIB-DGVM'. While important efforts have been made in this direction in the recent literature, fusing ecosystem science and community ecology certainly represents a central challenge in the construction of a new generation of Earth models (Fisher *et al.* 2010).

A second limitation is that biodiversity is only simplistically represented in the current generation of DGVMs. Usually, a pool of only 10 or so plant functional types (PFTs) are available for populating DGVMs (Sitch *et al.* 2003), just two of which occur in tropical forests: tropical broadleaf evergreen trees (woody vegetation with persistent leaves), and tropical broadleaf raingreen trees (semi-deciduous woody vegetation). Within a grid cell of c. 1° × 1° latitude/longitude, a fraction of each PFT is competing for space and resources. This simplification is easily understandable in view of the complexity of the task of modelling the interaction between a plant canopy and the atmospheric boundary layer (Jones 1992). However, what is known of the adaptive potential of organisms in changing environments (Davis, Shaw & Etterson 2005; Duputié et al. 2012) and of the evolutionary history of tropical tree families (Jaramillo et al. 2010; Wing et al. 2009) demands a critical reappraisal of over-simplistic approaches.

In this chapter, I examine lines of evidence for or against the Amazonian dieback scenario in light of ecological theory and palaeoenvironmental evidence. I then argue that a new generation of DGVMs must appropriately account for the physiology of tropical trees, including the contribution of both photosynthetic organs and the rest of the plants. I separate the contribution of photosynthetic organs (leaves) and of the rest of the plants (especially the stem and branches). Finally, I describe a possible implementation of this approach in an individual-based forest growth simulator.

## 6.2   The stability of Amazonian forests: historical insights

Tropical rain forests have been a dominant vegetation type on the Earth for much of the past 100 Ma. In his wonderful book on the evolution of tropical rain forests, Morley (2000) provided a synthesis of the fossil evidence for the tropical forest flora. Solid evidence now exists for the presence of multistoreyed angiosperm-dominated forests from the late Cretaceous (Morley 2011), or in the early Tertiary for the Neotropics (Burnham & Johnson 2004; Wing et al. 2009). This suggests that the rise to dominance of tropical rain forests preceded the Cretaceous–Tertiary transition. This claim was also supported by molecular dating of phylogenetic trees for two predominantly tropical forest clades, the Malpighiales (Davis, Shaw & Etterson 2005), and the Ericales (Sytsma et al. 2006). A continuous palynological record dating back to 65 Ma BP from Colombia has confirmed that at least some areas in northern South America have been dominated by tropical forest taxa for much of the period from the Early Paleocene to the Early Miocene (Jaramillo, Rueda & Mora 2006), although a lot of vegetational changes have taken place over this period (Jaramillo, Rueda & Mora 2006; see also Jaramillo et al. 2010; Rull 1999). Together with the evolution of C4 photosynthesis, the rise to dominance of tropical rain forests is probably one of the very few key evolutionary advances in the history of terrestrial vegetation over the past 100 Ma (Brodribb & Feild 2010; Christin et al. 2008; McAdam & Brodribb 2012; Morley 2011).

Focusing on the Quaternary, oxygen isotope data from Brazil speleothems spanning the past 200 ka demonstrate that the climate of South America has been altered by fluctuations in solar radiation, coupled with a large reorganisation of equatorial atmospheric circulation that led to a change in the position of the ITCZ (Cruz *et al.* 2009; Wang *et al.* 2007). Carbon isotope evidence from the Cariaco Basin, Venezuela, over the past 50 ka, suggests that the South American climate has been subject to large-scale oceanic shifts in the Atlantic meridional overturning circulation (Hughen *et al.* 2004). These climatic changes have been also traced in water level changes over the past 160 ka for Lake Pata, Brazil, close to the equator (Bush, Silman & Urrego 2002). Other areas of Amazonia appear to have been floristically quite stable over the past 50 ka, where the pollen cores show a dominance of arboreal pollen taxa, and little grass pollen, through much of this period (Burbridge, Mayle & Killeen 2004; Bush, Silman & Urrego 2004; Colinvaux, de Oliveira & Bush 1996; Haberle & Maslin 1999), except in an area that is today close to the forest–savanna ecotone: Serra dos Carajás, Brazil (Absy *et al.* 1991).

By far the most controversial climate-induced paleoecological event in South America is the one that occurred during the last glacial maximum (LGM), around 21 ka BP. There is evidence for a decline in precipitation and a decrease in temperature by up to 5 °C in some parts of this continent (Bush, Silman & Urrego 2004), in an atmosphere with $CO_2$ levels about half of those recorded today. Some authors have used this evidence to suggest that Amazonian forests were largely converted into savannas during the glacial periods. This fragmentation of Amazonian forests has been put forward as an explanation for the high diversity of this biome: many populations may have been maintained in allopatry through long periods in the Quaternary during which repeated episodes of forest fragmentation acted as a 'pump of speciation' (Bush 1994). Yet, there is no evidence for a widespread transition from a closed-canopy forest to a woodland savanna system either in the paleoecological record (Bush, Silman & Urrego 2004; Colinvaux *et al.* 2000; Haberle & Maslin 1999; Mayle *et al.* 2004, 2009) or in modelling studies (Cowling, Maslin & Sykes 2001). The pollen records reported by Colinvaux, de Oliveira and Bush (2000) and by Burbridge, Mayle and Killeen (2004) suggest that glacial-age Amazonian forests, with their mix of currently Andean and lowland Amazonian taxa, have no modern analogues. Pennington *et al.* (2000) proposed that in the LGM much of the current extent of the Amazonian forest was occupied by the now geographically restricted seasonally dry tropical forests. Together these studies suggest that a precipitation level of as much as 25% lower than today, and both lowered temperature and $CO_2$ concentration, did not result in a radical shift to an alternative stable state during the LGM. Rather, there was a smooth transition involving changes in the floristic assemblage, while maintaining a continuous canopy cover.

The LGM has often been perceived as the hallmark of past climatic changes. However, Amazonian paleoecology teaches us that tropical forests may have undergone the most radical transition much later, during the Holocene. Over 30 years ago, Servant *et al.* (1981) were the first to provide evidence for arid phases in Bolivia during the Holocene; much more evidence has accumulated recently. For instance, there is evidence of an important dry event at around 7–5 ka BP (Absy *et al.* 1991; Burbridge, Mayle & Killeen 2004; Mayle *et al.* 2004), and this has recently been confirmed with a larger array of techniques (Bird *et al.* 2011; van Breukelen *et al.* 2008). This period of increased drought occurrence may have played a prominent role in the history of human populations in this region, as suggested by evidence from crop domestication (Piperno 2011). Figure 6.1 shows one of the few palynological cores in French Guiana (Ledru 2001). The peak in the pollen of pioneer species (*Cecropia* and *Vismia*), lasting over two centuries between around 1500 and 1300 BP, was attributed to either a human disturbance or to a sustained climatic event (grey peak close to the C14 calibration point at 1570±50 BP, see also Bird *et al.* 2011 for a comparable drought around 1500 BP in Peru). The Holocene history of northeast Amazonia remains poorly documented, but recently Freycon *et al.* (2010) used soil carbon isotope composition to detect whether past vegetation may have been dominated by plants with a C4 photosynthetic pathway

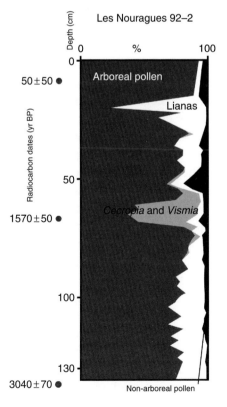

**Figure 6.1** A 3000-yr palynological record, from a peat bog at the Nouragues Ecological Research Station, French Guiana. Redrawn from Ledru (2001).

(essentially savanna grasses), which show a lower $^{13}C$ discrimination than arboreal taxa (predominantly of the C3 photosynthetic pathway). They showed that even forest sites close to coastal savannas today have remained forested during much of the Holocene. Together, this suggests that even though Amazonian forests have been through important climatic fluctuations during the Holocene, they have been quite resilient to these changes.

How does the history of tropical forests help shed light on their future? It is likely that the future environmental conditions of tropical America will be very different from that of the LGM. Precipitation will not necessarily be less than today, but the frequency of long droughts is likely to increase, a phenomenon that may have occurred episodically from 10 to 6 ka BP (Mayle *et al.* 2009). In addition, atmospheric $CO_2$ concentrations and temperature will increase (Salazar, Nobre & Oyama 2007), and deforestation will contribute to altering the regional climate (Poulter *et al.* 2010). Comparing LGM simulations with those of vegetation status under projected climates by the end of the twenty-first century, Cowling, Cox and Betts (2004) showed that the likely feedbacks responsible for maintaining the integrity of Amazonian forest cover in the past were a reduction in both evapotranspiration (related with reduced rainfall) and plant respiration (related with lower temperature). This combination of response leading to a lower net primary productivity (NPP) but also a lower metabolism is unlikely to hold in the future. For these reasons, Cowling, Cox and Betts (2004) suggested that the Amazonian forest is near its resilience threshold.

This analysis calls for a more in-depth study of the resilience concept. Resilience is the capacity of an ecosystem to absorb disturbance without shifting to an alternative state and losing ecological functions (Holling 1973). Thus resilience encompasses two processes: 'resistance', the ability of a system to withstand a disturbance, and 'recovery', the ability of the system to return to its initial, pre-disturbance, state. This distinction largely depends on how frequent the disturbances are: if the shocks occur frequently and stochastically, the impact of these shocks depend on the ecosystem's resistance. If the perturbations occur rarely, ecosystem stability will be measured by the rate at which the system returns to equilibrium (Ives & Carpenter 2007). The LGM scenario of a shift in floristic composition within a persistent tropical forest canopy cover is consistent with the view of a 'resistant' system. Forests have been able to reshuffle their floristic makeup so as to maintain fundamental ecological functions (water recycling, carbon storage, radiation balance). It also appears that tropical forests have an ability to recover from pronounced disturbances, even though this recovery may take centuries (Ledru 2001; Mayle *et al.* 2009). This prediction is consistent with the idea of biodiversity conferring 'insurance value' (Yachi & Loreau 1998). Some tree species are dominant today because they are adapted to current local environmental conditions. However, the large reservoir of species spanning a wide range of ecological functions enables the tropical forest system to navigate through a variety of pulse perturbations. Currently dominant species may decline in abundance under changing environmental conditions, but be replaced by other species that are rare today.

The consequence of this discussion is that the current classification of vegetation into a few PFTs ignores an important potential for the adaptation of ecological species assemblages to future climates. Current DGVMs therefore misrepresent the community-wide potential of the vegetation to adapt ecologically to novel environmental conditions. Next, I explore evidence in favour of this claim.

## 6.3   The leaf economics spectrum and the physiology of tropical trees

A great amount of work has been devoted to identifying PFTs within plants generally, and tropical tree species specifically, with the aim of simplifying the apparently overwhelming biological diversity of these ecosystems (Favrichon 1994; Picard & Franc 2003; Swaine & Whitmore 1988). The underlying theory of PFTs is that species in a given environment may be simply ranked along an axis of performance and persist in coexistence thanks to an ecological trade-off (Grime 1979; Swaine & Whitmore 1988). This idea is reminiscent of Robert MacArthur's model (1972) of a trade-off between ecological strategies with fast-growing species that die young (the r strategists) versus slow-growing species that survive for a long time (the K strategists). If this theory is valid, then functional traits should all covary along a single axis, and it is thought that carbon assimilation traits should thus suffice to describe the plant ecological strategy spectrum. This includes, in addition to competitive and successional traits, ecological traits that describe cold or drought tolerance (Harrison *et al.* 2010); drought tolerance is discussed further below.

Much of the physiological machinery implemented in current versions of DGVMs is based on a leaf-level view of plant physiology. Leaves are the most important organs for carbon fixation, and a general model of photosynthesis has been developed for them (Leuning *et al.* 1995; von Caemmerer 2000). Non-woody plants dominate a sizeable fraction of the planet's vegetation, and by focusing on leaf traits alone a universal way to classify plants into functional types becomes possible (Wright *et al.* 2004). As a result, an active field of research has been concerned with classifying plant species into PFTs using measurable leaf-level traits, or leaf functional traits (Cornelissen *et al.* 2003; Wright *et al.* 2004). These traits include such measures as total leaf area, leaf width, specific leaf area (leaf area per unit dry mass), elemental concentration in leaves (C, N, P and major elements like K, Ca, Mg, Al, Fe), and discrimination of stable isotopes of carbon and nitrogen ($\delta^{13}$C, $\delta^{15}$N). In addition, leaf mechanical properties have been included in these multi-factorial analyses, and the implications for defence have been discussed (Onoda *et al.* 2011; Read & Stokes 2006). These traits are easily collected across a large number of plants and facilitate the compilation of global datasets (Kattge *et al.* 2011).

Numerous reports of the cross-species variation of some of these traits have been published across biomes (Wright *et al.* 2004), or within tropical rain forests (Baraloto *et al.* 2009; Fyllas *et al.* 2009; Ometto *et al.* 2006). They point to a cross-biome universality of leaf traits. Wright *et al.* (2004) showed that, across biomes, species mean traits fell into a single universal surface in a foliar functional trait space, confirming the idea that some trade-off explains the covariation of functional strategies, thus defining the leaf economics spectrum. Recently Fyllas *et al.* (2009) have carried out an extensive study of regional-scale variation for a range of foliar functional traits in Amazonian tree species to test the pertinence of a leaf economics spectrum within tropical vegetation biomes. They conclude that variation in key foliar functional traits is associated with variation in tree growth. For instance, high fertility soils are associated with higher growth rates, lower leaf mass per area (LMA, the inverse of specific leaf area) and higher nutrient concentration per dry weight (N, P, K and Mg). Trees growing on more fertile soils have more nutrients (especially N and P) to invest into the photosynthetic apparatus, hence the correlation observed by Fyllas *et al.* (2009). This result provides strong, albeit correlative, support for developing DGVMs parameterised with foliar functional traits (Clark *et al.* 2011; Mercado *et al.* 2011). It is consistent with the broadly accepted assumption that PFTs can be defined by a simple suite of foliar traits.

The above PFT classification assumes that carbon assimilation is the major limiting factor in plant growth. However, short but stressful events may considerably compromise the fitness of populations, leading to an increased death rate and/or to reduced overall performance. The likelihood of sudden events that considerably reduce the population fitness has been explored in much greater detail for plants growing in the temperate zone where frost tolerance is an important dimension of the phenological timing of trees (Chuine 2000). In the tropics, one of the most important of these stressful events is the occurrence of prolonged drought periods (McDowell 2011). At an ecosystem scale, it has been demonstrated experimentally that droughts have a significant short-term impact on the ecosystem functioning of tropical forests (Markewitz *et al.* 2010). At the plant scale, stomatal closure is the main line of defence against drought, but beyond a certain point cell turgor will be lost, leading to leaf wilting (Nobel 2009). The ability of an ecosystem to withstand severe droughts depends on the ability of the species to resist wilting. It has thus become a major quest to find functional plant traits that would correlate with drought tolerance.

Recently, Bartlett, Scoffoni and Sack (2012) have provided a useful perspective on the issue of measuring leaf tolerance to drought. They have demonstrated that, across biomes, leaf water potential at wilting (or at turgor loss point, $\Pi_{tlp}$) is the best predictor of leaf drought tolerance. Leaf water potential at turgor loss point is a negative pressure (measured in MPa) since water is in tension within the leaf. Drought is measured by the soil negative pressure imposed upon the water column of the plant. If soil water potential falls below a threshold (often assumed to be $-1.5$ MPa), ecosystem-wide consequences for plant survival are to be expected. Several responses are possible in dry conditions. The plant may reduce its tolerance through osmotic regulation, leading to a reduction in $\Pi_{tlp}$ (Nobel 2009). This plasticity is limited, however (Wenhui & Prado 1998; Zhu & Cao 2009). Deciduous plants drop their leaves before they wilt, to save as much water as possible. Importantly, deciduousness in dry tropical forest species is not only aimed at maximising water use efficiency, but appears to be primarily a herbivore avoidance, or phenological escape, strategy (Janzen 1981; Marquis, Morais & Diniz 2002). Prado *et al.* (2004), in a detailed study of a range of cerrado plant species, have shown that during the dry season, evergreen species such as *Didymopanax vinosum* Cham. & Schlecht maintain their photosynthetic capacity (*A*) at the same time as regulating evapotranspiration (*E*) to levels comparable to that of the wet season. In contrast, deciduous species (e.g. *Bauhinia rufa* (Bongard) Stendel) regulate their water use efficiency (*A/E*) by reducing both *A* and *E*. The leaf turgor loss point is also often lower in evergreen species than the average community, although the relationship between deciduousness and tolerance to leaf wilting is not clear (Wenhui & Prado 1998).

Figure 6.2 represents the covariation of leaf water potential at the turgor loss point against the ratio of wet to dry mass of leaves. It summarises a number of interesting findings. First, the dry forest species of Hao *et al.* (2008) tend to have a lower $\Pi_{tlp}$ than the moist forest species of Zhu and Cao (2009), as also pointed out by Bartlett *et al.* (2012). There appears to be a relatively good correlation between $\Pi_{tlp}$ and the ratio of wet to dry mass of leaves ($r^2 = 0.63$). Second, a phylogenetically controlled comparison between dry forest species and woodland savanna species (the grey circles and grey triangles, respectively, in Figure 6.2) suggests that $\Pi_{tlp}$ is not necessarily lower in woodland savanna species than in adjacent dry forest species. Pending more detailed studies, this suggests that the phylogenetic signal is low for $\Pi_{tlp}$. Further genus-specific leaf tolerance studies, in *Cordia* (Choat, Sack & Holbrook 2007) and *Ficus* (Patiño *et al.* 1995), deserve to be mentioned in this respect. Third, Zhu and Cao's (2009) study confirms that osmotic regulation, leading to a drop of $\Pi_{tlp}$ between the wet and the dry season, is an important component of drought tolerance. Remarkably, the three liana species studied by Zhu and Cao (2009) show little to no osmotic regulation. Fourth, and

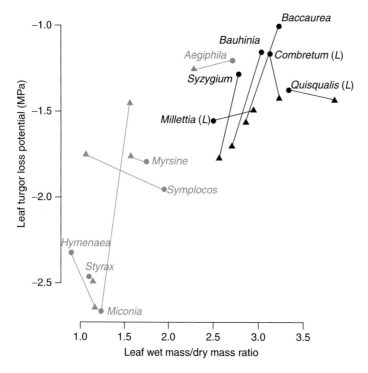

**Figure 6.2** Correlation between the leaf turgor loss potential ($\Pi_{tlp}$, in MPa) and the ratio of wet mass over dry mass for leaves. Grey symbols are from Hao *et al.* (2008), black symbols are from Zhu and Cao (2009). In Hao *et al.*'s (2008) study, six congeneric species pairs were compared, where each pair has one forest species (grey circles) and one cerrado species (grey triangles). In Zhu and Cao's (2009) study, six species were measured both in the wet season (black circles) and in the dry season (black triangles). Species denoted with (L) in Zhu and Cao's (2009) study are lianas.

finally, lianas' leaf water potential at the turgor loss point does not differ from that of trees, in spite of their propensity to keep their leaves even in semi-deciduous forests (Schnitzer & Bongers 2002).

Do some commonly measured leaf traits covary strongly with leaf tolerance to wilting? Niinemets (2001) has proposed that LMA should be a good correlate of drought tolerance because it is associated with leaf wall stiffness. However, Bartlett, Scoffoni and Sack (2012) showed that LMA is a poor predictor of $\Pi_{tlp}$ measurements globally, suggesting that leaf wall stiffness as an indicator of leaf drought tolerance does not hold globally across plants. In the few publications focusing on dry tropical environments, a relatively good correlation has been found between leaf drought tolerance and LMA (Bucci *et al.* 2004; Meinzer *et al.* 2008a; Poorter *et al.* 2009), but this evidence remains too thin to discount the possibility that $\Pi_{tlp}$ may represent an independent axis of variation in the leaf economy spectrum, and that drought tolerance is inadequately represented in the analysis by Wright *et al.* (2004). Besides, LMA is associated with other functions as well, and it is also a remarkably plastic trait (Poorter *et al.* 2009).

## 6.4   Whole-plant physiology of tropical trees

A second important issue relevant to the construction of PFTs is that tropical trees are not just leaf surfaces. Most of their carbon is held in self-supporting structures (trunks) and resource-foraging structures (roots). Leaf water is supplied through the xylem, and the whole plant water status is critically dependent on the health of woody tissue. Wood protection in particular may represent a non-negligible energetic investment for a tropical tree, as suggested by the variation in bark thickness across tree species (Brando *et al.* 2012; Paine *et al.* 2010). Much research has been conducted on wood structure, because tropical timber represents an important international economic market. Wood production is a critical allocation strategy for photosynthates, since growth in height leads to a competitive advantage in forested environments. Many wood functional traits may be measured that are likely to be even more important in predicting tree growth rates than leaf-level traits. For instance, just by looking at a wood core in the trunk of a tropical tree, critical demographic data may be inferred quite easily, at least if the tree shows an annual growth pattern (Rozendaal & Zuidema 2011; Worbes 2002).

Simple functional traits have been proposed for inclusion in DGVM development, such as wood density, or the distribution of conduit sizes (Chave *et al.* 2009; Patiño *et al.* 2009; Zanne *et al.* 2010). Wood density has generated a great deal of recent interest because it is believed to integrate a number of important stem processes (Baas *et al.* 2004). It has been speculated that wood density may correlate with the ability of a woody plant to withstand whole-plant water stress (Hacke *et al.* 2001; Jacobsen *et al.* 2005; see also below). Wood density is also clearly related to tree mechanical stability (Chave *et al.* 2009; van Gelder, Poorter & Sterck 2006), and correlates negatively with mortality rates across a broad range of forests (Kraft *et al.* 2010). Finally, wood density has been found to be strongly related to total stem sapflow, and thus total plant transpiration, in a limited number of studies (Bucci *et al.* 2004, 2008; McCulloh *et al.* 2011; Meinzer *et al.* 2008a).

In addition to causing leaf wilting, drought may cause irreversible damage to the plant as a result of cavitation in the xylem conduits (Cochard 2006; Tyree & Zimmermann 2002). Xylem failure during exceptional episodes of drought may occur more frequently in the future. Engelbrecht and Kursar (2003) have demonstrated that seedlings of a range of species respond very differently to drought stresses. Seedling drought tolerance may indeed be a critical element of the fitness of tree populations in seasonal climates, and a key explanation of patterns of plant distribution across environmental gradients (Engelbrecht *et al.* 2007). However, rapid changes in climate may also increase the risk of xylem failure of large trees. For instance, Zhang *et al.* (2009) have shown that larger individuals of the legume tree *Sclerolobium paniculatum* were more likely to show branch damage and to die than smaller trees under the same drought conditions (see Rood *et al.* 2000 for a temperate tree example). This shows that DGVMs should pay special attention to modelling xylem-failure induced mortality in trees, and not only mortality related to carbon starvation (see e.g. Fisher *et al.* 2010; McDowell 2011). An obvious trait to model the risk of xylem failure is the pressure at which a stem has lost 50% of its hydraulic conductivity ($P_{50}$). In their meta-analysis, Maherali *et al.* (2004) reported 41 $P_{50}$ measurements for moist tropical forest species (mostly from Tyree, Patiño & Becker 1998 and Zotz, Tyree & Cochard 1994), and only 19 for dry tropical forest species. They found that vulnerability to cavitation was on average almost three times larger in moist tropical forest than in dry tropical forest trees. Additional values not included in Maherali *et al.*'s (2004) compilation for dry and moist tropical forests confirm this first analysis (Brodribb *et al.* 2003; Bucci *et al.* 2006; Chen *et al.* 2009; Lopez *et al.* 2005; Markesteijn *et al.* 2011; Meinzer *et al.* 2003, 2008b; Zhu & Cao 2009; see Figure 6.3, and appendix). Figure 6.3 shows that moist tropical forest species appear to be more vulnerable to drought-induced xylem failure than dry forest or woodland savanna species. However, with the exception of Meinzer *et al.* (2003, 2008b), these previous studies have tended to ignore

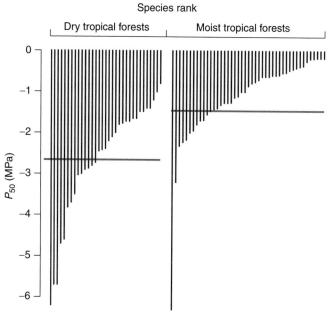

**Figure 6.3** Xylem vulnerability to cavitation (pressure at which 50% of the xylem hydraulic conductivity has been lost) for dry and moist tropical forests. This meta-analysis shows that dry forest species are on average half as vulnerable to xylem cavitation as moist tropical forest species. The mean values are drawn as grey horizontal lines (mean $P_{50} = -2.66$ MPa, $n = 33$, for dry tropical forests; mean $P_{50} = -1.41$ MPa, $n = 66$, for moist tropical forests). However, the range of variation is large and comparable in both biome types.

the species that dominate Amazonian forests. Thus this conclusion merits further scrutiny in this region. Xylem water potential at 50% loss of hydraulic conductivity varies a lot across species in both biomes, and spans almost the same range of variation. This is suggestive that, under a stronger drought, more species may be at risk in moist tropical forests than in dry tropical forests, yet the survivors may be enough to maintain a closed-canopy cover and a large fraction of the biomass stocks.

How should we account for non-leaf traits in the development of DGVMs? Under MacArthur's (1972) trade-off theory, whole-plant traits should covary in a predictable way and define simple plant ecological 'syndromes'. For instance, fast-growing trees should also invest less into wood construction costs because they invest more into photosynthesis (per dry mass). Although such a trade-off in allocation is expected across broad environmental gradients and across biomes, this pattern does not appear to hold within moist tropical forests. Baraloto et al. (2010) showed that leaf traits are not correlated with stem-related functional traits, and the leaf-investment and stem-investment strategies appeared to be uncorrelated. Thus, for PFTs based on leaf traits, it is impossible to predict how the plant will allocate carbon into wood production. Further, based on this analysis it is expected that species able to invest a lot in both wood and leaf construction can still persist in the ecosystem. Chen et al. (2009) arrived at a similar result, using more traits but only six species in the family Euphorbiaceae s.l. Fyllas, Quesada and Lloyd (2012) have taken this idea one step further through a global approach based on functional traits measured not only on leaves but also on whole plant traits, including wood traits. They conducted an ordination analysis on a suite of traits, much like Baraloto et al. (2010) but at a regional scale, and subsequently clustered the species into discrete groups using a K-mean cluster algorithm. They found that their species could be naturally clustered into four groups, possibly defining novel types of PFTs. These four groups correspond to a combination of light demand strategies (as measured by potential gas exchange rates) and overall tree stature. However, there was still large variation in species traits within each of these four PFTs. It should be noted that the uncoupling of leaf and stem traits remains a debated subject. Leaf and wood traits appear to be more correlated in xeric habitats than in moist forest ones. Indeed, the two studies where a convergence of wood and leaf traits was observed were conducted in woodland savanna and dry forest (Bucci et al. 2004; Mendez-Alonzo in press).

The special case of lianas merits a separate discussion. Tropical forests are remarkable for having a large abundance of lianas (Schnizter & Bongers 2002), which may increase in abundance with changing climates (Phillips et al. 2002). These lianas, as parasitic plants, do not need to invest as much carbon into wood construction. They have large conduits and a higher water conductivity leading to higher transpiration (Andrade *et al.* 2005; Feild & Balun 2008; Zhu & Cao 2009). Lianas thus represent a disproportionate amount of carbon turn-over (NPP) and of ecosystem transpiration in comparison with the biomass they hold (e.g. Restom & Nepstad 2001). They also have a distinctive response to drought, since many lianas of semideciduous forests keep their leaves during the dry season (Schnitzer & Bongers 2002; see also Figure 6.2). It would be important to further appraise the importance of accounting for the presence of lianas in DGVMs and to model their contribution to NPP and to ecosystem transpiration. Likewise, other life forms found almost exclusively in moist tropical forests, such as hemiepiphytes, may play an important ecosystem-level role (Patiño *et al.* 1995; Zotz, Tyree & Cochard 1994).

In conclusion, in spite of an enormous effort to better understand the physiology of tropical plants, a number of key points remain undocumented, especially regarding the drought tolerance of large tropical trees. As a result, current efforts to reduce these physiological behaviours to a few discrete groups have not met with great success. Most attempts to construct plant functional types have been restricted to leaf traits (Schulze *et al.* 1994; Wright *et al.* 2004), and available evidence now suggests that existing trait databases do not include appropriate proxies for xylem conductivity and for xylem vulnerability to cavitation. Comparing a range of species with respect to different ecological functions, it has often been found that traits sometimes covary but cannot easily be partitioned into discrete groups (Baraloto *et al.* 2010; Goldstein *et al.* 2008; Figure 6.3). This argument should not be over-looked when considering plant functional types as an operational concept in the building of dynamic vegetation models. It is possible that PFTs could be replaced with more detailed population-based models that couple the dynam-ics of the species assemblage with ecosystem processes, or that many more PFTs could be included to account for the observed variability in plant traits.

## 6.5  Discussion

The idea that the presence of a few species may help the persistence of ecological functions through environmental disturbances is far from novel in ecology and has been widely discussed in the ecosystem science literature. However, evidence for such a scenario is wanting in tropical forests because it is difficult to reconcile the long generation times of tree species, and the hypothetical nature of environmental change scenarios, with any experimen-tal test. Here, I have shown that the current generation of coupled biosphere–atmosphere Earth models still include too many uncertainties when it comes to making predictions about the future of Amazonian tropical forests. If the Amazon dieback scenario has spurred considerable controversy, evidence in its favour remains scarce, and existing models produce very different projec-tions for Amazonia at the end of the twenty-first century. However, global trends of an increase in temperature will probably be accompanied by stronger and/or more frequent droughts over Amazonia. Research on drought tolerance of Amazonian forests remains surprisingly scarce given the importance of the challenge, but available evidence suggests that both the leaves and the xylem of average moist tropical forest tree species are not as well adapted to drought as dry tropical forest and woodland savanna species. Thus, whether drought-tolerant trees will be able to supplant drought-intolerant ones within the moist tropical forest matrix, and given the short timeframe, remains an open question.

When building DGVMs, it is perhaps inevitable to use plant functional traits. A range of issues are associated with measuring and using these traits, as discussed above. Traits do not necessarily correlate directly with relevant physiological processes, and they may not be useful in a process-based model. Furthermore, plant functional traits cannot be considered as constant for species across their whole geographical range and/or environmental gradients. A recent detailed analysis of how whole-plant traits covary with environmental conditions has been published by Patiño *et al.* (2012). One of the strongest correlations in their dataset was for the decline of sapwood density with increasing soil fertility (see also Fyllas *et al.* 2009), a relationship also known by foresters. A remarkable experiment has been conducted in the Brazilian cerrado to further explore this question (Bucci *et al.* 2006). By fertilising the soil for 36 months for five tree species, the authors showed that only the addition of nitrogen had a significant effect, and that nitrogen addition resulted in a decline in both sapwood density and in vulnerability to cavitation (the trees growing in an N-enriched soil had lower $P_{50}$ values than the controls). The study of Bucci *et al.* (2006) therefore suggests that most of the traits discussed here are either directly correlated to demographic variables (such as stem growth rate) or are intrinsically variable. This variability, together with the adaptive potential of tree species, cannot be overemphasised. Such trait–environment covariation has never been included in DGVMs, in spite of their obvious importance. More experimental and empirical results are needed before generalisations are possible on this front.

It would be desirable to implement a finer-grained description of tropical forest vegetation dynamics, allowing for a more accurate description of interspecific and inter-individual variability. The problem raised here is one of parameter aggregation: it is often the case that by aggregating traits originally measured on individuals into a few discrete categories, the statistical properties of the entire dataset are altered. Although this problem has a remarkably long history in ecology (Iwasa, Andreasen & Levin 1987) and in forest model simulators (Hurtt *et al.* 1998; Ritchie & Hann 1997), it has been overlooked in recent attempts to develop DGVMs, in part owing to the lack of accessible databases on functional traits. One option for a new generation of DGVMs is to develop individual-based versions to account for the physiological processes at play in tropical forest ecosystems. Only the outline of such an approach is presented here, based on a previous development of an individual-based spatially explicit forest growth simulator described in Chave (1999) and called TROLL. In the original version of this dynamic forest growth simulator, each tree with a trunk diameter of 1 cm or above is simulated. At most, one individual can occupy a grid cell of 1 × 1 m, thus allowing a maximum number of 10 000 individuals per hectare. Individuals compete for free cell space as in cellular automata (Hurtt & Pacala 1995), but they also compete for light resources. Solar radiation above the canopy may be computed from geometrical considerations of solar movement, and it may be decomposed into a direct and a diffuse component (Leuning *et al.* 1995; Monteith & Unsworth 2007). In agreement with the Beer–Lambert law, light intensity in a forest declines exponentially from the top of the canopy to the ground level (Hirose 2005). To model this light attenuation, I took a discrete approach whereby the leaf density is computed in each voxel of side 1 m within the canopy, assuming a turbid medium approximation within each voxel (Le Roux *et al.* 2001). Death could result from a stochastic process, insufficient light availability (see also Pacala *et al.* 1996), carbon starvation (Fisher *et al.* 2010) or xylem embolism (Cochard 2006). The TROLL model also includes a detailed treefall gap formation module in which falling trees topple neighbours according to their relative height and size. Tree geometry is modelled explicitly by including, in addition to trunk dbh, total tree height, crown radius and crown depth. All of the parameters are defined for each species, hence there is no need to lump species into PFTs (but the intraspecific variability in ecological traits is ignored).

One challenge is to develop a leaf-level photosynthesis module averaged over sufficiently long time scales so as to avoid the issues of modelling the relationship between stomatal conductance $g_c$ to local environmental conditions (Lloyd & Farquhar 2008). This could be tackled by relating the mean ratio of intracellular to atmospheric $CO_2$ concentration, $c_i/c_a$, and carbon isotopic discrimination in leaves as modelled by $\delta^{13}C$ (Domingues, Martinelli & Ehleringer *et al.* 2007, 2010; Farquhar, Ehleringer & Hubick 1989). Indeed, carbon isotopic discrimination has been measured in a large range of trees empirically (Baraloto *et al.* 2010; Ometto *et al.* 2006). A second challenge is to include a detailed model of drought resistance, including the susceptibility of a plant's leaves and of its water column to sudden droughts. Empirical data to model leaf drought tolerance remains scarce, as reviewed above, but empirical evidence relating basic wood properties such as sapwood density and resistance to xylem cavitation is now strong and convincing. Finally, this model poses a serious computational challenge, which has been a major impediment to the development of global individual-based DGVMs in the past. To test this, I simulated the dynamics of a relatively small permanent plot (16 ha, 1 m spatial resolution). With these conditions, the TROLL model admits a maximum of 160 000 individuals at a time. Briefly, the test runs showed that species diversity can be maintained in the system while ecosystem variables (NPP, stem size distribution, biomass) reach an equilibrium within a few centuries. These results will be developed in a forthcoming work, but the point here is that such models are easily scalable using the impressive computer power available today. Importantly, they also offer an important means of performing direct and ecologically intuitive data assimilation.

To conclude, it is tempting to suggest that the oversimplification of plant functional types in existing DGVMs account, at least in part, for the predicted critical transition between forest and savanna in South America over the twenty-first century. Real ecosystems are species-rich, and some of their species (e.g. *Hymenaea courbaril* L.) thrive both in closed-canopy forests and in woodland savannas. Although they are scattered in the forest today, their fitness may be favoured by changing climates, and they would then rise to dominance in the decades to come. This floristic turnover, which cannot be modelled in the current generation of DGVMs, would help to maintain a closed canopy cover, and help minimise changes in ecosystem functions in the carbon, water and element cycles, and in the energy budget of the forest. Next generations of DGVMs should seek to bridge the divide between ecosystem science and community ecology, and account for biological diversity and for population processes.

## Acknowledgements

This work is dedicated to the memory of Sandra Patiño. It is a pleasure to acknowledge the useful comments from C. Canham and an anonymous referee, and M. Chave for redrawing Figure 6.1. I benefited from enlightening discussions with C. Baraloto, M. Bartlett, D. Coomes, T. Domingues, T. Kursar, J. Lloyd, C. Lusk, H. Muller-Landau, C.E.T. Paine, L. Poorter, L. Sack, S. Schnitzer, M. Servant, S. Sitch, S. Thomas, I. Wright and A. Zanne. This work has benefited from Investissement d'Avenir grants of the ANR (CEBA: ANR-10-LABX-0025; TULIP: ANR-10-LABX-0041), and from grants from ANR Biodiversité (BRIDGE project), Fondation pour la Recherche sur la Biodiversité (ATROPHY project), and CNES (TOSCA Biomass).

## Appendix 6.1

Compilation of values of xylem water potential at 50% loss of hydraulic conductivity ($P_{50}$) used to estimate the xylem vulnerability to cavitation, for tropical forest environments. Monocots, gymnosperms and mangrove species were excluded from this compilation.

| Species | Family | Forest type | $P_{50}$ (MPa) | Country | Reference |
|---|---|---|---|---|---|
| *Bursera simaruba* (L.) Sarg. | Burseraceae | Dry | −1 | Costa Rica | Brodribb *et al.* (2003) |
| *Calycophyllum candidissimum* (Vahl) DC | Rubiaceae | Dry | −2.87 | Costa Rica | Brodribb *et al.* (2003) |
| *Enterolobium cyclocarpum* (Jacq.) Griseb. | Fabaceae | Dry | −2.73 | Costa Rica | Brodribb *et al.* (2003) |
| *Hymenaea courbaril* L. | Fabaceae | Dry | −3 | Costa Rica | Brodribb *et al.* (2003) |
| *Quercus oleoides* Schltdl. & Cham. | Fagaceae | Dry | −3.03 | Costa Rica | Brodribb *et al.* (2003) |
| *Rehdera trinervis* (S.F. Blake) Moldenke | Verbenaceae | Dry | −2.8 | Costa Rica | Brodribb *et al.* (2003) |
| *Simarouba glauca* DC | Simaroubaceae | Dry | −2 | Costa Rica | Brodribb *et al.* (2003) |
| *Swietenia macrophylla* King | Meliaceae | Dry | −2.2 | Costa Rica | Brodribb *et al.* (2003) |
| *Blepharocalyx salicifolius* (Kunth) O. Berg | Myrtaceae | Dry | −1.72 | Brazil | Bucci *et al.* (2006) |
| *Caryocar brasiliense* Cambess. | Caryocaraceae | Dry | −1.48 | Brazil | Bucci *et al.* (2006) |
| *Ouratea hexasperma* (A. St.-Hil.) Baill. | Ochnaceae | Dry | −1.48 | Brazil | Bucci *et al.* (2006) |
| *Qualea parviflora* Mart. | Vochysiaceae | Dry | −1.65 | Brazil | Bucci *et al.* (2006) |
| *Schefflera macrocarpa* (Cham. & Schltdl.) Frodin | Araliaceae | Dry | −1.72 | Brazil | Bucci *et al.* (2006) |
| *Aleurites moluccana* (L.) Willd. | Euphorbiaceae | Moist | −2.17 | China | Chen *et al.* (2009) |
| *Bischofia javanica* Blume | Phyllanthaceae | Moist | −1.27 | China | Chen *et al.* (2009) |
| *Codiaeum variegatum* (L.) Rumph. ex A. Juss. | Euphorbiaceae | Moist | −2.23 | China | Chen *et al.* (2009) |
| *Drypetes indica* (Müll. Arg.) Pax & K. Hoffm. | Putranjivaceae | Moist | −2.32 | China | Chen *et al.* (2009) |
| *Hevea brasiliensis* (Willd. ex A. Juss.) Müll. Arg. | Euphorbiaceae | Moist | −1.27 | China | Chen *et al.* (2009) |
| *Macaranga denticulata* (Blume) Müll. Arg. | Euphorbiaceae | Moist | −1.14 | China | Chen *et al.* (2009) |
| *Acosmium cardenasii* H.S. Irwin & Arroyo | Fabaceae | Dry | −6.2 | Bolivia | Markesteijn *et al.* (2011) |
| *Anadenanthera colubrina* (Vell.) Brenan | Fabaceae | Dry | −5.7 | Bolivia | Markesteijn *et al.* (2011) |
| *Aspidosperma cylindrocarpon* Müll. Arg. | Apocynaceae | Dry | −2.9 | Bolivia | Markesteijn *et al.* (2011) |
| *Aspidosperma tomentosum* Mart. | Apocynaceae | Dry | −4.7 | Bolivia | Markesteijn *et al.* (2011) |
| *Astronium urundeuva* (Allemão) Engl. | Anacardiaceae | Dry | −1.8 | Bolivia | Markesteijn *et al.* (2011) |

| Species | Family | Moisture | Value | Country | Reference |
| --- | --- | --- | --- | --- | --- |
| *Bougainvillea modesta* Heimerl | Nyctaginaceae | Dry | −3.7 | Bolivia | Markesteijn *et al.* (2011) |
| *Casearia gossypiosperma* Briq. | Salicaceae | Dry | −4.6 | Bolivia | Markesteijn *et al.* (2011) |
| *Cecropia concolor* Willd. | Urticaceae | Dry | −0.8 | Bolivia | Markesteijn *et al.* (2011) |
| *Ceiba speciosa* (A. St.-Hil.) Ravenna | Malvaceae | Dry | −1.4 | Bolivia | Markesteijn *et al.* (2011) |
| *Centrolobium microchaete* (Mart. ex Benth.) H.C. Lima | Fabaceae | Dry | −1.2 | Bolivia | Markesteijn *et al.* (2011) |
| *Guibourtia hymenaefolia* (Moric.) J. Léonard | Fabaceae | Dry | −5.7 | Bolivia | Markesteijn *et al.* (2011) |
| *Solanum riparium* Pers. | Solanaceae | Dry | −2.1 | Bolivia | Markesteijn *et al.* (2011) |
| *Trichilia elegans* A. Juss. | Meliaceae | Dry | −3.5 | Bolivia | Markesteijn *et al.* (2011) |
| *Anacardium excelsum* (Kunth) Skeels | Anacardiaceae | Moist | −1.56 | Panama | Meinzer *et al.* (2003) |
| *Cordia alliodora* (Ruiz & Pav.) Oken | Boraginaceae | Moist | −3 | Panama | Meinzer *et al.* (2003) |
| *Ficus insipida* Willd. | Moraceae | Moist | −1.66 | Panama | Meinzer *et al.* (2003) |
| *Schefflera morototoni* (Aubl.) Maguire, Steyerm. & Frodin | Araliaceae | Moist | −1.68 | Panama | Meinzer *et al.* (2003) |
| *Chrysophyllum cainito* L. | Sapotaceae | Moist | −2.1 | Panama | Meinzer *et al.* (2008b) |
| *Ficus insipida* Willd. | Moraceae | Moist | −1.91 | Panama | Meinzer *et al.* (2008b) |
| *Manilkara bidentata* (A. DC.) A. Chev. | Sapotaceae | Moist | −2.65 | Panama | Meinzer *et al.* (2008b) |
| *Protium panamense* (Rose) I.M. Johnst. | Burseraceae | Moist | −1.73 | Panama | Meinzer *et al.* (2008b) |
| *Tachigali versicolor* Standl. & L.O. Williams | Fabaceae | Moist | −1.63 | Panama | Meinzer *et al.* (2008b) |
| *Tapirira guianensis* Aubl. | Anacardiaceae | Moist | −1.82 | Panama | Meinzer *et al.* (2008b) |
| *Trattinnickia aspera* (Standl.) Swart | Burseraceae | Moist | −1.07 | Panama | Meinzer *et al.* (2008b) |
| *Vochysia ferruginea* Mart. | Vochysiaceae | Moist | −1 | Panama | Meinzer *et al.* (2008b) |
| *Curatella americana* L. | Dilleniaceae | Dry | −1.4 | Venezuela | Sobrado (1996) |
| *Beureria cumanensis* O.E. Schulz | Boraginaceae | Dry | −3.82 | Venezuela | Sobrado (1997) |
| *Capparis aristiguetae* Iltis | Capparaceae | Dry | −2.45 | Venezuela | Sobrado (1997) |
| *Coursetia ferruginea* (Kunth) Lavin | Fabaceae | Dry | −2.42 | Venezuela | Sobrado (1997) |
| *Lonchocarpus pubescens* (Willd.) DC. | Fabaceae | Dry | −1.77 | Venezuela | Sobrado (1997) |
| *Morisonia americana* L. | Capparaceae | Dry | −2.39 | Venezuela | Sobrado (1997) |
| *Pithecellobium dulce* (Roxb.) Benth. | Fabaceae | Dry | −1.65 | Venezuela | Sobrado (1997) |

| Species | Family | Forest type | $P_{50}$ (MPa) | Country | Reference |
|---|---|---|---|---|---|
| *Aglaia glabrata* Teijsm. & Binn. | Meliaceae | Moist | −0.71 | Brunei | Tyree *et al.* (1998) |
| *Amyxa pluricornis* (Radlk.) Domke | Thymelaeaceae | Moist | −0.63 | Brunei | Tyree *et al.* (1998) |
| *Canarium caudatum* King | Burseraceae | Moist | −1.47 | Brunei | Tyree *et al.* (1998) |
| *Cotylelobium burckii* Heim | Dipterocarpaceae | Moist | −0.45 | Brunei | Tyree *et al.* (1998) |
| *Diospyros brachiata* King & Gamble | Ebenaceae | Moist | −0.42 | Brunei | Tyree *et al.* (1998) |
| *Diospyros hermaphroditica* Bakh. ex Steenis | Ebenaceae | Moist | −0.6 | Brunei | Tyree *et al.* (1998) |
| *Diospyros mindanaensis* Merr. | Ebenaceae | Moist | −0.79 | Brunei | Tyree *et al.* (1998) |
| *Dipterocarpus globosus* Vesque | Dipterocarpaceae | Moist | −0.18 | Brunei | Tyree *et al.* (1998) |
| *Dryobalanops aromatica* C.F. Gaertn. | Dipterocarpaceae | Moist | −0.26 | Brunei | Tyree *et al.* (1998) |
| *Heritiera sumatrana* Kosterm. | Malvaceae | Moist | −1.69 | Brunei | Tyree *et al.* (1998) |
| *Homalium moultonii* Merr. | Salicaceae | Moist | −6.3 | Brunei | Tyree *et al.* (1998) |
| *Isonandra lanceolata* Thwaites | Sapotaceae | Moist | −0.48 | Brunei | Tyree *et al.* (1998) |
| *Lophopetalum subobovatum* King | Celastraceae | Moist | −0.59 | Brunei | Tyree *et al.* (1998) |
| *Mallotus wrayi* King ex Hook. f. | Euphorbiaceae | Moist | −0.53 | Brunei | Tyree *et al.* (1998) |
| *Nephelium lappaceum* L. | Sapindaceae | Moist | −0.76 | Brunei | Tyree *et al.* (1998) |
| *Payena endertii* H.J. Lam | Sapotaceae | Moist | −0.63 | Brunei | Tyree *et al.* (1998) |
| *Pentace adenophora* Kosterm. | Malvaceae | Moist | −0.19 | Brunei | Tyree *et al.* (1998) |
| *Santiria mollis* Engl. | Burseraceae | Moist | −0.2 | Brunei | Tyree *et al.* (1998) |
| *Shorea faguetiana* Heim. | Dipterocarpaceae | Moist | −0.37 | Brunei | Tyree *et al.* (1998) |
| *Shorea mecistopteryx* Ridl. | Dipterocarpaceae | Moist | −0.63 | Brunei | Tyree *et al.* (1998) |
| *Shorea ovalis* Bl. | Dipterocarpaceae | Moist | −0.39 | Brunei | Tyree *et al.* (1998) |
| *Sindora leiocarpa* Backer ex K. Heyne; de Wit | Fabaceae | Moist | −0.86 | Brunei | Tyree *et al.* (1998) |
| *Stemonurus umbellatus* Becc. | Stemonuraceae | Moist | −0.18 | Brunei | Tyree *et al.* (1998) |
| *Syzygium ampullarium* (Stapf) Merr. & L.M. Perry | Myrtaceae | Moist | −0.6 | Brunei | Tyree *et al.* (1998) |

| Species | Family | | Value | Location | Reference |
|---|---|---|---|---|---|
| *Syzygium bankense* (Hassk.) Merr. & L.M. Perry | Myrtaceae | Moist | −1.26 | Brunei | Tyree et al. (1998) |
| *Syzygium muelleri* (Miq.) Miq. | Myrtaceae | Moist | −0.54 | Brunei | Tyree et al. (1998) |
| *Xerospermum laevigatum* Radlk. | Sapindaceae | Moist | −0.18 | Brunei | Tyree et al. (1998) |
| *Baccaurea ramiflora* Lour. | Phyllanthaceae | Moist | −2 | China | Zhu & Cao (2009) |
| *Bauhinia variegata* L. | Fabaceae | Moist | −1.55 | China | Zhu & Cao (2009) |
| *Combretum latifolium* Blume | Combretaceae | Moist | −1.11 | China | Zhu & Cao (2009) |
| *Millettia pachycarpa* Benth. | Fabaceae | Moist | −1.32 | China | Zhu & Cao (2009) |
| *Quisqualis indica* L. | Combretaceae | Moist | −1.42 | China | Zhu & Cao (2009) |
| *Syzygium szemaoense* Merr. & L.M. Perry | Myrtaceae | Moist | −1.95 | China | Zhu & Cao (2009) |
| *Cordia alliodora* (Ruiz & Pav.) Oken | Boraginaceae | Moist | −3.2 | Panama | Zotz et al. (1994) |
| *Ficus citrifolia* Mill. | Moraceae | Moist | −1.7 | Panama | Zotz et al. (1994) |
| *Ochroma pyramidale* (Cav. ex Lam.) Urb. | Malvaceae | Moist | −1 | Panama | Zotz et al. (1994) |
| *Ouratea lucens* (Kunth) Engl. | Ochnaceae | Moist | −1.8 | Panama | Zotz et al. (1994) |
| *Pseudobombax septenatum* (Jacq.) Dugand | Malvaceae | Moist | −1 | Panama | Zotz et al. (1994) |
| *Schefflera morototoni* (Aubl.) Maguire, Steyerm. & Frodin | Araliaceae | Moist | −1.4 | Panama | Zotz et al. (1994) |
| *Ouratea lucens* (Kunth) Engl. | Ochnaceae | Moist | −1.9 | Panama | Lopez et al. (2005) |
| *Swartzia simplex* (Sw.) Spreng. | Fabaceae | Moist | −2.8 | Panama | Lopez et al. (2005) |
| *Psychotria horizontalis* Sw. | Rubiaceae | Moist | −2.6 | Panama | Lopez et al. (2005) |
| *Hybanthus prunifolius* (Humb. & Bonpl.) Schultze-Menz. | Violaceae | Moist | −4.1 | Panama | Lopez et al. (2005) |
| *Prioria copaifera* Griseb. | Fabaceae | Moist | −0.8 | Panama | Lopez et al. (2005) |
| *Carapa guianensis* Aubl. | Meliaceae | Moist | −0.8 | Panama | Lopez et al. (2005) |
| *Ficus citrifolia* Mill. | Moraceae | Moist | −1.4 | Panama | Lopez et al. (2005) |
| *Bursera simaruba* (L.) Sarg. | Burseraceae | Moist | −3.2 | Panama | Lopez et al. (2005) |
| *Cordia alliodora* (Ruiz & Pav.) Oken. | Boraginaceae | Moist | −1.6 | Panama | Lopez et al. (2005) |

## References

Absy, M. L., Cleef, A., Fournier, M. *et al.* (1991) Mise en évidence de quatre phases d'ouverture de la forêt dense dans le Sud-Est de l'Amazonie au cours des 60,000 dernières années: première comparaison avec d'autres régions tropicales. *Comptes Rendus de l'Académie des Sciences Paris, Série II*, **312**, 673–678.

Agrawal A., Nepstad, D. & Chhatre, A. (2011) Reducing emissions from deforestation and forest degradation. *Annual Review in Environmental Resources*, **36**, 373–396.

Andrade, J. L., Meinzer, F. C., Goldstein, G. & Schnitzer, S.A. (2005) Water uptake and transport in lianas and co-occurring trees of a seasonally dry tropical forest. *Trees*, **19**, 282–289.

Baas, P., Ewers, F. W., Davis, S. D. & Wheeler, E. A. (2004). Evolution of xylem physiology. In *The Evolution of Plant Physiology* (eds. A. R. Hemsley & I. Poole), pp. 273–295. London, San Diego: Elsevier Academic Press.

Baraloto, C., Paine, C. E. T., Patiño, S. *et al.* (2009) Functional trait variation and sampling strategies in species-rich plant communities. *Functional Ecology*, **24**, 208–216.

Baraloto, C., Paine, C. E. T., Poorter, L. *et al.* (2010) Decoupled leaf and stem economics in rainforest trees. *Ecology Letters*, **13**, 1338–1347.

Bartlett, M. K., Scoffoni, C. & Sack, L. (2012) The determinants of leaf turgor loss point and prediction of drought tolerance of species and biomes: a global meta-analysis. *Ecology Letters*, **15**, 393–405.

Bird, B. W., Abbott, M. B., Rodbell, D. T. & Vuille, M. (2011) Holocene tropical South American hydroclimate revealed from lake sediment d18O record. *Earth and Planetary Science Letters*, **310**, 192–202.

Brando P. M., Nepstad, D. C., Balch, J. K. *et al.* (2012) Fire-induced tree mortality in a neotropical forest: the role of tree size, wood density and fire behavior. *Global Change Biology*, **18**, 630–641.

van Breukelen, M. R., Vonhof, H. B., Hellstrom, J. C., Wester, W. C. G. & Kroon, D. (2008) Fossil dripwater in stalagmites reveals Holocene temperatures and rainfall variation in Amazonia. *Earth and Planetary Science Letters*, **275**, 54–60.

Brodribb, T. J. & Feild, T. S. (2010) Leaf hydraulic evolution led a surge in leaf photosynthetic capacity during early angiosperm diversification. *Ecology Letters*, **13**, 175–183.

Brodribb, T. J., Holbrook, N. M., Edwards, E. J. & Gutierrez, M. V. (2003) Relations between stomatal closure, leaf turgor and xylem vulnerability in eight tropical dry forest trees. *Plant, Cell and Environment*, **26**, 443–450.

Bucci, S. J., Goldstein, G., Meinzer, F. C. *et al.* (2004) Functional convergence in hydraulic architecture and water relations of tropical savanna trees: from leaf to whole plant. *Tree Physiology*, **24**, 891–899.

Bucci, S. J., Scholz, F. G., Goldstein, G. *et al.* (2006) Nutrient availability constrains the hydraulic architecture and water relations of savannah trees. *Plant, Cell and Environment*, **29**, 2153–2167.

Bucci, S. J., Scholz, F. G., Goldstein, G. *et al.* (2008) Controls on stand transpiration and soil water utilization along a tree density gradient in a Neotropical savanna. *Agricultural and Forest Meteorology*, **148**, 839–849.

Burbridge, R. E., Mayle, F. E. & Killeen, T. J. (2004) Fifty-thousand-year vegetation and climate history of Noel Kempff Mercado National Park, Bolivian Amazon. *Quaternary Research*, **61**, 215–230.

Burnham, R. J. & Johnson, K. R. (2004) South American palaeobotany and the origins of Neotropical rainforests. *Philosophical Transactions of the Royal Society London Series B*, **359**, 1595–1610.

Bush, M. B. (1994) Amazonian speciation: a necessarily complex model. *Journal of Biogeography*, **21**, 5–17.

Bush, M. B., Miller, M. C., de Oliveira, P. E. & Colinvaux, P.A. (2002) Orbital forcing signal in sediments of two Amazonian lakes. *Journal of Paleolimnology*, **27**, 341–352.

Bush, M. B., Silman, M. R. & Urrego, D. H. (2004) 48,000 years of climate and forest change in a biodiversity hot spot. *Science*, **303**, 827–829.

von Caemmerer, S. (2000) *Biochemical Models of Leaf Photosynthesis*. Victoria, Australia: CSIRO Publishing.

Chave, J. (1999) Study of structural, successional and spatial patterns in tropical rain forests using TROLL, a spatially explicit forest model, *Ecological Modelling*, **124**, 233–254.

Chave, J., Coomes, D., Jansen, S. *et al.* (2009) Towards a worldwide wood economics spectrum. *Ecology Letters*, **12**, 351–366.

Chen, J. W., Zhang, Q., Li, X. S. & Cao, K. F. (2009) Independence of stem and leaf hydraulic traits in six Euphorbiaceae tree species with contrasting leaf phenology. *Planta*, **230**, 459–168.

Choat, B., Sack, L. & Holbrook, N. M. (2007) Diversity of hydraulic traits in nine Cordia species growing in tropical forests with contrasting precipitation. *New Phytologist*, **175**, 686–698.

Christin, P. A., Besnard, G., Samaritani, E. *et al.* (2008) Oligocene $CO_2$ decline promoted C4 photosynthesis in grasses. *Current Biology*, **18**, 37–43.

Chuine, I. (2000) A unified model for budburst of trees. *Journal of Theoretical Biology*, **207**, 337–347.

Clark, D. B., Mercado, L. M., Sitch, S. *et al.* (2011) The Joint UK Land Environment Simulator (JULES), Model description – Part 2: Carbon fluxes and vegetation *Geoscientific Model Development Discussions*, **4**, 641–688.

Cochard, H. (2006) Cavitation in trees. *Comptes Rendus de Physique*, **7**, 1018–1026.

Colinvaux, P. A., de Oliviera, P. E., Moreno, J. E., Miller, M. C. & Bush, M. B. (1996) A long pollen record from lowland Amazonia: forest and cooling in glacial times. *Science*, **274**, 85–88.

Colinvaux, P. A., de Oliveira, P. E. & Bush, M. B. (2000) Amazonian and neotropical plant communities on glacial time-scales: the failure of the aridity and refuge hypotheses. *Quaternary Science Review*, **19**, 141–169.

Cornelissen, J. H. C., Lavorel, S., Garnier, E. *et al.* (2003) A handbook of protocols for standardised and easy measurement of plant functional traits worldwide. *Australian Journal of Botany*, **51**, 335–380.

Cowling, S. A., Cox, P. M. & Betts, R. A. (2004) Contrasting simulated past and future responses of the Amazon rainforest to atmospheric change. *Philosophical Transactions of the Royal Society B*, **359**, 539–548.

Cowling, S. A., Maslin, M. A. & Sykes, M. T. (2001) Paleovegetation simulations of lowland Amazonia and implications for neotropical allopatry and speciation. *Quaternary Research*, **55**, 140–149.

Cox, P. M., Betts, R. A., Collins, M. *et al.* (2004) Amazonian forest dieback under climate-carbon cycle projections for the 21st century. *Theoretical Applied Climatology*, **78**, 137–156.

Cox, P. M., Betts, R. A., Jones, C. D., Spall, S. A. & Totterdell, I. J. (2000) Acceleration of global warming due to carbon-cycling feedbacks in a coupled climate model. *Nature*, **408**, 184–187.

Cramer, W., Bondeau, A., Schaphoff, S. *et al.* (2004) Tropical forests and the global carbon cycle: impacts of atmospheric carbon dioxide, climate change and rate of deforestation. *Philosophical Transactions of the Royal Society B*, **359**, 331–343.

Cruz, F. W., Wang, X., Auler, A. *et al.* (2009) Orbital and millennial-scale precipitation changes in Brazil from speleothem records. In *Past Climate Variability in South America and Surrounding Regions* (eds. F. Vimeux *et al.*) Developments in Paleoenvironmental Research 14. Berlin: Springer.

Davis, C. C., Webb, C. O., Wurdack, K. J., Jaramillo, C. A. & Donoghue M. A. (2005) Explosive radiation of Malpighiales supports a mid-Cretaceous origin of modern tropical rain forests. *American Naturalist*, **165**, E36–E65.

Davis, M. B., Shaw, R. G. & Etterson, J. R. (2005) Evolutionary responses to changing climates. *Ecology*, **86**, 1706–1714.

Domingues, T. F., Martinelli, L. A. & Ehleringer, J. R. (2007) Ecophysiological traits of plant functional groups in forest and pasture ecosystems from eastern Amazonia, Brazil. *Plant Ecology*, **193**, 101–112.

Domingues, T. F., Meir, P., Feldpausch, T. R. *et al.* (2010) Co-limitation of photosynthetic capacity by nitrogen and phosphorus in West Africa woodlands. *Plant, Cell & Environment*, **33**, 959–980.

Duputié, A., Massol, F., Chuine, I., Kirckpatrick, M. & Ronce, O. (2012) How do genetic correlations affect species range shifts in a changing environment? *Ecology Letters*, **15**, 251–259.

Engelbrecht, B. M. J. & Kursar, T. A. (2003) Comparative drought-resistance of seedlings of 28 species of co-occurring tropical woody plants. *Oecologia*, **136**, 383–393.

Engelbrecht, B. M. J., Comita, L. S., Condit, R. *et al.* (2007) Drought sensitivity shapes species distribution patterns in tropical forests *Nature*, **447**, 80–82.

Farquhar, G. D., Ehleringer, J. R. & Hubick, K. T. (1989) Carbon isotope discrimination and photosynthesis. *Annual Review of Plant Physiology and Plant Molecular Biology*, **40**, 503–537.

Favrichon, V. (1994) Classification des espèces arborées en groupes fonctionnels en vue de la réalisation d'un modèle de dynamique de peuplement en foret guyanaise. *Revue d'Écologie (Terre et Vie)*, **49**, 379–403.

Feild, T. S. & Balun, L. (2008) Xylem hydraulic and photosynthetic function of Gnetum (Gnetales) species from Papua New Guinea. *New Phytologist*, **177**, 665–675.

Fisher, R., McDowell, N., Purves, D. *et al.* (2010) Assessing uncertainties in a second-generation dynamic vegetation model

caused by ecological scale limitations. *New Phytologist*, **187**, 666–681.

Freycon, V., Krencker, M., Schwartz, D., Nasi, R. & Bonal, D. (2010) The impact of climate changes during the Holocene on vegetation in Northern French Guiana. *Quaternary Research*, **73**, 220–225.

Friedlingstein, P., Houghton, R. A., Marland, G. *et al.* (2010) Update on $CO_2$ emissions. *Nature Geosciences*, **3**, 811–812.

Fyllas, N. M., Patiño, S., Baker, T. R. *et al.* (2009) Basin-wide variations in foliar properties of Amazonian forests: Phylogeny, soils and climate. *Biogeosciences*, **6**, 2677–2708.

Fyllas, N. M., Quesada, C. A. & Lloyd, J. (2012) Deriving plant functional types for Amazonia for use in vegetation dynamics models. *Perspectives in Plant Ecology, Evolution, and Systematics*, **14**, 97–110.

Garreaud, R. D., Vuille, M., Compagnucci, R. & Marengo, J. (2009) Present-day South American climate. *Palaeogeography, Palaeoclimatology, Palaeoecology*, **281**, 180–195.

van Gelder, H. A., Poorter, L. & Sterck, F. J. (2006) Wood mechanics, allometry, and life-history variation in a tropical rain forest tree community. *New Phytologist*, **171**, 367–378.

Goldstein, G., Meinzer, F. C., Bucci, S. J. *et al.* (2008) Water economy of Neotropical savanna trees: six paradigms revisited. *Tree Physiology*, **28**, 395–404.

Grime, J. P. (1979) *Plant Strategies and Vegetation Processes*. Chichester: Wiley.

Haberle, S. G. & Maslin, M. A. (1999) Late Quaternary vegetation and climate change in the Amazon basin based on a 50,000 year pollen record from the Amazon Fan, ODP Site 932. *Quaternary Research*, **51**, 27–38.

Hacke, U. G., Sperry, J. S., Pockman, W. T., Davis, S. D. & McCulloh, K. A. (2001) Trends in wood density and structure are linked to prevention of xylem implosion by negative pressure. *Oecologia*, **126**, 457–461.

Hao, G. Y., Hoffmann, W. A., Scholtz, F. G. *et al.* (2008) Stem and leaf hydraulics of congeneric tree species from adjacent tropical savanna and forest ecosystems. *Oecologia*, **155**, 405–415.

Harrison, S. P., Prentice, I. C., Barboni, D. *et al.* (2010) Ecophysiological and bioclimatic foundations for a global plant functional classification. *Journal of Vegetation Science*, **21**, 300–317.

Hirose, T. (2005) Development of the Monsi-Saeki theory on canopy structure. *Annals of Botany*, **95**, 483–494.

Hirota, M., Holmgren, M., van Nes, E. H. & Scheffer, M. (2011) Global resilience of tropical forest and savanna to critical transitions. *Science*, **334**, 232–235.

Holling, C. S. (1973) Resilience and stability of ecological systems. *Annual Review of Ecology and Systematics*, **4**, 1–23.

Hughen, K. A., Lehman, S., Southon, J. *et al.* (2004) 14C activity and global carbon cycle changes over the past 50,000 years. *Science*, **303**, 202–207.

Huntingford, C., Fisher, R. A., Mercado, L. *et al.* (2008) Towards quantifying uncertainty in predictions of Amazon 'dieback'. *Philosophical Transactions of the Royal Society B*, **363**, 1857–1864.

Hurtt, G. C., Moorcroft, P. R., Pacala, S. W. & Levin, S. (1998) Terrestrial models and global change: challenges for the future. *Global Change Biology*, **4**, 581–590.

Hurtt, G. C. & Pacala, S. W. (1995) The consequences of recruitment limitation: Reconciling chance, history, and competitive differences between plants. *Journal of Theoretical Biology*, **176**, 1–12.

Ives, A. R. & Carpenter, S. R. (2007) Stability and diversity of ecosystems. *Science*, **317**, 58–62.

Iwasa, Y., Andreasen, V. & Levin, S. (1987) Aggregation in model ecosystems. I. Prefect aggregation. *Ecological Modelling*, **37**, 287–302.

Jacobsen, A. L., Ewers, F. W., Pratt, R. B., Paddock III, W. A. & Davis, S. D. (2005) Do xylem fibers affect vessel cavitation resistance? *Plant Physiology*, **139**, 546–556.

Janzen, D. H. (1981) Patterns of herbivory in a tropical deciduous forest. *Biotropica*, **13**, 271–282.

Jaramillo, C., Ochoa, D., Contreras, L. *et al.* (2010) Effects of rapid global warming at the Paleocene–Eocene boundary on Neotropical vegetation. *Science*, **330**, 957–961.

Jaramillo, C., Rueda, M. J. & Mora, G. (2006) Cenozoic plant diversity in the Neotropics. *Science*, **311**, 1893–1896.

Jones, H. G. (1992). *Plants and Microclimate*, 2nd edn. Cambridge: Cambridge University Press.

Kattge, J., Diaz, S., Lavorel, S. *et al.* (2011) TRY – a global database of plant traits. *Global Change Biology*, **17**, 2905–2935.

Kraft, N. J. B., Metz, M. R., Condit, R. S. & Chave, J. (2010) The relationship between wood density and mortality in a global tropical forest dataset. *New Phytologist*, **188**, 1124–1136.

Krinner, G., Viovy, N., de Noblet-Ducoudré, N. *et al.* (2005) A dynamic global vegetation model for studies of the coupled atmosphere–biosphere system. *Global Biogeochemical Cycles*, **19**, GB1015.

Le Quéré, C., Raupach, M. R., Canadell, J. G. *et al.* (2009) Trends in the sources and sinks of carbon dioxide. *Nature Geosciences*, **2**, 831–836.

Le Roux, X., Lacointe, A., Escobar-Gutierrez, A. & Le Dizès, S. (2001) Carbon-based models of individual tree growth: A critical appraisal. *Annals of Forest Science*, **58**, 469–506.

Ledru, M.-P. (2001) Late Holocene rainforest disturbance in French Guiana. *Review of Paleobotany and Palynology*, **115**, 161–176.

Leuning, R., Kelliher, F. M., De Pury, D. G. G. & Schulze, E. D. (1995) Leaf nitrogen, photosynthesis, conductance and transpiration: scaling from leaves to canopies. *Plant, Cell & Environment*, **18**, 1183–1200.

Lewis, S. L., Lloyd, J., Sitch, S., Mitchard, E. T. A & Laurance, W. F. (2009) Changing ecology of tropical forests: evidence and drivers. *Annual*

*Reviews of Ecology Evolution and Systematics*, **40**, 529–549.

Lloyd, J. & Farquhar, G. D. (2008) Effects of rising temperatures and [CO₂] on the physiology of tropical forest trees. *Philosophical Transactions of the Royal Society B*, **363**, 1811–1817.

Lopez, O. R., Kursar, T. A., Cochard, H. & Tyree, M. T. (2005) Interspecific variation in xylem variability to cavitation among tropical tree and shrub species. *Tree Physiology*, **25**, 1553–1562.

MacArthur, R. H. (1972) *Geographical Ecology: Patterns in the Distribution of Species*. Princeton: Princeton University Press.

Maherali, H., Pockman, W. T. & Jackson, R. B. (2004) Adaptive variation in the vulnerability of woody plants to xylem cavitation. *Ecology*, **85**, 2184–2199.

Malhi, Y., Aragão, L. E. O. C., Galbraith, D. *et al.* (2009) Exploring the likelihood and mechanism of a climate-change-induced dieback of the Amazon rainforest. *Proceedings of the National Academy of Sciences USA*, **106**, 20610–20615.

Marengo, J. (2004) Interdecadal and long-term rainfall variability in the Amazon basin. *Theoretical and Applied Climatology*, **78**, 79–96.

Markesteijn, L., Poorter, L., Paz, H. & Sack, L. (2011) Ecological differentiation in xylem cavitation resistance is associated with stem and leaf structural traits. *Plant, Cell and Environment*, **34**, 137–148.

Markewitz, D., Devine, S., Davidson, E. A., Brando, P. & Nepstad, D. C. (2010) Soil moisture depletion under simulated drought in the Amazon: impacts on deep root uptake. *New Phytologist*, **187**, 592–607.

Marquis, R. J., Morais, H. C. & Diniz, I. R. (2002), Interactions among Cerrado plants and their herbivores: unique or typical? In *The Cerrados of Brazil – Ecology and Natural History of a Neotropical Savanna* (eds. P. S. Oliveira & R. J. Marquis), pp. 306–328. New York: University Presses of California, Columbia and Princeton.

Mayle, F. E., Beerling, D. J., Gosling, W. D. & Bush, M. B. (2004) Responses of Amazonian ecosystems to climatic and atmospheric CO2 changes since the Last Glacial Maximum. *Philosophical Transactions of the Royal Society B*, **359**, 499–514.

Mayle, F. E., Burn, M. J., Power, M. & Urrego, D. H. (2009) Vegetation and fire at the Last Glacial Maximum in tropical South America. In *Past Climate Variability in South America and Surrounding Regions* (eds. F. Vimeux *et al.*) Developments in Paleoenvironmental Research 14. Berlin: Springer.

McAdam, S. A. & Brodribb, T. J. (2012) Stomatal innovation and the rise of seed plants. *Ecology Letters*, **15**, 1–8.

McCulloh, K. A., Meinzer, F. C., Sperry, J. S. *et al.* (2011) Comparative hydraulic architecture of tropical tree species representing a range of successional stages and wood density. *Oecologia*, **167**, 27–37.

McDowell, N. G. (2011) Mechanisms linking drought, hydraulics, carbon metabolism, and vegetation mortality. *Plant Physiology*, **155**, 1051–1059.

Meinzer, F. C., Campanello, P. I., Domec, J. C. *et al.* (2008a) Constraints on physiological function associated with branch architecture and wood density in tropical forest trees. *Tree Physiology*, **28**, 1609–1617.

Meinzer, F. C., James, S. A., Goldstein, G. & Woodruff, D. R. (2003) Whole water transport scales with sapwood capacitance in tropical forest canopy trees. *Plant, Cell & Environment*, **26**, 1147–1155.

Meinzer, F. C., Woodruff, D. A., Domec, J. C. *et al.* (2008b) Coordination of leaf and stem water transport properties in tropical forest trees. *Oecologia*, **156**, 31–41.

Mendez-Alonzo, R. *et al.* (in press) Coordination between leaf and stem economics in a tropical dry forest. *Ecology*.

Mercado, L. M., Patiño, S., Domingues, T. F. *et al.* (2011) Variations in Amazon forest productivity correlated with foliar nutrients and modelled rates of photosynthetic carbon supply. *Philosophical Transactions of the Royal Society B*, **366**, 3316–3329.

Monteith, J. L. & Unsworth, M. H. (2007) *Principles of Environmental Physics*, 3rd edn. Burlington, San Diego, London: Academic Press.

Moorcroft, P. R., Hurtt, G. C. & Pacala, S. W. (2001) A method for scaling vegetation dynamics: the ecosystem demography model (ED). *Ecological Monographs*, **71**, 557–586.

Morley, R. J. (2000) *Origin and Evolution of Tropical Rain Forests*. Chichester, New York: Wiley.

Morley, R. J. (2011) Cretaceous and Tertiary climate change and the past distribution of megathermal rainforests. In *Tropical Rainforest Responses to Climatic Change*, 2nd edn (eds. M. B. Bush, J. R. Flenley & W. D Gosling), pp. 1–34. Berlin-Heidelberg: Springer.

Murphy, B. P. & Bowman, D. M. J. S. (2012) What controls the distribution of tropical forest and savanna? *Ecology Letters*, **15**, 748–758.

Niinemets, U. (2001) Global-scale climatic controls of leaf dry mass per area, density, and thickness in trees and shrubs. *Ecology*, **82**, 453–469.

Nobel, P. S. (2009) *Physiochemical and Environmental Plant Physiology*, 5th edn. San Diego: Academic Press.

Ometto, J. P. H. B., Ehleringer, J. R., Domingues, T. F. *et al.* (2006) The stable carbon and nitrogen isotopic composition of vegetation in tropical forests of the Amazon Basin, Brazil. *Biogeochemistry*, **79**, 251–274.

Onoda, Y., Westoby, M., Adler, P. B. *et al.* (2011) Global patterns of leaf mechanical properties. *Ecology Letters*, **14**, 301–312.

Pacala, S. W., Canham, C. D., Saponara, J. *et al.* (1996) Forest models defined by field measurements, estimation, error analysis and dynamics. *Ecological Monographs*, **66**, 1–43.

Paine, C. E. T., Stahl, C., Courtois, E., Patiño, S. & Baraloto, C. (2010) Functional explanations for bark thickness in tropical forest trees. *Functional Ecology*, **24**, 1202–1210.

Patiño, S., Fyllas, N. M., Baker, T. R. *et al.* (2012) Coordination of physiological and structural traits in Amazon forest trees. *Biogeosciences*, **9**, 775–801.

Patiño, S., Lloyd, J., Paiva, R. *et al.* (2009) Branch xylem density variations across the Amazon Basin. *Biogeosciences*, **6**, 545–568.

Patiño, S., Tyree, M. T. & Herre, E. A. (1995) Comparison of hydraulic architecture of woody plants of differing phylogeny and growth form with special reference to free-standing and hemi-epiphytic Ficus species from Panama. *New Phytologist*, **129**, 125–134.

Pennington, R. T., Prado, D. E. & Pendry, C. A. (2000) Neotropical seasonally dry forests and Quaternary vegetation changes. *Journal of Biogeography*, **27**, 261–273.

Phillips, O. L., Martinez, R. V., Arroyo, L. *et al.* (2002) Increasing dominance of large lianas in Amazonian forests. *Nature*, **418**, 770–774.

Phillips, O. L., Aragão, L. E. O. C., Lewis, S. L. *et al.* (2009) Drought sensitivity of the Amazon rainforest. *Science*, **323**, 1344–1347.

Picard, N. & Franc, A. (2003) Are ecological groups of species optimal for forest dynamics modelling. *Ecological Modelling*, **163**, 175–186.

Piperno D. R. (2011) Prehistoric human occupation and impacts on Neotropical forest landscapes during the Late Pleistocene and Early/Middle Holocene. In *Tropical Rainforest Responses to Climatic Change*, 2nd edn (eds. M. B. Bush, J. R. Flenley & W. D Gosling). pp. 185–212. Berlin-Heidelberg: Springer.

Poorter, H., Niinemets, U., Poorter, L., Wright, I. J. & Villar, R. (2009) Causes and consequences of variation in leaf mass per area (LMA): a meta-analysis. *New Phytologist*, **182**, 565–588.

Poulter, B., Aragão, L., Heyder, U. *et al.* (2010) Net biome production of the Amazon basin in the 21st century. *Global Change Biology*, **16**, 2062–2075.

Prado, C. H. B. A., Wenhui, Z., Rojas, M. H. C. & Souza, G. M. (2004) Seasonal leaf gas exchange and water potential in a woody cerrado species community. *Brazilian Journal of Plant Physiology*, **16**, 7–16.

Purves, D. & Pacala, S. (2008) Predictive models of forest dynamics. *Science*, **320**, 1452–1453.

Read, J. & Stokes, A. (2006) Plant biomechanics in an ecological context. *American Journal of Botany*, **93**, 1546–1565.

Restom, T. G. & Nepstad, D. C. (2001) Contribution of vines to the evapotranspiration of a secondary forest in eastern Amazonia. *Plant and Soil*, **236**, 155–163.

Ritchie, M. W. & Hann D. W. (1997) Implications of disaggregation in forest growth and yield modeling. *Forest Science*, **43**, 223–233.

Rood, S. B., Patiño, S., Coombs, K. & Tyree, M. T. (2000) Branch sacrifice: cavitation-associated drought adaptation of riparian cottonwoods. *Trees*, **14**, 248–257.

Rozendaal, D. M. A. & Zuidema, P. A. (2011) Dendroecology in the tropics: a review. *Trees*, **25**, 3–16.

Rull, V. (1999) Palaeofloristic and palaeovegetational changes across the Paleocene-Eocene boundary in northern South America. *Review of Palaeobotany and Palynology*, **107**, 83–95.

Saatchi, S. S., Harris, N. L., Brown, S. *et al.* (2011) Benchmark map of forest carbon stocks in tropical regions across three continents. *Proceedings of the National Academy of Sciences USA*, **108**, 9899–9904.

Salazar, L. F., Nobre, C. A. & Oyama, M. D. (2007) Climate change consequences on the biome distribution in tropical South America. *Geophysical Research Letters*, **34**, L09708.

Schnitzer, S. A. & Bongers, F. (2002) The ecology of lianas and their role in forests. *Trends in Ecology & Evolution*, **17**, 223–230.

Schulze, E.-D., Kelliher, F. M., Korner, C., Lloyd, J. & Leuning, R. (1994) Relationships among maximum stomatal conductance, carbon assimilation rate and plant nitrogen nutrition: a global ecology scaling exercise. *Annual Review of Ecology and Systematics*, **25**, 629–660.

Servant, M., Fontes, J. C., Rieu, M. & Saliège, X. (1981) Phases climatiques arides holocènes dans le Sud-Ouest de l'Amazonie (Bolivie).

*Comptes Redus de l'Académie des Sciences Paris, Série II*, **292**, 1295–1297.

Shugart, H. H. (1984) *A Theory of Forest Dynamics*. New York: Springer.

Sitch, S., Smith, B., Prentice, I. C. *et al.* (2003) Evaluation of ecosystem dynamics, plant geography and terrestrial carbon cycling in the LPJ dynamic vegetation model. *Global Change Biology*, **9**, 161–185.

Sobrado, M. A. (1996) Embolism vulnerability of an evergreen tree. *Biologia Plantarum*, **38**, 297–301.

Sobrado, M. A. (1997) Embolism vulnerability in drought-deciduous and evergreen species of a tropical dry forest. *Acta Oecologica*, **18**, 383–391.

Staver, A. C., Archibald, S. & Levin, S. A. (2011) The global extent and determinants of savanna and forest as alternative stable states. *Science*, **334**, 230–232.

Swaine, M. D. & Whitmore, T. C. (1988) On the definition of ecological species groups in tropical rain forests. *Plant Ecology*, **75**, 81–86.

Sytsma, K. J., Walker, J. B., Schönenberger, J. & Anderberg, A. A. (2006) Phylogenetics, biogeography, and radiation of Ericales. *Annual BSA Meeting, Botany 2006*, Chicago, CA, Abstract volume 71.

Tyree, M. T., Patiño, S. & Becker, P. (1998) Vulnerability to drought-induced embolism of Bornean heath and dipterocarp forest trees. *Tree Physiology*, **18**, 583–588.

Tyree, M. T. & Zimmermann, M. H. (2002). *Xylem Structure and the Ascent of Sap*, 2nd edn (ed. T. E. Timell), pp. 283. Berlin: Springer-Verlag.

Wang, X., Auler, A. S., Edwards, R. L. *et al.* (2007) Wet periods in northeastern Brazil over the past 210 kyr linked to distant climate anomalies. *Nature*, **432**, 740–743.

Wenhui, Z. & Prado, C. H. B. A. (1998) Water relations balance parameters of 30 woody species from Cerrado vegetation in the wet and dry season. *Journal of Forestry Research*, **9**, 233–239.

Wing, S. L., Herrera, F., Jaramillo, C. A. *et al.* (2009) Late Paleocene fossils from the Cerrejón

Formation, Colombia, are the earliest record of Neotropical rainforest. *Proceedings of the National Academy of Sciences USA* **106**, 18627.

Worbes, M. (2002) One hundred years of tree-ring research in the tropics: a brief history and an outlook to future challenges. *Dendrochronologia*, **20**, 217–231.

Wright, I. J., Reich, P. B., Westoby, M. *et al.* (2004) The worldwide leaf economics spectrum. *Nature*, **428**, 821–827.

Yachi, S. & Loreau, M. (1998) Biodiversity and ecosystem productivity in a fluctuating environment: The insurance hypothesis. *Proceedings of the National Academy of Sciences USA*, **96**, 1453–1458.

Zanne, A. E., Westoby, M., Falster, D. S. *et al.* (2010) Angiosperm wood structure: Global patterns in vessel anatomy and their relation to wood density and potential conductivity. *American Journal of Botany*, **97**, 207–215.

Zhang, Y. J., Meinzer, F. C., Hao, G. Y. *et al.* (2009) Size-dependent mortality in a Neotropical savanna tree: the role of height-related adjustments in hydraulic architecture and carbon allocation. *Plant, Cell and Environment*, **32**, 1456–1466.

Zhu, S.-D. & Cao, K.-F. (2009) Hydraulic properties and photosynthetic rates in co-occurring lianas and trees in a seasonal tropical rainforest in southwestern China. *Plant Ecology*, **204**, 295–304.

Zotz, G., Tyree, M. T. & Cochard, H. (1994) Hydraulic architecture, water relations and vulnerability to cavitation of *Clusia uvitana* Pittier: a C3-CAM tropical hemiepiphyte. *New Phytologist*, **127**, 287–295.

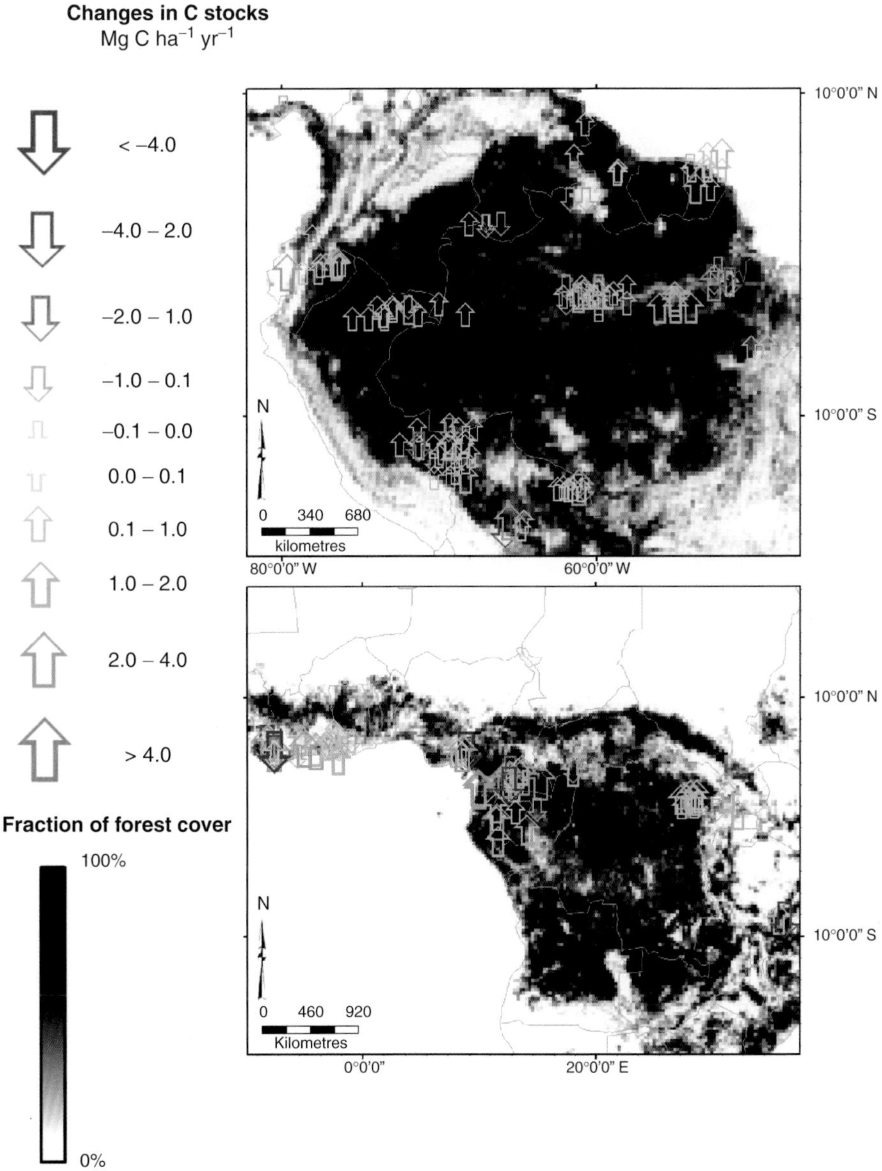
Changes in C stocks
Mg C ha−1 yr−1
< −4.0
−4.0 – 2.0
−2.0 – 1.0
−1.0 – 0.1
−0.1 – 0.0
0.0 – 0.1
0.1 – 1.0
1.0 – 2.0
2.0 – 4.0
> 4.0
Fraction of forest cover
100%
0%
10°0'0" N
10°0'0" S
N
0 340 680
kilometres
80°0'0" W
60°0'0" W
10°0'0" N
10°0'0" S
N
0 460 920
Kilometres
0°0'0"
20°0'0" E

**Figure 4.1** Locations of RAINFOR and AfriTRON network plots used in this study. For each we indicate whether they individually increased in biomass or decreased in biomass over the period monitored (ending prior to the 2005 drought for Amazonia).

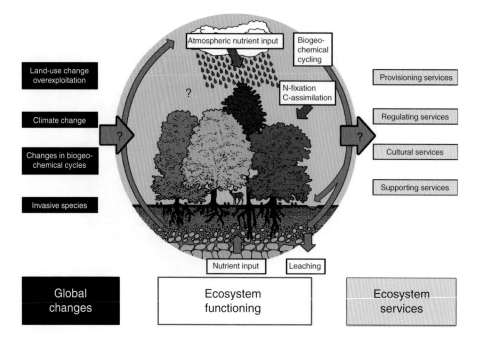

**Figure 8.1** Different drivers of global environmental change can have direct effects on the biodiversity of ecosystems and the ecological processes and functions. Changes in biodiversity can also affect ecosystem functioning. Alterations in biodiversity and functions may then translate into modifications of the delivery of ecosystem goods and services.

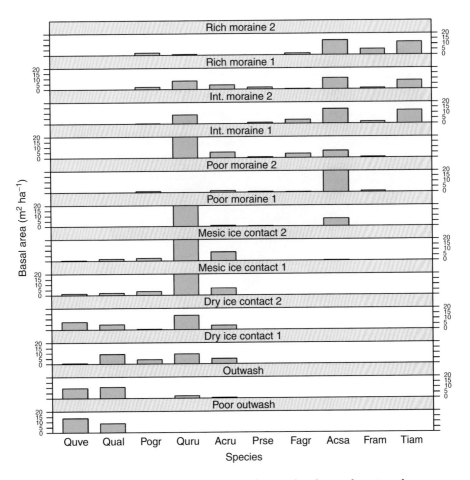

**Figure 11.1** Species basal area across our 12 primary sites in northwestern lower Michigan. The sites stratify a gradient in soil resource availability (water, calcium and nitrogen), generally increasing across sites from the bottom to the top of the graph. Abbreviations of species names are the first two letters of the genus and species and include: *Quercus velutina*, *Q. alba*, *Populus grandidentata*, *Q. rubra*, *Acer rubrum*, *Prunus serotina*, *Fagus grandifolia*, *A. saccharum*, *Fraxinus americana* and *Tilia americana*.

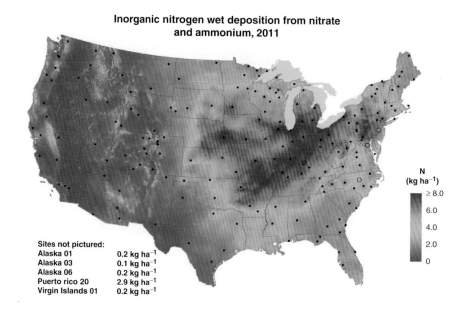

**Figure 11.2** Atmospheric wet deposition of ammonium and nitrate in the USA in 2011.

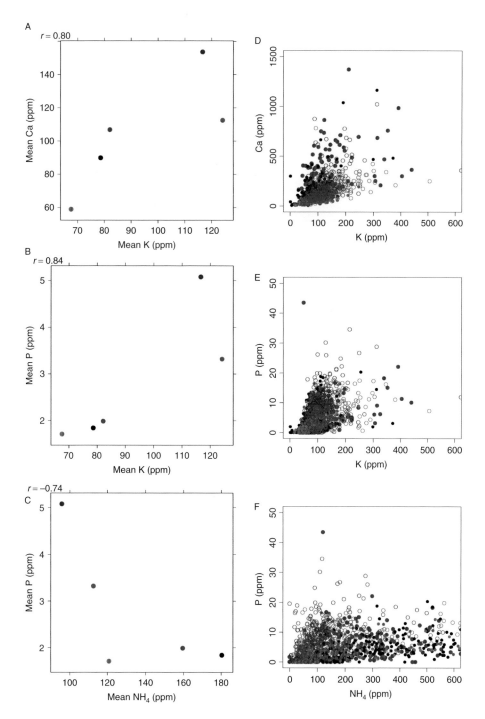

**Figure 11.4** Covariance among selected soil resources as site means (A) and at individual sample points (B–F). Each colour or shade corresponds with one of five of our research sites at La Selva Biological Station, Costa Rica.

**Figure 12.1** As in much of Amazonia, lowland forests of Madre de Dios, Peru appear as vast expanses of green canopy, incised by water bodies and deforestation (gold mining at A). Even a careful eye will pick out only the most basic variation in forest composition, such as swamp areas dominated by *Mauritia flexuosa* palm trees (B).

**Figure 12.3** This CAO image of the 50-hectare Center for Tropical Forest Science (CTFS) plot on Barro Colorado Island, Panama, shows (A) a natural colour composite as seen by the naked eye, and (B) spectroscopic analysis of three dominant chemical components throughout the canopy. In this case, the image was interpreted in terms of chlorophyll (reds), leaf mass per area (greens) and water content (blues). Note that the expression of chemical variation occurs primarily at the scale of individual crowns. White bar indicates approx. 30 m of distance.

**Figure 12.4** This three-dimensional CAO image of a Hawaiian tropical forest indicates that canopy chemical traits are differentially expressed among species, including (A) *Psidium cattleianum*, (B) *Mangifera indica* and (C) *Trema orientalis*. Species-level chemical signatures are created by low intraspecific variation, low inter-trait correlation and phylogenetic organisation in chemical traits.

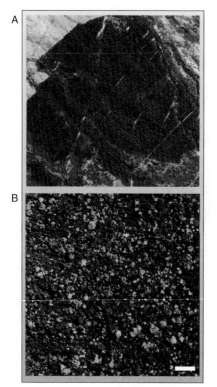

**Figure 12.5** CAO imagery taken over
(A) *Eucalyptus grandis* plantation and
(B) high-diversity lowland Amazon forest
indicates the role of chemical diversity in
expressing biological diversity. Chemicals
expressed here include chlorophyll, water
and phenols. Notice the near-constant
chemistry (colour) in the plantation canopy
and the crown-scale variation in chemical
signatures in the Amazon case. The near-
constant purple canopies in the left portion
of the Amazon image are small monotypic
stands of *Mauritia flexuosa* as seen in
Figure 12.1. White bar indicates 100 m of
distance.

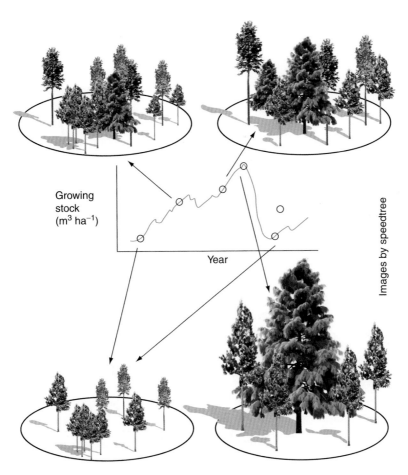

**Figure 13.2** Principle underlying forest gap models. Successional dynamics are simulated as the replacement of individual trees on small patches of land. The size of the patches is usually between 100 and 1000 $m^2$, commensurate with the maximum dimensions an individual tree can reach. Forest stand dynamics are calculated by averaging the properties across many (typically 50 to 200) such patches to reduce the influence of stochastic processes in the model (such as stochastic events in the establishment and mortality submodels). Figure drawn by Christof Bigler (ETH, Zurich). Tree pictures © Speedtree, http://www.speedtree.com.

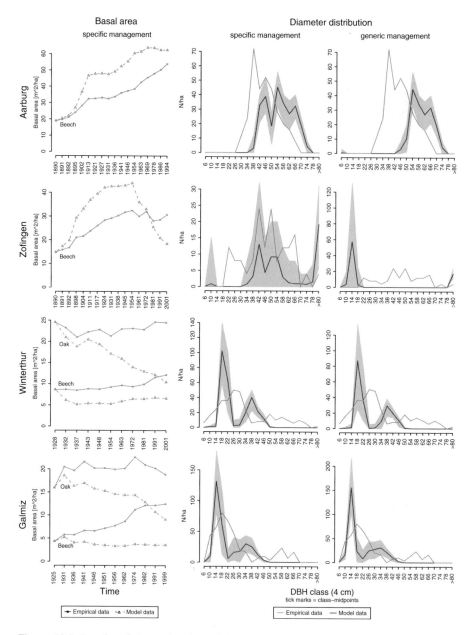

**Figure 13.5** Results of the evaluation of the FORCLIM model against measured long-term time series of basal area from managed stands in Switzerland, and comparison of the simulated diameter distribution against measured data for the last inventory. The shaded areas in the centre and right column indicate the 2.5 and 97.5 percentiles of the simulated data. From Rasche *et al.* (2011b).

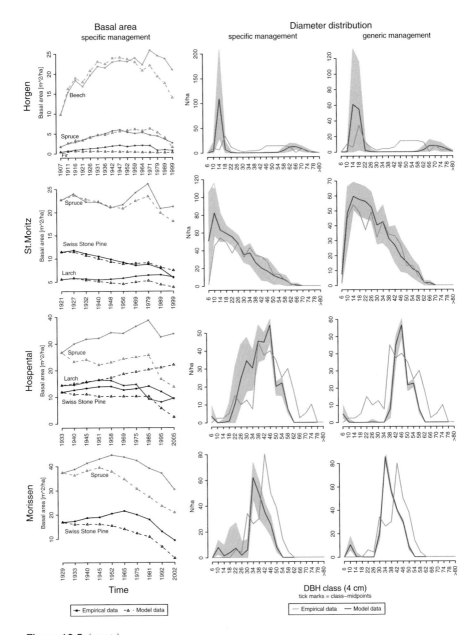

**Figure 13.5** (cont.)

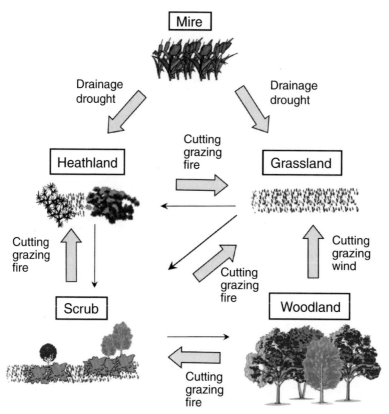

**Figure 15.7** Schematic diagram indicating the different ecosystem states and transitions in the New Forest, in relation to anthropogenic disturbance regime (after Newton 2011). Narrow arrows indicate successional changes, broad arrows indicate transitions induced by different forms of disturbance, which may be anthropogenic in origin. Some management interventions aimed at habitat restoration are not illustrated here; for example, mire communities can potentially be restored by reducing drainage, and heathland communities can be restored by removal of conifer plantations.

# CHAPTER SEVEN

# Traits, states and rates: understanding coexistence in forests

DREW W. PURVES and MARK C. VANDERWEL

*Computational Ecology and Environmental Science Group,*
*Microsoft Research Cambridge*

## 7.1 Introduction: why do tree species coexist?

The question of why there is more than one plant species on Earth is probably not one for ecology. Rather, it would appear to us at least that it is up to systems biology and evolutionary biology to explain why the enormous variation in structure and function exhibited by individual plants – a variation that makes sense given the huge range of physical environments that they occupy – occurs primarily as species-to-species variation, rather than as variation among ecotypes via local adaptation, or variation among individuals via phenotypic plasticity. However, given that plant species are so very different, the question of why we appear to observe the long-term co-occurrence of multiple species in the same region certainly is a question for ecology, so much so that the paradox of coexistence has remained central to community ecology for decades (e.g. Gause 1934; Grubb 1977; Hutchinson 1961; MacArthur 1970).

An important recent development has been the realisation, thanks to neutral theory, that the long-term co-occurrence of multiple taxonomic species is not, by itself, a paradox at all (Chave 2004; Hubbell 2001). We now know that it could take an enormous amount of time for a mixed community to drift to monodominance in any one region, if species were indistinguishable in terms of their traits. But this still leaves the challenge of explaining why we observe the long-term co-occurrence of species that are measurably different in traits that obviously affect fitness, such as growth, mortality and reproductive rates (see Purves & Turnbull 2010). Theoretical ecology has provided one kind of answer to this question, by identifying a suite of fundamental mechanisms that can maintain the coexistence of multiple species (Chesson 2000a). Although it is likely that there are new mechanisms still to be discovered, theoretical ecologists are almost entirely agreed that coexistence requires some form of negative feedback: if one species becomes too dominant, its performance declines, which in turn reduces its abundance; the opposite

*Forests and Global Change*, ed. David A. Coomes, David F. R. P. Burslem and William D. Simonson.
Published by Cambridge University Press. © British Ecological Society 2014.

occurs for species that drift to abundances that are too low (Chesson 2000a; and for forests see Dislich, Johst & Huth 2010). In the presence of such negative feedbacks, communities can exhibit stable coexistence of multiple species, where the community exhibits a typical mixture of species (or mixture of traits) that it tends to return to after perturbations. Without negative feedbacks between abundance and performance, one species would be expected to exhibit higher long-term fitness than all other species, and (assuming competition for limited resources prevents never-ending population growth) all other species would become locally extinct (Purves & Turnbull 2010). Importantly, negative feedbacks can maintain coexistence among species that differ in their baseline fitness (Chesson 2000a, b; and see Du, Zhou & Etienne 2011).

Despite all this theoretical work, we are still a long way from understanding exactly how coexistence occurs in reality (Adler, HilleRisLambers & Levine 2007; Leibold & McPeek 2006). There are a variety of different negative feedback mechanisms that could potentially promote coexistence. These includes the simplest mechanism: local, species-specific negative density dependence, NDD, whereby some aspect of performance declines as a species becomes locally more abundant (Chesson 2000a). NDD could be caused by species-specific pests and pathogens (Freckleton & Lewis 2006; Webb & Peart 1999) as well as by niche-like differences in resource use (pages 346–348 in Chesson 2000a; MacArthur 1970). But there are less intuitive mechanisms, including the temporal storage effect (where species performances vary randomly through time: Chesson 2000a), the spatial storage effect (where species performances vary randomly across space: Chesson 2000a), successional coexistence (where pioneer species coexist with late-successional species in disturbed landscapes: Pacala & Rees 1998), competition–colonisation trade-offs (where species with greater fecundity or dispersal ability coexist with those that are more competitively superior as adults: Tilman 1994), heteromyopia (where species compete with conspecifics over larger distances than they do with heterospecifics, something that might also be caused by pests and pathogens: Murrell & Law 2002) and coexistence due to species differences in intraspecific variation in performance (see Lichstein et al. 2007).

We do not know which of these potential negative feedback mechanisms tend to matter in different kinds of ecological communities, or if so, exactly how they operate. In part this reflects that, to solve problems analytically, theoretical community ecology has tended to employ 'toy' models that are difficult or impossible to relate to particular communities (e.g. the Lotka–Volterra competition equations, lottery models). Some sophisticated model-based analyses have been carried out for coexistence in actual communities – for example, Cáceres (1997) estimated the importance of the temporal storage effect (see below) for two species of *Daphnia*, and Levine and HilleRisLambers (2009) used a mixture of parameterised models and clever experimental manipulations to demonstrate that species-specific density dependence (see below) enabled the coexistence of multiple species of desert annual. But we are still left without an end-to-end understanding of coexistence for the vast majority of the world's communities, including forests. This is primarily because demonstrating a coexistence mechanism requires us not only to demonstrate a process that might enable coexistence, such as density-dependent seedling mortality (e.g. Comita *et al.* 2010; Johnson *et al.* 2012; Mangan *et al.* 2010; Webb & Peart 1999), but also to demonstrate that the nature and magnitude of that process affects the population dynamics of the species such that they coexist in the long term (discussed in: Freckleton & Lewis 2006; Harms *et al.* 2000).

Without a rigorous understanding of coexistence, it is difficult to see how we can predict and mitigate the effects of (say) altered land-use, habitat fragmentation, fire frequency, pollution, harvesting regimes, the appearance of new pathogens, and climate change, on forest biodiversity (Puettman, Coates & Messier 2008). However, if there is any area of ecology that has the potential to reach a usefully precise understanding of coexistence in a useful time frame, it must surely be forest ecology. Compared with almost any other kind of ecological community, there is a large degree of agreement about the key processes driving population dynamics in forests, at least at the local (stand) scale (Nyland 2007; Oliver & Larson 1996; Puettman, Coates & Messier 2008). For example, most forest scientists (a term that we use here to include those whose work is motivated primarily by questions of biodiversity, often referred to as 'forest ecologists'; and those whose work is primarily driven by questions of production forestry, often referred to as 'silviculturalists') would agree that, in order to model the dynamics of mixed-species, mixed-age forests, we need to recognise that forests are composed of individual trees differing in growth rate and size (requiring us to think in terms of size-structured populations), and that we need to recognise the existence of height-structured competition for light (requiring us to think about height and crown allometry) – both issues that are not necessarily important in all plant communities. And at the larger scale, forest scientists have long thought of forested landscapes in terms of 'metacommunities' (Leibold *et al.* 2004) – that is, as collections of local communities with different structural properties and different species composition, and at different stages of recovery from natural or anthropogenic disturbance (e.g. see Puettman, Coates & Messier 2008). In addition to this agreement in overall outlook, forest science benefits from a long tradition of building relatively realistic simulation models based on huge amounts of targeted field work (see Puettman, Coates & Messier 2008).

There are a large number of silvicultural models which are now routinely used to guide the production side of forest management (e.g. TASS / SYLVER / TIPSY: Di Lucca 1998; PROGNOSIS / FVS: Dixon 2002; Stage 1973). Because of the need to make defensible predictions, these models have been often (but not always!) constrained and validated against quantitative measurements taken from different individuals of different species. As a result, quantitative data for a surprisingly large number of tree species are freely available (e.g. the Functional Ecology of Trees Database, FET). However, the data that are freely available form just the tip of a much larger iceberg of incredibly valuable forest science data that are not – including much of the world's forest inventory data. In addition, there are forest gap models (e.g. JABOWA-FORET: Botkin, Wallis & Janak 1972, Shugart 1984; SORTIE and SORTIE-ND: Coates *et al.* 2003, Pacala *et al.* 1996; FORMIND and FORMIX: Huth & Ditzer 2000, Kohler & Huth 1998; for a review of gap models see Bugmann 2001). Gap models were first developed to address questions of species composition, especially secondary succession. These models track the fate of multiple individuals in mixed-species, mixed-age communities (in contrast to the even-aged monocultures focused on by silvicultural models) and have contributed some of the most realistic examples of simulated coexistence in ecology (Dislich, Johst & Huth 2010; Pacala *et al.* 1996).

Given this long history of quantitative empirical and modelling work in ecology, and given the importance of forests as repositories of biodiversity, it is not surprising that coexistence in forest communities has been and continues to be an active and influential research area in ecology (e.g. Clark *et al.* 2007; Connell 1971; Dislich, Johst & Huth 2010; Grubb 1977; Hubbell 2001; Janzen 1970; Kohyama 1993; Pacala *et al.* 1996). Into this crowded field (or forest?), this chapter is intended to contribute a general scheme for approaching questions of coexistence in any ecological community (the traits–states–rates scheme, TSR) which we think may be helpful in evaluating modelling and empirical studies of coexistence in forests. We then use the TSR scheme to begin to understand whether and how several coexistence mechanisms might occur within a particular forest landscape, using a simple but relatively realistic forest model (the Perfect Plasticity Approximation model, PPA: Purves *et al.* 2008; Strigul *et al.* 2008). Importantly, all of the parameters in our baseline PPA model (see below) were extracted from field data, allowing us to simulate the dynamics of eight actual species with realistic parameter values (Table 7.1). Then, we extend the baseline model to include additional coexistence mechanisms, carrying out a sensitivity analysis against the unknown parameters in each case (e.g. of the strength of species-specific density dependence acting on mortality: see below). This approach allows us to assess which of these mechanisms might plausibly maintain coexistence within this set of eight species in this forest community and, by extension,

**Table 7.1** Posterior means of PPA parameters for the eight most common species on mesic soils in the US Lake States (Wisconsin, Michigan, Minnesota), as extracted using the statistical methods and data described in Purves et al. (2008).

| Species[a] | Mortality[b] | | | Growth[c] | | Height[d] | | Crown[e] | Fecundity[f] | $\hat{Z}^*_j$[g] | | | $H_j^{20}$[h] |
|---|---|---|---|---|---|---|---|---|---|---|---|---|---|
| | $\mu_L$ | $\mu_D$ | $\kappa$ | $G_L$ | $G_D$ | $a$ | $\beta$ | $\phi$ | $F$ | pred | sim−s | sim+s | |
| Acer rubrum | 0.0023 | 0.0189 | 0.000096 | 0.3423 | 0.1507 | 4.3151 | 0.4642 | 0.1164 | 70.9874 | 30.7550 | 30.2971 | 22.9005 | 10.5384 |
| Acer saccharum | 0.0021 | 0.0180 | 0.000082 | 0.3079 | 0.0858 | 5.0258 | 0.4271 | 0.1200 | 70.9874 | 24.7022 | 24.9004 | 19.7654 | 10.9240 |
| Betula papyrifera | 0.0170 | 0.0433 | 0.000105 | 0.2047 | 0.0740 | 3.6832 | 0.5073 | 0.1207 | 70.9874 | 6.3621 | 6.5791 | 5.8033 | 7.5284 |
| Populus tremuloides | 0.0178 | 0.0660 | 0.000013 | 0.3817 | 0.1951 | 0.0880 | 4.6802 | 0.4612 | 70.9874 | 11.0864 | 11.2395 | 11.0716 | 11.9506 |
| Populus grandidentata | 0.0269 | 0.0664 | 0.000020 | 0.3992 | 0.2092 | 4.5595 | 0.4480 | 0.0952 | 70.9874 | 8.2704 | 8.4905 | 8.2686 | 11.5647 |
| Quercus rubra | 0.0029 | 0.0308 | 0.000310 | 0.3469 | 0.3246 | 4.0251 | 0.4756 | 0.1085 | 70.9874 | 32.9911 | 32.4180 | 21.8430 | 10.1133 |
| Tilia americana | 0.0027 | 0.0152 | 0.000179 | 0.2893 | 0.1315 | 3.1731 | 0.5506 | 0.1128 | 70.9874 | 32.3010 | 30.7637 | 20.8856 | 8.3417 |
| Abies balsamea | 0.0264 | 0.0288 | 0.000985 | 0.3698 | 0.1598 | 1.6649 | 0.7238 | 0.0985 | 70.9874 | 6.4223 | 8.4731 | 0.0000 | 7.0851 |

[a] Common names: Acer rubrum, red maple; Acer saccharum, sugar maple; Betula papyrifera, paper birch; Populus tremuloides, quaking aspen; Populus grandidentata, bigtooth aspen; Quercus rubra, red oak; Tilia americana, basswood; Abies balsamea, balsam fir.

[b] Mortality rate in the understorey ($yr^{-1}$: $\mu_D$) and in the canopy ($yr^{-1}$, = $\mu_L$+ $\kappa$ × dbh where dbh is diameter at breast height in cm).

[c] Diameter growth rate in the canopy and understorey (cm $yr^{-1}$; $G_L$ and $G_D$).

[d] Height (m, = $a$× dbh$\beta$).

[e] Crown radius (m, = $\phi$× dbh).

[f] Fecundity (ha$^{-1}$ $yr^{-1}$, $n_j$ = [F/10 000] × $ba_j$ where $ba_j$ is the stand basal area of canopy trees of species $j$ (units $m^2\ ha^{-1}$) and $n_j$ is the density of new recruits per year for species $j$).

[g] The metric $\hat{Z}^*_j$, the equilibrium canopy height for a monoculture of species $j$ (m), measures competitive ability for the late-successional niche, shown estimated using Equation (7.3) ('pred'; this equation ignores senescence), observed in simulations without senescence (i.e. $\kappa$ = 0, 'sim−s') or with senescence ($\kappa$ as given here; 'sim+s').

[h] The metric $H_j^{20}$, the height (m) of a 20-year-old open-grown tree, measures competitive ability for the early-successional niche.

suggest which mechanisms might plausibly be important in similar forests elsewhere (i.e. mesic temperate forests). The same approach means that, for those mechanisms that we find most plausible, we can assess the strength of the mechanism required to maintain coexistence among species, given observed differences in their baseline performance. In this way we hope to contribute to the development of a theory-informed baseline for further empirical and theoretical work on coexistence in forest communities worldwide.

## 7.2   Traits × states = rates

We introduce in Figure 7.1 a terminology and schematic for approaching coexistence in a changing environment. The figure is intended to convey four key ideas. First, there are traits of individuals, which by definition do not depend on the current state of the community. By trait, we mean any property of an individual which does not depend on the current state of the community, or which reacts so slightly to the state of the community that it does not affect population dynamics and hence coexistence. We believe this is the sense in which traits of species are understood by the majority of theoretical ecologists interested in general questions of coexistence. Trait is nearly

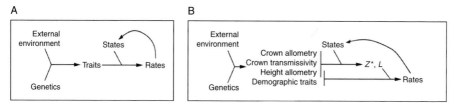

**Figure 7.1** The traits–states–rates (TSR) scheme for understanding coexistence (A), and as applied to the simplest form of the PPA model (B). A combination of the current states of the community, with the traits of individuals, implies a set of rates, which implies a new set of states, and so on. Coexistence occurs where this feedback actively maintains the presence of multiple species in the community, even after substantial perturbations away from equilibrium. In the PPA model (B) a set of static traits (crown allometry, crown transmissivity, height allometry) combine with the current states (a list of cohorts of trees of different size and species) to define a set of metrics (in the version illustrated in this figure, the canopy height $Z^*$ and the understorey light level $L$). These metrics then combine with demographic traits, as well as height allometry (which is needed to determine which cohorts are taller or shorter than $Z^*$), to set the growth, mortality and reproductive rate for each cohort. These rates imply a new set of states, i.e. a new set of cohorts. Both in the general case (A) and in the PPA (B), the traits themselves would be expected to result from a combination of the genetics of individuals, with the external environment. Coexistence occurs where the traits–states–rates feedback acts to actively maintain multiple species in the community.

synonymous with 'property' or 'characteristic' and, in many modelling applications, with 'species parameters', the point being that traits are unresponsive to population dynamics (although they may change in response to evolution or a change in the environment: Figure 7.1). And if we are willing to assume that the traits of individuals belonging to the same species are much more similar than those of individuals belonging to different species, then we can legitimately talk about species traits.

Second, there are the states of the community. Here, 'states' is synonymous with the term 'state variables' used by theoreticians. The state variables of a model of a community are simply the set of numbers that fully characterises the condition of that community in the model at any given point in time. This might mean simply the total population size of each species (e.g. the Lotka–Volterra competition equations, see below); but the states could include any important numbers that vary through time, for example representing soil nutrients, the abundance of pathogens, or how populations are currently broken down into different size categories (as in the PPA: see below).

Third, the traits and states combine, to imply a rate of change for each state variable. The set of rates implies a new set of states at some later time, for example one year later.

Fourth and finally, the traits themselves are not 'constants' but emerge from an interaction between the genetics of individuals and aspects of the external environment that are not affected by the current states of the community (e.g. climate). This final point is important because it encourages us to recognise that, in a changing world, properties of individuals that we might have hitherto treated as fixed, might themselves change, with knock-on effects for species composition, as well as forest structure, forest carbon dynamics and biogeochemistry (Körner 2004; Purves & Pacala 2008).

## 7.3   Traits, states and rates in the Lotka–Volterra competition equations

In this section we illustrate the TSR scheme with the Lotka–Volterra competition equations (hereafter LVC) for two species. It may seem strange to turn to the LVC, given that we have already stated that the fact that most theoretical understanding of use of toy models such as the LVC is a hindrance to understanding how coexistence (or the lack of it) operates in actual forest communities. However, we believe this walkthrough helps to clarify some key issues that would help in understanding coexistence in real forests. Later we use the TSR scheme to discuss the PPA which, compared with the Lotka–Volterra equations, bears a much closer relationship to how forests actually work. The LVC equations are:

$$\left(\frac{dx_1}{dt}\right) = \boxed{r_1}\,\textcircled{x_1}\left(1 - \left(\frac{\textcircled{x_1} + \boxed{\alpha_{12}}\,\textcircled{x_2}}{\boxed{K_1}}\right)\right) \qquad \boxed{\text{Trait}}$$

$$\textcircled{\text{State}}$$

$$\left(\frac{dx_2}{dt}\right) = \boxed{r_2}\,\textcircled{x_2}\left(1 - \left(\frac{\textcircled{x_2} + \boxed{\alpha_{21}}\,\textcircled{x_1}}{\boxed{K_2}}\right)\right) \qquad \left(\text{Rate}\right)$$

(7.1)

where $x_1$ and $x_2$ are the population densities of the two competing species; $K_1$ and $K_2$ are the carrying capacities of the species, defined as the density to which each species would equilibrate in the absence of the other species; $r_1$ and $r_2$ are the maximum per-capita growth rates of the species; and $\alpha_{12}$ and $\alpha_{21}$ are interaction coefficients that determine the per-capita effect of species 2 on the growth rate of species 1, and vice versa.

The symbol labelling in Equation (7.1) separates traits, states and rates. There are only two states, the population densities $x_1$ and $x_2$. These states change in time according to two rates, $\frac{dx_1}{dt}$ and $\frac{dx_2}{dt}$, which themselves are determined by an interaction between the states $x_1$ and $x_2$, and the traits: $K_1$, $K_2$, $r_1$, $r_2$, $\alpha_{12}$ and $\alpha_{21}$. Whatever the population density at any one time, the carrying capacity itself remains unchanged, qualifying $K_1$ as a trait. And although $K_1$ is the carrying capacity of *species* 1, it can also be described as a trait of each *individual* of species 1. To see how, focus for a moment on a particular individual of species 1. Next, imagine that all other individuals in the community are identical to that individual. Then, $K_1$ is the population density at which our focal individual would have an expected per-capita growth rate of exactly zero. In principle, this trait could be derived for any individual from any community, without reference to species identity; one could pick a random sapling from a forest, and ask: how many identical saplings would I need, to give this sapling an expected lifetime reproductive rate of exactly one? Also, it is important to note that $K_1$ does not depend on the states of the community (densities $x_1$ and $x_2$); but that nonetheless the value of $K_1$ would be expected to emerge from an interaction between the environment and the genetics of the individuals constituting species 1 (see Figure 7.1).

Another trait is $r_1$, the maximum per-capita growth rate of species 1, which is a trait because, although the *realised* per-capita growth rate of species 1 depends on $x_1$ and $x_2$ (see Eq. (7.1)), the *maximum* per-capita growth rate $r_1$ does not. And $r_1$ can be derived for any focal individual, because $r_1$ is defined as the expected number of new recruits that a focal individual could produce during its lifetime, in a community with no other individuals, and assuming no Allee effects. Finally, because the interaction coefficients $\alpha_{12}$ and $\alpha_{21}$ also do not depend on the current states of the community, they too are traits. However, these are in effect traits of a pair of individuals.

Having established the TSR scheme for the LVC we can use it to examine how coexistence works in the LVC, and how coexistence might be affected by environmental change. As every ecology student is taught, the LVC can give any of the following results: coexistence, exclusion of species 1 by species 2 (or vice versa), or founder control (where one species excludes the other, but which one wins depends on the initial condition). Importantly, the realised outcome depends only on the traits of the individuals that comprise species 1 and 2; for example, coexistence requires $K_1 > \frac{K_2}{\alpha_{12}}$ and $K_2 > \frac{K_1}{\alpha_{21}}$. Indeed, this is rather the point of the LVC, and (perhaps arguably) community ecology in general – to predict long-term outcomes at the community scale, from the traits of the individual interacting organisms.

As in all cases of interspecific coexistence, the coexistence case in the LVC requires that, if a particular species becomes too dominant (say, species 1 in this case), the lifetime reproductive rate of the individuals of species 1 declines relative to that of the individuals of species 2, which in turn implies that species 1 becomes less dominant over time (Chesson 2000a). To see how this arises from the TSR feedback, begin with a community at equilibrium. By definition, at equilibrium the rates are zero: that is, neither $x_1$ nor $x_2$ has a tendency to increase or decrease. The reason is that, at this point, when we combine the current states ($x_1$ and $x_2$) with the traits ($K_1, K_2, r_1, r_2, \alpha_{12}$ and $\alpha_{21}$) we come out with rates $dx_1/dt$ and $dx_2/dt$ equal to zero. Now, imagine artificially removing a few individuals of species 1, such that $x_1$ is lower. After this removal, when we combine the states and traits, we find that both rates will turn out positive (although with $dx_1/dt$ a bit more positive than $dx_2/dt$). This pair of positive rates implies that both species will increase, creating a new pair of values for $x_1$ and $x_2$. These new states will then combine once again with the traits, to provide yet another set of rates. And so on. Given long enough, everything will settle down again to the equilibrium, with both rates at zero. The run-through can be done from different starting points (e.g. one or other species at equilibrium and the other at zero) and for the coexistence case, the end result will always be the same. This is what is meant by 'stable coexistence' – both species persist in the community, even if the community is strongly perturbed away from equilibrium. Similar run-throughs can be done for the other cases (exclusion, founder control), and in all cases, the end result depends on the same TSR feedback.

## 7.4   Lotka–Volterra competition: response to environmental change

Next, consider, within the LVC, how a change in the external environment can affect the coexistence of species in the community. A change in the external environment affects the traits only. This change in traits, in turn, alters the outcome of the TSR feedback. Obviously, this introduces a natural time-lag between the environmental change and the change in the community, because the implications of the altered traits will take some time to make themselves known. Depending on the initial traits, and which traits change by how much and in what direction, the consequence of environmental change could be a relatively small change in the community, or a qualitative change into a new regime (Gause & Witt 1935). For example, if we had species coexistence to begin with, the coexistence might persist, but with altered abundances for the two species. Or, species coexistence might be destroyed by the regime shifting to one of exclusion or founder control. Alternatively, species coexistence could become enabled, for example via a shift from a regime where species 1 excluded species 2 to a regime where both species coexist. In this case, species 2 would have been absent from the community before the environmental change, but after the change the community (initially consisting only of species 1) would become suitable for invasion by species 2. According to the LVC, changes in traits can lead to a shift from any regime to any other, and even if the changes in traits are smooth, the shifts can sometimes be threshold-like (Gause & Witt 1935). Finally, 'environmental change' could be interpreted widely as any change in the value of one or more traits. For example, the appearance of a new disease might decrease the maximum growth rate, $r_1$, or nitrogen deposition might decrease the magnitude of competition and hence reduce the competition coefficients $\alpha_{12}$ and $\alpha_{21}$.

## 7.5   Lotka–Volterra competition: take-home messages for empirical forest ecology

Although somewhat abstract, the above walk-through of the LVC has some general implications for approaching coexistence in forest communities. The first take-home point is that to understand the coexistence of individuals with different traits, we need a way to scale from the traits of individuals to the long-term dynamics of the community, and, specifically, to explain how this scaling leads to the active maintenance of multiple species in the community, even when the system is perturbed away from equilibrium. If there are interspecific interactions, then the rates that determine the long-term dynamics of the community depend on how the species' traits combine with current states of the community. Thus, any attempt to explain coexistence in forests needs to: (1) explain which traits and states matter (and explain why the others can be ignored); (2) explain how these traits and states combine to determine demographic rates; (3) explain how this combination maintains multiple species, or multiple trait combinations, in the community.

The second take-home point is that the traits in the LVC do not correspond very well to the traits that are currently being focused on in a lot of empirical forest ecology. In this literature, the term 'trait' is currently being used almost exclusively to mean biophysical and ecophysiological metrics that can be measured instantaneously on an individual or a population. For example, wood density and leaf thickness (specific leaf area, SLA) can be measured on individuals observed at one time, and height allometry parameters can be fitted to data from multiple individuals from the same population, measured at one time. Such static traits may be of interest in themselves, and may be important in determining rates from states (e.g. canopy transmissivity and height allometry are important in gap models, and also in the PPA, see below). However, static traits by themselves cannot be sufficient for understanding coexistence, because coexistence is a property of population dynamics, i.e. a property of how things change through time. In the LVC the traits are either explicitly dynamic (the growth rate $r$), or have immediate impact on the dynamics via the LVC equations (the $\alpha$ values). To understand the coexistence of contrasting traits in forest communities, then, empirical forest ecology needs to focus on important traits that have a direct effect on demographic rates, and hence population dynamics. In the longer term it might be possible to understand the coexistence of (say) individuals with contrasting biophysical traits, but only if we could scale from the biophysical traits to the demographic traits (Sterck, Poorter & Schieving 2006; Ogle & Pacala 2009).

The third take-home point is that, even for a relatively simple model like the LVC, the exact way in which different traits determine the outcome of competition is far from obvious. This in turn implies that, unfortunately, explicit analytical or simulation modelling, rather than verbal argument, is required to work out whether and how species or individuals with different combinations of traits might coexist. It is notable that most discussions of species coexistence in forests do not include any analytical or simulation results that show coexistence can actually occur according to the proposed mechanism (something that we have tried to do in this chapter – see below). For example, empirical studies of Janzen–Connell effects (see Comita *et al.* 2010; Johnson *et al.* 2012; Mangan *et al.* 2010; Webb & Peart 1999) have yet to demonstrate that the nature and magnitude of the observed effects are sufficient to enable coexistence of the species involved (see Freckleton & Lewis 2006; Harms *et al.* 2000; Muller-Landau & Adler 2007).

## 7.6   Traits, states and rates in the perfect plasticity approximation model

We now use the TSR scheme to walk through a particular forest model – the PPA – to illustrate how we are beginning to understand the coexistence of contrasting traits within forest communities. The PPA is not the only model for which it would be possible to outline a TSR scheme (others include gap models and some silvicultural models). We chose the PPA because, like gap models, it has been developed with uneven-aged, multiple species communities in mind; but unlike gap models, it is a mean field model, where competition depends on a small number of stand-scale metrics (such as $Z^*$: see below). As a result, the PPA is somewhat easier to understand than gap models, and is partly analytically tractable. However, we would like to stress that our purpose is not to claim that the PPA will eventually prove to be the best way to approach coexistence in forests. Rather, we wish to illustrate in a general sense what a trait-based understanding of coexistence in forests might look like, and to generate some ideas that might be of interest to forest ecologists – all with a view to gaining a better understanding of coexistence in forest communities in the long term.

As explained above, we need to outline the traits, the states, and how these combine to determine the rates. For the PPA this outline goes as follows.

### PPA states

The full state of the PPA is dramatically 'higher dimensional' than are the LVC equations. Whereas LVC reduces each species just to its average population density (e.g. number of individuals per hectare), the PPA tracks, for each species, the average density of each size of tree (e.g. number of red maple individuals per hectare with dbh 12.3 cm). Thus the states can be expressed as a size distribution for each species. However, it is often more convenient to represent these states as a set of 'cohorts'. A cohort is a group of trees with identical properties (e.g. dbh, species) and an associated average spatial density (number per ha). So an example of a cohort would be: red maple, dbh 12.3 cm, 4.5 ha$^{-1}$. Size distributions (e.g. Figure 7.2B) or other summary metrics (e.g. stand basal area or stand biomass) can then be calculated as required by summing across those cohorts.

### PPA rates

Like any dynamic model, the PPA has to define how the states change through time according to a set of rates. If the stand is represented as cohorts (see above), then the rates need to define, for each cohort: (1) the realised growth rate, i.e. a rate of change in dbh; (2) the realised mortality rate, i.e. what fraction of the cohort is dying per unit time. In addition, it is necessary to define, for the stand, (3) a realised reproductive rate via which new cohorts are created. The idea behind simulating the PPA based on cohorts is as follows. Because the trees within a cohort are identical (and because the PPA assumes a 'well mixed' stand: Strigul et al. 2007), they have the same expected fate, so we can calculate the expected fate of an exemplar tree, then apply this fate to the whole cohort. For example, if for our red maple cohort the growth rate for the current time step was 0.18 cm, we would update the dbh to $12.3+0.18=12.48$ cm; and if the probability of mortality was 0.017, then we would update the density to $4.5 \times (1-0.017)=4.4235$ per ha. In simulations, then, we perform calculations for, and track the progress of, a set of cohorts, not a set of trees. For recruitment we can create one new cohort for each species per year (more could be used, if we wanted to incorporate variation in initial size, or permanent variation in performance among individuals within a species), and to set the initial dbh of each new cohort to 0. Thus the reproductive rate simply needs to specify the initial spatial density of new cohorts (the general definition of the PPA would allow seedlings to be treated differently to larger trees – but here we treat seedlings like very small trees, which grow and die following the same functions that apply to larger trees). The cohort makes simulations orders of magnitude faster, but it also makes the PPA unsuitable for addressing random variation in individual performance within a cohort (Clark *et al.* 2007), or fine-scale spatial processes (such as Heteromyopia; Murrel & Law 2002).

*PPA metrics*

The most important idea behind the PPA is that, to calculate rates from states, we can define a small set of stand-scale metrics that summarise competition for light. The first of these metrics, $Z^*$, is the canopy height, defined as the maximum height from the ground above which the canopy is still filled. Any leaves at a height greater than $Z^*$ are assumed to experience full light (and are referred to as in the canopy), whereas any leaves at a height less than $Z^*$ experience light that has already passed through a canopy of leaves (and are referred to as in the understorey). In the simplest version of the PPA (e.g. that used in Purves *et al.* 2008) the canopy height $Z^*$ is the only metric. The most natural second metric is the understorey light level $L$, defined as the fraction of light hitting the top of the canopy that is making it through to hit the understorey, where understorey is defined as all space less than a height $Z^*$ from the ground (see Adams, Purves & Pacala 2007a, b). We do not provide details of how to calculate the metrics $Z^*$ and $L$ here, but for the flat-top baseline model (see below) the calculations are very simple. In principle, it would be possible to calculate additional metrics, representing for example the spatial variation or seasonal timing of light, but the consequences of including such metrics in the PPA have yet to be explored.

Importantly, these metrics are calculated by combining the current *states*, with static *traits* relating to height and crown allometry, and crown transmissivity. Thus, the metrics can be calculated for a single stand at a single time. The metrics combine with *demographic traits* (e.g. maximum growth rate) to determine the rates outlined above.

*PPA traits*

The exact set of traits at play in the PPA depends on exactly how the model is configured. However, all instantiations of the PPA need to include a set of parameters to determine, for a tree of a given species and diameter: (1) static traits relating to height and crown allometry; (2) demographic traits defining how the rates depend on the metrics. Like the demographic traits in the LVC, the demographic traits in the PPA define both the maximum rates (maximum growth, maximum fecundity, minimum mortality rate) and the sensitivity of the rates to competition, i.e. to the metrics. Of course, the fact that traits involving growth, mortality, reproduction and allometry should appear in the PPA is itself not unique – indeed it is hard to imagine any understanding of competition and coexistence in forests that did not refer to these traits.

How are the rates calculated from the states and traits? If we use $T$ as general notation for traits, $S$ as a general notation for states, and $M$ as a general notation for the metrics, then we can write, for cohort $i$:

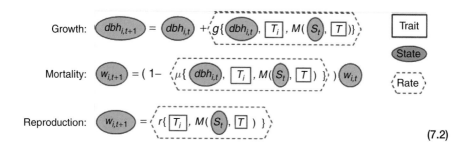

$$\text{(7.2)}$$

where reproduction applies only to those new cohorts $i$ that are added at time $t+1$, for which we set $dbh_i = 0$. Equation (7.2) is intended to illustrate the overall relationship between states, traits and rates in the PPA; but it also makes clear that there is a lot of flexibility in exactly how the PPA can be configured (as is the case for gap models). For example, any form of dependence of growth, mortality and reproductive output on dbh could be incorporated, and it could allow for any functional forms for height vs dbh, crown radius vs dbh, and crown transmissivity vs dbh. To qualify as a PPA model, all that is required is that competition occurs primarily via a small set of canopy metrics ($Z^*$, $L$ etc.), the calculation of which embodies an assumption of perfectly plastic competition for canopy space.

Applying these rates of change to the cohort gives a new set of cohorts reflecting the growth in the size of the trees comprising each cohort (Eq. (7.2) top), the mortality rate within each cohort (Eq. (7.2) middle) and the addition of new cohorts via reproduction (Eq. (7.2) bottom). This new set of cohorts implies new values for the metrics, which implies a new set of rates, which implies a new set of cohorts, and so on. Because competition is assumed to depend only on a small set of metrics, the equations governing the PPA are really quite simple compared with the high dimensionality of the PPA state space.

## 7.7   A baseline perfect plasticity approximation model

For the purposes of this study we defined a simple baseline version of the PPA, with a minimal level of complexity in all components (see Table 7.1). This baseline model is almost identical to that presented in Purves *et al.* (2008) and Adams, Purves and Pacala (2007), the only difference being a small senescence effect included here because we found that it made efficient numerical simulations much more stable. Specifically, without senescence we found equilibria that were reasonable, and stable, as expected from analytical analysis (Strigul *et al.* 2007); and short-term dynamics (up to 250 years) that were also reasonable (as shown in Purves *et al.* 2007). But beyond 250 years, we observed long-lived transients with unrealistic values for stand basal area (simulations not shown). The value of the senescence parameter $\kappa$ was also estimated from inventory data (Table 7.1).

The key assumptions of this baseline PPA model are: (1) individuals have perfectly flat discs for their crowns, which have radius proportional to dbh and which sit at the very top of the tree. Because of this assumption, each cohort is placed entirely into full light or into the understorey, depending solely on whether the individuals in that cohort are taller or shorter than $Z^*$; (2) height is predicted entirely from dbh using a species-specific power-law relationship; (3) dbh growth rate (cm yr$^{-1}$) has no dependency on dbh or understorey light, and so exhibits one of two species-specific values, $G_L$ for canopy trees and $G_D$ for understorey trees; (4) similarly for the annual mortality for understorey trees, which receive rate ($\mu_D$, yr$^{-1}$); (5) the annual mortality rate of canopy trees is a linear function of dbh such that $\mu = \mu + \kappa \cdot dbh$ where $\kappa$ is a species-specific parameter that sets the rate of senescence, i.e. how quickly mortality increases with size. Finally: (6) the annual recruitment rate for each species is assumed to be proportional to the total stand basal area of canopy trees of that species.

For this baseline model we obtained parameters for the eight most common species on mesic soils in the Lake States region of the USA (Wisconsin, Michigan and Minnesota) from US Forest Service 'FIA' data (Table 7.1). The data used were exactly those used for mesic soil in Purves *et al.* (2008). To estimate the parameters, we carried out a Bayesian analysis using 'Filzbach', a software library for carrying out robust and efficient maximum likelihood or Bayesian parameter estimation using Metropolis–Hastings Markov chain Monte Carlo sampling, in the languages C++ or C#. Filzbach is under development in the computational science lab at Microsoft Research Cambridge and is available for download, complete with a set of examples, via http://research. microsoft.com/science. The simulations presented here used only the posterior means for each parameter (Table 7.1).

## 7.8  A perfect plasticity approximation model for a monoculture
To understand the outcome of competition within the PPA it is first helpful to think about the dynamics of a monoculture (Strigul *et al.* 2007 provides a much longer and much more detailed treatment). The key behaviour of a PPA

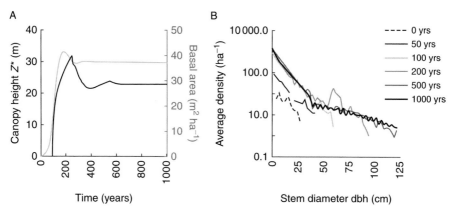

**Figure 7.2** The dynamics of a monoculture of red maple (*Acer rubrum*) simulated using the PPA forest model. The model was initialised with a very low density of small trees. Basal area (panel A, grey) rises very rapidly at first, then rises more slowly after the canopy height Z* (panel A, black) takes on a non-zero value. The increasing Z* pushes more trees into the understorey, which slows their growth rates, increases their mortality rates, and prevents them from contributing to recruitment. Through time the stand develops a stable size distribution (B) consisting of an exponential distribution with two different slopes, the first dictated by the ratio of growth to mortality for understorey trees (left of the kink in panel B), the second dictated by the ratio for canopy trees (right of the kink). The model used in this chapter included senescence (i.e. increased mortality rates for larger canopy trees). This results in a deficit of large trees, represented by the slight downward curvature in the size distribution for canopy trees.

monoculture is that the stand has an equilibrium set of states (the diameter distribution of cohorts, which can be used to calculate total stand density, basal area, etc.) to which it returns after any perturbation. This also implies that the stand has equilibrium values for competition metrics such as Z* and L. Around this equilibrium state, the stand can sometimes exhibit cycles, or even more complex behaviour – but for reasonable parameter values, stands tend to return to equilibrium rapidly, either monotonically or via damped oscillations (Figure 7.2A, B; and see Strigul *et al.* 2007).

Any population model that exhibits an equilibrium must include some form of negative feedback. That is, if the population grows larger than the equilibrium, there needs to be a tendency for individual performance to decline, such that the overall population growth rate becomes negative – and vice versa. To understand how this occurs within our baseline PPA model, begin with a stand at equilibrium (as we did with the LVC above). If we remove some canopy trees, the canopy height Z* will decrease. As a result, some trees that were formerly in the understorey will enter the canopy, not through the usual process of the trees growing up, but through the canopy coming down. These trees will now grow more quickly, die more slowly and contribute to stand recruitment. Therefore, the performance of the average tree in the stand will increase. As a result, the total stand basal area will increase, which will increase $Z^*$, eventually restoring $Z^*$ to its equilibrium value. The reverse would occur for tree removals, which would decrease $Z^*$ and increase average performance, making $Z^*$ increase again. During the return to equilibrium, the size distribution might wobble around a bit, and for a large perturbation $Z^*$ may go through another round of overshooting followed by damped oscillations; but the equilibrium $Z^*$ and size distribution will be restored, notwithstanding another major perturbation before equilibrium is reached. A stable $Z^*$ in turn implies a stable size distribution (Figure 7.2B).

For this simple model an approximate value of $Z^*$ at equilibrium for species $j$, denoted $\hat{Z}_j^*$, can be calculated from a combination of the static and demographic traits of species $j$, using a simple formula:

$$\hat{Z}_j^* \approx \alpha_j [\frac{G_{D,j}}{\mu_{D,j}}] \beta_j [\ln(2\pi\phi_j^2 F_j G_{L,j}^2 \mu_{L,j}^{-3})]^{\beta_j} \qquad (7.3)$$

where: $G_{L,j}$ and $G_{D,j}$ are canopy and understorey diameter growth rates (cm $yr^{-1}$); $\mu_{L,j}$ and $\mu_{D,j}$ are understorey mortality rates ($yr^{-1}$); $\phi$ is the crown allometry parameter (ratio of crown radius to dbh, m $cm^{-1}$); $F$ is a fecundity parameter (new recruits per unit basal area of canopy trees: see Table 7.1); and $\alpha_j$ and $\beta_j$ are height allometry parameters (see Table 7.1). This formula turns out to be useful when understanding coexistence within the PPA (see Adams, Purves & Pacala 2007a,b; Purves *et al.* 2008; Strigul *et al.* 2007; and below). Note that it depends only on the traits of species $j$.

## 7.9  Coexistence in the perfect plasticity approximation model

To begin it is important to separate stand-scale coexistence from landscape-scale coexistence. The former refers to coexistence that occurs within a single stand, which we formally define as a unit of land within which there is no spatial variation in states, traits or rates. Landscape-scale coexistence refers to coexistence among a set of stands, which may differ in their physical environments, their history (e.g. some stands have been disturbed recently) and/or their disturbance regimes (some stands are perturbed more often). Landscape scale coexistence is touched on only briefly towards the end of the chapter.

### 7.9.1   Stand-scale coexistence via differential crown transparency

Previous analyses of PPA models with only the $Z^*$ metric (Adams, Purves & Pacala 2007a,b; Strigul *et al.* 2007) have shown that within-stand coexistence does not occur at all. Specifically, where the only metric measuring competition for light is $Z^*$, the species with the greatest $\hat{Z}_j^*$ (i.e. equilibrium canopy height in monoculture) eventually drives all other species to extinction. Referring to the explanation of the dynamics of a PPA monoculture above, it is relatively easy to see why. In a mixed species stand, if the current $Z^*$ is below $\hat{Z}_j^*$ for both species, then both species increase; if $Z^*$ is above $\hat{Z}_j^*$ for both species, then both species decline; but if $Z^*$ is somewhere in between, then the species with the greater $\hat{Z}_j^*$ will increase, while the other species continues to decrease. The end point is that $Z^*$ equilibrates at the greater of the two $\hat{Z}_j^*$ values, and the other species declines to zero. There is a strong analogy here to the LVC, in that the outcome of competition can be predicted from the traits; and that the way the traits combine is highly non-intuitive. The prediction that the species with the greatest $\hat{Z}_j^*$ tends to win in competition has been tested for four different soil types in the US Lake States with some success (Purves *et al.* 2008).

Extensions of the model beyond the simplest case do allow for stand-scale coexistence. Adams, Purves and Pacala (2007a,b) consider the simple PPA model, but with interspecific variation in canopy transmissivity, which in turn allows for variation in the understorey light level $L$. The growth and mortality rates of individuals then become a continuous function of the light that they receive, which is taken to be full light (1.0) for trees taller than $Z^*$, and $L$ (0–1) for trees shorter than $Z^*$. The value of $L$ can be calculated as a weighted mean over the transmissivity of the canopy trees. In this model then, trees can suffer competition for light because the canopy is tall (high $Z^*$) and/or because the understorey is very dark (low $L$).

Within this model all four of the classical Lotka–Volterra outcomes become possible: dominance by either species, founder control, or coexistence (Adams, Purves & Pacala 2007a, b; and see Dybzinski & Tilman 2009). Imagine two competing species $j$ and $k$. The outcome can be understood quite simply, in terms of an *effective* $\hat{Z}_j^*(L)$, defined as the equilibrium canopy height a species would reach in monoculture, if we imposed an understorey light level $L$. At any one time, competition will tend to favour whichever species has the greatest effective $\hat{Z}_j^*$ given the current understorey light level. Now, the actual understorey light level must be between the crown transmissivity of the two species – call these $L_j$ and $L_k$. So, we can compare the effective $\hat{Z}_j^*$ for each species in its own understorey light level (i.e. $\hat{Z}_j^*(L_j)$ and $\hat{Z}_k^*(L_k)$) and in the competitor's light level (i.e. $\hat{Z}_j^*(L_k)$ and $\hat{Z}_k^*(L_j)$). If one species has the greater $\hat{Z}_j^*$ at both light levels then that species will win: e.g. species $j$ would win if $\hat{Z}_j^*(L_j) > \hat{Z}_k^*(L_j)$ and $\hat{Z}_j^*(L_k) > \hat{Z}_k^*(L_k)$. Alternatively, if each species has the greatest $\hat{Z}_j^*$ in its own light level, i.e. if $\hat{Z}_j^*(L_j) > \hat{Z}_k^*(L_j)$ and $\hat{Z}_k^*(L_k) > \hat{Z}_j^*(L_k)$, then we have founder control, where a monoculture of either species cannot be invaded by the other. In this configuration, each species in effect 'engineers' the understorey light level that favours itself. But, if each species has the greatest $\hat{Z}_j^*$ in the light level of the other species, i.e. $\hat{Z}_j^*(L_k) > \hat{Z}_k^*(L_k)$ and $\hat{Z}_k^*(L_j) > \hat{Z}_j^*(L_j)$, then both species can invade an equilibrium stand of the other species, implying that both species coexist. In this case, each species tends to create an understorey light environment that favours the other species. As a result, both species coexist, and the understorey light equilibriates to value between $L_j$ and $L_k$.

It remains to be seen whether this form of coexistence occurs in reality. On current evidence it seems likely to be rather uncommon, for two reasons. First, this form of coexistence requires that species perform worse, relative to other species, in the understorey light level that they themselves create. For species occupying the late successional niche, i.e. those species that are evolved to replace themselves in undisturbed stands, this seems a rather strange direction for evolution to have taken, even more so because, for late successionals, individual adult trees will often find themselves casting shade over their own progeny. The second reason for thinking that this form of coexistence might be rare is that empirical evidence suggests that, if anything, the species that cast the deepest shade are the best adapted to deal with deep shade, even among species that would generally be thought of as late successional (Canham 1994). For the same two reasons, it perhaps seems more likely that founder control via this mechanism (i.e. species becoming dominant by creating an understorey light level that favours themselves) would be relatively common in nature. However, it is important to bear in mind that the above discussion is based on the PPA which, among other assumptions, treats light as a 'mean field' property within a stand. In reality, trees create spatially heterogeneous light environments within a stand, something that could allow species to coexist.

To examine the possibility of coexistence via canopy shading within the PPA, we extended our baseline PPA model to make the growth and mortality of understorey individuals a function of the current understorey light level $L$. Beginning with the baseline PPA, we added an adjustment on the growth and mortality of trees of species $j$, as follows. For trees of species $j$ we made growth, and expected lifespan, linear functions of the understorey light level as follows:

$$\Delta G = G_D + [G_L - G_D][(L - v_j)/(1 - v_j)]$$
$$\mu = \{\mu_D^{-1} + [(\mu_L + \kappa \, dbh)^{-1} - \mu_D^{-1}][(L - v_j)/(1 - v)]\}^{-1} \qquad (7.4)$$

where $\Delta G$ is the diameter growth rate and $\mu$ is the annual probability of mortality. Under this formulation, when $L = v_j$, growth and mortality rate are equal to the parameters $G_D$ and $\mu_D$; whereas when $L = 1$, growth and mortality are equal to their values in full light ($G_L$, and $\mu_L + \kappa \cdot dbh$, where $\kappa$ sets the senescence effect). The logic behind this approach is that within the FIA data, we define a species-specific average light level for understorey trees, $v_j$. Understorey trees should exhibit the average understorey growth rates (i.e. $G_L$, which is estimated from the data) when exposed to this average light level – but exhibit different values when growing in light levels that differ from $v_j$. For example, when growing under a monoculture of species $k$, understorey trees of species $j$ would experience $L_k$, not $v_j$. This approach allowed us to simulate competition among pairs of species that differed in their baseline parameters (as given in Table 7.1), but also in $v$ and $L$.

We did not have sufficient information to rigorously estimate $v$ and $L$ for any species. Instead, we carried out a simple sensitivity analysis of competition between two species (red maple and sugar maple) where we: (1) fixed $v$ and $L$ for red maple from appropriate literature values (Canham *et al.* 1994); and (2) carried out 100 separate simulations, with the $v$ and $L$ for sugar maple varying from 0.20 to 5.0 times that of red maple. We repeated this using red oak in place of sugar maple. This procedure allowed for a wide variety of relative performances of the two species in different understorey light levels, maximising our chances of seeing coexistence in at least some cases. Even so, red maple's greater overall competitive ability (i.e. greater $\hat{Z}_j^*$), meant that it still outcompeted sugar maple (or red oak) in all simulations.

### 7.9.2   Two does not imply many

Before moving on to consider other forms of coexistence that might occur within the PPA, it is worth pointing out that in general, showing that a mechanism can lead to the coexistence of two species does not imply that the mechanism could maintain more than two species. That is, showing theoretically that two species with contrasting properties can coexist according to a particular mechanism does not necessarily imply that a whole suite of species, with a range of properties, can coexist according to that same mechanism. Theoreticians tend to stop at two-species coexistence, not because it implies multiple species coexistence, but because multi-species coexistence is hard to demonstrate and even harder to understand.

We mention this here because we believe that coexistence via differential canopy shading could not maintain any more than two species. The reason is that competition occurs via only two metrics ($Z^*$, $L$), which in general is likely to allow for the coexistence of no more than two species. The simpler model with only one metric ($Z^*$, no variation in $L$) leads to dominance by one species, and it is possible that a PPA model with a larger number of metrics (e.g. seasonal variation in light) might support a larger suite of species. There appears to be a strong analogy here to Tilman's $R^*$ and resource ratio theories (Tilman 1982): these predict that the maximum number of locally coexisting species is equal to the number of resources (see page 191 in Dybzinski & Tilman 2009), which in Tilman's theories behave similarly to the metrics in the examples discussed here. Two other commonly discussed mechanisms that appear to support two, but never or rarely more than two coexisting species, are the competition–colonisation trade-off (Adler & Mosquera 2000; Coomes & Grubb 2003) and the successional niche (Pacala & Rees 1998).

## 7.10   Stand-scale coexistence via species-specific density dependence

A more general mechanism of coexistence that can maintain the coexistence of multiple (i.e. more than two) species, and which has received a great deal of attention in the theoretical ecology literature, is species-specific negative density dependence (e.g. see Chesson 2000a). According to this mechanism, the performance of the individuals of any focal species $j$ declines as $j$ becomes more common relative to other species, preventing any one species from excluding all others. This mechanism can enable the coexistence of species with substantially different baseline fitness (defined as fitness in some reference community, e.g. an empty stand), in which case the inferior species attain lower abundances at equilibrium (Chesson 2000a). However, as the difference in baseline fitness becomes larger, we would expect that the strength of density dependence required to maintain coexistence increases.

Let's consider the potential mechanisms that might induce species-specific density dependence in forests. One possibility is differences in species resource use (Gause 1934; MacArthur 1970; Wright 2002). For example, some species might rely on episodic rainfall available in shallow soil, whereas others might rely on more reliable stores of water in deeper soil layers; or species could utilise different sources of nutrients. In both cases, individuals would suffer more competition from conspecifics than they would from heterospecifics. A second general mechanism is species-specific pests and pathogens (Wright 2002). If species become more common, this might lead to a disproportionate increase in the abundance of species-specific pests, reducing performance. The idea that this might lead to coexistence has become known as the Janzen–Connell hypothesis (Janzen 1970; Connell 1971; and see Muller-Landau & Adler 2007). As originally discussed, the Janzen–Connell hypothesis was explicitly spatial, with performance being reduced only in the neighbourhood of conspecifics. Nowadays the mechanism is probably best thought of more generally, as also including diffuse effects where, over a large area, a higher average abundance leads to higher average pest load and therefore a lower average performance (Muller-Landau & Adler 2007).

To illustrate how this form of coexistence might occur in forests, we returned to our baseline PPA model and introduced different strengths of species-specific negative density dependence. We did this by adjusting growth, mortality, or reproduction of an individual of species $j$, relative to that expected from the baseline model, such that the rate declined as the total crown area of that species, $A_j$ (units ha per ha) increased. This adjustment was over and above the effect of $Z^*$. To provide a tangible measure of density dependence, we parameterised the model such that the parameter setting the strength of density dependence ($\lambda$) refers to performance in a stand fully stocked with conspecifics (total crown area for that species = ground area) relative to a mixed stand (total crown area for that species = 0.20 × ground area). For example, for tree (more properly, cohort) $k$, with species $j$, the adjustment was $G'_k = G_k - (1 - \lambda)G_k \left[\frac{Aj - 0.20}{1.0 - 0.20}\right]$ where $G_k$ is the rate from the baseline model, and $G'_k$ is the growth rate after the adjustment for density dependence. This way, $\lambda = 0.50$ implies that trees of species $j$ grow half as quickly in a stand fully stocked with $j$, compared with a reference stand that is only partially stocked with $j$. For mortality, $\lambda = 0.50$ implies that the expected lifespan of trees in the fully stocked stand is half that in the partially stocked stand.

The results, shown in Figure 7.3, are exactly in line with general theoretical expectations about species-specific density dependence. Without any density dependence, the stand quickly becomes a monoculture of one species (Figure 7.3(A–C), far left of each panel). This was expected in this case because we have no known coexistence mechanism operating within the stand. And as expected, the winning species is red maple. Red maple dominance also occurs if the density dependence is too weak to compensate for red maple's

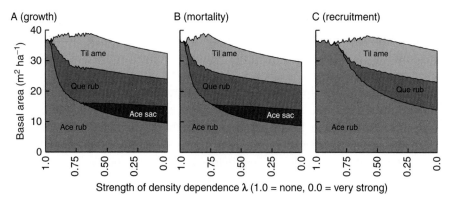

Figure 7.3 According to the PPA model, species-specific density dependence can enable the local coexistence of multiple late-successional species in undisturbed stands. Each panel shows the composition (basal area of each species) of a simulated stand after 3500 years, for 100 separate simulations differing only in the strength of density dependence. Stands were initialised with a low density of eight species (Table 7.1). In all simulations, species composition equilibrated well before 3500 years and remained extremely stable thereafter (not shown). Density dependence adjusted the growth, mortality (expected lifespan) or recruitment rate of each species $j$, as a linear function of the total crown area of species $j$. The parameter $\lambda$ can be described as performance in a stand dominated by conspecifics relative to that in a mixed stand (see main text).

superior baseline performance (Figure 7.3(A–C), left portion of each panel). But for density dependence stronger than a critical value, the stand supports three or more coexisting species at equilibrium (Figure 7.3(A–C): the fact that in all cases the stand goes from a monoculture to a three-species mixture, without going through a two-species mixture, is interesting and surprising, but not discussed further here). Stronger density dependence can support up to four coexisting species (Figure 7.3(A,B) far right of each panel). These four species (red maple, sugar maple, red oak, and basswood) were those identified in Purves *et al.* (2008) as being significantly late-successional in reality, and have the greatest $\hat{Z}_j^*$ values as calculated either from the parameters in Purves *et al.* (2008) or from the parameters used here (Table 7.1). That is, these four species are the only real contenders for the late-successional niche. The implication is that this simple form of species-specific negative density dependence might allow for the stand-scale coexistence of multiple late-successional species, but cannot rescue pioneers that are outcompeted at the stand scale without major disturbance (the two aspen species), or are uncompetitive for the late-successional niche for other reasons (e.g. Balsam fir has very high canopy mortality rates according to our parameters because it suffered from a spruce budworm (*Choristoneura fumiferana*) outbreak during the time the inventory data were collected: see Purves *et al.* 2008).

As Figure 7.3 shows, for both growth and mortality the threshold for three species to coexist occurs at around $\lambda = 0.85$. That is, if trees grew only 15% more slowly (or had expected lifespan 15% lower) in a fully stocked compared with a partially stocked stand, all three species could coexist, despite substantial differences in baseline performance. The results for density dependence acting on growth were very similar to those for mortality (Figure 7.3(A) vs (B)). This makes sense given that $\hat{Z}_j^*$, which sets the species' competitive abilities for the late successional niche, is strongly dependent on the *ratio* of understorey growth to understorey mortality, $\frac{G_{D,j}}{\mu_{D,j}}$, but much more weakly dependent on canopy growth, canopy mortality, or reproduction (Eq. (7.3)). Therefore halving growth (and thus halving understorey growth) will have similar effects to doubling mortality (and therefore doubling understorey mortality) – because both will lead to a halving of the ratio $\frac{G_{D,j}}{\mu_{D,j}}$. Coexistence also occurred via density dependence acting on recruitment (Figure 7.3(C)). The required strength of density dependence was greater compared with growth or mortality (which again makes sense given Eq. (7.3)), but was well within reasonable values ($\lambda = 0.73$). Recent work based on FIA data has shown that negative density dependence on recruitment is pervasive across species in the United States, particularly in areas of relatively high species diversity (Johnson *et al.* 2012). It remains to be seen whether the same strength of density dependence could maintain the coexistence of multiple species in the hyper-diverse trop-ical forests, where most of the empirical work on the Janzen–Connell effect has been carried out.

To help understand how this form of coexistence occurs, we can return once again to our traits–states–rates feedback. Begin with a mixed-species stand at equilibrium. Within this stand, the current states (the list of cohorts in the stand) combine with some static traits (height and crown allometry) to imply the canopy metric $Z^*$, which is perceived equally by all species. A separate combination of states with static traits (this time just crown allometry) deter-mines the total crown area in the stand, for each species $j$, $A_j$. These metrics ($Z^*$ and the $A$ values) combine with demographic traits, to determine the rates of growth, mortality and reproduction. Note that the demographic traits for each species now include $\lambda$, which sets the strength of density dependence. At equilibrium, the growth, mortality and reproductive rates combine to give a total, net change of zero in the population density of each species.

Now imagine perturbing this community away from equilibrium by switch-ing the species identity of some individuals from species $i$ to species $j$. Assuming the species are fairly similar, this will have little effect on $Z^*$ and so, in the baseline version of the PPA, the replacement would have no effect on the population dynamics of the species. However, in the presence of negative density dependence, the replacements will reduce $A_i$ and increase $A_j$. Individuals of species $i$ had a realised lifetime reproductive rate of 1.0 before this change, and because this lifetime reproductive rate is negatively correlated with $A_i$, it must be that a decrease in $A_i$ makes the lifetime repro-ductive rate of $i$ greater than 1, whereas the reverse is true for species $j$, i.e. the lifetime reproductive rate for species $j$ must become less than 1.0. As a result, $i$ will become more common, $j$ will become less common, and the community moves back towards equilibrium.

## 7.11   Coexistence through temporal variation: the temporal storage effect

The temporal storage effect occurs owing to random temporal variation in species performances – for example, where there are good and bad years for some species for some aspects of performance due to interannual variation in the climate. This kind of temporal variation can lead to coexistence, not because random variation *per se* causes coexistence, but because the temporal variation makes each species compete more with itself than it does with other species. This occurs because a greater number of individuals are present at times when recent performance has been better than average for their own species, such that individuals find themselves competing with conspecifics more often than would be expected from the long-term average abundances of the different species (Chesson 2000a).

There is relatively strong evidence that the storage effect occurs in some populations of annual plants (Pake & Venable 1995) and aquatic organisms with an annual life-cycle (Cáceres 1997), and the requirements for it to work imply that it might be common in short-lived species. Within forests, temporal variation in performance certainly occurs, and can be considerable for recruitment even for non-masting species (e.g. Clark *et al.* 2004). But it is not clear that it is likely to lead to the coexistence of multiple species at the stand level. Specifically, if individuals compete primarily for light, then the degree of competition experienced by individuals is likely to be much more strongly related to overall stand structure, as captured by canopy metrics such as $Z^*$ and $L$, than it is to the abundance of conspecifics. The canopy metrics could vary through time because of interannual environmental variation, but the effects of this variation would be felt equally by all individuals. For example, a good year for species $j$ might increase the abundance of $j$ and thereby temporarily increase $Z^*$; but this increase would reduce the average performance of all species, not just species $j$. Moreover, the canopy metrics tend not to vary very much anyway, both because they exhibit stable equilibria (i.e. they tend to head back towards their equilibrial values after perturbation) and because stand structure represents a legacy of past performance that tends to average out over the lifetime of individual trees.

To confirm these expectations we introduced different strengths of species-specific temporal variation in growth, mortality or recruitment, into our baseline PPA model (Figure 7.4, top panels). We drew a random effect $\varepsilon_j$ for each species $j$ for each PPA time step (5 years). Within that time step, we applied the effect multiplicatively to either the growth rate, expected lifespan, or recruitment rate, of all cohorts of species $j$. For example, for the growth of cohort $k$ with species $j$, we would apply $G'_k = e_j G_k$ where $G_k$ is the rate from the baseline model, and $G'_k$ is the growth rate after the adjustment for temporal variation. Each effect was drawn from a uniform distribution, such that $\varepsilon_j$ varied randomly from $1 - \omega$ to $1 + \omega$. To vary the strength of temporal variation, we varied $\omega$ from zero (no interannual variation) to nearly 1.0 (corresponding to very large temporal variation in performance). The temporal variation in performance did induce temporal variation in $Z^*$, although as expected variation in $Z^*$ was much less than the variation in performance itself (not shown). Moreover, the total stand basal area, and $Z^*$, were lower for larger magnitudes of variation (Figure 7.4, top). But we observed no coexistence.

## 7.12   Stand-scale coexistence: other possibilities

The stand-scale coexistence mechanisms considered above – differential crown transparency, species-specific density dependence and temporal storage effect – are by no means the only possible ones. We cannot provide a full list here, far less analyse each in detail, but we briefly discuss three. The first

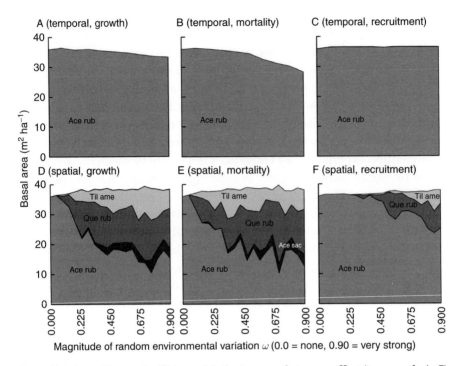

**Figure 7.4** According to the PPA model, the temporal storage effect (top panels A–C) does not readily induce the local coexistence of multiple species in undisturbed stands, but the spatial storage effect (bottom panels D–F) does. Each of the top panels shows the composition (basal area of each species) of a simulated stand after 3500 years, for 100 simulations differing only in the magnitude of random temporal variation in performance. Each of the bottom panels shows the species composition of a landscape of 50 stands, for 20 different landscapes differing in the magnitude of random spatial variation in performance (i.e. 1000 simulations in all). In all cases random variation occurred via multiplicative adjustments on growth, mortality (expected lifespan), or recruitment rate of each species $j$. The parameter $\omega$ sets the magnitude of the random variation (performance relative to the baseline PPA model varied from $1-\omega$ to $1+\omega$ : see main text).

possibility is coexistence due to differential leaf phenology. As mentioned above, in principle coexistence could occur due to differential crown transmissivity creating different understorey light levels $L$ (see Subsection 7.9.1, above). In the same way, it is possible that coexistence could be enabled by species creating different seasonal timings of understorey light, such as between evergreen and deciduous species or deciduous species that leaf out on different dates.

A second possibility is coexistence among species that can and species that cannot reproduce in the understorey. Obviously, all else being equal understorey reproduction is advantageous, such that species with this ability would

outcompete those without it. However, we would expect the ability to reproduce in the understorey to come at the cost of other aspects of performance
affecting competitive ability for canopy space (e.g. lower understorey growth
rates, shorter stature); in which case there could be a 'niche' for understorey
specialist species that never (or rarely) capture space in the canopy
(Kohyama & Takada 2009). A third possibility for within-stand coexistence is
coexistence due to fine-scale spatial and/or temporal partitioning among
species within the stand. An example might be species specialising in recruiting in certain micro-environments (see Grubb 1977; this would be a within-
stand version of the spatial storage effect – see below), or coexisting via a
competition–colonisation trade-off (Clark *et al.* 2004). The PPA is not well
suited to addressing this kind of fine-scale coexistence because it is a mean-
field model (the assumption of perfect plasticity removes the signature of
horizontal space: Purves *et al.* 2008; Strigul *et al.* 2007) and even defines a stand
as a unit of forest with a spatially homogenous environment – but these
mechanisms could be addressed with gap models. Coexistence according to
these mechanisms is likely to share some properties with coexistence via
species-specific density dependence (Figure 7.3).

## 7.13   Landscape-scale coexistence: environmental heterogeneity and successional coexistence

We now step up a scale to consider a landscape consisting of multiple stands.
We examine two mechanisms that have long been recognised by forest
scientists as important in potentially enabling species coexistence at the
landscape scale: the spatial storage effect and successional coexistence. This
is not to suggest that these two are the only mechanisms that can enable
landscape-scale coexistence. For example, we do not touch on the competition–colonisation trade-off (Coomes & Grubb 2003). More generally, fragmented landscapes, supporting partially connected metacommunities, can
exhibit a wide variety of interesting, complex dynamics (Leibold *et al.* 2004).
For example, in a fragmented landscape a species with greater seed dispersal
ability might be expected to lose a larger fraction of seeds to the matrix and
thus be disadvantaged: but dispersal in landscapes can have much more
complex effects where seeds are dispersed by animals that preferentially
deliver seeds to patches rather than the matrix, to patches with certain
species compositions (e.g. jays preferentially burying acorns under pines) or
to edges rather than interiors (Montoya *et al.* 2008; Purves & Dushoff 2005).
Thus, at the very least, fragmentation is likely to alter the identity of the
dominant species, but it may also enable coexistence mechanisms that are not
fully understood at present. It should nonetheless be possible to understand
such coexistence mechanisms in terms of how the TSR feedback actively
maintains the presence of multiple species within the landscape as a whole.

The spatial storage effect occurs where stand-to-stand variation in the physical environment (for example soil) creates a situation where different species tend to dominate different stands. Even if this mechanism led to exclusion (i.e. a lack of coexistence) in every individual stand, it could support the presence of multiple species in the landscape as a whole. In the theoretical literature this is known as the spatial storage effect (Chesson 2000a), but long before this coexistence mechanism was understood theoretically it was recognised that tree species exhibit strong correlations with the physical environment at scales ranging from continental to local (e.g. Cowles 1899; Whittaker 1956, 1960). However, we still have little understanding of how these correlations emerge, in terms of the response of demographic traits (such as growth, mortality and reproduction) to environmental gradients; and via interactions between different species.

We extended our baseline PPA model to allow for the spatial storage effect by simulating forested landscapes subject to random, species-specific, stand-to-stand variation in either growth, mortality, or reproduction (Figure 7.4, bottom panels). The approach was identical to that used to address random temporal variation (see legend to Figure 7.4), except that we did a single draw of each species-specific random effect $\varepsilon_j$ for each stand, after which we held it constant. We found that a small amount of spatial variation in growth or mortality led to the coexistence of the four late-successional 'contenders' red maple, sugar maple, red oak and basswood at the landscape scale (Figure 7.4 (D), (E)). This result confirms, for spatial variation at the landscape scale, the contention that species-specific random variation could potentially be important in maintaining the coexistence of tree species (Clark *et al.* 2007). The consequences of spatial variation in growth were very similar to those of variation in mortality (Figure 7.4(D) vs (E)). Once again this result can be understood in terms of the formula for $\hat{Z}_j^*$ (Eq. (7.3)) which shows that $\hat{Z}_j^*$ responds similarly to proportional changes in growth and in mortality (see the discussion of species-specific density dependence above). Spatial variation in recruitment was less effective in inducing coexistence (Figure 7.4(F)), which again, is expected from the fact that $\hat{Z}_j^*$ shows only a weak response to reproduction (Eq. 7.3; this formula for $\hat{Z}_j^*$ can also be used to predict the species composition of the landscape numerically, without the need for simulations, not shown here).

In understanding the implications of the spatial storage effect in isolation, it is important to picture the landscape that it implies, namely a patchwork of monocultures. In our simulations there was no dispersal among different stands, and, as expected given that no local coexistence mechanisms were in place, each stand became dominated by just one species (not shown). Intuition would suggest that dispersal among patches would lead to individual stands becoming much more mixed (via mass effect and source–sink dynamics: Chesson 2000b) – but Lichstein and Pacala (2011) show that in a landscape with no disturbance (as in our simulations), stands remain highly dominated by the locally superior species even with relatively large amounts of dispersal among stands. This suggests that, at the landscape scale, NDD and the spatial storage effect might be distinguished as follows: the local storage effect should lead to patches that are largely dominated by a single species, with that pattern of dominance stable through time; whereas NDD should lead to locally mixed stands. Going beyond this generalisation to actually quantify the relative contribution of each mechanism would, however, require detailed fieldwork and modelling.

How does the spatial storage effect lead to long-term coexistence in this case? Stated differently, why does the landscape exhibit a typical species composition that it tends to return to after perturbation? For this coexistence mechanism, it is much easier to consider the landscape simply as a set of stands, each dominated by just one species. Start with an equilibrium landscape, where each stand is dominated by the species with the greatest local $\hat{Z}_j^*$. Then find some stands currently dominated by species $i$ and switch the species identities of the trees in those stands to $j$. After this perturbation, and assuming some dispersal among stands, the altered stands will become re-invaded by species $i$. Thus $i$ will increase at the cost of $j$, and the landscape equilibrium will be restored.

The final coexistence mechanism that we consider is successional coexistence. It is well known that this form of coexistence occurs in landscapes where stands are regularly affected by disturbances that remove a large fraction of the stand biomass. In such landscapes, there can be a niche for 'pioneer' species (hereafter referred to as early-successionals) that are specialised to colonising and dominating stands immediately after disturbance (e.g. through high fecundity, adaptations to dispersal, fast diameter growth rate, tall stature; all at the cost of understorey survival and maximum lifespan: e.g. Pacala *et al.* 1996). The PPA can help in understanding how traits combine to determine competitive ability for the early successional niche (Purves *et al.* 2008), and Lichstein *et al.* (2011) show formally that a disturbed landscape of PPA stands can support the stable coexistence of early- vs late-successionals. However, coexistence *among* early successionals is a different question, and is likely to behave somewhat differently from coexistence among late-successionals. For example, species performance in disturbed stands is not strongly dependent on mortality because young trees in the canopy generally survive very well. Consequently, species-specific density dependence on mortality (or spatial variation in mortality) might not matter very much to early-successionals (in contrast to late-successionals: Figures 7.3, 7.4). On the other hand, fecundity, which is apparently the least important aspect of performance for late-successionals (Figures 7.3, 7.4), is likely to be critical for early-successionals. This can be seen in the variety of reproductive strategies adopted by species adapted to fire disturbance, such as clonal sprouting in quaking aspen, or serotiny in jack pine (*Pinus banksiana*) cones.

## 7.14    Summary

This overview of coexistence in forests is incomplete in that we consider only a subset of the possible coexistence mechanisms, and in that we focus on one particular model (the PPA). Nonetheless several main conclusions emerge about the mechanisms that might plausibly maintain the coexistence of the species considered here, in the region for which the PPA was initially developed. Local coexistence of late-successionals due to the temporal storage effect (at least in terms of relatively short-term temporal variation), or species differences in canopy transmissivity, appears to be unlikely. In contrast, a small amount of local species-specific density dependence (as might occur because of pests and pathogens) and/or species-specific spatial variation in performance (as might occur in different local climatic conditions) can apparently induce the coexistence of several late-successional species, despite relatively large differences in their baseline competitive abilities (Table 7.1). In this region, the identity of the dominant species at the stand level is correlated with soil (Burns & Honkala 1990a, b), suggesting that at least some coexistence occurs because of the spatial storage effect; whereas the fact that most older stands contain multiple late-successional species suggests that some form of local density dependence is preventing stands becoming monocultures of the locally superior species. Finally, the coexistence of late- with early-successionals is undoubtedly occurring and relatively well understood; but the mechanisms that might be maintaining coexistence among multiple early-successional species remain to be explored. More generally we hope that our use of the TSR scheme, and selected analytical results (e.g. Eq. (7.3)), to understand how coexistence might be occurring among named species, in a named region, via simple but realistic simulations parameterised from inventory data, provides a glimpse of what a fuller understanding of species coexistence in forested landscapes might look like.

In the meantime, various forms of global change will continue to affect forest communities. As outlined at the beginning of this chapter, toy models like the Lotka–Volterra can help us to conceptualise these effects: environmental change (broadly defined) affects traits, and therefore the rates, and therefore the states, of the communities (Gause & Witt 1935). But even within a fairly simple model of forests like the PPA, there are many ways in which this could play out. For example, climate change (or other perturbations) could alter allometries, mortality rates, growth rates, pests and pathogens (and hence local density dependence); or disturbance could alter landscape dynamics. The net result could be to increase or decrease the number of species coexisting in any one location, and/or to alter the identity of those coexisting species. To work out which, as we have tried to explain and illustrate here, we need to scale from the altered traits, via demography, to the long-term population dynamics that ultimately determine coexistence.

## References

Adams, T. A., Purves, D. W. & Pacala, S. W. (2007a) Understanding height-structured competition in forests: is there an $R^*$ for light? *Proceedings of the Royal Society Series B*, **274**, 3039–3048.

Adams, T. A., Purves, D. W. & Pacala, S. W. (2007b) Understanding height-structured competition in forests: is there an $R^*$ for light? (erratum) *Proceedings of the Royal Society Series B*, **275**, 591.

Adler, F. R. & Mosquera, J. M. (2000) Is space necessary? Interference competition and limits to biodiversity. *Ecology*, **81**, 3226–3232.

Adler, P. B., HilleRisLambers, J. & Levine, J. M. (2007) A niche for neutrality. *Ecology Letters*, **10**, 95–104.

Botkin, D. B., Wallis, J. R. & Janak, J. F. (1972) Some ecological consequences of a computer model of forest growth. *Journal of Ecology*, **60**, 849–872.

Bugmann, H. (2001) A review of forest gap models. *Climatic Change*, **51**, 259–305.

Burns, R. M. & Honkala, B. H. (1990a) *Silvics of North America: Conifers*. Washington, DC: USDA Forest Service.

Burns, R. M. & Honkala, B. H. (1990b) *Silvics of North America: Hardwoods*. Washington, DC: USDA Forest Service.

Cáceres, C. (1997) Temporal variation, dormancy, and coexistence: a field test of the storage effect. *Proceedings of the National Academy of Science USA*, **94**, 9171–9175.

Canham, C. D. (1994) Causes and consequences of resource heterogeneity in forests: interspecific variation in light transmission by canopy trees. *Canadian Journal of Forest Research*, **24**, 337–349.

Chave, J. (2004) Neutral theory and community ecology. *Ecology Letters*, **7**, 241–253.

Chesson, P. (2000a) Mechanisms of maintenance of species diversity. *Annual Review of Ecology and Systematics*, **31**, 343–366.

Chesson, P. (2000b) General theory of competitive coexistence in spatially-varying environments. *Theoretical Population Biology*, **58**, 211–237.

Clark, J. S., Dietz, M., Chakraborty, S. *et al.* (2007) Resolving the biodiversity paradox. *Ecology Letters*, **10**, 647–659.

Clark, J. S., LaDeau, S. & Ibanez, I. (2004) Fecundity of trees and the colonization-competition hypothesis. *Ecological Monographs*, **74**, 415–442.

Coates, K. D., Canham, C. D., Beaudet, M., Sachs, D. L. & Messier, C. (2003) Use of a spatially explicit individual-tree model (SORTIE/BC) to explore the implications of patchiness in structurally complex forests. *Forest Ecology and Management*, **186**, 297–310.

Comita, L. S., Muller-Landau, H. C., Aguilar, S. & Hubbell, S. P. (2010) Asymmetric density dependence shapes species abundances in a tropical tree community. *Science*, **329**, 330–332.

Connell, J. H. (1971) On the role of natural enemies in preventing competitive exclusion in some marine animals and in rain forest trees. In *Dynamics of Populations* (eds. B. J. den Boer & G. R. Gradwell), pp. 298–310. Wageningen: Centre for Agricultural Publishing and Documentation.

Coomes, D. A. & Grubb, P. J. (2003) Colonization, tolerance, competition and seed-size variation within functional groups. *Trends in Ecology & Evolution*, **18**, 283–291.

Cowles, H. C. (1899) The ecological relations of the vegetation on the sand dunes of Lake

Michigan. Part I: Geographical relations of the dune floras. *Botanical Gazette*, **27**, 95–117.

Di Lucca, C. M. (1998) TASS/SYLVER/TIPSY: systems for predicting the impact of silvicultural practices on yield, lumber value, economic return and other benefits. In *Stand Density Management Conference: Using the Planning Tools* (ed. C. R. Bamsey), pp. 7–16. Edmonton: Clear Lake Ltd.

Dislich, C., Johst, K. & Huth, A. (2010) What enables coexistence in plant communities? Weak versus strong species traits and the role of local processes. *Ecological Modelling*, **221**, 2227–2236.

Dixon, G. E. (2002) *Essential FVS: A User's Guide to the Forest Vegetation Simulator*. Internal Report. Fort Collins, CO: USDA Forest Service, Forest Management Service Center.

Du, X., Zhou, S. & Etienne, R. S. (2011) Negative density dependence can offset the effect of species competitive asymmetry: a niche-based mechanism for neutral-like patterns. *Journal of Theoretical Biology*, **278**, 127–134.

Dybzinski, R. & Tilman, D. (2009) Competition and coexistence in plant communities. In *The Princeton Guide to Ecology* (ed. S. Levin). Princeton, NJ: Princeton University Press.

Freckleton, R. P. & Lewis, O. T. (2006) Pathogens, density dependence and the coexistence of tropical trees. *Proceedings of the Royal Society Series B*, **273**, 2909–2916.

Gause, G. F. (1934) *The Struggle for Existence*. Baltimore: William and Wilkins.

Gause, G. F. & Witt, A. A. (1935) Behavior of mixed populations and the problem of natural selection. *American Naturalist*, **69**, 596–609.

Grubb, P. J. (1977) The maintenance of species-richness in plant communities: the importance of the regeneration niche. *Biological Reviews*, **52**, 107–145.

Harms, K. E., Wright, S. J., Calderon, O., Hernandez, A. & Herre, E. A. (2000) Pervasive density-dependent recruitment enhances seedling diversity in a tropical forest. *Nature*, **404**, 493–495.

Hubbell, S. P. (2001) *The Unified Neutral Theory of Biodiversity and Biogeography*. Princeton, NJ: Princeton University Press.

Hutchinson, G. E. (1961) The paradox of the plankton. *American Naturalist*, **882**, 137–145.

Huth, A. & Ditzer, T. (2000) Simulation of the growth of a Dipterocarp lowland rain forest with FORMIX3. *Ecological Modelling*, **134**, 1–25.

Kohler, P. & Huth, A. (1998) The effect of tree species grouping in tropical rain forest modelling – Simulation with the individual based model FORMIND. *Ecological Modelling*, **109**, 301–321.

Kohyama, T. (1993) Size-structured tree populations in gap-dynamic forest – the forest architecture hypothesis for the stable coexistence of species. *Journal of Ecology*, **81**, 131–143.

Kohyama, T. & Takada, T. (2009) The stratification theory for plant coexistence promoted by one-sided competition. *Journal of Ecology*, **97**, 463–471.

Körner, C. (2004) Through enhanced tree dynamics carbon dioxide enrichment may cause tropical forests to lose carbon. *Philosophical Transactions of the Royal Society Series B*, **359**, 493–498.

Janzen, D. H. (1970) Herbivores and the number of tree species in tropical forests. *American Naturalist*, **104**, 501–508.

Johnson, D. J., Beaulieu, W. T., Bever, J. D. & Clay, K. (2012) Conspecific negative density dependence and forest diversity. *Science*, **336**, 904–907.

Leibold, M. A., Holyoak, M., Mouquet, N. *et al.* (2004) The metacommunity concept: a framework for multi-scale community ecology. *Ecology Letters*, **7**, 601–613.

Leibold, M. A. & McPeek, M. A. (2006) Coexistence of the niche and neutral perspectives in community ecology. *Ecology*, **87**, 1399–1410.

Levine, J. M. & HilleRisLambers, J. (2009) The importance of niches for the maintenance of species diversity. *Nature*, **461**, 254–257.

Lichstein, J. W., Dushoff, J., Levin, S. A. & Pacala, S. W. (2007) Intraspecific variation and species coexistence. *American Naturalist*, **170**, 807–818.

Lichstein, J.W. & Pacala, S.W. (2011) Local diversity in heterogeneous landscapes: quantitative assessment with a height-structured forest metacommunity model. *Theoretical Ecology*, **4**, 269–281.

MacArthur, R. (1970) Species packing and competitive equilibrium for many species. *Theoretical Population Biology*, **1**, 1–11.

Mangan, S.A., Schnitzer, S.A., Herre, E.A. *et al.* (2010) Negative plant-soil feedback predicts tree-species relative abundance in a tropical forest. *Nature*, **466**, 752–755.

Muller-Landau, H.C. & Adler, F.R. (2007) How seed dispersal affects interactions with specialized natural enemies and their contribution to diversity maintenance. In *Seed Dispersal: Theory and its Application in a Changing World* (eds. A.J. Dennis, E.W. Schupp, R.J. Green & D.W. Westcott) pp. 407–426. Wallingford: CAB International.

Murrell, D.J. & Law, R. (2002) Heteromyopia and the spatial coexistence of similar competitors. *Ecology Letters*, **6**, 48–59.

Montoya, D., Zavala, M.A., Rodríguez, M.A. & Purves, D.W. (2008) Animal versus wind dispersal and the robustness of tree species to deforestation. *Science*, **320**, 1502–1504.

Nyland, R.D. (2007) *Silviculture: Concepts and Applications*. Boston: Waveland Press.

Ogle, K. & Pacala, S.W. (2009) A modeling framework for inferring tree growth and allocation from physiological, morphological, and allometric traits. *Tree Physiology*, **29**, 587–605.

Oliver, C.D. & Larson, B.C. (1996) *Forest Stand Dynamics*. New York: Wiley.

Pacala, S.W., Canham, C.D., Saponara, J., Silander, J.A. & Kobe, R.K. (1996) Forest models defined by field measurements: estimation, error analysis and dynamics. *Ecological Monographs*, **66**, 1–43.

Pacala, S.W. & Rees, M. (1998) Models suggesting field experiments to test two hypotheses explaining successional diversity. *American Naturalist*, **152**, 729–737.

Pake, C. & Venable, D.L. (1995) Is coexistence of Sonoran desert annual plants mediated by temporal variability reproductive success. *Ecology*, **76**, 246–261.

Puettman, K.J., Coates, D. & Messier, C.C. (2008) *A Critique of Silviculture*. Washington: Island Press.

Purves, D.W. & Dushoff, J. (2005) Directed seed dispersal and metapopulation response to habitat loss and disturbance: application to *Eichhornia paniculata*. *Journal of Ecology*, **93**, 658–669.

Purves, D.W., Lichstein, J.W., Strigul, N. & Pacala, S.W. (2008) Predicting and understanding forest dynamics using a simple tractable model. *Proceedings of the National Academy of Sciences USA*, **105**, 17018–17022.

Purves, D.W. & Pacala, S.W. (2008) Predictive models of forest dynamics. *Science*, **320**, 1452–1453.

Purves, D.W. & Turnbull, L.A. (2010) Different but equal: the implausible assumption at the heart of neutral theory. *Journal of Animal Ecology*, **79**, 1215–1225.

Shugart, H.H. (1984) *A Theory of Forest Dynamics: The Ecological Implications of Forest Succession Models*. New York: Springer-Verlag.

Stage, A.R. (1973) *Prognosis Model for Stand Development. Research Paper INT-137*. Ogden, UT: USDA Forest Service, Intermountain Forest and Range Experiment Station.

Sterck, F.J., Poorter, L. & Schieving, F. (2006) Leaf traits determine the growth-survival trade-off across rain forest tree species. *The American Naturalist*, **167**, 758–765.

Strigul, N., Pristinski, D., Purves, D.W., Dushoff, J. & Pacala, S.W. (2007) Scaling from trees to forests: tractable macroscopic equations for forest dynamics. *Ecological Monographs*, **78**, 523–545.

Tilman, D. (1982) *Resource Competition and Community Structure*. Monographs in

Population Biology Vol. 17. Princeton, NJ: Princeton University Press.

Tilman, D. (1994) Competition and biodiversity in spatially structured habitats. *Ecology*, **75**, 2–16.

Webb, C. O. & Peart, D. R. (1999) Seedling density dependence promotes coexistence of Bornean rain forest trees. *Ecology*, **80**, 2006–2017.

Whittaker, R. H. (1956) Vegetation of the great smoky mountains. *Ecological Monographs*, **26**, 1–80.

Whittaker, R. H. (1960) Vegetation of siskiyou mountains, Oregon and Washington. *Ecological Monographs*, **30**, 279–338.

Wright, S. J. (2002) Plant diversity in tropical forests: a review of mechanisms of species coexistence. *Oecologia*, **130**, 1–14.

CHAPTER EIGHT

# The functional role of biodiversity in the context of global change

MICHAEL SCHERER-LORENZEN

*Faculty of Biology – Geobotany, University of Freiburg*

## 8.1  Introduction

The various drivers of environmental global change, namely changes in land-use, climate and biogeochemical cycles, or the spread of invasive species, can have major impacts on the biological diversity of different ecosystems, including forests (Sala *et al.* 2000). Ongoing biodiversity loss has prompted concerns that the functioning of ecosystems and the services that humans derive from the environment may be compromised (Daily 1997; Millennium Ecosystem Assessment 2005). These losses and ecosystem degradation have substantial costs for society, as recently shown by The Economics of Ecosystems and Biodiversity study (TEEB 2009). The challenge of understanding the influence of biodiversity on ecosystem functioning (BEF) initiated a new interdisciplinary research area that emerged only two decades ago (Schulze & Mooney 1993), and the science of BEF has become one of the most active fields in ecology since then, as documented by a number of books and reviews (Hooper *et al.* 2005; Kinzig, Pacala & Tilman 2002; Loreau *et al.* 2001; Loreau, Naeem & Inchausti 2002; Naeem 2002; Naeem *et al.* 2009; Scherer-Lorenzen *et al.* 2005a; Schulze & Mooney 1993), and meta-analyses (Balvanera *et al.* 2006; Cardinale *et al.* 2006, 2007, 2011). A recent meta-analysis, for example, listed 574 independent experimental manipulations of species richness, published in 192 peer-reviewed papers, reporting 1417 observations on how species richness affects ecosystem processes (Cardinale *et al.* 2011).

Although there are still many open questions to be solved, a strikingly consistent pattern emerged from these studies: increasing diversity of communities is commonly associated with an increased mean (and a decreased variance) of many process rates (Hooper *et al.* 2005). Both theoretical and experimental developments suggest that these diversity–functioning relationships result from three mechanisms: *niche complementarity*, the *sampling effect* and *ecological insurance*. Niche complementarity occurs where a more diverse community, composed of a mixture of specialised species differing in structure and function, is able to exploit the available resources better than any given monoculture, leading to higher productivity and/or lower levels of

*Forests and Global Change*, ed. David A. Coomes, David F. R. P. Burslem and William D. Simonson. Published by Cambridge University Press. © British Ecological Society 2014.

unconsumed resources (Loreau & Hector 2001; Tilman, Lehman & Thomson 1997). The sampling effect recognises that more diverse communities are more likely to contain high-performing species, which dominate the community and its effects on ecosystem processes (Aarssen 1997; Huston 1997). The concept of ecological insurance stresses that, when subject to unpredictable perturbations, more diverse communities are more likely to contain species that can cope with the new conditions (Lawton & Brown 1993; Yachi & Loreau 1999). In essence, a new ecological framework has developed that underlines the active role of the biota and its diversity in governing environmental conditions within ecosystems, with cascading effects on the delivery of ecosystem services and human well-being (de Groot *et al.* 2010; Hillebrand & Matthiessen 2009; Naeem 2002).

While biodiversity certainly matters for ecosystem functioning, global changes are also influencing environmental conditions and ecological processes directly. Classical examples for forests include alterations of biogeochemical cycles after tree harvesting (Bormann *et al.* 1968) or acid rain input (Schulze 1989). A recent analysis has shown that the consequences of biodiversity loss are of comparable magnitude to the effects of such other global change drivers (Hooper *et al.* 2012). Disentangling the direct effects of environmental change on ecosystem functioning from those mediated by biodiversity change remains a challenge (Figure 8.1). Hence, forest ecologists now face three important questions:

- What are the impacts of global changes on forest biodiversity and ecosystem functioning?
- What is the functional role of biodiversity in forests? Which biological mechanisms are responsible?
- What are the consequences for ecosystem services?

In this review, I will focus on the second question, surveying the literature published since the publication of *Forest Diversity and Function* some years ago, which synthesised knowledge about biodiversity effects on ecosystem functioning in temperate and boreal forest ecosystems (Scherer-Lorenzen, Körner & Schulze 2005a).

## 8.2   A historical perspective

Although the aim is to cover the most recent literature, it is worth recalling that the question of whether tree diversity influences forest properties is an old one. It is related to the search for principles in the comparison between pure and mixed stands for the sustainable production of wood. Hans Pretzsch has explored the literature by the founding fathers of forest management and sustainability, and has discovered a lively debate about this issue in the early days of forestry science (Pretzsch 2005). I mention some of these old statements

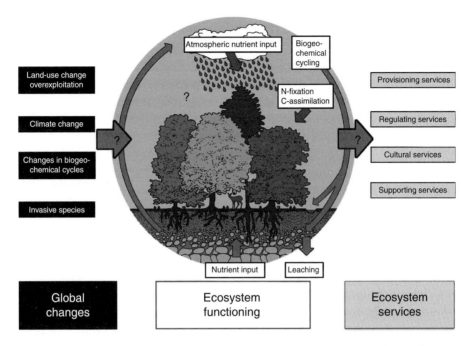

**Figure 8.1** Different drivers of global environmental change can have direct effects on the biodiversity of ecosystems and the ecological processes and functions. Changes in biodiversity can also affect ecosystem functioning. Alterations in biodiversity and functions may then translate into modifications of the delivery of ecosystem goods and services. See plate section for colour version.

to show how the perspective has changed, depending on the economic circumstances of those times, which I briefly introduce. The translation from German to English was taken from Pretzsch (2005), if not otherwise mentioned.

During the eighteenth and nineteenth centuries, wood was the only source of heating energy for both households and pre-industrial processes, including mining. Hence, the overall forest productivity was more important than the production of certain timber types (Körner 2005). Wood was also the most important construction material for houses and ships. In consequence, forests in mid-Europe were heavily overexploited and degraded. Important parts of local economies, such as silver mining, were endangered owing to scarcity of wood. Von Carlowitz (1713) proposed the concept of sustainability. Large areas were afforested, mainly with fast-growing species, such as spruce or pine in pure stands. Local experiences were often generalised, without the possibility of independent evaluation. In this context Georg Ludwig Hartig (1764–1837) argued against mixed-species plantations:

... the mixing of deciduous and coniferous species is not advantageous, as the coniferous trees generally tend to displace deciduous ones and because one type of tree impedes the growth of the other; so that no mixed deciduous and coniferous forests should be established with intent.

(Hartig (1791), p. 134.)

All mixed stands with coniferous and deciduous species should be converted into pure stands of the constituent species, as soon as circumstances permit.

(Hartig (1804), p. 40.)

Heinrich Cotta (1763–1844) argued the opposite:

Endeavours to establish pure stands everywhere are based on an old and highly detrimental prejudice [...]. Since not all tree species utilise resources in the same manner, growth is more lively in mixed stands and neither insects nor storms can do as much damage; also, a wider range of timber will be available everywhere to satisfy different demands.

(Cotta (1828), p. 115.)

Cotta therefore appears to be the founder of the resource complementarity principle, identifying ecological differences among species as the mechanism resulting in increased productivity and stability in mixed versus pure stands. He recognised this principle earlier than Charles Darwin, who is claimed to have been the first to discover that biodiversity influences ecosystem function and who gave it an evolutionary basis (Hector & Hooper 2002; McNaughton 1993). Another proponent of mixed forestry was Karl Gayer (1822–1907) who wrote:

The mixed forest does not only produce more, but also more valuable commercial timber than that grown in pure stands.

(Gayer (1886), p. 31.)

Also of that era, Alfred Möller (1860–1922) searched for the underlying mechanisms of positive mixing effects on timber production and showed that canopy stratification, i.e. architectural complementarity, matters:

... if we design stands of shade-intolerant and shade-tolerant tree species, [...] the potential for timber production is raised even more; the reason being that it is now possible to go considerably farther in the stratification of age classes than in the design of pure stands with only a single layer.

(Möller (1922), pp. 41–42.)

By the twentieth century, wood had been almost completely replaced by fossil fuels as energy sources. The mass production of industrial wood with standardised sizes and qualities was demanded by the forest industries. Afforestations with fast-growing species in monoculture prevailed until the middle of the century. The first scientific evaluations of long-term silvicultural experiments that were established in the late nineteenth century, with one- and two-species mixtures, led to a differentiated and hypothesis-driven view on the mixed-species issue: pure stands were often more productive than mixtures, depending on soil conditions. During the late twentieth century, concerns about the ecological sustainability of monocultures and their resistance and resilience to perturbations raised interest in mixed tree communities in forestry (Cannell *et al.* 1992; Kelty, Larson & Oliver 1992; Olsthoorn *et al.* 1999; Rothe & Binkley 2001). These discussions, further stimulated by policy processes such as the UN Convention on Biological Diversity (CBD), the UN Framework Convention on Climate Change (UNFCCC), the Ministerial Conference on the Protection of Forests in Europe (MCPFE), and the EU Habitats Directive, initiated a trend in many industrialised nations to convert monocultures into structured mixed stands, hoping that increasing species diversity would enhance functioning and increase stability.

Matthew J. Kelty and colleagues made the important point that species interactions are the key to understand mixing effects:

It is not possible to make general statements that mixed-species stands are better or worse than monocultures for all purposes. The nature of the interactions among species controls the differences in production and other ecological processes between mixtures and monocultures of the component species. It is not helpful to ascribe positive aspects of mixtures to a vaguely defined synergism; it is necessary to understand competition and other interactions among species, relative to local site conditions, in order to apply results of studies to management situation in an appropriate way.

(Kelty & Cameron (1995), p. 322.)

By the twenty-first century, the concept of multifunctionality of forests was expanded by including ecosystem services that go beyond the more classical forest functions, such as timber production, protective function, stability and recreation. In light of the biodiversity–ecosystem function debate, ecological arguments for the protection and sustainable use of diverse forest ecosystems are now increasingly used. In particular, within the framework of the UN CBD, arguments for the protection and sustainable management of forest ecosystems were compiled, showing that biodiversity matters, especially in the face of changing climate:

The available scientific evidence strongly supports the conclusion that the capacity of forests to resist change, or recover following disturbance, is dependent on biodiversity at multiple scales.

(Thompson *et al.* (2009), p. 7.)

Maintaining and restoring biodiversity in forests promotes their resilience to human-induced pressures and is therefore an essential 'insurance policy' and safeguard against expected climate change impacts [...] Increasing the biodiversity in planted and semi-natural forests will have a positive effect on their resilience capacity and often on their productivity (incl. carbon storage).

(Thompson *et al.* (2009), p. 7.)

Plantations and modified natural forests will face greater disturbances and risks for large-scale losses due to climate change than primary forests, because of their generally reduced biodiversity.

(Thompson *et al.* (2009), p. 7.)

In summary, there have long been opposing views on the question of whether mixed (and thus more diverse) forests are better for society, or whether forestry should concentrate on a monoculture-based strategy. Basic ideas about potential mechanisms driving some of the observed mixture effects were formulated almost 200 years ago, but still resonate today (see below). For a long time, statements about the functional effects of tree diversity were mostly based on expert knowledge and anecdotal evidence from few case studies. A systematic evaluation of the available scientific information about the role of forest biodiversity has started only recently.

## 8.3   The scientific evidence

Driven by the increasing interest in biodiversity–ecosystem functioning relationships since the 1990s, a number of authors started to compile the available knowledge about biodiversity effects in forests. I will summarise the main findings of these reviews first and follow this by a targeted discussion of the scientific approaches adopted in some of these studies.

### 8.3.1   Recent reviews

To avoid misunderstandings arising from unclear definitions, the explanatory variable 'biodiversity' needs defining in the context of forest BEF research. Despite the obvious importance of the many different facets of biodiversity for ecosystem functioning, this review focuses on the effects of changing tree species richness, because of its dominance in the current literature. However, there have also been reports summarising the relevance of genetic, functional or landscape diversity for ecosystems, which I will mention first. The few available reviews suggest that genetic diversity within tree species might indeed be an important factor for ecosystem functioning, especially in relation to stability measures, owing to the role of genetic diversity in adapting to environmental changes (Müller-Starck, Ziehe & Schubert 2005; Thompson *et al.* 2009).

  Functional diversity has come more and more into focus as an explanatory variable for many ecological processes because it can link the variability in morphological, physiological and phenological characteristics of species or individuals to ecosystem functions (Petchey, O'Gorman & Flynn 2009). Therefore, the diversity of such functional traits is central in the search for mechanisms of any BEF relationship. The recent developments to compile information about functional traits of tree species, such as the global TRY database (see http://www.try-db.org) and other related initiatives (Naeem & Bunker 2009), are therefore a very valuable and necessary tool to advance our understanding of the role of biodiversity.

Diversity at the ecosystem or landscape scale is certainly a very relevant aspect of biodiversity for forest ecosystems, which often cover large areas with huge underlying environmental variability. Thompson *et al.* (2009) raised the interesting question of whether species-level beta diversity (spatial turnover in species composition) may have any effect on ecosystem resilience in the face of environmental change. In the review by Cavard *et al.* (2011), it was shown that mixed or mosaic forest landscapes support avian diversity in unmanaged boreal forests.

Several reviews explore the question of whether tree diversity influences ecosystem functioning in natural or semi-natural forests. Early reviews focused on the relationship between tree species richness and some measure of productivity and element cycling across biomes, e.g. within the SCOPE programme and the Global Biodiversity Assessment (Mooney *et al.* 1995, 1996). These correlative studies concluded that there is no clear relationship between forest biodiversity and processes at the ecosystem level such as growth or wood production, or fluxes of water, carbon or nutrients in species-poor boreal systems (Pastor *et al.* 1996) or temperate systems (Schulze *et al.* 1996). When effects were observed, they were mainly governed by indirect influences acting via the chemical composition of foliage affecting litter decomposition, with the presence of particular species accounting for much of the effect. Similarly, no effects of tree diversity on biomass production were expected for tropical forests under constant conditions (Orians, Dirzo & Cushman 1996; Wright 1996). Assuming an asymptotic diversity–productivity relationship, it was argued that most tropical forests with their extraordinary diversity are far beyond the point where a loss of tree species richness would affect productivity. Interestingly, the unified neutral theory of biodiversity and biogeography by Stephen P. Hubbell also suggests no such diversity–productivity relationship in highly species-rich tropical forests, because of ecological equivalence in resource use, at least within the large group of shade-tolerant species dominating such forests (Hubbell 2006). These early researchers also acknowledged that observational studies were inadequate to test these assumptions on a mechanistic level, and that a combination of long-term observations and surveys, manipulative experiments and modelling would be needed to gain further insights into the functional consequences of biodiversity.

In 2005, in an attempt to merge knowledge about mixing effects from the forestry sector and the BEF community, we synthesised the available literature about tree diversity effects on a variety of ecosystem processes and characteristics, including productivity, resource use and biogeochemical cycles, herbivore and pathogen load, and stability against disturbances (Scherer-Lorenzen, Körner & Schulze 2005a). It became clear that there are several ways that tree diversity may influence ecosystem functioning. Interestingly, the strongest positive effects were related to some aspects of stand stability. For example, a meta-analysis on the occurrence of and damage by insect herbivores clearly showed that in most cases, lower tree species diversity results in greater insect pest abundance, density or damage (Jactel, Brockerhoff & Duelli 2005). Similarly, susceptibility to fungal pathogens is often greatest in low diversity mixtures, although 'lucky monocultures' that somehow escape disease do exist (Pautasso, Holdenrieder & Stenlid 2005). On the other hand, the review by Dhôte (2005) did not suggest a greater resistance of complex forests to strong winds, which has often been suggested. Hence, there was less evidence for coherent and consistent patterns. In other words, a variety of different effects have been found depending on the environmental conditions, the forest type, the identity of the dominating species or the processes under study (Scherer-Lorenzen, Körner & Schulze 2005b).

Thompson *et al.* (2009), in their synthesis of biodiversity–resilience–stability relationships in forests, listed only 20 studies that tested the relationship between species richness and some measure of productivity, which is a tiny fraction compared with those studies in grasslands. Out of these studies, which included both experimental (direct planting or removal experiments) and observational approaches, 15 reported a positive diversity–productivity relationship and 5 a neutral or negative one (although one study was wrongly placed in the positive group). They thus concluded that diverse and complex forests are generally more productive and provide more services than those with low species richness. Similarly, their analyses of several case studies supported the idea that diverse forests are more resilient owing to a large and robust species pool, turnover of species and some redundancy of functional species providing insurance against environmental perturbations. They also suggested a negative relationship between species diversity and the invasibility of forests, especially by pests and pathogens.

Complementing the review of Thompson *et al.* (2009), Nadrowski, Wirth and Scherer-Lorenzen (2010) analysed 31 studies, mainly published after 2007, which reported tree diversity effects at the stand level. In contrast to Thompson *et al.* (2009) and to some of the contributions in Scherer-Lorenzen, Körner and Schulze (2005a), this meta-analysis only considered studies covering a large diversity gradient, omitting the many reports that compared monocultures with two-species mixtures. This study also separated the effects of different kinds of diversity gradients, namely richness (i.e. species richness gradient with different tree species, as a measure of taxonomic diversity), dilution (i.e. monoculture of only one species, and species richness gradient including that species in all mixtures), genetic diversity,

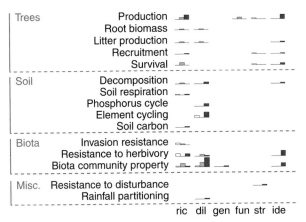

**Figure 8.2** Results of a qualitative meta-analysis of tree diversity effects on ecosystem functioning in forests by Nadrowski, Wirth and Scherer-Lorenzen (2010). Diversity gradients were separated into richness (ric), dilution (dil), genetic diversity (gen), functional diversity (fun), and structural diversity (str). Identity effects (ide) were also reported. Ecosystem functions were grouped into functional syndromes (Trees: functions related to tree productivity and population dynamics; Soil: functions related to soil parameters; Biota: functions related to communities of biota other than trees; Misc.: miscellaneous functions). Bars show the distribution of negative (white), neutral or unimodal (light grey) or positive (dark grey) effects. Absence of a bar means that there was no study reporting such a result. Reprinted from Nadrowski, Wirth and Scherer-Lorenzen (2010), with permission from Elsevier.

functional diversity and structural (i.e. architectural canopy) diversity. The large number of different response variables reported were grouped into 15 categories, which were further divided into three main functional classes: functions and processes related to tree productivity and population dynamics of trees, those related to communities of biota other than trees, and those related to soil parameters (Nadrowski, Wirth & Scherer-Lorenzen, 2010). As shown in Figure 8.2, there are several examples of positive BEF relationships in forests, especially related to productivity, associated biodiversity and soil parameters, although neutral or negative effects have also been reported. Quite often, however, diversity effects cannot be clearly separated from confounding factors such as environmental heterogeneity, especially in observational studies, as mentioned above (Vilà *et al.* 2005). In addition, effects of species identity (i.e. precisely which species were present) were often stronger than pure richness effects (i.e. how many species were present). Nevertheless, it is important to stress the fact that none of the studies analysed more than one independent ecosystem function, and species identity effects are likely to differ depending on the function considered (Nadrowski, Wirth & Scherer-Lorenzen 2010). From the perspective of forest multifunctionality, diversity may still matter in such systems with strong identity effects. This aspect should more often be kept in mind in the debate about the relative importance of richness versus identity effects.

A recent review by Cavard *et al.* (2011) on the importance of unmanaged mixed boreal and northern temperate forests for biodiversity conservation showed that understorey plant species richness is generally higher in mixed than in pure forests, because of the provision of greater microhabitat diversity in the presence of different tree species. These effects were mostly attributable to the presence of both early successional broadleaved species and late successional conifer species within mixed stands, differing in their specific effects on light availability and soil conditions. Avian diversity may also benefit from higher tree diversity if certain bird species prefer or require different tree species within a stand or within the landscape. Soil fauna effects were much more variable, with only few studies documenting positive effects of mixed versus pure stands, e.g. for earthworms and oribatid mites. Additionally, diversity of ectomycorrhizae was often positively related to host tree species diversity, presumably because some ectomycorrhizae species are associated with multiple hosts. In general, however, the authors found very little evidence for the existence of certain taxa uniquely associated to mixed forests, i.e. for mixedwood-indicator species. In most cases, therefore, increasing tree diversity resulted in additive species identity effects, rather than in some kind of synergistic diversity effects where biodiversity in mixed stands would be higher than in the corresponding monocultures taken together. In other words, non-tree biodiversity in mixed forests mostly reflected the accumulation of species associated with each tree species.

Another relevant review to our question of interest was published by Díaz *et al.* (2009), who discussed means to incorporate biodiversity and its functional implications in initiatives to mitigate climate change. Since forests, including their soils, are the largest pool of terrestrial carbon, forest biodiversity may play an important role in long-term C storage and sequestration. Thus, biodiversity should not only be considered in international conventions for its intrinsic value, but also for its potential to enhance or reduce the effectiveness of C sequestration measures. The authors first review the theoretical background of biodiversity effects on C gain and losses, followed by a compilation of available evidence and recommendations to include biodiversity aspects in the design of mitigation actions. Clearly, the best option to preserve and enhance long-term C storage is the conservation of primary forests, with their ability to maintain C stocks, biodiversity and ecosystem services. On the relationship between forest biodiversity and C-related processes, they conclude that 'mixed forestry systems might be more stable in the face of environmental variability and directional change than monocultures, and they might sequester C more securely in the long term' (Díaz *et al.* 2009, p. 164). They admit that the evidence for this recommendation, which is based on the idea of niche complementarity and complementary resource use among heterospecific individuals, is still inconclusive for forests. Nevertheless, experience from polycultures or agroforestry systems shows that mixed systems may additionally provide a larger variety of other goods and services, and constitute a buffer against environmental change and pest damage. Thus, adopting mixed systems might be an important step forward in designing ecological and socially accepted C-sequestration projects, especially in developing countries.

### 8.3.2    Approach-specific analyses

Most of the BEF studies – reviewed in the publications mentioned in Section 8.1 – deal with fast-growing systems, such as grasslands or laboratory mesocosms. The vast majority of these studies adopt an experimental approach, manipulating certain aspects of diversity in model ecosystems while keeping environmental conditions as constant as possible. However, performing biodiversity experiments with trees is challenging, and the pros and cons have been discussed elsewhere (Leuschner, Jungkunst & Fleck 2009; Scherer-Lorenzen *et al.* 2005c). To gain a full understanding of the functional role of biodiversity, a series of different and complementary approaches are needed, including analyses of silvicultural experiments, comparative studies of natural ecosystems or of forest inventory networks, and modelling approaches. In the following section, I will present examples of these different approaches, with the aim of stimulating thought about the design and execution of different kinds of BEF studies in forest ecosystems.

*8.3.2.1 Silvicultural experiments and plantation forestry*
Concerns about the ecological sustainability of monocultures, their resistance and resilience against perturbations and the socio-economic consequences raised interest in mixed tree communities in forestry during the late twentieth century (Cannell, Malcolm & Robertson 1992; Kelty, Larson & Oliver 1992; Olsthoorn *et al.* 1999; Rothe & Binkley 2001). Most of this knowledge was gained by studying plantation forests, which are usually dominated by one or very few commercially important tree species and which strongly differ from natural forests in structure and function. As a consequence, silvicultural trials mostly include only two species, in mixture and in monoculture. Only recently have the potential benefits of including biodiversity been analysed and promoted. Owing to the enormous number of publications from silvicultural experiments and plantations involving only a few species, I restrict the following section to reviews summarising these results, and to a few exemplary studies that cover a larger diversity gradient.

Forrester *et al.* (2006) reviewed the literature on the effects of planting nitrogen-fixing species into *Eucalyptus* plantations, and confirmed the well-known fertilisation effect of N-fixation that results in greater productivity of the mixtures. Piotto (2008) compared tree growth in pure and mixed plantations across several species and regions, albeit with a clear focus on tropical systems. This meta-analysis with 14 published studies representing 46 different tree species showed slight positive mixing effects on tree diameter growth, while height growth remained unaffected. Confirming the results of Forrester *et al.* (2006), mixtures with N-fixing species had the strongest effect on growth of the non-fixing species. Out of the 14 experiments, only 5 compared monocultures with mixtures of more than two species, but none covered an entire gradient of different diversities. Piotto concluded that beside other beneficial effects with respect to a broader range of environmental services (such as protection, biodiversity conservation or restoration of degraded land), mixed plantations – especially those including N-fixing species – may have the potential to increase productivity and shorten rotation lengths, and should therefore be adopted more widely by silviculturalists.

Bauhus and Schmerbeck (2010) reviewed the available literature on tree diversity effects on production functions (biomass, non-wood forest products) and regulating functions (water, carbon and nutrient cycles, and resilience), and discussed potential underlying mechanisms for diversity effect, including niche complementarity due to canopy and belowground stratification, and facilitation (mostly due to admixture of nitrogen-fixing species). They concluded that there might be great potential to increase the number of ecosystem functions and services of plantations through silvicultural management that promotes biodiversity. However, such beneficial effects might not be realised in every situation, strongly depending on site conditions, the species involved and the specific local management. They also pointed to the fact that there might be trade-offs between the effects of mixing tree species. For example, enhanced biomass production in mixed situations may come at the cost of higher water consumption (Forrester *et al.* 2010), which may increase the susceptibility of the trees to drought, and which may in turn reduce groundwater recharge and drinking water availability in many semi-arid regions of the world.

Other forest ecologists have also emphasised the importance of local abiotic and biotic circumstances in driving mixture effects. For example, Pretzsch and colleagues systematically compiled the available datasets from many silvicultural trials and found that the presence of positive mixture effects on productivity, leading to transgressive overyielding, was very much dependent on soil fertility and climate (Pretzsch 2005; Pretzsch & Schütze 2009; Pretzsch *et al.* 2010). For European mixtures of spruce (*Picea abies*) and beech (*Fagus sylvatica*), for instance, growth of spruce can be enhanced by admixing beech at nutrient-poor sites, because of enhanced nutrient availability through addition of beech litter promoting decomposition and mineralisation

(Rothe & Binkley 2001). At nutrient-rich sites, in contrast, beech can profit from admixing spruce because of reduced intraspecific competition for light. At the stand level, the overall mixing effects thus change along such fertility gradients, with obvious implications for the management of such stands. These studies also show a big advantage of BEF studies with trees over other experimental systems: it is often much easier to trace back diversity effects from the stand to the individual tree level, showing that the causes of beneficial effects might strongly differ between the species involved. In addition, the study of trees allows the inclusion of mortality into the mechanistic BEF framework (Potvin & Dutilleul 2009; Potvin & Gotelli 2008), which is often impossible in herbaceous and microbial systems.

Ecosystem processes other than tree growth and timber yields have received less attention in the analysis of silvicultural experiments, maybe with the exception of damaging organisms such as insect herbivores (Jactel, Brockerhoff & Duelli 2005) or pathogens (Pautasso, Holdenrieder & Stenlid 2005). Vehviläinen, Koricheva and Ruohomaki (2007, 2008) and Koricheva et al. (2006) performed meta-analyses based on reports on herbivore abundance and pathogen damage, as well as predatory arthropods in long-term forest experiments, mainly from boreal and temperate forests. They found that more diverse stands were not consistently less vulnerable than pure stands, and that species composition was often more important than species richness.

Very few silvicultural mixing trials or commercial plantations cover diversity gradients of more than two species. As one exception, Firn, Erskine and Lamb (2007) analysed plantations of different species in Australia that developed into highly diverse systems after some decades of growth and different thinning treatments, thus representing a hybrid between natural and experimental community studies. In contrast to the results from many grassland biodiversity experiments, productivity decreased with increasing tree diversity, whereas the availability of soil resources such as N and P increased. They concluded that the patterns were mainly driven by the presence of dominant species, representing a 'sampling effect'. However, the thinning treatments were confounded with species identity, so that both recruitment of species diversity and biomass production could have been influenced by the thinning regime. In contrast, Erskine, Lamb and Bristow (2006) found a significant positive effect of tree diversity on productivity, measured as basal area increment, in much younger tropical plantations in the same region of Australia, which were already established as plantations of different species diversity and composition. These two contrasting examples show that different results can emerge depending on the experimental design, stand age or spatial scale of the study system, which underlines the complex nature of BEF relationships in forests.

A recent review compiled the knowledge about the effect of mixing tree species on tree nutrition and nutrient dynamics (Richards *et al.* 2010). It argued that variables influencing productivity, such as the supply, capture and efficiency of use of resources, can be influenced by interspecific interactions in mixed stands through morphological and physiological changes. There is accumulating evidence that mixing often positively affects litter decomposition and soil-nutrient mineralisation (Hättenschwiler 2005), hence influencing nutrient supply to the plants; meta-analyses of Richards *et al.* (2010) showed that in the majority of cases, a shift to greater aboveground N and P content of species occurred if growing in mixtures, indicating an increase of the resources captured from a site. This could result from changes in spatial, temporal and chemical patterns of root dynamics. Leaf N concentrations also increased for a given species if growing with N-fixing trees, suggesting higher photosynthetic rates and nutrient use efficiency. Nutrient use efficiencies were also often different in mixed stands, with evidence for both higher and lower values. Changes in canopy photosynthetic capacities, in C allocation or in foliar nutrient residence times have been seen as responsible. In summary, this review revealed that several pathways are obviously involved that lead to changes in tree nutrition and productivity in mixed compared with pure stands.

In essence, silvicultural species and mixing trials provide a great wealth of information about the ecology and physiology of tree species and their suitability for plantation forestry, aiming at the maximisation of timber yields. They can also help to elucidate the underlying mechanisms of mixing effects, because they often follow a rigid experimental design that allows a direct comparison of tree performance under intra- and interspecific competition in otherwise similar environmental conditions (Jones, McNamara & Mason 2005). Some of these experiments have already run for several decades, so dynamic temporal responses can be followed, although these older experiments are often not well replicated and data availability is sometimes poor. In addition, they often include different management treatments, so that responses of pure and mixed stands to thinning, for example, can be studied in more detail, allowing the formulation of silvicultural recommendations for mixed stands. On the other hand, a clear drawback of these experiments for BEF-related issues is the preponderance of comparisons between monocultures and two-species mixtures, often with a 50:50 mixing ratio only. Without the establishment of more diverse mixtures, providing longer and more continuous gradients of tree species, as well as the comparison of several different species combinations, it is impossible to determine thresholds in the diversity-functioning trajectory, or to distinguish between richness and compositional effects. To be more valuable for BEF research, other functions beside those directly linked to timber yield should also be included in the monitoring design of these experiments.

### 8.3.2.2  Forest biodiversity experiments

Forests are underrepresented in experimental BEF research. For example, only 8% of all ecosystems included in the meta-analyses of Cardinale *et al.* (2006) are temperate forests, and experimental manipulation did not include trees, but other organisms such as decomposer groups. Ecologists have recently begun to establish tree diversity experiments, similar to those with other model ecosystems such as grasslands or mesocosms, despite the longevity of forest systems and the associated difficulties of conducting manipulative experiments in these settings (Scherer-Lorenzen *et al.* 2005c). Building upon the ideas and results of such experiments with fast-growing model systems, as well as similar experiments involving trees (e.g. exploring the possibility of mimicking succession in developing sustainable agroforestry systems: Ewel, Mazzarino & Berish 1991), model forest communities with different numbers of tree species, functional groups or genotypes were planted. The basic features of these tree diversity experiments, including methodological and design considerations, have already been published (Scherer-Lorenzen *et al.* 2005c). At the time of that publication, a total of seven independent experiments were set up. Since then, a global network of such tree diversity experiments (TreeDivNet: see www.treedivnet.ugent.be) has been developed, established and financed by different and independent groups. At these sites, tree communities of differing tree diversity have been established by planting, with gradients of tree species richness, genetic diversity, number of functional groups, or continuous gradients of functional diversity. In total, these experiments now cover more than 600 hectares, composed of almost 2900 plots. More than 630 000 individual stems have been manually planted. All experiments follow the same basic approach but differ in some details of their design. For example, at some sites, patch planting has been done to avoid out-competition of slow-growing species by fast ones, i.e. to ensure full mixing of species within very long time spans (Scherer-Lorenzen *et al.* 2007b). At other sites, in contrast, individual-based mixing of species in combination with a high planting density has been adopted to allow for early species interactions. Some experiments have rather small plot sizes (e.g. 12.25–25 m$^2$), while others have 1–4 hectare plots and try to mimic forest microclimate within single plots. Some of the experiments are already 10 years old, whereas others have been planted only recently. Thus, mainly processes important during the initial phase of forest establishment can be studied currently, while processes that change with ongoing forest maturation, or are relevant in mature forests, can only be addressed at later stages. This is one of the largest experimental platforms in ecosystem research worldwide, specifically designed to elucidate the functional significance of forest biodiversity.

In the meantime, the first results have now been published (Table 8.1). In the oldest forest biodiversity experiment, established in 1999 in southwestern Finland, Vehviläinen and Koricheva (2006) analysed browsing patterns of voles and moose, testing the 'associational resistance hypothesis'. This hypothesis states that herbivory is reduced in plant communities composed of several different species, whereas herbivory damage is higher in species-poor or monospecific communities (Jactel, Brockerhoff & Duelli 2005). It has mostly been confirmed for specialised herbivores that may capitalise on the huge availability of their preferred feeding plant, which is less diluted in species-poor communities than in more diverse ones. In contrast, generalist species may benefit from a larger variety of feeding plants in mixed stands, leading to higher herbivory with increasing plant diversity (referred to as the 'associational susceptibility hypothesis'). Owing to the very different life histories of voles and moose, including differences in body size and feeding specialisation, foraging patterns and movement ability, tree species diversity and composition had contrasting effects on these two herbivores. While the response of the more specialised voles did indeed support the predictions of the associational resistance hypothesis, with higher damage in monocultures, moose browsing tended to be lower in one- and two-species mixtures (Vehviläinen & Koricheva 2006). However, the presence and abundance of particular tree species (such as birch, which are preferred fodder plants for moose) and the population dynamics of voles strongly influenced the observed patterns in herbivory. Consequently, the authors concluded that 'diversification of forest stands may have very different effects on mammalian browsing depending on the herbivores present, their densities, and the tree species used in reforestation (Vehviläinen & Koricheva 2006, p. 497).

The second-oldest BEF experiment with trees was established in 2001 in Sardinilla, Panama, spanning a gradient of one, three and six tree species. Owing to the fast growth under these tropical conditions, this experiment currently is the one with the highest number of published studies, and it is the first one yielding results on tree growth, mortality and productivity (Healy, Gotelli & Potvin 2008; Potvin & Dutilleul 2009; Potvin & Gotelli 2008), and on litter decomposition, nutrient dynamics and soil respiration (Murphy et al. 2008; Oelmann et al. 2009; Scherer-Lorenzen et al. 2007a; Zeugin et al. 2010). The implications of these different ecosystem processes for carbon storage was summarised recently (Potvin et al. 2011). In essence, after only 3 to 8 years of growth, tree diversity affected many of the processes studied, although not in a consistent way. For example, wood and litter production tended to be higher in mixtures than in monocultures, with a particular three-species mixture outperforming all other communities, including the corresponding

**Table 8.1** Overview of experimental studies on BEF relationships in tree biodiversity experiments, published since 2005.

| Reference | Biome | Ecosystem variables | Diversity gradient (tree species richness) | Diversity effects | Direction of effects |
|---|---|---|---|---|---|
| Vehviläinen & Koricheva 2006 | Boreal | Moose browsing | 1, 2, 3, 5 | + | ↗ |
| Vehviläinen & Koricheva 2006 | Boreal | Vole damage | 1, 2, 3, 5 | * | ↗ |
| Don et al. 2007 | Temperate | Vole damage | 2, 4, 6 | * | ↗ |
| Scherer-Lorenzen et al. 2007 | Tropical | Litter production | 1, 3, 6 | * | ↘↗ |
| Scherer-Lorenzen et al. 2007 | Tropical | Litter decomposition | 1, 3, 6 | – | ↗ |
| Healy, Gotelli & Potvin 2008 | Tropical | Biomass production | 1, 3, 6 | * | ↘↗ |
| Healy, Gotelli & Potvin 2008 | Tropical | Mortality | 1, 3, 6 | * | ↘ |
| Murphy et al. 2008 | Tropical | Soil respiration | 1, 3, 6 | * | ↘↗ |
| Potvin & Gotelli 2008, Potvin & Dutilleul 2009 | Tropical | Tree growth | 1, 3, 6 | * | ↗ |
| Potvin & Gotelli 2008, Potvin & Dutilleul 2009 | Tropical | Basal area | 1, 3, 6 | – | |
| Potvin & Gotelli 2008, Potvin & Dutilleul 2009 | Tropical | Tree mortality | 1, 3, 6 | – | |
| Oelmann et al. 2009 | Tropical | Aboveground N, P, K, Ca, Mg pools | 1, 3, 6 | + | ↘↗ |
| Oelmann et al. 2009 | Tropical | Aboveground biomass | 1, 3, 6 | * | ↘↗ |
| Huxham et al. 2010 | Tropical | Aboveground biomass (mangroves) | 1, 2, 3 | + | ↗ |
| Zeugin et al. 2010 | Tropical | Aboveground N pools | 1, 3, 6 | – | |
| Zeugin et al. 2010 | Tropical | Aboveground P pools | 1, 3, 6 | + | ↘↗ |
| Zeugin et al. 2010 | Tropical | Aboveground biomass | 1, 3, 6 | – | |
| Zeugin et al. 2010 | Tropical | N use efficiency | 1, 3, 6 | – | |

**Table 8.1** (cont.)

| Reference | Biome | Ecosystem variables | Diversity gradient (tree species richness) | Diversity effects | Direction of effects |
|---|---|---|---|---|---|
| Zeugin et al. 2010 | Tropical | P use efficiency | 1, 3, 6 | * | ↘↗ |
| Ruiz-Jaen & Potvin 2011 | Tropical | Aboveground carbon storage | 6, 9, 18 | * | ↗ |
| Potvin et al. 2011 | Tropical | Aboveground carbon storage | 1, 3, 6 | – | |
| Potvin et al. 2011 | Tropical | Aboveground carbon storage, controlled for mortality | 1, 3, 6 | * | ↗↗ |
| Potvin et al. 2011 | Tropical | Net primary production | 1, 3, 6 | – | |
| Potvin et al. 2011 | Tropical | Litter production | 1, 3, 6 | – | |
| Potvin et al. 2011 | Tropical | Coarse woody debris production | 1, 3, 6 | – | |
| Potvin et al. 2011 | Tropical | Herb layer biomass | 1, 3, 6 | – | |
| Potvin et al. 2011 | Tropical | Coarse woody debris decomposition | 1, 3, 6 | * | ↗ |
| Potvin et al. 2011 | Tropical | Soil organic carbon concentration, soil organic carbon pools, soil $\delta^{13}C$ | 1, 3, 6 | – | |
| Potvin et al. 2011 | Tropical | Loss in soil organic carbon | 1, 3, 6 | * | ↗↗ |
| Potvin et al. 2011 | Tropical | Ecosystem carbon gain | 1, 3, 6 | – | |
| Both et al. 2012 | Subtropical | Herb layer performance and richness | 1, 2, 4 | – | |
| Both et al. 2012 | Subtropical | Exotic herb layer cover | 1, 2, 4 | * | ↗ |
| Geißler et al. 2012 | Subtropical | Kinetic energy of rainfall | 1, 4 | – | |
| Lang et al. 2012 | Subtropical | Tree sapling growth, biomass allocation and architecture | 1, 2, 4 | – | |

| | | | | | |
|---|---|---|---|---|---|
| Lang et al. 2012 | Subtropical | Tree sapling pruning and branch turnover | 1, 2, 4 | * | ↗ |
| Lei, Scherer-Lorenzen & Bauhus 2012a | Temperate | Fine root length, surface area and morphology | 1, 2, 3, 4 | – | ↗ |
| Lei, Scherer-Lorenzen & Bauhus 2012b | Temperate | Fine root biomass production | 1, 2, 3, 4 | * | ↗ |
| Lei, Scherer-Lorenzen & Bauhus 2012b | Temperate | Fine root biomass mortality | 1, 2, 3, 4 | * | ↗ |
| Lei, Scherer-Lorenzen & Bauhus 2012b | Temperate | Root biomass of non-woody vegetation | 1, 2, 3, 4 | * | ↗ |

* Significant effects with $p < 0.05$
+ Trends with $p < 0.1$
– No effects with $p > 0.1$
↗ Positive diversity effects
↘ Negative diversity effects
↗ or ↘↗ Unimodal relationship

monocultures (Oelmann *et al.* 2009; Potvin *et al.* 2011; Scherer-Lorenzen *et al.* 2007a; Zeugin *et al.* 2010). This mixture of a fast-growing species forming the upper canopy (*Luhea seemannii*), a moderately growing species in the middle canopy (*Anacardium excelsum*) and a slow-growing, late successional species in the lower canopy (*Tabebuia rosea*) developed a pronounced aboveground strat- ification. Hence, complementarity in light acquisition might have been the underlying mechanism of this overyielding mixture. Similarly, deviation from expected yield approaches of data on aboveground nutrient pools also showed some significant complementarity effects in three- and six-species mixtures, while selection effects were small and non-significant (Oelmann *et al.* 2009; Zeugin *et al.* 2010). In contrast, other ecosystem processes and functions such as litter decomposition (Scherer-Lorenzen *et al.* 2007a), root and microbial biomass (Murphy *et al.* 2008) were unaffected by overall changes in tree diversity. Many processes under study showed a unimodal relationship with highest performance at the intermediate three-species level, and a slight decrease at the six-species level. But this decrease may have been because all of the six-species replicates were, by chance, located on the most poorly drained soils, leading to longer periods of water logging and corresponding lower growth and higher mortality (Healy, Gotelli & Potvin 2008). Generally, environmental heterogeneity had major influences on the response variables measured, as well as species identity effects, with both aspects usually explaining more variation than did diversity (Healy, Gotelli & Potvin 2008). These results therefore reinforce the finding of other authors, suggesting that a few functionally important traits may strongly control the performance of mixed tree plantations, so that no general positive or negative mixture effects should be expected, unless there are sampling effects (Bauhus & Schmerbeck 2010; Ewel & Mazzarino 2008). An elegant example of how such strong species-specific influences result in increasing perform- ance with increasing diversity through sampling effects comes from a man- grove diversity experiment in Kenya, where mixtures containing one species (*Avicennia marina*) had higher biomass production than those without it (Huxham *et al.* 2010). Nevertheless, the Sardinilla experiment in Panama also showed that the common focus on diversity effects on variables such as pool sizes of carbon or nutrients and related fluxes themselves may actually hide more subtle effects on the functional links among those variables. Structural equation modelling has shown that the links among these pools and fluxes become significantly stronger as diversity increases (Potvin *et al.* 2011). Thus, increasing the diversity of trees in plantation forestry may indeed affect ecosystem functioning, but the effects may vary substantially. It has to be kept in mind, however, that the time span of this and other BEF experiments with trees is still very short, and that the relative strength of diversity effects may still increase with time, as has been shown for grassland experiments.

The largest European tree diversity experiment BIOTREE, established in 2002/2003, is now also providing first insights into BEF relationships in the early phase after tree establishment (Scherer-Lorenzen *et al.* 2007b). Browsing by voles was negatively affected by increasing tree species richness very shortly after planting (Don *et al.* 2007). Increasing neighbourhood diversity resulted in higher fine root production and mortality after 6 years of growth, indicating higher turnover rates in species-rich communities (Lei, Scherer-Lorenzen & Bauhus 2012b). Fine root exploitation measured as root length and surface area, in contrast, remained unaffected by tree diversity (Lei, Scherer-Lorenzen & Bauhus 2012a). The two dominant conifer species (Norway spruce and Douglas fir) benefited most from growing with inferior competitors (European beech and sessile oak) and showed overyielding in root production. In addition, the spatial distribution of roots within the soil layer changed, which may finally result in pronounced niche differentiation among the coexisting species. Interestingly, root biomass of non-woody vegetation was lower in species-rich plots, which suggests that the often observed problems with afforestation resulting from competition between the ground-layer vegetation and tree saplings may be more easily overcome by planting species-rich tree communities (Lei, Scherer-Lorenzen & Bauhus 2012b).

First results have now also been published from a diversity experiment with 3-year-old tree saplings in subtropical China. For example, tree sapling diversity had no effect on herb layer performance and richness, except for cover of exotic herb species (Both *et al.* 2012). Similarly, growth, biomass allocation and crown architectural traits were not affected by tree species richness, but by species composition and identity (Lang *et al.* 2012). However, pruning and branch turnover were enhanced with increasing diversity, indicating that saplings are able to adapt their crown architecture to changes in their local neighbourhood. The authors concluded that this dynamic branch demography could be caused by proceeding niche differentiation with regard to the light harvesting system. An interesting but rarely measured ecosystem property was analysed by Geißler *et al.* (2012), who showed that the kinetic energy of rainfall – which strongly controls erosion processes – depends largely on tree sapling density and the canopy architecture of the species. However, mixing tree saplings with different architectural traits had no effect on the kinetic energy in comparison with saplings grown in monoculture.

The pros and cons of biodiversity experiments that adopt the 'synthetic community approach' have already been discussed widely, especially with respect to applying the results to 'real world', natural situations (Díaz *et al.* 2003; Lepš 2004; Schmid & Hector 2004; Schmid *et al.*, 2002; Srivastava & Vellend 2005). For tree diversity experiments, the potentials, challenges and limitations were presented in detail by Scherer-Lorenzen *et al.* (2005c) and Leuschner, Jungkunst and Fleck (2009). The main advantage of this approach lies in its experimental creation of a diversity gradient independent of environmental heterogeneity and assembly filters. Thus, diversity can be treated as an explanatory variable, whereas ecosystem processes can be regarded as response variables. Of course, some environmental heterogeneity cannot be avoided given the relative large areas required, influencing the results and underlying the need to document site factors carefully (Healy, Gotelli & Potvin 2008). Nevertheless, the ability of this design to quantify the effect of diversity *per se* against a background of various other influencing factors and covariates (species identity, environment, management etc.) – called maximisation of 'orthogonality' by Nadrowski, Wirth and Scherer-Lorenzen (2010) – is its main strength. This is only possible if diversity is weakly correlated with these factors (i.e. orthogonal). Additionally, the easy logistics with many nearby stands allow for the quantification of a wide range of ecosystem functions (high 'comprehensiveness'; Nadrowski, Wirth & Scherer-Lorenzen 2010). The obvious disadvantages of forest experiments are the currently relative young age and the long time needed for establishment and occurrence of first species interactions. As plantations, they are not representative of natural, highly structured and multi-aged forest ecosystems, but rather of commercial timber plantations (low 'representativity'; Nadrowski, Wirth & Scherer-Lorenzen 2010). Finally, the large areas needed (although some small-scale tree diversity experiments have also been successfully established, focusing on early interactions among saplings) are logistically and financially challenging, although cooperation with climate change mitigation, forest rehabilitation or conservation initiatives might aid in setting up more such experiments (Díaz *et al.* 2009; Hector *et al.* 2011).

### 8.3.2.3 *Observational studies that compare natural forests differing in diversity*

Observational studies along longer gradients of tree diversity can be done with two different approaches (*sensu* Snedecor & Cochran 1980): either sample surveys with a random or grid-based selection of plots across a specific region, or comparative studies where a similar number of plots per diversity level are deliberately chosen. Forest inventories are a good example of the first approach, and they have also been used to study tree diversity effects. The second, comparative approach has recently been used in some BEF studies in forests.

Using information from forest inventories    Forest inventories at the national or regional level, as well as existing databases from permanent forest monitoring networks, are an extremely data-rich and valuable tool to analyse correlations between forest diversity and ecosystem processes. However, only a few published inventory-based diversity-functioning studies exist (Table 8.2), even though National Forest Inventories are available for many

**Table 8.2** *Examples of forest inventory analyses on BEF relationships in natural forests*

| Reference | Biome | Ecosystem variables | Diversity gradient | Diversity effects | Direction of effects |
|---|---|---|---|---|---|
| Caspersen & Pacala 2001 | Boreal and temperate | Productivity | 1, 4, 8, 13 | * | ↗ |
| Enquist & Niklas 2001 | Global | Total standing tree biomass | Up to 275 species per 0.1 ha | – | |
| Vilà et al. 2003 | Mediterranean | Stemwood production | 1, 2, 3, 4, 5 | * | ↗ |
| Vilà 2004 | Mediterranean | Litter production and C stocks | 1, 2, 3, 4, 5 | * | ↗ |
| Vilà et al. 2005 | Mediterranean | Stemwood production | 1, 2, 3, 4, 5 SR | * | ↗ |
| Moser & Hansen 2009 | Temperate | Tree growth | Shannon index | * | ↗ |
| Moser & Hansen 2009 | Temperate | Aspen forest | | | ↗ |
| Moser & Hansen 2009 | Temperate | Sugar maple–beech–yellow birch forest | | * | ↗ |
| Vilà et al. 2007 | Mediterranean | Stemwood production | 1, 2, 3, 4, ≥5 SR | * | ↗ |
| Vilà et al. 2007 | Mediterranean | Stemwood production | 1, 2, 3 FG | * | ↗ |
| Liang et al. 2007 | Temperate | Growth | 1– >10 | * | ↗ |
| Liang et al. 2007 | Temperate | Recruitment | 1– >10 | * | ↗ |
| Liang et al. 2007 | Temperate | Mortality | 1– >10 | – | |
| Paquette & Messier 2010 | Boreal and temperate | Productivity | 1–13 SR | * | ↗ |
| Paquette & Messier 2010 | Boreal and temperate | Productivity | 0–1.8 FDis | * | ↗ |
| Woodall et al. 2011 | Boreal, temperate and subtropical | Aboveground live and dead C storage | 0.1–.0 SCPR | – | |
| Woodall et al. 2011 | Boreal, temperate and subtropical | Aboveground live and dead C storage | 99th percentile | * | ↗ |

**Table 8.2** (cont.)

| Reference | Biome | Ecosystem variables | Diversity gradient | Diversity effects | Direction of effects |
|---|---|---|---|---|---|
| Gamfeldt et al. 2013 | Boreal, temperate | Tree biomass production | 1–10 | * | ↗↘ |
| Gamfeldt et al. 2013 | Boreal, temperate | Soil carbon storage | 1–10 | * | ↗ |
| Gamfeldt et al. 2013 | Boreal, temperate | Bilberry production | 1–10 | * | ↗↗ |
| Gamfeldt et al. 2013 | Boreal, temperate | Game production potential | 1–10 | * | ↗↘ |
| Gamfeldt et al. 2013 | Boreal, temperate | Understorey plant species richness | 1–10 | * | ↗ |
| Gamfeldt et al. 2013 | Boreal, temperate | Dead wood | 1–10 | * | ↗ |

FG: number of functional groups; SR: number of tree species; FD: continuous measure of functional diversity, with FDis = functional dispersion (Laliberté & Legendre 2010); SCPR: species composition purity ratio, ranging from 0.1 (highly mixed stands) to 1.0 (pure stands) (Woodall et al. 2011)

* Significant effects with $p < 0.05$

- No effects with $p > 0.1$

↗ Positive diversity effects

↘ Negative diversity effects

↗↘ or ↘↗ Unimodal relationship

countries. Most of these inventories focus on production functions of the forest, but some also regularly record other ecosystem characteristics.

Caspersen and Pacala (2001) analysed the 24 670 plots from the United States FIA database and reported positive relationships between diversity and productivity, but they could not disentangle the confounding effects of site quality and diversity on productivity. This positive correlation was found for both tree species richness *per se*, and successional diversity, as measures of forest biodiversity. Using the FIA dataset of the eastern United States only, Woodall *et al.* (2011) found no overall response of live or dead tree above-ground carbon to decreasing 'species composition purity ratio' (i.e. with increasing tree species richness). However, by using the mean 99th percentile of tree carbon, they could show that for many tree species assemblages an increase of tree diversity increased maximum carbon storage. They conclude that this result highlights the opportunity to increase yields or other functions such as C-storage by identifying particular combinations of species that outperform pure stands. Analysing an even smaller subset of the US FIA dataset, Moser and Hansen (2009) found opposing diversity effects in two contrasting forest types in one ecoregion: while an increase in Shannon diversity resulted in lower tree growth in aspen forests growing in more northerly and colder sites, the opposite effect was found for sugar maple–beech–yellow birch forests growing in warmer regions, indicating that diversity effects can be highly dependent on species composition or site conditions. Vilà (2004) could isolate a residual positive effect of diversity on litter carbon stocks of Spanish forests, but found no effect on productivity. Vilà *et al.* (2003, 2005, 2007) observed increasing wood production with increasing tree species richness in Catalonian forests with different independent datasets (with 2107, 5069 and 10 644 plots), at least in early successional stages. However, once the confounding effects of environmental and structural variables were included, either the positive diversity–productivity correlation was no longer significant, or the variability explained by diversity was very low. More recently, Paquette and Messier (2010) analysed 12 324 plots in boreal and temperate bioclimatic domains of Québec, eastern Canada. For the first time, this study revealed strong, positive and significant effects of tree diversity on productivity after climatic and environmental variables were controlled for. Using multi-sample structural equation modelling (SEM), the authors demonstrated that the diversity effects were mainly mediated through functional differences among species, especially in the more stressful boreal environments. They concluded that complementary resource use may also operate in long-lived forest communities, especially in less productive systems. In contrast, competitive exclusion and dominance of particular species may prevail under more favourable and stable conditions, leading to only weak or no diversity–productivity relationships. Additionally, the authors proposed that a reduced span of functional diversity among species growing in more fertile sites, i.e. a higher degree of functional redundancy, may also reduce the possibility of detecting any diversity effects in such forests. A very recent study by Gamfeldt *et al.* (2013) reported that multiple ecosystem services, such as production of tree biomass, soil carbon storage, berry production, game production, understorey plant species richness and presence of dead wood were all positive to positively hump-shaped related to tree species richness in Swedish production forests.

Such inventory analyses can capitalise on the huge number of permanent monitoring plots existing in many countries. Working with and interpreting inventory-based analyses also provides a good opportunity for fruitful co-operations between scientists from ecology and forestry. However, the effects of a large number of covariables must be statistically disentangled (Vilà *et al.* 2005). In addition, tree diversity is only a 'by-product' because the selection of plots has not been based on a diversity criterion, but rather on representativeness of forest types, or on grid-based sampling schemes. Hence, there is a strong sampling bias in low-diversity stands (see e.g. Vilà *et al.* 2007). Comparison of results obtained from different inventories is sometimes difficult because different monitoring designs are in use, e.g. plot-based versus plot-less designs. Finally, based on personal experiences, access to data is not as easy as one would expect, with several inventory-specific legal or administrative restrictions. Nevertheless, this wealth of information should be more rigorously used in BEF research, and the study by Paquette and Messier (2010) provides an excellent framework for the analysis of such large datasets and the inclusion of confounding variables. Up to now, these inventory studies even reveal the strongest and most consistent pattern of tree diversity effects: there is accumulating evidence for a general positive relationship between tree species richness and productivity (Table 8.2).

Comparative studies    Comparative studies analysing relationships between tree diversity and ecosystem function are surprisingly scarce (Table 8.3), although they offer the advantage of comparing complex communities under natural conditions. More importantly, there is currently no systematic set-up of observational studies allowing the quantification of the biodiversity–ecosystem functioning relationship in forests.

Results from a first case study in central European beech forests (Leuschner, Jungkunst & Fleck 2009) show that increasing the number of tree species from pure beech to five-species mixtures has variable effects on different ecosystems functions. For example, total standing aboveground biomass was negatively related to tree diversity (Jacob, Leuschner & Thomas 2010a), while root biomass remained unaffected (Meinen, Hertel & Leuschner 2009a), although root production and thus turnover rates were higher in diverse stands

**Table 8.3** *Examples of observational/comparative studies on BEF relationships in natural forests, published since 2005.*

| Reference | Biome | Ecosystem variables | Diversity gradient (tree species richness) | Diversity effects | Direction of effects |
|---|---|---|---|---|---|
| Cesarz et al. 2007 | Temperate | Earthworm diversity and density | 1, 3, 5 | * | ↗ |
| Mölder, Bernhardt-Römermann & Schmidt 2008 | Temperate | Herb-layer diversity | 1, 3, 5 | * | ↗ |
| Schuldt et al. 2008 | Temperate | Spider diversity | 1, 3, 5 | – | |
| Guckland et al. 2009a | Temperate | Litter production | 1, 3, 5 | – | |
| Guckland et al. 2009a | Temperate | Soil nutrients | 1, 3, 5 | * | ↘ |
| Guckland et al. 2009a | Temperate | Organic carbon in humus layer | 1, 3, 5 | * | ↗ |
| Guckland, Flessa & Prenzel 2009b | Temperate | Methane uptake | 1, 3, 5 | – | |
| Meinen, Hertel & Leuschner 2009a | Temperate | Root standing biomass | 1, 3, 5 | – | |
| Meinen, Hertel & Leuschner 2009b | Temperate | Root production and turnover | 1, 3, 5 | * | ↗ |
| Sobek et al. 2009a | Temperate | Leaf damage on beech | 1, 3, 5 | * | ↗ |
| Sobek et al. 2009a | Temperate | Galls and mines frequency | 1, 3, 5 | – | |
| Sobek et al. 2009a | Temperate | Predator diversity | 1, 3, 5 | */– | ↗ |
| Sobek et al. 2009b | Temperate | Beetle diversity | 1, 3, 5 | * | ↗ |
| Sobek et al. 2009c | Temperate | Abundance of bees and wasps | 1, 3, 5 | * | ↗ |
| Talkner et al. 2009 | Temperate | Phosphorus pools | 1, 3, 5 | * | ↗ |
| Talkner et al. 2009 | Temperate | P turnover rates | 1, 3, 5 | * | ↗ |
| Krämer & Hölscher 2009 | Temperate | Throughfall | 1, 3, 5 | * | ↗ |
| Krämer & Hölscher 2009 | Temperate | Stemflow | 1, 3, 5 | * | ↗ |
| Krämer & Hölscher 2009 | Temperate | Interception | 1, 3, 5 | – | |
| Guckland, Corre & Flessa 2010 | Temperate | Mineral nitrogen production | 1, 3, 5 | * | ↗ |
| Guckland, Corre & Flessa 2010 | Temperate | Soil N$_2$O production | 1, 3, 5 | * | ↗ |
| Jacob, Leuschner & Thomas 2010a | Temperate | Tree aboveground productivity | 1, 3, 5 | * | ↗ |
| Jacob et al. 2010b | Temperate | Litter decomposition | 1, 3, 5 | – | |

Table 8.3 (cont.)

| Reference | Biome | Ecosystem variables | Diversity gradient (tree species richness) | Diversity effects | Direction of effects |
|---|---|---|---|---|---|
| Ruiz–Jaen & Potvin 2010 | Tropical | Tree carbon storage | 30–61 | * | ↗ |
| Schuldt et al. 2010 | Subtropical | Herbivory | 25–69 | * | ↗ |
| Thoms et al. 2010 | Temperate | Soil microbial diversity | 1, 3, 5 | – | |
| Both et al. 2011 | Subtropical | Herb-layer productivity | 25–69 | – | |
| Brassard et al. 2011 | Boreal | Root productivity | 1, 3 | * | ↗ |
| Haas et al. 2011 | Subtropical | Pathogen infection | 1–12 | * | ↘ |
| Lang & Polle 2011 | Temperate | Root cation and S concentrations | 1, 3, 5 | * | ↗ |
| Lang & Polle 2011 | Temperate | Root N and P concentrations | 1, 3, 5 | – | |
| Lang & Polle 2011 | Temperate | Ectomycorrhizal fungal diversity | 1, 3, 5 | * | |
| Schuldt et al. 2011 | Subtropical | Spider abundance and diversity | 25–69 | * | ↗ |
| Schuldt et al. 2011 | Subtropical | Spider foraging guild richness | 25–69 | * | ↗ |
| Vockenhuber et al. 2011 | Temperate | Herb-layer diversity | 2–9 | * | ↗ |
| Zeng et al. 2011 | Subtropical | Genetic diversity of understorey shrub | 39–69 | – | |
| Schuldt et al. 2012 | Subtropical | Spider assemblages structure | 25–69 | – | |
| Brassard et al. 2013 | Boreal | Fine root productivity | 1–4 | – | |
| Brassard et al. 2013 | Boreal | Fine root productivity | Evenness | * | ↗ |

* Significant effects with $p < 0.05$
– No effects with $p > 0.1$
↗ Positive diversity effects
↘ Negative diversity effects

(Meinen, Hertel & Leuschner 2009b). The latter finding was recently confirmed for mixed stands in boreal forests (Brassard *et al.* 2011, 2013). Positive associations with tree diversity were found for herb-layer diversity (Mölder, Bernhardt-Römermann & Schmidt 2008), beetle diversity (Sobek *et al.* 2009b), earthworm diversity (Cesarz *et al.* 2007), predator diversity during some phenological stages (Sobek *et al.* 2009a), and abundance of pollinators and predatory wasps and their natural enemies (Sobek *et al.* 2009c). No diversity effects, in contrast, were observed for spider diversity (Schuldt *et al.* 2008), the presence of galls and mines (Sobek *et al.* 2009a), soil microbial diversity (Thoms *et al.* 2010), ectomycorrhizal fungal diversity (Lang & Polle 2011) or methane uptake (Guckland, Flessa & Prenzel 2009b). Aspects of nutrient cycling also showed mixed results: with increasing tree species richness and decreasing abundance of beech, litter decomposition remained constant (Jacob *et al.* 2010b), whereas organically bound P pool sizes (Talkner *et al.* 2009), annual $N_2O$ and mineral nitrogen production increased (Guckland, Corre & Flessa 2010), although the latter was confounded with the clay content of the soil. Phosphorus-turnover times in organic surface layers were shorter in mixed than in pure beech stands, presumably influenced by the presence of certain tree species. Stand-level concentrations of cations in roots were also higher in mixed communities (Lang & Polle 2011), along with a generally increased overall nutrient availability (Guckland *et al.* 2009a). These examples from that study site clearly showed that the identity and abundance of the tree species present are the major determinants of the processes under study, associated with a 'dilution' of beech with increasing species richness. In addition, covariation of some soil properties with tree diversity makes it difficult to distinguish direct diversity effects on processes from those mediated by the environment. Subsequent studies in the same area, but with a different sampling design (see Leuschner, Jungkunst & Fleck 2009) essentially supported the abovementioned results: tree diversity explains some variation in several ecosystem functions and processes, together with environmental factors and tree species identity (e.g. Vockenhuber *et al.* 2011).

A similar, integrated observational study was recently established in the extremely diverse subtropical forests of China, with 27 comparative study plots differing in tree diversity and successional stage (Bruelheide *et al.* 2011). First results indicate that herb-layer productivity (Both *et al.* 2011), genetic diversity of an understorey shrub (Zeng *et al.* 2011), and spider assemblage structure and variability (Schuldt *et al.* 2012) were not affected by tree diversity, while herbivory increased with tree diversity, supporting the 'associational susceptibility hypothesis' (Schuldt *et al.* 2010). In contrast, the 'enemies hypothesis', which predicts higher predator abundance and diversity with increasing plant diversity, could not be supported as spider abundance and richness rather decreased with increasing tree diversity (Schuldt *et al.* 2011).

Similar results were found in a large-scale study in mixed evergreen and redwood forests in California, USA: increasing tree species diversity resulted in lower infection risk with an invasive pathogen (*Phytophthora ramorum*), which is in line with a dilution effect where risk is reduced with increasing diversity owing to lower competency of alternative hosts (Haas *et al.* 2011). In tropical Panama, Ruiz-Jaen and Potvin (2010) showed that species richness accounted for a larger portion of the variability in tree carbon storage (19%) than abiotic variables (1%) or spatial patterns (13%), despite large differences in spatial and environmental conditions. In addition to richness, dominance of species was also responsible for the observed effects.

Such observational and comparative approaches explicitly incorporate environmental variation into the study design because of inevitable abiotic differences between the sampled sites, thus 'moving functional biodiversity research to the real world' (Solan *et al.* 2009). As a consequence, such across-habitat or across-locality comparisons have to explicitly include site conditions as covariables in order to detect any potential effects that diversity exhibits within a site (Scherer-Lorenzen 2005; Schmid & Hector, 2004; Vilà *et al.* 2005). Careful selection of study sites according to pre-defined criteria related to the underlying cause of diversity differences (e.g. soil types and hydrological conditions) is crucial (Leuschner, Jungkunst & Fleck 2009). Nevertheless, 'no other approach is suitable (i) for dealing explicitly with adult trees, (ii) for addressing stands with a near-natural canopy and root system architecture, (iii) for investigating stands with an intact food web structure, and (iv) for measuring stocks of carbon and nutrients in soil and biomass at a quasi steady-state' (Leuschner, Jungkunst & Fleck, 2009, p. 4). Thus, this approach certainly maximises representativity and the applicability for ecosystem managers. As drawbacks, the potential role of site history and past management must be considered, as well as the practical difficulty of finding suitable species combinations to fulfil all criteria (Leuschner, Jungkunst & Fleck 2009).

Overall, dealing with observational data can be very challenging when it comes to building a model, because of the many confounding – known or unknown – variables. In addition, standard analysis approaches such as step-wise regression may produce misleading results from observational analyses that would not be repeatable because of model selection uncertainty (Burnham & Anderson 2002).

### 8.3.2.4 Modelling approaches
As in many other fields of ecology, modelling and simulation approaches are also a valuable tool for BEF research, and they have helped greatly in sharpening the ideas of underlying mechanisms (see e.g. Loreau 1998; Mouquet, Moore & Loreau 2002; Pacala & Tilman 2002; Tilman, Lehman & Thomson

1997; Yachi & Loreau 1999). Surprisingly, few modelling efforts have been done so far concerning the BEF relationships in forest ecosystems. Bunker *et al.* (2005), for example, performed a simulation study with different extinction scenarios on effects on carbon storage in tropical rainforest communities, resulting in very different relationships between diversity and C-storage depending on the traits of species lost. Applying the forest succession model FORCLIM, Morin *et al.* (2011) showed that tree species richness promotes productivity in European temperate forests across a large climatic gradient, mostly through strong complementarity for light use between species. These examples show that by using several different modelling tools, such as forest growth models, process-based succession models, structural equation modelling or mixed-effect models, it should be possible to gain a more mechanistic understanding of potential diversity effects in forests (e.g. Bolker *et al.* 1995; Pacala & Deutschman 1995). As a new challenge ahead, we should try to mechanistically link forest models with global change models, with the aim of predicting global forest biodiversity–ecosystem functioning relationships under different global change scenarios.

### 8.3.2.5 *Multidisciplinarity and multifunctionality studies*

A single approach to studying the functional significance of biodiversity is insufficient, especially in forest ecosystems with their complex structure and longevity. Different approaches have their advantages and disadvantages, maximising either 'orthogonality', 'comprehensiveness' or 'representativity', *sensu* Nadrowski, Wirth and Scherer-Lorenzen (2010). Thus, significant advances in understanding the diversity-functioning relationship in forests depend on studies that carefully disentangle the interactions between site quality, stand origin, management, and different measures of diversity and function (Scherer-Lorenzen *et al.* 2005b), combining and integrating different scientific approaches. For example, in a recent meta-analysis of studies that examined mixing effects of different tree species (although including many studies with only two species grown in pure and mixed stands), Zhang *et al.* (2012) showed that polycultures generally had almost 25% higher productivity than monocultures. Interestingly, they could demonstrate that different measures of diversity (evenness and species richness), stand age and heterogeneity of some life history traits (shade tolerance) substantially explained the observed variation in productivity. Variation in other traits (nitrogen fixation, growth habits), biome and stand origin (planted versus naturally established), in contrast, had only negligible effects.

Equally important is a focus on forest multifunctionality. It has been shown that biodiversity effects differ among different functions, and that higher levels of biodiversity are required to deliver several ecosystem services simultaneously under different environmental conditions, times and places

(Gamfeldt, Hillebrand & Jonsson 2008; Hector & Bagchi 2007; Isbell *et al.* 2011; Zavaleta *et al.* 2010). As forest ecosystems provide a multitude of functions and services, it is thus desirable to simultaneously measure as many variables as possible, such as carbon sequestration, water cycling, nutrient retention, habitat provision and timber production.

An example of such an integrating venture is the European project FunDivEUROPE (Functional significance of forest biodiversity in Europe: see www.fundiveurope.eu), which combines the analysis of several tree diversity experiments with the set-up and monitoring of comparative study plots differing in tree diversity in six European forest types, complemented by an in-depth analysis of forest inventory datasets and modelling approaches. Since European forests are relatively species-poor, it would be extremely helpful for our understanding of functional biodiversity effects in forests, if similar and complementing projects with a focus on multidisciplinarity and multifunctionality could be initiated in other regions of the globe, especially in highly diverse temperate, subtropical or tropical biomes.

## 8.4  Conclusions

In the past few years, interest in the effects of forest biodiversity on ecosystem functioning has strongly increased, and several studies have reported a large number of responses to changing tree diversity. Following this review, a few key conclusions can be drawn:

- Species identity and the functional traits of dominant tree species often have strong impact on ecosystem functions. However, functional differences between tree species are the basis for any relationship between biodiversity and ecosystem processes, emphasising the value of trait-based approaches for understanding the biotic control of ecosystem processes, because of the potential causal link between traits, niche differentiation and ecosystem processes. Traits, however, are not static, and intraspecific variability and phenotypic plasticity should be taken into account.
- Tree diversity influences ecosystems functioning to variable extents, but some trends are now obvious: tree growth and biomass production as well as the abundance and diversity of associated organisms are often positively associated with increasing tree diversity. Other ecological functions and processes, such as those related to biogeochemical cycling, seem to be less sensitive to changes in tree diversity and are more strongly controlled by site conditions, especially in observational studies. Hence, a careful quantification of confounding variables, in combination with structural equation modelling or redundancy analyses, provides a tool to statistically analyse BEF relations and to separate diversity effects from those mediated by the environment or management.

- Species interactions leading to complementarity, facilitation and other mechanisms determining resilience are likely to be important in forest ecosystems. Mixtures composed of shade-tolerant and shade-intolerant species appear to be those with highest niche occupancy. Nevertheless, experimental tests and rigorous quantification of such mechanisms in diverse forest ecosystems are extremely scarce.

Areas in need of further research and development include:

- Documenting BEF relationships in natural forests, along gradients of species loss.
- Enforcing the important role of long term, continuous studies giving the longevity of forest ecosystems.
- Developing further the experimental platforms for BEF research in forests (such as TreeDivNet), especially taking functional diversity into account (e.g. Baraloto *et al.* 2010).
- Studying the role of genetic, functional, structural and landscape diversity for ecosystem functioning, to complement the current focus on species diversity, including evenness as an important aspect of diversity in the study designs.
- Adapting and using different modelling tools to mechanistically analyse BEF patterns and to predict changes of these patterns under global change scenarios.
- Elucidating the underlying mechanisms of BEF relationships, including at the individual tree level.
- Identifying and quantifying functional response and effect traits of trees, to understand the response of forests to environmental change, and to support the search for BEF mechanisms.
- Enlarging the BEF concept to multi-trophic interactions within forests, with the mutual dependencies between the producer, consumer and decomposer subsystems.
- Integrating the role of spatial patterns in determining BEF relationships, both at the individual (e.g. canopy stratification, neighbour interactions) and the ecosystem scale (e.g. patch dynamics).
- Identifying potential trade-offs between mixture effects, including several different functions and services that forest ecosystems provide (i.e. multifunctionality).
- Developing further the knowledge base that underpins the domestication and cultivation of tree species, which may result in the development of commercial mixtures of species with 'good ecological combining abilities' (*sensu* Harper 1977).
- Developing new silvicultural options for mixed-species stands that implement forest biodiversity as an element of adaptation strategies.

- Promoting knowledge transfer between different stake-holders involved: ecologists, silviculturalists, foresters, ecosystem or forest managers, and the local communities.

I hope that this review has shown that the study of biodiversity–ecosystem functioning relationships in forests is a dynamic, interesting and important field of research, with many open questions still to be resolved. In the face of ongoing global changes, knowledge about changes in forest biodiversity, their functional consequences and their impacts on the delivery of ecosystem services (Figure 8.1) is crucial for the conservation and sustainable use of these ecosystems that control a large portion of the global biogeochemical cycles, harbour a myriad of species and are so important for human society.

## Acknowledgements

I am grateful to David Coomes (Cambridge) and David Burslem (Aberdeen) for their kind invitation to present ideas about the diversity–ecosystem functioning relationship in forest ecosystems at the 2011 Symposium 'Forests and Global Change' of the British Ecological Society. I also thank the BES for its financial support. Many of the ideas presented here were discussed in depth with the members of the research projects FunDivEUROPE, BACCARA, BIOTREE and BEF China, and of the TreeDivNet community; and I am especially grateful to Christian Wirth (Leipzig), Kris Verheyen (Ghent), Jürgen Bauhus (Freiburg), Bart Muys (Leuven), Hervé Jactel (Bordeaux), Catherin Potvin (Montreal), Andy Hector (Zurich), Julia Koricheva (London), Helge Bruelheide (Halle), Markus Fischer (Bern) and Ernst-Detlef Schulze (Jena), among many others. I also acknowledge helpful comments by A. Hector, C. E. T. Paine, J. Chamagre and one anonymous reviewer on an earlier version of this paper. FunDivEUROPE and BACCARA are funded within the 7th Framework Programme of the European Commission (contracts 265171 and 226299, respectively). BEF China is funded by the German Science Foundation (DFG FOR 891) and the National Science Foundation of China (NSFC 30710103907 and 30930005).

## References

Aarssen, L. W. (1997) High productivity in grassland ecosystems: effects by species diversity or productive species? *Oikos*, **80**, 183–184.

Balvanera, P., Pfisterer, A. B., Buchmann, N. *et al.* (2006) Quantifying the evidence for biodiversity effects on ecosystem functioning and services. *Ecology Letters*, **9**, 1146–1156.

Baraloto, C., Marcon, E., Morneau, F. O., Pavoine, S. & Roggy, J.-C. (2010) Integrating functional diversity into tropical forest plantation designs to study ecosystem processes. *Annals of Forest Science*, **67**, 303.

Bauhus, J. & Schmerbeck, J. (2010) Silvicultural options to enhance and use forest plantation biodiversity. In *Ecosystem Goods and Services from Plantation Forests* (eds.

J. Bauhus, P. van der Meer & M. Kanninen), pp. 96–139. London, Washington, DC: Earthscan.

Bolker, B. M., Pacala, S. W., Bazzaz, F. A., Canham, C. D. & Levin, S. A. (1995) Species diversity and ecosystem response to carbon dioxide fertilization: conclusions from a temperate forest model. *Global Change Biology*, **1**, 373–381.

Bormann, F. H., Likens, G. E., Fisher, D. W. & Pierce, R. S. (1968) Nutrient loss accelerated by clear-cutting of a forest ecosystem. *Science*, **159**, 882.

Both, S., Fang, T., Baruffol, M. *et al.* (2012) Effects of tree sapling diversity and nutrient addition on herb-layer invasibility in communities of subtropical species. *Open Journal of Ecology*, **2**, 1–11.

Both, S., Fang, T., Böhnke, M. *et al.* (2011) Lack of tree layer control on herb layer characteristics in a subtropical forest, China. *Journal of Vegetation Science*, **22**, 1120–1131.

Brassard, B. W., Chen, H. Y. H., Bergeron, Y. & Pare, D. (2011) Differences in fine root productivity between mixed- and single-species stands. *Functional Ecology*, **25**, 238–246.

Brassard, B. W., Chen, H. Y. H., Cavard, X. *et al.* (2013) Tree species diversity increases fine root productivity through increased soil volume filling. *Journal of Ecology* **101**, 210–219.

Bruelheide, H., Böhnke, M., Both, S. *et al.* (2011) Community assembly during secondary forest succession in a Chinese subtropical forest. *Ecological Monographs*, **81**, 25–41.

Bunker, D. E., DeClerck, F., Bradford, J. C. *et al.* (2005) Species loss and aboveground carbon storage in a tropical forest. *Science*, **310**, 1029–1031.

Burnham, K. P. & Anderson, D. R. (2002) *Model Selection and Multimodel Inference: A Practical Information-Theoretic Approach*. New York: Springer.

Cannell, M. G. R., Malcolm, D. C. & Robertson, P. A. (1992) *The Ecology of Mixed-Species Stands of Trees*. Oxford: Blackwell Scientific Publications.

Cardinale, B. J., Matulich, K. L., Hooper, D. U. *et al.* (2011) The functional role of producer diversity in ecosystems. *American Journal of Botany*, **98**, 572–592.

Cardinale, B. J., Srivastava, D. S., Duffy, E. *et al.* (2006) Effects of biodiversity on the functioning of trophic groups and ecosystems. *Nature*, **443**, 989–992.

Cardinale, B. J., Wright, J. P., Cadotte, M. W. *et al.* (2007) Impacts of plant diversity on biomass production increase through time because of species complementarity. *Proceedings of the National Academy of Sciences USA*, **104**, 18123–18128.

Caspersen, J. P. & Pacala, S. W. (2001) Successional diversity and forest ecosystem function. *Ecological Research*, **16**, 895–903.

Cavard, X., Macdonald, S. E., Bergeron, Y. & Chen, H. Y. H. (2011) Importance of mixedwoods for biodiversity conservation: Evidence for understory plants, songbirds, soil fauna, and ectomycorrhizae in northern forests. *Environmental Review*, **19**, 142–161.

Cesarz, S., Fahrenholz, N., Migge-Kleian, S., Platner, C. & Schaefer, M. (2007) Earthworm communities in relation to tree diversity in a deciduous forest. *European Journal of Soil Biology*, **43**, S61–S67.

Cotta, J. H. (1828) *Anweisung zum Waldbau*. Dresden, Leipzig: Arnoldische Buchhandlung.

Daily, G. C. (1997) *Nature's Services – Societal Dependence on Natural Ecosystems*. Washington DC, Covelo: Island Press.

de Groot, R. S., Alkemadeb, R., Braatc, L., Heina, L. & Willemen, L. (2010) Challenges in integrating the concept of ecosystem services and values in landscape planning, management and decision making. *Ecological Complexity*, **7**, 260–272.

Dhôte, J.-F. (2005) Implication of forest diversity in resistance to strong winds. In *Forest Diversity and Function: Temperate and Boreal Systems* (eds. M. Scherer-Lorenzen,

C. Körner & E.-D. Schulze), pp. 291–307. Berlin, Heidelberg, New York: Springer.

Díaz, S., Symstad, A.J., Stuart Chapin, I.F., Wardle, D.A. & Huenneke, L.F. (2003) Functional diversity revealed by removal experiments. *Trends in Ecology & Evolution*, **18**, 140–146.

Díaz, S., Wardle, D.A. & Hector, A. (2009) Incorporating biodiversity in climate change mitigation initiatives. *Biodiversity, Ecosystem Functioning, and Human Wellbeing: An Ecological and Economic Perspective* (eds. S. Naeem, D.E. Bunker, A. Hector, M. Loreau & C. Perrings), pp. 149–166. Oxford: Oxford University Press.

Don, A., Arenhövel, W., Jacob, R., Scherer-Lorenzen, M. & Schulze, E.-D. (2007) Anwuchserfolg von 19 verschiedenen Baumarten bei Erstaufforstungen – Ergebnisse eines Biodiversitätsexperiments. *Allgemeine Jagd- und Forstzeitung*, **178**, 164–172.

Enquist, B.J. & Niklas, K.J. (2001) Invariant scaling relations across tree-dominated communities. *Nature*, **410**, 655–660.

Erskine, P.D., Lamb, D. & Bristow, M. (2006) Tree species diversity and ecosystem function: Can tropical multi-species plantations generate greater productivity? *Forest Ecology and Management*, **233**, 205–210.

Ewel, J.J. & Mazzarino, M.J. (2008) Competition from below for light and nutrients shifts productivity among tropical species. *Proceedings of the National Academy of Sciences USA*, **105**, 18836–18841.

Ewel, J.J., Mazzarino, M.J. & Berish, C.W. (1991) Tropical soil fertility changes under monocultures and successional communities of different structure. *Ecological Applications*, **1**, 289–302.

Firn, J., Erskine, P.D. & Lamb, D. (2007) Woody species diversity influences productivity and nutrient availability in tropical plantations. *Oecologia* **154**, 521–533.

Forrester, D.I., Bauhus, J., Cowie, A.L. & Vanclay, J.K. (2006) Mixed-species plantations of *Eucalyptus* with nitrogen-fixing trees: a review. *Forest Ecology and Management*, **233**, 211–230.

Forrester, D.I., Theiveyanathan, S., Collopy, J.J. & Marcar, N.E. (2010) Enhanced water use efficiency in a mixed *Eucalyptus globulus* and *Acacia mearnsii* plantation. *Forest Ecology and Management*, **259**, 1761–1770.

Gamfeldt, L., Hillebrand, H. & Jonsson, P.R. (2008) Multiple functions increase the importance of biodiversity for overall ecosystem functioning. *Ecology*, **89**, 1223–1231.

Gamfeldt, L., Snall, T., Bagchi, R. *et al.* (2013) Higher levels of multiple ecosystem services are found in forests with more tree species. *Nature Communications* **4**, 1340.

Gayer, K. (1886) *Der gemischte Wald, seine Begründung und Pflege, insbesondere durch Horst- und Gruppenwirtschaft.* Berlin: Paul Parey.

Geißler, C., Lang, A.C., von Oheimb, G. *et al.* (2012) Impact of tree saplings on the kinetic energy of rainfall – The importance of stand density, species identity and tree architecture in subtropical forests in China. *Agricultural and Forest Meteorology*, **156**, 31–40.

Guckland, A., Brauns, M., Flessa, H., Thomas, F.M. & Leuschner, C. (2009a) Acidity, nutrient stocks and organic matter content in soils of a temperate deciduous forest with different abundance of European beech (*Fagus sylvatica* L.). *Journal of Plant Nutrition and Soil Science*, **172**, 500–511.

Guckland, A., Corre, M.D. & Flessa, H. (2010) Variability of soil N cycling and N2O emission in a mixed deciduous forest with different abundance of beech. *Plant and Soil*, **336**, 25–38.

Guckland, A., Flessa, H. & Prenzel, J. (2009b) Controls of temporal and spatial variability of methane uptake in soils of a temperate deciduous forest with different abundance of European beech (*Fagus sylvatica* L.). *Soil Biology & Biochemistry*, **41**, 1659–1667.

Haas, S.E., Hooten, M.B., Rizzo, D.M. & Meentemeyer, R.K. (2011) Forest species diversity reduces disease risk in a generalist plant pathogen invasion. *Ecology Letters*, **14**, 1108–1116.

Harper, J. L. (1977) *Population Biology of Plants*. London: Academic Press.

Hartig, G. L. (1791) *Anweisung zur Holzzucht für Förster*. Marburg: Neue Akademische Buchhandlung.

Hartig, G. L. (1804) *Anweisung zur Taxation und Beschreibung der Forste*. Gießen: Heyer.

Hättenschwiler, S. (2005) Effects of tree species diversity on litter quality and decomposition. *Forest Diversity and Function. Temperate and Boreal Systems* (eds. M. Scherer-Lorenzen, C. Körner & E.-D. Schulze), pp. 149–164. Berlin, Heidelberg, New York: Springer.

Healy, C., Gotelli, N. J. & Potvin, C. (2008) Partitioning the effects of biodiversity and environmental heterogeneity for productivity and mortality in a tropical tree plantation. *Journal of Ecology*, **96**, 903–913.

Hector, A. & Bagchi, R. (2007) Biodiversity and ecosystem multifunctionality. *Nature*, **446**, 188–190.

Hector, A. & Hooper, R. (2002) Darwin and the first ecological experiment. *Science*, **295**, 639–640.

Hector, A., Philipson, C., Saner, P. *et al.* (2011) The Sabah Biodiversity Experiment: a long-term test of the role of tree diversity in restoring tropical forest structure and functioning. *Philosophical Transactions of the Royal Society B: Biological Sciences*, **366**, 3303–3315.

Hillebrand, H. & Matthiessen, B. (2009) Biodiversity in a complex world: consolidation and progress in functional biodiversity research. *Ecology Letters*, **12**, 1405–1419.

Hooper, D. U., Adair, E. C., Cardinale, B. J. *et al.* (2012) A global synthesis reveals biodiversity loss as a major driver of ecosystem change. *Nature*, **486**, 105–108.

Hooper, D. U., Chapin, F. S. I., Ewel, J. J. *et al.* (2005) Effects of biodiversity on ecosystem functioning: a consensus of current knowledge and needs for future research. *Ecological Monographs*, **75**, 3–36.

Hubbell, S. P. (2006) Neutral theory and the evolution of ecological equivalence. *Ecology*, **87**, 1387–1398.

Huston, M. A. (1997) Hidden treatments in ecological experiments: re-evaluating the ecosystem function of biodiversity. *Oecologia*, **110**, 449–460.

Huxham, M., Kumara, M. P., Jayatissa, L. P. *et al.* (2010) Intra- and interspecific facilitation in mangroves may increase resilience to climate change threats. *Philosophical Transactions of the Royal Society B: Biological Sciences*, **365**, 2127–2135.

Isbell, F., Calcagno, V., Hector, A. *et al.* (2011) High plant diversity is needed to maintain ecosystem services. *Nature*, **477**, 199–202.

Jacob, M., Leuschner, C. & Thomas, F. M. (2010a) Productivity of temperate broad-leaved forest stands differing in tree species diversity. *Annals of Forest Science*, **67**, 503.

Jacob, M., Viedenz, K., Polle, A. & Thomas, F. (2010b) Leaf litter decomposition in temperate deciduous forest stands with a decreasing fraction of beech (*Fagus sylvatica*). *Oecologia* **164**, 1083–1094.

Jactel, H., Brockerhoff, E. & Duelli, P. (2005) A test of the biodiversity-stability theory: meta-analysis of tree species diversity effects on insect pest infestations, and re-examination of responsible factors. In *Forest Diversity and Function: Temperate and Boreal Systems* (eds. M. Scherer-Lorenzen, C. Körner & E.-D. Schulze), pp. 235–262. Berlin, Heidelberg, New York: Springer.

Jones, H. E., McNamara, N. & Mason, W. L. (2005) Functioning of mixed-species stands: evidence from a long-term experiment. *Forest Diversity and Function. Temperate and Boreal Systems* (eds. M. Scherer-Lorenzen, C. Körner & E.-D. Schulze), pp. 111–130. Berlin, Heidelberg, New York: Springer.

Kelty, M. J. & Cameron, I. R. (1995) Plot design for the analysis of species interactions in mixed stands. *Commenwealth Forestry Review*, **74**, 322–332.

Kelty, M. J., Larson, B. C. & Oliver, C. D. (1992) *The Ecology and Silviculture of Mixed-Species*

*Forests*. Dordrecht, Boston, London. Kluwer Academic Publishers.

Kinzig, A. P., Pacala, S. W. & Tilman, D. (2002) The functional consequences of biodiversity: Empirical progress and theoretical extensions. In *Monographs in Population Biology* (eds. S. A. Levin & H. S. Horn), p. 365. Princeton, Oxford: Princeton University Press.

Kirui, B., Huxham, M., Kairo, J. & Skov, M. (2008) Influence of species richness and environmental context on early survival of replanted mangroves at Gazi Bay, Kenya. *Hydrobiologia* **603**, 171–181.

Koricheva, J., Vehviläinen, H., Riimaki, J. *et al.* (2006) Diversification of tree stands as a means to manage pests and diseases in boreal forests: Myth or reality? *Canadian Journal of Forest Research*, **36**, 324–336.

Körner, C. (2005) An introduction to the functional diversity of temperate forest trees. *Forest Diversity and Function. Temperate and Boreal Systems* (eds. M. Scherer-Lorenzen, C. Körner & E.-D. Schulze), pp. 13–38. Berlin, Heidelberg, New York: Springer.

Krämer, I. & Hölscher, D. (2009) Rainfall partitioning along a tree diversity gradient in a deciduous old-growth forest in Central Germany. *Ecohydrology* **2**, 102–114.

Laliberté, E. & Legendre, P. (2010) A distance-based framework for measuring functional diversity from multiple traits. *Ecology*, **91**, 299–305.

Lang, A. C., Härdtle, W., Baruffol, M. *et al.* (2012) Mechanisms promoting tree species co-existence: Experimental evidence with saplings of subtropical forest ecosystems of China. *Journal of Vegetation Science*, **23**, 837–846.

Lang, C. & Polle, A. (2011) Ectomycorrhizal fungal diversity, tree diversity and root nutrient relations in a mixed Central European forest. *Tree Physiology*, **31**, 531–538.

Lawton, J. H. & Brown, V. K. (1993) Redundancy in ecosystems. In *Biodiversity and Ecosystem Function* (eds. E.-D. Schulze & H. A. Mooney),

pp. 255–270. Berlin, Heidelberg, New York: Springer.

Lei, P., Scherer-Lorenzen, M. & Bauhus, J. (2012a) Belowground facilitation and competition in young tree species mixtures. *Forest Ecology and Management*, **265**, 191–200.

Lei, P., Scherer-Lorenzen, M. & Bauhus, J. (2012b) The effect of tree species diversity on fine-root production in a young temperate forest. *Oecologia*, **169**, 1105–1115.

Lepš, J. (2004) What do the biodiversity experiments tell us about consequences of plant species loss in the real world? *Basic and Applied Ecology*, **5**, 529–534.

Leuschner, C., Jungkunst, H. F. & Fleck, S. (2009) Functional role of forest diversity: Pros and cons of synthetic stands and across-site comparisons in established forests. *Basic and Applied Ecology*, **10**, 1–9.

Liang, J. J., Buongiorno, J., Monserud, R. A., Kruger, E. L. & Zhou, M. (2007) Effects of diversity of tree species and size on forest basal area growth, recruitment, and mortality. *Forest Ecology and Management*, **243**, 116–127.

Loreau, M. (1998) Biodiversity and ecosystem function: a mechanistic model. *Proceedings of the National Academy of Sciences USA*, **95**, 5632–5636.

Loreau, M. & Hector, A. (2001) Partitioning selection and complementarity in biodiversity experiments. *Nature*, **412**, 72–76.

Loreau, M., Naeem, S. & Inchausti, P. (2002) *Biodiversity and Ecosystem Functioning: Synthesis and Perspectives*. Oxford, New York: Oxford University Press.

Loreau, M., Naeem, S., Inchausti, P. *et al.* (2001) Biodiversity and ecosystem functioning: current knowledge and future challenges. *Science*, **294**, 804–808.

McNaughton, S. J. (1993) Biodiversity and function of grazing ecosystems. In *Biodiversity and Ecosystem Function* (eds. E.-D. Schulze & H. A. Mooney), pp. 361–383. Berlin, Heidelberg, New York: Springer.

Meinen, C., Hertel, D. & Leuschner, C. (2009a) Biomass and morphology of fine roots in temperate broad-leaved forests differing in tree species diversity: is there evidence of below-ground overyielding? *Oecologia*, **161**, 99–111.

Meinen, C., Hertel, D. & Leuschner, C. (2009b) Root growth and recovery in temperate broad-leaved forest stands differing in tree species diversity. *Ecosystems* **12**, 1103–1116.

Millennium Ecosystem Assessment (2005) *Ecosystems and Human Well-being: Biodiversity Synthesis*. Washington: World Resources Institute.

Mölder, A., Bernhardt-Römermann, M. & Schmidt, W. (2008) Herb-layer diversity in deciduous forests: raised by tree richness or beaten by beech? *Forest Ecology and Management* **256**, 272–281.

Möller, A. (1922) *Der Dauerwaldgedanke. Sein Sinn und seine Bedeutung*. Berlin: Verlag Julius Springer.

Mooney, H. A., Cushman, J. H., Medina, E., Sala, O. E. & Schulze, E.-D. (1996) *Functional Roles of Biodiversity: A Global Perspective*. Chichester, New York, Brisbane, Toronto, Singapore: John Wiley & Sons.

Mooney, H. A., Lubchenco, J., Dirzo, R. & Sala, O. E. (1995) Biodiversity and ecosystem functioning: ecosystem analyses. In *Global Biodiversity Assessment* (eds. V. H. Heywood & R. T. Watson), pp. 327–452. Cambridge: Cambridge University Press.

Morin, X., Fahse, L., Scherer-Lorenzen, M. & Bugmann, H. (2011) Tree species richness promotes productivity in temperate forests through strong complementarity between species. *Ecology Letters*, **14**, 1211–1219.

Moser, W. K. & Hansen, M. (2009) The relationship between diversity and productivity in selected forests of the Lake States Region (USA): relative impact of species versus structural diversity. In *Proceedings of the Eighth Annual Forest Inventory and Analysis Symposium 2006* (eds. R. E. McRoberts, G. A. Reams, P. C. Van Deusen & W. H. McWilliams), pp. 149–157. Washington, DC: US Department of Agriculture, Forest Service.

Mouquet, N., Moore, J. L. & Loreau, M. (2002) Plant species richness and community productivity: why the mechanism that promotes coexistence matters. *Ecology Letters*, **5**, 56–65.

Müller-Starck, G., Ziehe, M. & Schubert, R. (2005) Genetic diversity parameters associated with viability selection, reproductive efficiency, and growth in forest tree species. In *Forest Diversity and Function. Temperate and Boreal Systems* (eds. M. Scherer-Lorenzen, C. Körner & E.-D. Schulze), pp. 87–108., Berlin, Heidelberg, New York: Springer.

Murphy, M., Balser, T., Buchmann, N., Hahn, V. & Potvin, C. (2008) Linking tree biodiversity to belowground process in a young tropical plantation: Impacts on soil $CO_2$ flux. *Forest Ecology and Management*, **255**, 2577–2588.

Nadrowski, K., Wirth, C. & Scherer-Lorenzen, M. (2010) Is forest diversity driving ecosystem function and service? *Current Opinion in Environmental Sustainability*, **2**, 75–79.

Naeem, S. (2002) Ecosystem consequences of biodiversity loss: the evolution of a paradigm. *Ecology*, **83**, 1537–1552.

Naeem, S. & Bunker, D. E. (2009) TraitNet: furthering biodiversity research through the curation, discovery, and sharing of species trait data. In *Biodiversity, Ecosystem Functioning, and Human Wellbeing* (eds. S. Naeem, D. E. Bunker, A. Hector, M. Loreau & C. Perrings), pp. 281–289. Oxford: Oxford University Press.

Naeem, S., Bunker, D. E., Hector, A., Loreau, M. & Perrings, C. (eds.) (2009) *Biodiversity, Ecosystem Functioning, and Human Wellbeing*. Oxford: Oxford University Press.

Oelmann, Y., Potvin, C., Mark, T. *et al.* (2009) Tree mixture effects on aboveground nutrient pools of trees in an experimental plantation in Panama. *Plant and Soil*, **326**, 199–212.

Olsthoorn, A. F. M., Bartelink, H. H., Gardiner, J. J. *et al.* (1999) Management of mixed-species forests: silviculture and economics. In *IBN Scientific Contributions*. Wageningen: DLO Institute for Forestry and Nature Research (IBN-DLO).

Orians, G. H., Dirzo, R. & Cushman, J. H. (1996) Impact of biodiversity on tropical forest ecosystem processes. In *Functional Roles of Biodiversity: A Global Perspective* (eds. H. A. Mooney, J. H. Cushman, E. Medina, O. E. Sala & E.-D. Schulze), pp. 213–244. Chichester, New York, Brisbane: John Wiley & Sons.

Pacala, S. & Tilman, D. (2002) The transition from sampling to complementarity. In *The Functional Consequences of Biodiversity: Empirical Progress and Theoretical Extensions* (eds. A. P. Kinzig, S. W. Pacala & D. Tilman), pp. 151–166. Princeton, Oxford: Princeton University Press.

Pacala, S. W. & Deutschman, D. H. (1995) Details that matter – the spatial distribution of individual trees maintains forest ecosystem function. *Oikos*, **74**, 357–365.

Paquette, A. & Messier, C. (2010) The effect of biodiversity on tree productivity: from temperate to boreal forests. *Global Ecology and Biogeography*, **20**, 170–180.

Pastor, J., Mladenoff, D. J., Haila, Y., Bryant, J. & Payette, S. (1996) Biodiversity and ecosystem processes in boreal regions. In *Functional Roles of Biodiversity. A Global Perspective* (eds. H. A. Mooney, J. H. Cushman, E. Medina, O. E. Sala & E. D. Schulze), pp. 33–69. Chichester, New York, Brisbane: John Wiley & Sons.

Pautasso, M., Holdenrieder, O. & Stenlid, J. (2005) Susceptibility to fungal pathogens of forests differing in tree diversity. In *Forest Diversity and Function: Temperate and Boreal Systems* (eds. M. Scherer-Lorenzen, C. Körner & E.-D. Schulze), pp. 263–289. Berlin, Heidelberg, New York: Springer.

Petchey, O. L., O'Gorman, E. J. & Flynn, D. F. B. (2009) A functional guide to functional diversity measures. In *Biodiversity, Ecosystem Functioning, and Human Wellbeing* (eds. S. Naeem, D. E. Bunker, A. Hector, M. Loreau & C. Perrings), pp. 49–59. Oxford: Oxford University Press.

Piotto, D. (2008) A meta-analysis comparing tree growth in monocultures and mixed plantations. *Forest Ecology and Management*, **255**, 781–786.

Potvin, C. & Dutilleul, P. (2009) Neighborhood effects and size-asymmetric competition in a tree plantation varying in diversity. *Ecology*, **90**, 321–327.

Potvin, C. & Gotelli, N. J. (2008) Biodiversity enhances individual performance but does not affect survivorship in tropical trees. *Ecology Letters*, **11**, 217–223.

Potvin, C., Mancilla, L., Buchmann, N. *et al.* (2011) An ecosystem approach to biodiversity effects: Carbon pools in a tropical tree plantation. *Forest Ecology and Management*, **261**, 1614–1624.

Pretzsch, H. (2005) Diversity and productivity in forests: evidence from long-term experimental plots. In *Forest Diversity and Function. Temperate and Boreal Systems* (eds. M. Scherer-Lorenzen, C. Körner & E.-D. Schulze), pp. 41–64. Berlin, Heidelberg, New York: Springer.

Pretzsch, H., Block, J., Dieler, J. *et al.* (2010) Comparison between the productivity of pure and mixed stands of Norway spruce and European beech along an ecological gradient. *Annals of Forest Science*, **67**, 712.

Pretzsch, H. & Schütze, G. (2009) Transgressive overyielding in mixed compared with pure stands of Norway spruce and European beech in Central Europe: evidence on stand level and explanation on individual tree level. *European Journal of Forest Research*, **128**, 183–204.

Richards, A. E., Forrester, D. I., Bauhus, J. & Scherer-Lorenzen, M. (2010) The influence of mixed tree plantations on the nutrition of individual species: a review. *Tree Physiology*, **30**, 1192–1208.

Rothe, A. & Binkley, D. (2001) Nutritional interactions in mixed species forests: a synthesis. *Canadian Journal of Forest Research*, **31**, 1855–1870.

Ruiz-Jaen, M. C. & Potvin, C. (2010) Tree diversity explains variation in ecosystem function in a neotropical forest in Panama. *Biotropica*, **42**, 638–646.

Ruiz-Jaen, M. C. & Potvin, C. (2011) Can we predict carbon stocks in tropical ecosystems from tree diversity? Comparing species and functional diversity in a plantation and a natural forest. *New Phytologist*, **189**, 978–987.

Sala, O. E., Chapin, F. S., Armesto, J. J. *et al.* (2000) Biodiversity – Global biodiversity scenarios for the year 2100. *Science*, **287**, 1770–1774.

Scherer-Lorenzen, M. (2005) Biodiversity and ecosystem functioning: basic principles. *Biodiversity: Structure and Function*. In *Encyclopedia of Life Support Systems (EOLSS)* (eds. W. Barthlott, K. E. Linsenmair & S. Porembski). Oxford: EOLSS Publisher.

Scherer-Lorenzen, M., Bonilla, J.-L. & Potvin, C. (2007a) Tree species richness affects litter production and decomposition rates in a tropical biodiversity experiment. *Oikos*, **116**, 2108–2124.

Scherer-Lorenzen, M., Körner, C. & Schulze, E.-D. (2005a) *Forest Diversity and Function: Temperate and Boreal Systems. Ecological Studies*. Berlin, Heidelberg, New York: Springer.

Scherer-Lorenzen, M., Körner, C. & Schulze, E.-D. (2005b) The functional significance of forest diversity: a synthesis. In *Forest Diversity and Function: Temperate and Boreal Systems* (eds. M. Scherer-Lorenzen, C. Körner & E.-D. Schulze), pp. 377–389. Berlin, Heidelberg, New York: Springer.

Scherer-Lorenzen, M., Potvin, C., Koricheva, J. *et al.* (2005c) The design of experimental tree plantations for functional biodiversity research. In *Forest Diversity and Function. Temperate and Boreal Systems* (eds. M. Scherer-Lorenzen, C. Körner & E.-D. Schulze), pp. 347–376. Berlin, Heidelberg, New York: Springer.

Scherer-Lorenzen, M., Schulze, E.-D., Don, A., Schumacher, J. & Weller, E. (2007b) Exploring the functional significance of forest diversity: A new long-term experiment with temperate tree species (BIOTREE). *Perspectives in Plant Ecology, Evolution and Systematics*, **9**, 53–70.

Schmid, B. & Hector, A. (2004) The value of biodiversity experiments. *Basic and Applied Ecology*, **5**, 535–542.

Schmid, B., Hector, A., Huston, M. A. *et al.* (2002) The design and analysis of biodiversity experiments. In *Biodiversity and Ecosystem Functioning: Synthesis and Perspectives* (eds. M. Loreau, S. Naeem & P. Inchausti), pp. 61–75., Oxford, New York: Oxford University Press

Schuldt, A., Baruffol, M., Böhnke, M. *et al.* (2010) Tree diversity promotes insect herbivory in subtropical forests of south-east China. *Journal of Ecology*, **98**, 917–926.

Schuldt, A., Both, S., Bruelheide, H. *et al.* (2011) Predator diversity and abundance provide little support for the Enemies Hypothesis in forests of high tree diversity. *PLoS ONE*, **6**, e22905.

Schuldt, A., Bruelheide, H., Härdtle, W. & Assmann, T. (2012) Predator assemblage structure and temporal variability of species richness and abundance in forests of high tree diversity. *Biotropica*, **44**, 793–800.

Schuldt, A., Fahrenholz, N., Brauns, M. *et al.* (2008) Communities of ground-living spiders in deciduous forests: Does tree species diversity matter? *Biodiversity and Conservation*, **17**, 1267–1284.

Schulze, E.-D. (1989) Air pollution and forest decline in a spruce (*Picea abies*) forest. *Science*, **244**, 776–783.

Schulze, E.-D., Bazzaz, F. A., Nadelhoffer, K. J., Koike, T. & Takatsuki, S. (1996) Biodiversity and ecosystem function of temperate deciduous broad-leaved forests. In *Functional Roles of Biodiversity: A Global Perspective* (eds. H. A. Mooney, J. H. Cushman, E. Medina, O. E. Sala & E.-D. Schulze), pp. 71–98. Chichester, New York, Brisbane: John Wiley & Sons.

Schulze, E.-D. & Mooney, H. A. (1993) Biodiversity and ecosystem function. In *Ecological Studies*. Berlin, Heidelberg, New York: Springer

Snedecor, G. W. & Cochran, W. G. (1980) *Statistical Methods*. Ames, Iowa: Iowa State University Press.

Sobek, S., Scherber, C., Steffan-Dewenter, I. & Tscharntke, T. (2009a) Sapling herbivory, invertebrate herbivores and predators across a natural tree diversity gradient in Germany's largest connected deciduous forest. *Oecologia*, **160**, 279–288.

Sobek, S., Steffan-Dewenter, I., Scherber, C. & Tscharntke, T. (2009b) Spatiotemporal changes of beetle communities across a tree diversity gradient. *Diversity and Distributions*, **15**, 660–670.

Sobek, S., Tscharntke, T., Scherber, C., Schiele, S. & Steffan-Dewenter, I. (2009c) Canopy vs. understory: Does tree diversity affect bee and wasp communities and their natural enemies across forest strata? *Forest Ecology and Management*, **258**, 609–615.

Solan, M., Godbold, J. A., Symstad, A., Flynn, D. F. B. & Bunker, D. E. (2009) Biodiversity-ecosystem function research and biodiversity future: early bird catches the worm or a day late and a dollar short? In *Biodiversity, Ecosystem Functioning, and Human Wellbeing: An Ecological and Economic Perspective* (eds. S. Naeem, D. E. Bunker, A. Hector, M. Loreau & C. Perrings), pp. 30–45. Oxford: Oxford University Press.

Srivastava, D. S. & Vellend, M. (2005) Biodiversity-ecosystem function research: Is it relevant to conservation? *Annual Review of Ecology, Evolution, and Systematics*, **36**, 267–294.

Talkner, U., Jansen, M. & Beese, F. O. (2009) Soil phosphorus status and turnover in central-European beech forest ecosystems with differing tree species diversity. *European Journal of Soil Science*, **60**, 338–346.

TEEB (2009) *The Economics of Ecosystems and Biodiversity for National and International Policy Makers. Summary: Responding to the Value of Nature 2009.* Wesseling: European Communities.

Thompson, I., Mackey, B., McNulty, S. & Mosseler, A. (2009) *Forest Resilience, Biodiversity, and Climate Change. A Synthesis of the Biodiversity/Resilience/Stability Relationship in Forest Ecosystems.* Montreal: Secretariat of the Convention on Biological Diversity.

Thoms, C., Gattinger, A., Jacob, M., Thomas, F. M. & Gleixner, G. (2010) Direct and indirect effects of tree diversity drive soil microbial diversity in temperate deciduous forest. *Soil Biology & Biochemistry*, **42**, 1558–1565.

Tilman, D., Lehman, C. & Thomson, K. (1997) Plant diversity and ecosystem productivity: theoretical considerations. *Proceedings of the National Academy of Sciences USA*, **94**, 1857–1861.

Vehviläinen, H. & Koricheva, J. (2006) Moose and vole browsing patterns in experimentally assembled pure and mixed forest stands. *Ecography*, **29**, 497–506.

Vehviläinen, H., Koricheva, J. & Ruohomäki, K. (2007) Tree species diversity influences herbivore abundance and damage: meta-analysis of long-term forest experiments. *Oecologia*, **152**, 287–298.

Vehviläinen, H., Koricheva, J. & Ruohomaki, K. (2008) Effects of stand tree species composition and diversity on abundance of predatory arthropods. *Oikos*, **117**, 935–943.

Vilà, M. (2004) Biodiversity correlates with regional patterns of forest litter pools. *Oecologia*, **139**, 641–646.

Vilà, M., Inchausti, P., Vayreda, J. *et al.* (2005) Confounding factors in the observational productivity-diversity relationship in forests. In *Forest Diversity and Function. Temperate and Boreal Systems* (eds. M. Scherer-Lorenzen, C. Körner & E.-D. Schulze), pp. 65–86. Berlin, Heidelberg, New York: Springer.

Vilà, M., Vayreda, J., Comas, L. *et al.* (2007) Species richness and wood production: a positive association in Mediterranean forests. *Ecology Letters*, **10**, 241–250.

Vilà, M., Vayreda, J., Gracia, C. & Ibáñez, J. J. (2003) Does tree diversity increase wood production in pine forests? *Oecologia*, **135**, 299–303.

Vockenhuber, E. A., Scherber, C., Langenbruch, C. *et al.* (2011) Tree diversity and environmental context predict herb species richness and cover in Germany's largest connected deciduous forest. *Perspectives in Plant Ecology Evolution and Systematics*, **13**, 111–119.

von Carlowitz, H. C. (1713) *Sylvicultura oeconomica, oder hauβwirthliche Nachricht und Naturmäβige Anweisung zur wilden Baum-Zucht* Leipzig: Braun.

Wiedemann, E. (1951) *Ertragskundliche und waldbauliche Grundlagen der Forstwirtschaft*, Frankfurt/Main: Sauerländer.

Woodall, C. W., D'Amato, A. W., Bradford, J. B. & Finley, A. O. (2011) Effects of stand and inter-specific stocking on maximizing standing tree carbon stocks in the eastern United States. *Forest Science*, **57**, 365–378.

Wright, S. J. (1996) Plant species diversity and ecosystem functioning in tropical forests. In *Biodiversity and Ecosystem Processes in Tropical Forests* (eds. G. H. Orians, R. Dirzo & J. H. Cushman), pp. 11–31. Berlin, Heidelberg: Springer.

Yachi, S. & Loreau, M. (1999) Biodiversity and ecosystem productivity in a fluctuating environment: the Insurance Hypothesis.

*Proceedings of the National Academy of Sciences USA*, **96**, 57–64.

Zavaleta, E., Pasari, J. R., Hulvey, K. B. & Tilman, D. (2010) Sustaining multiple ecosystem functions in grassland communities requires higher biodiversity. *Proceedings of the National Academy of Sciences USA* **107**, 1443–1446.

Zeng, X., Michalski, S. G., Fischer, M. & Durka, W. (2011) Species diversity and population density affect genetic structure and gene dispersal in a subtropical understory shrub. *Journal of Plant Ecology*, **5**, 270–278.

Zeugin, F., Potvin, C., Jansa, J. & Scherer-Lorenzen, M. (2010) Is tree diversity an important driver for phosphorus and nitrogen acquisition of a young tropical plantation? *Forest Ecology and Management*, **260**, 1424–1433.

Zhang, Y., Chen, H. Y. H. & Reich, P. B. (2012) Forest productivity increases with evenness, species richness and trait variation: a global meta-analysis. *Journal of Ecology*, **100**, 742–749.

# CHAPTER NINE

# Exploring evolutionarily meaningful vegetation definitions in the tropics: a community phylogenetic approach

ARY T. OLIVEIRA-FILHO
*Instituto de Ciências Biológicas, Universidade Federal de Minas Gerais*
R. TOBY PENNINGTON
*Tropical Biology Group, Royal Botanic Garden Edinburgh*
JAY ROTELLA
*Ecology, Montana State University*
and
MATT LAVIN
*Plant Sciences and Plant Pathology, Montana State University*

## 9.1 Introduction

In considering how forests will react to global change, understanding the distinctions between vegetation types is important. If we are to pinpoint the species that might thrive in Amazonia if the rain forest there 'dies back' because of drying and more seasonal climates, then characterising the vegetation types growing currently in seasonally dry areas of the Neotropics is critical. This is one motivation for this paper. Another is to add impetus to the preservation of dry-adapted vegetation because it is highly threatened and relatively neglected by conservationists compared with rain forests.

Our approach is not to re-visit the labyrinthine debates of vegetation defined by subtleties of taxonomic composition and relative abundance of species (e.g. Mucina 1997; Poore 1955). Instead, we use an approach that asks whether major biome settings, as defined by physiognomies of their component plants and ecological factors (e.g. presence of fire), represent distinctive theatres of evolution for constituent woody floras. We build upon an approach developed to study the phylogenetic structure of local communities at small spatial scales (e.g. Webb *et al.* 2002) and apply it at near-continental scales. If certain kinds of dry-adapted vegetation represent evolutionary theatres, then detecting lineages repeatedly moving between biomes (e.g. ecological speciation) is expected to be less common than detecting clades of species that are all confined to one kind of dry-adapted vegetation (phylogenetic niche conservatism; Crisp *et al.* 2009; Donoghue 2008).

*Forests and Global Change*, ed. David A. Coomes, David F. R. P. Burslem and William D. Simonson.
Published by Cambridge University Press. © British Ecological Society 2014.

## 9.2   Problems with definitions of seasonally dry vegetation in the neotropics: an example

The widely cited land cover map of South America by Eva *et al.* (2004) provides an accurate representation of many vegetation types. In certain seasonally dry areas, however, physiognomically similar but floristically distinct vegetation might be difficult to distinguish using remote-sensed data. For example, Eva *et al.* (2004) classify the deciduous woodlands of the Chaco region of central South America and the deciduous woodlands of the caatinga of northeastern Brazil as one and the same. The physiognomies of these are indeed similar in that they both comprise short-statured woodlands that are deciduous during the dry season. The Chaco, however, experiences severe winter frosts and has floristic affinities with temperate vegetation rather than with the caatinga (Prado 1991; Prado & Gibbs 1993). Eva *et al.*'s classification of deciduous forests has been used in attempts to model the fate of Amazonian rain forests under drying climates (e.g. Malhi *et al.* 2009). However, because the chaco and caatinga harbour biologically different vegetation types, doubt is cast on any conclusions drawn regarding the future nature of forests in Amazonia.

## 9.3   The caatinga and cerrado

Northeastern and central Brazil harbour large expanses of two kinds of seasonal woody vegetation, the 'caatinga' and 'cerrado,' which are used to define two adjacent phytogeographic domains (Figure 9.1) and particular vegetation types within them.

The Caatinga Phytogeographic Domain is mostly occupied by caatinga, which is the largest expanse of seasonally dry tropical forests and woodlands (SDTFs) in the Neotropics, a vegetation type where woody species are largely deciduous and there is a notable presence of succulent species (Queiroz 2006; Santos *et al.* 2012). Caatinga SDTFs occupy generally fertile and shallow soils and lose most (>60%) leaf biomass during the dry season. Because the growing season is relatively short and erratic (Ab'Sáber 1974; Oliveira, Jarenkow & Rodal 2006), grass productivity is low and the vegetation is not commonly prone to fire during the dry season. This last attribute is consistent with the commonly high abundance of large statured to arborescent Cactaceae, which are ill-adapted to survive burning (Linares-Palomino, Oliveira-Filho & Pennington 2011; Pennington, Lavin & Oliveira-Filho 2009).

The Cerrado Phytogeographic Domain comprises the largest New World expanse of savanna woodlands known as the cerrado (Ratter, Bridgewater & Ribeiro 2006; Figure 9.1). The cerrado savannas generally occur on poor and deep soils, retain much leaf biomass during the dry season (usually over 50%) and have abundant grass cover that forms during the relatively more productive growing season (Oliveira-Filho & Ratter 2002). Such high productivity of grasses renders this vegetation fire-prone during the dry season.

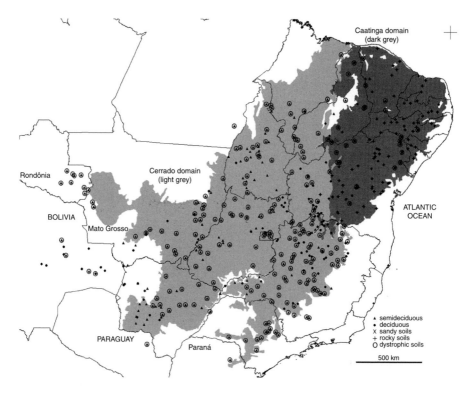

**Figure 9.1** The distribution of the 466 floristic study sites from eastern and southern Brazil and adjacent Bolivia and Paraguay. The Caatinga Phytogeographical Domain (dark grey area) includes 149 sample sites, whereas the Cerrado Phytogeographical Domain (light grey area) has 317. Floristic study sites occurring to the south and east of the shaded areas represent satellites of SDTFs or caatinga (bullets) and savanna woodlands or cerrado (triangles). Floristic study sites marked with crosshairs indicate those on shallow rocky soils. Study sites marked by X indicate those on sandy soils. Otherwise sites are located on mostly deep loamy soils with high moisture retention capacity. Floristic study sites encircled are those on nutrient poor (dystrophic) soils. The Caatinga Domain contains most of the sites on rocky or sandy substrates whereas the Cerrado Domain harbours most sites with nutrient-poor (dystrophic) soils. The upper right cross represents –2.00 latitude and –35.00 longitude.

We suggest that the different general ecologies of the caatinga and cerrado impose constraints on woody plant evolution. This idea stems from the findings that SDTFs rich in succulent plants (represented by the caatinga) and tropical savanna woodlands (represented by the cerrado) each harbour distinct clades of woody species (e.g. Duputie, Salick & McKey 2011; Lavin 2006; Lavin *et al.* 2004; Pennington, Lavin & Oliveira-Filho 2009; Queiroz & Lavin 2011; Schrire, Lavin & Lewis 2005; Simon *et al.* 2009). These molecular phylogenetic studies often involve molecular clock analyses, which reveal that clades of species endemic to geographically localised nuclei of SDTFs often have age estimates of up to several to many millions of years (e.g. Särkinen *et al.* 2011), whereas clades of species confined to tropical savannas are often not so geographically localised or have younger age estimates.

This evolutionary distinction of SDTFs and tropical savanna woodlands might be due to the ecology that causes the degree of seasonality. A relatively long, pronounced and erratic dry season in SDTFs does not impose a disturbance in a caatinga-like plant community (Pennington, Lavin & Oliveira-Filho 2009), but it might in a tropical savanna woodland, which is less seasonally dry (Oliveira, Jarenkow & Rodal 2006). This disturbance would take the form of drought-related mortality of plants that occurs in a similar manner to the effect of drought in tropical rain forests (see Meir & Woodward 2010). The resistance to mortality and therefore persistence over evolutionary time scales of resident plant lineages and communities in SDTFs, which are adapted to extreme drought, reduces the chance of successful establishment by immigrant propagules. In savanna woodlands and tropical rain forests, periods of drought and fire, with consequent mass mortality of local resident plants, might occasionally offer a marked opportunity for colonising species to establish successfully at a rate higher than in SDTFs.

To move beyond an approach that examines phylogenies of single clades and to test more broadly the hypothesis that these two kinds of seasonal tropical woody vegetations impose profound constraints on woody plant evolution, floristic data taken from the caatinga (representative of SDTFs) and neighbouring cerrado (representative of tropical savanna woodlands) were subjected to a community phylogenetic analysis. In addition to determining the extent of community phylogenetic structuring between these two vegetation types, an underlying ecology related to seasonality was identified as the potential cause of such structuring. Because ecological studies in tropical vegetation suggest that phylogenetic structuring of herbaceous plant lineages might be different from that of woody plant groups (e.g. Tuomisto *et al.* 2003a, b), our findings might be most relevant to detecting ecologies that shape phylogenetic patterns of woody plant diversity.

## 9.4    Materials and methods

We used a community phylogenetic approach to test the hypothesis that the ecologies that cause the difference between SDTFs and savanna woodlands profoundly structure phylogenetic beta diversity (e.g. Graham & Fine 2008). This differs from other applications of community phylogenetics such as the detection of phylogenetic aggregation (evidence of ecological filtering; e.g. Graham & Fine 2008) or overdispersion (evidence of competitive exclusion; e.g. Cadotte *et al.* 2010; Webb *et al.* 2002; or biotic interchange; e.g. Kissling *et al.* 2012). Our approach attempts to address which environmental variables shape phylogenetic beta diversity. It is important to note, however, that if any variable is found not to shape phylogenetic diversity at the spatial scale of our analyses, this does not mean that is not important at other scales or locations. For example, if the degree of sandiness was not found to be an important explanatory variable for shaping phylogenetic beta diversity, this would suggest only that taxa above the species level (e.g. genera) do not tend to be confined to sandy soils even if the degree of sandiness locally structures vegetation physiognomy (e.g. Fine & Kembel 2010; Queiroz 2006; Santos *et al.* 2012).

The woody plant diversity within the Caatinga Domain (e.g. Queiroz 2006) and Cerrado Domain (e.g. Ratter, Bridgewater & Ribeiro 2006; Simon *et al.* 2009) was represented by 466 floristic study sites (Figure 9.1, shaded regions). Each of these comprised a homogeneous type of woody vegetation on a uniform substrate for which a floristic checklist was developed (www.montana.edu/mlavin/data/ary_site_matrix.txt). These 466 sites were variable in size (e.g. 5–15 ha) because each included the full extent of a homogeneous type of woody vegetation within a circle having a 10 km diameter (Oliveira-Filho 2010; see TreeAtlan website: www.icb.ufmg.br/treeatlan/; Santos *et al.* 2012). The 466 sites included 1716 species, which are assumed to represent much of the ecological and taxonomic diversity of arborescent species within the Caatinga and Cerrado Domains. Pseudoreplication was assumed to be minimal because different vegetation and substrate types were often sampled at close geographical proximity (e.g. Figure 9.1). The Caatinga Domain was sampled in 149 sites and the Cerrado Domain in 317 sites. The floristic checklists developed for each of these forest or woodland sites were transformed into an occupancy matrix of 466 sites by 1716 species (www.montana.edu/mlavin/data/ary_species_matrix.txt; which was rendered into a site by genus matrix: www.montana.edu/mlavin/data/ary_genus_matrix.txt). Although forest and woodland sites were of variable size, these floristic checklist data were considered to be valuable in addressing the hypothesis that ecological differences between SDTFs (e.g. caatinga) and tropical savanna woodland (e.g. cerrado) can strongly shape patterns of woody plant beta diversity above the species level.

### 9.4.1   Response variable

Mean nearest taxon distance (Webb *et al.* 2002; Webb, Ackerly & Kembel 2008) was the phylogenetic community distance modelled during this study. This metric involves the mean of the branch lengths that separate inter-site pairs of most closely related species (a species at one site is matched with its closest relative at another site until all species in two sites are paired). The reasons for this choice include: (1) if an ecology structures patterns of beta diversity above the species level, the sites occupying similar ecologies ought to share many more conspecifics, congeneric and confamilial taxa (or any level above that of species) than expected by chance, and the mean nearest taxon distance best detects this; and (2) of all the community phylogenetic metrics available (e.g.

PhyloSor, UniFrac, mean pairwise phylogenetic distances), the mean nearest taxon metric is not narrowly scaled between 0 and 1 (as are PhyloSor and UniFrac) and shows the greatest range of variation, much more so than do the mean pairwise phylogenetic distances (Figure 9.2). Indeed, mean nearest taxon distances correspond well to Bray–Curtis distances derived from the differences in shared genera, whereas mean pairwise phylogenetic distances do not (Figure 9.2). This is important given that differences in shared higher-level taxa can serve as a phylogenetic proxy (e.g. Hamilton *et al.* 2011). Community phylogenetic distances were generated using the R statistical program version 2.15 (R development core team 2012) with the package 'picante' 1.3–0 (Kembel *et al.* 2012). The 'comdistnt' function in 'picante' uses the species occupancy matrix and the community phylogeny to produce a community phylogenetic distance matrix for all pairwise comparisons of sample sites. Mean nearest taxon distances did not incorporate abundances because only occupancy (presence or absence) was scored for a species at each site. This phylogenetic distance incorporated conspecifics shared between site comparisons because we wanted to measure phylogenetic beta diversity at and above the species level with one composite metric.

The community phylogeny of 1716 species was generated with Phylomatic (Webb & Donoghue 2005) and Phylocom version 4.2 (Webb, Ackerly & Kembel 2008) using the angiosperm backbone tree (svn.phylodiversity.net/tot/mega-trees/R20100701.new). The taxonomic list submitted to Phylomatic followed the Angiosperm Phylogeny Group III classification (Angiosperm Phylogeny Group 2009; www.montana.edu/mlavin/data/ary_phylomatic_list.txt). Branch lengths in the community phylogeny were scaled to millions of years (Ma) using the branch-length-adjustment (bladj) option in Phylocom, which invoked the age estimates of Wikstrom, Savolainen and Chase (2001; svn. phylodiversity.net/tot/megatrees/ages) to constrain minimum ages of specified nodes (see www.montana.edu/mlavin/data/ary_bladj_tree.nex).

### 9.4.2 Explanatory variables

Alternative ecological site classifications (or categorical variables) to that involving the Caatinga or Cerrado Domains were evaluated (Figure 9.1). These included leaf loss (deciduous, with over 60% leaf loss during the dry season, or semideciduous, less than 60% leaf shedding), climatic regime ('semi-arid' with over 160 days of water deficit or 'seasonal' if less) and three substrate classifications (rocky versus deep soils; sandy, sandy-loamy or loamy soils; and eutrophic, mesotrophic or dystrophic soils; Table 9.1; Oliveira-Filho 2009; Oliveira-Filho & Ratter 2002). Quantitative variables included geographic distance (Manhattan distances, derived from summing the differences in latitude and longitude as reported in decimal degrees), elevation (m), distance from the ocean (km), 'mean duration of water deficit' extracted from climate diagrams

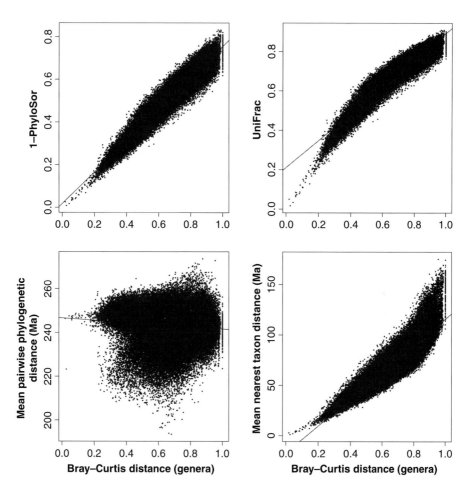

**Figure 9.2** Relationships of different community phylogenetic distances (*y* axis) to the differences in shared genera (*x* axis) for the 108 345 pairwise comparisons (data points) of the 466 floristic study sites. Regression lines ('abline' function in R) are fitted for descriptive purposes. Bray–Curtis distances derived from differences in shared genera among survey sites serve as a proxy for a phylogenetic distance. PhyloSor (phylogenetic Sorensen's similarity) represents the fraction of branch-length shared between two communities (1 – PhyloSor converts similarity into a distance). UniFrac is the unique (non-shared) fraction of phylogenetic branch-lengths between two sites. Mean pairwise phylogenetic distance (scaled in millions of years, Ma) represents the mean distance of two randomly drawn species, one from each of the pairwise site comparisons. Mean nearest taxon distance (scaled in Ma) represents the mean distance between closest inter-site pairs of species.

(Walter 1985) as number of days, and 19 bioclimatic variables produced by WorldClim 1.4, a high-resolution (1 km) set of global climate layers created by Hijmans *et al.* (2005). Of these bioclimatic variables, 11 were temperature- and 8 were precipitation-related (Table 9.2).

**Table 9.1** *Model ranking involving alternative classifications of SDTFs and tropical savanna woodlands that occur in east central Brazil (Oliveira-Filho 2009). The higher the model ranking, the greater the expected community phylogenetic differences between categories. For leaf loss, deciduous, an attribute generally of SDTFs, refers to over 60% leaf fall during the dry season whereas semideciduous, an attribute generally of tropical savannas, refers to 30–60% leaf fall during the dry season. Domain refers to the phytogeographical province (shaded areas in Figure 9.1). For regime, semi-arid, an attribute generally of SDTFs, refers to over 160 days per year of a water deficit. na = not applicable. Model ranking was identical when the response variable was Bray–Curtis distances of species occupancy (presence–absence), as indicated by Mantel $R^2$ values in the last column (for all reported $R^2$, p = 0.001).*

| Explanatory variable of nearest taxon distance | AIC | ΔAIC | Weight | Mantel $R^2$ | Mantel $R^2$ (Bray–Curtis) |
|---|---|---|---|---|---|
| Leaf loss: deciduous versus semideciduous | 944 114 | 0 | 1 | 0.37 | 0.50 |
| Domain: Caatinga versus Cerrado | 958 896 | 14 782 | 0 | 0.28 | 0.41 |
| Substrate: rocky versus deep soils | 969 500 | 25 386 | 0 | 0.21 | 0.23 |
| Regime: semi-arid versus seasonal | 977 818 | 33 703 | 0 | 0.14 | 0.23 |
| Substrate: eu-, meso-, versus dystrophic | 980 332 | 36 218 | 0 | 0.12 | 0.18 |
| Substrate: loamy, sandy-loamy, versus sandy | 986 672 | 42 558 | 0 | 0.07 | 0.09 |
| Intercept only | 994 743 | 50 629 | 0 | na | |

## 9.4.3   Model evaluation

All explanatory variables were evaluated with correlation tables and model-selection approaches to identify those that most succinctly characterise the ecology that explains phylogenetic beta diversity. The hypothesis being tested is that an ecological measure related to the degree of seasonality that differentiates SDTFs from tropical savanna woodlands is important in shaping patterns of woody plant beta diversity above the species level. If so, a pair of sites that are in close geographical proximity, but that greatly differ in factors that affect the degree of seasonality, will be compositionally different with respect to shared species and higher level taxa. In contrast, geographically proximal sites that are similar in the ecologies that affect the degree of seasonality will be expected to be compositionally much more similar in shared species and higher level taxa.

The explanatory variables were evaluated with multivariate- and distance-modelling approaches. Principal components (PCO) analysis was used to array

**Table 9.2** *Model ranking involving each continuous explanatory variable with an interaction of the deciduousness category (deciduous versus semideciduous). Scores for the model without this interaction are reported for comparison. The higher the model ranking, the greater the expected difference between categories with respect to the specified continuous variable. The highest ranking model involving geographical distance, for example, reveals that no matter how geographically close a deciduous and semideciduous site, the pair will be very different in phylogenetic composition. The high ranking model involving water deficit suggests that a pair of sites classified as deciduous and semideciduous are expected to differ most with respect to the number of days of water deficit compared with the other precipitation and temperature variables. For all reported $R^2$ values of models with an interaction of deciduousness category, $p = 0.001$. The top two models here were also the top two when Bray–Curtis distance derived from species occupancies was the explanatory variable.*

| Explanatory variable of nearest taxon distance | With interaction of deciduousness category | | | | | Without interaction | |
|---|---|---|---|---|---|---|---|
| | AIC | ΔAIC | Weight | Mantel $R^2$ | P | ΔAIC | Mantel $R^2$ |
| Geographical distance (Manhattan) | 926 575 | 0 | 1 | 0.47 | 0.001 | 45 641 | 0.19 |
| Water deficit (number of days) | 937 138 | 10 562 | 0 | 0.41 | 0.001 | 56 099 | 0.11 |
| Annual precipitation (mm) | 938 454 | 11 878 | 0 | 0.40 | 0.001 | 52 926 | 0.13 |
| Precipitation during the wettest month (mm) | 938 973 | 12 397 | 0 | 0.40 | 0.001 | 56 227 | 0.10 |
| Precipitation during the wettest quarter (mm) | 939 319 | 12 744 | 0 | 0.40 | 0.001 | 54 965 | 0.11 |
| Annual temperature range (°C) | 939 843 | 13 268 | 0 | 0.40 | 0.001 | 62 777 | 0.05 |
| Isothermality (ratio) | 940 199 | 13 623 | 0 | 0.39 | 0.001 | 64 773 | 0.03 |
| Precipitation seasonality (std deviation) | 940 787 | 14 212 | 0 | 0.39 | 0.001 | 63 335 | 0.04 |
| Distance from the ocean (km) | 940 935 | 14 360 | 0 | 0.39 | 0.001 | 63 276 | 0.04 |
| Precipitation during the coldest month (mm) | 941 141 | 14 566 | 0 | 0.39 | 0.001 | 65 809 | 0.02 |
| Precipitation during the driest quarter (mm) | 941 392 | 14 817 | 0 | 0.39 | 0.001 | 66 543 | 0.02 |
| Precipitation during the driest month (mm) | 942 150 | 15 575 | 0 | 0.38 | 0.001 | 67 224 | 0.01 |
| Annual minimum temperature (°C) | 942 558 | 15 983 | 0 | 0.38 | 0.001 | 66 445 | 0.02 |
| Temperature seasonality (std deviation) | 942 828 | 16 253 | 0 | 0.38 | 0.001 | 67 432 | 0.01 |
| Precipitation during the warmest month (mm) | 942 967 | 16 392 | 0 | 0.38 | 0.001 | 66 987 | 0.01 |

**Table 9.2** (cont.)

| Explanatory variable of nearest taxon distance | With interaction of deciduousness category | | | | | Without interaction | |
|---|---|---|---|---|---|---|---|
| | AIC | ΔAIC | Weight | Mantel $R^2$ | P | ΔAIC | Mantel $R^2$ |
| Mean temperature during the warmest month (°C) | 943 177 | 16 602 | 0 | 0.38 | 0.001 | 67 663 | 0.01 |
| Mean temperature during the wettest month (°C) | 943 244 | 16 669 | 0 | 0.38 | 0.001 | 67 682 | 0.00 |
| Mean temperature during the driest month (°C) | 943 379 | 16 804 | 0 | 0.38 | 0.001 | 67 687 | 0.00 |
| Annual temperature maximum (°C) | 943 608 | 17 032 | 0 | 0.38 | 0.001 | 67 900 | 0.00 |
| Mean annual temperature (°C) | 943 647 | 17 072 | 0 | 0.38 | 0.001 | 67 925 | 0.00 |
| Mean temperature during the cold period (°C) | 943 690 | 17 114 | 0 | 0.38 | 0.001 | 67 970 | 0.00 |
| Elevation (m) | 943 864 | 17289 | 0 | 0.37 | 0.001 | 67 952 | 0.00 |
| Intercept only | 994 743 | 68167 | 0 | na | na | na | na |

sample sites in two dimensions using mean nearest taxon distances. Generalised additive modelling was then used to fit or 'surf' each of the explanatory variables onto this two-dimensional array (e.g. using data points from the first and second PCO axis as the response variable). These operations were performed with the R base packages, as well as 'vegan' version 2.0–4 (Oksanen *et al.* 2012) and 'labdsv' version 1.5–0 (Roberts 2012). Distance models were evaluated by generalised additive modelling. In both multivariate and distance approaches, models were ranked according to Akaike's information criterion (AIC, Akaike 1973). The model with the lowest AIC value was considered the best. The relative plausibility of each model was evaluated by examining differences between the AIC value for the best model and values for every other model ($\Delta$AIC, Burnham & Anderson 2002; Johnson & Omland 2004). Models with $\Delta$AIC < 2 are considered strongly supported by the data, and models with $\Delta$AIC > 10 can be considered to have essentially no support from the data. We measured the relative likelihood of models given the data and the model list using Akaike weights ($w_i$), which are normalised values that sum to 1 across all models. Distance and PCO model analysis, ranking and selection among all subsets were performed with the R base packages, as well as 'ecodist' 1.2.7 (Goslee & Urban 2007), 'MuMIn' 1.7.7 (Bartoń 2012), and 'pgirmess' 1.5.3 (Giraudoux 2012).

## 9.5   Results

The 149 Caatinga Domain sites harboured 1151 arborescent species, whereas the 317 Cerrado Domain sites included 1221 species. Notably, the 200 deciduous sites (i.e. SDTFs or caatinga-like vegetation) comprised 1465 arborescent species whereas the 266 semideciduous sites (savanna woodland or cerrado-like vegetation) included 814 species. These findings reveal how floristically diverse the STDFs or deciduous enclaves and satellites actually are (Figure 9.1; bullets outside the dark grey shading).

The caatinga and cerrado vegetations are floristically distinct at the family, genus and species level. For example, the families Cactaceae and Vochysiaceae show great diversity imbalance across the caatinga and cerrado. Arborescent Cactaceae (e.g. *Cereus*) are found in nearly all caatinga and very few cerrado sites, and vice versa for the Vochysiaceae (e.g. *Qualea*). *Cereus kroenleinii* (Cactaceae) was found in 95 of the 149 caatinga sites (64%) and in only 14 of the 317 cerrado sites (4%), for example. In contrast, *Qualea grandiflora* (Vochysiaceae) occurred in 241 of the 317 cerrado sites (76%) yet was sampled in just 5 of the 149 caatinga sites (3%). Such floristic differences are commonly found at taxonomic levels at and above the species, as evinced by the following results of the community phylogenetic analysis.

Of the categorical variables that serve to distinguish SDTFs from tropical savanna woodlands, the deciduousness classification (deciduous versus semideciduous) was much more explanatory than Caatinga versus Cerrado Phytogeographical Domain (Figure 9.1), regime (semi-arid versus seasonal) or substrate type (Table 9.1). This was true regardless of whether distance or multivariate approaches were used. For example, the first PCO axis (Figure 9.3) was much better explained by classifying sites as deciduous or

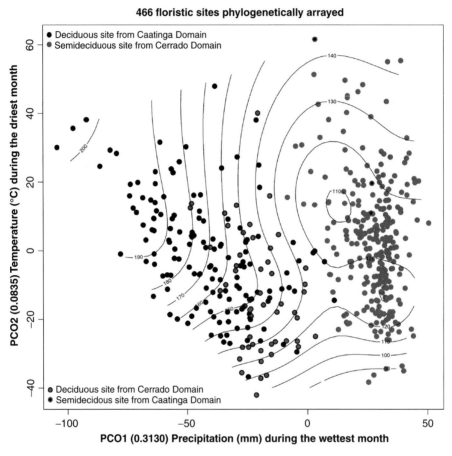

**Figure 9.3** Principal coordinates (PCO) analysis with the 466 floristic study sites ordinated along the first two axes with mean nearest taxon distances (the proportion of variation captured by each axis is reported). Explanatory variables having the strongest relationship to each of first two axes are reported. Number of days in water deficit is fitted to this surface (gradient lines ranging from 90 to 200 days) using a generalised additive model, as implemented in the surf function of the R package 'labdsv' (annual precipitation and precipitation during the wettest month have a strong inverse correlation with number of days of water deficit). Fitted temperature values during the driest month range from 18.5 °C at the lowest values of the second axis to 25.5 °C at the highest.

semideciduous rather than caatinga or cerrado. Most importantly, all of the continuous variables were much more explanatory when interacting with site classification, especially with the deciduous versus semideciduous categories (Table 9.2). This reveals that no matter how geographically proximal or climatically similar two sites are, if they differ in a certain suite of ecological variables that determine the degree of leaf deciduousness, then they will tend to be phylogenetically distinct with respect to community composition of arborescent plants (Table 9.2). From an alternative perspective, the continuous variables 'number of days per year of a water deficit,' 'annual precipitation' and 'precipitation during the wettest month' differ more between the deciduous and semideciduous sites than did any other continuous variables (Table 9.2).

Phylogenetic beta diversity (spatial turnover in clade composition) shows a contrasting pattern to species beta diversity (spatial turnover in species composition) within and among deciduous and semideciduous sites (Figure 9.4). Bray–Curtis distances of species composition reveal that within-deciduous-site comparisons involve many that differ completely in species composition (Figure 9.4; grey open circles to the extreme right in A). In general, Bray–Curtis distances between deciduous sites tend to be shifted to the right relative to Bray–Curtis distances between semideciduous sites (Figure 9.4; grey open circles in B), which suggests that species beta diversity is higher among deciduous sites. Phylogenetic beta diversity, in contrast, differs little when making within-deciduous and within-semideciduous-site comparisons.

## 9.6  Discussion

Our results strongly suggest that an ecology related to leaf deciduousness profoundly shapes patterns of beta diversity at and above the species level. Deciduous vegetation, where typically well over 60% of leaf biomass is shed during the dry season, as opposed to semideciduous vegetation where often less than 50% of leaf biomass is shed (Oliveira-Filho 2009), comprises woody plant lineages that have evolved to be well adapted to arid conditions. That the ecology of leaf deciduousness profoundly structures phylogenetic beta diversity means that the ability to inhabit a deciduous or semideciduous setting is more likely to be inherited rather than readily evolved (Tables 9.1 and 9.2, where top models hold regardless of whether the explanatory variable is Bray–Curtis distances derived from species occupancies or nearest taxon distances derived from the community phylogeny). This is evidence of phylogenetic niche conservatism (e.g. Donoghue 2008), which was detected with a limited number of taxon phylogenies of clades inhabiting SDTFs or tropical woody savanna (summarised in Pennington, Lavin & Oliveira-Filho 2009; Pennington *et al.* 2011) and is detected here with a community phylogeny of an entire woody flora.

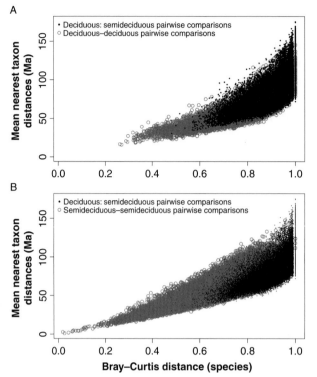

Figure 9.4 Mean nearest taxon distances as a function of Bray–Curtis distances derived from species occupancies. A: Open grey circles represent pairwise site comparisons within deciduous vegetation. B: Open grey circles represent pairwise site comparisons within semideciduous vegetation. The black data points in both panels are identical and represent pairwise comparisons involving both deciduous and semideciduous sites.

Although many ecological variables were analysed in this study, it may well be that seasonality of precipitation primarily interacts with substrate conditions to determine the degree of leaf deciduousness and thus explains why the degree of deciduousness is a better explanatory variable than any one of the bioclimatic or other variables. The reasoning is that shallow, rocky or sandy soils with little water retention capacity are common in deciduous settings (SDTFs; Hugget 1995). Precipitation is more erratic and of shorter duration among the deciduous sites. The generally more fertile (eutrophic) soils of these sites, however, facilitate opportunistic leaf regeneration during the short and unpredictable growing periods (e.g. Queiroz 2006). Selection in SDTFs therefore favours arborescent species adapted to shedding and re-growing leaves opportunistically as a function of precipitation. This is the case for the legume family, the most species-rich family in this study (e.g. Queiroz 2009), where deciduousness is facilitated by a high nitrogen metabolism (McKey 1994). In contrast, nutrient-poor soils with a capacity to retain more water are common at semideciduous sites. These sites often have deep loamy soils regardless of how old and nutrient-poor they are (e.g. Oliveira & Ratter 2002). Selection here favours woody plant lineages that tend to shed leaves less often. Grasses and similar life forms tend to accumulate in savanna woodland (semideciduous) sites where soil water is generally more available or precipitation is higher during a longer growing season.

Oliveira-Filho, Jarenkow and Rodal (2006) and Santos *et al.* (2012) have established that the above ecological variables related to the degree of deciduousness have been important in shaping plant communities in eastern Brazil. The finding that this ecology related to leaf deciduousness structures the phylogenetic beta diversity of woody plants is revealed here for the first time. The phylogenetic community structuring is found to be important even among the enclaves and satellites of deciduous sites within the cerrado, which were initially identified by their sharing of a few distinctive widespread species (e.g. Linares-Palomino, Oliveira & Pennington 2011; Pennington, Pendry & Prado 2000; Prado 2000; Prado & Gibbs 1993). Genus- and family-level similarities among these SDTF enclaves and satellites, and the main body of the caatinga SDTF, should not be overlooked.

Our results suggest that these ecological differences between physiognomically similar types of seasonal tropical woody vegetation have the capacity to structure woody plant biodiversity over millions of years. This is consistent with molecular clock findings that suggest that lineages confined to individual nuclei of SDTFs have local persistence times measuring in the millions of years (Figure 9.1; e.g. Lavin 2006; Pennington, Lavin & Oliveira-Filho 2009; Pennington *et al.* 2010, 2011; Queiroz & Lavin 2011). Similarly, lineages confined to savanna woodlands (e.g. cerrado) may have originated *c.* 4–7 million years ago coinciding with the rise of C4 grasses (Pennington, Lewis & Ratter 2006; Simon *et al.* 2009).

## 9.7   The influence of geographic distance

The importance of the deciduous and semideciduous site classification underscores the interaction of this ecology with geographic distance in shaping patterns of woody plant biodiversity (Table 9.2). This analysis suggests that the enclaves of SDTFs (caatinga-like) within the Cerrado Domain (Figure 9.1; bullets indicate deciduous sites including those outside the Caatinga Domain) have a community phylogenetic composition more similar to caatinga SDTFs. Furthermore, only pairwise comparisons within just deciduous or semideciduous sites show a pattern of distance decay (Figure 9.5; top panel). This strength of distance decay is indicative of the degree of dispersal limitation within a metacommunity (*sensu* Hubbell 2001) or the immigration rate among local communities belonging to a single metacommunity. The strength of the distance decay may thus be a signature of biome integrity. This within-biome distance decay was predicted (see Section 9.4.3). That is, sites differing in ecological factors that determine the degree of leaf deciduousness will be different no matter how geographically proximal, whereas sites similar in degree of deciduousness

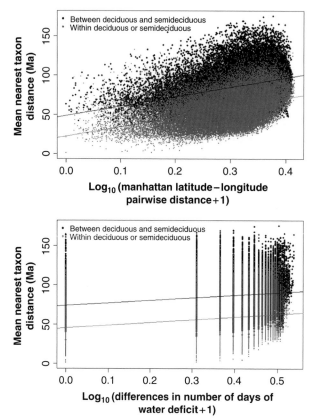

**Figure 9.5** A distance model detailing the interaction of a high-ranking model that shows the interaction of geographical distance or the differences in number of days of water deficit as a function of specific site comparisons (grey-shaded data points for within type comparisons, black data points for between type comparisons). Generalised additive modelling reveals that these top two continuous explanatory variables (Table 9.2) each interacting with site classification (Table 9.1; deciduous versus semideciduous) have a Mantel $R^2 = 0.47$.

will be much more compositionally similar when geographically proximal (Figure 9.5: top panel).

The above prediction came in part from the finding that geographically structured phylogenies are common to clades confined to nuclei of SDTFs (e.g. Duno de Stefano *et al.* 2010; Lavin 2006; Pennington *et al.* 2010, 2011; Queiroz and Lavin 2011) but less common for clades confined to savanna woodlands (e.g. Pennington, Lavin & Oliveira-Filho 2009; Schrire *et al.* 2009). This prediction also stems from floristic data, from South America (e.g. Linares-Palomino, Oliveira-Filho & Pennington 2011) and Mexico (e.g. Trejo & Dirzo 2002), which show that sites from both within and between distinct nuclei of SDTFs often share few species. Our finding that deciduous sites might have a higher turnover in species composition compared with semideciduous sites (Figure 9.4) is consistent with the finding that the cerrado vegetation (and perhaps savanna woodlands in general) is dominated by an oligarchy of woody species (Ratter *et al.* 2003), whereas nuclei of SDTFs, including the caatinga vegetation, are not (Pennington, Lewis & Ratter 2006; Trejo & Dirzo 2002). In sum, we are suggesting both that the ecology related to leaf deciduousness can structure woody plant phylogenetic beta diversity, and that variations in such an ecology among biomes (e.g. deciduous versus semideciduous) determine a biome-specific geographic distance decay pattern with respect to community phylogenetic distances.

## 9.8  Future prospects

A woody plant lineage growing in SDTFs has little expectation of a long growing season during a typical year, and it must have inherited abilities to detect when to grow and produce leaves opportunistically and when to senesce or go dormant. A plant's ability to be highly deciduous is thus an ecological trait of consequence in a highly seasonal climate. Although our current knowledge of trait variation in leaf deciduousness among the 1716 arborescent species in this study is limited, the eventual inclusion of leaf deciduousness as a trait scored from states assigned to individual species (cf. Ackerly 2004) could provide an alternative quantitative measure of the degree of deciduousness for each site compared with our current qualitative classification into deciduous and semideciduous. Such a quantitative perspective of leaf deciduousness is worth investigating.

This study was motivated by the need to distinguish among the kinds of seasonally dry tropical woodlands and related vegetation because they are some of the most threatened tropical biomes in the world (Pennington, Lewis & Ratter 2006). We believe that nuclei of SDTFs, which include the caatinga, have assembled under low rates of resident mortality via adaptation to low rates of fire, a temperature regime that precludes frost, and a precipitation regime that includes extensive and erratic drought (e.g. over 120 days of water deficit; Figure 9.3) on substrates with little capacity for water retention. SDTFs form a distinct metacommunity or biome compared with adjacent seasonal vegetations, such as tropical savanna woodlands (e.g. cerrado) or temperate deciduous forests and woodlands (e.g. chaco). Regrettably, SDTFs have not been circumscribed correctly, which can lead to misleading conservation recommendations. Olson et al.'s (2001, p. 933) delineation of terrestrial ecoregions, for example, which is explicitly described as 'an innovative tool for conserving biodiversity', considers chaco vegetation, which receives regular frost and has a flora with temperate zone affinities, as a 'tropical and subtropical dry broadleaf forest' along with SDTFs, such that occur in the caatinga and the Pacific coast of Mesoamerica. Olson et al. also classify caatinga SDTFs as part of a separate biome of 'deserts and xeric shrublands'. Perhaps because of these inadequate biome definitions, it is notable that terrestrial ecoregions suggested as priority for conservation fail to include some highly threatened, endemic rich areas of seasonally dry tropical woodlands (e.g. inter-Andean valleys in Bolivia and southern Peru; Olson & Dinerstein 2002). Such prioritisation has been very influential for major actors in conservation such as WWF.

The methods we propose here can help in the delimitation of SDTFs as a metacommunity and permit better conservation planning. In the selection of future study sites that fit the global characterisation of SDTFs (Schrire, Lavin & Lewis 2005), we predict that SDTFs will eventually be shown to include the Sonoran Desert, the Chihuahuan Desert, the Tamaulipan matorral, the Monte of the southern Andean region, the Somalia–Masai region of the Horn of Africa, the Karoo–Namib of southwestern Africa and perhaps the Sindian–Nubian region of southwestern Asia. All these areas, like the Brazilian caatinga, are characterised by a low-statured forest or shrub-dominated woodland often rich in cacti or other succulent plant groups whose constituents are drought-tolerant and where dry plant material never accumulates to levels that render it prone over geological time scales to fires frequent enough to be a major ecological force. Unfortunately, the proposed metacommunity of SDTFs is now subject to high degrees of human-related disturbance, so a global characterisation of this threatened vegetation type would go a long way to assisting conservation efforts that identify and prioritise its remaining fragments for management and protection.

## Acknowledgements

Marty Wojciechowski assisted in the development of the legume supertree that was included in the Phylomatic angiosperm backbone tree. Cam Webb kindly facilitated our use of Phylocom and Phylomatic, and Dave Roberts our use of the R package, labdsv. Domingos Cardoso, Kyle Dexter and an anonymous reviewer provided comments that improved the presentation of this manuscript.

## References

Ab'Sáber, A. N. (1974) O domínio morfoclimático semi-árido das caatingas brasileiras. *Geomorfologia*, **43**, 1–39.

Ackerly, D. D. (2004) Adaptation, niche conservatism, and convergence: comparative studies of leaf evolution in the California chaparral. *The American Naturalist*, **163**, 654–671.

Akaike, H. (1973) Information theory and an extension of the maximum likelihood principle. In *International Symposium on Information Theory* (eds. B. N. Petran & F. Csàaki), pp. 267–281. Budapest: Akadèemiai Kiadi.

Angiosperm Phylogeny Group (2009) An update of the Angiosperm Phylogeny Group classification for the orders and families of flowering plants: APG III. *Botanical Journal of the Linnean Society*, **161**, 105–121.

Bartoń, K. (2012) MuMIn: multi-model inference. R package version 1.7.7 (http://CRAN.R-project.org/package=MuMIn).

Burnham, K. P. & Anderson, D. R. (2002) *Model Selection and Multi-Model Inference: A Practical Information-Theoretic Approach*. New York: Springer.

Cadotte, M. W., Davies, T. J., Regetz, J. *et al.* (2010) Phylogenetic diversity metrics for ecological communities: integrating species richness, abundance and evolutionary history. *Ecology Letters*, **13**, 96–105.

Crisp, M. D., Arroyo, M.T.K., Cook, L. G. *et al.* (2009) Phylogenetic biome conservatism on a global scale. *Nature*, **458**, 754–756.

Donoghue, M. J. (2008) A phylogenetic perspective on the distribution of plant diversity. *Proceedings of the National Academy of Sciences USA*, **105**, 11549–11555.

Duno de Stefano, R., Fernández-Concha, G. C., Can-Itza, L. L. & Lavin, M. (2010) The morphological and phylogenetic distinctions of *Coursetia greenmanii* (Leguminosae): taxonomic and ecological implications. *Systematic Botany*, **35**, 289–295.

Duputie, A., Salick, J. & McKey, D. (2011) Evolutionary biogeography of Manihot (Euphorbiaceae), a rapidly radiating neotropical genus restricted to dry environments. *Journal of Biogeography*, **38**, 1033–1043.

Eva, H. D., Belward, A. S., de Miranda, E. E. *et al.* (2004) A land cover map of South America. *Global Change Biology*, **10**, 731–744.

Fine, P. V. A. & Kembel, S. (2010) Phylogenetic community structure and phylogenetic turnover across space and edaphic gradients in western Amazonian tree communities. *Ecography* **14**, DOI: 10.1111/j.1600–0587.2010.06548.x.

Giraudoux, P. (2012) pgirmess: Data Analysis in Ecology. R Package Version 1.5.3 (http://CRAN.R-project.org/package=pgirmess).

Goslee, S. C. & Urban, D. L. (2007) The ecodist package for dissimilarity-based analysis of ecological data. *Journal of Statistical Software*, **22**, 1–19 (http://cran.r-project.org/package=ecodist).

Graham, C. H. & Fine, P. V. A. (2008) Phylogenetic beta diversity: linking ecological and evolutionary processes across space in time. *Ecology Letters*, **11**, 1265–1277.

Hamilton, T. L., Vogl, K., Bryant, D. A., Boyd, E. S. & Peters, J. W. (2011) Environmental constraints defining the distribution, composition, and evolution of chlorophototrophs in thermal features of Yellowstone National Park. Geobiology doi: 10.1111/j.1472–4669.2011.00296.x.

Hijmans, R. J., Cameron, S. E., Parra, J. L., Jones, P. G. & Jarvis, A. (2005) Very high resolution interpolated climate surfaces for global land areas. *International Journal of Climatology*, **25**, 1965–1978.

Hubbell, S. P. (2001) *The Unified Neutral Theory of Biodiversity and Biogeography*. Princeton, NJ: Princeton University Press.

Hugget, R. J. (1995) *Geoecology: An Evolutionary Approach.*, London: Routledge.

Johnson, J. B. & Omland, K. S. (2004) Model selection in ecology and evolution. *Trends in Ecology & Evolution*, **19**, 101–108.

Kembel, S., Ackerly, D., Blomberg, W. K. *et al.* (2012) *picante: phylocom integration, community analyses, null-models, traits and evolution in R*, version 1.3–0 (http://cran.r-project.org/package=picante).

Kissling, W. D., Eiserhardt, W. L., Baker, W. J. *et al.* (2012) Cenozoic imprints on the phylogenetic structure of palm species assemblages worldwide. *Proceedings of the National Academy of Sciences USA*, published online before print April 23, 2012, doi: 10.1073/pnas.1120467109.

Lavin, M. (2006) Floristic and geographic stability of discontinuous seasonally dry tropical forests explains patterns of plant phylogeny and endemism. In *Neotropical Savannas and Seasonally Dry Forests: Plant Biodiversity, Biogeographic Patterns and Conservation* (eds. R. T. Pennington, J. A. Ratter & G. P. Lewis), pp. 433–447. Boca Raton, FL: CRC Press.

Lavin, M., Schrire, B. D., Lewis, G. *et al.* (2004) Metacommunity processes rather than continental tectonic history better explain geographically structured phylogenies in legumes. *Philosophical Transactions of the Royal Society, Series B*, **359**, 1509–1522.

Linares-Palomino, R., Oliveira Filho, A. T. & Pennington, R. T. (2011) Neotropical seasonally dry forests: diversity, endemism, and biogeography of woody plants. In *Seasonally Dry Tropical Forests* (eds. R. Dirzo, H. S. Young, H. A. Mooney & G. Ceballos), pp. 3–22. Washington, DC: Island Press.

Malhi, Y., Aragao, L. E. O. C., Galbraith, D. *et al.* (2009) Exploring the likelihood and mechanism of a climate-change-induced dieback of the Amazon rainforest.

*Proceedings of the National Academy of Sciences USA*, **106**, 20610–20615.

McKey, D. (1994) Legumes and nitrogen: the evolutionary ecology of a nitrogen-demanding lifestyle. In *Advances in Legume Systematics, Part 5, The Nitrogen Factor* (eds. J. I. Sprent & D. McKey), pp. 211–228. London: Royal Botanic Gardens Kew.

Meir, P. & Woodward, I. F. (2010) Amazonian rain forests and drought: response and vulnerability. *New Phytologist*, **187**, 553–557.

Mucina, P. (1997) Nomenclature and the code: a few concluding remarks. *Folia Geobotanica*, **32**, 421–422.

Oksanen, J., Guillaume Blanchet, F., Kindt, R. *et al.* (2012) vegan: Community Ecology Package. R Package Version 2.0–4 (http://CRAN.R-project.org/package=vegan).

Oliveira-Filho, A. T. (2009) Classificação das fitofisionomias da América do Sul extra-Andina: proposta de um novo sistema – prático e flexível – ou uma injeção a mais de caos? *Rodriguésia*, **60**, 237–258.

Oliveira-Filho, A. T. (2010) *TreeAtlan 2.0, Flora arbórea da América do Sul cisandina tropical e subtropical: Um banco de dados envolvendo biogeografia, diversidade e conservação.* Universidade Federal de Minas Gerais. (http://www.icb.ufmg.br/treeatlan/).

Oliveira-Filho, A. T., Jarenkow, J. A. & Rodal, M. J. N. (2006) Floristic relationships of seasonally dry forests of eastern South America based on tree species distribution patterns. In *Neotropical Savannas and Seasonally Dry Forests: Plant Biodiversity, Biogeographic Patterns and Conservation* (eds. R. T. Pennington, J. A. Ratter & G. P. Lewis), pp. 159–192. Boca Raton, FL: CRC Press.

Oliveira-Filho, A. T. & Ratter, J. A. (2002) Vegetation physiognomies and woody flora of the Cerrado Biome. In *The Cerrados of Brazil: Ecology and Natural History of a Neotropical Savanna* (eds. P. S. Oliveira & R. J. Marquis), pp. 91–120. New York: Columbia University Press.

Olson, D., Dinerstein, E., Wikramanayake, E. *et al.* (2001) Terrestrial ecoregions of the world – a new map of life on Earth. *Bioscience*, **51**, 933–938.

Olson, D. & Dinerstein, E. (2002) The Global 200: priority ecoregions for global conservation. *Annals of the Missouri Botanical Garden*, **89**, 199–224.

Pennington, R. T., Daza, A., Reynel, C. & Lavin, M. (2011). *Poissonia eriantha* (Leguminosae) from Cuzco, Peru: an overlooked species underscores a pattern of narrow endemism common to seasonally dry neotropical vegetation. *Systematic Botany* **36**, 59–68.

Pennington, R. T., Lavin, M. & Oliveira-Filho, A. (2009) Woody plant diversity, evolution and ecology in the tropics: perspectives from seasonally dry tropical forests. *Annual Review of Ecology, Evolution, and Systematics*, **40**, 437–457.

Pennington, R. T., Lavin, M., Särkinen, T. *et al.* (2010) Contrasting plant diversification histories within the Andean biodiversity hotspot. *Proceedings of the National Academy of Sciences USA*, **107**, 13783–13787.

Pennington, R. T., Lewis, G. & Ratter, J. A. (2006) An overview of the plant diversity, biogeography and conservation of neotropical savannas and seasonally dry forests. In *Neotropical Savannas and Seasonally Dry Forests: Plant Biodiversity, Biogeographic Patterns and Conservation* (eds. R. T. Pennington, J. A. Ratter & G. P. Lewis), pp. 1–29. Boca Raton, FL: CRC Press.

Pennington, R. T., Prado, D. A. & Pendry, C. (2000) Neotropical seasonally dry forests and Pleistocene vegetation changes. *Journal of Biogeography*, **27**, 261–273.

Poore, M. E. D. (1955) The use of phytosociological methods in ecological investigations: I. The Braun–Blanquet system. *Journal of Ecology*, **43**, 226–244.

Prado, D. E. (1991) *A critical evaluation of the floristic links between Chaco and Caatinga vegetation in South America.* Unpublished PhD thesis. University of St Andrews, UK.

Prado, D. E. & Gibbs, P. E. (1993) Patterns of species distribution in the dry seasonal forests of South America. *Annals of the Missouri Botanical Garden*, **80**, 902–927.

Prado, D. E. (2000) Seasonally dry forests of tropical South America: from forgotten ecosystems to a new phytogeographic unit. *Edinburgh Journal of Botany*, **57**, 437–461.

Queiroz, L. P. (2009) *Leguminosas da caatinga*. Universidade Estadual de Feira de Santana, Feira de Santana.

Queiroz, L. P. de (2006) The Brazilian caatinga: phytogeographical patterns inferred from distribution data of the Leguminosae. In *Neotropical Savannas and Seasonally Dry Forests: Plant Biodiversity, Biogeographic Patterns and Conservation* (eds. R. T. Pennington, J. A. Ratter & G. P. Lewis), pp. 121–157. Boca Raton, FL: CRC Press.

Queiroz, L. P. de & Lavin, M. (2011) Coursetia (Leguminosae) from eastern Brazil: nuclear ribosomal and chloroplast DNA sequence analysis reveal the monophyly of three caatinga-inhabiting species. *Systematic Botany*, **36**, 69–79.

R Development Core Team (2012) *R: A language and environment for statistical computing. R Foundation for Statistical Computing*. Vienna, Austria. ISBN 3-900051-07-0, URL http://www.R-project.org.

Ratter, J. A., Bridgewater, S., Atkinson, R. & Ribeiro, J. F. (2003) Analysis of the Brazilian cerrado vegetation III: comparison of the woody vegetation of 376 areas. *Edinburgh Journal of Botany*, **60**, 57–109.

Ratter, J. A., Bridgewater, S. & Ribeiro, J. F. (2006) Biodiversity patterns of woody vegetation of the Brazilian cerrado. In *Neotropical Savannas and Seasonally Dry Forests: Plant Biodiversity, Biogeographic Patterns and Conservation* (eds. R. T. Pennington, J. A. Ratter & G. P. Lewis), pp. 31–66. Boca Raton, Florida: CRC Press.

Roberts, D. W. (2012) labdsv: Ordination and multivariate analysis for ecology. Version 1.5-0 (http://cran.r-project.org/package=labdsv).

Santos, R. M., Oliveira-Filho, A. T., Eisenlohr, P. V. et al. (2012) Identity and relationships of the Arboreal Caatinga among other floristic units of seasonally dry tropical forests (SDTFs) of north-eastern and Central Brazil. *Ecology and Evolution*, Open Access: doi: 10.1002/ece3.91.

Särkinen, T., Pennington, R. T., Lavin, M., Simon, M. F. & Hughes, C. E. (2011) Evolutionary islands in the Andes: persistence and isolation explains high endemism in Andean dry tropical forests. *Journal of Biogeography*: doi:10.1111/j.1365-2699.2011.02644.x.

Schrire, B., Lavin, M., Forest, F. & Barker, N. (2009) Phylogeny of the tribe Indigofereae (Leguminosae–Papilionoideae): geographically structured more in succulent-rich and temperate settings than in grass-rich environments. *American Journal of Botany*, **96**, 816–852.

Schrire, B. D., Lavin, M. & Lewis, G. P. (2005) Biogeography of the Leguminosae. In *Legumes of the World* (eds. G. Lewis, B. Schrire, B. Mackinder & M. Lock), pp. 21–54. London: Royal Botanic Gardens, Kew.

Simon, M. F., Grether, R., Queiroz, L. P. de et al. (2009) Recent assembly of the Cerrado, a neotropical plant diversity hotspot, by in situ evolution of adaptations to fire. *Proceedings of the National Academy of Sciences USA*, **106**, 20359–20364.

Trejo, I. & Dirzo, R. (2002) Floristic diversity of Mexican seasonally dry tropical forests. *Biodiversity Conservation*, **11**, 2063–2084.

Tuomisto, H., Ruokolainen, K., Aguilar, M. & Sarmiento, A. (2003a) Floristic patterns along a 43-km long transect in an Amazonian rain forest. *Journal of Ecology*, **91**, 743–756.

Tuomisto, H., Ruokolainen, K. & Yli-Halla, M. (2003b) Dispersal, environment, and floristic variation of western Amazonian forests. *Science*, **299**, 241–244.

Walter, H. (1985) *Vegetation of the Earth and Ecological Systems of the Geo-biosphere*, 3rd edn. Berlin: Springer-Verlag.

Webb, C. O., Ackerly, D. D., McPeek, M. A. & Donoghue, M. J. (2002) Phylogenies and community ecology. *Annual Review of Ecology and Systematics*, **33**, 475–505.

Webb, C. O. & Donoghue, M. J. (2005) Phylomatic: tree assembly for applied phylogenetics. *Molecular Ecology Notes*, **5**, 181–183.

Webb, C. O., Ackerly, D. D. & Kembel, S. W. (2008) Phylocom: software for the analysis of phylogenetic community structure and trait evolution. *Bioinformatics*, **24**, 2098–2100. http://www.phylodiversity.net/phylocom/.

Wikstrom, N., Savolainen, V. & Chase, M. W. (2001) Evolution of angiosperms: Calibrating the family tree. *Proceedings of the Royal Society of London, Series B*, **268**, 2211–2220.

CHAPTER TEN

# Drought as a driver of tropical tree species regeneration dynamics and distribution patterns

LIZA S. COMITA

*Department of Evolution, Ecology, and Organismal Biology, Ohio State University Smithsonian Tropical Research Institute, Panamá*

and

BETTINA M. J. ENGELBRECHT

*Smithsonian Tropical Research Institute, Panamá Bayreuth Centre for Ecology and Environmental Research, University of Bayreuth*

## 10.1 Introduction

Tropical forests harbour the most diverse plant communities on Earth. This high diversity makes it particularly challenging to understand and predict how these communities will be altered by changing climatic conditions. However, doing so is imperative since, like other systems, tropical forests have experienced and are predicted to experience increases in $CO_2$ and temperature, as well as large shifts in precipitation patterns (Bawa & Markham 1995; IPCC 2007; Malhi & Phillips 2004). Nonetheless, studies of how tropical species will respond to climate change are scarce (e.g. Colwell *et al.* 2008; Miles, Grainger & Phillips 2004).

One of the main consequences of global climate change projected for the tropics is shifts in rainfall patterns (Hulme & Viner 1998). Models have predicted changes in annual rainfall up to 3000 mm per year, and changes in dry season length of up to several months in the tropics (Cox *et al.* 2000; Hulme & Viner 1998; Neelin *et al.* 2006). Projections differ hugely among tropical regions, and both increases and decreases are expected (Hulme & Viner 1998; IPCC 2007; Neelin *et al.* 2006). Global climate models are converging on projecting significant decreases in mean rainfall in Central and South America, while increases are expected in tropical Africa and Southeast Asia, although considerable uncertainty in rainfall projections still exists (IPCC 2007). Increases in extreme weather events (e.g. droughts, intense precipitation) are also expected in tropical regions (IPCC 2007). Increased frequency of

El Niño events (Timmermann *et al.* 1999) would also affect rainfall patterns in the tropics, since El Niño is associated with extreme climatic events including drought and flooding. At regional scales, changes in climate are also likely to result from land-use change, with large-scale deforestation and habitat fragmentation leading to drier conditions (Costa & Foley 2000; Hoffmann, Schroeder & Jackson 2003; Malhi *et al.* 2008).

Predicting how changing precipitation patterns will affect tropical forests depends on a clear understanding of how tree species are affected by water availability. Tree species' responses to water availability play a significant role in influencing their distribution patterns and abundance (Baltzer *et al.* 2008; Comita & Engelbrecht 2009; Engelbrecht *et al.* 2007). This in turn shapes patterns of community composition and diversity across landscapes (Pyke *et al.* 2001; ter Steege *et al.* 2006; Toledo *et al.* 2011) and ultimately influences ecosystem functioning (Bunker *et al.* 2005; Hooper & Vitousek 1997). Thus, shifts in water availability are likely to have significant consequences for tropical forests.

Adult trees have exhibited increased mortality rates in response to severe experimental and natural droughts in tropical forests (e.g. Allen *et al.* 2010; Ashton 1993; Becker & Wong 1993; Condit, Hubbell & Foster 1995; da Costa *et al.* 2010; Nakagawa *et al.* 2000; Nepstad *et al.* 2007; Phillips *et al.* 2010; Williamson *et al.* 2000; Potts 2003; Slik 2004), suggesting that substantial changes in rainfall patterns will influence tropical forests through alterations to current tree composition. However, even small changes in climate may alter tropical forest communities through effects on juvenile plants. Most tropical tree species spend tens to potentially hundreds of years in the forest understorey as seedlings or small saplings (Delissio *et al.* 2002; Hubbell 1998) whose ability to persist in the face of multiple stresses (e.g. pest pressure, light, water and nutrient limitation) determines their chances of reaching the reproductive stage. Seedlings and small saplings are thought to be more susceptible to changes in water availability than larger individuals, owing to their relatively shallow roots which do not reach deep, moist soil layers (Cao 2000; Engelbrecht & Kursar 2003; Gibbons & Newbery 2003) and to asymmetric competition with adults for soil moisture (Lewis & Tanner 2000). Impacts of changing precipitation patterns on juvenile plants are likely to alter future forest composition, since early life stages are considered a bottleneck in the life cycle of trees (Harper 1977) and since processes affecting seedling recruitment and survival are hypothesised to play a major role in the maintenance of high levels of diversity in tropical tree communities (Chesson & Warner 1981; Connell 1971; Grubb 1977; Janzen 1970).

In order to gain a better understanding of how shifts in precipitation patterns due to climate change will alter tropical forests, we examine how tropical tree species respond to variation in water availability and how that translates into species distributions and patterns of diversity. Here we focus specifically on how regeneration dynamics are affected by low water availability (i.e. drought). We review recent experimental and observational studies from tropical forests, and present new data from our own ongoing studies in the forests of central Panama. We largely restrict our review to studies assessing effects of water availability on seedlings in the field, because of the limitations of greenhouse and laboratory experiments (see Box 10.1).

---

**BOX 10.1  Field versus pot experiments on seedling responses to drought**

Field experiments are best suited for examining the ecological importance of variation in water availability in natural habitats, whereas isolated effects of individual factors and how they specifically influence plants are generally best explored under controlled conditions in the laboratory or in the greenhouse. Field experiments allow for the evaluation of the effects of individual factors in the context of all other processes influencing species performance in the natural habitat, thus giving a more realistic picture of the ecological importance of a factor. For example, low light levels in the understorey may limit seedling performance in the field so that plants cannot take advantage of added moisture. Additionally, working under field conditions assures that environmental variations are within the ranges relevant in the habitat. With adequate experimental design and interpretation, these aspects outweigh the problem of limited experimental control of water availability in field experiments, especially in the light of a number of substantial problems associated specifically with drought experiments in potted plants, many of which are avoided in field experiments:

- The rate of drying in pots is mainly given by water depletion by the plants, which in turn is proportional to the transpiration rates of the plants (Jarvis & Jarvis 1963). Larger individuals and/or species with high transpiration rates deplete the available water faster and are therefore subjected to drought stress earlier than smaller/less transpiring plants – potentially leading to the erroneous conclusion that they are more drought-sensitive. This may be especially pronounced when comparing deciduous and evergreen plants with vastly different leaf areas. In contrast to pot experiments, in the field, asymmetric competition for water from the surrounding trees overrides water depletion from any target seedling, so that drying rates are independent of seedling size and transpirational behaviour.

**BOX 10.1 (cont.)**

- Maintaining low, relevant and constant water availability treatments across species (and potential additional treatments, such as light) is rather complicated in pot experiments owing to the interaction of plant size/behaviour (which are in turn influenced by many treatments) and soil water content, i.e. drought intensity.
- It is well known that root restriction in containers can change allocation patterns and limit growth. Since root allocation and extension influence plant access to water and water uptake, this may significantly affect plant water relations.
- The limited soil volume available to plants in pots additionally implies that they cannot evade drought by developing deeper/more extended root systems, and thus gaining access to additional water.
- The rate and direction of drying in pots are usually substantially different from field conditions (e.g. faster drying and no progressive drying from the top to lower soil layers). Gradual acclimation to drought conditions over time is known to be important for plant performance under drought. Given the substantially different drying dynamics, drought responses in pots may not reflect processes in the field.

In particular, the first two issues substantially complicate designing and analysing comparative studies of effects of water availability in pots. Methods used in agricultural and physiological work to control substrate water potential, such as the use of polyethylene glycol (Burlyn & Kaufmann 1973; Turkan *et al.* 2005; also see Snow & Tingey 1985), do not allow plants to reach the low water potentials that critically influence survival and growth of many tropical species (<< –3 MPa, e.g. Baltzer *et al.* 2008; Kursar *et al.* 2009; Markesteijn *et al.* 2010). In pot experiments, soil water status has to be very carefully monitored and either differentially transpired water replaced across treatments (e.g. Sack 2004), or measurements of plant performance or physiological processes be related to measurements of soil or plant water status, rather than to duration of the dry treatment (Baltzer *et al.* 2009; Bonal & Guehl 2001; Kursar *et al.* 2009; ter Steege 1994). If soil water availability is not maintained constant across species and treatments (and/or carefully monitored) the desired effect of more specific control in greenhouse or laboratory experiments is lost, and the power of the experiment may be severely limited. Although the potential problems mentioned above can be dealt with, they are frequently not adequately accounted for, rendering the interpretation of the data difficult.

Throughout this chapter we use the term *drought resistance* as 'the capacity of a plant to withstand periods of dryness' (Larcher 2003), i.e. the ability to survive drought while minimising reductions in growth, and ultimately fitness. When using the term *drought resistance*, we refer to performance under drought conditions *relative* to performance under 'optimal' irrigated conditions, assessed in field experiments (see Engelbrecht & Kursar 2003). This approach allows the differentiation of the effects of low water availability, including both direct and indirect effects, from non-drought related factors that may additionally reduce performance and induce mortality during dry periods, e.g. pest pressure or low light conditions (Engelbrecht, Kursar & Tyree 2005). The term *drought resistance* is thus equivalent to response ratios (Hedges, Gurevitch & Curtis 1999). In contrast, we use the term *drought performance* simply to describe the performance of plants during dry periods, which is the outcome of all drought and non-drought related factors acting on the plants.

## 10.2    Regeneration dynamics in experimental field manipulations of water availability

In this section we review studies in which levels of water availability were experimentally manipulated. The majority of these studies involved irrigation to supplement precipitation, typically during dry periods, because removing water from a natural system is associated with substantial logistical difficulties, and the required structures may have indirect effects on regeneration (e.g. shading and seed rain exclusion through panels and gutters).

### 10.2.1    Germination

Seeds of most tropical woody species are desiccation-sensitive (i.e. recalcitrant; Daws, Garwood & Pritchard 2005, 2006; Vazquez-Yanes & Orozco-Segovia 1993). Nevertheless, water availability is unlikely to be a major factor limiting seed survival and germination for these species, because the peak of seed dispersal and germination often occurs in the wet season when water is abundant (Daws, Garwood & Pritchard 2005; Garwood 1983). Consistent with this, supplemental irrigation had no overall effect on seed germination in 12 species in an Amazonian rainforest (Paine, Harms & Ramos 2009). Similarly, in a study that simulated various patterns of rainfall in a seasonal tropical forest in Mexico, seed germination and seedling establishment rates differed little among rainfall treatments for three focal species (Blain & Kellman 1991). However, differential seed responses to water potential have been suggested to be important for determining habitat preferences of pioneer species, which have desiccation-tolerant seeds that germinate after gap formation (Daws *et al.* 2008), as well as for species associated with drier terra firme habitats (Paine, Harms & Ramos 2009). In addition, short dry stretches can occur during the wet season (Burslem, Grubb & Turner 1996; Engelbrecht *et al.* 2006) and may lead to the desiccation of drought-sensitive seeds, which could affect their viability (Daws *et al.* 2007). Additionally, decreasing wet season duration could delay seed germination, giving seedlings less time to establish sufficient root systems before the start of the dry season. This may adversely affect seedlings' ability to withstand their first dry season, but such effects remain to be explored.

## 10.2.2    Growth and survival

A number of field studies examining the effects of supplemental irrigation on seedling growth and survival in tropical forests have accumulated over the past several years (Table 10.1). These studies focused on the forest understorey and were mostly, but not exclusively, conducted in seasonal moist forests in Central Panama. They clearly indicate widespread water limitation of seedling performance during the dry season: growth and/or survival generally increase with supplemental irrigation in the dry season compared with seedlings under naturally dry conditions (Figures 10.1 and 10.2) (Brenes-Arguedas, Coley & Kursar 2009; Bunker & Carson 2005; Engelbrecht & Kursar 2003; Engelbrecht *et al.* 2007; Fisher, Howe & Wright 1991; Paine, Harms & Ramos 2009; Yavitt & Wright 2008). For example, irrigation had a significant positive effect on height growth of both naturally regenerating and experimentally seeded species in Peru, and a positive effect on survival of the experimentally seeded species (Paine, Harms & Ramos 2009). Similarly, irrigation increased survival and growth of transplanted seedlings of 28 woody species relative to performance under severe dry season conditions (Figure 10.2) (Engelbrecht & Kursar 2003). Survival increased in 82% of the 28 species (with a significant effect in 57%), and growth increased in 92% (with a significant effect in 89%). Perhaps most strikingly, in several studies (Bunker & Carson 2005; Engelbrecht & Kursar 2003; Paine, Harms & Ramos 2009), growth rates shifted from negative (i.e. leaf and biomass loss) under dry season conditions, to positive in irrigated plots (Figure 10.1). The effects of dry season drought on seedlings growing in gaps have been examined in only a handful of studies. Consistent with understorey effects, dry season irrigation increased seedling growth and survival in gaps in a single species study in Panama (Fisher, Howe & Wright 1991), but watering at the end of the dry season did not increase growth in gaps for three species studied in the Bolivian Amazon (Poorter & Hayashida-Oliver 2000). Overall, for most species studied there is a clear trend for increased performance with supplemental irrigation during dry periods, indicating that they are indeed water-limited; however, the occurrence and magnitude of the effects are not entirely consistent across studies (see Box 10.2 for a discussion of the reasons contributing to such differences).

**Table 10.1** *Effect of experimental manipulation of soil moisture availability in the field on seedling performance of woody tropical species.*

Unless noted in footnotes, moisture was manipulated through supplementary irrigation; studies are sorted by habitat (understorey, gap), and by the average annual rainfall at the study site. A positive effect signifies overall higher performance at higher soil moisture, and none, no significant overall effect. Numbers in parentheses give the number of species exhibiting a positive effect of irrigation, a negligible effect or a negative effect, respectively. The total number of species in the study is given as well. The habitat in which the study was conducted is given as understorey (U) and gaps (G). Studies were conducted on seedlings that were naturally regenerating (NR), transplanted (T) or sown (SS). Average annual rainfall (mm) at the study sites is provided (rounded to 100 mm). Where additional experimental treatments were applied, data refer to otherwise non-manipulated treatments only. Experiments in different habitats and/or sites within a study were treated separately. Where possible, overall positive or negative effects are based on statistical analyses provided in the paper. Where the comparison was not specifically analysed, we estimated the effect based on the effect sizes and standard errors given in the papers as data values, graphs or text. Effects on individual species are based on the sign of the effect (positive or negative), with species exhibiting a negligible effect (performance dry /performance irrigated ~ 1; based on data or graphs) noted separately. BCNM, Barro Colorado Natural Monument.

| Dry season | | Wet season | | Annual | | Number of species | Habitat | Approach | Annual rainfall | Country | Site | Study |
|---|---|---|---|---|---|---|---|---|---|---|---|---|
| Growth | Survival | Growth | Survival | Growth | Survival | | | | | | | |
| Understorey: | | | | | | | | | | | | |
| n.a. | **pos** (14;4;5) | n.a. | **none**[1] | **pos** (14;3;7) | n.a. | 24[2] | U | T | 1700 | Panama | Gunn Hill | Brenes-Arguedas et al. (2009) |
| **pos** (26;2;0) | **pos** (23;5;0) | n.a. | n.a. | n.a. | n.a. | 28 | U | T | 2600[3] | Panama | BCNM | Engelbrecht & Kursar (2003) |
| **none** (10;0;0) | **pos** (7;1;2) | **none** (2;6;2) | **none** (3;5;2) | **none** (5;2;3) | **none** (8;2;0) | 10 | U | NR | 2600 | Panama | BCNM | Bunker & Carson (2005)[13] |
| **pos** (1;0;0) | **pos** (1;0;0) | n.a. | n.a. | n.a. | n.a. | 1 | U | T | 2600 | Panama | BCNM | Fisher et al. (1991) |
| **pos**[4] (3;0;0) | n.a. | **none**[4] (1;1;1) | n.a. | n.a. | n.a. | 3 | U | NR | 2600 | Panama | BCNM | Yavitt & Wright (2008) |
| n.a. | **pos** (20;0;0) | n.a. | n.a. | n.a. | n.a. | 20[5] | U | T | 2800[3] | Panama | BCNM | Engelbrecht et al. (2007) |
| n.a. | **pos** (2;2;0) | n.a. | n.a. | n.a. | n.a. | 4 | U | T | 2600 | Panama | BCNM[6] | Asquith & Mejia-Chang (2005) |
| n.a. | n.a. | n.a. | n.a. | **none** (1;3;0) | **pos**[7] (2;2;0) | 4 | U | T | 2600 | Panama | BCNM | Tanner & Barberis (2007) |

**Table 10.1** (cont.)

| Dry season | | Wet season | | Annual | | Number of species | Habitat | Approach | Annual rainfall | Country | Site | Study |
|---|---|---|---|---|---|---|---|---|---|---|---|---|
| Growth | Survival | Growth | Survival | Growth | Survival | | | | | | | |
| n.a. | n.a. | n.a. | n.a. | n.a. | pos[8] (1;1;0) | 2 | U | NR | 2600 | Panama | BCNM | Mulkey, Wright & Smith (1993) |
| pos[1] | pos[1] | n.a. | n.a. | none[1] | none[1] | 12 | U | SS | 2600 | Peru | Los Amigos | Paine et al. (2009) |
| pos[1] | none[1] | n.a. | n.a. | pos[1] | none[1] | Unknown[9] | U | NR | 2600 | Peru | Los Amigos | Paine et al. (2009) |
| n.a. | none (9;6;8) | n.a. | none[1] | pos (13;1;10) | n.a. | 24[2] | U | T | 3000 | Panama | Lorenzo | Brenes-Arguedas et al. (2009) |
| **Gaps:** | | | | | | | | | | | | |
| pos (1;0;0;) | pos (1;0;0;) | n.a. | n.a. | n.a. | n.a. | 1 | G | T | 2600 | Panama | BCNM | Fisher et al. (1991) |
| n.a. | n.a. | n.a. | pos[10] (6;0;0) | n.a. | n.a. | 6 | G | SS | 2600[3] | Panama | BCNM | Engelbrecht et al. (2005) |
| n.a. | n.a. | n.a. | n.a. | n.a. | pos (1;1;0) | 2 | G | NR | 2600 | Panama | BCNM | Mulkey, Wright & Smith (1993) |
| n.a. | n.a. | n.a. | n.a. | n.a. | none (0;1;0) | 1[11] | U, G[12] | NR | 2600 | Panama | BCNM | Mulkey & Wright (1996) |

[1] No data for individual species provided
[2] 23 species for survival
[3] Rainout shelters and supplementary irrigation were combined
[4] Based on height growth
[5] Species not considered in Engelbrecht and Kursar (2003)
[6] Various island and mainland sites
[7] Data over 4 years
[8] Data over 3 years
[9] 1856 seedlings, number of species not known
[10] Survival over 10 days with experimental manipulation
[11] Only refers to species not considered in Mulkey et al. (1993)
[12] Habitat not specified
[13] Only high irrigation treatment considered

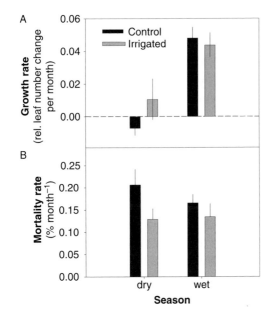

**Figure 10.1** Effect of supplementary irrigation in the dry and wet season on growth (A) and mortality (B) of naturally regenerating seedlings of 10 woody species in the understorey of a lowland tropical moist forest on Barro Colorado Island (BCI), Panama. Growth rates were significantly lower in the dry season than in the wet season. Growth was not significantly affected by irrigation, although a consistent trend of higher growth under irrigated conditions was seen in all species. Mortality rates did not differ between seasons, but in the dry season irrigation led to significantly lower mortality rates. Data are means ±1 SE. Drawn from data in Bunker and Carson (2005; the high irrigation treatment).

In the wet season, water availability is unlikely to be limiting. Consistent with this idea, supplementary irrigation has been shown to have generally no effect on growth and survival of seedlings in the moist forest understorey during the wet season (Figure 10.1) (Bunker & Carson 2005; Brenes-Arguedas, Coley & Kursar 2009; Fisher, Howe & Wright 1991). However, small seedlings of pioneer species growing in gaps were found to have increased mortality during short dry spells of only a couple of days in dry versus irrigated conditions in the wet season (Engelbrecht *et al.* 2006).

Supplemental irrigation can result in higher *annual* growth and survival rates (Tanner & Barberis 2007 for survival; Brenes-Arguedas, Coley & Kursar 2009 for growth), but this is not necessarily the case (Bunker & Carson 2005; Tanner & Barberis 2007 for growth). For example, Bunker and Carson (2005) found increased seedling survival in irrigated treatments during the dry season for 10 woody species in Panama, but no differences in survival across the full year. Thus, under some circumstances, other factors affecting performance in the wet season may cancel out positive effects of increased water availability in the dry season (Bunker & Carson 2005; Tanner & Barberis 2007).

### 10.2.3   Seedling size/age effects

Smaller plants are generally considered to be more vulnerable to drought stress than larger ones (Bunker & Carson 2005; Paine, Harms & Ramos 2009). Within species, the impact of low water availability indeed decreases with seedling size, which is determined by seedling age as well as genetic factors

**Box 10.2  Reasons for differential outcomes of supplemental irrigation studies**

Although there is a clear overall trend of higher seedling growth and survival with supplemental irrigation in the dry season, growth and survival are not necessarily simultaneously affected, and the size and significance of the effects vary among studies (Table 10.1). Several factors probably contribute to these differences, some of them ecologically meaningful, others due simply to differences in experimental design.

First, even at a single site, experiments conducted in years with differing drought severities are likely to yield different results, with more pronounced effects in drier years. Furthermore, drought intensity and soil properties vary locally and regionally, such that the same level of supplemental irrigation will probably have stronger effects on seedling growth and survival at sites where water is more limiting. The lack of an ecologically meaningful measure of water availability or drought intensity that is easy (and inexpensive) to measure and is comparable across sites and years currently hinders meaningful comparisons among forests and years. This also precludes a meta-analysis of such studies, allowing only a descriptive review of the literature (see Tables 10.1–10.3). To advance understanding of the effects of water availability and the extent of drought impacts, future studies must include a measure of soil water availability that is independent of plant species and size. Rainfall data alone are not sufficient, since differences in topography or soil characteristics, as well as evapotranspiration, also modulate soil water availability. Profiles of soil water potentials through the rooting zone of the seedlings will provide the most meaningful information. They can be assessed, for example, with psychrometers, the 'filter paper technique', or by gravimetric (or volumetric) soil water content, calibrated to soil water potentials through soil retention curves (e.g. Bonal & Guehl 2000; Engelbrecht & Kursar 2003; Markesteijn *et al.* 2010; Rascher *et al.* 2004).

Furthermore, variation in seedling drought resistance among species can lead to strong sampling effects in studies that examine only a few species (see Westoby 2002). Often, study species are not explicitly chosen with respect to (or randomly with respect to) their drought resistance (or a preliminary indicator thereof), so that a study may be inadvertently restricted to either drought-resistant or drought-sensitive species. This may result in hugely different outcomes when trying to generalise from the study species to the community, or when trying to infer differences across sites or years. Thus, care must be taken when interpreting experiments that include only a small subset of species from the community. Future studies should aim to use explicit species sampling schemes to adequately take into account the large interspecific variation in species' drought responses.

Additionally, differences in experimental study results can be due to differences in irrigation effects. Quantifying the strength of water

**Box 10.2 (cont.)**

limitation requires that drought stress is completely alleviated, i.e. species do not experience any drought stress in the supplemental irrigation treatment. This can be astonishingly hard to achieve experimentally, and may require very different amounts of irrigation in different sites and years. For example, in an irrigation study in a forest on the dry side of the Isthmus of Panama in the dry season, soil moisture did not show any appreciable increase despite water supplementation equivalent to the amount of average rainy-season rainfall (>200 mm), presumably owing to intense competition from neighbouring trees (the study had to be abandoned; Engelbrecht, unpublished data). Experiments that do not completely alleviate drought stress may reveal some effects, if water limitation exists, but will not quantify its full extent. In such cases, experiments are essentially simulating the effect of a less intense dry season or drought event, which may produce unexpected results. For example, in the irrigation study of Bunker *et al.* (2005), several species showed decreased growth at intermediate irrigation, but increased growth at high irrigation. Adjusting irrigation levels so that adequate and comparable water levels are achieved is especially critical in studies comparing irrigation effects across sites or years. Again, careful monitoring of soil water availability is critical.

In field irrigation studies, both effects on growth, but not survival (Bunker & Carson 2005; Yavitt & Wright 2008), and effects on survival, but not growth (Tanner & Barberis 2007), have been found. Effects on growth, but not survival, can be easily understood, since even slight drought stress at plant water potentials well above lethal levels (and even before wilting) can lead to decreased growth rates due to decreased turgor, stomatal closure limiting photosynthesis and generally inhibited metabolic processes (Hsiao 1973). Thus, in such studies, drought intensities (i.e. the extent and/or length of low water potentials) were simply not strong enough to induce death in the study species, an ecologically meaningful result. In contrast, effects on survival, but not on growth, are harder to explain, because, as described above, growth reductions *should* occur considerably before lethal water potentials are reached. One possible reason for detecting only survival effects is that growth rates can only be quantified for individuals that survive over the census interval. Studies that have few intermittent growth measurements may not detect lower growth before death since growth measurements exclude seedlings that show strong negative growth (e.g. leaf loss, stem dieback) and consequently die relatively quickly (i.e. before the first growth measurements are taken). Therefore, studies addressing effects of drought on growth should census plants frequently enough to avoid such effects.

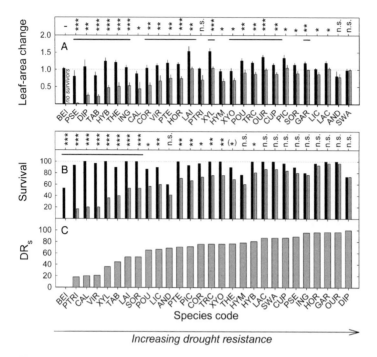

**Figure 10.2** Interspecific variation in drought effects on growth and survival in transplanted seedlings of 28 co-occurring woody species in the understorey of a lowland tropical forest in Central Panama. (A) Leaf-area change, relative to initial leaf area, in transplanted seedlings under dry and irrigated conditions, (B) survival under dry and irrigated conditions, and (C) drought resistance ($DR_s$) calculated as percent survival in dry conditions (grey) relative to irrigated conditions (black). Results of $t$-tests in (A) and of Fisher's exact test in (B) for treatment differences within species are given as: ***$P < 0.0001$, **$P < 0.005$, *$P < 0.05$, (*) $P = 0.05$, n.s. $P > 0.05$ (not significant). Horizontal bars mark those species for which treatment differences were significant ($P < 0.05$) after stepwise Bonferroni adjustment. When deciduous species are excluded, growth and survival responses to drought are positively correlated with each other. Redrawn from Engelbrecht and Kursar (2003). With permission from Springer Science and Business Media.

and environmental conditions. This is most directly shown by decreases in the effect of irrigation with seedling age or size (Bunker & Carson 2005; Paine, Harms & Ramos 2009; Poorter & Hayashida-Oliver 2000), and supported by observational studies (e.g. Delissio & Primack 2003). Across species, however, comparative irrigation studies of 28 understorey species (Engelbrecht & Kursar 2003) and six gap species (Engelbrecht *et al.* 2007) found no differences in drought resistance between species with larger vs. smaller seedlings. Increases of drought resistance with plant size or age are usually attributed to smaller and/or younger plants having smaller roots systems and less access to deeper soil layers with higher water availability (Cao 2000; Gibbons &

Newbery 2003), although the evidence for differences in rooting depth leading to the size dependence of drought resistance is limited (see Section 10.3).
Within species, smaller seedlings may additionally, or alternatively, be less
hardy (owing to unsuitable local conditions or genetics) and therefore more
vulnerable to drought-induced mortality.

### 10.2.4    Interspecific variation

Comparative experimental studies clearly indicate that the strength of the
effect of drought on seedling performance varies widely among species, under-
scoring their differential capacity to withstand periods of low water availability
(Brenes-Arguedas, Coley & Kursar 2009; Bunker & Carson 2005; Engelbrecht &
Kursar 2003; Engelbrecht *et al.* 2007; Tanner & Barberis 2007). For example,
among 48 native tree and shrub species in the forest understorey in Central
Panama, performance in dry relative to irrigated conditions (i.e. drought resistance) varied from 0% to 100% (Figure 10.2) (Engelbrecht & Kursar 2003;
Engelbrecht *et al.* 2007). As discussed below, the wide variation of drought
resistance among species is consistent with the large variation among species
in physiological and morphological traits relevant to plant water relations. We
later review how these large interspecific differences in drought resistance have
pronounced effects on population dynamics and species distribution patterns.

### 10.3    Mechanisms determining interspecific variation in seedling drought responses

Various traits and mechanisms have been suggested to underlie differences in
drought resistance among seedlings of tropical tree species. Mechanisms are
broadly divided into two categories: *desiccation avoidance* and *desiccation tolerance* (Larcher 2003). Mechanisms of desiccation avoidance are those that
prevent or delay species from experiencing low tissue water potentials
(the thermodynamic state of water, measured as pressure or suction in pascal,
with lower (i.e. more negative) values indicating a lower 'availability' of
water). Efficient mechanisms of desiccation avoidance minimise the decrease
of plant water potentials under drought conditions. These traits include (1)
maximising water uptake through deep and/or extended root systems; (2)
water storage in stems, leaves or roots; and (3) minimising transpirational
water loss through early stomatal closure and efficient cuticles, or drought
deciduousness (leaf shedding).

Mechanisms of desiccation tolerance allow plants to continue functioning
or, under more severe conditions, to survive despite a decrease of plant water
potentials. These mechanisms include (4) mechanisms at the leaf (and meristem) level, e.g. maintaining cell turgor through high osmotic potentials and
rigid cell walls, and maintaining vital cell processes through protection of
membranes, enzymes and DNA, and (5) mechanisms in the water-conducting

tissues (xylem) that promote a high resistance to xylem cavitation, thus allowing plants to maintain water transport under conditions of low water availability.

The two groups of mechanisms have traditionally been treated as alternative strategies, even implying a trade-off between the two (Larcher 2003). However, all terrestrial vascular plants exhibit all of these mechanisms (with the exception of deciduousness) – all have roots, stomata and cuticles, water-containing tissues and water-conducting tissues, and are able to withstand some degree of water loss. Indeed, the evolution of these characters in vascular plants is the basis of their ecological success on land. What species differ in is the efficiency of the different mechanisms (and the expression of the associated traits) and how they combine to allow each species to withstand periods of low water availability.

The variation in drought resistance of species within and across systems may be governed by the variation in the efficiency of one dominant trait or a combination of several traits. For example, in Mediterranean systems, rooting depth has been shown to determine the drought survival of seedlings (Padilla & Pugnaire 2007). On the other hand, different combinations of traits may lead to the same integrated drought resistance. Evaluating the role and importance of potentially relevant traits (or their combination) in driving the variation in species' responses to drought in a community requires directly relating them to species' drought resistance. Apart from trait values, we need quantitative, comparative assessments of drought resistance via controlled experiments or, if such data are not available, comparative data on species performance or distribution with respect to drought intensity.

Numerous studies on the physiology of water relations of tropical woody plants have revealed enormous variation among species in water uptake, stomatal reactions, deciduousness, water storage and hydraulic architecture, resulting in differences in plant water balance and potentials (e.g. Bonal & Guehl 2001; Brodribb et al. 2003; Jackson et al. 1995; Markesteijn et al. 2011; Tyree & Ewers 1996). However, studies allowing for the rigorous evaluation of the importance of various traits and mechanisms in shaping plant drought resistance, and their performance and distribution under drought conditions, remain scarce. This is due to a scarcity of relevant comparative datasets on species performance responses to drought (i.e. drought resistance) combined with complementary data on the potentially relevant traits for the same set of species. Even datasets that combine trait data with quantitative data on species distribution patterns with respect to water availability remain scarce (but see Baltzer et al. 2008; Markesteijn & Poorter 2009), and to our knowledge no datasets exist that directly relate traits to comparative field performance under drought conditions. In the following we summarise the evidence for the importance of different mechanisms for drought resistance of tropical seedlings from the few available comparative studies.

Differences in *rooting depth and volume*, which determine access to soil water, have long been suggested to be main drivers of variation in seedling drought performance across species in tropical forests. In Mediterranean systems, rooting depth has indeed been shown to be decisive in shaping seedling survival over dry periods (Padilla & Pugnaire 2007). However, seedling size, root–shoot ratio, rooting depth, and 'rooting depth per leaf area' were all unrelated to variation in seedling drought resistance among 28 understorey and 6 pioneer species in Central Panama (Engelbrecht *et al.* 2006; Engelbrecht *et al.* unpublished data; Kursar, Engelbrecht & Tyree 2003). Survival under irrigated versus control conditions was unrelated to root–shoot ratios in another study in Panama (Mulkey, Wright & Smith 1993), and dry season mortality in a moist forest in Thailand was unrelated to rooting depth (Marod *et al.* 2002). Similarly, in a comparison of dry and moist forest species, Markesteijn and Poorter (2009) found no relationship between rooting depth, or root length per leaf area, and species abundance in the two forest types, and even a decrease in root volume with stronger association to dry sites – despite various differences in biomass allocation to roots and root structure. In contrast, in a study comparing four Neotropical forests (in Costa Rica, Panama, Brazil and Peru), seedlings had deeper roots relative to leaf area at the most seasonal site (Paz 2003). The accumulating evidence suggests that under field conditions access to soil water resources through deep and/or extended root systems is not a decisive mechanism driving the variation among species in drought performance responses of tropical seedlings. However, root traits may vary across forest systems.

Plants can store water in their leaves, stems or roots, a characteristic that in tropical woody plants is mainly expressed in dry forests (Borchert 1994). Across species in a moist forest in Panama, leaf water content was not related to species' drought resistance (Engelbrecht *et al.*, unpublished data), and in Bolivia, contrary to expectation, root water content increased with association to moist vs. dry forests (Markesteijn & Poorter 2009). The limited data therefore do not support an important role of water storage in drought responses of tropical seedlings, but more data, especially including stem water storage, are clearly needed.

Plants can minimise their transpirational water loss through early stomatal closure, an effective cuticle, or shedding their leaves during periods of low water availability, i.e. drought deciduousness. During the dry season, plants in the forest understorey exhibit reduced *stomatal conductance*, i.e. they close their stomata (Cao 2000; Engelbrecht, Wright & De Steven 2002; Mulkey *et al.* 1992; Mulkey, Wright & Smith 1993; Veenendaal *et al.* 1996; Wright *et al.* 1992). However, comparative data on stomatal responses to drought in tropical seedlings, and how they relate to performance under drought conditions, remain exceedingly rare. In a detailed study of seedlings of three tropical tree species during a soil drying cycle in a growth chamber, Bonal and Guehl (2001) showed tremendous differences among species. In one species, stomata were extremely sensitive to soil drying, immediately reducing stomatal conductance with initiation of soil drying and reaching zero stomatal conductance at relatively high soil water contents. The most contrasting species maintained the stomata open until soil water contents were reduced to rather low levels (almost a third of saturation contents) and only reached full closure at much lower soil water contents than the other species. The differences in stomatal behaviour directly affected leaf water potentials, which remained high in the species with early stomatal closure, but decreased strongly with soil water content in the species whose stomata remained open, with the intermediate species showing intermediate leaf water potentials. We would expect that the species with sensitive stomatal response to drying would have the lowest growth rate, but the highest survival, whereas the species with delayed stomatal closure should exhibit faster growth, but lower survival. For growth, this pattern was indeed found, but the intermediate species showed even higher growth than both other species. Drought survival was not assessed in the study. In field studies in the tropics, stomatal conductance during the dry season in dry control versus irrigated plots was unrelated to survival (Mulkey, Wright & Smith 1993), and similarly, stomatal reaction to decreasing soil water contents did not reflect distribution patterns with respect to water availability (ter Steege 1994). Assessing stomatal responses to soil drought requires careful monitoring of soil and/or plant water status, especially for studies conducted in potted plants (see Box 10.1; also see Bonal & Guehl 2001). In cases where water status is not monitored (e.g. Slot & Poorter 2007), clear interpretation of results becomes difficult. At present, further research on the importance of stomatal responses for drought resistance of tropical trees is needed.

*Cuticular conductance* for water vapour in leaves is generally low, and when stomata are open it contributes little to overall plant water loss. However, as stomata close, cuticular water loss becomes increasingly important, and at stomatal closure it constitutes all of the plant water loss (Kerstiens 1996a, b). Differences in cuticular conductance might therefore be important for drought survival under severe drought stress, and thus species with lower cuticular conductance may be more drought-resistant. In seedlings of 20 tropical tree species, cuticular conductance (assessed as minimum leaf conductance) varied four-fold and differed significantly among species. However, it was not related to species' drought resistance (Engelbrecht *et al.*, unpublished data).

*Deciduous* trees generally occur under drier conditions in tropical forests (e.g. Malhi *et al.* 2009; Poorter, Bongers & Lemmens 2004). Leaf shedding decreases transpirational water loss and may therefore contribute to higher drought resistance (Borchert 1994; Reich & Borchert 1984). Even species whose adults are evergreen may have seedlings that shed their leaves under drought conditions (Engelbrecht & Kursar 2003). Unexpectedly, variation in deciduousness among species was unrelated to seedling drought resistance in Central Panama (Engelbrecht & Kursar 2003). Poorter and Markesteijn (2008) found longer survival times of deciduous species in pot experiments. However, such longer drought survival times of deciduous species in pots come with the caveat that soil drying can be substantially delayed for such species because of the reduced transpirational water loss, thus exposing them to less intense drought conditions (see Box 10.1). Rigorous evidence for an important role of deciduousness for drought performance of tropical seedlings is therefore still lacking.

The current evidence on individual traits associated with mechanisms of *desiccation avoidance*, presented above, does not support the idea that the traits individually are important in determining interspecific variation in drought resistance among seedlings of tropical woody plants. The effectiveness of the combined mechanisms of desiccation avoidance in a plant can be evaluated by assessing its leaf water potential under conditions of low water availability. If mechanisms of desiccation avoidance are important, leaf water potentials should remain high, whereas low leaf water potentials indicate that desiccation was not effectively avoided. Thus midday leaf water potentials provide an integrated measure of the effectiveness of mechanisms of desiccation avoidance. Midday leaf water potentials of 20 species in the dry season in Panama ranged from −1.2 to −3.2 MPa, but were not related to drought resistance (Engelbrecht *et al.*, unpublished data). This provides further support that *desiccation avoidance* does not govern seedling drought resistance in tropical forests.

An integrated measure of *desiccation tolerance* is lethal leaf water potential. If plants already die with minimal desiccation, i.e. at high water potentials, mechanisms of desiccation tolerance are not well developed, whereas low lethal water potentials indicate high desiccation tolerance. In a screenhouse study, Kursar *et al.* (2009) assessed lethal leaf water potential (and leaf water content) as the value at which 50% of the individuals of a species die (equivalent to LD 50). Across 19 species, lethal leaf water potential showed a highly significant negative correlation with species' drought resistance (independently assessed in a field experiment, Figure 10.3A; also see Tyree *et al.* 2003), and it also varied between species found in high vs. low rainfall areas (Figure 10.3B; Kursar *et al.* 2009). Specifically, drought-sensitive species die at high leaf water potentials whereas drought-resistant species can withstand

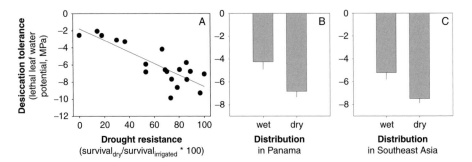

**Figure 10.3** Desiccation tolerance, assessed as lethal leaf water potentials, correlates with seedling drought resistance assessed experimentally in the field in Panama (A; $n = 19$, $R^2 = 0.70$, $P < 0.0001$). Lethal leaf water potentials are significantly higher in wet forest species than moist forest species in Panama (B; $t$-test, $P < 0.005$, data for 25 species), and significantly higher in species restricted to wet aseasonal forests than in species occurring in drier seasonal forests on the Malay–Thai Peninsula in Southeast Asia (C; $t$-test, $P < 0.005$, data for 24 species). (A, B) Redrawn from Kursar *et al.* (2009); and (C) redrawn from Baltzer *et al.* (2008).

low water potentials. Additionally, across seedlings of 24 species, Baltzer *et al.* (2008) found significantly lower lethal leaf water potentials (and water contents) in species that occur in seasonally dry forests than in species restricted to wet evergreen forest south of the Kangar–Pattani Line (KPL) on the Malay–Thai Peninsula in Southeast Asia (Figure 10.3C). Combined, these datasets provide strong support for the idea that mechanisms of desiccation tolerance that allow plants to maintain tissue function or viability despite low water contents play an important role in determining variation in drought resistance across woody seedlings in tropical moist forests worldwide.

Which mechanisms of desiccation tolerance are actually important? Mechanisms at both the leaf level (mesophylls and epidermis) and in the xylem tissue may contribute. Wilting at lower water potentials (i.e. more negative turgor loss points), higher solute concentrations at full turgor (i.e. more negative solute potentials) and more rigid cell walls (i.e. higher bulk modulus of elasticity) are associated with lower lethal leaf water potentials and with species occurring in drier seasonal forests (Baltzer *et al.* 2008). These results demonstrate that there are strong inherent differences in leaf-level tissue characteristics consistent with mechanisms leading to higher desiccation tolerance in species in drier sites. Osmotic adjustments and changes in cell wall elasticity are known to occur under drought conditions (Tyree & Jarvis 1982; Eamus & Prior 2001), and interspecific differences in the acclimation potential of these parameters may additionally contribute to differences in lethal leaf water potentials. The extent to which compatible solutes, i.e. solutes not involved in primary metabolism (Arndt *et al.* 2001; Chen & Murata 2002; Merchant *et al.* 2006), play a role in the desiccation tolerance of tropical seedlings through stabilising macromolecules has not yet been addressed.

Maintaining the functionality of the xylem, the water-conducting tissue, under drought conditions is critical initially to maintain transpirational water flow and photosynthesis, and under more advanced drought conditions to supply leaf and meristem tissues with sufficient water to stay above lethal water potentials. Under decreasing stem water potentials (increasing tension), xylem vessels cavitate and embolisms (air bubbles) form, which interrupt the water flow and thus reduce the stem hydraulic conductance (Tyree & Sperry 1989). Vulnerability to cavitation varies enormously among species of tropical plants (Brodribb *et al.* 2003; Choat, Sack & Holbrook 2007; Markesteijn *et al.* 2011; Tyree & Ewers 1996). No direct data are available to relate comparative xylem vulnerability of tropical seedlings to their desiccation tolerance (i.e. lethal leaf water potential or content). However, Kursar *et al.* (2009) found that leaf specific hydraulic conductivity (the hydraulic conductivity of the stem per leaf area) declined with increasing desiccation tolerance. Leaf specific hydraulic conductivity is usually positively related to xylem vulnerability (e.g. Markesteijn *et al.* 2011), in turn suggesting that species with higher xylem vulnerability are indeed less desiccation-tolerant. This is further supported by the finding of a significant increase in seedling wood density with the degree of association to dry forests in Bolivia (Markesteijn & Poorter 2009). High wood density is associated with small diameter xylem vessels that have higher resistance to xylem embolism than large vessels (Hacke *et al.* 2001).

To summarise, strong evidence has accumulated over the past several years that mechanisms of desiccation tolerance are decisive in determining differential seedling responses to drought, with both leaf and xylem level processes being relevant. However, contrary to longstanding assumptions and results from other ecosystems, currently there is no convincing empirical evidence that mechanisms of desiccation avoidance are important for shaping differences in seedling drought resistance in tropical moist and wet forests. These results will be important to consider when selecting 'soft traits' indicative of plant drought responses.

## 10.4   Effects of temporal and spatial variation in water availability on tropical tree regeneration

We can gain further insights into how species are affected by water availability by examining how current variation in water availability affects seedling dynamics and species distributions. In tropical forests, annual rainfall and dry season intensity vary widely and lead to pronounced spatial and temporal variation in water availability (Walsh 1996). Plant responses to this variation can provide insight into how sensitive or resilient tropical species and communities will be to changes in precipitation, and can provide key baseline information that can be used in quantitative models of species distributions and forest composition under specific climate scenarios.

### 10.4.1   Temporal variation in water availability

In many tropical forests – including moist and wet ones – rainfall is seasonal, with one or two dry seasons per year (Walsh 1996). Even in aseasonal equatorial forests, dry periods of more than two weeks occur and can affect plants (e.g. Becker 1992; Burslem, Grubb & Turner 1996; Walsh & Newbery 1999). In addition to seasonal variation, there is large interannual variation in total and seasonal rainfall in the tropics. Extreme wet and dry years are often related to the El Niño–Southern Oscillation. In the moist and wet tropics, severe droughts often occur in association with El Niño climatic events (Allan, Lindesay & Parker 1996; Walsh & Newbery 1999). For example, the El Niño event of 1982–83 resulted in an unusually severe dry season and elevated tree mortality rates at Barro Colorado Island (BCI), Panama (Condit, Hubbell & Foster 1995), and the 1997–98 El Niño event caused widespread droughts in Southeast Asia (Bebber, Brown & Speight 2004). Even in the absence of El Niño conditions, pronounced regional droughts can occur, such as the 2005 drought in the Amazon basin (Phillips *et al.* 2009). In contrast, La Niña years generally have above average rainfall and lower solar irradiance owing to increased cloud cover (Wright 2005).

### 10.4.2   Effects of seasonal variation in water availability

Two alternative hypotheses can be proposed concerning seasonal effects on tropical seedlings. First, seedling performance may be higher in the dry season than in the wet season, because light, the most limiting resource in the understorey of tropical forests, occurs at higher levels in the dry season (Russo *et al.* 2012; Wright 2005), and at the same time, pest pressure may be lower, although that is not always the case (Coley 1983; Wolda 1978). Alternatively, seedling performance may be higher in the wet season, because low water availability limits growth and survival in the dry season so that seedlings are not able to take advantage of higher light levels. Evidence has now accumulated that seedling performance does indeed vary substantially between seasons. Table 10.2 lists studies examining effects of temporal variation in water availability on seedling performance. The majority of these studies support the latter hypothesis, that seedling performance is negatively affected by dry season water limitation.

In nearly all studies, seedling growth and/or survival were higher in the wet season than in the dry season (Table 10.2). This is consistent with studies that

**Table 10.2** *Effect of temporal variation in soil moisture availability on seedling performance of woody tropical species.*

A positive effect signifies overall higher performance at higher soil moisture conditions (i.e. in the wet season or in wet years), a negative effect lower performance at higher soil moisture, and none, no significant overall effect (as in Table 10.1). Numbers in parentheses give the number of species exhibiting a positive effect of a wetter period, a negligible effect, or a negative effect, respectively. Studies are sorted by habitat (understorey, gap), and by the average annual rainfall (mm) at the study site. BDFFP, Biological Dynamics of Forest Fragments Project. See Table 10.1 for further explanations.

| Growth | Survival | Number of species | Habitat | Approach | Rainfall | Country | Site | Study |
|---|---|---|---|---|---|---|---|---|
| Seasonal effects[1,2]: | | | | | | | | |
| n.a. | **pos** (2;0;0) | 2 | U | T | 1000 | Benin | Kandi | Biaou *et al.* (2011) |
| n.a. | **none** (2;0;0) | 2 | U | T | 1100 | Benin | Bassila | Biaou *et al.* (2011) |
| n.a. | pos[3] | >53[4] | U[5] | NR | 1100 | Ghana | Pinkwae | Lieberman & Li (1992) |
| **pos** (2;0;0) | **pos** (2;0;0) | 2 | U | T | 1300 | Ghana | Tinte Bepo Forest Reserve | Veenendaal *et al.* (1996) |
| **none** (0;4;0) | **pos** (3;1;0) | 4 | U | T | 1600[6] | Costa Rica | Guanacaste Conservation Area | Gerhardt (1996) |
| **none** (0;4;0) | **pos** (4;0;0) | 4 | U | T | 1600[7] | Costa Rica | Guanacaste Conservation Area | Gerhardt (1996) |
| n.a. | **pos** (7;3;2) | 12 | U | NR | 1700 | Thailand | Mae Klog | Marod *et al.* (2002) |
| n.a. | **pos** (14;4;5) | 24 | U | T | 1700 | Panama | Gunn hill | Brenes-Arguedas *et al.* (2009) |
| **pos** (2.1.0) | n.a. | 3 | U | T | 1800 | Bolivia | El Tigre | Poorter & Hayashida-Oliver (2000) |
| n.a. | none (0;1;0) | 1 | U | NR | 2200 | Mexico | Santa Gertrudis | Cruz-Rodriguez & López-Mala (2004) |
| n.a | **pos** (3;1;0) | 4 | U | NR | 2300 | Panama | Casarete[8] | Lopez & Kursar (2007) |
| **pos** (23;5;8) | **pos** (26;0;7) | 36[9] | U | NR | 2600 | Panama | BCNM | Comita & Engelbrecht (2009) |
| **pos** (10;0;0) | **none** (4;4;2) | 10[10] | U | NR | 2600 | Panama | BCNM | Bunker & Carson (2005) |
| n.a. | **pos** (5;2;0) | 7 | U | T | 2600 | Panama | BCNM | Myers & Kitajima (2007) |

**Table 10.2** (cont.)

| Growth | Survival | Number of species | Habitat | Approach | Rainfall | Country | Site | Study |
|---|---|---|---|---|---|---|---|---|
| pos (1;0;0) | n.a. | 1 | U | T | 2600 | Panama | BCNM | Fisher et al. (1991) |
| none[11] (1;1;1) | | 3 | U | NR | 2600 | Panama | BCNM | Yavitt & Wright (2008) |
| none (0;3;0) | pos[12] (3;0;0) | 3 | U | NR | 2600 | Malaysia | Pantai Aceh Forest Reserve | Turner (1990) |
| neg (2;0;4) | pos (5;0;1) | 6 | U | NR | 2800 | Malaysia | Danum Valley | Bebber, Brown & Speight (2004) |
| n.a. | pos[3] | 3 | U | NR | 2800 | Malaysia | Danum Valley | Bebber, Brown & Speight (2002) |
| n.a. | none (9;3;11) | 24 | U | T | 3000 | Panama | Lorenzo | Brenes-Arguedas et al. (2009) |
| n.a. | pos (1;0;0) | 1 | U | NR | 5000 | Cameroon | Korup National Park | Green & Newbery (2002) |
| none | pos[3] | 64[4] | UG[13] | NR | 800 | Jamaica | Hellshire Hills | McLaren & McDonald (2003) |
| pos (2;0;0) | n.a. | 2 | UG[13] | T | 2200 | Brazil | BDFFP | Lewis & Tanner (2000) |
| n.a. | pos (1;1;0) | 2 | G | T | 1100 | Benin | Kandi | Biaou et al. (2011) |
| n.a. | none (0;1;1) | 2 | G | T | 1100 | Benin | Bassila | Biaou et al. (2011) |
| pos (2;0;0) | none (2;0;0) | 2 | G | T | 1300 | Ghana | Tinte Bepo Forest Reserve | Veenendaal et al. (1996) |
| pos (2;1;0) | n.a. | 3 | G | T | 1800 | Bolivia | El Tigre | Poorter & Hayashida-Oliver (2000) |
| pos (1;0;0) | n.a. | 1 | G | T | 2600 | Panama | BCNM | Fisher, Howe & Wright (1991) |
| pos[12] (6;0;0) | pos (5;1;0)[14] | 6 | G | SS | 2600 | Panama | BCNM | Pearson et al. (2003) |
| none (0;1;0) | pos[12] (1;0;0) | 1 | G | NR | 2600 | Malaysia | Pantai Aceh Forest Reserve | Turner (1990) |

| Wet versus dry years: | | species | | | rainfall | country | site | reference |
|---|---|---|---|---|---|---|---|---|
| n.a. | pos[3] | 12 | NR | U | 1700 | Thailand | Mae Klog Water shed research station | Marod et al. (2002) |
| n.a. | none[15] (0;1;0) | 1 | NR | U | 2300 | Panama | Casarete[8] | Lopez & Kursar (2007) |
| pos[16] (19;3;7) | pos[16] (3;32;1) | 36[17] | NR | U | 2600 | Panama | BCI | Comita & Engelbrecht (this study) |
| n.a. | none (0;3;0) | 3 | NR | U | 2600 | Panama | BCI | Engelbrecht et al. (2002) |
| n.a. | pos[18] (1;0;0) | 1 | NR | U | 2600 | Panama | BCI | Gilbert et al. (2001) |
| none[15] | pos[3] | 7 | NR | U | 2700 | Malaysia | Lambir Hills, Borneo | Delissio & Primack (2002) |

[1] The wet season usually refers to the one following the first dry season, the initial wet season was excluded
[2] In aseasonal sites, data refer to dry and wet periods
[3] No data for individual species provided
[4] Community level study
[5] Stratified random transects, assumed to be predominantly located in the understorey
[6] Evergreen site
[7] Deciduous site
[8] Seasonally flooded forest
[9] Growth for 33 species
[10] Refers to the 10 most abundant species with species specific data
[11] Refers to height growth
[12] Excluding initial wet season
[13] Understorey and gaps pooled cannot be distinguished from the data provided
[14] Based on results for medium-sized gaps
[15] No consistent differences between wet and dry years
[16] Year with lowest vs. year with highest dry season rainfall; negligible effect for species if <10% difference
[17] Growth for 29 species
[18] After initial year

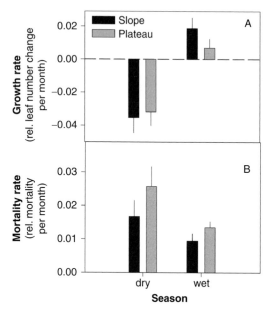

**Figure 10.4** Spatial and temporal differences in the performance of naturally regenerating seedlings in the understorey of a tropical moist forest in Panama. Seedlings were monitored in dry plateau and wet slope sites in the dry and the wet season. Relative growth rates (A) were significantly lower in the dry season than in the wet season, but did not differ between habitats. Mortality rates (B) were higher in the dry than in the wet season and higher in the dry plateau than in moist slope sites. Both growth and mortality varied significantly among species (see text). Data are means ±1 SE for 36 species for mortality, and 33 species for growth. Redrawn from Comita and Engelbrecht (2009). With permission from the Ecological Society of America (ESA).

have found that plants in tropical forests can be exposed to considerable drought stress. At the height of the dry season, widespread wilting has been observed (Chiariello, Field & Mooney 1987; Engelbrecht *et al.*, unpublished data), and leaf water potentials down to –4.8 MPa have been measured in moist tropical sites during the dry season (Eamus & Prior 2001; Engelbrecht *et al.*, unpublished data; Tobin, Lopez & Kursar 1999; Veenendaal *et al.* 1996), levels far below the conventional wilting point (–1.5 MPa, Larcher 2003) and comparable to midsummer values in savanna datasets or Mediterranean climates (e.g. Eamus & Prior 2001).

In an extensive survey of seasonal growth and survival of seedlings of 36 woody species on Barro Colorado Island, Panama (Comita & Engelbrecht 2009), overall seedling mortality was significantly higher in the dry season than the wet season, particularly in the drier plateau habitat (Figure 10.4). Growth rates also differed significantly between seasons, with overall negative growth (i.e. leaf loss) in the dry season and positive growth in the wet season (Figure 10.4). This was partially, but not exclusively, due to drought-deciduous species. When examining performance of species separately, 80% of species showed higher growth and 65% higher survival in the wet season than in the dry season (Comita & Engelbrecht 2009). The magnitude of the differences in seasonal growth and survival varied among species, and some species showed a pronounced opposite trend, reflecting the wide variation in drought resistance among species. This study was conducted in a year with a relatively severe dry season, and patterns may differ among years with differing precipitation (see Section 10.4.3 below). However, monthly survival (but not growth) rates were consistently lower in the dry season in three years with different rainfall regimes (Comita & Engelbrecht, unpublished data). The findings of these and other studies (Table 10.2) are consistent with widespread water limitation of seedling growth and drought-induced mortality during the dry season in seasonal tropical forests.

Drought has even been shown to be an important driver of seedling mortality in seasonally flooded forests, where inundation during the wet season is often thought to be the most extreme stress with which seedlings have to contend. In a study of four species in seasonally flooded forests in Darien, Panama, seedling mortality per month was three times as great in the dry season as in the wet season (Lopez & Kursar 2007). Similarly, decreased seedling growth and increased seedling mortality in response to drought has been observed for tree species in Amazonian floodplain forests (reviewed in Parolin *et al.* 2010).

Despite the fact that the majority of species examined exhibit lower seedling performance in the dry season, depending on species' drought resistance, dry season strength and microsite conditions, some species appear to be able to take advantage of higher light conditions and lower pest pressure in the dry season (e.g. Comita & Engelbrecht 2009; Yavitt & Wright 2008). In particular, drought-resistant species and individuals located in moist microsites should stand to benefit from dry season conditions.

Not only do rates of seedling mortality vary between seasons, but the agents of mortality can differ completely between wet and dry seasons. For example, in a study of 12 species in Thailand, drought and fire caused mortality in the dry season, whereas wet season mortality was caused by pathogens, insect herbivores and physical damage, as well as additional unknown causes (Marod *et al.* 2002). Furthermore, the importance of different agents for accumulated annual mortality differed substantially among species: whereas in one species all mortality was due to drought, in other species pathogens or physical damage were the main causes of death. These results highlight the differential selection pressures in the dry and wet season, and indicate that the importance of different mortality agents is likely to shift under altered precipitation regimes.

### 10.4.3   Effects of interannual variation in precipitation

Year-to-year variation in total rainfall and dry season severity has also been shown to influence seedling dynamics (Table 10.2). For example, strong interannual variation in seedling mortality was found in a 5-year study in Thailand (Marod *et al.* 2002) and could be attributed to differences in annual rainfall: seedling survival was lowest in the driest year and highest when annual rainfall was highest. Further evidence for the role of water availability in driving these patterns comes from the fact that these differences in annual survival were related to dry season mortality, which varied substantially among years (3.2–8.7% per month), but not to wet season mortality, which was relatively stable across years (11.6–13.8% per month).

A number of studies have specifically compared seedling performance in years with and without El Niño-related droughts. In northwest Borneo, higher seedling mortality and stem-dieback was observed over a 2-year census interval with a severe El Niño-associated drought compared with earlier (baseline) census intervals (Delissio & Primack 2003). In a 3-year study of *Prioria copaifera*, the dominant species in a seasonally flooded forest, seedling mortality was higher during a long El Niño dry season compared with a mild dry season, but seedling mortality rates were highest in a 'normal' dry season (Lopez & Kursar 2007).

At our study site in Central Panama, we monitored growth and survival of naturally occurring seedlings of 36 species over three years that differed substantially in precipitation patterns (Comita & Engelbrecht, unpublished data). The first year of the study, 2003, had a particularly severe dry season associated with an El Niño event (Figure 10.5A). Dry season rainfall in 2004 was also below average, but higher than in 2003. In contrast, dry season rainfall in 2005 was above average. Interestingly, wet season rainfall, as well as total annual rainfall, showed the opposite pattern, with precipitation highest in 2003 and lowest in 2005, thereby allowing us to separate out effects of dry season vs. total annual rainfall on seedling performance (Figure 10.5B).

We found that dry season survival was lowest in 2003 and 2004, years with below average dry season rainfall, and highest in 2005, the year with above average dry season rainfall (Figure 10.5B). Over the three years, wet season mortality rates similarly mirrored rainfall in the wet season, with the highest wet season survival in 2003 (the year with the highest wet season rainfall) and the lowest wet season survival in 2005 (the year with the lowest wet season rainfall). Interestingly, *annual* survival rates did not differ significantly among years (Figure 10.5C), in part owing to the opposing trends in dry and wet season mortality, but also owing to mixed responses of the 36 focal species (Figure 10.6), which were driven by differences in species' drought resistance (discussed below). These results demonstrate how a lack of community-level variation in seedling performance can mask large differences among species in responses to water availability. Ignoring such variation would lead to incorrect predictions about how species composition and diversity would shift in response to climate change. In addition, these results and others (e.g. Lopez & Kursar 2007, discussed above) suggest that while drought stress during severe dry seasons, such as those associated with El Niño events, often negatively affects seedling performance, annual mortality rates may not be strongly affected since non-drought-related mortality agents can also cause

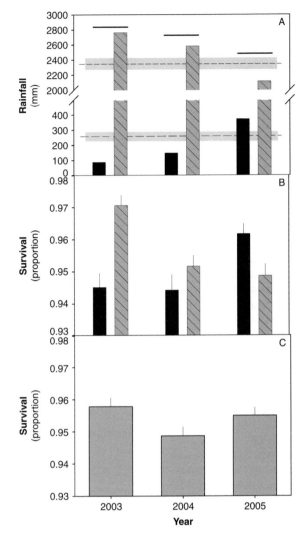

**Figure 10.5** Rainfall and survival of seedlings of 36 species in lowland tropical forest on BCI, Panama, in three years that differed in precipitation patterns. Cumulative dry and wet season rainfall (black bars and grey hatched bars, respectively) varied widely among the three years (A), as did total annual rainfall (bold horizontal lines). Dashed horizontal lines depict the 30-average seasonal rainfall ± 1 SE for the dry season (lower line) and wet season (upper line). (B) The proportion of seedlings surviving the 4-month dry season (black bar) and the 8-month wet season (grey hatched bar). Monthly survival rates were higher in the wet season than in the dry season in all three years (not shown). (C) The proportional annual seedling survival. Mean and SE values of the proportion surviving are corrected for differences in leaf number (within species) to account for changes in the size of surviving seedlings over time. Data in (A) are from ESP (2011).

high mortality rates. As a result, across years differing in precipitation patterns, the relationship between water availability and seedling performance is far from straightforward, further complicating attempts to predict how regeneration dynamics will respond to changing climate.

### 10.4.4    Spatial variation in water availability

Annual rainfall varies widely across tropical regions. For example, across the Amazon basin, as well as in tropical West Africa, annual rainfall varies from about 1000 mm to more than 4000 mm (Sombroek 2001; Poorter *et al.* 2004; Quesada *et al.* 2009; Swaine 1996). Sharp rainfall gradients can also occur over

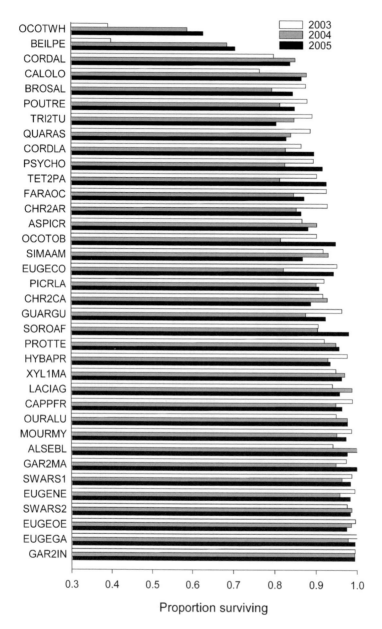

**Figure 10.6** Annual survival rates of naturally regenerating seedlings of 36 species on Barro Colorado Island, Panama, in three years that differed in precipitation (see Figure 10.5A). Values of proportion surviving are corrected for differences in leaf number (within species) to account for changes in the size of surviving seedlings over time.

relatively short distances. Across the Isthmus of Panama, rainfall varies from *c.* 1600 mm on the Pacific coast to *c.* 3100 mm on the Caribbean coast, over a distance of only 65 km (ACP 2011), and results in pronounced differences in soil moisture availability (Engelbrecht *et al.*, unpublished data). Such rainfall gradients are usually, but not always, associated with changes in dry season length (e.g. Clinebell *et al.* 1995; Davidar *et al.* 2007).

At local scales, soil moisture varies with topographic position, slope angle and position, soil texture (e.g. % clay), and canopy openness, leading some plants to experience significantly higher or lower water availability than individuals located only tens or hundreds of metres away. In particular, ridges and plateaus tend to have drier soils than slopes and valleys (Becker *et al.* 1988; Daws *et al.* 2002; Gibbons & Newbery 2003; Markesteijn *et al.* 2010), sandy soils are more drought-prone than loamy soils (Larcher 2003) and understorey sites drier than gaps (Becker *et al.* 1988; Poorter & Hayashida-Oliver 2000; Veenendaal *et al.* 1996). In the following, we will first discuss effects of local-scale variation in water availability on seedling performance, and then review available data on effects of larger-scale variation in rainfall.

### 10.4.5   Effects of local-scale variation in soil moisture

Since soil moisture varies with topography and soil properties, differences in seedling performance among local habitats may be driven in large part by differences in soil water availability. It is important to note, however, that additional factors, including light and nutrient availability, and pest pressure, can vary among soil types or with topography (e.g. Fine, Mesones & Coley 2004; Gunatilleke *et al.* 2006; John *et al.* 2007; Palmiotto *et al.* 2004; Russo *et al.* 2012) so care must be taken when interpreting results of observational studies. Table 10.3 lists studies that have compared seedling performance between habitats that vary in soil moisture.

Differences in habitat soil moisture may initially shape regeneration through effects on germination and early seedling establishment. For example, seedling emergence and dry season survival of first year seedlings were higher in moist slope sites than in drier plateau sites on Barro Colorado Island, Panama (Daws *et al.* 2005). However, during the wet season, mortality was elevated on slopes, presumably owing to damage from overland water flow during intense rainfall or higher pathogen attack in the wetter slope sites. Thus, wetter habitats can be either beneficial or detrimental to early seedlings, depending on whether drought or physical damage and pathogen attack are more important causes of mortality.

The performance of later seedling stages has also been shown to vary among topographic habitat types. Higher mortality in drier plateau sites than in wetter slope sites was observed in the 50-ha Forest Dynamics Plot on Barro Colorado Island, with the difference between habitats particularly

**Table 10.3** *Effect of spatial variation in soil moisture availability on seedling performance of woody tropical species.*

*A positive effect signifies overall higher performance at higher soil moisture conditions (i.e. wetter habitats or sites), a negative effect lower performance at higher soil moisture, and none, no significant overall effect. Numbers in brackets give the number of species exhibiting a positive effect of a moister habitat, a negligible effect, or a negative effect, respectively. The habitat comparison, based on topography, soils or rainfall regime, is specified for local-scale studies, and the rainfall regimes at the study sites for regional-scale comparisons. Studies are sorted by habitat (understorey, gap), and by the average annual rainfall (mm) at the study site.*

| Dry season[1] Growth | Survival | Wet season Growth | Survival | Annual Growth | Survival | Comparison | Number of species | Habitat | Approach[11] | Rainfall | Country | Site | Study |
|---|---|---|---|---|---|---|---|---|---|---|---|---|---|
| **Local scale:** | | | | | | | | | | | | | |
| n.a. | **pos**[2] | n.a. | **neg**[2] | n.a. | n.a. | topography: plateau–slope | >58[3] | U | NR | 2600 | Panama | BCNM | Daws et al. (2005) |
| **none** (17;1;15)[4] | **pos** (23;6;7)[4] | **pos** (22;1;10)[4] (27;1;8) | **pos** (27;1;8) | **none** (20;2;11)[4] | **pos** (27;2;7)[4] | topography: plateau–slope | 36[5] | U | NR | 2600 | Panama | BCNM | Comita & Engelbrecht (2009) |
| **none**[2] | **none**[2] | **none**[2] | **none**[2] | n.a. | n.a. | ridge–slope–valley | 6 | U | NR | 2800 | Malaysia | Danum Valley | Bebber, Brown & Speight (2004) |
| n.a. | n.a. | n.a. | n.a. | **none** (0;3;3) | **none** (0;3;3) | soil type and topography: ridges–valleys | 6 | U | T | 3000 | Malaysia | Lambir | Palmiotto et al. (2004) |
| n.a. | n.a. | n.a. | n.a. | **none** (1;3;0) | **none**[6] (0;3;1) | continuous moisture gradient[7] | 4 | U[7] | T | 3600 | Madagascar | Tampolo | de Gouvenain et al. (2007) |
| n.a. | n.a. | n.a. | n.a. | **pos** (2;2;0) | **pos** (3;1;0) | topography: ridgetop–valley | 4 | U | T | 5000 | Sri Lanka | Sinhajara | Ashton et al. (1995) |
| n.a. | n.a. | n.a. | n.a. | **none** (2;2;2) | **pos** (3;3;0) | soil type and topography: ridges–valleys | 6 | G | T | 3000 | Malaysia | Lambir | Palmiotto et al. (2004) |
| n.a. | n.a. | n.a. | n.a. | **none** (1;3;0) | **none** (0;3;1) | continuous moisture gradient | 4 | G | T | 3600 | Madagascar | Tampolo | de Gouvenain et al. (2007) |
| n.a. | n.a. | n.a. | n.a. | **pos** (4;0;0) | **none** (0;2;2) | topography: ridgetop–valley | 4 | G[8] | T | 5000 | Sri Lanka | Sinhajara | Ashton et al. (1995) |

regional/large scale

| | | | | | | | | | | | | |
|---|---|---|---|---|---|---|---|---|---|---|---|---|
| n.a. | **pos** (2;0;0) | n.a. | **none** (1;0;1) | **pos** (2;0;0) | **pos** (2;0;0) | long–short dry season/dry woodland | 2 | U | T | 1000 vs. 1200[9] | Benin | Kandi | Biaou et al. (2011) |
| n.a. | **pos** (2;0;0) | n.a. | **none** (1;0;1) | **pos** (2;0;0) | **pos** (2;0;0) | long–short dry season/dry woodland | 2 | G | T | 1000 vs. 1200[9] | Benin | Bassila | Biaou et al. (2011) |
| n.a. | **pos** (14;4;5) | n.a. | **none** (9;3;11) | **neg** (4;0;20) | n.a. | rainfall: low–high moist/wet forest | 24[10] | U | T | 1700 vs. 3000 | Panama | Gunn Hill-Lorenzo | Brenes-Arguedas et al. (2009) |
| none | pos | none | none | none | pos | rainfall: low–high moist/wet forest | 36 | U | T | 1600 vs. 3000 | Panama | Cardenas – Lorenzo | Engelbrecht (unpub. data) |

[1] In aseasonal sites, data refer to dry and wet period

[2] No data for individual species provided

[3] Community-level study

[4] Considered negligible effect if <10% difference

[5] Growth for 33 species

[6] Data over 2 years

[7] Results refer to extremes of moisture and light gradient

[8] Results refer to gap centres

[9] 5 vs. 7 months dry season

[10] 23 species for survival

[11] NR = Naturally regenerating, T = transplanted

pronounced in the dry season (Figure 10.4), suggesting that differences between the two habitats in seedling performance was due primarily to water availability (Comita & Engelbrecht 2009). In particular, species whose adult trees are associated with the moist slope habitats showed higher mortality in the plateau versus the slope habitat in the dry season. On the other hand, species whose adults are associated with drier plateau habitats showed no difference in seedling mortality rates between the habitats, regardless of season (Comita & Engelbrecht 2009). The fact that differential mortality between the two habitats was most pronounced for species associated with moist sites, specifically in the dry season, again suggests that water availability was indeed a key driver of patterns of seedling performance.

The importance of water availability, rather than nutrients, in driving differences in species' performance among topographic habitats was convincingly shown in a transplant study in Malaysian Borneo (Palmiotto et al. 2004). For four out of six species studied, seedling growth rates varied significantly between drier ridges and wetter gullies, habitats that also differ in soil water holding capacity and nutrient status. Two of the species showed higher growth and two lower growth in gullies, indicating interspecific variation in resource requirements. The importance of varying water availability (and/or the development of anoxic conditions) for the observed habitat differences was confirmed by the fact that phosphorus additions had no significant effect on growth rates (despite elevated soil and tissue P concentrations). In the same study, seedling survival was significantly higher in the wetter gullies than on the drier ridge tops for three of the study species, but only when they were growing in gap sites. In summary, available data indicate that variation in water availability can play a substantial direct role in driving local performance differences among habitats.

### 10.4.6    Effects of regional variation in rainfall

Regional-scale variation in water availability may also influence seedling performance. A comparison of dynamics of naturally occurring seedlings at four tropical forest sites with different rainfall regimes (BCI, Panama; Pasoh, Malaysia; Nouragues, French Guinea; and Yasuní, Ecuador) showed that the most seasonal site (BCI) had the highest annual mortality rates (Metz et al. 2008). However, the second highest mortality rate occurred at the wettest, aseasonal site (Yasuní), and within-site spatial and temporal variation in seedling demographic rates exceeded differences among sites (Metz et al. 2008). Such comparisons are useful at the community level, but do not allow for comparisons of the performance of individual species under varying rainfall conditions, because of corresponding shifts in species composition.

Large-scale transplant experiments are therefore necessary to assess variation of seedling performance under different rainfall regimes (Table 10.3). In a transplant experiment with 24 woody plant species across a rainfall gradient in Panama ranging from *c.* 1700 mm to 3000 mm, Brenes-Arguedas *et al.* (2009) found overall very similar annual mortality rates for seedlings planted at the dry and the wet site (2.3% vs. 2.5% per month). At both sites, mortality was considerably higher in the seedlings' first dry season than in the subsequent wet season, but this effect was especially pronounced at the dry site. Overall leaf production at the dry site was double that at the wet site. However, these overall effects average out pronounced differences among the species that were related to their distribution with respect to rainfall, with each group having the highest survival in their place of origin: species occurring in dry areas exhibited higher survival at the dry site, and species restricted to moist sites had higher survival at the wet site. For growth, both groups had higher leaf production at the dry site, but the difference was especially pronounced for species restricted to wet sites. The pronounced mortality in the dry season in the dry site, which was alleviated through irrigation, shows that low water availability directly leads to mortality at that site. However, other results of the study hint towards the importance of additional factors in shaping performance differences between the sites. Understorey light levels and nutrients were higher in the dry site (Brenes-Arguedas *et al.* 2008, 2011), probably contributing to the considerably higher growth rates at that site. Additionally, leaf damage was higher at the wet site, further reducing growth rates there (Brenes-Arguedas, Coley & Kursar 2009). Because forest structure, understorey light levels, pathogen and herbivore pressure, and soil nutrients vary among forests and along rainfall gradients, it is challenging to separate out the effect of drought in such experiments. However, they give a realistic picture of the integrated responses of seedling performance and dynamics to the complex shifts of environmental factors with changing rainfall regimes, and are therefore highly relevant for understanding consequences of global climate change.

Two additional multi-species datasets from transplant experiments across rainfall gradients in tropical wet to moist forest, another one from Panama and one from Southeast Asia, also found strong differences in survival of seedlings of woody species between sites with different rainfall regimes, but neither found growth differences (Engelbrecht, unpublished data; Baltzer & Davies, personal communication). A comparison between transplanted seedlings at two woodland sites with different dry season lengths in Benin showed consistent results (Biaou *et al.* 2011): survival was considerably higher at the mesic than at the dry site, with an especially pronounced effect on the drought-sensitive species, but growth again did not differ between sites.

## 10.5    Species' drought resistance, regeneration dynamics, and species distributions and diversity

The studies reviewed above indicate that periods of low water availability typically have negative effects on seedling performance at the community level, but, at the same time, there exists huge variation among species in their responses. Variation in species' drought resistance – as quantified from irrigation experiments – has been shown to determine how individual species respond to natural variation in water availability. For example, Comita and Engelbrecht (2009) found that survival rates in drier plateau habitats were significantly positively correlated with species' drought resistance in the dry season (where drought resistance was measured in independent experiments; Engelbrecht et al. 2007). However, this was not the case in either the wet season or in wetter slope habitats. Similar patterns were found for growth rates (after excluding drought-deciduous species; Comita & Engelbrecht 2009). These results provide strong evidence that direct effects of low water availability lead to low survival and growth of seedlings of drought-sensitive species in drier habitats.

Species' drought resistance also determines how species respond to interannual variation in water availability. Overall, seedling survival rates were positively related to species' drought resistance in all three years of our study of naturally occurring seedlings in central Panama (Figure 10.7, Comita & Engelbrecht, unpublished data; described above in Section 10.4.3). However, the relationship was significantly stronger in the year with the driest dry season, indicating that drought-sensitive species do indeed have reduced survival in drought years (Figure 10.7). Interestingly, growth rates showed a positive relationship with species' drought resistance in years with below average dry season rainfall, but a negative relationship in the year with above average dry season rainfall (Figure 10.7). These results suggest that, despite their lower survival, drought-sensitive species are able to coexist with drought-resistant species owing to their higher growth in years when water is not as limiting. This is consistent with results from a regional-scale study that found that species occurring on the wetter side of the Isthmus of Panama had higher growth rates and were better able to take advantage of increased light availability when water was not limiting, compared with species occurring on the drier side (Brenes-Arguedas et al. 2011). Similarly, in a study of saplings and trees ≥1 cm dbh in Southeast Asia, species restricted to wet aseasonal forests had higher growth rates than species occurring in dry seasonal forests (Baltzer et al. 2007).

These studies suggest that variation in tropical tree species' drought resistance, combined with variation in water availability, plays a large and direct role in determining where and when species can successfully regenerate. This, in turn, suggests a key role for drought resistance in shaping distribution patterns of tropical tree species. Indeed, it has long been recognised that

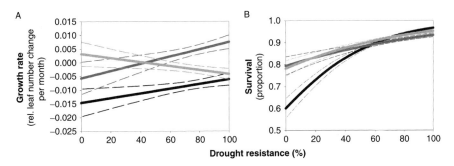

**Figure 10.7** Relationship between species' drought resistance and (A) annual seedling growth and (B) survival in three years with different rainfall patterns on Barro Colorado Island, Panama. Data are for 2003 (black, very strong dry season), 2004 (dark grey, below average dry season rainfall) and 2005 (light grey, above average dry season rainfall). Data are means (solid lines), and 1 SE (dashed lines). All relationships were significant, and there was a significant growth × year and survival × year interaction. Mean and SE values of growth rates and proportion surviving are corrected for differences in leaf number (within species) to account for changes in the size of surviving seedlings over time. Drought resistance was independently assessed in a field irrigation experiment (Figure 10.2C; Engelbrecht *et al.* 2007).

water availability is a major correlate of distributions and diversity patterns of plant species (e.g. Currie & Paquin 1987; Hawkins *et al.* 2003; Kreft & Jetz 2007; Whittaker & Niering 1975). In lowland tropical forests, numerous regional-scale studies have found that diversity, species composition and species distributions strongly correlate with annual rainfall or dry season intensity (e.g. Bongers *et al.* 1999; Bongers, Poorter & Hawthorne 2004; Clinebell *et al.* 1995; Condit 1998; Davidar, Puyravaud & Leigh 2005; Gentry 1988; Hall & Swaine 1981; Hawkins *et al.* 2003; Holdridge *et al.* 1971; Medina 1999; Pyke *et al.* 2001; Slik *et al.* 2003; ter Steege *et al.* 2006). In addition, tropical forests undergo pronounced temporal shifts in species abundance and distribution on scales of decades, as well as thousands of years, that are associated with changes in rainfall patterns (e.g. Condit, Hubbell & Foster 1996; Enquist & Enquist 2011; Feeley *et al.* 2011; Mayle & Power 2008). Moreover, at local scales, many tropical plants show associations with topographic habitat types that vary in soil moisture (e.g. Harms *et al.* 2001; Newbery *et al.* 1996; Svenning 1999; Valencia *et al.* 2004; Webb & Peart 2000).

Despite obvious correlations with water availability, other factors, such as soil nutrients, light availability, pest pressure or historical mechanisms, can covary with water availability and therefore could be responsible for observed correlations between water availability and species' distributions (Baltzer *et al.* 2008; Brenes-Arguedas *et al.* 2009; Givnish 1999; ter Steege *et al.* 2003; Veenendaal & Swaine 1998). However, two recent studies strongly suggest a

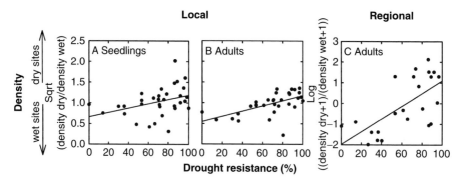

**Figure 10.8** Relationship between species drought resistance and local and regional distribution patterns in lowland tropical forests in Central Panama. There was a significant relationship with drought resistance for local density in dry plateau vs. wetter slope sites for (A) seedlings ($R^2 = 0.14$, $P = 0.035$), and for (B) trees $\geq 1$ cm dbh ($R^2 = 0.34$, $P = 0.0004$) in the BCI 50-ha Forest Dynamics Plot. There was also a significant relationship between drought resistance and the density of adults in a plot on the dry side vs. on the wet side of the Isthmus of Panama (C) ($R^2 = 0.44$, $P = 0.0006$). Redrawn from Engelbrecht *et al.* (2007).

direct, causal role of water availability in shaping tropical tree species' distributions at regional and local scales. Engelbrecht *et al.* (2007) examined distribution patterns of 48 tree and shrub species and found that species' drought resistance, assessed experimentally at the seedling stage, was significantly correlated with species distributions at the regional scale across 122 inventory plots spanning a strong rainfall gradient from the Pacific to the Caribbean side of the Isthmus of Panama (Figure 10.8). At the local scale, within a single large plot (50 ha) in the centre of the rainfall gradient, the distributions of species across topographic habitat types that vary in soil moisture (plateau vs. slope) were also significantly related to species' drought resistance both at the seedling and adult stage (Figure 10.8). In addition, it was shown that these correlations did not arise indirectly through species' responses to variation in light or nutrients (Engelbrecht *et al.* 2007). Similarly, Baltzer *et al.* (2008) found that species' distributions along a climatic gradient spanning the Malay–Thai Peninsula were related to experimentally assessed species' desiccation tolerance, not to historical factors, as had previously been suggested. Specifically, species whose distributions included seasonally dry forests were more desiccation-tolerant and showed different associated physiological characteristics than species restricted to wet aseasonal forests (see Section 10.3 above). Together, these studies provide strong evidence that species' drought resistance interacts with water availability to shape distribution patterns at local and regional scales in the tropics.

Water availability also plays a significant role in shaping patterns of diversity within and among tropical forests. In general, species diversity increases with precipitation and decreases with dry season length across tropical forests (Bongers, Poorter & Hawthorne 2004; Clinebell *et al.* 1995; Condit 1998; Davidar, Puyravaud & Leigh 2005; Gentry 1988; Hall & Swaine 1981; Hawkins *et al.* 2003; Holdridge *et al.* 1971; Medina 1999; Pyke *et al.* 2001; ter Steege *et al.* 2003). On local scales, habitats with high soil moisture tend to support higher tree species richness than drier habitats, although light and nutrient availability also vary with topography (e.g. Gunatilleke *et al.* 2006; Hubbell & Foster 1983; Hubbell *et al.* 1999). Experimental studies support the idea that water availability plays a direct role in shaping such patterns through effects on seedling diversity. In an irrigation experiment in Peru, watered plots had a higher density and higher species richness than unwatered plots, for both sown and naturally occurring seedlings (Paine, Harms & Ramos 2009). Similarly, irrigation had a significant, positive effect on seedling species richness in Panama (Bunker & Carson 2005). These results suggest that drought stress leads to the loss of drought-sensitive species through mortality, and thus decreases species diversity. Additionally, density-dependent mortality due to species-specific pests may be higher in wetter habitats, thus allowing for the coexistence of more species (Givnish 1999).

## 10.6   Conclusions and future research directions

Several conclusions can be drawn from the studies reviewed above. First, water availability is clearly an important driver of regeneration dynamics under current climatic conditions, particularly in seasonal tropical forests and during drought events. This is demonstrated by patterns of seedling recruitment, growth and survival in response to seasonal, interannual and spatial variation in water availability, as well as by experiments that show increased performance in response to supplemental watering during dry periods. Second, although low water availability (i.e. drought) tends to have negative consequences on seedling performance at the community level, there exists huge variation among species in their responses to drought. Variation in drought resistance among tropical woody plant species is governed by differences in physiological traits, primarily those that allow species to tolerate low water availability (i.e. mechanisms of desiccation tolerance). Third, the variation among species in drought resistance, and resulting variation in regeneration dynamics, plays a significant role in shaping differences in species distribution and diversity patterns across rainfall gradients (i.e. changes in annual precipitation and dry season length) at regional scales, and across local soil moisture gradients (associated with topography or soils).

How will altered precipitation patterns due to climate change affect tropical forests, given the relationship between water availability, regeneration dynamics and species distributions? First, increases in dry season length or increases in the severity or frequency of drought events are expected to reduce recruitment, growth and survival of seedlings of drought-sensitive species, particularly in dry habitats and at the dry end of their ranges. As a result, within tropical tree communities, we anticipate a decrease in the abundance of drought-sensitive species, and a restriction of those species to wetter microsites (e.g. slopes and depressions). Failure to regenerate may eventually lead to local extinction of drought-sensitive species, resulting in a loss of diversity within the local community, and a contraction of species ranges at the regional scale, which will increase the probability of extinction at larger scales.

On the other hand, increased rainfall or decreased dry season length will not necessarily increase seedling performance at the community level or favour drought-sensitive species. The irrigation experiments reviewed above found that, although increased water availability increases seedling perform-ance in the dry season, such effects do not necessarily add up to higher growth and survival over the course of the entire year. This is because other mortality agents may become increasingly important with higher water availability (e.g. pathogen and herbivore damage, and light and nutrient availability), and may compensate for decreased drought-related mortality. In addition, increases in the intensity of precipitation events, i.e. strong rainfall, may wash away seeds and young seedlings and also physically damage established seedlings and saplings. Thus, under increased rainfall, the 'winners' are more likely to be determined by resistance to physical damage and pest pressure or their competitive ability than by their drought resistance. Increased rainfall that leads to flooding would also favour tropical tree species that can tolerate anoxic conditions (Parolin *et al.* 2010).

If changing precipitation patterns mainly affect regeneration, such changes to tree community composition and diversity may not be observable for tens to hundreds of years or longer, since tropical trees species are very long-lived. However, if drought events or intense rainfalls are severe enough to increase adult tree mortality (e.g. Phillips *et al.* 2010), effects could be evident on a much shorter time scale. Increased adult mortality would additionally affect regeneration through increased formation of light gaps, which would favour pioneer species (Slik 2004).

To accurately predict how tropical tree species and communities will respond to changing precipitation through effects on regeneration, there are several areas of research that still need to be undertaken. First, the majority of studies of tropical tree species' response to water availability come from a relatively small number of sites, with the majority being con-ducted in lowland, seasonal, moist forests in the Neotropics. Studies from additional tropical areas (e.g. dry and wet forests, aseasonal and montane, Neotropical vs. Palaeotropical) are needed to further our understanding of the differences in drought responses and drought resistance among communities and regions. It is important to note that careful monitoring of water availability will be necessary to allow for meaningful cross-site comparisons.

Second, there is a dearth of quantitative data on how water availability interacts with other abiotic factors (i.e. light, nutrients, temperature and $CO_2$), and how it influences biotic interactions (e.g. pathogen or herbivore attack). These factors undoubtedly influence species performance and distributions, and are known to vary often with water availability (e.g. Givnish 1999; Swaine 1996; Veenendaal et al. 1996). However, how such interactions affect regeneration dynamics in tropical forest communities, and the ramifications for species distributions and diversity, remain to be explored.

Third, an improved mechanistic understanding of tropical tree species' physiological responses to drought is needed to develop meaningful proxies and identify 'soft traits' that correlate with species' drought resistance. This is particularly important for making projections of species' responses and effects on ecosystem functions in tropical forests, where the high diversity precludes detailed studies of all species in the community.

Fourth, although it is clear that there is wide variation among tropical tree species in drought resistance, little is known about variation within species, in terms of either phenotypic plasticity or genetic variation. Such information is key for assessing the potential of species to adapt to changing climate and to predict when and where species will be most affected (Williams et al. 2008). Furthermore, estimates of tropical tree species' migration potentials are needed to determine whether species will be able to track climate across the landscape (Clark et al. 2003).

Finally, efforts to predict the future of tropical forests under global climate change are currently hampered by the fact that existing climate change models can only predict precipitation patterns with extremely high uncertainty (IPCC 2007), particularly at regional to local spatial scales (e.g. Malhi et al. 2009).

In conclusion, our results highlight the sensitivity of tropical forest trees to variation in water availability. Thus, shifts in precipitation patterns will undoubtedly influence the population dynamics and distributions of individual species, with likely consequences for community composition, diversity and ecosystem functioning. The full extent of these changes remains unclear, but the resilience of these ecosystems will depend in large part on the degree to which large, contiguous, intact swaths of tropical forest are preserved.

## Acknowledgements
We thank the BCI 50-ha plot field crew for assisting with data collection in the field. Previously unpublished data presented here were collected with funds from the Center for Tropical Forest Sciences at the Smithsonian Tropical

Research Institute, the US National Science Foundation (DEB-0075102), and the German Research Foundation (DFG). L. S. Comita acknowledges the support of a fellowship from the National Center for Ecological Analysis and Synthesis, a centre funded by NSF (grant no. EF-0553768), the University of California, Santa Barbara, and the State of California.

## References

ACP (2011) ACP Physical Monitoring Downloads. http://striweb.si.edu/esp/physical_monitoring/download_acp.htm

Allan, R., Lindesay, J. & Parker, D. E. (1996) *El Niño, Southern Oscillation and Climatic Variability*. Silver Spring, MD: Aubrey Books Intl Ltd.

Allen, C. D., Macalady, A. K., Chenchouni, H. *et al.* (2010) A global overview of drought and heat-induced tree mortality reveals emerging climate change risks for forests. *Forest Ecology and Management*, **259**, 660–684.

Arndt, S. K., Clifford, S. C., Wanek, W., Jones, H. G. & Popp, M. (2001) Physiological and morphological adaptations of the fruit tree *Ziziphus rotundifolia* in response to progressive drought stress. *Tree Physiology*, **21**, 705–715.

Ashton, P. S. (1993) The community ecology of Asian rainforests, in relation to catastrophic events. *Journal of Biosciences*, **18**, 501–514.

Ashton, P. H. S., Gunatilleke, C. V. S. & Gunatilleke, I. (1995) Seedling survival and growth of four *Shorea* species in a Sri Lankan rainforest. *Journal of Tropical Ecology*, **11**, 263–279.

Asquith, N. M. & Mejia-Chang, M. (2005) Mammals, edge effects, and the loss of tropical forest diversity. *Ecology* **86**, 379–390.

Baltzer, J. L., Davies, S. J., Bunyavejchewin, S. & Noor, N.S.M. (2008) The role of desiccation tolerance in determining tree species distributions along the Malay–Thai Peninsula. *Functional Ecology*, **22**, 221–231.

Baltzer, J. L., Davies, S. J., Noor, N.S.M., Kassim, A. R. & LaFrankie, J. V. (2007) Geographical distributions in tropical trees: can geographical range predict performance and habitat association in co-occurring tree species? *Journal of Biogeography*, **34**, 1916–1926.

Bawa, K. S. & Markham, A. (1995) Climate change and tropical forests. *Trends in Ecology & Evolution*, **10**, 348–349.

Bebber, D., Brown, N. & Speight, M. (2002) Drought and root herbivory in understorey *Parashorea* Kurz (Dipterocarpaceae) seedlings in Borneo. *Journal of Tropical Ecology*, **18**, 795–801.

Bebber, D. P., Brown, N. D. & Speight, M. R. (2004) Dipterocarp seedling population dynamics in Bornean primary lowland forest during the 1997–8 El Niño–Southern Oscillation. *Journal of Tropical Ecology*, **20**, 11–19.

Becker, P. (1992) Seasonality of rainfall and drought in Brunei Darussalam. *Brunei Museum Journal*, **7**, 99–109.

Becker, P., Rabenold, P. E., Idol, J. R. & Smith, A. P. (1988) Water potential gradients for gaps and slopes in a Panamanian tropical moist forests dry season. *Journal of Tropical Ecology*, **4**, 173–184.

Becker, P. & Wong, M. (1993) Drought-induced mortality in tropical heath forest. *Journal of Tropical Forest Science*, **5**, 416–419.

Biaou, S. S. H., Holmgren, M., Sterck, F. J. & Mohren, G. M. J. (2011) Stress-driven changes in the strength of facilitation on tree seedling establishment in West African woodlands. *Biotropica*, **43**, 23–30.

Blain, D. & Kellman, M. (1991) The effect of water supply on tree seed germination and seedling survival in a tropical seasonal forest in Veracruz, Mexico. *Journal of Tropical Ecology*, **7**, 69–83.

Bonal, D. & Guehl, J. M. (2001) Contrasting patterns of leaf water potential and gas exchange responses to drought in seedlings of tropical rainforest species. *Functional Ecology*, **15**, 490–496.

Bongers, F., Poorter, L. & Hawthorne, W. D. (2004)
The forests of Upper Guinea: gradients in
large species composition. In *Biodiversity of
West African forests. An Ecological Atlas of Woody
Plant Species* (eds. L. Poorter, F. Bongers,
F. N. Kouame & W. D. Hawthorne), pp. 41–52.
Oxford, UK: CABI Publishing.

Bongers, F., Poorter, L., Van Rompaey, R. &
Parren, M. P. E. (1999) Distribution of twelve
moist forest canopy tree species in Liberia
and Cote d'Ivoire: response curves to a
climatic gradient. *Journal of Vegetation Science*,
**10**, 371–382.

Borchert, R. (1994) Soil and stem water storage
determine phenology and distribution of
tropical dry forest trees. *Ecology*, **75**,
1437–1449.

Brenes-Arguedas, T., Coley, P. D. & Kursar, T. A.
(2009) Pests vs. drought as determinants of
plant distribution along a tropical rainfall
gradient. *Ecology*, **90**, 1751–1761.

Brenes-Arguedas, T., Rios, M., Rivas-Torres, G. *et al.*
(2008) The effect of soil on the growth
performance of tropical species with
contrasting distributions. *Oikos*, **117**,
1453–1460.

Brenes-Arguedas, T., Roddy, A. B., Coley, P. D. &
Kursar, T. A. (2011) Do differences in
understory light contribute to species
distributions along a tropical rainfall
gradient? *Oecologia*, **166**, 443–456.

Brodribb, T. J., Holbrook, N. M., Edwards, E. J. &
Gutierrez, M. V. (2003) Relations between
stomatal closure, leaf turgor and xylem
vulnerability in eight tropical dry forest
trees. *Plant, Cell and Environment*, **26**, 443–450.

Bunker, D. E. & Carson, W. P. (2005) Drought
stress and tropical forest woody seedlings:
effect on community structure and
composition. *Journal of Ecology*, **93**, 794–806.

Bunker, D. E., DeClerck, F., Bradford, J. C. *et al.*
(2005) Species loss and aboveground carbon
storage in a tropical forest. *Science*, **310**,
1029–1031.

Burlyn, E. M. & Kaufmann, M. R. (1973) The
osmotic potential of Polyethylene Glycol
6000. *Plant Physiology*, **51**, 914–916.

Burslem, D. F. R. P., Grubb, P. J. & Turner, I. M.
(1996) Responses to simulated drought and
elevated nutrient supply among shade-
tolerant tree seedlings of lowland tropical
forest in Singapore. *Biotropica*, **28**, 636–648.

Cao, K. F. (2000) Water relations and gas
exchange of tropical saplings during a
prolonged drought in a Bornean heath
forest, with reference to root architecture.
*Journal of Tropical Ecology*, **16**, 101–116.

Chen, T. H. H. & Murata, N. (2002) Enhancement
of tolerance of abiotic stress by metabolic
engineering of betaines and other
compatible solutes. *Current Opinion in Plant
Biology*, **5**, 250–257.

Chesson, P. L. & Warner, R. R. (1981)
Environmental variability promotes
coexistence in lottery competitive systems.
*American Naturalist*, **117**, 923–943.

Chiariello, N. R., Field, C. B. & Mooney, H. A.
(1987) Midday wilting in a tropical pioneer
tree. *Functional Ecology*, **1**, 3–11.

Choat, B., Sack, L. & Holbrook, N. M. (2007)
Diversity of hydraulic traits in nine *Cordia*
species growing in tropical forests with
contrasting precipitation. *New Phytologist*,
**175**, 686–698.

Clark, J. S., Lewis, M., McLachlan, J. S. &
HilleRisLambers, J. (2003) Estimating
population spread: what can we forecast
and how well? *Ecology*, **84**, 1979–1988.

Clinebell, R. R., Phillips, O. L., Gentry, A. H.,
Stark, N. & Zuuring, H. (1995) Prediction of
Neotropical tree and liana species richness
from soil and climatic data. *Biodiversity and
Conservation*, **4**, 56–90.

Coley, P. D. (1983) Herbivory and defensive
characteristics of tree species in a lowland
tropical forest. *Ecological Monographs*, **53**,
209–233.

Colwell, R. K., Brehm, G., Cardelus, C. L.,
Gilman, A. C. & Longino, J. T. (2008) Global
warming, elevational range shifts, and
lowland biotic attrition in the wet tropics.
*Science*, **322**, 258–261.

Comita, L. S. & Engelbrecht, B. M. J. (2009)
Seasonal and spatial variation in water

availability drive habitat associations in a tropical forest. *Ecology*, **90**, 2755–2765.

Condit, R. (1998) Ecological implications of changes in drought patterns: Shifts in forest composition in Panama. *Climatic Change*, **39**, 413–427.

Condit, R., Hubbell, S. P. & Foster, R. B. (1995) Mortality rates of 205 neotropical tree and shrub species and the impact of a severe drought. *Ecological Monographs*, **65**, 419–439.

Condit, R., Hubbell, S. P. & Foster, R. B. (1996) Changes in tree species abundance in a Neotropical forest: Impact of climate change. *Journal of Tropical Ecology*, **12**, 231–256.

Connell, J. H. (1971) On the role of natural enemies in preventing competitive exclusion in some marine animals and in rain forest trees. In *Dynamics of Populations* (eds. P. J. den Boer & G. R. Gradwell), pp. 298–312. Wageningen, The Netherlands: Centre for Agricultural Publishing and Documentation.

Costa, M. H. & Foley, J. A. (2000) Combined effects of deforestation and doubled atmospheric $CO_2$ concentrations on the climate of Amazonia. *Journal of Climate*, **13**, 18–34.

Cox, P. M., Betts, R. A., Jones, C. D., Spall, S. A. & Totterdell, I. J. (2000) Acceleration of global warming due to carbon-cycle feedbacks in a coupled climate model. *Nature*, **408**, 184–187.

Cruz-Rodríguez, J. A. & López-Mala, L. (2004) Demography of the seedling bank of *Manilkara zorpota* (L). Royen in a subtropical rain forest of Mexico. *Plant Ecology*, **172**, 227–235.

Currie, D. J. & Paquin, V. (1987) Large-scale biogeographical patterns of species richness of trees. *Nature*, **329**, 326–327.

da Costa, A. C. L., Galbraith, D., Almeida, S. *et al.* (2010) Effect of 7 yr of experimental drought on vegetation dynamics and biomass storage of an eastern Amazonian rainforest. *New Phytologist*, **187**, 579–591.

Davidar, P., Puyravaud, J. P. & Leigh, E. G. (2005) Changes in rain forest tree diversity, dominance and rarity across a seasonality gradient in the Western Ghats, India. *Journal of Biogeography*, **32**, 493–501.

Davidar, P., Rajagopal, B., Mohandass, D. *et al.* (2007) The effect of climatic gradients, topographic variation and species traits on the beta diversity of rain forest trees. *Global Ecology and Biogeography*, **16**, 510–518.

Daws, M. I., Bolton, S., Burslem, D., Garwood, N. C. & Mullins, C. E. (2007) Loss of desiccation tolerance during germination in neo-tropical pioneer seeds: Implications for seed mortality and germination characteristics. *Seed Science Research*, **17**, 273–281.

Daws, M. I., Crabtree, L. M., Dalling, J. W., Mullins, C. E. & Burslem, D. (2008) Germination responses to water potential in Neotropical pioneers suggest large-seeded species take more risks. *Annals of Botany*, **102**, 945–951.

Daws, M. I., Garwood, N. C. & Pritchard, H. W. (2005) Traits of recalcitrant seeds in a semi-deciduous tropical forest in Panama: some ecological implications. *Functional Ecology*, **19**, 874–885.

Daws, M. I., Garwood, N. C. & Pritchard, H. W. (2006) Prediction of desiccation sensitivity in seeds of woody species: A probabilistic model based on two seed traits and 104 species. *Annals of Botany*, **97**, 667–674.

Daws, M. I., Mullins, C. E., Burslem, D., Paton, S. R. & Dalling, J. W. (2002) Topographic position affects the water regime in a semideciduous tropical forest in Panama. *Plant and Soil*, **238**, 79–90.

Daws, M. I., Pearson, T. R. H., Burslem, D., Mullins, C. E. & Dalling, J. W. (2005) Effects of topographic position, leaf litter and seed size on seedling demography in a semi-deciduous tropical forest in Panama. *Plant Ecology*, **179**, 93–105.

de Gouvenain, R. L., Kobe, R. K. & Silander, J. A. (2007) Partitioning of understorey light and dry-season soil moisture gradients among seedlings of four rain-forest tree species in Madagascar. *Journal of Tropical Ecology*, **23**, 569–579.

Delissio, L. J. & Primack, R. B. (2003) The impact of drought on the population dynamics of canopy-tree seedlings in an aseasonal Malaysian rain forest. *Journal of Tropical Ecology*, **19**, 489–500.

Delissio, L. J., Primack, R. B., Hall, P. & Lee, H. S. (2002) A decade of canopy-tree seedling survival and growth in two Bornean rain forests: Persistence and recovery from suppression. *Journal of Tropical Ecology*, **18**, 645–658.

Eamus, D. & Prior, L. (2001) Ecophysiology of trees of seasonally dry tropics: Comparisons among phenologies. *Advances in Ecological Research,* **32**, 113–197.

Engelbrecht, B. M. J., Comita, L. S., Condit, R. *et al.* (2007) Drought sensitivity shapes species distribution patterns in tropical forests. *Nature*, **447**, 80–82.

Engelbrecht, B. M. J., Dalling, J. W., Pearson, T. R. H. *et al.* (2006) Short dry spells in the wet season increase mortality of tropical pioneer seedlings. *Oecologia*, **148**, 258–269.

Engelbrecht, B. M. J. & Kursar, T. A. (2003) Comparative drought-resistance of seedlings of 28 species of co-occurring tropical woody plants. *Oecologia*, **136**, 383–393.

Engelbrecht, B. M. J., Kursar, T. A. & Tyree, M. T. (2005) Drought effects on seedling survival in a tropical moist forest. *Trees-Structure and Function*, **19**, 312–321.

Engelbrecht, B. M. J., Wright, S. J. & De Steven, D. (2002) Survival and ecophysiology of tree seedlings during El Niño drought in a tropical moist forest in Panama. *Journal of Tropical Ecology*, **18**, 569–579.

Enquist, B. J. & Enquist, C. A. F. (2011) Long-term change within a Neotropical forest: assessing differential functional and floristic responses to disturbance and drought. *Global Change Biology*, **17**, 1408–1424.

ESP (2011) BCI Physical Monitoring Downloads. http://striweb.si.edu/esp/physical_monitoring/download_bci.htm

Feeley, K. J., Davies, S. J., Perez, R., Hubbell, S. P. & Foster, R. B. (2011) Directional changes in the species composition of a tropical forest. *Ecology*, **92**, 871–882.

Fine, P. V. A., Mesones, I. & Coley, P. D. (2004) Herbivores promote habitat specialization by trees in Amazonian forests. *Science*, **305**, 663–665.

Fisher, B. L., Howe, H. F. & Wright, S. J. (1991) Survival and growth of *Virola surinamensis* yearlings: water augmentation in gap and understory. *Oecologia*, **86**, 292–297.

Garwood, N. C. (1983) Seed germination in a seasonal tropical forest in Panama: a community study. *Ecological Monographs*, **53**, 159–181.

Gentry, A. H. (1988) Changes in plant community diversity and floristic composition on environmental and geographical gradients. *Annals of the Missouri Botanical Garden*, **75**, 1–34.

Gerhardt, K. (1996) Effects of root competition and canopy openness on survival and growth of tree seedlings in a tropical seasonal dry forest. *Forest Ecology and Management*, **82**, 33–48.

Gibbons, J. M. & Newbery, D. M. (2003) Drought avoidance and the effect of local topography on trees in the understorey of Bornean lowland rain forest. *Plant Ecology*, **164**, 1–18.

Gilbert, G. S., Harms, K. E., Hamill, D. N. & Hubbell, S. P. (2001) Effects of seedling size, El Niño drought, seedling density, and distance to nearest conspecific adult on 6-year survival of *Ocotea whitei* seedlings in Panama. *Oecologia*, **127**, 509–516.

Givnish, T. J. (1999) On the causes of gradients in tropical tree diversity. *Journal of Ecology*, **87**, 193–210.

Green, J. J. & Newbery, D. M. (2002) Reproductive investment and seedling survival of the mast-fruiting rain forest tree, *Microberlinia bisulcata* A.Chev. *Plant Ecology*, **162**, 169–183.

Grubb, P. J. (1977) The maintenance of species-richness in plant communities: the importance of regeneration niche. *Biological Reviews of the Cambridge Philosophical Society*, **52**, 107–145.

Gunatilleke, C. V. S., Gunatilleke, I. A. U. N., Esufali, S. *et al.* (2006) Species-habitat associations in a Sri Lankan dipterocarp forest. *Journal of Tropical Ecology*, **22**, 371–384.

Hacke, U. G., Sperry, J. S., Pockman, W. T., Davis, S. D. & McCulloch, K. A. (2001) Trends in wood density and structure are linked to prevention of xylem implosion by negative pressure. *Oecologia*, **126**, 457–461.

Hall, J. B. & Swaine, M. D. (1981) *Distribution and Ecology of Vascular Plants in a Tropical Rain Forest: Forest Vegetation in Ghana*. Geobotany Vol. 1. The Hague, Netherlands; Boston, MA: Dr W. Junk Publishers.

Harms, K. E., Condit, R., Hubbell, S. P. & Foster, R. B. (2001) Habitat associations of trees and shrubs in a 50-ha Neotropical forest plot. *Journal of Ecology*, **89**, 947–959.

Harper, J. L. (1977) *Population Biology of Plants*. London: Academic Press.

Hawkins, B. A., Field, R., Cornell, H. V. et al. (2003) Energy, water, and broad-scale geographic patterns of species richness. *Ecology*, **84**, 3105–3117.

Hedges, L. V., Gurevitch, J. & Curtis, P. S. (1999) The meta-analysis of response ratios in experimental ecology. *Ecology*, **80**, 1150–1156.

Hoffmann, W. A., Schroeder, W. & Jackson, R. B. (2003) Regional feedbacks among fire, climate, and tropical deforestation. *Journal of Geophysical Research*, **108**, ACL4-1–11.

Holdridge, L. R., Grenke, W. C., Hatheway, W. H., Liang, T. & Tosi, J. A. (1971) *Forest Environments in Tropical Life Zones*. Oxford: Pergamon Press.

Hooper, D. U. & Vitousek, P. M. (1997) The effects of plant composition and diversity on ecosystem processes. *Science*, **277**, 1302–1305.

Hsiao, T. C. (1973) Plant responses to water stress. *Annual Review of Plant Physiology*, **24**, 519–570.

Hubbell, S. P. (1998) The maintenance of diversity in a Neotropical tree community: conceptual issues, current evidence, and challenges ahead. In *Forest Biodiversity Research, Monitoring and Modeling: Conceptual Background and Old World Case Studies* (eds. D. F. & J. A. Comiskey), pp. 17–44. Pearl River, NY: Parthenon Publishing.

Hubbell, S. P. & Foster, R. B. (1983) Diversity of canopy trees in a Neotropical forest and implications for conservation. In *Tropical Rain Forest: Ecology and Management* (eds. S. L. Sutton, T. C. Whitmore & A. C. Chadwick), pp. 25–41. Oxford: Blackwell Scientific.

Hubbell, S. P., Foster, R. B., O'Brien, S. T. et al. (1999) Light-gap disturbances, recruitment limitation, and tree diversity in a Neotropical forest. *Science*, **283**, 554–557.

Hulme, M. & Viner, D. (1998) A climate change scenario for the tropics. *Climatic Change*, **39**, 145–176.

IPCC (2007) *Climate Change 2007: Impacts, Adaptation and Vulnerability. Contribution of Working Group II to the Fourth Assessment Report of the Intergovernmental Panel on Climate Change*. Cambridge: Cambridge University Press.

Jackson, P. C., Cavelier, J., Goldstein, G., Meinzer, F. C. & Holbrook, N. M. (1995) Partitioning of water resources among plants of a lowland tropical forest. *Oecologia*, **101**, 197–203.

Janzen, D. H. (1970) Herbivores and number of tree species in tropical forests. *American Naturalist*, **104**, 501–528.

Jarvis, P. G. & Jarvis, M. S. (1963) The water relations of tree seedlings I. Growth and water use in relations to soil water potential. *Physiologia Plantarum*, **16**, 215–235.

John, R., Dalling, J. W., Harms, K. E. et al. (2007) Soil nutrients influence spatial distributions of tropical tree species. *Proceedings of the National Academy of Sciences USA*, **104**, 864–869.

Kerstiens, G. (1996a) Cuticular water permeability and its physiological significance. *Journal of Experimental Botany*, **47**, 1813–1832.

Kerstiens, G. (1996b) Diffusion of water vapour and gases across cuticles and through stomatal pores presumed closed. *Plant Cuticles* (ed. G. Kerstiens), pp. 121–134. Oxford: BIOS Scientific Publisher Ltd.

Kreft, H. & Jetz, W. (2007) Global patterns and determinants of vascular plant diversity.

*Proceedings of the National Academy of Sciences USA*, **104**, 5925–5930.

Kursar, T. A., Engelbrecht, B. M. J., Burke, A. *et al.* (2009) Tolerance to low leaf water status of tropical tree seedlings is related to drought performance and distribution. *Functional Ecology*, **23**, 93–102.

Kursar, T. A., Engelbrecht, B. M. J. & Tyree, M. T. (2003) Soil moisture release curves for two tropical forests having similar rainfall but distinct tree communities. *Ecological Society of America Annual Meeting Abstracts*, **88**, 193–194.

Larcher, W. (2003) *Physiological Plant Ecology*, 4th edn. Berlin: Springer.

Lewis, S. L. & Tanner, E. V. J. (2000) Effects of above- and belowground competition on growth and survival of rain forest tree seedlings. *Ecology*, **81**, 2525–2538.

Lieberman, D. & Li, M. (1992) Seedling recruitment patterns in tropical dry forest in Ghana. *Journal of Vegetation Science*, **3**, 375–382.

Lopez, O. R. & Kursar, T. A. (2007) Interannual variation in rainfall, drought stress and seedling mortality may mediate monodominance in tropical flooded forests. *Oecologia*, **154**, 35–43.

Malhi, Y., Aragao, L., Galbraith, D. *et al.* (2009) Exploring the likelihood and mechanism of a climate-change-induced dieback of the Amazon rainforest. *Proceedings of the National Academy of Sciences USA*, **106**, 20610–20615.

Malhi, Y. & Phillips, O. L. (2004) Tropical forests and global atmospheric change: a synthesis. *Philosophical Transactions of the Royal Society Series B: Biological Sciences*, **359**, 549–555.

Malhi, Y., Roberts, J. T., Betts, R. A. *et al.* (2008) Climate change, deforestation, and the fate of the Amazon. *Science*, **319**, 169–172.

Markesteijn, L., Iraipi, J., Bongers, F. & Poorter, L. (2010) Seasonal variation in soil and plant water potentials in a Bolivian tropical moist and dry forest. *Journal of Tropical Ecology*, **26**, 497–508.

Markesteijn, L. & Poorter, L. (2009) Seedling root morphology and biomass allocation of 62 tropical tree species in relation to drought- and shade-tolerance. *Journal of Ecology*, **97**, 311–325.

Markesteijn, L., Poorter, L., Paz, H., Sack, L. & Bongers, F. (2011) Ecological differentiation in xylem cavitation resistance is associated with stem and leaf structural traits. *Plant, Cell and Environment*, **34**, 137–148.

Marod, D., Kutintara, U., Tanaka, H. & Nakashizuka, T. (2002) The effects of drought and fire on seed and seedling dynamics in a tropical seasonal forest in Thailand. *Plant Ecology*, **161**, 41–57.

Mayle, F. E. & Power, M. J. (2008) Impact of a drier Early–Mid-Holocene climate upon Amazonian forests. *Philosophical Transactions of the Royal Society Series B*, **363**, 1829–1838.

McLaren, K. P. & McDonald, M. A. (2003) The effects of moisture and shade on seed germination and seedling survival in a tropical dry forest in Jamaica. *Forest Ecology and Management*, **183**, 61–75.

Medina, E. (1999) Tropical forests: diversity and function of dominant lifeforms. In *Handbook of Functional Plant Ecology* (eds. F. Pugnaire & M. I. Vallejo), pp. 407–448. New York: Marcel Dekker.

Merchant, A., Tausz, M., Arndt, S. K. & Adams, M. A. (2006) Cyclitols and carbohydrates in leaves and roots of 13 *Eucalyptus* species suggest contrasting physiological responses to water deficit. *Plant, Cell and Environment*, **29**, 2017–2029.

Metz, M. R., Comita, L. S., Chen, Y. Y. *et al.* (2008) Temporal and spatial variability in seedling dynamics: a cross-site comparison in four lowland tropical forests. *Journal of Tropical Ecology*, **24**, 9–18.

Miles, L., Grainger, A. & Phillips, O. (2004) The impact of global climate change on tropical forest biodiversity in Amazonia. *Global Ecology and Biogeography*, **13**, 553–565.

Mulkey, S. S., Smith, A. P., Wright, S. J., Machado, J. L. & Dudley, R. (1992) Contrasting leaf phenotypes control seasonal variation in water-loss in a tropical forest shrub. *Proceedings of the National Academy of Sciences USA*, **89**, 9084–9088.

Mulkey, S. S. & Wright, S. J. (1996) Influence of seasonal drought on the carbon balance of tropical forest plants. In *Tropical Forest Plant Ecophysiology* (eds. S. S. Mulkey, R. L. Chazdon & A. P. Smith), pp. 217–243. New York: Chapman & Hall.

Mulkey, S. S., Wright, S. J. & Smith, A. P. (1993) Comparative physiology and demography of 3 Neotropical forest shrubs: alternative shade-adaptive character syndromes *Oecologia*, **96**, 526–536.

Myers, M. A. & Kitajima, K. (2007) Carbohydrate storage enhances seedling shade and stress tolerance in a neotropical forest. *Journal of Ecology*, **95**, 383–395.

Nakagawa, M., Tanaka, K., Nakashizuka, T. *et al.* (2000) Impact of severe drought associated with the 1997–1998 El Niño in a tropical forest in Sarawak. *Journal of Tropical Ecology*, **16**, 355–367.

Neelin, J. D., Munnich, M., Su, H., Meyerson, J. E. & Holloway, C. E. (2006) Tropical drying trends in global warming models and observations. *Proceedings of the National Academy of Sciences USA*, **103**, 6110–6115.

Nepstad, D. C., Tohver, I. M., Ray, D., Moutinho, P. & Cardinot, G. (2007) Mortality of large trees and lianas following experimental drought in an Amazon forest. *Ecology*, **88**, 2259–2269.

Newbery, D. M., Campbell, E. J. F., Proctor, J. & Still, M. J. (1996) Primary lowland dipterocarp forest at Danum Valley, Sabah, Malaysia. Species composition and patterns in the understorey. *Vegetatio*, **122**, 193–220.

Padilla, F. M. & Pugnaire, F. I. (2007) Rooting depth and soil moisture control Mediterranean woody seedling survival during drought. *Functional Ecology*, **21**, 489–495.

Paine, C. E. T., Harms, K. E. & Ramos, J. (2009) Supplemental irrigation increases seedling performance and diversity in a tropical forest. *Journal of Tropical Ecology*, **25**, 171–180.

Palmiotto, P. A., Davies, S. J., Vogt, K. A. *et al.* (2004) Soil-related habitat specialization in dipterocarp rain forest tree species in Borneo. *Journal of Ecology*, **92**, 609–623.

Parolin, P., Lucas, C., Piedade, M. T. F. & Wittmann, F. (2010) Drought responses of flood-tolerant trees in Amazonian floodplains. *Annals of Botany*, **105**, 129–139.

Paz, H. (2003) Root/shoot allocation and root architecture in seedlings: Variation among forest sites, microhabitats, and ecological groups. *Biotropica*, **35**, 318–332.

Pearson, T. R. H., Burslem, D. F. R. P., Goeriz, R. E. & Dalling, J. W. (2003) Regeneration niche partitioning in neotropical pioneers: effects of gap size, seasonal drought, and herbivory on growth and survival. *Oecologia*, **137**, 456–465.

Phillips, O. L., Aragao, L., Lewis, S. L. *et al.* (2009) Drought sensitivity of the Amazon rainforest. *Science*, **323**, 1344–1347.

Phillips, O. L., van der Heijden, G., Lewis, S. L. *et al.* (2010) Drought-mortality relationships for tropical forests. *New Phytologist*, **187**, 631–646.

Poorter, L., Bongers, F., Kouame, F. N. & Hawthorne, W. D. (2004) *Biodiversity of West African Forests: An Ecological Atlas of Woody Plant Species*. Oxford: CABI Publishing.

Poorter, L., Bongers, F. & Lemmens, R. H. M. J. (2004) West African forests; introduction. In *Biodiversity of West African Forests. An Ecological Atlas of Woody Plant Species* (eds. L. Poorter, F. Bongers, F. N. Kouame & W. D. Hawthorne), pp. 5–14., Oxford: CABI Publishing.

Poorter, L. & Hayashida-Oliver, Y. (2000) Effects of seasonal drought on gap and understorey seedlings in a Bolivian moist forest. *Journal of Tropical Ecology*, **16**, 481–498.

Poorter, L. & Markesteijn, L. (2008) Seedling traits determine drought tolerance of tropical tree species. *Biotropica*, **40**, 321–331.

Potts, M. D. (2003) Drought in a Bornean everwet rain forest. *Journal of Ecology*, **91**, 467–474.

Pyke, C. R., Condit, R., Aguilar, S. & Lao, S. (2001) Floristic composition across a climatic gradient in a neotropical lowland forest. *Journal of Vegetation Science*, **12**, 553–566.

Quesada, M., Sanchez-Azofeifa, G. A., Alvarez-Anorve, M. *et al.* (2009) Succession and management of tropical dry forests in the Americas: Review and new perspectives. *Forest Ecology and Management*, **258**, 1014–1024.

Rascher, U., Bobich, E. G., Lin, G. H. *et al.* (2004) Functional diversity of photosynthesis during drought in a model tropical rainforest – the contribution of leaf area, photosynthetic electron transport and stomatal conductance to reduction in net ecosystem carbon exchange. *Plant, Cell and Environment*, **27**, 1239–1256.

Reich, P. B. & Borchert, R. (1984) Water stress and tree phenology in a tropical dry forest in the lowlands of Costa Rica. *Journal of Ecology*, **72**, 61–74.

Russo, S. E., Zhang, L. & Tan, S. (2012) Covariation between understorey light environments and soil resources in Bornean mixed dipterocarp rain forest. *Journal of Tropical Ecology* **28**, 33–44.

Sack, L. (2004) Responses of temperate woody seedlings to shade and drought: do trade-offs limit potential niche differentiation? *Oikos*, **107**, 110–127.

Slik, J. W. F. (2004) El Niño droughts and their effects on tree species composition and diversity in tropical rain forests. *Oecologia*, **141**, 114–120.

Slik, J. W. F., Poulsen, A. D., Ashton, P. S. *et al.* (2003) A floristic analysis of the lowland dipterocarp forests of Borneo. *Journal of Biogeography*, **30**, 1517–1531.

Slot, M. & Poorter, L. (2007) Diversity of tropical tree seedling responses to drought. *Biotropica*, **39**, 683–690.

Snow, M. D. & Tingey, D. T. (1985) Evaluation of a system for the imposition of plant water stress. *Plant Physiology* **77**, 602–607.

Sombroek, W. (2001) Spatial and temporal patterns of Amazon rainfall – Consequences for the planning of agricultural occupation and the protection of primary forests. *Ambio*, **30**, 388–396.

Svenning, J. C. (1999) Microhabitat specialization in a species-rich palm community in Amazonian Ecuador. *Journal of Ecology*, **87**, 55–65.

Swaine, M. D. (1996) Rainfall and soil fertility as factors limiting forest species distributions in Ghana. *Journal of Ecology*, **84**, 419–428.

Tanner, E. V. J. & Barberis, I. M. (2007) Trenching increased growth, and irrigation increased survival of tree seedlings in the understorey of a semi-evergreen rain forest in Panama. *Journal of Tropical Ecology*, **23**, 257–268.

ter Steege, H. (1994) Flooding and drought tolerance in seeds and seedlings of two *Mora* species segregated along a soil hydrological gradient in the tropical rain-forest of Guyana. *Oecologia*, **100**, 356–367.

ter Steege, H., Pitman, N., Sabatier, D. *et al.* (2003) A spatial model of tree alpha-diversity and tree density for the Amazon. *Biodiversity and Conservation*, **12**, 2255–2277.

ter Steege, H., Pitman, N. C. A., Phillips, O. L. *et al.* (2006) Continental-scale patterns of canopy tree composition and function across Amazonia. *Nature*, **443**, 444–447.

Timmermann, A., Oberhuber, J., Bacher, A. *et al.* (1999) Increased El Niño frequency in a climate model forced by future greenhouse warming. *Nature*, **398**, 694–697.

Tobin, M. F., Lopez, O. R. & Kursar, T. A. (1999) Responses of tropical understory plants to a severe drought: Tolerance and avoidance of water stress. *Biotropica*, **31**, 570–578.

Toledo, M., Poorter, L., Pena-Claros, M. *et al.* (2011) Climate is a stronger driver of tree and forest growth rates than soil and disturbance. *Journal of Ecology*, **99**, 254–264.

Turkan, I., Bor, M., Ozdemir, F. & Koca, H. (2005) Differential responses of lipid peroxidation and antioxidants in the leaves of drought-tolerant *P. acutifolius* Gray and drought-sensitive *P. vulgaris* L. subjected to polyethylene glycol mediated water stress. *Plant Science*, **168**, 223–231.

Turner, I. M. (1990) The seedling survivorship and growth of three *Shorea* species in a

Malaysian tropical rain forest. *Journal of Tropical Ecology*, **6**, 469–478.

Tyree, M. T., Engelbrecht, B. M. J., Vargas, G. & Kursar, T. A. (2003) Desiccation tolerance of five tropical seedlings in Panama. Relationship to a field assessment of drought performance. *Plant Physiology*, **132**, 1439–1447.

Tyree, M. T. & Ewers, F. W. (1996) Hydraulic architecture of woody tropical plants. In *Tropical Forest Plant Ecophysiology* (eds. S. S. Mulkey, R. L. Chazdon & A. P. Smith), pp. 217–243. New York: Chapman & Hall.

Tyree, M. T. & Jarvis, P. G. (1982) Water in tissues and cells. *Encyclopedia of Plant Physiology* (eds. O. L. Lange, P. S. Nobel, C. B. Osmond & H. Ziegler), pp. 36–71. Berlin: Spring-Verlag.

Tyree, M. T. & Sperry, J. S. (1989) Vulnerability of xylem to cavitation and embolism. *Annual Review of Plant Physiology and Plant Molecular Biology*, **40**, 19–38.

Valencia, R., Foster, R. B., Villa, G. *et al.* (2004) Tree species distributions and local habitat variation in the Amazon: large forest plot in eastern Ecuador. *Journal of Ecology*, **92**, 214–229.

Vazquez-Yanes, C. & Orozco-Segovia, A. (1993) Patterns of seed longevity and germination in the tropical rainforest. *Annual Review of Ecology and Systematics*, **24**, 69–87.

Veenendaal, E. M. & Swaine, M. D. (1998) Limits to tree species distribution in lowland tropical rainforests. *Dynamics of Tropical Communities: 37th Symposium of the British Ecological Society*. (eds. D. M. Newbery, H. H. T. Prins & N. Brown), pp. 163–191. Oxford: Blackwell Scientific.

Veenendaal, E. M., Swaine, M. D., Agyeman, V. K. *et al.* (1996) Differences in plant and soil water relations in and around a forest gap in West Africa during the dry season may influence seedling establishment and survival. *Journal of Ecology*, **84**, 83–90.

Walsh, R. P. D. (1996) Climate. In *The Tropical Rainforest: An Ecological Study* (ed. P. W. Richards), pp. 159–205. Cambridge: Cambridge University Press.

Walsh, R. P. D. & Newbery, D. M. (1999) The ecoclimatology of Danum, Sabah, in the context of the world's rainforest regions, with particular reference to dry periods and their impact. *Philosophical Transactions of the Royal Society Series B*, **354**, 1869–1883.

Webb, C. O. & Peart, D. R. (2000) Habitat associations of trees and seedlings in a Bornean rain forest. *Journal of Ecology*, **88**, 464–478.

Westoby, M. (2002) Choosing species to study. *Trends in Ecology & Evolution*, **17**, 587.

Whittaker, R. H. & Niering, W. A. (1975) Vegetation of the Santa Catalina Mountains, Arizona 5. Biomass, production, and diversity along elevation gradient. *Ecology*, **56**, 771–790.

Williams, S. E., Shoo, L. P., Isaac, J. L., Hoffmann, A. A. & Langham, G. (2008) Towards an integrated framework for assessing the vulnerability of species to climate change. *Plos Biology*, **6**, 2621–2626.

Williamson, G. B., Laurance, W. F., Oliveira, A. A. *et al.* (2000) Amazonian tree mortality during the 1997 El Niño drought. *Conservation Biology*, **14**, 1538–1542.

Wolda, H. (1978) Seasonal fluctuations in rainfall, food and abundance of tropical insects. *Journal of Animal Ecology*, **47**, 369–381.

Wright, S. J. (2005) The El Niño Southern Oscillation influences tree performance in tropical rainforests. In *Tropical Rainforests: Past, Present, and Future* (eds. E. Bermingham, R. E. Dickinson & C. Moritz), pp. 295–310. Chicago and London: University of Chicago Press.

Wright, S. J., Machado, J. L., Mulkey, S. S. & Smith, A. P. (1992) Drought acclimation among tropical forest shrubs (*Psychotria*, Rubiaceae). *Oecologia*, **89**, 457–463.

Yavitt, J. B. & Wright, S. J. (2008) Seedling growth responses to water and nutrient augmentation in the understorey of a lowland moist forest, Panama. *Journal of Tropical Ecology*, **24**, 19–26.

CHAPTER ELEVEN

# Tree performance across gradients of soil resource availability

RICHARD K. KOBE, THOMAS W. BARIBAULT
and ELLEN K. HOLSTE
*Department of Forestry, Michigan State University*

## 11.1   Introduction

Whether in the temperate zone or tropics, tree species composition and forest productivity are strongly associated with soil characteristics (e.g. Figure 11.1). Although these community- and ecosystem-level processes necessarily arise from variation in individual tree performance, the influences of specific soil resources on particular tree demographic processes have yet to be fully elucidated (Kobe 1996).

It is important, for several reasons, to understand how soil resources govern tree performance. First, and perhaps most salient to the theme of this volume, human activity exerts a potentially strong effect on soil resource availability through atmospheric deposition of nitrogen (N) (Figure 11.2), which accelerates soil acidification and the leaching of phosphorus (P) and base cations (calcium (Ca), magnesium (Mg), and potassium (K)) (Izuta *et al.* 2004; Matson *et al.* 1999; Perakis *et al.* 2006). Inorganic N deposition takes two major forms: nitrate ($NO_3^-$) from the combustion of fossil fuels and ammonium ($NH_4^+$) from agricultural activity. Background levels of N deposition are typically <1 kgN ha$^{-1}$ yr$^{-1}$, as measured in remote non-industrialised areas of the world (Hedin *et al.* 1995). In North America, N deposition can be more than 20 kgN ha$^{-1}$ yr$^{-1}$ (Gradowski & Thomas 2008; Weathers *et al.* 2006). Levels in Europe are much higher, with maximum levels reaching at least 43.5 kgN ha$^{-1}$ yr$^{-1}$ recently (Stevens *et al.* 2011) and 75 kgN ha$^{-1}$ yr$^{-1}$ in the 1990s (Dise & Wright 1995). Atmospheric deposition of N is not exclusively a temperate issue, and levels of N deposition are expected to increase in the tropics with further industrial and agricultural development (Matson *et al.* 1999). Even though soil N levels are higher in tropical than temperate forests, additional inputs of N through deposition could lead to lower plant diversity and increased bulk carbon storage, as well as losses of base cations and P (Cusack *et al.* 2011; Lu *et al.* 2010; Matson *et al.* 1999).

Forest soils weather and acidify over time even in the absence of N deposition, leading to sustained losses of base cations and P, and concomitant increases in Al and Fe concentrations (Chadwick *et al.* 1999; Hedin, Vitousek & Matson

*Forests and Global Change*, ed. David A. Coomes, David F. R. P. Burslem and William D. Simonson. Published by Cambridge University Press. © British Ecological Society 2014.

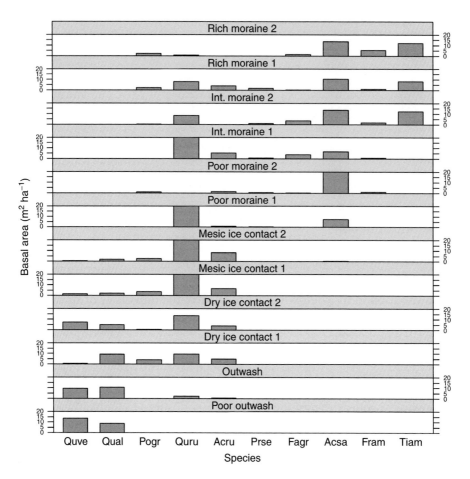

**Figure 11.1** Species basal area across our 12 primary sites in northwestern lower Michigan. The sites stratify a gradient in soil resource availability (water, calcium and nitrogen), generally increasing across sites from the bottom to the top of the graph. Abbreviations of species names are the first two letters of the genus and species and include: *Quercus velutina, Q. alba, Populus grandidentata, Q. rubra, Acer rubrum, Prunus serotina, Fagus grandifolia, A. saccharum, Fraxinus americana* and *Tilia americana*. See plate section for colour version.

2003; Porder & Chadwick 2009; Porder, Clark & Vitousek 2006; Walker & Syers 1976). With an emphasis on P dynamics, Walker and Syers (1976) presented a framework for these processes and a conceptual basis for the predominance of N limitation in younger temperate soils and P limitation in the typically older soils of the lowland tropics. However, Walker and Syers (1976, p. 2) also state: '… levels of other essential elements [besides P] such as Ca, Mg, and K also decline to low values, pH levels are low, and the vegetation changes to species tolerant of the impoverished conditions …'. Coupled element losses with soil

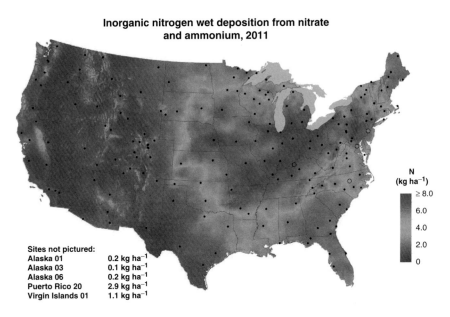

**Inorganic nitrogen wet deposition from nitrate and ammonium, 2011**

N
(kg ha$^{-1}$)

≥ 8.0

6.0

4.0

2.0

0

Sites not pictured:
Alaska 01          0.2 kg ha$^{-1}$
Alaska 03          0.1 kg ha$^{-1}$
Alaska 06          0.2 kg ha$^{-1}$
Puerto Rico 20     2.9 kg ha$^{-1}$
Virgin Islands 01  1.1 kg ha$^{-1}$

National Atmospheric Deposition Program/National Trends Network
http://nadp.isws.illinois.edu

**Figure 11.2** Atmospheric wet deposition of ammonium and nitrate in the USA in 2011. See plate section for colour version.

development argue for an examination of a broad suite of potentially limiting soil resources rather than simply N in temperate and P in lowland tropical forests.

A second important motivation for understanding the relationship between tree performance and soil resources is that mineral nutrients constrain forest productivity and consequently ecosystem services including wood, fibre and biofuels production, and sequestration of atmospheric $CO_2$ (Malhi *et al.* 2004). For example, an increase in the terrestrial carbon (C) sink in response to higher atmospheric $CO_2$ could be constrained by N and other elements (Hungate *et al.* 2003), despite increased belowground C allocation to acquire more N when trees experience elevated atmospheric $CO_2$ (Drake *et al.* 2011). Ultimately, C sequestration depends on changes in forest biomass through time. Thus, understanding tree growth and mortality responses to soil resources could aid in more mechanistically scaling C storage to broader regions (Bugmann & Bigler 2011; Coomes *et al.* 2012).

Third, nutrient limitation is magnified by harvesting because of the removal of minerals in biomass. This has long been recognised (Federer *et al.* 1989; Whitmore 1984), but the extent of the problem may be an underappreciated aspect of anthropogenic global change (Canham, Chapter 5 of this volume). Tree harvests, particularly those that include removal of bark and leaves, can deplete mineral nutrients, including P (Ilg, Wellbrock & Lux 2009; Vanguelova *et al.* 2010) and base cations (Adams *et al.* 2000; Federer *et al.* 1989; Vanguelova *et al.* 2010) in temperate forests, base cations in subtropical forest plantations (e.g. Hernandez *et al.* 2009) and P in tropical forests (Whitmore 1984). Soil resource depletion may also accelerate when the return interval of normally infrequent natural disturbances (e.g. wind, fire) shortens (Keppel, Buckley & Possingham 2010; Uriarte *et al.* 2004; Wanthongchai, Bauhus & Goldammer 2008).

Fourth, soil resources could mediate the effects of climate change on geographic distributions of species. For example, as tree species approach their range limits defined by precipitation and temperature, the proportion of sites in which a species is found declines but not the species' relative abundance within sites where it is present; this suggests that edaphic characteristics associated with particular sites allow for species presence even at climatic range limits (Canham & Thomas 2010). Similarly, soil fertility associated with bedrock type determined the rate and species composition of postglacial colonisation by woody plants; pollen records indicate the absence of *Picea* sp. and *Abies* sp., and dominance by *Pinus contorta*, on infertile rhyolitic soils after glaciation, despite a suitable regional climate for *Picea* and *Abies* species (Whitlock 1993). In addition, nutrient imbalances can interact with extremes in temperature, precipitation and other environmental factors to impair tree vigour (St Clair, Sharpe & Lynch 2008).

Here, we review several facets of how soil resources influence tree performance, with a focus on variation in species composition and tree growth across soil resource gradients. We consider a broad array of mineral nutrients, beyond the typical emphasis on N in temperate forests and P in tropical forests. The review also touches on soil water because it often covaries with mineral nutrient availability. While we present a broad global view, a recurring theme is recent research that our group and collaborators have conducted across natural soil resource gradients in temperate oak/northern hardwood forests in the northwestern lower peninsula of Michigan, USA, and wet tropical forests at La Selva Biological Station in Costa Rica (McDade *et al.* 1994) (Table 11.1).

## 11.2   Forest composition and productivity across soil resource gradients

Across a broad geographic range in eastern North America, from at least Wisconsin (Bray & Curtis 1957; Kotar 1986) to Massachusetts (Spurr 1956), *Acer saccharum* (sugar maple), *Fraxinus americana* (white ash) and *Tilia americana* are typically associated with mesic sites of higher nutrient availability. In contrast, oaks (*Quercus velutina* (black oak) and *Q. alba* (white oak)) and pines (*Pinus banksiana*, *P. rigida* and *P. strobus*) tend to occur on drier sites with lower

**Table 11.1** *Characteristics of the two primary study sites.*

|  | Temperate | Tropical |
|---|---|---|
| Location | 44° N 85° W | 10° N 84° W |
| Precipitation | 700 mm | 4300 mm |
| Sites (n) | 13 | 5 |
| Range, total P | 25.7–47.4 mg kg$^{-1}$ | 1.71–5.08 mg kg$^{-1}$ |
| Range, NH$_4$ + NO$_3$ | 4.03–31.3 mg kg$^{-1}$ | 158.5–290.9 mg kg$^{-1}$ |
| Range, Ca | 70–1160 mg kg$^{-1}$ | 58.9–153.6 mg kg$^{-1}$ |
| Range, K | 22.9–33.8 mg kg$^{-1}$ | 67.6–124.3 mg kg$^{-1}$ |
| Species composition | *A. saccharum, Q. rubra, A. rubrum, Q. alba*, 17 others | >150 species |
| Stand ages | ~80 to 100 years | Mostly old growth |

nutrient availability (e.g. Host & Pregitzer 1991; Whitney 1991). These same patterns of association are evident at our field sites in northern Michigan (Figure 11.1).

Whereas temperate forest communities are clearly aggregated by site quality, the typically higher species richness in tropical forests may obscure any neat site-based delineation of community types. Nevertheless, several studies have demonstrated associations between tree species composition and soil or habitat type in highly diverse tropical forests (Sollins 1998; Webb & Peart 2000). Across three neotropical forests, the distribution of 36–51% of species was significantly associated with soil nutrients, with base cations exerting stronger influence than N and P (John *et al.* 2007). At La Selva Biological Station in Costa Rica, at least 30% of tree species are associated with soil type or topographic position (Clark *et al.* 1999 ). In Bornean mixed Dipterocarp forest, 73% of species were significantly aggregated on one of four soil types (Russo *et al.* 2005).

Tree growth and forest productivity are often correlated with multiple resources across natural fertility gradients, so it remains a challenge to determine which particular resource(s) are limiting (Baribault, Kobe & Rothstein 2010). Moreover, covariance in species composition, ecosystem net primary productivity and soil resource availability obscure causation. Productivity is positively related to natural gradients of soil N availability in temperate (Baribault, Kobe & Rothstein 2010; Pastor *et al.* 1984; Zak, Host & Pregitzer 1989) and sometimes in tropical forests (Johnson 2006), especially those of higher elevation (e.g. Adamek, Corre & Hölscher 2009; Tanner, Kapos & Franco 1992). In lowland tropical forests, higher productivity occurs on sites of greater soil P (Aragão *et al.* 2009; Vitousek & Farrington 1997). To date, however, few studies have examined elements other than N and P in both temperate and tropical forests.

Recently, these broad-scale patterns of temperate N limitation and tropical P limitation have been further investigated, resulting in challenges to their generality (e.g. Baribault *et al.* 2010; Gradowski & Thomas 2008; Joshi *et al.* 2003; Wright *et al.* 2011). At our temperate sites in northern Michigan, wood production was most strongly correlated with exchangeable Ca and leaf production with soil N (Baribault, Kobe & Rothstein 2010). In central Ontario, an area of high atmospheric N deposition, tree diameter growth was correlated with P, Ca and K (Gradowski & Thomas 2006). At our tropical sites in Costa Rica, K is most strongly correlated with tree growth (Baribault, Kobe & Finley 2012), which is consistent with a fertilisation experiment in Panama (Wright *et al.* 2011).

The covariance among species composition, production and resources could arise also from vegetative feedbacks on soils rather than solely resource effects on production and composition. This coupling is especially difficult to resolve for N, because decomposition of organic matter rather than mineral weathering is the major source of plant available N. Across a deposition gradient in both elevation and atmospheric N in the northeastern US, N mineralisation is strongly correlated with aboveground net primary production (ANPP), but ANPP is unrelated to mineral N availability, which is governed by both mineralisation and atmospheric deposition (Joshi *et al.* 2003). These results suggest that ANPP influences N mineralisation rather than the reverse. Nitrogen resorption from fine roots (Kunkle, Walters & Kobe 2009) and senescent leaves (Kobe, Lepczyk & Iyer 2005), and direct N absorption by leaves (Sparks *et al.* 2009), could partially decouple N metabolism from soil N availability (Migita, Chiba & Tange 2007). Soil exchangeable base cation levels also can be altered by the presence of certain species. For example, *Acer saccharum* or *Tilia americana* in the northeastern US enhance levels of exchangeable cations (Dijkstra & Smits 2002; Finzi, Van Breemen & Canham 1998; Fujinuma, Bockheim & Balster 2005), further promoting the regeneration of these species (Kobe, Likens & Eager 2002). In the wet tropics, species-specific chemical feedbacks influence seedling growth and survivorship (McCarthy-Neumann & Kobe 2010), but the particular chemicals involved in the feedback remain uncharacterised.

## 11.3   Resource variation and covariation
### 11.3.1   Spatial heterogeneity

Forest soil nutrients are heterogeneously distributed across multiple spatial scales from the biome level (N vs. P limitation) to plant-level scales (e.g. Figure 11.3) (Farley & Fitter 1999; Lechowicz & Bell 1991; Mou, Mitchell & Jones 1997). Heterogeneity can arise abiotically from parent material, climate and topography, or biotically through plant–soil feedbacks (Holste *et al.*, unpublished ms; Jenny 1941). Mineral weathering releases P, base cations

(A) **Total extractable P availability**

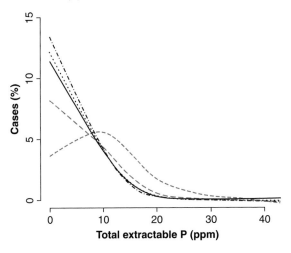

(B) **Nutrient heterogeneity of volcanic soil**

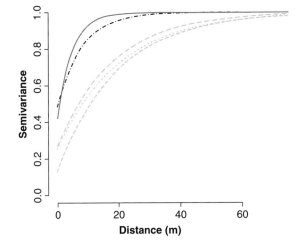

**Figure 11.3** (A) Soil P availability without respect to spatial structure across the five study sites in Costa Rica. More weathered volcanic substrates = black; solid, dotted, dot-dash. Alluvial substrates = grey; dashed, long-dash. (B) The spatial distribution of soil nutrients across a weathered, volcanic site. (Inorganic N ($NO_3^-$ + $NH_4^+$) = dark grey, solid; total extractable P = black, dot-dash; K = grey, long-dash; Mg = grey, dotted; Ca = grey, dashed). From E. K. Holste et al. (unpublished ms).

(Ca, K and Mg) and micronutrients into exchangeable pools, where ions may be occluded (i.e. bound) to other chemicals or soil colloids, leached through the soil, immobilised by soil microbes or taken up by plants (McGroddy, Silver & Oliveira 2004; Schlesinger et al. 1996; Walker & Syers 1976), thereby creating patches differing in resource availability. Individuals of different plant species or functional groups (e.g. leguminous species), together with fungi and bacteria, can form patches of similar resource levels through zones of depletion around roots, senesced tissue chemistry and other plant–soil feedbacks (e.g. McCarthy-Neumann & Kobe 2010; Schenk 2006; Townsend, Asner & Cleveland 2008; Ushio, Kitayama & Balser 2010; Weber & Bardgett 2011). Patches of N and C concentrations can arise from the accumulation and decomposition of organic residues and/or through biological N fixation by microorganisms (Franklin & Mills 2009; Gallardo, Parama & Covelo 2006). The effects of these processes accumulate over time (e.g. Jenny 1941), creating a spatially heterogeneous resource environment for individual seedlings and trees.

The sessile nature of plants makes the spatial structure of resources particularly important to the study of plant–resource interactions (Stuefer 1996). For example, even though our five tropical sites span a gradient of P and base cations, all sites contain sampling points with similarly low levels of P; what distinguishes the high fertility sites is a greater number of sample points with high P levels (Figure 11.3A). Thus, an unlucky seedling could establish in a low-P locale on a relatively fertile site. The spatial scale at which resource heterogeneity emerges is also crucial when considered in the context of plant size and horizontal rooting extent. Across our sites, different resources had characteristic spatial structure, with total N and extractable P exhibiting spatial autocorrelation at finer scales than the base cations (e.g. Figure 11.3B). From a seedling's perspective, N and P would be patchier than base cations (Hutchings *et al.* 2003). Conversely, fine-scale heterogeneity may be less relevant to a mature tree with a root system large enough to integrate both nutrient rich and poor patches. Similarly, both ectomycorrhizal and arbuscular mycorrhizal fungi are capable of integrating into common networks of large spatial extent that could effectively homogenise nutrient availability for all trees connected to the network (e.g. Simard 2009, van der Heijden & Horton 2009).

## 11.3.2   Covariance among soil resources

Resources often covary in nature, which makes it difficult to isolate their effects. We intensively sampled soils across our sites at La Selva to characterise spatial structure and covariance in soil resources (Holste *et al.*, unpublished ms). When considered as site means, the base cations (Ca, Mg, K) strongly covaried with each other and with total extractable P (Figure 11.4A), all of which were negatively correlated with N ($NH_4$ shown). High levels of N and low levels of P are common on older tropical soils (Vitousek & Denslow 1986). The two younger sites of alluvial soils had higher mean extractable P and base cations and lower N than the older sites (consistent with Walker & Syers 1976). When considered as individual sample points, a greater area of resource space is spanned and correlations are weaker (e.g. Yavitt *et al.* 2009), providing greater potential to isolate resource effects.

Taking into account the spatial dependency of individual sampling points reveals a *positive* correlation between local N (measured as sum of $NH_4^+$ and $NO_3^-$) and P availability (Guhaniyogi *et al.*, in review), a correlation of opposite sign to that found between site means. A positive correlation

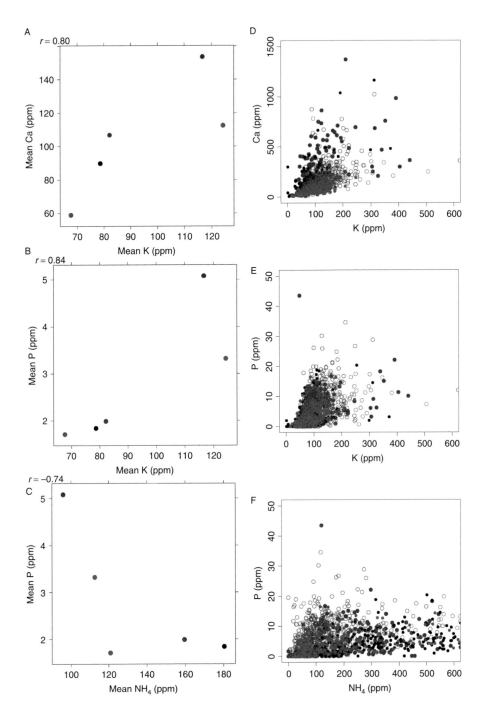

**Figure 11.4** Covariance among selected soil resources as site means (A) and at individual sample points (B–F). Each colour or shade corresponds with one of five of our research sites at La Selva Biological Station, Costa Rica. See plate section for colour version.

between N and P availability at a fine spatial scale is consistent with the hypothesis that extracellular phosphatases, which are 8–32% N, increase P availability through hydrolysation of ester–$PO_4^-$ bonds in soil organic P (Houlton *et al.* 2008; Pant & Warman 2000; Treseder & Vitousek 2001). This mechanism could explain the high species prevalence of atmospheric $N_2$ fixation in the tropics, despite presumed P limitation. In contrast to the fine-scale correlation between N and P, the correlations of base cations with N and P are not consistent across space (Guhaniyogi *et al.*, in review); species-specific variation in tree feedbacks on base cations (Finzi, Van Breemen & Canham 1998) may disrupt consistent correlations between base cations versus N and P.

### 11.3.3    Effects of soil resources on interceptance of irradiance

Transmittance of radiation through tree canopies generally decreases with increasing nutrient and water availability (Table 11.2, Figure 11.5) (Coomes & Grubb 2000; Iversen & Norby 2008; Will *et al.* 2002; Xia & Wan 2008), which arises as a consequence of both greater leaf production within species (Dölle & Schmidt 2009) and replacement of species with others that differ in transmission of irradiance (Canham *et al.* 1994; Lefrancois, Beaudet & Messier 2008). Nitrogen and P probably constrain leaf production – and thus shading – arising from the relatively high demands for N and P in photosynthetic machinery (Evans 1989; Reich, Oleksyn & Wright 2009). Across our fertility gradient in Michigan, the strongest correlate of leaf production is soil N availability (Baribault, Kobe & Rothstein 2010). However, in the absence of

**Table 11.2** *Understorey irradiance in low versus high fertility sites.*

| Irradiance – high fertility | Irradiance – low fertility | Measured nutrient(s) | Forest type (location) | Study |
|---|---|---|---|---|
| 2.5 | 7.5[a] | P | Cool temperate evergreen (New Zealand) | Coomes *et al.* (2009) |
| 1.5 | 11.0[a] | N, Ca, water | Oak–northern hardwood (eastern US) | Baribault & Kobe (2011) |
| 15 | 30.0[b] | N | Boreal (British Columbia, Can.) | Kranabetter & Simard (2008) |
| 2.8 | 3.2[b] | N, P, base cations | Lowland wet tropical (Borneo) | Dent & Burslem (2009) |
| 5.15 | 6.22[c] | N, P, base cations | Lowland wet tropical (Borneo) | Russo *et al.* (2010) |

[a] % diffuse irradiance
[b] % full sun
[c] mol m$^{-2}$ day$^{-1}$

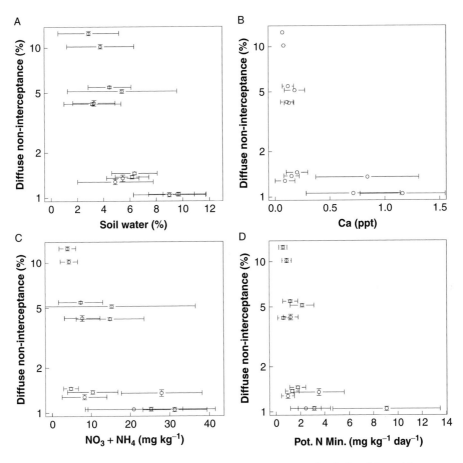

Figure 11.5 Canopy openness (% diffuse non-interceptance) relationships with measured soil resources. Error bars show standard error for both axes, with diffuse non-interceptance presented on a log scale. Pot. N Min., potential nitrogen mineralisation. ppt = parts per thousand. From Baribault and Kobe (2011).

fertilisation experiments, it is difficult to discern whether higher levels of N availability result from or cause higher leaf production or if they act in cyclical reinforcement, as much N is mineralised from decomposing leaves. Nevertheless, consistent with field observations, in a greenhouse experiment, seedling leaf mass (as a fraction of whole plant mass) increased with N fertilisation (Kobe, Iyer & Walters *et al.* 2010).

The positive correlation between leaf area index and water availability probably arises from a fundamentally different mechanism. Lower leaf area would limit water loss, which is especially important in drought-prone sites (Runyon *et al.* 1994). Variation among sites in leaf area could arise from species replacement or intraspecific variation in leaf area index (Dent & Burslem 2009; Lefrancois, Beaudet & Messier 2008; Simioni *et al.* 2004).

An important implication of these relationships is that light competition between neighbouring trees would be expected to be more severe under higher water and mineral nutrient availability (Coomes & Grubb 2000). Similarly, constraints of understorey irradiance on seedling/sapling growth, and on survivorship, increase with water and mineral nutrient availability. These relationships may provide a simple way to include the effects of soil resources in dynamic vegetation models, such as PPA (Purves & Vanderwel, Chapter 7 of this volume). Another implication is that there may be greater diversity of light-based niches in forest ecosystems growing on soils of high fertility (Coomes *et al.* 2009).

## 11.4   Effects of soil resources on processes determining tree species composition

### 11.4.1   The growth–survival trade-off extended to soil resources

In both temperate and tropical forests, there is now a well-documented interspecific trade-off between survivorship under low light versus rapid growth under high light (Kitajima 1994; Kobe 1999; Kobe *et al.* 1995), which could explain the dominance of different species across gradients of light availability (Pacala *et al.* 1996). Similarly, an interspecific trade-off of seedling growth at high soil resources versus survivorship at low soil resources provides a compelling explanation for variation in tree species composition across soil resource gradients (Russo *et al.* 2007; Schreeg, Kobe & Walters 2005). Based on a transplant experiment in our sites in northern Michigan, the species associated with lower fertility sites (*Quercus velutina* and *Q. rubra*) survived well under low fertility but grew relatively slowly under average irradiance conditions in higher fertility morainal sites, with irradiance tending to decrease with site fertility (Figure 11.5). In contrast, the species associated with higher fertility (*Acer saccharum*, *Fraxinus americana* and *Prunus serotina*) tended to survive poorly under low fertility and probably were filtered from these sites as juveniles (Figure 11.6).

We found no evidence for an interspecific trade-off between low versus high-fertility sapling growth (Kobe 2006), even though this trade-off is sometimes assumed by forest gap models (e.g. Bugmann & Cramer 1998). Consistent with these results, Baraloto, Bonal and Goldberg (2006) found no evidence to support a growth-based trade-off between low-fertility white sand and higher-fertility clay in French Guiana. Nevertheless, our relatively simple models of temperate sapling growth as functions of sapling size, irradiance, foliar N and water explained 74–90% of the variance in radial growth, indicating a high degree of determinism, in contrast to the results for seedlings in the southern Appalachians (Clark *et al.* 2003). The interactions of N and water with irradiance also were consistent across species, with water influencing

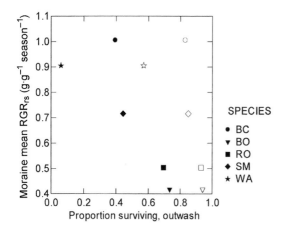

**Figure 11.6** Among species, there is a trade-off between survivorship under low fertility conditions (on outwash) versus growth under high fertility (moraines). Open symbols show proportion surviving over 1 year while closed symbols show survival scaled to 5 years. BC = black cherry (*Prunus serotina*), BO = black oak (*Quercus velutina*), RO = red oak (*Q. rubra*), SM = sugar maple (*Acer saccharum*) and WA = white ash (*Fraxinus americana*). RGR = Relative growth rate. From Schreeg, Kobe and Walters (2005).

growth at all light levels and N only at higher light levels. This supports that irradiance and water can be simultaneously limiting to growth.

Notably, no study to date has identified the particular resource(s) that cause poor survivorship under lower-fertility soils. However, across broad precipitation gradients, seedling survivorship responses to water deficits can explain species distributions (Comita and Engelbrecht, Chapter 10 of this volume). Species specialising on low fertility and drier sandstone ridges also have higher water use efficiency than species associated with higher-fertility alluvial sites in Borneo; greater water use efficiency may come at the cost of lower growth rates under high fertility (Baltzer *et al.* 2005), which is consistent with an edaphic growth–survival trade-off. Nevertheless, different resources could limit survivorship in different species of seedlings. For our sites in Michigan, we suspect that soil water deficits are an important contributor to poor survivorship, especially for shallowly rooted *P. serotina* (Schreeg, Kobe & Walters 2005). Low levels of soil Ca could cause low survivorship of *A. saccharum*, mediated through Ca effects on fine root growth (Park *et al.* 2008; Reich *et al.* 1997), mycorrhizal fungi colonisation, and photosynthesis (St Clair & Lynch 2005), and improved carbon balance/growth (Bigelow & Canham 2007; Dauer *et al.* 2007; Kobe, Likens & Eager 2002; Kulmatiski *et al.* 2007; Zaccherio & Finzi 2007).

Evidence for a high-fertility growth versus low-fertility survival trade-off also extends to tropical tree species. Across 960 Bornean tree species, average growth on more fertile soils was negatively correlated with average survivorship on the lowest-fertility sandy loam soil (Russo *et al.* 2007). Among five species in a shadehouse experiment, survival under the lowest resource conditions (shade and sandstone soil) was negatively correlated with maximum growth, which tended to occur under high light and the higher-fertility alluvial soil (Dent & Burslem 2009). In contrast, Baraloto, Bonal and Goldberg (2005) found little evidence for performance trade-offs for seedlings transplanted across soil types in French Guiana, probably because soils had little influence on relative growth rates and survivorship.

Interactions between herbivores and soil type could give rise to and/or reinforce the high-fertility growth/low fertility survivorship trade-off. For example, in the Peruvian Amazon, when seedlings are protected from herbivores, high-fertility species survive as well as low-fertility species under low-fertility conditions. In the absence of herbivore protection, the high-fertility species survive relatively poorly under low-fertility conditions in comparison with low-fertility species (Fine, Mesones & Coley 2004). In this way, the growth–survival trade-off arises from a trade-off between growth and defence allocation. We are not aware of similar studies in temperate forests.

To identify potential limiting resources in a wet tropical forest, we developed models of seedling growth as functions of irradiance and soil mineral nutrients for 94 woody species at La Selva, based on extant seedlings (Holste, Kobe & Vriesendorp 2011). Our results for seedling growth (Holste, Kobe & Vriesendorp 2011) and survivorship (Kobe & Vriesendorp 2011) generally are consistent with a light-based growth–survival trade-off (Holste, Kobe & Vriesendorp 2011), which could be magnified through interactions with natural enemies (Kobe & Vriesendorp 2011; McCarthy-Neumann & Kobe 2008). Both irradiance and soil nutrients had greater positive effects on the growth of light-demanding species that survived poorly under low light (e.g. Figure 11.7). The growth results are conservative because we would expect soil effects to manifest more strongly under high light, and all of our seedlings

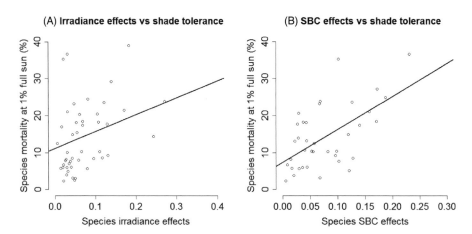

Figure 11.7 Species-specific shade tolerance (measured as probability of mortality under 1% full sun) versus growth effects of (A) irradiance and (B) base cations (SBC, sum of base cations) for seedlings at La Selva Biological Station. Each point represents one species; only species with significant growth responses to resources are shown. From Holste *et al.* (2011).

occurred at <7% canopy openness. Modelling seedling mortality responses to soil nutrients, planned for the near future, will enable a more direct test of a soil resource-based growth–survival trade-off.

Despite limited irradiance in the understorey (Holste, Kobe & Vriesendorp 2011), the percentage of species for which there was a significant growth response to soil resources was similar to that of irradiance (Figure 11.8). Moreover, the magnitude of soil resource effects approached that of irradiance (Figure 11.9). These results are consistent with other studies that have

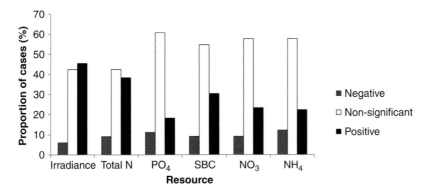

**Figure 11.8** Percentage of species for which growth was significantly correlated with each measured soil resource for seedlings from La Selva Biological Station. SBC = Sum of base cations. From Holste *et al.* (2011).

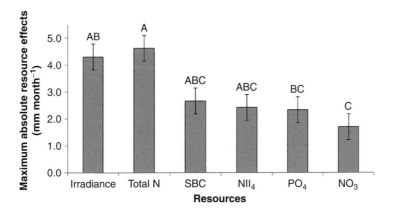

**Figure 11.9** Mean resource effects on growth across species for seedlings from La Selva Biological Station. All resource effects were assessed as absolute values (i.e. only magnitude and not direction of resource effects were incorporated) and are scaled by mean initial seedling height to express responses in mm of height growth per month. Error bars represent standard error while letters A, B, C correspond to significantly different pairwise comparisons at $P = 0.05$. SBC = Sum of base cations. From Holste, Kobe and Vriesendorp (2011).

found increased growth in response to soil resources (including water) in shaded conditions of the forest understorey in both temperate (Kobe 2006; Walters & Reich 1997) and tropical forests (Yavitt & Wright 2008). Among soil resources, sum of base cations (SBC) and N had similar or greater magnitudes of effect than P, even though P is generally considered the most limiting soil nutrient in lowland tropical forests (Hedin *et al.* 2009). This is consistent with accumulating empirical evidence (see Lawrence 2003) where N and base cations may be directly limiting to seedling growth and/or influence the acquisition of other elements through phosphatase production or mycorrhizal colonisation. Arbuscular mycorrhizal fungi can improve nutrient uptake and defend against pathogens and herbivores (Borowicz 2001). Base cation availability, particularly Ca, is correlated with the growth of seedlings colonised by mycorrhizal fungi (Burslem *et al.* 1995; Denslow, Vitousek & Schultz 1987; Juice *et al.* 2006; St Clair & Lynch 2005).

Similarly, since N is a key component of photosynthesis, understorey seedlings might benefit from increased N availability through increased chlorophyll and light capture (Fahey, Battles & Wilson 1998) and/or RuBisCO and initial $CO_2$ fixation (Evans 1989). As the central atom in the chlorophyll molecule, Mg also might benefit light capture (Shabala & Hariadi 2005), and even under low light conditions (<1% PAR), seedling growth increased in response to $Mg^+$ additions in a controlled greenhouse study (Burslem *et al.* 1995). Therefore, irradiance and soil nutrients may simultaneously limit seedling growth. In contrast, however, we did not find support for N-limitation of growth under low irradiance in temperate saplings (see section 4.1 and Kobe 2006).

## 11.4.2 Net competitive interactions strengthen with site fertility

The interspecific trade-off between high-fertility growth and low-fertility survival (Figure 11.6) manifests in seedlings. Implicit in this trade-off is that the seedlings of low-fertility species are outcompeted at higher-fertility sites because their understoreys have lower levels of irradiance (Figure 11.5) and the low-fertility species tend to be shade-intolerant (Kobe *et al.* 1995).

Similarly, during later life history stages, low-fertility species are filtered from higher-fertility sites owing to stronger net competitive interactions, probably for irradiance (Baribault & Kobe 2011). Net competitive interactions are measured phenomenologically as neighbourhood effects on large tree growth, and these are more prevalent at high fertility for our sites in Michigan (Table 11.3). Neighbourhood interactions were important for four of the five species dominant at sites with high resource availability but were only weakly correlated with growth for one (*A. rubrum*) of the five species dominant at intermediate/lower-resource sites.

Table 11.3 *Effects of neighbourhood and soil resources on the growth of trees (>10 cm dbh) across a fertility gradient in northwestern lower Michigan (condensed from Baribault & Kobe 2011). Species are ordered by site association, starting from high to low fertility. The direction of significant correlations of growth to neighbourhood, and/or soil resources are indicated with '+' or '–' symbols. ΣN is the sum of inorganic pools of N (NH$_4^+$ and NO$_3^-$).*

| Species | Predominant site type | Shade tolerance | Neighbourhood | H$_2$O | ΣN | Ca |
|---------|----------------------|-----------------|---------------|--------|-----|-----|
| Acsa | Moraine | Very tolerant | – | | + | |
| Tiam | Moraine | Tolerant | | | | |
| Fram | Moraine | Intolerant | – | | | |
| Prse | Int. moraine | Moderate | – | | | + |
| Fagr | Poor moraine | Very tolerant | – | | + | |
| Acru | Ice-contact | Moderate | – | – | | |
| Pogr | Ice-contact | Intolerant | | | | + |
| Quru | Ice-contact | Intolerant | – | | | |
| Quve | Outwash | Intolerant | | | | |
| Qual | Outwash | Intolerant | – | | | |

These neighbourhood interactions probably arose from competition for irradiance as shading increases with site fertility. Furthermore, the negative correlation of growth to soil water in three species (*Q. alba*, *Q. rubra* and *A. rubrum*) common at lower-fertility sites was likely to be due to increased shading as soil water (and mineral nutrients) increased across the fertility gradient. These and other shade-intolerant species are sensitive to competitive interactions with other species, as indicated by displacement along soil resource gradients between conditions for optimal growth and where the species reaches its highest abundance (Canham *et al.* 2006). Greater shading at high fertility could arise from changes in species composition (Canham *et al.* 1994) as well as mineral nutrient effects on leaf production within species (Chen *et al.* 2010). Stronger neighbourhood effects on high- versus low-fertility sites, presumably driven by irradiance, do not conflict with greater competition for soil resources under lower-fertility sites; belowground competition could be fierce, but neighbourhood seems to more effectively characterise above- rather than belowground competition.

## 11.5   Tree growth responses to soil resources

In both our temperate and tropical sites, base cations have emerged as strong correlates of productivity and tree growth. In our temperate sites, aboveground net primary production of wood (ANPP$_W$) was most strongly correlated with Ca availability, but the relationship reached asymptotic production at relatively low soil Ca levels with only the four lowest-fertility sites in the dynamic range for $ANPP_W$ (Figure 11.10, Baribault, Kobe & Rothstein 2010). $ANPP_W$ was more weakly correlated with N availability (sum of $NH_4^+$ and $NO_3^-$) and water, relationships that were consistent with previous studies on similar sites (Pastor *et al.* 1984; Zak, Host & Pregitzer 1989; Reich *et al.* 1997). Had we measured only N and/or soil water, we would have overlooked the stronger relationship between $ANPP_W$ and Ca. Leaf production, in contrast, was most strongly correlated with N (Figure 11.11). At the individual tree level, soil

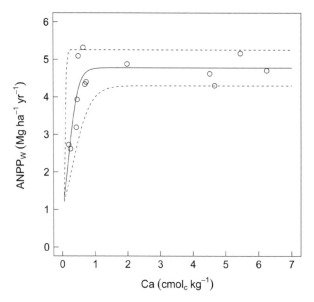

**Figure 11.10** Aboveground net primary production of wood as a function of soil exchangeable Ca for sites in northwestern lower Michigan. From Baribault, Kobe and Rothstein (2010).

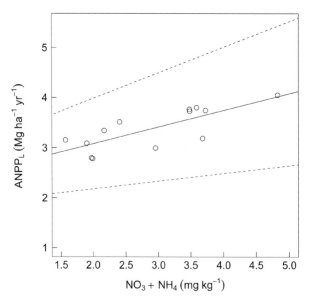

**Figure 11.11** Leaf production in relationship to sum of inorganic N pools for sites in northwestern lower Michigan. From Baribault *et al.* (2010).

resource effects on growth are not as pronounced (Table 11.3), probably because most species had restricted distributions across sites (Figure 11.1) and did not experience the full range of variation in soil resources. Nevertheless, individual tree diameter growth was positively correlated with N for one species, Ca for another, and water for two additional species (Table 11.3).

As different nutrients have different physiological roles, and plants adjust allocation to acquire limiting resources (e.g. Bloom, Chapin & Mooney 1985; Canham *et al.* 1996; Kobe, Iyer & Walters 2010), multiple resources could be simultaneously limiting (e.g. Kobe 2006). Typically, studies in north temperate forests are designed to test for N limitation alone (Magill *et al.* 2004), N versus P limitation (Finzi 2009; Will *et al.* 2006), base cation limitation alone (Long, Horsley & Hall 2011) or base cation versus P limitation (Gradowski & Thomas 2008). Relatively few studies (e.g. Bigelow & Canham 2007; Kulmatiski *et al.* 2007) explicitly test both N and base cations. Increased tree growth in response to experimental additions of nutrients, or across natural fertility gradients, may result from alleviation of direct limitation in structural tissues and metabolic processes, or a reduction of indirect limitation mediated by a secondary resource.

Consistent with multiple resource limitation, many temperate forest fertilisation experiments with different nutrient treatments result in significant growth or productivity responses (Park *et al.* 2008). Calcium fertilisation elicits positive growth responses in seedlings (Kobe, Likens & Eager 2002; Zaccherio & Finzi 2007), saplings (Juice *et al.* 2006; St Clair & Lynch 2005), and canopy adults (Gradowski & Thomas 2008). Similarly, N fertilisation leads to increased specific leaf area, foliar N content, photosynthetic rates, and tree growth or ANPP (Finzi 2009; Henderson & Jose 2005; Will *et al.* 2006). Excessive N levels, however, can reduce growth and survivorship (Magill *et al.* 2004), potentially regulated through soil pH reduction and base cation leaching (e.g. Högberg, Högberg & Myrold 2007). Within even the same ecosystems, fertilisation with base cations (e.g. Ca and K) may increase tree growth, while additional fertilisation with other resources (e.g. $PO_4$ and N) increases growth even further (Kulmatiski *et al.* 2007; Røsberg, Frank & Stuanes 2006), supporting multiple soil resource limitation.

At our field sites in Costa Rica, the growth of trees ≥5 cm dbh was related to K, Ca and P (Baribault, Kobe & Finley 2012). Across all trees, mean basal area increment was correlated with both P and K (Figure 11.12). However, this relationship is based on species from very different functional groups (palms, non-legume dicots, legumes) and adult stature (canopy, subcanopy, smaller than subcanopy (<subcanopy)), which could have different resource requirements.

To provide finer resolution, we examined growth–soil resource relationships for separate functional group × adult stature categories (Table 11.4).

Table 11.4 *Summary of relationships between site mean basal area increment and soil resources. From Baribault, Kobe and Finley (2012).*

| Functional group | Adult stature | P | K | Ca |
|---|---|---|---|---|
| All | All | $R^2 = 0.958$ <br> $P = 0.0004$ | $R^2 = 0.790$ <br> $P = 0.044$ | – |
| Arecaceae | Subcanopy | $R^2 = 0.868$ <br> $P = 0.021$ | – | – |
| Arecaceae | < subcanopy | $R^2 = 0.961$ <br> $P = 0.003$ | – | $R^2 = 0.843$ <br> $P = 0.028$ |
| Non-legume dicots | Canopy | – | $R^2 = 0.864$ <br> $P = 0.022$ | |
| Non-legume dicots | < canopy | – | $R^2 = 0.822$ <br> $P = 0.034$ | $R^2 = 0.816$ <br> $P = 0.036$ |
| Fabaceae | Canopy | – | | |
| Fabaceae | < canopy | – | | |

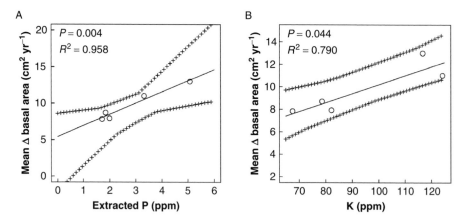

Figure 11.12 Site mean basal area increment versus soil P and K for trees in five mapped stands at La Selva Biological Station, Costa Rica. Hatched lines represent uncertainty in the relationship between mean basal area and the soil resource arising from uncertainty in estimating soil resource levels. From Baribault, Kobe and Finley (2012).

Among the Arecaceae, growth was related to P for both subcanopy and <subcanopy groupings; the growth of the <subcanopy grouping also was related to Ca. However, growth was not related to P for any other grouping, suggesting that the relationship between growth and P for all stems was strongly

influenced by palms. For non-leguminous dicots, the most abundant group in our plots, growth was related to K and Ca. Finally, the growth of legumes was not related to any of the measured resources. A plausible explanation for legume escape from P limitation is diversion of fixed $N_2$ to production of rhizosphere phosphatase (Olander & Vitousek 2000; Wang *et al.* 2007). Site mean legume growth was also unrelated to soil base cations, although we cannot identify a clear mechanism that explains how $N_2$ fixation could alleviate base cation limitation.

Other tropical studies support the importance of base cations, in addition to P, in governing tropical tree growth (Townsend *et al.* 2011). Among the strongest support is a fertilisation experiment that was conducted on Barro Colorado Island, Panama (Wright *et al.* 2011). The experiment maintained factorial N, P and K additions for 11 years and found that K additions reduced stand-level fine root biomass, decreased allocation to seedling root mass, increased seedling height growth, and together with N, increased growth of saplings and poles. Addition of P resulted in marginally higher fine litter production (Wright *et al.* 2011). In Dipterocarp forests in Borneo, basal area and biomass growth were strongly correlated with extractable P and cation exchange capacity, with many components of ANPP correlated with K; multiple linear regression suggested the importance of both P and Ca (Paoli & Curran 2007). In the Venezuelan Amazon, fine root growth was stimulated by additions of Ca and P in *terra firma* forests and by N and/or P in forests subject to flooding (Cuevas & Medina 1988). In similar *terra firma* forests, net photosynthetic capacity was correlated with N and P, especially among early successional species; but at low foliar N and P concentrations, Ca was the only significant correlate with maximum photosynthesis (Reich, Ellsworth & Uhl 1995). Similarly, within a given climate range, productivity in *Eucalyptus* plantations was positively correlated with soil base cations and P (Ryan *et al.* 2008). Across the RAINFOR plots in Amazonia, effective cation exchange capacity is more strongly correlated with forest biomass growth rates than any metric of P or any other nutrient (Table 11.2 in Quesada *et al.* 2009), despite interpretation of results as evidence of P limitation. Thus multiple lines of evidence, including direct measurements of tree growth, fine root growth and maximum photosynthetic rates, support the potential importance of base cations.

## 11.6    Conclusions and summary

**Soil resources are tremendously heterogeneous at multiple spatial scales**, from fine-scale variation within sites, to sites across the landscape, to variation among biomes. In our temperate sites, which originally were delineated as distinct forest ecosystem types (Host & Pregitzer 1991), there is surprisingly greater within-site variability in soil resources than canopy openness (Figure 11.5). This result is generally consistent with the high spatial variability in temperate soils, even in agricultural ecosystems where soils have been mixed through ploughing and cropping for more than 100 years (Robertson *et al.* 1997). In Costa Rica, all sites from our presumed fertility gradient overlapped at the low end of resource levels, and a right skew in distribution distinguished the high-resource sites (Figure 11.3A). Thus, from the perspective of individual seedlings and smaller trees, even those separated by only a few metres, soil resource environments may be equally or more heterogeneous than light environments. An important practical implication is that characterising soil resource availability to seedlings may necessitate fine spatial scale sampling.

**Base cations also could limit tree performance in both temperate and tropical forests**, but have not received as much study as N and P. Particular elements could be limiting because of peculiarities in soil mineralogy; for example, sulphur generally does not limit productivity, but it can constrain the productivity response of *Pinus contorta* forests to N fertilisation in British Columbia (Kishchuk *et al.* 2002). However, numerous lines of evidence point to a broader importance of base cations beyond mineralogical peculiarity, including loss of base cations with soil development (Walker & Syers 1976), correlations with seedling and tree growth (Baribault, Kobe & Rothstein 2010; Holste, Kobe & Vriesendorp 2011; Wright *et al.* 2011) and associations with species distributions (Gunatilleke *et al.* 1997).

**Particular nutrients may limit different aspects of tree performance**, an expectation that follows from element-specific roles in physiological function. By extension, different tree species or functional groups also may be limited by particular elements. For example, sapling growth was correlated with various soil properties for different species in the northeastern US, but each species' growth correlated with a different attribute (Bigelow & Canham 2002). In our own field studies, without regard to species, we found that Ca was the strongest correlate of wood production at our Michigan sites, whereas N was most strongly correlated with leaf production (Baribault, Kobe & Rothstein 2010). In our tropical sites, different resources influenced the growth of different species groups in mature trees (Baribault, Kobe & Finley 2012). Seedling growth in the understorey also was correlated with different elements for different species (Holste, Kobe & Vriesendorp 2011). In a wet tropical forest in Panama, N additions increased fruit and flower litter, and K and P enhanced decomposition, suggesting indirect effects of the latter (Kaspari *et al.* 2008). In the same region, P addition increased litter production, K addition decreased stand-level allocation to fine roots and increased seedling height growth, and K together with N increased growth of saplings and pole-sized trees (Wright *et al.* 2011).

**Trees have mechanisms to actively manage access to mineral nutrients, which often occurs in concert with microbial symbionts**.

In temperate forests, *Acer saccharum*, *Tilia americana* and *Fraxinus americana* enhance base cation availability in superficial soil layers via Ca uptake from deeper soil strata, subsequent decomposition of litter and fine-roots with higher Ca concentrations (Dijkstra & Smits 2002; Fujinuma *et al.* 2005; Park *et al.* 2008), and by increasing Ca weathering at various soil depths (Dijkstra *et al.* 2003). In turn, elevated Ca levels could promote the growth and survival of seedlings (e.g. Juice *et al.* 2006; Kobe, Likens & Eager 2002; St Clair & Lynch 2005) and mature trees (Gradowski & Thomas 2008) of these species.

Increased root mass under low nutrients has been assumed to reflect increased root absorptive surface area, but this change was largely driven by increases in non-structural carbohydrates (NSC) in a greenhouse study of seven species of temperate tree seedlings (Kobe, Iyer & Walters 2010). NSC could increase access to soil resources by providing an energy source for decomposers in the rhizosphere and for mycorrhizal fungi (Cardon *et al.* 2002; Dijkstra & Cheng 2007; Phillips & Fahey 2006), the colonisation of which is cued by NSC levels (Graham, Duncan & Eissenstat 1997).

Nutrient effects on tropical seedling and tree growth also may be mediated through mycorrhizae. At our research sites at La Selva, K and Ca were correlated with average tree growth across sites (Table 11.4), and base cations (the sum of Ca, K and Mg) were correlated with individual seedling growth (Figures 11.9 and 11.10). Base cations may improve access to other limiting nutrients via mycorrhizae (Burslem *et al.* 1995; Denslow, Vitousek & Schultz 1987). In addition, results from our tropical sites are consistent with the idea that fixed N may be allocated to phosphatase production (Dodd *et al.* 1987), which breaks down recalcitrant bonds and increases P availability.

**Finally it is crucial to understand relationships between tree performance and soil resources on several pressing contemporary fronts**. Changes in climate will affect geographic distributions of tree species (Canham & Thomas 2010; McLachlan, Clark & Manos 2005), but changes in species ranges are likely to be mediated through site variation in soil resource availability (Canham & Thomas 2010), perhaps constrained by an interspecific trade-off in low-fertility survival versus high-fertility growth.

Soil resources also are at the nexus of C sequestration and storage. Regardless of exactly which resources are involved, higher-fertility soils support higher net primary production (NPP). But higher NPP may not translate into greater C storage because rates of tree mortality may also be higher on higher-productivity sites (Coomes *et al.* 2012; Quesada *et al.* 2009; Stephenson & van Mantgem 2005).

Human activity also directly affects soil resource availability through atmospheric deposition of N. If N constrains tree growth, either singly or in combination with other resources, then atmospheric N deposition would enhance forest productivity. On the other hand, if base cations constrain aspects of forest productivity, the acceleration of base cation losses through atmospheric N deposition could lead to decreased productivity. To better predict forest responses to a myriad of global changes, it is crucial to better understand how soil resources influence tree performance.

## Acknowledgements

This research was supported by NSF (DEB 0743609, 0958943) and Michigan AgBioResearch (NRSP-3, National Atmospheric Deposition Program). We thank the numerous assistants in the lab and field who contributed to data.

## References

Adamek, M., Corre, M. D. & Hölscher, D. (2009) Early effect of elevated nitrogen input on above-ground net primary production of a lower montane rain forest, Panama. *Journal of Tropical Ecology*, **25**, 637.

Adams, M. (2000) Impact of harvesting and atmospheric pollution on nutrient depletion of eastern US hardwood forests. *Forest Ecology and Management*, **138**, 301–319.

Aragão, L. E. O. C., Malhi, Y., Metcalfe, D. B. *et al.* (2009) Above- and below-ground net primary productivity across ten Amazonian forests on contrasting soils. *Biogeosciences*, **6**, 2759–2778.

Baltzer, J. L., Thomas, S. C., Nilus, R. & Burslem, D. F. R. P. (2005) Edaphic specialization in tropical trees: physiological correlates and responses to reciprocal transplantation. *Ecology*, **86**, 3063–3077.

Baraloto, C., Bonal, D. & Goldberg, D. E. (2006) Differential seedling growth response to soil resource availability among nine neotropical tree species. *Journal of Tropical Ecology*, **22**, 487.

Baraloto, C., Goldberg, D. E. & Bonal, D. (2005) Performance trade-offs among tropical tree seedlings in contrasting microhabitats. *Ecology*, **86**, 2461–2472.

Baribault, T. W. & Kobe, R. K. (2011) Neighbour interactions strengthen with increased soil resources in a northern hardwood forest. *Journal of Ecology*, **99**, 1358–1372.

Baribault, T. B., Kobe, R. K. & Finley, A. O. (2012) Tropical tree growth is correlated with soil phosphorus, potassium, and calcium, though not for legumes. *Ecological Monographs*, **82**, 189–203.

Baribault, T. W., Kobe, R. K. & Rothstein, D. E. (2010) Soil calcium, nitrogen, and water are correlated with aboveground net primary production in northern hardwood forests. *Forest Ecology and Management*, **260**, 723–733.

Bigelow, S. W. & Canham, C. D. (2002) Community organization of tree species along soil gradients in a north-eastern USA forest. *Journal of Ecology*, **90**, 188–200.

Bigelow, S. W. & Canham, C. D. (2007) Nutrient limitation of juvenile trees in a northern hardwood forest: Calcium and nitrate are preeminent. *Forest Ecology and Management*, **243**, 310–319.

Bloom, A. J., Chapin, F. S. I. & Mooney, H. A. (1985) Resource limitation in plants – an economic analogy. *Annual Review of Ecology and Systematics*, **16**, 363–392.

Borowicz, V. A. (2001) Do arbuscular mycorrhizal fungi alter plant–pathogen relations? *Ecology*, **82**, 3057–3068.

Bray, J. R. & Curtis, J. T. (1957) An ordination of the upland forest communities of southern Wisconsin. *Ecological Monographs*, **27**, 325.

Bugmann, H. & Bigler, C. (2011) Will the $CO_2$ fertilization effect in forests be offset by reduced tree longevity? *Oecologia*, **165**, 533–544.

Bugmann, H. & Cramer, W. (1998) Improving the behaviour of forest gap models along drought gradients. *Forest Ecology and Management*, **103**, 247–263.

Burslem, D. F. R. P., Grubb, P. J. & Turner, I. M. (1995) Responses to nutrient addition among tree seedlings of lowland in Singapore tropical rain forest. *Journal of Ecology*, **83**, 113–122.

Canham, C. D., Berkowitz, A. R., Kelly, V. R. et al. (1996) Biomass allocation and multiple resource limitation in tree seedlings. *Canadian Journal of Forest Research*, **26**, 1521–1530.

Canham, C. D., Finzi, A. C., Pacala, S. W. & Burbank, D. H. (1994) Causes and consequences of resource heterogeneity in forests: interspecific variation in light transmission by canopy trees. *Canadian Journal of Forest Research*, **24**, 337–349.

Canham, C. D., Papaik, M. J., Uriarte, M. et al. (2006) Neighborhood analyses of canopy tree competition along environmental gradients in New England forests. *Ecological Applications*, **16**, 540–554.

Canham, C. D. & Thomas, R. Q. (2010) Frequency, not relative abundance, of temperate tree species varies along climate gradients in eastern North America. *Ecology*, **91**, 3433–3440.

Cardon, Z., Czaja, A., Funk, J. & Vitt, P. (2002) Periodic carbon flushing to roots of *Quercus rubra* saplings affects soil respiration and rhizosphere microbial biomass. *Oecologia*, **133**, 215–223.

Chadwick, O. A., Derry, L. A., Vitousek, P. M., Huebert, B. J. & Hedin, L. O. (1999) Changing sources of nutrients during four million years of ecosystem development. *Nature*, **397**, 491–497.

Chen, F.-S., Zeng, D.-H., Fahey, T. J., Yao, C.-Y. & Yu, Z.-Y. (2010) Response of leaf anatomy of *Chenopodium acuminatum* to soil resource availability in a semi-arid grassland. *Plant Ecology*, **209**, 375–382.

Clark, D. B., Palmer, M. W. & Clark, D. A. (1999) Edaphic factors and the landscape-scale distributions of tropical rain forest trees. *Ecology*, **80**, 2662–2675.

Clark, J. S., Mohan, J., Dietze, M. & Ibanez, I. (2003) Coexistence: how to identify trophic trade-offs. *Ecology*, **84**, 17–31.

Coomes, D. A. & Grubb, P. J. (2000) Impacts of root competition in forests and woodlands: a theoretical framework and review of experiments. *Ecological Monographs*, **70**, 171–207.

Coomes, D. A., Holdaway, R. J., Kobe, R. K., Lines, E. R. & Allen, R. B. (2012) A general integrative framework for modelling woody biomass production and carbon sequestration rates in forests. *Journal of Ecology*, **100**, 42–64.

Coomes, D. A., Kunstler, G., Canham, C. D. & Wright, E. (2009) A greater range of shade-tolerance niches in nutrient-rich forests: an explanation for positive richness–productivity relationships? *Journal of Ecology*, **97**, 705–717.

Cuevas, E. & Medina, E. (1988) Nutrient dynamics within Amazonian forests. *Oecologia*, **76**, 222–235.

Cusack, D. F., Silver, W. L., Torn, M. S. & McDowell, W. H. (2011) Effects of nitrogen additions on above- and belowground carbon dynamics in two tropical forests. *Biogeochemistry*, **104**, 203–225.

Dauer, J. M., Chorover, J., Chadwick, O. A. et al. (2007) Controls over leaf and litter calcium concentrations among temperate trees. *Biogeochemistry*, **86**, 175–187.

Denslow, J. S., Vitousek, P. M. & Schultz, J. C. (1987) Bioassays of nutrient limitation in a tropical rain forest soil. *Oecologia*, **74**, 370–376.

Dent, D. H. & Burslem, D. F. R. P. (2009) Performance trade-offs driven by morphological plasticity contribute to habitat specialization of Bornean tree species. *Biotropica*, **41**, 424–434.

Dijkstra, F. A., Breemen, N. van, Jogmans, A. G., Davies, G. R. & Likens, G. E. (2003) Calcium weathering in forested soils and the effect of different tree species. *Biogeochemistry*, **62**, 253–275.

Dijkstra, F. A. & Cheng, W. (2007) Interactions between soil and tree roots accelerate long-term soil carbon decomposition. *Ecology Letters*, **10**, 1046–1053.

Dijkstra, F. A. & Smits, M. M. (2002) Tree species effects on calcium cycling: the role of calcium uptake in deep soils. *Ecosystems*, **5**, 0385–0398.

Dise, N. & Wright, R. F. (1995) Nitrogen leaching from European forests in relation to nitrogen deposition. *Forest Ecology and Management*, **71**, 153–161.

Dodd, J. C., Burton, C. C., Burns, R. G. & Jeffries, P. (1987) Phosphatase activity associated with the roots and the rhizosphere of plants infected with vesicular-arbuscular mycorrhizal fungi. *New Phytologist*, **107**, 163–172.

Dölle, M. & Schmidt, W. (2009) Impact of tree species on nutrient and light availability: evidence from a permanent plot study of old-field succession. *Plant Ecology*, **203**, 273–287.

Drake, J. E., Gallet-Budynek, A., Hofmockel, K. S. *et al.* (2011) Increases in the flux of carbon belowground stimulate nitrogen uptake and sustain the long-term enhancement of forest productivity under elevated $CO_2$. *Ecology Letters*, **14**, 349–357.

Evans, J. R. (1989) Photosynthesis and nitrogen relationships in leaves of C3 plants. *Oecologia*, **78**, 9–19.

Fahey, T. J., Battles, J. J. & Wilson, G. F. (1998) Responses of early successional northern hardwood forests to changes in nutrient availability. *Ecological Monographs*, **68**, 183–212.

Farley, R. A. & Fitter, A. H. (1999) Temporal and spatial variation in soil resources in a deciduous woodland. *Journal of Ecology*, **87**, 688–696.

Federer, C. A., Hornbeck, J. W., Tritton, L. M. *et al.* (1989) Long-term depletion of calcium and other nutrients in eastern US forests. *Environmental Management*, **13**, 593–601.

Fine, P. V. A., Mesones, I. & Coley, P. D. (2004) Herbivores promote habitat specialization by trees in Amazonian forests. *Science*, **305**, 663–665.

Finzi, A. C. (2009) Decades of atmospheric deposition have not resulted in widespread phosphorus limitation or saturation of tree demand for nitrogen in southern New England. *Biogeochemistry*, **92**, 217–229.

Finzi, A. C., Van Breemen, N. & Canham, C. D. (1998) Canopy tree–soil interactions within temperate forests: species effects on soil carbon and nitrogen. *Ecological Applications*, **8**, 440–446.

Franklin, R. B. & Mills, A. L. (2009) Importance of spatially structured environmental heterogeneity in controlling microbial community composition at small spatial scales in an agricultural field. *Soil Biology and Biochemistry*, **41**, 1833–1840.

Fujinuma, R., Bockheim, J. & Balster, N. (2005) Base-cation cycling by individual tree species in old-growth forests of upper Michigan, USA. *Biogeochemistry*, **74**, 357–376.

Gallardo, A., Parama, R. & Covelo, F. (2006) Differences between soil ammonium and nitrate spatial pattern in six plant communities. Simulated effect on plant populations. *Plant and Soil*, **279**, 333–346.

Gradowski, T. & Thomas, S. C. (2006) Phosphorus limitation of sugar maple growth in central Ontario. *Forest Ecology and Management*, **226**, 104–109.

Gradowski, T. & Thomas, S. C. (2008) Responses of *Acer saccharum* canopy trees and saplings to P, K and lime additions under high N deposition. *Tree Physiology*, **28**, 173–185.

Graham, J. H., Duncan, L. W. & Eissenstat, D. M. (1997) Carbohydrate allocation patterns in citrus genotypes as affected by phosphorus nutrition, mycorrhizal colonization and mycorrhizal dependency. *New Phytologist*, **135**, 335–343.

Gunatilleke, C. V. S., Gunatilleke, I. A. U. N., Perera, G. A. D., Burslem, D. F. R. P. & Ashton, P. M. S. (1997) Responses to nutrient addition of eight closely related species of *Shorea* in Sri Lanka. *Journal of Ecology*, **85**, 301–311.

Hedin, L. O., Armesto, J. J., Johnson, A. H., Mar, N. & Johnson, H. (1995) Patterns of nutrient loss from unpolluted, old-growth temperate forests: evaluation of biogeochemical theory. *Ecology*, **76**, 493–509.

Hedin, L. O., Vitousek, P. M. & Matson, P. A. (2003) Nutrient losses over four million years of tropical forest development. *Ecology*, **84**, 2231–2255.

Hedin, L. O., Brookshire, E. N. J., Menge, D. N. L. & Barron, A. R. (2009) The nitrogen paradox in tropical forest ecosystems. *Annual Review of Ecology, Evolution, and Systematics*, **40**, 613–635.

van der Heijden, M. G. A. & Horton, T. R. (2009) Socialism in soil? The importance of mycorrhizal fungal networks for facilitation in natural ecosystems. *Journal of Ecology*, **97**, 1139–1150.

Henderson, D. E. & Jose, S. (2005) Production physiology of three fast-growing hardwood species along a soil resource gradient. *Tree Physiology*, **25**, 1487–1494.

Hernández, J., Pino, A. del, Salvo, L. & Arrarte, G. (2009) Nutrient export and harvest residue decomposition patterns of a *Eucalyptus dunnii* Maiden plantation in temperate climate of Uruguay. *Forest Ecology and Management*, **258**, 92–99.

Högberg, M. N., Högberg, P. & Myrold, D. D. (2007) Is microbial community composition in boreal forest soils determined by pH, C-to-N ratio, the trees, or all three? *Oecologia*, **150**, 590–601.

Holste, E. K., Kobe, R. K. & Vriesendorp, C. F. (2011) Seedling growth responses to soil resources in the understory of a wet tropical forest. *Ecology*, **92**, 1828–1838.

Host, G. & Pregitzer, K. (1991) Ecological species groups for upland forest ecosystems of northwestern Lower Michigan. *Forest Ecology and Management*, **43**, 87–102.

Houlton, B. Z., Wang, Y.-P., Vitousek, P. M. & Field, C. B. (2008) A unifying framework for dinitrogen fixation in the terrestrial biosphere. *Nature*, **454**, 327–330.

Hungate, B. A., Dukes, J. S., Shaw, M. R., Luo, Y. & Field, C. B. (2003) Atmospheric science. Nitrogen and climate change. *Science*, **302**, 1512–1513.

Hutchings, M. J., John, E. A. & Wijesinghe, D. K. (2003) Toward understanding the consequences of soil heterogeneity for plant populations and communities. *Ecology*, **84**, 2322–2334.

Ilg, K., Wellbrock, N. & Lux, W. (2009) Phosphorus supply and cycling at long-term forest monitoring sites in Germany. *European Journal of Forest Research*, **128**, 483–492.

Iversen, C. M. & Norby, R. J. (2008) Nitrogen limitation in a sweetgum plantation: implications for carbon allocation and storage. *Canadian Journal of Forest Research*, **38**, 1021–1032.

Izuta, T., Yamaoka, T., Nakaji, T. *et al.* (2004) Growth, net photosynthesis and leaf nutrient status of *Fagus crenata* seedlings grown in brown forest soil acidified with $H_2SO_4$ or $HNO_3$ solution. *Trees*, **18**, 677–685.

Jenny, H. (1941) *Factors of Soil Formation: A System of Quantitative Pedology*. New York: McGraw Hill.

John, R., Dalling, J. W., Harms, K. E. *et al.* (2007) Soil nutrients influence spatial distributions of tropical tree species. *Proceedings of the National Academy of Sciences USA*, **104**, 864–869.

Johnson, D. W. (2006) Progressive N limitation in forests: review and implications for long-term responses to elevated $CO_2$. *Ecology*, **87**, 64–75.

Joshi, A. B., Vann, D. R., Johnson, A. H. & Miller, E. K. (2003) Nitrogen availability and forest productivity along a climosequence on Whiteface Mountain, New York. *Canadian Journal of Forest Research*, **1891**, 1880–1891.

Juice, S. M., Fahey, T. J., Siccama, T. G. *et al.* (2006) Response of sugar maple to calcium addition to northern hardwood forest. *Ecology*, **87**, 1267–1280.

Kaspari, M., Garcia, M. N., Harms, K. E. *et al.* (2008) Multiple nutrients limit litterfall and decomposition in a tropical forest. *Ecology Letters*, **11**, 35–43.

Keppel, G., Buckley, Y. M. & Possingham, H. P. (2010) Drivers of lowland rain forest community assembly, species diversity and forest structure on islands in the tropical South Pacific. *Journal of Ecology*, **98**, 87–95.

Kishchuk, B. E., Weetman, G. F., Brockley, R. P. & Prescott, C. E. (2002) Fourteen-year growth response of young lodgepole pine to repeated fertilization. *Canadian Journal of Forest Research*, **160**, 153–160.

Kitajima, K. (1994) Relative importance of photosynthetic traits and allocation patterns as correlates of seedling shade tolerance of 13 tropical trees. *Oecologia*, **98**, 419–428.

Kobe, R. K. (1996) Intraspecific variation in sapling mortality and growth predicts geographic variation in forest composition. *Ecological Monographs*, **66**, 181–201.

Kobe, R. K. (1999) Light gradient partitioning among tropical tree species through differential seedling mortality and growth. *Ecology*, **80**, 187.

Kobe, R. K. (2006) Sapling growth as a function of light and landscape-level variation in soil water and foliar nitrogen in Northern Michigan. *Oecologia*, **147**, 119–133.

Kobe, R. K., Iyer, M. & Walters, M. B. (2010) Optimal partitioning theory revisited: nonstructural carbohydrates dominate root mass responses to nitrogen. *Ecology*, **91**, 166–179.

Kobe, R. K., Lepczyk, C. A. & Iyer, M. (2005) Resorption efficiency decreases with increasing green leaf nutrients in a global data set. *Ecology*, **86**, 2780–2792.

Kobe, R. K., Likens, G. E. & Eagar, C. (2002) Tree seedling growth and mortality responses to manipulations of calcium and aluminum in a northern hardwood forest. *Canadian Journal of Forest Research*, **966**, 954–966.

Kobe, R. K., Pacala, S. W., Silander, J. A. J. & Canham, C. D. (1995) Juvenile tree survivorship as a component of shade tolerance. *Ecological Applications*, **5**, 517–532.

Kobe, R. K. & Vriesendorp, C. F. (2011) Conspecific density dependence in seedlings varies with species shade tolerance in a wet tropical forest. *Ecology Letters*, **14**, 503–510.

Kotar, J. (1986) Soil–habitat type relationships in Michigan and Wisconsin. *Journal of Soil and Water Conservation*, **41**, 348–350.

Kranabetter, J. M. & Simard, S. W. (2008) Inverse relationship between understory light and foliar nitrogen along productivity gradients of boreal forests. *Canadian Journal of Forest Research*, **38**, 2487–2496.

Kulmatiski, A., Vogt, K. A., Vogt, D. J. *et al.* (2007) Nitrogen and calcium additions increase forest growth in northeastern USA spruce–fir forests. *Canadian Journal of Forest Research*, **37**, 1574–1585.

Kunkle, J. M., Walters, M. B. & Kobe, R. K. (2009) Senescence-related changes in nitrogen in fine roots: mass loss affects estimation. *Tree Physiology*, **29**, 715–723.

Lawrence, D. (2003) The response of tropical tree seedlings to nutrient supply: meta-analysis for understanding a changing tropical landscape. *Journal of Tropical Ecology*, **19**, 239–250.

Lechowicz, M. J. & Bell, G. (1991) The ecology and genetics of fitness in forest plants. II. Microspatial heterogeneity of the edaphic environment. *Journal of Ecology*, **79**, 687–696.

Lefrançois, M.-L., Beaudet, M. & Messier, C. (2008) Crown openness as influenced by tree and site characteristics for yellow birch, sugar maple, and eastern hemlock. *Canadian Journal of Forest Research*, **38**, 488–497.

Long, R. P., Horsley, S. B. & Hall, T. J. (2011) Long-term impact of liming on growth and vigor of northern hardwoods. *Canadian Journal of Forest Research*, **1307**, 1295–1307.

Lu, X., Mo, J., Gilliam, F. S., Zhou, G. & Fang, Y. (2010) Effects of experimental nitrogen additions on plant diversity in an old-growth tropical forest. *Global Change Biology*, **16**, 2688–2700.

Magill, A., Aber, J., Currie, W. *et al.* (2004) Ecosystem response to 15 years of chronic nitrogen additions at the Harvard Forest LTER, Massachusetts, USA. *Forest Ecology and Management*, **196**, 7–28.

Malhi, Y., Baker, T. R., Phillips, O. L. *et al.* (2004) The above-ground coarse wood productivity of 104 Neotropical forest plots. *Global Change Biology*, **10**, 563–591.

Matson, P. A., McDowell, W. H., Townsend, A. R. & Vitousek, P. M. (1999) The globalization of N deposition: ecosystem consequences in tropical environments. *Biogeochemistry*, **46**, 67–83.

McCarthy-Neumann, S. & Kobe, R. K. (2008) Tolerance of soil pathogens co-varies with shade tolerance across species of tropical tree seedlings. *Ecology*, **89**, 1883–1892.

McCarthy-Neumann, S. & Kobe, R. K. (2010) Conspecific plant-soil feedbacks reduce survivorship and growth of tropical tree seedlings. *Journal of Ecology*, **98**, 396–407.

McDade, L. A., Bawa, K. S., Hespenheide, H. A. & Hartshorn, G. S. (1994) *Ecology and Natural History of a Neotropical Rain Forest*. Chicago, IL: University of Chicago Press.

McGroddy, M. E., Silver, W. L. & Oliveira, R. C. D. (2004) The effect of phosphorus availability on decomposition dynamics in a seasonal lowland Amazonian forest. *Ecosystems*, **7**, 172–179.

McLachlan, J. S., Clark, J. S. & Manos, P. S. (2005) Molecular indicators of tree migration capacity under rapid climate change. *Ecology*, **86**, 2088–2098.

Migita, C., Chiba, Y. & Tange, T. (2007) Seasonal and spatial variations in leaf nitrogen content and resorption in a *Quercus serrata* canopy. *Tree Physiology*, **27**, 63–70.

Mou, P., Mitchell, R. J. & Jones, R. H. (1997) Root distribution of two tree species under a heterogeneous nutrient environment. *The Journal of Applied Ecology*, **34**, 645–656.

Olander, L. P. & Vitousek, P. M. (2000) Regulation of soil phosphatase and chitinase activity by N and P availability. *Biogeochemistry*, **49**, 175–190.

Pacala, S., Canham, C., Saponara, J. *et al.* (1996) Forest models defined by field measurements: estimation, error analysis and dynamics. *Ecological Monographs*, **66**, 1–43.

Pant, H. K. & Warman, P. R. (2000) Enzymatic hydrolysis of soil organic phosphorus by immobilized phosphatases. *Biology and Fertility of Soils*, **30**, 306–311.

Paoli, G. D. & Curran, L. M. (2007) Soil nutrients limit fine litter production and tree growth in mature lowland forest of southwestern Borneo. *Ecosystems*, **10**, 503–518.

Park, B. B., Yanai, R. D., Fahey, T. J. *et al.* (2008) Fine root dynamics and forest production across a calcium gradient in northern hardwood and conifer ecosystems. *Ecosystems*, **11**, 325–341.

Pastor, J., Aber, J. A., McClaugherty, C. A. & Meillilo, J. M. (1984) Aboveground production and N and P cycling along a nitrogen mineralization gradient on Blackhawk Island, Wisconsin. *Ecology*, **65**, 256–268.

Perakis, S. S., Maguire, D. A., Bullen, T. D. *et al.* (2006) Coupled nitrogen and calcium cycles in forests of the Oregon Coast range. *Ecosystems*, **9**, 63–74.

Phillips, R. P. & Fahey, T. J. (2006) Tree species and mycorrhizal associations influence the magnitude of rhizosphere effects. *Ecology*, **87**, 1302–1313.

Porder, S. & Chadwick, O. A. (2009) Climate and soil-age constraints on nutrient uplift and retention by plants. *Ecology*, **90**, 623–636.

Porder, S., Clark, D. A. & Vitousek, P. M. (2006) Persistence of rock-derived nutrients in the wet tropical forests of La Selva, Costa Rica. *Ecology*, **87**, 594–602.

Quesada, C. A., Lloyd, J., Schwarz, M. *et al.* (2009) Regional and large-scale patterns in Amazon forest structure and function are mediated by variations in soil physical and chemical properties. *Biogeosciences Discussions*, **6**, 3993–4057.

Reich, P. B., Oleksyn, J. & Wright, I. J. (2009) Leaf phosphorus influences the photosynthesis-nitrogen relation: a cross-biome analysis of 314 species. *Oecologia*, **160**, 207–212.

Reich, P. B., Ellsworth, D. S. & Uhl, C. (1995) Leaf carbon and nutrient assimilation and conservation in species of differing successional status in an Amazonian forest. *Functional Ecology*, **9**, 65–76.

Reich, P. B., Grigal, D. F., Aber, J. D. & Gower, S. T. (1997) Nitrogen mineralization and productivity in 50 hardwood and conifer stands on diverse soils. *Ecology*, **78**, 335–347.

Robertson, G. P., Klingensmith, K. M., Klug, M. J. *et al.* (1997) Soil resources, microbial activity, and primary production across an agricultural ecosystem. *Ecological Applications*, **7**, 158–170.

Runyon, J., Waring, R. H., Goward, S. N. & Welles, J. M. (1994) Environmental limits on net primary production and light-use efficiency across the Oregon transect. *Ecological Applications*, **4**, 226–237.

Russo, S. E., Brown, P., Tan, S. & Davies, S. J. (2007) Interspecific demographic trade-offs and soil-related habitat associations of tree species along resource gradients. *Journal of Ecology*, **96**, 192–203.

Russo, S. E., Cannon, W. L., Elowsky, C., Tan, S. & Davies, S. J. (2010) Variation in leaf stomatal traits of 28 tree species in relation to gas exchange along an edaphic gradient in a Bornean rain forest. *American Journal of Botany*, **97**, 1109–1120.

Russo, S. E., Davies, S. J., King, D. A. & Tan, S. (2005) Soil-related performance variation and distributions of tree species in a Bornean rain forest. *Journal of Ecology*, **93**, 879–889.

Ryan, M., Binkley, D. & Stape, J. (2008) Why don't our stands grow even faster? Control of production and carbon cycling in eucalypt plantations. *Southern Forests: A Journal of Forest Science*, **70**, 99–104.

Røsberg, I., Frank, J. & Stuanes, A. O. (2006) Effects of liming and fertilization on tree growth and nutrient cycling in a Scots pine ecosystem in Norway. *Forest Ecology and Management*, **237**, 191–207.

Schenk, H. J. (2006) Root competition: beyond resource depletion. *Journal of Ecology*, **94**, 725–739.

Schreeg, L. A., Kobe, R. K. & Walters, M. B. (2005) Tree seedling growth, survival, and morphology in response to landscape-level variation in soil resource availability in northern Michigan. *Canadian Journal of Forest Research*, **35**, 263–273.

Shabala, S. & Hariadi, Y. (2005) Effects of magnesium availability on the activity of plasma membrane ion transporters and light-induced responses from broad bean leaf mesophyll. *Planta*, **221**, 56–65.

Simard, S. W. (2009) The foundational role of mycorrhizal networks in self-organization of interior Douglas-fir forests. *Forest Ecology and Management*, **258**, S95–S107.

Simioni, G., Gignoux, J., Le Roux, X., Appé, R. & Benest, D. (2004) Spatial and temporal variations in leaf area index, specific leaf area and leaf nitrogen of two co-occurring savanna tree species. *Tree Physiology*, **24**, 205–16.

Sollins, P. (1998) Factors influencing species composition in tropical lowland rain forest: does soil matter ? *Ecology*, **79**, 23–30.

Sparks, J. P. (2009) Ecological ramifications of the direct foliar uptake of nitrogen. *Oecologia*, **159**, 1–13.

Spurr, S. H. (1956) Forest associations in the Harvard Forest. *Ecological Monographs*, **26**, 245–262.

St Clair, S. B. & Lynch, J. P. (2005) Base cation stimulation of mycorrhization and photosynthesis of sugar maple on acid soils are coupled by foliar nutrient dynamics. *The New Phytologist*, **165**, 581–590.

St Clair, S. B., Sharpe, W. E. & Lynch, J. P. (2008) Key interactions between nutrient limitation and climatic factors in temperate forests: a synthesis of the sugar maple literature. *Canadian Journal of Forest Research*, **38**, 401–414.

Stephenson, N. L. & van Mantgem, P. J. (2005) Forest turnover rates follow global and regional patterns of productivity. *Ecology Letters*, **8**, 524–531.

Stevens, C., Duprè, C., Gaudnik, C. *et al.* (2011) Changes in species composition of European acid grasslands observed along a gradient of nitrogen deposition. *Journal of Vegetation Science*, **22**, 207–215.

Stuefer, J. F. (1996) Potential and limitations of current concepts regarding the response of clonal plants to environmental heterogeneity. *Vegetatio*, **127**, 55–70.

Tanner, E. V. J., Kapos, V. & Franco, W. (1992) Nitrogen and phosphorus fertilization effects on Venezuelan montane forest trunk growth and litterfall. *Ecology*, **73**, 78–86.

Townsend, A. R., Asner, G. P. & Cleveland, C. C. (2008) The biogeochemical heterogeneity of tropical forests. *Trends in Ecology & Evolution*, **23**, 424–431.

Townsend, A. R., Cleveland, C. C., Houlton, B. Z., Alden, C.B. & White, J.W. (2011) Multi-element regulation of the tropical forest carbon cycle. *Frontiers in Ecology and the Environment*, **9**, 9–17.

Treseder, K. K. & Vitousek, P. M. (2001) Effects of soil nutrient availability on investment in acquisition of N and P in Hawaiian rain forests. *Ecology*, **82**, 946–954.

Uriarte, M., Canham, C. D., Thompson, J. & Zimmerman, J. K. (2004) Neighborhood analysis of tree growth and survival in a hurricane-driven tropical forest. *Ecological Monographs*, **74**, 591–614.

Ushio, M., Kitayama, K. & Balser, T. C. (2010) Tree species-mediated spatial patchiness of the composition of microbial community and physicochemical properties in the topsoils of a tropical montane forest. *Soil Biology and Biochemistry*, **42**, 1588–1595.

Van Breemen, N., Finlay, R., Lundström, U. *et al.* (2000) Mycorrhizal weathering: A true case of mineral plant nutrition? *Biogeochemistry*, **49**, 53–67.

Vanguelova, E., Pitman, R., Luiro, J. & Helmisaari, H.-S. (2010) Long term effects of whole tree harvesting on soil carbon and nutrient sustainability in the UK. *Biogeochemistry*, **101**, 43–59.

Vitousek, P. M. (2004) *Nutrient Cycling and Limitation: Hawaii as a Model System*. Princeton, NJ: Princeton University Press.

Vitousek, P. M. & Denslow, J. S. (1986) Nitrogen and phosphorus availability in treefall gaps of a lowland tropical rainforest. *Journal of Ecology*, **74**, 1167–1178.

Vitousek, P. M. & Farrington, H. (1997) Nutrient limitation and soil development: Experimental test of a biogeochemical theory. *Biogeochemistry*, **37**, 63–75.

Walker, T. W. & Syers, J. K. (1976) The fate of phosphorus during pedogenesis. *Geoderma*, **15**, 1–19.

Walters, M. B. & Reich, P. B. (1997) Growth of *Acer saccharum* seedlings in deeply shaded understories of northern Wisconsin: effects of nitrogen and water availability. *Canadian Journal of Forest Research*, **27**, 237–247.

Wang, L., Mou, P. P., Huang, J. & Wang, J. (2007) Spatial heterogeneity of soil nitrogen in a subtropical forest in China. *Plant and Soil*, **295**, 137–150.

Wanthongchai, K., Bauhus, J. & Goldammer, J. (2008) Nutrient losses through prescribed burning of aboveground litter and understorey in dry dipterocarp forests of different fire history. *Catena*, **74**, 321–332.

Weathers, K. C., Simkin, S. M., Lovett, G. M. & Lindberg, S. E. (2006) Empirical modeling of atmospheric deposition in mountainous landscapes. *Ecological Applications*, **16**, 1590–1607.

Webb, C. O. & Peart, D. R. (2000) Habitat associations of trees and seedlings in a Bornean rain forest. *Journal of Ecology*, **88**, 464–478.

Weber, P. & Bardgett, R. D. (2011) Influence of single trees on spatial and temporal patterns of belowground properties in native pine forest. *Soil Biology and Biochemistry*, **43**, 1372–1378.

Whitlock, C. (1993) Postglacial vegetation and climate of Grand Teton and Southern Yellowstone National Parks. *Ecological Monographs*, **63**, 173–198.

Whitmore, T. C. 1984. *Tropical Rain Forests of the Far East* 2nd edn. Oxford: Oxford University Press.

Whitney, G. G. (1991) Relation of plant species to substrate, landscape position, and aspect in north central Massachusetts. *Canadian Journal of Forest Research*, **21**, 1245–1252.

Will, R., Markewitz, D., Hendrick, R. *et al.* (2006) Nitrogen and phosphorus dynamics for 13-year-old loblolly pine stands receiving complete competition control and annual N fertilizer. *Forest Ecology and Management*, **227**, 155–168.

Will, R. E., Munger, G. T., Zhang, Y. & Borders, B. E. (2002). Effects of annual fertilization and complete competition control on current annual increment, foliar development, and growth efficiency of different aged *Pinus taeda* stands. *Canadian Journal of Forest Research*, **32**, 1728–1740.

Wright, S. J., Yavitt, J. B., Wurzburger, N. *et al.* (2011) Potassium, phosphorus or nitrogen limit root allocation, tree growth and litter production in a lowland tropical forest. *Ecology*, **92**, 1616–1625.

Xia, J. & Wan, S. (2008) Global response patterns of terrestrial plant species to nitrogen addition. *The New Phytologist*, **179**, 428–439.

Yavitt, J. B., Harms, K. E., Garcia, M. N. *et al.* (2009) Spatial heterogeneity of soil chemical properties in a lowland tropical moist forest, Panama. *Australian Journal of Soil Research*, **47**, 674–687.

Yavitt, J. B. & Wright, S. J. (2008) Seedling growth responses to water and nutrient augmentation in the understorey of a lowland moist forest, Panama. *Journal of Tropical Ecology*, **24**, 19–26.

Zaccherio, M. T. & Finzi, A. C. (2007) Atmospheric deposition may affect northern hardwood forest composition by altering soil nutrient supply. *Ecological Applications*, **17**, 1929–1941.

Zak, D. R., Host, G. E. & Pregitzer, K. S. (1989) Regional variability in nitrogen mineralization, nitrification, and overstory biomass in northern Lower Michigan. *Canadian Journal of Forest Research*, **19**, 1521–1526.

# PART III

# Detecting and modelling global change

# A chemical-evolutionary basis for remote sensing of tropical forest diversity

GREGORY P. ASNER

*Carnegie Institution for Science*

## 12.1  Introduction

One of ecology's fundamental pursuits centres on explaining controls over the distribution of species. Interest in species distributions is also increasing in the context of global change. There is a growing emphasis on providing information to decision-makers on where to protect and restore ecosystems and the species they harbour. Nowhere does this seem more obvious, or more pressing, than in tropical forests. Land-use change continues to strike deep into tropical forest regions, and climate change has come to the forefront in tropical forest conservation and planning. Temperature, precipitation and other climatic factors are shifting in some regions, or they are becoming highly variable (Cox *et al.* 2004; Williams, Jackson & Kutzbach 2007), and these changes are placing species in novel conditions that will force them to adapt, move or die (Asner, Loarie & Heyder 2010; Loarie *et al.* 2009).

We currently have few tools for mapping species distributions in tropical forests under these changing conditions, and our ability to monitor distributional changes remains limited despite their critical importance to ecology and conservation. Today, our understanding of species distributions comes from contrasting, and geographically limited, information sources. On the one hand, we have incredibly dense information at small scales of up to 50 hectares or so (Condit *et al.* 2005; Hubbell & Foster 1986). This information is key to understanding local-scale community patterns (Harms *et al.* 2001), but sparsely distributed plots cannot resolve ecological and biogeographic processes operating at the scales of long-range dispersal, migration or landscape evolution. On the other hand, we have longer-range, transect-based information on species occurrence, which does not provide the comprehensive inventories required for ecological modelling, although it is critical to basic conservation planning (http://fieldmuseum.org/explore/department/ecco). Emerging satellite-based methods, especially when combined with field observations, are beginning to fill in the geographic void with predictions of community patch-matrix patterns (Higgins *et al.* 2011; Turner *et al.*

*Forests and Global Change*, ed. David A. Coomes, David F. R. P. Burslem and William D. Simonson.
Published by Cambridge University Press. © British Ecological Society 2014.

**Figure 12.1** As in much of Amazonia, lowland forests of Madre de Dios, Peru appear as vast expanses of green canopy, incised by water bodies and deforestation (gold mining at A). Even a careful eye will pick out only the most basic variation in forest composition, such as swamp areas dominated by *Mauritia flexuosa* palm trees (B). See plate section for colour version.

2003), but current approaches do not constitute direct measurements of species distributions or diversity levels. With mainstream technologies, it is not possible to monitor spatially explicit change in species distributions and biological diversity, which is likely to be non-random over landscape, regional and global scales.

From above, tropical forests look like monotonous green carpets, at least until a river or forest clearing is encountered to expose water, soils and man-made materials (Figure 12.1). A few species are conspicuous and identifiable, like some palm (e.g *Mauritia*) or flowering trees (e.g. *Tabebuia*), but things generally seem green and hard to differentiate. Being able to identify species, or to map gradients in species richness, in the canopy of tropical forests would represent a substantial scientific advance, facilitating unprecedented forms of conservation and resource planning. Aerial photographs have been used for years to estimate the cover and abundance of conspicuous temperate or plantation species (e.g. Swetnam, Allen & Betancourt 1999), and some of that capability has been transferred to high-resolution spaceborne cameras (Thenkabail *et al.* 2004). Yet standard imaging cameras have yielded little information on species distributions or richness in tropical canopies.

Here I explore new possibilities for mapping canopy species diversity in humid tropical forests based on both the traits expressed among canopy taxa and the technologies needed to access information on those traits. I refer specifically to the Carnegie Airborne Observatory (CAO; http://cao.ciw.edu) because I developed it to focus mapping measurements on the plant traits that might best express the diversity of canopies in tropical forests. I also consider the ecological and evolutionary basis for trait-based remote sensing, with emphasis on the chemical attributes of canopy species. The ultimate purpose of the CAO and its biodiversity monitoring capabilities is to track compositional and/or functional changes in ecosystems, particularly under conditions of rapid global change.

## 12.2   Canopy chemistry: a window into biodiversity?

Canopy chemistry may represent a window into mapping biological diversity in tropical forests. Plants synthesise a wide variety of leaf compounds utilising numerous chemical elements and, for purposes here, it is convenient to group them into three functional categories: (i) light capture and growth, (ii) longevity and defence, and (iii) maintenance and metabolism (Table 12.1). While not independent, these groups are easily recognised by plant physiologists and ecologists, and thus can be traced throughout the scientific literature. Light capture–growth compounds include photosynthetic pigments such as chlorophylls and carotenoids, nitrogen and phosphorus, as well as the immediate products of photosynthesis such as soluble carbon compounds (Chapin III 1991; Evans 1989; Niinemets *et al.* 1999). Longevity compounds include lignin and cellulose that are structurally tough, lasting much of a leaf's lifetime (Melillo, Aber & Muratore 1982), while the defence category extends this list to more dynamic polyphenols (Coley, Kursar & Machado 1993). Maintenance–metabolism elements are those required in small quantities to support and mediate myriad functions within the leaf, but

**Table 12.1** *A portfolio of chemical compounds and elements provides a multi-dimensional signature of foliar investment in light capture and growth, longevity and defence, and maintenance and metabolism.*

| Light capture and growth | Longevity and defence | Maintenance and metabolism |
| --- | --- | --- |
| Anthocyanins | Carbon (C) | Potassium (K) |
| Chlorophylls | Hemi-cellulose | Calcium (Ca) |
| Carotenoids | Cellulose | Magnesium (Mg) |
| Nitrogen (N) | Lignin | Zinc (Zn) |
| Phosphorus (P) | Phenols | Manganese (Mn) |
| Water | Tannins | Boron (B) |
| Soluble carbon | | Iron (Fe) |

few are considered to be highly specialised. An overarching or synthetic structural trait is leaf mass per area (LMA); while not a chemical *per se*, LMA is linked to growth traits (Wright *et al.* 2004; Poorter *et al.* 2009).

Much work has focused on the ecological significance of these foliar compounds and elements. Biogeochemists tend to look at nitrogen, phosphorus and base cations (Ca, Mg, K), as well as lignin, in mediating productivity and decomposition (Aber & Melillo 1991; Schlesinger 1991). Physiologists often consider photosynthetic compounds and nutrients affecting trade-offs among growth-related processes (Peterson *et al.* 1999; Wright, Reich & Westoby 2001). Here I take a broad view, thinking of the leaf chemical portfolio as expressing strategic trade-offs among investments in light capture–growth, longevity–defence and maintenance–metabolic needs. By doing so, we can treat the chemical portfolios as 'signatures'. If chemical signatures are organised phylogenetically, then this might reflect variation in biological diversity at some taxonomic level. However, if the chemical phylogenetic signal is highly conserved, then closely related species may have similar chemical signatures, described broadly by Ackerly (2009) and for defence compounds by Agrawal (2007). Or if chemical phylogenies are highly dispersed, then species may prove to be chemically distinct from one another within a community (Kursar *et al.* 2009). Independent of phylogeny, ensembles of chemical signatures – compared among taxa at the community level – will probably describe functional diversity among tropical forest canopies. Without such chemical information, one might mistake many tropical forests as functionally similar or floristically monotonous when using chemical remote-sensing methods to map them.

## 12.3    Factors suggesting evolution in canopy chemical traits

There are a number of issues to consider when assessing whether or not canopy chemical traits, and particularly chemical signatures, exist among taxa. These include intraspecific variation, inter-trait correlation and chemical phylogenetic organisation. Depending upon the patterns that exist, chemically based windows to biodiversity mapping may or may not emerge.

### 12.3.1    Intraspecific variation

Temperate forest ecologists sometimes observe such high intraspecific variation that it would surprise them to find substantial chemical signature differentiation among taxa. However, in the temperate zone, such as in boreal or mixed deciduous forests with relatively few tree taxa (Latham & Ricklefs 1993), species are often adapted to span a wide range of climate conditions. They span these variable conditions while negotiating nitrogen-limited substrates spread over huge geographic areas (Vitousek & Howarth 1991). Variable climate and low nitrogen availability are associated with higher intraspecific plasticity in leaf traits (Karlsson & Nordell 1998; Niinemets,

Valladares & Ceulemans 2003; Reich, Walters & Ellsworth 1997). As a result, variation in the chemistry of a temperate species might be heavily driven by environmental factors, with adaptations centred more on increasing intra-specific variation among relatively fewer species to negotiate environmental gradients in space and time, thereby trumping phylogenetic expression of chemical variation.

In humid tropical forests, growth conditions are generally good, and although rock-derived nutrient availability may be low, especially for phosphorus and calcium (Vitousek & Sanford Jr. 1986; Vitousek, Turner & Kitayama 1995), production often remains high (Clark *et al.* 2001). High net primary production is maintained because nitrogen flows in relative abun-dance in many humid forests (Martinelli *et al.* 1999), and canopy species have evolved to recapture other nutrients even before discarded foliage reaches the soil surface (Vitousek 1982, 1984). However, good growth conditions are also associated with herbivory and parasitism in humid tropical forests, and it is in these environments where some of the strongest expressions of taxonomic order in canopy chemistry can be found, beginning with observations of rela-tively low intraspecific variation. For LMA, the within-species variation for thousands of taxa averages just 16% (Asner *et al.* 2011b), albeit only if samples are taken from upper, sunlit positions in the canopies.[1] Observations of low intraspecific variation of LMA at the top of tropical forest canopies are mirrored in many leaf chemical traits (Figure 12.2). Light capture–growth traits vary within species by an average of about 20%, depending upon the trait, in the upper canopy (Asner *et al.* 2009). Longevity–defence compounds also display low intraspecific variation, although often higher for phenols. Elements supporting maintenance and multiple metabolic functions (i.e. Mn, B, Zn) often display the highest levels of within-species variation (Figure 12.2).

### 12.3.2  Inter-trait correlation

Determining whether consistent combinations of leaf chemicals – or signatures – exist also requires an understanding of potential relationships between the contributing compounds and elements. Strong correlation between traits reduces the complexity and diversity of chemical signatures, whereas orthogonality among traits increases them. Growth factors such as chlorophylls, nitrogen and phosphorus are, on average, about 50–60% inter-correlated (Wright *et al.* 2004), and these correlations may be more strongly expressed when nitro-gen is limiting growth, thereby down-regulating all growth-related chemicals

---

[1] Without this control, variability in LMA and nearly all other growth compounds and nutrients is dominated by variation in lighting and shading conditions. Sticking with the upper canopy provides critically important control for comparative and phylogenetic analy-sis, and it is also extremely important in the effort to measure leaf traits with remote-sensing technology that is most sensitive to upper canopy foliage.

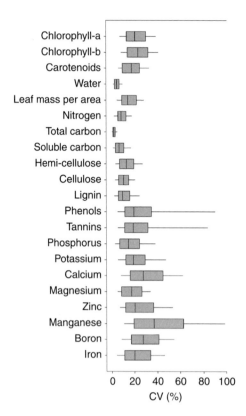

**Figure 12.2** Intraspecific variation of foliar chemistry (expressed as a percentage coefficient of variation, CV, within species) is generally low in the upper canopy of humid tropical forests. This example shows mean and standard deviation (box plot), as well as minimum and maximum (whisker lines), for 21 leaf traits collected from sunlight positions in more than 200 species in the Peruvian Amazon. Adapted from Asner and Martin (2011).

(Cordell *et al.* 2001). However, outside the circle of the most growth-related traits, it can take 15 or more statistical degrees of freedom to explain the covariation among 21 light–growth, longevity–defence and maintenance–metabolism traits (Asner & Martin 2011; Asner, Martin & Suhaili 2012). It is not clear whether this occurs primarily in tropical forests, or if it is common among plants or canopy species. Nonetheless, for humid tropical forests, the measurements demonstrate the multidimensionality of leaf chemical signatures, and these patterns are highly suggestive of multivariate trait evolution.

### 12.3.3    Taxonomic organisation

A taxonomically nested pattern for a chemical trait would suggest some evolutionary basis to that trait, and such patterns have been uncovered in recent studies in Hawaiian (Asner & Martin 2009), Amazonian (Asner & Martin 2011; Fyllas *et al.* 2009), Australian (Asner *et al.* 2009) and Malaysian (Asner, Martin & Suhaili 2012) tropical forest canopies. There is often strong taxonomic organisation among leaf traits in humid tropical forest canopies, starting with LMA: Asner *et al.* (2011b) found that 70% of the LMA variation among 2873 canopy individuals, collected from a wide range of humid tropical forests, could be explained to the species level. This finding for LMA extends to foliar chemicals: Fyllas *et al.* (2009) found that up to 50% of variation in about eight canopy foliar chemicals collected throughout Amazonia could be attributed to phylogeny, independent of site conditions. In a detailed site-level study in the Peruvian Amazon, Asner and Martin (2011) extended that finding to 21 traits among 600 coexisting canopies, finding that nearly 90% of the chemical variation among canopies could be attributed to taxonomic affiliation. This pattern has repeated itself at many sites throughout the global humid tropics (Carnegie Spectranomics Database; http://Spectranomics.ciw.edu).

## 12.4   Expressions of functional and biological diversity in hyperspectral imagery

As described, tropical forest canopies contain foliage with emergent, predictable chemical properties, including relatively low intraspecific variation, low inter-trait correlation when considering chemicals beyond the core growth-related compounds, and demonstrable taxonomic organisation. This combination may facilitate biodiversity assessment using remotely sensed data because these emergent chemical patterns mediate canopy spectral properties as measured with certain types of remote-sensing instruments. Many research groups have reported taxonomic variation associated with leaf and canopy spectral properties (e.g. Castro-Esau, Sanchez-Azofeifa & Caelli 2004; Féret & Asner 2011; Sanchez-Azofeifa *et al.* 2009; Williams 1991). In particular, a rich history of study in imaging spectroscopy (also known as hyperspectral remote sensing) has demonstrated that many of the chemicals can be measured remotely (reviews by Kokaly *et al.* 2009; Ustin *et al.* 2009). Further, Asner *et al.* (2011a) recently quantified the relationship between spectral and chemical data for thousands of tropical forest canopies. Another synthesis is not my goal here. Instead, with the aid of CAO imagery, I present evidence for canopy chemical diversity among tropical forest individuals, and discuss how chemical diversity is linked to biological diversity.

The CAO includes two high-fidelity imaging spectrometers that measure light reflected from canopies in up to 480 narrow spectral bands. By computing a principal components analysis of the CAO spectrometer data, and then classifying the results by spectral features, I have uncovered evidence for taxon-specific spectral signatures, such as for the well-known 50-hectare Center for Tropical Forest Science (CTFS; http://www.ctfs.si.edu) plot on Barro Colorado Island, Panama (Figure 12.3). The image reveals the possibility that spectral – and thus chemical – diversity exists in the canopy on very short distance scales of individual crowns. If this were not the case, then colours in the image would appear speckled and randomly distributed. Instead, spectral diversity is expressed crown by crown, and where variation does exist within a crown, close inspection of the original imagery indicates the presence of partial crown mortality, lianas or shadowing.

**Figure 12.3** This CAO image of the 50-hectare Center for Tropical Forest Science (CTFS) plot on Barro Colorado Island, Panama, shows (A) a natural colour composite as seen by the naked eye, and (B) spectroscopic analysis of three dominant chemical components throughout the canopy. In this case, the image was interpreted in terms of chlorophyll (reds), leaf mass per area (greens) and water content (blues). Note that the expression of chemical variation occurs primarily at the scale of individual crowns. White bar indicates approx. 30 m of distance. See plate section for colour version.

This crown-based pattern in tropical forest spectroscopy can be extended to a taxon-specific interpretation such as shown for an area of lowland rain forest on the Island of Hawaii (Figure 12.4). Combining this image with detailed ground and laboratory analysis, we found that the crowns with similar spectral signatures were of the same species more than 70% of the time (Féret & Asner 2011, 2013). For example, each red crown in Figure 12.4 is the invasive tree *Psidium cattleianum*. Field-based chemical interpretation of the map indicates that the spectra are driven by differences in LMA, chlorophyll, nitrogen, phenols and water content among species.

Finally, evidence suggesting a direct link between spectral and biological diversity in tropical forests is emerging in new comparative analyses of CAO data taken over different forests. For example, a monotypic stand of *Eucalyptus grandis* maintains a nearly constant spectroscopy (Figure 12.5A). Note the expression of low intraspecific variation by near constant colour; where there is variation, it is caused by shadows among crowns. In contrast, a high-diversity Amazonian forest shows a kaleidoscope of spectral variation (Figure 12.5B). Here, it is again observed that the results are expressed at the crown level. Areas of near-constant canopy spectroscopy in the left portion of the image (shown in purple) turn out to be near-monotypic stands of *Mauritia flexuosa* (see also Figure 12.1). That is, even in high-diversity landscapes, one

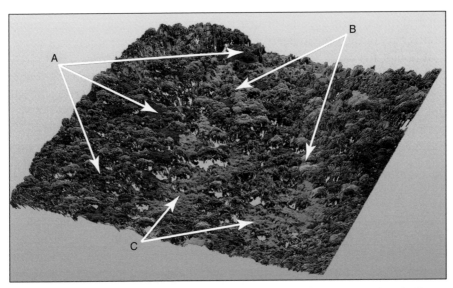

**Figure 12.4** This three-dimensional CAO image of a Hawaiian tropical forest indicates that canopy chemical traits are differentially expressed among species, including (A) *Psidium cattleianum*, (B) *Mangifera indica* and (C) *Trema orientalis*. Species-level chemical signatures are created by low intraspecific variation, low inter-trait correlation and phylogenetic organisation in chemical traits. See plate section for colour version.

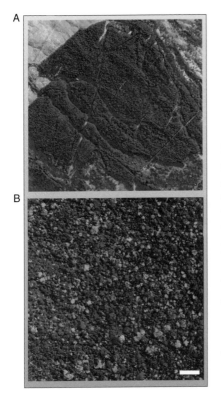

**Figure 12.5** CAO imagery taken over (A) *Eucalyptus grandis* plantation and (B) high-diversity lowland Amazon forest indicates the role of chemical diversity in expressing biological diversity. Chemicals expressed here include chlorophyll, water and phenols. Notice the near-constant chemistry (colour) in the plantation canopy and the crown-scale variation in chemical signatures in the Amazon case. The near-constant purple canopies in the left portion of the Amazon image are small monotypic stands of *Mauritia flexuosa* as seen in Figure 12.1. White bar indicates 100 m of distance. See plate section for colour version.

can find cold spots of spectral diversity expressing local areas of lower canopy biodiversity in the CAO imagery.

Although for years we have known that spectral properties are directly controlled by the foliar chemical properties in forest vegetation, only now are we getting a top-down look at the degree to which these patterns occur and how they may be related to tropical forest biodiversity. These are the first quantitative glimpses, and the degree to which species dictate the chemistry and spectroscopy of forest canopies is still far from understood. Much more study is needed to advance the role of this new observational capability in scientific, conservation and forest management contexts.

## 12.5   Ecological and evolutionary causes for chemical signatures

What ecological and evolutionary processes give rise to individual canopies and species having unique spectral and chemical signatures within a community? Some new information, combined with long-standing theories, provides important clues.

In humid tropical forests, geologic and topographic variation is often associated with changes in plant species composition (Gentry 1988; Higgins *et al.* 2011; Phillips *et al.* 2003), and in some regions such as Amazonia, floristic changes are connected to differences in soil cations, phosphorus availability and texture (ter Steege *et al.* 2006; Tuomisto *et al.* 1995, 2003). Floristic variation also occurs with geographically varying climate regimes. Critically, the observed compositional turnover is often paralleled by changes in average (community-level) chemical concentrations in canopy foliage (Asner & Martin 2011; Fyllas *et al.* 2009). That is, we see both a change in floristics and a change in the average chemical make-up of the canopies when crossing soil- and climate-mediated thresholds and boundaries. On either side of these thresholds, convergence in the canopy chemical signatures among coexisting species can be viewed as a syndrome, and we know that soil-mediated chemical syndromes occur among growth-related traits, especially for leaf nitrogen and phosphorus. For example, high-fertility soils harbour species with higher nutrient concentrations in their foliage; opposite patterns are often found in species found in low-nutrient conditions (Townsend *et al.* 2007; Townsend, Asner & Cleveland 2008). We also see community-scale shifts in foliar trait syndromes related to longevity–defence and maintenance–metabolism (e.g. phenols and carbon fractions), although these patterns can be more subtle (Asner & Martin 2011). Moreover, plant species tend to display suppressed levels of phenotypic plasticity in foliar longevity-and-defence compounds in resource-poor conditions (Stamp 2003). It seems that abiotic resources are key factors mediating plant evolutionary strategies, setting spatially explicit templates for the types of defence that may evolve (Kursar & Coley 2003). Furthermore, although growth (e.g. nitrogen) and defence (e.g. lignin) traits are often viewed as correlated in temperate forest ecosystems (Melillo, Aber & Muratore 1982), we can find a clear disconnect between them in tropical canopies (Asner & Martin 2011; Fyllas *et al.* 2009). This provides a critical insight: it suggests that evolution in highly competitive, high-production environments, such as humid tropical forests, leads to highly diverse, uncorrelated foliar chemical strategies. Why?

The environmental factors supporting elevated productivity in tropical forests (abundant nitrogen, light, water) are also correlated with pest and pathogen pressure (Ayres 1993; Mattson 1980), and the diversity of herbivores, parasites, viruses and other leaf-attacking lifeforms may well have led to the pronounced radiation of host strategies designed to combat, accommodate and outlast these threats in order to increase survival and fitness. This builds directly on the seminal work of Janzen (1970) and Connell (1970), who argued for the existence of pest- and pathogen-mediated density dependence in plant seedling establishment and recruitment. They suggested that, by host-specific co-evolution, herbivores and other leaf-threatening lifeforms maintain very low densities of conspecific plants locally. Janzen also proposed that tropical plants found in low-nutrient environments allocate heavily to chemical defences to protect foliage, whereas plants found on higher-nutrient soils invest more in chemicals yielding higher growth rates. Key work by Coley (1983) also suggests that light-gap species maintain chemical traits that are different from those found in shaded understorey environments. So while soil nutrient status fosters the community-scale foliar chemical syndromes described earlier, host-specific growth and defence strategies create unique chemical signatures among plant species coexisting within a community. Add to this the possibility for highly competitive plant-to-plant interactions and evolved syndromes for light and nutrients (Coley 1993; Coley & Barone 1996; Fine, Mesones & Coley 2004), and a multi-scale kaleidoscope of chemical traits emerges, as we observe in CAO imagery of humid tropical forests.

How diverse are chemical signatures among coexisting canopy species? Does each have a unique combination of chemical traits? At some level, the answer is yes, but intraspecific variation – as low as it can be at times – still leaves a buffer of chemical variability for each species, making it hard to answer these questions. Species-specificity is also dependent upon the number of traits considered within a chemical signature: combining traits results in increased differentiation among species, but does this have ecological or evolutionary meaning? The CAO imagery again provides some clues. In the Hawaiian image example (Figure 12.4), the forest is dominated by a relatively recent compilation of exotic species introduced from forests of Oceania, Asia, Central and South America (Mascaro *et al.* 2008; Zimmerman *et al.* 2007). The forest thus harbours species with chemical traits established in far-flung communities evolved under diverse environmental conditions and biogeographic histories. Perhaps as a result, each canopy species is very distinct and separable in the imagery. In the Peruvian Amazon image, the canopy comprises species evolved in similar, late-Holocene climate conditions (Williams, Jackson & Kutzbach 2007). There was thus a shared environment for chemical trait evolution, but the species also come from differing pre-Holocene biogeographic origins (Hoorn *et al.* 2010). Chemical diversity is high and many species are chemically distinct, yet the imagery suggests greater overlap among coexisting canopies (i.e. a shared syndrome) than we find in the Hawaiian forest canopy occupied by species from very diverse evolutionary and biogeographic backgrounds.

These tantalising hints suggest that canopy biodiversity maps based on chemical plant traits could unlock doors to understanding forest function and community assembly, and how species have evolved under contrasting environmental regimes. Far more work is needed to measure the spectral patterns and to interpret them chemically and in terms of biological diversity. Yet this early evidence suggests a novel pathway forward to unravelling the secrets of the ecology and evolution of tropical forest communities.

## 12.6   Biodiversity mapping and global change

There is a pressing need to take biodiversity mapping and monitoring beyond the plot or transect scale. The velocity of climate and land-use changes is now likely to exceed the migration potential of many species and functional groups of species (Asner, Loarie & Heyder 2010; Loarie *et al.* 2009), and this process has already begun to rearrange the composition of our biosphere (Parmesan 2006; Wake, Hadly & Ackerly 2009). In short, our biosphere is in a state of non-equilibrium change (Biggs, Carpenter & Brock 2009; Schimel, Asner & Moorcroft 2013). Without leaps forward in the area of biodiversity monitoring, changes in biospheric composition will go unaccounted, and thus will have unknown impact on prognostic studies of the future global environment. New technologies such as imaging spectroscopy are key to making sure biodiversity change is quantified, but technology represents only part of the solution going forward. New and innovative approaches are needed to take advantage of the developing technologies. I propose that the best approaches will be seated in an understanding of the underlying evolutionary drivers of trait-based diversification among species. More generally, mapping compositional and functional changes at the regional level will require effort among experts from multiple fields including engineering, chemistry and evolutionary biology. The required interdisciplinary links still need forging, yet the effort is central to advancing biodiversity monitoring for conservation planning, ecosystem management and resource policy development in this century of rapid global change.

## Acknowledgements

I thank the many colleagues who have influenced my thinking on the topics presented here. I thank Roberta Martin, Alan Townsend and two anonymous reviewers for comments on the manuscript, and David Burslem and David Coomes for organising the writers and for editing. The Carnegie Airborne Observatory is made possible by the Andrew Mellon Foundation, Avatar Alliance Foundation, Gordon and Betty Moore Foundation, Grantham Foundation for the Protection of the Environment, John D. and Catherine T. MacArthur Foundation, Margaret A. Cargill Foundation, Mary Anne Nyburg Baker and G. Leonard Baker Jr, W. M. Keck Foundation and William R. Hearst III.

## References

Aber, J. D. & Melillo, J. M. (1991) *Terrestrial Ecosystems*. Philadelphia: Saunders College Publishing.

Ackerly, D. (2009) Conservatism and diversification of plant functional traits: Evolutionary rates versus phylogenetic signal. *Proceedings of the National Academy of Sciences USA*, **106**, 19699–19706.

Agrawal, A. A. (2007) Macroevolution of plant defense strategies. *Trends in Ecology & Evolution*, **22**, 103–109.

Asner, G., Martin, R. & Suhaili, A. (2012) Sources of canopy chemical and spectral diversity in lowland Bornean forest. *Ecosystems*, **15**, 504–517.

Asner, G. P., Loarie, S. R. & Heyder, U. (2010) Combined effects of climate and land-use change on the future of humid tropical forests. *Conservation Letters*, **3**, 395–403.

Asner, G. P. & Martin, R. E. (2009) Airborne spectranomics: Mapping canopy chemical and taxonomic diversity in tropical forests. *Frontiers in Ecology and the Environment*, **7**, 269–276.

Asner, G. P. & Martin, R. E. (2011) Canopy phylogenetic, chemical and spectral assembly in a lowland Amazonian forest. *New Phytologist*, **189**, 999–1012.

Asner, G. P., Martin, R. E., Ford, A. J., Metcalfe, D. J. & Liddell, M. J. (2009) Leaf chemical and spectral diversity of Australian tropical forests. *Ecological Applications*, **19**, 236–253.

Asner, G. P., Martin, R. E., Knapp, D. E. et al. (2011a) Spectroscopy of canopy chemicals in humid tropical forests. *Remote Sensing of Environment*, **115**, 3587–3598.

Asner, G. P., Martin, R. E., Tupayachi, R. et al. (2011b) Taxonomy and remote sensing of leaf mass per area (LMA) in humid tropical forests. *Ecological Applications*, **21**, 85–98.

Ayres, M. P. (1993) Plant defense, herbivory, and climate change. In *Biotic Interactions and Global Change* (eds. P. M. Kareiva, J. G. Kingsolver & R. B. Huey), pp. 75–94. Sunderland, MA: Sinauer Associates.

Biggs, R., Carpenter, S. R. & Brock, W. A. (2009) Turning back from the brink: Detecting an impending regime shift in time to avert it. *Proceedings of the National Academy of Sciences USA*, **106**, 826–831.

Castro-Esau, K. L., Sanchez-Azofeifa, G. A. & Caelli, T. (2004) Discrimination of lianas and trees with leaf-level hyperspectral data. *Remote Sensing of Environment*, **90**, 353–372.

Chapin III, F. S. (1991) Integrated responses of plants to stress. *BioScience*, **41**, 29–36.

Clark, D. A., Brown, S., Kicklighter, D. W. et al. (2001) Net primary production in tropical forests: An evaluation and synthesis of existing field data. *Ecological Applications*, **11**, 371–384.

Coley, P. D. (1983) Herbivory and defensive characteristics of tree species in a lowland tropical forest. *Ecological Monographs*, **53**, 209–234.

Coley, P. D. (1993) Gap size and plant defenses. *Trends in Ecology and Evolution*, **8**, 1–2.

Coley, P. D. & Barone, J. A. (1996) Herbivory and plant defenses in tropical forests. *Annual Review of Ecology and Systematics*, **27**, 305–335.

Coley, P. D., Kursar, T. A. & Machado, J.-L. (1993) Colonization of tropical rain forest leaves by epiphylls: effects of site and host-plant leaf lifetime. *Ecology*, **74**, 619–623.

Condit, R., Ashton, P., Balslev, H. *et al.* (2005) Tropical tree alpha-diversity: Results from a worldwide network of large plots. *Science*, **55**, 565–582.

Connell, J. H. (1970) On the role of natural enemies in preventing competitive exclusion in some marine animals and in rain forest trees. In *Dynamics of Population* (eds. P. J. Den Boer & G. R. Gradwell). Wageningen: Pudoc.

Cordell, S., Goldstein, G., Meinzer, F. C. & Vitousek, P. M. (2001) Regulation of leaf life-span and nutrient-use efficiency of *Metrosideros polymorpha* trees at two extremes of a long chronosequence in Hawaii. *Oecologia (Berlin)*, **127**, 198–206.

Cox, P. M., Betts, R. A., Collins, M. *et al.* (2004) Amazonian forest dieback under climate-carbon cycle projections for the 21st century. *Theoretical and Applied Climatology*, **78**, 137–156.

Evans, J. R. (1989) Photosynthesis and nitrogen relationships in leaves of C3 plants. *Oecologia*, **78**, 9–19.

Féret, J.-B. & Asner, G. P. (2011) Spectroscopic classification of tropical forest species using radiative transfer modeling. *Remote Sensing of Environment*, **115**, 2415–2422.

Féret, J.-B. & Asner, G. P. (2013) Tree species discrimination in tropical forests using airborne imaging spectroscopy. *IEEE Transactions on Geoscience and Remote Sensing*, **51**, 73–84.

Fine, P. V. A., Mesones, I. & Coley, P. D. (2004) Herbivores promote habitat specialization by trees in Amazonian forests. *Science*, **305**, 663–665.

Fyllas, N., Patiño, S., Baker, T. *et al.* (2009) Basin-wide variations in foliar properties of Amazonian forest: phylogeny, soils and climate. *Biogeosciences*, **6**, 2677–2708.

Gentry, A. H. (1988) Changes in plant community diversity and floristic composition on environmental and geographical gradients. *Annals of the Missouri Botanical Garden*, **75**, 1–34.

Harms, K. E., Condit, R., Hubbell, S. P. & Foster, R. B. (2001) Habitat associations of trees and shrubs in a 50-ha neotropical forest plot. *Journal of Ecology*, **89**, 947–959.

Higgins, M., Ruokolainen, K., Tuomisto, H. *et al.* (2011) Geological control of floristic composition in Amazonian forests. *Journal of Biogeography*, **38**, 2136–2149.

Hoorn, C., Wesselingh, F. P., ter Steege, H. *et al.* (2010) Amazonia through time: Andean uplift, climate change, landscape evolution, and biodiversity. *Science*, **330**, 927–931.

Hubbell, S. P. & Foster, R. B. (1986) Biology, chance, and history and the structure of tropical rainforest tree communities. In *Community Ecology* (eds. J. Diamond & T. J. Case), pp. 314–329. New York: Harper and Row.

Janzen, D. H. (1970) Herbivores and the number of tree species in tropical forests. *American Naturalist*, **104**, 501–528.

Karlsson, P. S. & Nordell, K. O. (1998) Intraspecific variation in nitrogen status and photosynthetic capacity within mountain birch populations. *Ecography*, **11**, 293–297.

Kokaly, R. F., Asner, G. P., Ollinger, S. V., Martin, M. E. & Wessman, C. A. (2009) Characterizing canopy biochemistry from imaging spectroscopy and its application to ecosystem studies. *Remote Sensing of Environment*, **113**, S78–S91.

Kursar, T. A. & Coley, P. D. (2003) Convergence in defense syndromes of young leaves in tropical rainforests. *Biochemical Systematics and Ecology*, **31**, 929–949.

Kursar, T.A., Dexter, K.G., Lokvam, J. et al. (2009) The evolution of antiherbivore defenses and their contribution to species coexistence in the tropical tree genus Inga. Proceedings of the National Academy of Sciences USA, **106**, 18073–18078.

Latham, R.E. & Ricklefs, R.E. (1993) Global patterns of tree species richness in moist forests: energy-diversity theory does not account for variation in species richness. Oikos, **67**, 325–333.

Loarie, S.R., Duffy, P.B., Hamilton, H. et al. (2009) The velocity of climate change. Nature, **462**, 1052–1057.

Martinelli, L.A., Piccolo, M.C., Townsend, A.R. et al. (1999) Nitrogen stable isotopic composition: tropical vs. temperate forests. Biogeochemistry, **46**, 45–65.

Mascaro, J., Becklund, K.K., Hughes, R.F. & Schnitzer, S.A. (2008) Limited native plant regeneration in novel, exotic-dominated forests on Hawai'i. Forest Ecology and Management, **256**, 593–606.

Mattson, W.J. (1980) Herbivory in relation to plant nitrogen content. Annual Review of Ecology and Systematics, **11**, 119–161.

Melillo, J.M., Aber, J.D. & Muratore, J.F. (1982) Nitrogen and lignin control of hardwood leaf litter decomposition dynamics. Ecology, **63**, 621–626.

Niinemets, U., Tenhunen, J.D., Canta, N.R. et al. (1999) Interactive effects of nitrogen and phosphorus on the acclimation potential of foliage photosynthetic properties of cork oak, Quercus suber, to elevated atmospheric $CO_2$ concentrations. Global Change Biology, **5**, 455–470.

Niinemets, U., Valladares, F. & Ceulemans, R. (2003) Leaf-level phenotypic variability and plasticity of invasive Rhododendron ponticum and non-invasive Ilex aquifolium co-occurring at two contrasting European sites. Plant, Cell and Environment, **26**, 941–956.

Parmesan, C. (2006) Ecological and evolutionary responses to recent climate change. Annual Review of Ecology, Evolution, and Systematics, **37**, 637–669.

Peterson, A.G., Ball, J.T., Luo, Y. et al. (1999) The photosynthesis-leaf nitrogen relationship at ambient and elevated atmospheric carbon dioxide: A meta-analysis. Global Change Biology, **5**, 331–346.

Phillips, O.L., Vargas, P.N., Lorenzo, A. et al. (2003) Habitat association among Amazonian tree species: a landscape-scale approach. Journal of Ecology, **91**, 757–775.

Poorter, H., Niinemets, U., Poorter, L., Wright, I.J. & Villar, R. (2009) Causes and consequences of variation in leaf mass per area (LMA): a meta-analysis. New Phytologist, **182**, 565–588.

Reich, P.B., Walters, M.B. & Ellsworth, D.S. (1997) From tropics to tundra: Global convergence in plant functioning. Proceedings of the National Academy of Sciences USA, **94**, 13730–13734.

Sanchez-Azofeifa, G.A., Castro, K., Wright, S.J. et al. (2009) Differences in leaf traits, leaf internal structure, and spectral reflectance between two communities of lianas and trees: Implications for remote sensing in tropical environments. Remote Sensing of Environment, **113**, 2076–2088.

Schimel, D.S., Asner, G.P., & Moorcroft, P.R. (2013) Observing changing ecological diversity in the Anthropocene. Frontiers in Ecology and the Environment, **11**, 129–137.

Schlesinger, W.H. (1991) Biogeochemistry, An Analysis of Global Change. San Diego, CA: Academic Press.

Stamp, N. (2003) Out of the quagmire of plant defense hypotheses. The Quarterly Review of Biology, **78**, 23–55.

Swetnam, T.W., Allen, C.D. & Betancourt, J.L. (1999) Applied historical ecology: Using the past to manage for the future. Ecological Applications, **9**, 1189–1206.

ter Steege, H., Pitman, N.C.A., Phillips, O.L. et al. (2006) Continental-scale patterns of canopy tree composition and function across Amazonia. Nature, **443**, 444–447.

Thenkabail, P.S., Enclona, E.A., Ashton, M.S., Legg, C. & De Dieu, M.J. (2004) Hyperion, IKONOS, ALI, and ETM plus sensors in the study of African rainforests. *Remote Sensing of Environment*, **90**, 23–43.

Townsend, A. R., Asner, G. P. & Cleveland, C. C. (2008) The biogeochemical heterogeneity of tropical forests. *Trends in Ecology and the Environment*, **23**, 424–431.

Townsend, A. R., Cleveland, C. C., Asner, G. P. & Bustamante, M. M. C. (2007) Controls over foliar N:P ratios in tropical rain forests. *Ecology*, **88**, 107–118.

Tuomisto, H., Poulsen, A. D., Ruokolainen, K. *et al.* (2003) Linking floristic patterns with soil heterogeneity and satellite imagery in Ecuadorian Amazonia. *Ecological Applications*, **13**, 352–371.

Tuomisto, H., Ruokolainen, K., Kalliola, R. *et al.* (1995) Dissecting Amazonian biodiversity. *Science*, **269**, 63–66.

Turner, W., Spector, S., Gardiner, N. *et al.* (2003) Remote sensing for biodiversity and conservation. *Trends in Ecology and Evolution*, **18**, 306–314.

Ustin, S. L., Gitelson, A. A., Jacquemoud, S. *et al.* (2009) Retrieval of foliar information about plant pigment systems from high resolution spectroscopy. *Remote Sensing of Environment*, **113**, S67–S77.

Vitousek, P. M. (1982) Nutrient cycling and nutrient use efficiency. *American Naturalist*, **119**, 553–572.

Vitousek, P. M. (1984) Litterfall, nutrient cycling, and nutrient limitation in tropical forests. *Ecology*, **65**, 285–298.

Vitousek, P. M. & Howarth, R. W. (1991) Nitrogen limitation on land and in the sea – How can it occur? *Biogeochemistry*, **13**, 87–115.

Vitousek, P. M. & Sanford Jr, R. L. (1986) Nutrient cycling in moist tropical forest. *Annual Review of Ecology and Systematics*, **17**, 137–167.

Vitousek, P. M., Turner, D. R. & Kitayama, K. (1995) Foliar nutrients during long-term soil development in Hawaiian montane rain forest. *Ecology*, **76**, 712–720.

Wake, D. B., Hadly, E. A. & Ackerly, D. D. (2009) Biogeography, changing climates and niche evolution. *Proceedings of the National Academy of Sciences USA*, **106**, 19631–19637.

Williams, D. L. (1991) A comparison of spectral reflectance properties at the needle, branch, and canopy level for selected conifer species. *Remote Sensing of Environment*, **35**, 79–93.

Williams, J. W., Jackson, S. T. & Kutzbach, J. E. (2007) Projected distributions of novel and disappearing climates by 2100 AD. *Proceedings of the National Academy of Sciences USA*, **104**, 5738–5742.

Wright, I. J., Reich, P. B. & Westoby, M. (2001) Strategy shifts in leaf physiology, structure and nutrient content between species of high- and low-rainfall and high- and low-nutrient habitats. *Functional Ecology*, **15**, 423–434.

Wright, I. J., Reich, P. B., Westoby, M. *et al.* (2004) The worldwide leaf economics spectrum. *Nature*, **428**, 821–827.

Zimmerman, N., Hughes, R. F., Cordell, S. *et al.* (2007) Patterns of primary succession of native and introduced plants in lowland wet forests in Eastern Hawaii. *Biotropica*, doi:10.1111/j.1744-7429.2007.00371.x.

# CHAPTER THIRTEEN

# Forests in a greenhouse atmosphere: predicting the unpredictable?

HARALD BUGMANN

*Forest Ecology, ETH Zurich*

## 13.1 Introduction

Forest ecosystems are of key importance from the global to the local level, as they provide a multitude of goods and services upon which humanity depends (MEA 2005). Globally, forests are an important element of many biogeochemical cycles, among others the carbon cycle, with direct implications for atmospheric greenhouse gas concentrations as well as for the energy balance at the land surface (e.g. albedo); also, they harbour a considerable amount of terrestrial biodiversity. In many countries worldwide, forests continue to be an important element in the resource base of human livelihoods, including wood for construction and energy use, food and fibre, and many other products. Both regionally and locally, forests are important for mitigating soil erosion or protecting mountain settlements from rockfall and snow avalanches (IUCN 2008).

Humanity is facing the task of reducing carbon emissions from the burning of fossil fuels by *c.* 80% over the coming decades (IPCC 2007). Therefore, the role of forests will most likely increase in the future as an energy base as well as for the sustainable production of fibre; it has long been known that any petrochemically based good could be produced from wood compounds (Goldstein 1975). For all these reasons, understanding the factors and processes that shape the structure, composition and functioning of forest ecosystems is not only of scientific interest, but also of great practical importance in the context of the management of these systems in the face of multiple, often conflicting demands by human societies. Indeed, the dynamics of forest ecosystems at decadal to centennial time scales (subsequently referred to as 'long-term forest dynamics') have long fascinated and puzzled laypeople as well as scientists.

Forests may not be more complex than other ecosystems such as coral reefs (Sale 1991) or tidal communities (Dethier 1984), but they are more difficult to study because their dynamics are characterised by large spatial and temporal scales. Some species of trees, the dominant life form in forests, can grow up to a height of more than 100 m (Franklin & Dyrness 1973), and some have the

*Forests and Global Change*, ed. David A. Coomes, David F. R. P. Burslem and William D. Simonson.
Published by Cambridge University Press. © British Ecological Society 2014.

capability to live for more than 4500 years (Schulman 1958). Thus, scientific tools and methods are challenged when it comes to characterising, analysing and understanding the long-term dynamics of forest ecosystems, as most of the scientific approaches that we employ operate over short temporal scales and small areas, with a few exceptions. For example, in palaeo-ecology (Delcourt & Delcourt 1991) very long time scales are covered, but usually for individual sites and with a rather limited temporal resolution. By contrast, novel remote-sensing tools such as LiDAR (light detection and ranging; Goodwin, Coops & Culvenor 2006) can greatly expand our capability of measuring high-resolution data over large areas, but for the foreseeable future these will remain snapshots in a very long temporal sequence of forest development. Thus, forest dynamics is a field where the scientific method is likely to meet its limits, i.e. where we may encounter phenomena that we cannot measure or analyse adequately and thus cannot fully understand, purely for reasons of scale.

The marked human-induced changes of the land surface and of climate, commonly referred to as elements of 'global change' (MEA 2005; IPCC 2007), are one of the key problems for humanity, as they threaten the livelihoods of a large fraction of the human population via changes in the delivery of forest ecosystem goods and services, including changes in water availability leading to forest dieback and soil erosion. Given the importance of forests and their goods and services, it is of utmost importance that the scientific community is able to make robust and reliable assessments of the future long-term development of forest ecosystems at multiple spatial scales, from the local to the global. Hence, we are scientifically challenged by a task that is very much needed but difficult to achieve.

In this contribution, I will reflect on three things. First, how can we address the challenges outlined above in terms of spatial and temporal scales? Second, what are we actually doing when we, as scientists, are assessing the future state and fate of forest ecosystems – are we attempting to predict the future? And third, how successful have we been to date? For the latter question, I will focus on a case study, i.e. individual-based models of forest succession, which are quantitative, computer-based tools that have been used in multiple instances to assess changes of species composition and stand structure over time, and a range of other ecosystem goods and services derived from these properties.

## 13.2   How can we address the challenges?

Science started with observational studies, in our context observations on patterns and processes in forest ecosystems, and they have taken us a long way in putting together the puzzle of how forest ecosystems 'work'. However, global change will most likely take us at an unprecedented speed into domains of climate space that lack an analogue in the past. Therefore, observational data that necessarily refer to the past or the current behaviour of forests cannot normally be used as robust analogues for the future, even if they are cast into a quantitative framework such as the Holdridge Life Zone model (Holdridge 1967), which was widely used until the early 1990s for making projections of future vegetation at the global scale (e.g. Smith, Leemans & Shugart 1992). Observations are highly useful for improving our understanding of ecological processes, but they are limited in their power when it comes to making extrapolations under novel environmental conditions.

Experiments can be more helpful in the global change context, as they allow us to set abiotic and biotic conditions to mimic anticipated future conditions, e.g. by laboratory or free-air experiments adjusting $CO_2$ concentrations (e.g. Lee, Barrott & Reich 2011), by heating the soil *in situ* (e.g. Martin *et al.* 2010), or by setting temperature, radiation and precipitation values according to future scenarios in greenhouses or open-top chambers (e.g. Pieper *et al.* 2011). This allows us to study the response of ecosystems to expected future conditions, albeit with clear limitations. For example, owing to time constraints and particularly the need to produce results within the first 2–3 years of a study, experimental treatments normally impose a step change of environmental conditions on the ecosystem, rather than (more realistic) gradual changes, thus raising questions about the representativeness of the treatment for real-world conditions of the future. In addition, only the initial response can be measured, whereas there is ample evidence for a down-regulation of most responses after several years (Leuzinger *et al.* 2011). In the context of forests, it is particularly problematic that for logistical reasons, small (i.e. typically young) trees need to be investigated, and the treatment cannot be maintained to elucidate the long-term response, i.e. to study the subjects until they have grown to adult size. Thus, scaling of experimental results to longer time scales and mature individuals is required, which is a non-trivial task (*cf.* Bugmann *et al.* 2000).

This should not imply, however, that observational and experimental studies are inadequate in a global change context. As the third pillar of the scientific method beyond observations and experiments, dynamic models of ecological processes can be developed to synthesise our knowledge about ecosystems and the patterns and processes that determine their dynamics (Figure 13.1). Such models can then be used to test whether observational or experimental data are reproduced by simulation results. If the model is successful in such exercises, this increases our confidence that model applications under novel conditions will yield robust results. Yet, it is clear that although such tests are necessary, they certainly do not represent a sufficient condition to show the applicability of any model under global change conditions (assuming that the latter do not have a past or present-day analogue).

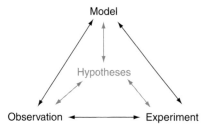

**Figure 13.1** Schematic of the tight relationship between scientific hypotheses, observations, experiments and modelling. Hypotheses give rise to observations, the setting up of new experiments, or they influence the development of models, which in turn can be viewed as hypotheses (see text). In turn, observations, experimental results and simulation results from models give rise to new hypotheses about the way nature works.

Furthermore, data assimilation techniques can be quite powerful for increasing the robustness and reliability of computer models. Originally developed in numerical weather prediction (for an early overview, see Evensen 1992), they proved to be very useful, particularly since vast amounts of data (i.e. global weather observations) are becoming available continuously. This is not so obvious for forest properties, many of which are difficult to obtain in spite of novel techniques such as remote sensing; still, data assimilation techniques are increasingly applied in models of terrestrial systems (*cf.* Hartig *et al.* 2012). Although they offer the big advantage that disparate data sources can be combined, the general paucity of vegetation data requires us to balance two very different uses of data: on the one hand for actively improving model quality (data assimilation, model parameterisation); on the other hand for independently assessing model quality (model testing).

Scientists who are developing dynamic models usually call the latter kind of exercise 'model validation', although it is fundamentally impossible to prove the validity of any scientific work – we can only test hypotheses and either falsify them, or fail to falsify them (Popper 1934). It is important to recognise that the latter does not constitute proof of the validity of the hypothesis. In this context, 'model validation' would be better viewed as an attempt to avoid falsification, and I thus prefer the terms 'model corroboration', 'model evaluation' or 'model testing'.

A model is a deliberate simplification of reality that is set up to explain a range of phenomena, based upon certain objectives. As such, a model can be viewed as a special case of a (potentially very complicated) hypothesis that acknowledges limited understanding. Let us consider this in more detail. The simple hypothesis 'bacterial populations grow exponentially' is equivalent to the exponential model, which immediately yields testable and falsifiable predictions (*sensu* Popper 1934). However, most models of ecological phenomena, such as long-term forest dynamics, are much more complex than the exponential equation and thus do not yield one single prediction. As such, they are not testable *per se*, and they are certainly not falsifiable because we know that they are not accurate representations of reality – this is what gave rise to the famous quote 'all models are wrong, but some models are useful' (Box & Draper 1987). Still, such models can be employed to simulate a range of (forest) properties in space and time; the simulation results represent hypotheses in their own right that can be tested against empirical data (e.g. forest biomass or species composition along environmental gradients). If the model fails to depict such ecosystem properties accurately, we conclude that our scientific understanding as embodied in the model is inadequate; in the case of an accurate match between model outputs and measurements, our confidence in the usefulness of the model increases.

Model-based projections of future ecosystem dynamics are extrapolations that cannot be tested now – in the year 2100, we will know more about their appropriateness ('validity'). Yet, such simulation results have gained political importance, for example in the context of the IPCC; thus scientists who develop models of long-term ecosystem dynamics need to pay particular attention to rigorous model testing under the widest possible range of past and/or current conditions as well as against experimental data.

In Section 13.4, I will review successes, failures, pitfalls and work that remains to be done in one of these fields, dealing with forest succession and the pertinent modelling approaches. However, before turning to that topic, I would like to reflect on what we are actually doing when we apply dynamic models of ecological processes in 'impact assessments'.

## 13.3   What are we doing when we try to 'predict' the future?

In Ancient Rome, Cato Censorius (234–149 BC) is said to have finished every speech in the Senate, irrespective of its subject, with the words 'ceterum censeo Carthaginem esse delendam' ('Furthermore, I think that Carthage should be destroyed [by us]'). He did this to the point where his colleagues eventually took that decision, which led to the Third Punic War. I do not intend to start a war in science, but I cannot help pointing out that in global change science, we are not always precise with our use of language (Bugmann 2003), which may lead to misunderstandings particularly when our findings are picked up by stake-holders and enter the public debate via the media.

I propose that it would be beneficial if we used distinct terminology for dealing with the levels of (un)certainty in our knowledge (Table 13.1). I particularly suggest that we should use the term 'predict' (or 'prediction') to refer to things about which we can be *certain*, such as the timing of the next eclipse of the Sun. We should use 'forecast' to refer to things that we can say with a certain *probability* only, such as a weather forecast, which implies, for example, a certain probability of rain on the next day; thus, forecasting carries the notion of a likelihood. When we are not able to attach a probability to our

**Table 13.1** *Terms, their definitions based on the compilation from the Merriam–Webster Dictionary (from Bugmann 2003) and some examples.*

| Term | Definition | Example |
|------|------------|---------|
| Prediction | Commonly denotes inference from facts or accepted laws of nature, implying certainty | Astronomers predict an eclipse |
| Forecast | Adds the implication of anticipating eventualities and differs from predict in being concerned with probabilities | Forecasting snow |
| Projection | An estimate of future possibilities | Projected world population in 2050 |
| Scenario | An account or synopsis of a possible course of action or events | |

statements (as is often the case in global change science), we should use the terms 'projection' or 'scenario', which indicate a *possibility*, and this is what we are addressing in most cases: scenarios of future $CO_2$ concentrations, future climate or future forest responses are *possible* developments. Climate scientists have begun to attach probabilities to the output of climate models; but fortunately, this is commonly and correctly (although slightly redundantly) referred to as 'probabilistic forecasting' (e.g. Weigel & Mason 2011).

Unfortunately, in the scientific literature we often see statements such as 'the model predicts …'; I think such statements are inappropriate for two reasons. First, we as scientists use a model to make 'predictions', whereas the model as such does not 'predict'; it is only a tool in our hands and does not act independently. Second, simulation results could be considered to be 'predictions' only if they were not afflicted with uncertainty. The fact that a model's simulation results are a logical and *certain* consequence of the model's assumptions, parameter values and input variables does not imply that it would be justified to ignore all the underlying uncertainties. Particularly in global change science, uncertainties about model formulations abound, from general circulation models (e.g. parameterisation of clouds) to crop or forest models (e.g. long-term $CO_2$ effects), and thus simulation results – at the very least in the ecological sciences – should never be viewed as predictions (Table 13.1).

Calling simulation results 'predictions' may even be dangerous when communicating with stake-holders (Bugmann 2003), because the term 'predict' may then be interpreted in the context of the ecological dynamics that are being studied rather than in the context of a specific model. Hence, under such circumstances 'model predictions' quickly turn into 'predictions of the future behaviour of a specific ecosystem', and this would most likely be inappropriate.

Lastly, and on a somewhat less acute note, I would like to insist that 'modelling' and 'simulation' are not the same thing – 'modelling' is the activity of developing a simplified picture of reality, be it as a verbal, graphical, mathematical or other sort of model. When such a model is transferred to a computer and implemented using a programming language or simulation software, we can use this implementation to produce simulation results. Hence, data generated by a computer model are always 'simulated', not 'modelled'; the real system is being modelled, and when the model equations are solved numerically on a computer, this leads to simulation results.

## 13.4   How successful have we been to date in forest succession modelling?

At the 1969 meeting of the Ecological Society of America, a novel approach for the modelling of forest succession was presented (Siccama et al. 1969), which was based on tracking the fate of individual trees on small patches of land that at some point become dominated by one or a few big specimens; when these trees die, they leave a gap in the forest – thus the name 'forest gap models' (Figure 13.2; cf. Shugart 1984). Essentially, these are models of tree population dynamics and the interactions between tree populations, which give rise to emergent properties (Grimm et al. 2005) at the stand (or ecosystem) level such as aboveground biomass, species composition or the frequency distribution of tree diameters at various spatial scales. It is noteworthy that this individual-based (or 'agent-based', to use more recent terminology) concept led to a wide array of offspring well before the beginning of the 1990s (cf. Grimm & Railsback 2005).

The fact that individual-based models of forest succession produce emergent properties at the population and ecosystem levels is a distinct advantage over other approaches such as matrix models (e.g. Ralston et al. 2003), which must be parameterised using data at the population or ecosystem level. The rich array of patterns that are simulated as emergent properties by individual-based models yields multiple opportunities for model testing. If a model matches many observed patterns simultaneously (such as species composition, leaf area index and basal area) without having been parameterised to this end, this greatly increases our confidence in the model. This is the main reason why many insights on the factors shaping the long-term dynamics of real forests have been gained from individual-based models (cf. Shugart 1998), on which I therefore focus below.

Three publications (Botkin, Janak & Wallis 1970, 1972a,b) marked the beginning of what was going to become an enormous radiation of the individual-based approach to forest succession modelling, leading to several hundred forest gap models being developed worldwide and across all major forest biomes. Technical reviews of the structure of forest gap models and

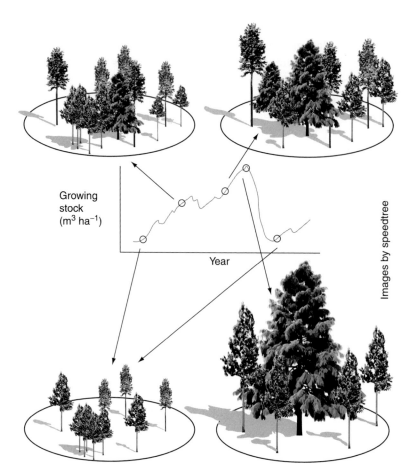

**Figure 13.2** Principle underlying forest gap models. Successional dynamics are simulated as the replacement of individual trees on small patches of land. The size of the patches is usually between 100 and 1000 m$^2$, commensurate with the maximum dimensions an individual tree can reach. Forest stand dynamics are calculated by averaging the properties across many (typically 50 to 200) such patches to reduce the influence of stochastic processes in the model (such as stochastic events in the establishment and mortality submodels). Figure drawn by Christof Bigler (ETH, Zurich). Tree pictures © Speedtree, http://www.speedtree.com. See plate section for colour version.

their development since the early 1970s can be found elsewhere (e.g. Bugmann 2001; Bugmann *et al.* 1996; Liu & Ashton 1995; Shugart 1984, 1998). Here, I will review these developments at a meta-level, with a focus on the issues of model testing as a basis for model applications under novel climatic conditions. I think the phases of the use of forest gap models can be categorised, by and large, by decade.

In the 1970s, the major emphasis after the seminal papers by Daniel Botkin and colleagues, which dealt with the Hubbard Brook forest as a case study, was on the adaptation of the approach for other ecosystems such as southern Appalachian forests (Shugart & West 1977), eucalypt forests in Australia (Shugart & Noble 1981) or tropical rain forests (Doyle 1981). At that time, model tests were limited in scope for two reasons. First, since no extrapolations beyond current conditions were attempted (with a few exceptions, e.g. Botkin, Janak & Wallis 1973), it was sufficient to show that the model reproduced current vegetation features reasonably well. Second, the long-term nature of forest dynamics makes it difficult to determine the exact setup of a simulation study that is geared towards reproducing, for example, the current diameter structure of any particular forest. This is so because current forest properties depend largely on the disturbance history of the forest (including insect attacks, wildfires and windthrow events as well as past management impacts, etc.), which in most cases is not known sufficiently well. Therefore, disagreements between simulation results and reality may not necessarily indicate a faulty model, but could equally well indicate an incomplete and inadequate knowledge of the history of the forest stand over the past decades to centuries. This led researchers to be satisfied with qualitative agreement between simulation results and measured data (e.g. the right species are simulated to dominate the forest; aboveground biomass is in broad agreement with expectations; or the shape of the diameter distribution appears reasonable).

In the 1980s, beyond further radiation of the approach (including among others the western United States: Kercher & Axelrod 1984; and Europe: Kienast 1987, Leemans & Prentice 1989), the models were increasingly used to study the impacts of future climate change on forest dynamics. For example, Solomon and Tharp (1985) and Solomon (1986) were aware of the novel terrain they explored, and made two attempts to increase the confidence one could place in such applications.

First, Solomon and Tharp (1985) confronted simulation results with pollen records of the Holocene to check whether their model, FORENA, was capable of tracking long-term, climate-induced changes in forest vegetation (Figure 13.3). Their approach was incomplete because the drivers of the model, i.e. climatic data, were inferred from the pollen record against which the simulation results were compared, making the reasoning somewhat circular. In addition, it is not obvious how to quantitatively and unequivocally compare measured *pollen frequencies* deposited in sediment, which derive from a certain catchment area, with simulated species-specific *stand biomass* that refers to one point in the landscape. For these two reasons, such tests constitute relatively weak evidence for a model's utility in the global change context.

Second, Solomon (1986) expanded the range of applicability of the FORENA model from a single site or a small number of sites within a small region

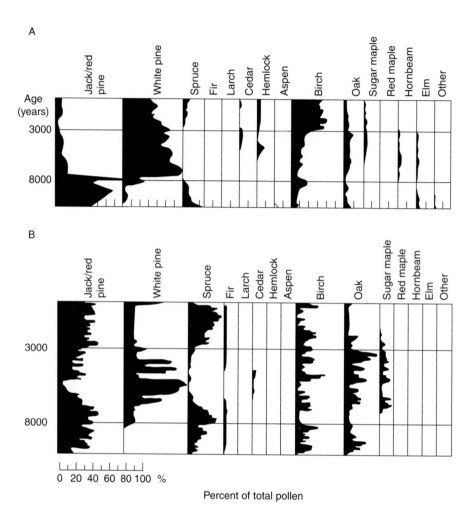

**Figure 13.3** Comparison of measured pollen frequencies (A) with pollen data simulated by the succession model FORENA (B). The latter were derived from simulated biomass by applying linear conversion factors. From Solomon and Tharp (1985).

(which had been the focus of previous work) to a larger array of sites arranged along a very extended climatic gradient, ranging from the boreal-tundra ecotone in Canada to warm-wet forests in southern Georgia (USA). The underlying rationale was that a model that is to project future forest dynamics reliably at a given site must be capable of reproducing current forest properties under the widest possible range of climates. Again, this is a necessary but not a sufficient condition to show the applicability of a model for future conditions. Similar, though less rigorous, tests and model applications were conducted by other researchers, such as Pastor and Post (1988), and Dale and Franklin (1989).

In the 1990s, model applications for impact assessment of climate change continued (e.g. Kienast 1991; Kräuchi & Kienast 1993). Simultaneously a period of reflection and (self-)criticism started, leading some authors to question the validity of what they perceived to be a highly empirical approach. These authors suggested that detailed knowledge from ecophysiology and biophysics should be injected into the models (e.g. Bonan, Shugart & Urban 1990; Friend *et al.* 1997; Martin 1992), thus greatly increasing their complexity (Figure 13.4). Others complained that through the continuous addition of details (and the passing on of computer code from one laboratory to the other), the models had become complicated to an extent that compromised their rigorous analysis (Bugmann 1996). Still others claimed that the good model performance shown in many studies at the site level was entirely due to misconceived functions that determined the distribution ranges of species (e.g. Loehle & LeBlanc 1996), such that what one got (in terms of model output) was what one put in (in terms of model parameters), rendering the models completely inappropriate for impact assessments of climate change.

The reactions to these criticisms focused on three lines of development. First, the 'hybrid' model approach begun by Martin (1992), Bonan (1993) and Friend *et al.* (1997) was explored in greater detail, eventually leading to current-day stand models such as FORMIND (Köhler & Huth 2007) or PICUS (Seidl, Rammer & Lexer 2011). Second, focusing on exploring competition between individual trees, models were developed that consider tree properties in three dimensions (e.g. Pacala, Canham & Silander 1993), thus inducing great model complexity but making the models useful for addressing a wide array of basic and applied ecological questions (e.g. Deutschman *et al.* 1997; Pacala & Rees 1998). Third, several researchers tried to develop improved but still simple formulations of ecological processes shaping forest dynamics and their climatic drivers, including FORSKA (Prentice, Sykes & Cramer 1993) and FORCLIM (Bugmann & Solomon 2000), eventually leading to the development of dynamic global vegetation models (DGVMs) such as LPJ-GUESS (Smith, Prentice & Sykes 2001), which in turn are hybrids between global biogeochemistry models (such as LPJ; Sitch *et al.* 2003) and forest gap models such as FORSKA.

In the 2000s, partly based upon a workshop and publication (Bugmann, Reynolds & Pitelka 2001) that aimed to outline the way ahead with the development of forest gap models (particularly Price *et al.* 2001 for tree regeneration; Norby *et al.* 2001 for growth processes; and Keane *et al.* 2001 for tree mortality), more rigorous tests of simulation results against measured data followed. These tests increasingly considered long-term data series from various sources, including ecological relevés (e.g. Risch, Heiri & Bugmann 2005) as well as growth-and-yield plots from forest science (e.g. Wehrli *et al.* 2005). Also, the focus of model application moved from projecting the

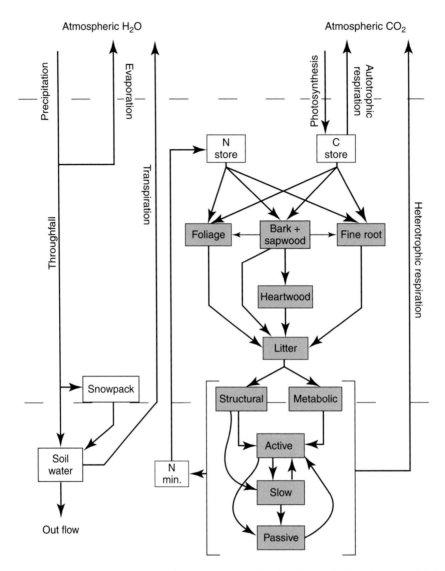

**Figure 13.4** Model structure of HYBRID v3.0 (Friend *et al.* 1997), showing the high level of detail that is considered in terms of tree growth, compared with a handful of simple equations in most earlier forest-gap models (see review by Bugmann 2001).

development of unmanaged forests (e.g. Bugmann 1997; Prentice, Sykes & Cramer 1991; and many others) to the inclusion of more or less detailed management submodels, such that the fate of managed stands could be evaluated (e.g. Lindner 2000; Rasche *et al.* 2011a; Figure 13.5).

These developments over the past *c.* 10 years were confronted with novel problems in terms of model evaluation. First, hybrid models such as LPJ-GUESS are not easy to parameterise at the species level (e.g. Miller *et al.*

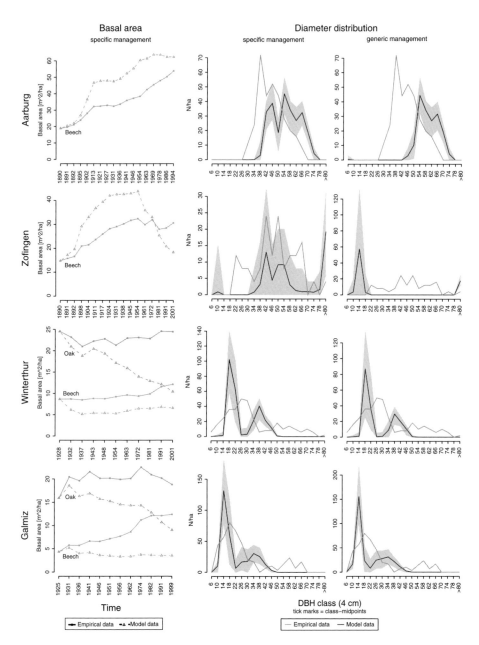

**Figure 13.5** Results of the evaluation of the FORCLIM model against measured long-term time series of basal area from managed stands in Switzerland, and comparison of the simulated diameter distribution against measured data for the last inventory. The shaded areas in the centre and right column indicate the 2.5 and 97.5 percentiles of the simulated data. From Rasche *et al.* (2011b). See plate section for colour version.

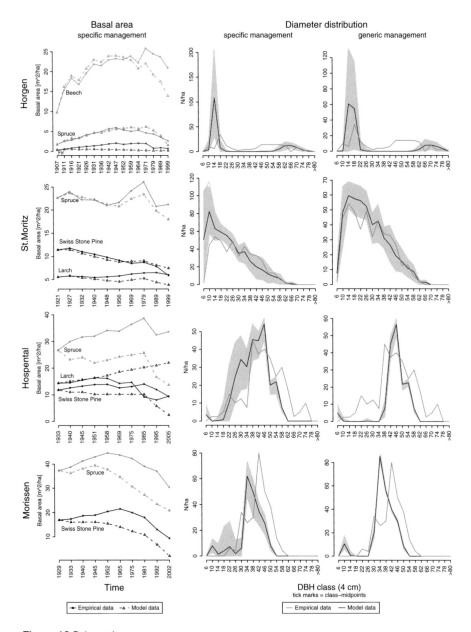

**Figure 13.5** (cont.)

2008) because tree physiology is known well for the most abundant and/or commercially important tree species only, leaving some flexibility with parameter estimation for other species; unless a certain amount of parameter 'tuning' is used, simulation results may not correspond to expectations (A. Wolf, personal communication). Also, since the focus of the application of these models has been on regional to continental scales (e.g. Morales *et al.* 2007), their main concern was not with local accuracy, but rather whether the distribution ranges of the species (or plant functional types) were captured adequately, and whether the fluxes of carbon and water between the biosphere and the atmosphere were simulated accurately. It is not entirely clear yet whether a model that is adequate at one scale (such as the continental scale in the case of LPJ-GUESS) must sacrifice accuracy at another scale (here, the local scale), following the principles laid out by Levins (1966), or whether it is possible to develop an approach that matches a range of patterns at widely disparate scales (*cf.* O'Neill *et al.* 1986), which would be an asset from the point of view of pattern-oriented modelling (Grimm *et al.* 2005).

Second, when subjecting succession models to tests against empirical time-series data from managed forests, one initialises the model with the first data point of the observations (inventory) and then compares the simulation results against reality for the last inventory (and possibly for the intermediate inventories as well). However, most empirical data series are short relative to the time scale of forest dynamics, such that for a 20- to 40-yr record the best estimator of the last inventory may simply be the initial state. As a consequence, any model that simulates little change (no matter what kind of change it simulates) is probably going to perform well, thus greatly reducing the discriminatory power of the dataset. Hence, the length of the data series is of key importance, and century-long datasets would be required – however, they are quite rare (but *cf.* Lindner, Sievänen & Pretzsch 1997 and Rasche *et al.* 2011a; Figure 13.5). In addition, when stand dynamics of managed forests are simulated, this usually implies that the management *per se* has a strong impact on observed forest dynamics (as most of these plots were set up to study optimal management for the maximisation of yield), thus lowering the degree to which ecological processes can play out in the simulation (as well as in reality). For example, most mortality in inventoried stands is due to the chainsaw, making it very difficult to test the mortality submodel of forest gap models adequately. An alternative approach is to use data from unmanaged forests (i.e. strict forest reserves; *cf.* Heiri 2009), but in most cases these data series do not span more than 40–50 years; one of the longest available data series is from permanent plots in the Bialowieza forest (Poland), dating back 'merely' to 1936 (Bernadzki *et al.* 1998).

## 13.5  Challenges

The diversity of approaches that are currently being used to make projections of future forest dynamics is positive, in my view. There are a number of competing approaches, with different advantages and disadvantages, thus providing multiple opportunities for learning from each other. While 'mainstream thinking' today probably goes in the direction of favouring 'mechanistic', physiologically based approaches (such as PICUS, HYBRID or LPJ-GUESS), there are several reasons and recent experiences that suggest it may be necessary to re-consider the fundamental assumptions upon which models of long-term forest dynamics are based, as follows.

First, models that are simulating photosynthesis and respiration explicitly are based on the assumption that the carbon source (i.e. photosynthesis and $CO_2$ concentration) is limiting plant performance and, ultimately, carbon storage, rather than plant growth as such (*cf.* Körner 1998). This is in sharp contrast to more empirically based models, where growth is simulated based upon environmental factors that are reducing an optimal growth rate, irrespective of the level of carbon assimilation (so-called sink limitation). It is evident that models that are based on the source limitation approach will simulate a strong $CO_2$ effect on vegetation (e.g. Cramer *et al.* 2001), whereas those based on the sink limitation approach will inevitably feature a small or no $CO_2$ effect at all in the long term. Yet, the debate whether source or sink limitation is dominating global vegetation processes is not resolved.

Second, the question of whether models of long-term forest dynamics are producing the right answers for the right reasons is not resolved either. For example, regarding the 'mechanistic' models, it appears that global NPP and carbon storage in biomass are simulated correctly by some of these models not because they correctly simulate the carbon gain of the different plant functional types, which would lead to competitive advantages or disadvantages, but because the bioclimatic limits determine the distribution of plant types, rather than any mechanistic model formulations (Leuzinger *et al.* 2013). Similarly, regarding the 'empirical' models, replacing the empirically not well-founded approaches for modelling tree mortality (Wunder *et al.* 2006) by empirically derived mortality submodels does not necessarily lead to an improved simulation of forest succession (case study with FORCLIM; J. Wunder *et al.*, unpublished). It appears that errors in the current mortality formulation are balanced and counteracted by errors in other parts of the model, thus clearly indicating the need for further model improvements to increase the robustness of the overall model.

Lastly, processes may exist that should be reflected in models of long-term forest dynamics, but that currently are not incorporated through negligence or lack of adequate data. Among these is the trade-off between growth rate (early in tree life) and longevity, a phenomenon that has been well known to foresters for a very long time, but with few quantitative data available to formulate or test model assumptions. Bigler and Veblen (2009) provided data for three conifer species, clearly showing that those individuals that grew fast in the first 50 years of their life tended to die prematurely. When this finding was used in the FORCLIM model to test the implications for a possible reduction of longevity in $CO_2$-fertilised trees (Bugmann & Bigler 2011), there was no net $CO_2$ fertilisation effect on aboveground biomass at most of the studied sites in the long term. This example shows that scaling from short-term, small-scale findings (here, $CO_2$ fertilisation experiments) to long-term, large-scale ecosystem responses can be difficult, because additional processes may become important that are easily forgotten.

## 13.6  Conclusions

Over the past 40 years, the field of forest succession modelling has advanced substantially. These tools proved to be useful in basic ecology, among others in the context of evaluating the relative importance of various ecological processes in shaping long-term forest dynamics, or in confirming the utility of Gleason's (1939) successional theory that emphasises the 'individualistic behaviour of vegetation'. Furthermore, the current generation of forest succession models is also highly useful in applied ecology, as they are much more reliable than their predecessors for projecting the effects of changes in climate and management on forest properties and ecosystem goods and services across the twenty-first century. For example, whereas the models of the 1980s projected widespread forest dieback owing to increases in temperature or to decreases in precipitation, this view has been refined, suggesting that only drought-induced mortality is likely to be widespread (cf. Allen et al. 2010), whereas temperature increases are most likely to lead to gradual shifts in forest properties only (cf. Didion et al. 2011). Such information is important, for example, for deriving adaptive management strategies (Millar et al. 2007).

Thus, the critical reflections of this chapter should not be taken to indicate that nothing could be said about the behaviour of forests in a greenhouse atmosphere. Overall, I think that in spite of the remaining limitations, forest succession models as representations of the current state of knowledge and their outputs are to be taken seriously, although perhaps not literally. I definitely think that simulation studies provide useful projections of future forest trajectories and as such are highly relevant for informing stake-holders about the future that they are possibly (not probably, and not certainly!) facing. Even though the 'theory of forest dynamics' (to quote the title of the book by Shugart 1984) as it is embodied in succession models of the various kinds may not be completely accurate, it is good enough to make projections based on the current generation of the models. 'All models are wrong, but some models are useful' (Box & Draper 1987); many models of long-term forest dynamics are certainly useful in the context of assessments of global change impacts.

# References

Allen, C. D., Macalady, A. K., Chenchouni, H. *et al.* (2010) A global overview of drought and heat-induced tree mortality reveals emerging climate change risks for forests. *Forest Ecology and Management*, **259**, 660–684.

Bernadzki, E., Bolibok, L., Brzeziecki, B., Zajaczkowski, J. & Zybura, H. (1998) Compositional dynamics of natural forests in the Bialowieza National Park, northeastern Poland. *Journal of Vegetation Science*, **9**, 229–238.

Bigler, C. & Veblen, T. T. (2009) Increased early growth rates decrease longevities of conifers in subalpine forests. *Oikos*, **118**, 1130–1138.

Bonan, G. B. (1993) Do biophysics and physiology matter in ecosystem models? *Climatic Change*, **24**, 281–285.

Bonan, G. B., Shugart, H. H. & Urban, D. L. (1990) The sensitivity of some high-latitude boreal forests to climatic parameters. *Climatic Change*, **16**, 9–29.

Botkin, D. B., Janak, J. F. & Wallis, J. R. (1970) *A Simulator for Northeastern Forest Growth*. Research Report 3140, Yorktown Heights, NY: IBM Thomas J. Watson Research Center.

Botkin, D. B., Janak, J. F. & Wallis, J. R. (1972a) Some ecological consequences of a computer model of forest growth. *Journal of Ecology*, **60**, 849–872.

Botkin, D. B., Janak, J. F. & Wallis, J. R. (1972b) Rationale, limitations and assumptions of a northeastern forest growth simulator. *IBM J. Res. Development*, **16**, 101–116.

Botkin, D. B., Janak, J. F. & Wallis, J. R. (1973) Estimating the effects of carbon fertilization on forest composition by ecosystem simulation. In *Carbon and the Biosphere* (eds. G. M. Woodwell & E. V. Pecan), pp. 328–344. Washington, DC: US Department of Commerce

Box, G. E. P. & Draper, N. R. (1987) *Empirical Model-Building and Response Surfaces*. New York, NY: John Wiley & Sons.

Bugmann, H. (1996) A simplified forest model to study species composition along climate gradients. *Ecology*, **77**, 2055–2074.

Bugmann, H. (1997) An efficient method for estimating the steady-state species composition of forest gap models. *Canadian Journal of Forest Research*, **27**, 551–556.

Bugmann, H. (2001) A review of forest gap models. *Climatic Change*, **51**, 259–305.

Bugmann, H. (2003) Predicting the ecosystem effects of climate change. In *Models in Ecosystem Science* (eds. C. D. Canham, W. K. Lauenroth & J. S. Cole), pp. 385–409. Princeton, NJ: Princeton University Press.

Bugmann, H. & Bigler, C. (2011) Will the $CO_2$ fertilization effect in forests be offset by reduced tree longevity? *Oecologia*, **165**, 533–544.

Bugmann, H., Lindner, M., Lasch, P. *et al.* (2000) Scaling issues in forest succession modelling. *Climatic Change*, **44**, 265–289.

Bugmann, H. K. M., Reynolds, J. F. & Pitelka, L. F. (eds.) (2001) How much physiology is needed in forest gap models for simulating long-term vegetation response to global change? *Climatic Change*, **51**, 249–557.

Bugmann, H. & Solomon, A. M. (2000) Explaining forest composition and biomass across multiple biogeographical regions. *Ecological Applications*, **10**, 95–114.

Bugmann, H., Yan, X., Sykes, M. T. *et al.* (1996) A comparison of forest gap models: Model structure and behaviour. *Climatic Change*, **34**, 289–313.

Cramer, W., Bondeau, A., Woodward, F. *et al.* (2001) Global response of terrestrial ecosystem structure and function to $CO_2$ and climate change: results from six dynamic global vegetation models. *Global Change Biology* **7**, 357–373.

Dale, V. H. & Franklin, J. F. (1989) Potential effects of climate change on stand development in the Pacific Northwest. *Canadian Journal of Forest Research*, **19**, 1581–1590.

Delcourt, H. R. & Delcourt, P. A. (1991) *Quaternary Ecology: A Paleoecological Perspective*. New York: Springer Science & Business.

Dethier, M. N. (1984) Disturbance and recovery in intertidal pools: maintenance of mosaic patterns. *Ecological Monographs*, **54**, 99–118.

Deutschman, D. H., Levin, S. A., Devine, C. & Buttel, L. A. (1997) Scaling from trees to forests: analysis of a complex simulation model. *Science*, **277**, 1688.

Didion, M., Kupferschmid, A. D., Wolf, A. & Bugmann, H. (2011) Ungulate herbivory modifies the effects of climate change on mountain forests. *Climatic Change*, **109**, 647–669.

Doyle, T. W. (1981) The role of disturbance in the gap dynamics of a montane rain forest: an application of a tropical forest succession model. In *Forest Succession: Concepts and Application* (eds. D. C. West, H. H. Shugart & D. B. Botkin), pp. 56–73. New York: Springer

Evensen, G. (1992) Using the extended Kalman filter with a multilayer quasi-geostrophic ocean model. *Journal of Geophysical Research*, **97**, 17905–17924.

Franklin, J. F. & Dyrness, C. T. (1973) *Natural Vegetation of Oregon and Washington*. Reprinted 1988, Corvallis, OR: Oregon State University Press.

Friend, A. D., Stevens, A. K., Knox, R. G. & Cannell, M.G.R. (1997) A process-based, terrestrial biosphere model of ecosystem dynamics (Hybrid v3.0). *Ecological Modelling*, **95**, 249–287.

Gleason, H. A. (1939) The individualistic concept of the plant association. *American Midland Naturalist*, **21**, 92–110.

Goldstein, J. S. (1975) Potential for converting wood into plastics: chemicals from wood may regain importance as the cost of petroleum continues to rise. *Science*, **189**, 847–852.

Goodwin, N. R., Coops, N. C. & Culvenor, D. S. (2006) Assessment of forest structure with airborne LiDAR and the effects of platform altitude. *Remote Sensing of Environment*, **103**, 140–152.

Grimm, V. & Railsback, S. F. (2005) *Individual-based Modeling and Ecology*. Princeton NJ: Princeton University Press.

Grimm, V., Revilla, E., Berger, U. *et al.* (2005) Pattern-oriented modeling of agent-based complex systems: lessons from ecology. *Science*, **310**, 987–991.

Hartig, F., Dyke, J., Hickler, T., *et al.* (2012) Connecting dynamic vegetation models to data – an inverse perspective. *Journal of Biogeography*, **39**, 2240–2252.

Heiri, C. (2009) Stand dynamics in Swiss forest reserves: an analysis based on long-term forest reserve data and dynamic modeling. Unpublished PhD thesis No. 18388, Swiss Federal Institute of Technology Zurich.

Holdridge, L. R. (1967) *Life Zone Ecology*. San José, Costa Rica: Tropical Science Center.

IPCC (2007) Synthesis report. *Fourth Assessment Report of the Intergovernmental Panel on Climate Change* (eds. R. K. Pachauri & A. Reisinger). Geneva, Switzerland: IPCC.

IUCN (2008) Forest environmental services. In *Encyclopedia of Earth* (ed. J. Cutler). Washington, DC: Environmental Information Coalition, National Council for Science and the Environment.

Keane, R. E., Austin, M., Field, C. *et al.* (2001) Tree mortality in gap models: application to climate change. *Climatic Change*, **51**, 509–540.

Kercher, J. R. & Axelrod, M. C. (1984) Analysis of SILVA: a model for forecasting the effects of $SO_2$ pollution and fire on western coniferous forests. *Ecological Modelling*, **23**, 165–184.

Kienast, F. (1987) *FORECE – A Forest Succession Model for Southern Central Europe*. Oak Ridge, TN: Oak Ridge National Laboratory, ORNL/TM-10575.

Kienast, F. (1991) Simulated effects of increasing $CO_2$ on the successional characteristics of Alpine forest ecosystems. *Landscape Ecology*, **5**, 225–238.

Köhler, P. & Huth, A. (2007) Impacts of recruitment limitation and canopy disturbance on tropical tree species richness. *Ecological Modelling*, **203**, 511–517.

Körner, C. (1998) A re-assessment of high elevation treeline position and their explanation. *Oecologia*, **115**, 445–459.

Kräuchi, N. & Kienast, F. (1993) Modelling subalpine forest dynamics as influenced by a changing environment. *Water, Air and Soil Pollution*, **68**, 185–197.

Lee, T. D., Barrott, S. H. & Reich, P. B. (2011) Photosynthetic responses of 13 grassland species across 11 years of free-air $CO_2$ enrichment is modest, consistent and independent of N supply. *Global Change Biology*, **17**, 2893–2904.

Leemans, R. & Prentice, I. C. (1989) *FORSKA, A General Forest Succession Model*. Uppsala: Institute of Ecological Botany.

Leuzinger, S., Lou, Y. Q., Beier, C. *et al.* (2011) Do global change experiments overestimate impacts on terrestrial ecosystems? *Trends in Ecology & Evolution*, **26**, 236–241.

Leuzinger, S., Manusch, C., Bugmann, H. & Wolf, A. (2013) A sink-limited growth model improves biomass estimation along boreal and alpine tree lines. *Global Ecology and Biogeography*, in press (DOI: 10.1111/geb.12047).

Levins, R. (1966) The strategy of model building in population biology. *American Scientist*, **54**, 421–431.

Lindner, M. (2000) Developing adaptive forest management strategies to cope with climate change. *Tree Physiology*, **20**, 299–307.

Lindner, M., Sievänen, R. & Pretzsch, H. (1997) Improving the simulation of stand structure in a forest gap model. *Forest Ecology and Management*, **95**, 183–195.

Liu, J. & Ashton, P. S. (1995) Individual-based simulation models for forest succession and management. *Forest Ecology and Management*, **73**, 157–175.

Loehle, C. & LeBlanc, D. (1996) Model-based assessments of climate change effects on forests: a critical review. *Ecological Modeling*, **90**, 1–31.

Martin, M., Gavazov, K., Körner, C., Hättenschwiler, S. & Rixen, C. (2010) Reduced early growing season freezing resistance in alpine treeline plants under elevated atmospheric $CO_2$. *Global Change Biology*, **16**, 1057–1070.

Martin, P. (1992) EXE: A climatically sensitive model to study climate change and $CO_2$ enrichment effects on forests. *Australian Journal of Botany*, **40**, 717–735.

MEA (2005) *Millennium Ecosystem Assessment*. Global Assessment Reports Vol. 1–3. Washington, DC: Island Press.

Millar, C. I., Stephenson, N. L. & Stephens, S. L. (2007) Climate change and forests of the future: managing in the face of uncertainty. *Ecological Applications*, **17**, 2145–2151.

Miller, P. A., Giesecke, T., Hickler, T. *et al.* (2008) Exploring climatic and biotic controls on Holocene vegetation change in Fennoscandia. *Journal of Ecology*, **96**, 247–259.

Morales, P., Hickler, T., Rowell, D. P., Smith, B. & Sykes, M. T. (2007) Changes in European ecosystem productivity and carbon balance driven by regional climate model output. *Global Change Biology*, **13**, 108–122.

Norby, R. J., Ogle, K., Curtis, P. S. *et al.* (2001) Aboveground growth and competition in forest gap models: An analysis for studies of climatic change. *Climatic Change*, **51**, 415–447.

O'Neill, R. V., DeAngelis, D. L., Waide, J. B. & Allen, T. F. H. (1986) *A Hierarchical Concept of Ecosystems*. Princeton, NJ: Princeton University Press,

Pacala, S. W., Canham, C. D. & Silander Jr, J. A. (1993) Forest models defined by field measurements: I. The design of a northeastern forest simulator. *Canadian Journal of Forest Research*, **23**, 1980–1988.

Pacala, S. W. & Rees, M. (1998) Models suggesting field experiments to test two hypotheses explaining successional diversity. *American Naturalist*, **152**, 729–737.

Pastor, J. & Post, W. M. (1988) Response of northern forests to $CO_2$-induced climate change. *Nature*, **334**, 55–58.

Pieper, S. J., Lowen, V., Gill, M. & Johnstone, J. F. (2011) Plant responses to natural and experimental variations in temperature in Alpine tundra, Southern Yukon, Canada. *Arctic, Antarctic and Alpine Research*, **43**, 442–456.

Popper, K. (1934) *Logik der Forschung*. Vienna: Julius Springer-Verlag.

Prentice, I. C., Sykes, M. T. & Cramer, W. (1991) The possible dynamic response of northern forests to global warming. *Global Ecology and Biogeography Letters*, **1**, 129–135.

Prentice, I. C., Sykes, M. T. & Cramer, W. (1993) A simulation model for the transient effects of climate change on forest landscapes. *Ecological Modelling*, **65**, 51–70.

Price, D. T., Zimmermann, N. E., van der Meer, P. J. *et al.* (2001) Regeneration in gap models: priority issues for studying forest responses to global change. *Climatic Change*, **51**, 475–508.

Ralston, R., Buongiorno, J., Schulte, B. & Fried, J. (2003). Non-linear matrix modeling of forest growth with permanent plot data: the case of uneven-aged Douglas-fir stands. *International Transactions in Operations Research*, **10**, 461–482.

Rasche, L., Fahse, L., Zingg, A. & Bugmann, H. (2011a) Getting a virtual forester fit for the challenge of climatic change. *Journal of Applied Ecology*, **48**, 1174–1186.

Rasche, L., Fahse, L., Zingg, A. & Bugmann, H. (2011b) Ein virtueller Förster lernt durchforsten – Sukzessionsmodelle in der Ertragsforschung? In *Tagungsband der Jahrestagung der Sektion Ertragskunde des deutschen Verbandes der forstlichen Versuchsanstalten* (ed. J. Nagel), pp. 207–212. Göttingen.

Risch, A., Heiri, C. & Bugmann, H. (2005) Simulating structural forest patterns with a forest gap model: a model evaluation. *Ecological Modelling*, **181**, 161–172.

Sale, P. F. (ed.) (1991) *The Ecology of Fishes on Coral Reefs*. San Diego, CA: Academic Press.

Schulman, E. (1958) Bristlecone pine, oldest known living thing. *National Geographic Magazine*, **113**, 354–372.

Seidl, R., Rammer, W. & Lexer, M. J. (2011) Climate change vulnerability of sustainable forest management in the Eastern Alps. *Climatic Change*, **106**, 225–254.

Shugart, H. H. (1984) *A Theory of Forest Dynamics. The Ecological Implications of Forest Succession Models*. New York: Springer.

Shugart, H. H. (1998) *Terrestrial Ecosystems in a Changing Environment*. Cambridge: Cambridge University Press.

Shugart, H. H. & Noble, I. R. (1981) A computer model of succession and fire response of the high-altitude *Eucalyptus* forest of the Brindabella Range, Australian Capital Territory. *Australian Journal of Ecology*, **6**, 149–164.

Shugart, H. H. & West, D. C. (1977) Development of an Appalachian deciduous forest succession model and its application to assessment of the impact of the chestnut blight. *Journal of Environmental Management*, **5**, 161–179.

Siccama, T. G., Botkin, D. B., Bormann, F. H. & Likens, G. E. (1969) Computer simulation of a northern hardwood forest. *Bulletin of the Ecological Society of America*, **50**, 93.

Sitch, S., Smith, B., Prentice, I. C. *et al.* (2003) Evaluation of ecosystem dynamics, plant geography and terrestrial carbon cycling in the LPJ dynamic global vegetation model. *Global Change Biology*, **9**, 161–185.

Smith, B., Prentice, I. C. & Sykes, M. T. (2001) Representation of vegetation dynamics in the modelling of terrestrial ecosystems: comparing two contrasting approaches within European climate space. *Global Ecology & Biogeography*, **10**, 621–637.

Smith, T. M., Leemans, R. & Shugart, H. H. (1992) Sensitivity of terrestrial carbon storage to $CO_2$-induced climate change: Comparison of four scenarios based on general circulation models. *Climatic Change*, **21**, 367–384.

Solomon, A. M. (1986) Transient response of forests to $CO_2$-induced climate change: simulation modeling experiments in eastern North America. *Oecologia*, **68**, 567–579.

Solomon, A. M. & Tharp, M. L. (1985) Simulation experiments with late quaternary carbon storage in mid-latitude forest communities. In *The Carbon Cycle and Atmospheric $CO_2$: Natural Variations Archean to Present*. Geophysical Monograph Vol. 32 (eds. E. T. Sundquist & W. S. Broecker), pp. 235–250. Washington, DC: American Geophysical Union

Wehrli, A., Zingg, A., Bugmann, H. & Huth, A. (2005) Using a forest patch model to predict the dynamics of stand structure in Swiss mountain forests. *Forest Ecology and Management*, **205**, 149–167.

Weigel, A. P. & Mason, S. J. (2011) The generalized discrimination score for ensemble forecasts. *Monthly Weather Review*, **139**, 3069–3074.

Wunder, J., Bigler, C., Reineking, B., Fahse, L. & Bugmann, H. (2006) Optimisation of tree mortality models based on growth patterns. *Ecological Modelling*, **197**, 196–206.

# CHAPTER FOURTEEN

# Detecting and projecting changes in forest biomass from plot data

HELENE C. MULLER-LANDAU, MATTEO DETTO,
RYAN A. CHISHOLM, STEPHEN P. HUBBELL and
RICHARD CONDIT

*Smithsonian Tropical Research Institute, Panama*

## 14.1 Introduction

Increasing atmospheric carbon dioxide, changing climates, nitrogen deposition and other aspects of anthropogenic global change are hypothesised to be changing forest productivity and biomass stocks in tropical forests and elsewhere (Clark 2004; Lewis, Malhi & Phillips 2004; Lewis *et al.* 2009a; Luo, 2007; Myeni *et al.* 1997). These hypotheses continue to be much debated, with contrary views on the plausibility of particular mechanisms and on the status of current evidence for or against them (Clark 2007; Friedlingstein *et al.* 2006; Holtum & Winter 2010; Körner 2009; Wright 2005, 2010). The influence of atmospheric and climate change on forest biomass is of particular interest because of the potential for positive or negative feedbacks. Increases in forest biomass and associated carbon pools would slow the rise in atmospheric carbon dioxide, producing a negative feedback, whereas decreases in forest biomass would have the opposite effect. Uncertainty surrounding these feedbacks is considerable at the global scale, with important implications for global carbon budgets (Luo 2007).

In view of this, it is essential to know whether forests are experiencing changes in productivity and biomass in excess of those typical for their age. Successional forests, those regrowing after disturbances, increase in biomass over time, with the trajectory and duration of this increase varying with forest type (Bormann & Likens 1979; Odum 1969). In the absence of global change, such forests are expected to eventually reach a dynamic equilibrium in which biomass gains from growth and recruitment are balanced by biomass losses from tree death and branchfall, and these old-growth forests thus experience no directional changes in biomass (Odum 1969; Yang, Luo & Finzi 2011). Accordingly, detection of directional changes in biomass in old-growth forests is generally considered evidence of global change influences. When and where such changes are detected, the next critical question concerns

*Forests and Global Change*, ed. David A. Coomes, David F. R. P. Burslem and William D. Simonson.
Published by Cambridge University Press. © British Ecological Society 2014.

prediction of future net carbon fluxes and ultimate carbon stocks of such altered forests.

Detecting influences of global change on forest biomass is complicated by the fact that biomass is always changing on small spatial scales even in old-growth forests. In old-growth forests, gap-phase dynamics mean that forests in most areas and at most times are increasing modestly in biomass as trees grow, while a few are experiencing large decreases in biomass where one or more large trees have died ('slow in, rapid out', in the words of Körner 2003). It is only on a landscape scale that we expect the biomass of old-growth forests to be at equilibrium in the absence of global change or other tempo-ral climate variability (note that this applies only to biomass; soil carbon stocks, for example, may show long-term directional change even in old-growth forests). Regional and global climate cycles could lead forests to be out of equilibrium even on landscape scales at any given time. Thus, detecting global change in old-growth forests requires a large enough sam-ple size with adequate distribution in space and time to be able to confi-dently distinguish global change influences from the natural gap-dynamic cycle and cyclical climate variation. The question of what constitutes an adequate sample size has been addressed in the recent literature (Fisher *et al.* 2008; Gloor *et al.* 2009).

Because of the large area of old-growth forests in the tropics, and their high carbon density, potential alteration of their biomass stocks is of partic-ular importance to the global carbon cycle (Saugier, Roy & Mooney 2001; Schimel 1995). Many studies have evaluated changes in biomass stocks in tropical forests using recensuses of field plots (Baker *et al.* 2004; Chave *et al.* 2008; Lewis *et al.* 2009b; Phillips *et al.* 1998, 2008), and some have also examined changes in coarse woody productivity (Lewis *et al.* 2004; Phillips, 1996). Field measurements of tropical forest biomass stocks have focused largely on aboveground woody biomass of trees. Generally biomass is esti-mated from measurements of trees greater than 10 cm in diameter at breast height (dbh) and from allometric relationships. These trees constitute the vast majority of biomass stocks in these forests, with smaller trees and shrubs, lianas and herbaceous vegetation making up a small minority that few studies have measured directly. Belowground biomass pools (roots, etc.) can also be estimated from allometric relationships, typically by assuming that they are proportional to aboveground biomass. Empirical evidence suggests that this is true on average, although there is considerable variation among sites in the observed proportions (Wolf, Field & Berry 2011; Yang & Luo 2011). More precise methods of estimating above- and belowground biomass rely on destructive techniques that disturb the forest and prohibit repeat measurements and assessments of change. Soil carbon pools are also hypothesised to be affected by global change (Luo 2007; Rustad *et al.* 2001), but to date there have been few studies of repeated measurement of soil carbon in the tropics.

In this contribution, we address the issues of how to detect and project biomass change in old-growth forests from plot data, focusing on tropical forests. We focus solely on aboveground biomass (hereafter referred to simply as 'biomass'), the pool for which the most data are available. We first evaluate some key contributions to uncertainty and bias in estimates of biomass change from plot data. We specifically examine the scaling of sampling error with plot area and census interval, and the potential for biases resulting from different kinds of measurement errors and data entry errors and their interaction with error-correction routines. We then discuss alternative approaches to projecting future biomass of old-growth forests, and present a new approach based on Markov chain models of small plot biomass transitions. Throughout, we use the 50-ha forest dynamics plot on Barro Colorado Island (BCI) as a case study. We close with recommendations for future work.

## 14.2   Estimating biomass change
### 14.2.1   Sampling errors in biomass change

A major contributor to uncertainty in biomass change estimates from plot data in old-growth forests is sampling error. On small scales, some areas are expected to have strong decreases in biomass due to deaths of big trees, whereas most areas are expected to witness no such mortality and thus will have smaller increases in biomass that reflect tree growth. Samples based on larger plot areas and longer census intervals are expected to encompass more representative distributions of these changes. Quantification of sampling uncertainty is important for developing confidence intervals on estimates of biomass change, and associated tests of whether observed changes are significantly different from zero.

It is important to note that sampling errors are inherently unbiased. A measurement is by definition biased if its expected value, i.e. the mean of the distribution of its values, is different from the true value. For any random sample, the expectation of the sample mean is the true mean. Statements by Fisher *et al.* (2008) and Körner (2009) that the sample mean of biomass change is biased because of the 'slow in, rapid out' phenomenon are incorrect and reflect a misunderstanding of the meaning of bias. The 'slow in, rapid out' phenomenon can indeed lead to an asymmetric (skewed) sampling distribution, in which the median exceeds the mean, but the mean of this distribution is still the true mean provided the plots are an unbiased sample of the landscape. One real concern is that the 'slow in, rapid out' phenomenon could exacerbate biases associated with non-random plot placement across the landscape. For example, biomass change estimates will be biased in the positive direction if site selection is biased towards locations that experience less disturbance during the census interval (Körner 2009).

Fisher *et al.* (2008) and Gloor *et al.* (2009) recently explored the influence of sampling error on true power to reject the null hypothesis of no change in biomass given the potential for large-scale disturbances. These studies use simulation analyses to explore the importance of clustered disturbances combined with the 'slow in, rapid out' nature of biomass change, and the sample size needed to confidently reject a null hypothesis of no change. The studies come to contrasting conclusions on the sufficiency of available evidence to reject the hypothesis of no change, reflecting two key differences in assumptions. Fisher *et al.* (2008) underestimate the available sample size in time – assuming one-year census intervals, when in fact intervals were more typically 10 years. Fisher *et al.* (2008) also use a flawed procedure to fit the size distribution of disturbance events, and thus almost certainly overestimate the probability of large disturbance events. Gloor *et al.* (2009) corrected these errors, and concluded that sample sizes in area and time were sufficient to demonstrate that average biomass change in 135 forest plots, typically 1 ha or larger, across the Amazon basin is significantly positive, under the assumptions that plots were an unbiased sample of the landscape and that individual plot biomass change estimates were unbiased. It is important to note that these results are sensitive to the frequency of large disturbance events, and that there are very limited existing data relevant to estimating these frequencies.

Quantification of sampling errors is of considerable interest, in part for tests of whether observed changes are significantly different from zero. Here, we first examine how sampling uncertainty scales with plot area and time period for individual plots, an issue that is critical to determining the appropriate weighting when plot size and census interval vary. We then address the issue of sampling uncertainty for mean biomass change in ensembles of plots.

*14.2.1.1 Spatial and temporal scaling of sampling uncertainty for single plots*
Spatial and temporal autocorrelation in biomass change, or its absence, is critical to the scaling of sampling errors in biomass change. In the absence of such autocorrelation, the variance of the observed change in biomass per area is expected to decrease in proportion to 1/(area × time), because area × time is the effective total sample size. (Therefore, the standard deviation and the coefficient of variation, CV, are expected to decline in proportion to 1/sqrt(area × time).) When spatial and/or temporal autocorrelation is present, however, uncertainty will decrease more slowly with increasing area (for contiguous or nearby plots) and time interval. Previous studies of the spatial scaling of uncertainty in biomass (not biomass change) have found that the

coefficient of variation declines with area to the power −0.43 between 0.05 and 6 ha for biomass of trees >10 cm in Paracou, French Guiana (Wagner *et al.* 2010), and to the power −0.37 between 0.125 and 4 ha for biomass of trees >35 cm in Tapajos, Brazil (reanalysis of the data plotted as Figure 14.4 in Keller *et al.* (2001)). Earlier studies have examined similar questions for basal area (e.g. Higuchi, dos Santos & Jardim 1982). The difference from scaling with a power of −0.5 suggests some spatial autocorrelation in biomass at these scales and sites. Wagner *et al.* (2010) further found that the CV of biomass productivity and biomass losses scaled with area to the power −0.429 and −0.451, respectively, suggesting that net biomass change would be likely to scale with similar exponents, again reflecting some spatial autocorrelation.

We used the 25-year, 50-ha dataset for the BCI forest dynamics plot to examine the spatial and temporal scaling of uncertainty in biomass change at this site. We found that the decrease in the standard deviation with increasing plot size from 0.025 to 1 ha matched the theoretical expectation if there is no spatial autocorrelation, with the standard error of biomass change declining almost exactly with 1/sqrt(area), i.e. with area to the power −0.5 (Figure 14.1A). Linear regression of the log-transformed standard deviation on log-transformed area produces an estimated slope of −0.493 (95% CI −0.496 to −0.491). This is consistent with the lack of spatial structure in biomass change at these scales: the semivariogram is flat (results not shown), as is the wavelet power spectrum (Figure 14.2A). Temporal autocorrelation also appeared to be unimportant on the time scales considered, as the standard deviation declined with the inverse square root of census interval in accordance with the theoretical prediction for the case of no autocorrelation (Figure 14.1B).

Bootstrapping over subplots can be used to quantify sampling uncertainty for single plots. Since the biomass change on the plot is known more exactly, this bootstrapping procedure is technically estimating sampling uncertainty associated with the stochastic process operating within this plot (and that could potentially have produced other outcomes) (e.g. Chave *et al.* 2008). When dividing a plot into subplots for the purposes of within-plot bootstrapping, it is essential that the subplot scale be greater than the integral length scale, the scale at which the spatial semivariogram plateaus, i.e. there should be no spatial autocorrelation between subplots. Violation of this could lead to artificially low confidence intervals. On BCI, as Chave *et al.* (2008) previously reported for this and other large plots, the confidence intervals are insensitive to the subplot scale for subplot sizes between 0.025 and 1 ha (Figure 14.2B), consistent with the lack of spatial structure at these scales (Figure 14.2A). The sampling uncertainty for the full 50-ha plot that is estimated by bootstrapping over subplots is exactly consistent with the spatial scaling of sampling uncertainty for smaller areas (Figure 14.1A).

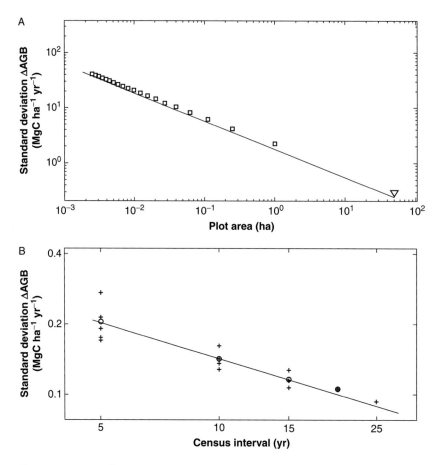

Figure 14.1 Sampling uncertainty in estimated biomass change as a function of plot area and census interval for the 50-ha plot on Barro Colorado Island, Panama, quantified here as the standard deviation of the biomass change over replicate plots and/or census intervals of the relevant size. (A) Observed standard deviations for square plots of different area (squares) and the standard deviation of the estimate for the whole plot obtained from bootstrapping over subplots (triangle) for the 2005–2010 census interval, compared with the expected decline with square root of area (line). (B) Standard deviations for the entire 50-ha plot from bootstrapping over 10 × 10 m subplots for census intervals of different length using the six censuses between 1985 and 2010 (plus signs), and the average of the standard deviations for any census interval (circles), compared with the expected decline with the square root of time (line).

One perhaps obvious limitation of plot-based assessments of the spatial scaling of sampling error in biomass change is that they provide no informa-tion on how error scales over larger areas than the largest sample taken. This is because differences in habitat, land-use history, climate or other factors may exist beyond the sampled area, which could cause the variogram to rise at

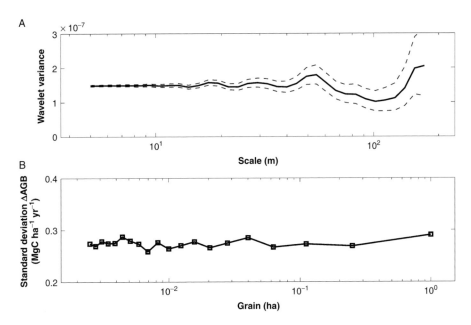

**Figure 14.2** The spatial structure of biomass change on the BCI 50-ha plot. (A) The wavelet power spectrum, with 95% confidence intervals (dashed line), shows little significant spatial structure or autocorrelation. (B) The bootstrapped standard deviation (1000 bootstraps) of biomass change estimates on BCI is insensitive to the spatial grain over which bootstrapping is done, as expected given the lack of spatial structure at these scales.

a different rate than within the sampled area. For example, although we found no spatial autocorrelation of biomass change within the BCI 50-ha plot, we expect that there might be spatial autocorrelation at larger scales within central Panama due to spatially structured variation in rainfall, soil type and past land-use. We also expect that other sites of similar scale might show very different patterns of spatial and temporal scaling of sampling errors. In particular, sites that have experienced recent large-scale patchy disturbances (unlike BCI) might show significant spatial and temporal auto-correlation in biomass and biomass change, and thus slower declines in sampling error with area and time. Parallel issues regarding how patterns change with spatial scale have long been a focus of research on diversity; e.g. the distinction between alpha, beta and gamma diversity (MacArthur & Wilson 1967; Ricklefs 2004).

### 14.2.1.2 Sampling uncertainty for ensembles of plots

If samples are available from different plots within a landscape or region, it becomes possible to estimate landscape biomass or biomass change within an appropriate statistical framework. Biomass change estimates may come from plots of different areas and census intervals of different lengths. If the plots are randomly situated in the landscape, then the best unbiased estimate of the overall landscape biomass change is obtained by taking a weighted mean of the individual site estimates, where each weight is proportional to the reciprocal of the variance of the corresponding site estimate. Let $X(a,t)$ be a random variable representing the biomass estimate at a randomly chosen site of area $a$ and census interval $t$. Then the variance of $X(a,t)$ is

$$\mathrm{var}(X(a,t)) = \frac{1}{t}\left(\sigma^2 + \frac{\tau^2}{a}\right)$$

where $\sigma^2$ is the between-site (landscape) variance and $\tau^2$ is the within-site variance (e.g. between individual hectares within the site). In practice, the variances may be difficult to estimate. The formula above assumes that temporal autocorrelation in biomass change can be ignored. If temporal autocorrelation is substantial, then plots should be weighted more evenly with respect to census interval, with the exact weighting depending on the form of temporal autocorrelation.

The proper weighting of plots varying in area thus depends critically on the relative size of the variance within sites ($\tau^2$) and the variance among sites ($\sigma^2$). In the limit that landscape variance is much larger than within-site variance (very heterogeneous landscapes), the weighting formula reduces to simply $t$, meaning equal weighting if the census intervals are equal across sites, regardless of plot area. In the limit that landscape variance is much smaller than within-site variance and within-site variance is identical across plots (very homogeneous landscapes), the weighting formula reduces to $ta$. Intermediate situations call for weighting by the product of time and of area to a power between zero and one, e.g. $t\sqrt{a}$.

The choice of weightings can make a small but noticeable difference in the mean change across plots (Table 14.1), emphasising the importance of choosing an appropriate weighting scheme or at least testing the robustness of results to different plausible weighting schemes (as done by Baker *et al.* 2004). Of course, if information on underlying landscape heterogeneity is available and if the available plots are not proportionally representative of this heterogeneity, weighting should also take account of this, if possible. De Gruijter *et al.* (2006) provides an excellent treatment of the broader issues surrounding sampling design in environmental monitoring.

One approach to determining the best weighting for biomass change estimates is to search empirically for the weighting that minimises trends in residuals plots of site biomass change versus site area and census interval (Phillips *et al.* 2009; Lewis *et al.* 2009b). Specifically, one graphs the product of weights and squared residuals vs area and vs time. This approach is in principle excellent; however, to produce useful results it requires sufficiently large numbers of sites of different areas and census intervals, a condition that is rarely met in practice. (For example, the vast majority of plots used in the abovementioned papers are 1 ha in area, and there are too few plots at other areas to gain much insight into the best weighting by area.) Combining the datasets from all the references in Table 14.1 provides a somewhat better basis for choosing a weighting with area, and suggests that the ideal weighting would be the product of time and of area to a power between 0 and 1. Weighting by $t$ or $ta$ leads to significant trends in the residuals plots, while weighting by $t\sqrt{a}$ (among others) produces no significant trends.

Once the appropriate weighting has been determined, confidence intervals for sampling uncertainty for an ensemble of sites can be estimated by bootstrapping over plots or sites (e.g. Phillips *et al.* 2009). If multiple plot data are available, it is possible to bootstrap at both the within-plot and between-plot levels to produce a confidence interval on the landscape biomass change estimate, providing that appropriate weighting schemes are used on the between-plot bootstrapped data. It is important to note that this only captures uncertainty due to sampling error.

### 14.2.2    Influences of measurement errors and data 'cleaning' procedures

Measurement errors are ubiquitous and inescapable in field data collection. Variation in the height of the measuring tape or caliper on the stem and variation in the hydration status of the stem introduce random errors into stem diameter measurements. Further, error in positioning the measuring tape to be exactly perpendicular to the long axis of the stem can lead to systematic overestimation of diameter. Additional and potentially larger errors enter during data recording and data entry, including digit switching, missed or added digits, and switching data between two trees. Careful field and data entry procedures can reduce the incidence of such errors, but never completely eliminate them. All these errors, hereafter referred to simply as measurement errors, introduce uncertainty into estimates of standing biomass and biomass change. Further, because of the non-linear relationship between diameter and biomass, random errors in diameter can and do induce systematic errors in biomass. In tropical forests, trees with buttresses or other types of irregular trunks present additional challenges for accurate and precise measurements of biomass and biomass growth (Clark 2002; Phillips *et al.* 2002; Sheil 1995).

Most studies have attempted to minimise the influence of measurement errors and changing height of measurement on buttressed trees through what we will call data cleaning procedures. These typically include screening data

**Table 14.1** Estimated mean change in aboveground biomass of trees 10 cm or more in diameter. Estimates are for different datasets under alternative schemes for weighting data points as a function of plot area and census interval, with 95% confidence intervals, with 95% confidence intervals for sampling uncertainty only; that is, confidence intervals based on bootstrapping over plots (or sites in Phillips et al. 1998). If there is no spatial autocorrelation in biomass change, the best unbiased estimator of overall biomass change is based on weighting by area × time (assuming plots are an unbiased sample of the landscape). If there is strong spatial structure in biomass change such that landscape variance among plots greatly exceeds sampling variance within plots, then the best unbiased estimated is based on weighting by time (see text). Numbers were recalculated from the datasets provided with the original publications, to be in units of MgC ha⁻¹ yr⁻¹, with carbon stocks calculated as 47% of dry biomass, and to include only trees greater than or equal to 10 cm in diameter. Note that numbers in the original publications were in some cases based on analyses assuming carbon was 50% dry biomass; were for total biomass, not just carbon; included estimated carbon stocks in lianas, small trees and belowground biomass; involved different weightings; and/or include other sources of error in confidence intervals.

| Publication | Region | Dates | Number of plots | Total ha-yrs | Tree AGB change (MgC ha$^{-1}$ yr$^{-1}$) | | | |
| --- | --- | --- | --- | --- | --- | --- | --- | --- |
| | | | | | Unweighted | Weighted by time | Weighted by time × area | Weighted by time × sqrt(area) |
| Phillips et al. 1998 | Pantropic | 1947–1997 | 68 | 2350 | 0.33 (0.15,0.52) | 0.18 (0.02,0.34) | 0.12 (−0.10,0.31) | 0.15 (0.00,0.30) |
| Phillips et al. 1998 | Neotropics | 1956–1997 | 50 | 1621 | 0.48 (0.26,0.71) | 0.41 (0.23,0.57) | 0.15 (−0.11,0.35) | 0.26 (0.07,0.45) |
| Phillips et al. 1998 | Lowland Neotropics | 1956–1997 | 45 | 1577 | 0.46 (0.21,0.71) | 0.35 (0.17,0.54) | 0.14 (−0.12,0.35) | 0.23 (0.03,0.43) |
| Phillips et al. 1998 | Amazon | 1956–1997 | 40 | 877 | 0.41 (0.18,0.67) | 0.38 (0.19,0.56) | 0.24 (0.10,0.43) | 0.31 (0.15,0.48) |
| Baker et al. 2004 | Amazon | 1980–2003 | 59 | 864 | 0.57 (0.37,0.77) | 0.50 (0.28,0.70) | 0.46 (0.25,0.65) | 0.48 (0.28,0.68) |
| Chave et al. 2008 | Pantropic | 1985–2005 | 10 | 3156 | 0.22 (−0.02,0.45) | 0.23 (−0.03,0.51) | 0.24 (−0.06,0.56) | 0.24 (−0.04,0.54) |
| Phillips et al. 2009 | Amazon | 1972–2006 | 123 | 2410 | 0.44 (0.30,0.57) | 0.39 (0.28,0.50) | 0.45 (0.33,0.56) | 0.41 (0.31,0.51) |

| Source | Region | Years | | | | | | |
|---|---|---|---|---|---|---|---|---|
| Phillips et al. 2009 | Amazon | 1972–2007 | 136 | 2607 | 0.29 (0.14,0.44) | 0.35 (0.23,0.47) | 0.42 (0.30,0.53) | 0.37 (0.26,0.49) |
| Lewis et al. 2009b | Africa – raw[1] | 1968–2007 | 79 | 1206 | 0.54 (0.07,0.98) | 0.54 (0.19,0.90) | 0.63 (0.27,0.94) | 0.57 (0.25,0.89) |
| Lewis et al. 2009b | Africa – corrected[1] | 1968–2007 | 79 | 1206 | 0.60 (0.12,1.05) | 0.66 (0.32,0.99) | 0.74 (0.37,1.05) | 0.68 (0.35,0.99) |
| Lewis et al. 2009b | Africa – mean[1] | 1968–2007 | 79 | 1206 | 0.59 (0.11,1.02) | 0.64 (0.31,0.97) | 0.75 (0.37,1.06) | 0.67 (0.35,0.99) |
| Lewis et al. 2009b | Africa – perturbed[1] | 1968–2007 | 79 | 1206 | 0.55 (0.11,0.95) | 0.59 (0.28,0.89) | 0.67 (0.33,0.95) | 0.61 (0.32,0.90) |
| Lewis et al. 2009b | Pantropic[2] | 1947–2007 | 156 | 5483 | 0.53 (0.27,0.76) | 0.49 (0.30,0.67) | 0.35 (0.15,0.58) | 0.43 (0.27,0.60) |
| All combined | Pantropic[3] | 1947–2007 | 251 | 8243 | 0.36 (0.18,0.53) | 0.34 (0.23,0.47) | 0.32 (0.17,0.47) | 0.34 (0.23,0.45) |

[1] Lewis et al. (2009b) presented four different sets of results corresponding to four different procedures for dealing with changes in the point of measurement.

[2] Lewis et al. (2009b) report Pantropical results obtained by combining the results of Baker et al. (2004) for the Amazon, Lewis et al. (2009b) Africa corrected, the undisturbed Chave et al. (2008) (excluding Lenda and Edoro to avoid double-counting, as these are also in Lewis et al. 2009b) and the Phillips et al. (1998) Asia plots.

[3] Our Pantropical compilation includes the Lewis et al. (2009b) Africa raw data, the Phillips et al. (2009) Amazon data through 2007, the undisturbed Chave et al. (2008 ) data (excluding the Lenda and Edoro plots to avoid double-counting), and the Phillips et al. (1998) non-Amazon plots.

for outliers that are considered so unlikely as to almost certainly be errors, and substituting a corrected value for these outliers; we will refer to these steps as data screening and gap-filling, respectively. In addition, most studies in which points of diameter measurement change on some trees between censuses have devised algorithms to 'correct' the diameter change on these trees. The data cleaning steps that are taken typically seem reasonable, but multiple alternative procedures meet the 'reasonable' test. Where authors have, to their credit, examined multiple alternatives, they often find that these produce different results (Chave *et al.* 2003; Lewis *et al.* 2009a). Such sensitivity analyses are laudable, but do not shed light on which alternative is best. Choice among data cleaning procedures should ideally be based on analyses of the potential for the data cleaning itself to introduce errors and biases. For studies of forest change, systematic errors are arguably of more concern than random errors.

To demonstrate the potential influences of different data cleaning procedures on estimates of biomass change, we estimated biomass change over two census intervals on BCI using a variety of procedures to deal with extreme outliers, hemiepiphytes (strangler figs) and trees whose point of measurement changed. The estimated aboveground biomass (AGB) change between 1985 and 1990 is greatly affected by the choice of data cleaning procedures: it varies from −0.61 (95% confidence interval, CI, −1.22, −0.05) MgC ha$^{-1}$ yr$^{-1}$ if the raw 'uncorrected' data are analysed, to +1.31 (0.83, 1.70) if using a gap-filling procedure for AGB-change outliers and stems that have point-of-measurement changes (Table 14.2). The high sensitivity to data cleaning procedures for this census interval in part reflects the large number of problematic cases in this census interval, owing to changes in details of census procedures (especially with respect to buttressed trees) and changes in field personnel between these two censuses. The estimated AGB change between 2005 and 2010, when detailed census procedures and supervisory personnel were consistent across both censuses, is considerably less sensitive to the data correction method used, but still varies from −0.47 (−0.98, −0.08) to −0.07 (−0.54, 0.27) MgC ha$^{-1}$ yr$^{-1}$ (Table 14.2). In the earlier census interval, the choice of data cleaning procedure makes the difference between significant biomass decline and significant biomass increase. In the later interval, it makes a difference between statistically significant biomass decline and no significant biomass change.

Clearly, then, procedures for data screening, gap-filling and modelling growth in trees with changing points of measurement are critically important to estimating biomass change in tropical forests. Many previous authors have discussed the potential qualitative impact of different types of measurement errors or measurement procedures (Clark 2002; Phillips *et al.* 2002; Sheil 1995). Here, we focus on just two issues – issues that our analyses show are

Table 14.2 *Effects of alternative data cleaning routines on AGB change estimates (95% CI) for the BCI 50-ha plot for 1985–1990 and 2005–2010. Census methodology and supervisory personnel changed somewhat between the 1985 and 1990 census, and not at all between 2005 and 2010. Plot census methods are described in Condit (1998). See Appendix 14.1 for details on the AGB calculations. Three classes of problematic measurements were screened: (1) hemiepiphytes (strangler figs) for which diameter measurements do not reflect basal area; (2) stems that were extreme outliers in biomass change; and (3) stems whose height of measurement changed. Biomass changes for hemiepiphytes were simply set to zero. Biomass changes for the other classes of screened individuals were either set to zero or changed to the value obtained from a biomass growth model fitted to non-screened data.*

| Screened stems and their treatment | | | | |
|---|---|---|---|---|
| Hemiepiphytes[1] | \|ΔAGB\| outliers[2] | POM change[3] | ΔAGB 1985–1990 (MgC ha⁻¹ yr⁻¹) | ΔAGB 2005–2010 (MgC ha⁻¹ yr⁻¹) |
| | | | −0.61 (−1.22 −0.05) | −0.46 (−1.04 −0.08) |
| ΔAGB =0 | | | −0.58 (−1.26 −0.04) | −0.47 (−0.98 −0.08) |
| ΔAGB =0 | ΔAGB =0 | | 0.04 (−0.48 0.47) | −0.43 (−0.99 −0.08) |
| ΔAGB =0 | Model growth[4] | | 0.13 (−0.31 0.55) | −0.43 (−0.89 −0.06) |
| ΔAGB =0 | ΔAGB =0 | ΔAGB =0 | 0.49 ( 0.04 0.89) | −0.28 (−0.78 0.07) |
| ΔAGB =0 | Model growth[4] | Model growth[4] | 1.31 ( 0.83 1.70) | −0.07 (−0.54 0.27) |

[1] Hemiepiphytes encompass six species of strangler figs: *Ficus bullenei, F. citrifolia, F. colubrinae, F. costaricana, F. pertusa* and *F. popenoei*. In total, there were 36 individuals of these species that were alive in one or more censuses between 1985 and 2010, and between 12 and 20 alive in any given census.

[2] Stems that had a rate of change in biomass (increase or decrease) of more than 2 MgC yr⁻¹, and that were not recorded as stem breaks or point of measurement changes.

[3] Change in the point of measurement between the two censuses greater than 0.2 m.

[4] AGB change substituted with the value obtained from the fits of non-screened trees to a third-order polynomial model $Y = a_3 X^3 + a_2 X^2 + a_1 X + a_0$ where $Y = \log(AGB_{t+1} - AGB_t)$ and $X = \log(AGB_t)$. All individuals of all species (except the hemiepiphytes) were combined in this model; individuals were binned into 50 classes of equal numbers of elements, and the logs of the class-wise arithmetic means were regressed against each other to fit the coefficients $a_i$.

particularly important to determination of biomass change in this forest (Table 14.2). First, we examine the impact of ordinary measurement errors and data cleaning procedures and their interaction on estimates of biomass and biomass change. Second, we discuss issues surrounding measurement and modelling of growth in buttressed trees, or more generally, all trees whose diameter is measured above the standard 1.3 m and whose height of measurement may change substantially over time. In both cases, we focus especially on the potential to introduce systematic errors (i.e. biases) in estimates of biomass and biomass change.

### 14.2.2.1 Ordinary measurement errors and data cleaning

Most past studies of biomass change have used some sort of data cleaning procedure to identify presumed erroneous values and 'correct' them. Past approaches to error identification most typically involved absolute cutoffs for diameter growth rates, with more extreme values considered unrealistic and thus necessarily erroneous. For example, diameter increases of more than $35 \text{ mm yr}^{-1}$, $40 \text{ mm yr}^{-1}$ or $45 \text{ mm yr}^{-1}$, or decreases of more than $5 \text{ mm yr}^{-1}$, have been flagged for correction (Chave *et al.* 2003, 2008; Lewis *et al.* 2009b; Phillips *et al.* 2009). Where multiple census data are available, these presumed errors are corrected by interpolation or extrapolation where possible. In other cases, they are set to the mean (Chave *et al.* 2008; Phillips *et al.* 2009) or median (Lewis *et al.* 2009b) diameter growth rates for trees in the same diameter class. Despite the ubiquity of such procedures, we know of no study that has systematically evaluated their potential influence on estimates of forest biomass change. On first principles, these procedures may well reduce certain kinds of random and systematic errors – but as we show below, this reduction may come at the cost of the introduction of other systematic errors. How large are the systematic errors introduced by data cleaning? Is data cleaning a worthwhile procedure given potential trade-offs between correcting one kind of error and introducing another?

A key problem of error identification is that it is difficult, if not impossible, to design error detection criteria that exactly balance the correction of positive and negative errors in diameter growth, and thus avoid inducing systematic biases. It is often easier to identify large negative errors, because large decreases in measured diameters are biologically implausible unless there are concurrent observations of stem breaks. In contrast, large positive errors may go undetected because it is possible for some individuals to grow very quickly. If measurement errors are symmetric, but negative errors are more likely to be detected and corrected, then this introduces a positive bias on biomass change estimates. Identifying appropriate thresholds to balance positive and negative error correction in diameter growth exactly is possible in principle but very difficult in practice. Thus, such thresholds will almost inevitably introduce systematic errors in estimates of biomass change.

A key problem in gap-filling erroneous measurements is to ensure that the corrections do not introduce systematic errors in statistics of interest. There is a large existing literature on gap-filling methods and their relative performance in terms of bias and root mean square error, RMSE (e.g. Moffat *et al.* 2007), including analyses specific to individual tree growth (Sironen, Kangas & Maltamo 2010; Sironen *et al.* 2008). Nearest-neighbour imputation methods, in which the missing value is substituted with the mean from the $k$ nearest neighbours as defined by distance in a space of traits of interest (e.g. diameter, forest type), emerge as particularly useful, with minimal bias and RMSE (Sironen, Kangas & Maltamo 2010). The most common gap-filling method applied in tropical biomass studies – substituting the mean diameter growth for similarly sized trees – is in some sense a very limited application of this method, in which size class is the only distance metric considered. However, gap-filling with mean diameter growth for reference populations is problematic when the goal is calculation of biomass growth, because of the non-linear relationship between diameter and biomass and the skewed distribution of growth rates among individuals. Thus, for example, gap-filling with mean diameter growth leads to systematic 10% overestimation of individual tree biomass growth in a test with BCI data, even though this method produces unbiased estimates of diameter growth. In contrast, substituting with mean biomass growth will produce unbiased estimates of biomass growth – but systematically underestimate diameter growth. Because mean growth is typically larger than median growth, substituting median biomass growth will underestimate biomass gain (e.g. by 40% in a test with BCI data). The use of median diameter growth could overestimate or underestimate biomass growth, depending on the statistics of the target population. In sum, the gap-filling algorithms that have been employed to date in tropical forest biomass change studies have almost certainly introduced systematic errors that bias resulting estimates of total biomass change.

The importance of the resulting systematic errors will vary depending not only on the algorithm, but also on patterns of diameter growth at the site. Here, we examine what biases result from commonly used (1) error detection and (2) gap-filling algorithms when applied to the BCI data for 2005–2010.

First, we consider the effects of absolute diameter growth thresholds for error identification. On BCI, the 30 stems that decreased in diameter by less than 5 mm yr$^{-1}$ between 2005 and 2010 together account for a decrease of 0.153 MgC ha$^{-1}$ yr$^{-1}$, whereas the 25 stems that grew by more than 40 mm yr$^{-1}$ together contribute an increase of 0.133 MgC ha$^{-1}$ yr$^{-1}$, together contributing net biomass change of −0.019 MgC ha$^{-1}$ yr$^{-1}$. (These calculations exclude stems that had a change in point of measurement or a break below the measuring point.) Changing all their growth rates to the mean biomass growth rates for similar diameter stems increases net biomass change by 0.019 MgC ha$^{-1}$ yr$^{-1}$.

Second, we examine the most commonly used gap-filling procedure – mean diameter growth. As mentioned previously, this tends to overestimate mean biomass growth of individual trees on BCI by 10%. Suppose that this correction is applied to 1% of trees (Phillips *et al.* 2009 apply such a correction to 0.9% of trees in their analyses). Applying this correction to 1% of stems on BCI upwardly biases biomass growth estimates by less than 0.005 MgC ha$^{-1}$ yr$^{-1}$, assuming no bias in error detection. Thus, on BCI, unbalanced error detection is more problematic than biased gap-filling algorithms in terms of the size of resulting biases in biomass change, but both overall biases are relatively small. This suggests, consistent with the results in Table 14.2, that data cleaning for trees whose diameter is measured at the standard height is not a major source of systematic errors at least for the BCI 2005 and 2010 census data (although it may be important in other cases, e.g. the BCI 1985–1990 data). (Trees measured at non-standard heights, which we examine in the next section, appear to be a much bigger source of errors.)

Although effects on BCI are modest, we argue that there remains a need for improvement in data cleaning procedures for studies of biomass change. There are three distinct types of approaches that would yield unbiased estimates of biomass changes. The first approach would be to apply unbiased error detection and gap-filling algorithms. This approach could draw on the large literature on such issues in forestry and other disciplines (Moffat *et al.* 2007; Sironen *et al.* 2010). Analyses should specifically evaluate bias (e.g. Sironen *et al.* 2010). Application of these algorithms, especially for error detection, will have to be tailored to individual sites and their growth patterns. A second approach would be to analyse biomass change using Bayesian methods that explicitly included probability distributions of measurement errors, and explicitly modelled observed growth as the convolution of true growth and measurement errors. Such models would greatly benefit from incorporation of data that specifically constrained the measurement error distribution, such as remeasurement data. Metcalf *et al.* (2009) provide an excellent example of this approach, applied to analyses of tree growth. A third approach would be to eschew data cleaning altogether, and instead quantify the impact of measurement errors on statistics of interest, and then correct those statistics accordingly after they are calculated from uncorrected data. This last approach is in many ways the simplest, and should be successful in eliminating systematic errors. It will, however, leave potentially large random errors.

We now apply this last approach to BCI, where a large dataset on remeasurements of the same stems allows us to quantitatively assess the impacts of measurement errors on biomass. In the 1995, 2000 and 2005 censuses, diameters of 1562 randomly chosen stems were independently remeasured within 30 days of the original measurement. Rüger *et al.* (2011) fitted this error distribution with a sum of two normal distributions (both centred at zero; these errors were purely random not systematic). The first distribution, which has 97.24% of the weight, describes small errors that are proportional to tree diameter (standard deviation sd = 0.927 mm + 0.0038*dbh mm); the second describes larger errors that are independent of diameter (sd = 25.6 mm). We used a Monte Carlo approach to assess the impact of such measurement errors on biomass and biomass change. In particular, we assumed that the 2005 and 2010 BCI census data represent the true diameters, and we examined how applying additional measurement errors drawn from the measured distribution of measurement errors changed estimates of biomass and biomass change. We found that adding such measurement errors led to slight overestimation of biomass, by an average of 0.14% (bootstrapped 95% CI 0.07, 0.21), with no significant effect on biomass change. Thus, for BCI at least, simply ignoring all measurement errors, and leaving data uncorrected, is expected to have a trivial *systematic* impact on estimates of biomass and biomass change – although the uncorrected measurement errors will introduce random errors. Clearly, if measurement error rates were higher, as they may be at some other sites, the impact of measurement errors alone would be larger, and may induce larger systematic errors. For example, if the dbh measurements of 1% of stems in the BCI data have a pair of adjacent digits switched, this results in 1.7% systematic overestimation of biomass. One could quantify the resulting systematic errors through exercises such as these to correct estimates of total biomass and total biomass change calculated from uncorrected individual measurements.

### 14.2.2.2 The special challenge of buttressed trees

One of the greatest potential sources of error in estimates of biomass change is the measurement and analysis of buttressed trees (Clark 2002; Sheil 1995). We use 'buttressed trees' to refer to all trees whose diameters are measured at heights above 1.5 m because of buttresses or irregular trunks, and whose heights of measurement are likely to increase over time. The standard measurement height is 1.3 m, and stems with small irregularities only in this area are measured slightly above or below the standard point (1–1.5 m). Thus, we chose 1.5 m as a threshold to capture mainly trees with buttresses or irregular trunks. Trees measured at heights above 1.5 m constituted 59% of estimated tree biomass on BCI in the 2010 census, although these trees represented just 1.4% of stems. Thus, estimates of biomass change and productivity for BCI are very sensitive to the algorithms used to calculate biomass changes for these trees.

Diameter–biomass relationships are likely to differ for buttressed trees, yet these differences are not reflected in current allometric equations. Individual tree biomass is typically estimated from allometric equations relating diameter, wood density and sometimes tree height to biomass, with diameter measured either at 1.3 m height or 'above buttresses' (Chave *et al.* 2005). Because trunk diameter generally declines (i.e. tapers) with increasing height, we would expect that trees whose diameter is measured at a height above 1.3 m will have smaller diameters for the same biomass, or equivalently, higher biomass for the same diameter. Consequently, biomass–diameter relationships for buttressed trees are expected to deviate systematically from those for non-buttressed trees, when the diameters in the former case are measured above buttresses and above 1.3 m height, while diameters in the latter case are measured exactly at 1.3 m height. Surprisingly, we know of no study that has tested for such systematic differences, nor any published dataset that would allow such tests to be made.

As a consequence, buttressed trees represent a large potential source of systematic error in estimates of biomass and biomass change. The application of the same biomass allometry equations to buttressed and unbuttressed trees is likely to lead to systematic underestimation of biomass in buttressed trees, and systematic overestimation in unbuttressed trees. These two opposite types of errors will cancel exactly at the plot level if the frequency of buttressed trees in the plot matches the frequency of buttressed trees in the dataset used to develop the biomass allometry equations, and if diameters of buttressed trees are measured in the same way in both datasets. Plot-level biomass will tend to be systematically overestimated in stands with lower frequencies of buttressed trees, and systematically underestimated in stands with higher frequencies of buttressed trees, assuming diameters of buttressed trees are measured in a consistent manner across the plots and in the biomass calibration dataset.

The lack of standard methods for determining measurement heights on buttressed trees creates additional potential for systematic error. For example, if diameters of buttressed trees are measured at greater heights in the plot than in the biomass calibration dataset, then biomass will be systematically underestimated even if the frequency of buttressed trees is identical. Such differences in measurement methods for buttressed trees are quite likely. For one-time measurements such as those for calibrating biomass equations, diameters are typically measured directly above buttresses, which presumably means within 10–20 cm of the top of buttresses. In permanent plots where repeat censuses are planned, diameters are typically measured at greater heights to ensure that the measurement point will remain above buttresses in the next census; an oft-used rule is to measure 50 cm above the top of the buttress (Condit 1998). In general, there is no quantitative, generally accepted, standard definition of the top of the buttress, or of the distance above the top of the buttress at which diameters should be measured, and thus it is to be expected that different field teams and technicians would make diameter measurements at different heights given the same tree form. The emergence of a universal standard (perhaps 50 cm above as in Condit 1998), applied to both biomass calibration equations and plot censuses, would remove this potential source of systematic error.

On BCI, the proportion of trees measured at heights above 1.5 m has increased greatly over time (Table 14.3). We know that some of these shifts reflect changes in measurement procedures: in the first census, all trees were

**Table 14.3** *Number, frequency, and proportion estimated aboveground biomass of tree stems measured above 1.5 m height in the Barro Colorado Island forest dynamics plots in different censuses.*

| Census year | Number | Stems with height of measurement >1.5 m | | |
| | | Proportion of total stems ≥1 cm | Proportion of total stems ≥10 cm | Proportion of total biomass[1] |
| --- | --- | --- | --- | --- |
| 1982 | 0 | 0.00% | 0.0% | 0.0% |
| 1985 | 1302 | 0.48% | 6.0% | 28.4% |
| 1990 | 2076 | 0.72% | 9.3% | 48.5% |
| 1995 | 2456 | 0.92% | 10.8% | 53.0% |
| 2000 | 2786 | 1.12% | 12.3% | 53.7% |
| 2005 | 2872 | 1.17% | 12.8% | 54.3% |
| 2010 | 3373 | 1.37% | 14.8% | 58.6% |

[1] Here biomass was calculated by substituting the observed maximum height diameter measurement directly into the biomass allometry equation (no data cleaning, no taper).

measured at 1.3 m even if this was around buttresses, whereas in the second census buttressed trees were measured directly above buttresses, and in the third census, the protocol was changed to place measurement points on buttressed trees high enough that they would be expected to remain above buttresses in the following census even after growth. It is more difficult to interpret the continued, more modest, increases in the proportion of stems measured at height above 1.5 m between 1990 and 2010. These increases are likely in part to reflect increasing conservatism on the part of the field crew, as they sought for ever more round points on the bole, or heights that are ever more certain not to be affected by buttresses in the subsequent census, as well as the fact that measurement points are moved up but never down. However, there is also the possibility that there has been some real increase in buttressed trees, and/or heights of buttresses on trees, on BCI. Regardless of the causes of the increase in height of measurement, the increasing frequency of diameter measurements at heights above 1.5 m would be expected to introduce a negative bias on estimated biomass change on BCI, because of the way the diameter measurements interact with the biomass allometry equation. A larger and larger proportion of trees fall into the category of systematic underestimation of biomass, while an ever smaller proportion fall into the category of systematic overestimation of biomass.

In principle, it should be possible to correct for the biases in biomass and biomass change that are associated with measurements of diameters at heights above 1.3 m. One possibility would be to replace 'diameter at 1.3 m or above buttresses' with 'diameter at 1.3 m, measured or estimated based on taper' in biomass allometry equations. Taper equations, such as those used by Metcalf *et al.* (2009), could be used to calculate equivalent diameters at 1.3 m height from diameters measured above buttresses. Given the right taper functions, we would expect that biomass–diameter datasets constructed under this definition would show no systematic differences between buttressed and non-buttressed trees. If there were no systematic differences, then one could construct and apply biomass allometry equations without regard to the frequency of buttressed trees. Indeed, in this case, equations could be constructed simply from data on non-buttressed trees, which might be the more practical approach, as older datasets on biomass of buttressed trees do not necessarily include necessary information on the height of diameter measurement for buttressed trees.

We use the BCI dataset for 2005–2010 to illustrate the potential impact of measurement practices for buttressed trees on estimates of biomass and biomass change (Table 14.4). In the 2010 census, 962 stems were measured at two heights. If we use the diameter measurement at the lower height in the biomass allometry equation, total biomass is 4.2 MgC ha$^{-1}$ larger than if we use the measurement at the greater height (Table 14.4). Inferring diameter at 1.3 m based on taper should in principle make the biomass estimates less sensitive to the exact measurement height, decreasing the difference between these estimates. We used the taper equation $DBH = De^{\alpha(h - 1.3)}$, where $D$ is the measured diameter and $h$ is the height of the measurement, a function previously fitted to empirical data on diameters in similar height ranges for five tropical tree species by Metcalf *et al.* (2009), and values of $\alpha$ that spanned the range for these five species. At higher taper values, biomass estimates were substantially higher (Table 14.4). Biomass estimates were essentially identical between minimum and maximum height diameter measurements for $\alpha = 0.055$, which suggests that this value might best represent average taper in these trees. However, use of realistic taper functions and resulting estimates of equivalent diameters at 1.3 m height with currently available biomass equations (themselves based on dbh or diameter 'above buttresses') will invariably lead to systematic overestimation of biomass, with the degree of overestimation dependent on the relative representation of diameter measurements above buttresses in the biomass calibration datasets.

The treatment of buttressed trees had an even bigger relative effect on estimates of biomass change for BCI (Table 14.4). When we used measured diameters directly in the biomass equation (taper = 0 in Table 14.4), estimates of biomass change varied from −0.56 to 0.31 MgC ha$^{-1}$ yr$^{-1}$ depending on the choice of point of measurement (POM): the largest decrease was found when the minimum POM was used in each census, and the largest increase when the same POM was used (where available) and the maximum POM otherwise. Using the diameter from the same POM across two censuses provides better estimates

**Table 14.4** *Effect of treatment of diameters measured at non-standard heights on estimates of aboveground tree biomass and biomass change on Barro Colorado Island, Panama. Diameter measurements were available at two (or rarely more) measurement heights for 948 stems in 2005 and 962 stems in 2010 (less than 0.4% of all stems in each census), generally in cases where the measurement point was being moved upwards to ensure that it would remain above buttresses in the next census. The standard treatment for biomass in most studies is to use the lowest available good diameter measurement above buttresses or irregularities (here 'minimum'), and to insert this diameter measurement directly into the allometry equations (here taper = 0). The standard for estimates of biomass change is to use the same height of measurement across the two censuses if available, and the lowest good measurement when there are multiple options (here 'same and min'). The default in the BCI database is always to use the maximum diameter measurement available ('maximum'). Alternatively, a taper equation can be used to estimate equivalent diameter at 1.3 m height, and this equivalent diameter can be used in the biomass equation. We use the taper equation $D_{1.3} = D_i e^{-\alpha(h_i-1.3)}$, which Metcalf et al. (2009) previously fitted to empirical data on diameters in similar height ranges for five tropical tree species; values of $\alpha$ are chosen to span the range for these five species. No other data cleaning was done. Details of methods for calculating biomass are given in Appendix 14.1.*

| | Taper parameter ($\alpha$, units of m$^{-1}$) | | | | | |
|---|---|---|---|---|---|---|
| POM choice | 0 | 0.01 | 0.02 | 0.03 | 0.06 | 0.12 |
| **AGB (MgC ha$^{-1}$) in 2010** | | | | | | |
| Minimum[1] | 147.2 | 153.0 | 159.3 | 166.2 | 190.8 | 262.3 |
| Maximum[2] | 143.0 | 149.4 | 156.4 | 164.0 | 191.3 | 271.6 |
| **ΔAGB 2005–2010 (MgC ha$^{-1}$ yr$^{-1}$)** | | | | | | |
| Minimum[1] | −0.559 | −0.458 | −0.340 | −0.206 | 0.322 | 2.171 |
| Maximum[2] | −0.463 | −0.389 | −0.307 | −0.216 | 0.123 | 1.238 |
| Same and min[3] | 0.217 | 0.197 | 0.175 | 0.152 | 0.074 | −0.122 |
| Same and max[4] | 0.312 | 0.275 | 0.234 | 0.188 | 0.016 | −0.521 |

[1] Where diameter measurements were available from multiple heights in a given census, the diameter with the *minimum* height of measurement was used. Under this rule, 1540 stems had a change in diameter measurement height between 2005 and 2010.

[2] Where diameter measurements were available from multiple heights in a given census, the diameter with the *maximum* height of measurement was used. Under this rule, 1374 stems had a change in diameter measurement height between 2005 and 2010.

[3] Where the stem was alive in both censuses, diameter measurements that were made at the *same* height in both censuses were used when available. In other cases, the diameter with the *minimum* height of measurement in that census was used. Under this rule, 976 stems had a change in diameter measurement height between 2005 and 2010.

[4] Where the stem was alive in both censuses, diameter measurements that were made at the *same* height in both censuses were used when available. In other cases, the diameter with the *maximum* height of measurement in that census was used. Under this rule, 976 stems had a change in diameter measurement height between 2005 and 2010.

of the biomass change of the individual trees in question, but introduces systematic errors in biomass change at the plot level, because trees are then measured at different heights relative to the tops of upwardly growing buttresses in the different censuses. When we calculated equivalent diameter at 1.3 m based on taper equations, and used this diameter in the biomass allometry equations, biomass change went from negative to positive as the taper parameter $a$ increased (Table 14.4). This result is consistent with the fact that the later census had a higher proportion of trees with higher POMs. There was no single taper value for which all four POM choices led to similar values for biomass change; overall the standard deviation among the values was lowest for $a = 0.05$, at which point the mean estimate was 0.076 MgC ha$^{-1}$ yr$^{-1}$.

   In the absence of better allometric data for buttressed trees, it is difficult if not impossible to say which measurement and analysis protocols produce the best estimates of plot-level biomass and biomass change, but it is clear that current standard practices introduce systematic errors. Given that virtually all tree boles taper, we recommend that height of measurement be recorded for any diameter measurement taken at a non-standard height. Explicit treatment of height of diameter measurement in future biomass allometry measurements, combined with data on height of diameter measurements, would allow large reductions in systematic errors associated with buttressed trees. Studies of trunk taper on buttressed species in the range of heights typically used for measurement would also be useful. Ideally, analyses should incorporate information on taper as well as diameter measurements at one or more non-standard heights to infer true biomass growth (Metcalf *et al.* 2009). In the long run, an even better approach might be to measure trees with buttresses and those liable to develop buttresses at a standard height that remained above buttresses on most if not all trees (e.g. 5 m, 8 m), and combine these with allometric equations for biomass of buttressed trees based on diameter measurements at such heights. Such an approach is already used in Finland, where standard forest inventory practices include measurements of diameters at 6 m height, measurements that are taken from the ground using a device called the Finnish caliper.

## 14.3   Projecting biomass change

Observations of biomass change in forests provide critical evidence regarding the question of current effects of global change on forests, but they do not provide clear insights into future biomass change. The simplest assumption – that change in a given forest will continue at the most recently observed rate – is obviously wrong when projecting for 50 or more years. The next simplest assumption, of linear extrapolation based on two or more rates of change, is also obviously wrong on longer time scales. Another approach is clearly needed to project how biomass will change in the medium and long term. In general, there are two broad classes of strategies that can be employed: phenomenological models and mechanistic models.

In the following subsection, we present a phenomenological approach for short- and medium-term projections of biomass, based on Markov chain models and observed small-scale biomass transition probabilities.

### 14.3.1    Markov chain models of biomass change

A Markov chain model captures stochastic transitions between states (here, tree biomass in small forest plots) with a matrix of transition probabilities. First-order Markov chain models were first used to model successional changes in species composition and/or vegetation type in the 1970s (e.g. Horn 1975; Usher 1979; Waggoner & Stephens 1970). Their application in this context was criticised for the models' inability to capture historical and spatial dependence of succession (Facelli & Pickett 1990). In particular, the simplest Markov chain models assume that (1) transition probabilities depend only on the current state not on past states (the memory-less property); (2) transition probabilities do not vary in time or space (stationarity); and (3) transitions in different cells are independent (spatial independence). More complex models can relax these assumptions, but the data needed to parameterise them increase accordingly, and even the most basic models require extensive data on observed transitions for parameterisation (Facelli & Pickett 1990). Thus, Markov chain models were superseded as more mechanistic gap models of succession were developed for temperate forests, models that simultaneously predicted changes in species composition, forest structure and forest dynamics (Shugart 1984). However, these mechanistic models require extensive, species-level information on individual growth, mortality, and recruitment and how this varies with gap age, or in later models, neighbourhood (Pacala *et al.* 1996). Similar models have been constructed at the functional type level for some tropical forests (e.g. Chave 1999), but we lack the information needed to build such mechanistic models for most sites. This suggests a reconsideration of the 'black box' approach of Markov chain models, especially in cases where extensive transition data are available to parameterise such models.

A Markov chain model for forest biomass can be parameterised from recensus data from a large plot or many small plots. With this approach, the data on biomass and biomass change within small subplots are used to parameterise a linear matrix model that describes the dynamics of the probability distribution of biomass. This approach captures gap dynamics, as small subplots can transition in and out of low-biomass states with realistic probabilities based on the observed relationship of biomass to biomass change. Kellner *et al.* (2009) used this approach to model transitions in canopy height, a proxy for forest biomass, parameterising their model with airborne LiDAR data for large areas. We argue that such models provide a useful basis for projecting biomass distributions (and thus mean biomass) forward into the future under the assumption that transition probabilities continue as currently observed.

To parameterise a Markov chain model for biomass change, we first divide the range of observed biomass densities into $N$ classes. Let $\mathbf{V}(t)$ be a vector of length $N$, with elements $v_i(t)$ corresponding to the proportion of subplots having biomass density in class $i$ at time $t$. Let $\mathbf{M}$ be a transition probability matrix, whose elements $m_{ij}$ give the probability that a subplot that was in state $j$ transitions to state $i$ in one time step. Then, $\mathbf{V}(t + 1) = \mathbf{MV}(t)$. (That is, following the standard rules of matrix multiplication, each element $v_i(t+1) = \sum_j m_{ij}v_j(t)$.) Provided $\mathbf{M}$ is not singular, there exists a single equilibrium probability distribution $\mathbf{V}^*$ such that $\mathbf{V}^* = \mathbf{M}\,\mathbf{V}^*$, and this equilibrium can be obtained analytically from the first eigenvector of $\mathbf{M}$ (Anderson & Goodman 1957). That is, over time, given a fixed transition probability matrix $\mathbf{M}$, any and every initial frequency distribution that is non-zero will converge on the equilibrium.

We parameterised a Markov chain model for the biomass density of 10 m × 10 m subplots on the Barro Colorado Island 50-ha plot. We first divided the 50-ha plot into contiguous 10 m × 10 m subplots (5000 in total), and calculated total biomass in each subplot by summing estimated biomass of each tree within it. Individual tree biomass was calculated from uncorrected diameter data for the highest diameter for each stem in each census using a pantropical allometric equation (Chave *et al.* 2005) (details in Appendix 14.1). We log-transformed total biomass in each subplot (to achieve normality), and used a two-dimensional Gaussian kernel density estimator with fixed width to estimate the continuous joint probability distribution (Haan 1999; Scott 1992; Silverman 1986) for log biomass density at census $t$ and census $t + 1$. This resulted in estimates of $p_{ij}$, the probability that a given 10 m × 10 m plot is in biomass density class $j$ at one time step and in biomass density class $i$ during the next time step. The Gaussian kernel estimator essentially obtains a smoothed version of the empirically observed joint probability surface (Figure 14.3). The transition matrix is calculated as the conditional probability from the joint probability density function:

$$m_{ij} = \frac{p_{ij}}{p_j} = \frac{p_{ij}}{\sum_k p_{kj}} \tag{14.1}$$

where $p_j$ is the marginal probability that a subplot has biomass density class $j$ in the first census interval. The matrix $\mathbf{M}$ is independent of $t$ because of the memory-less property of Markov chains.

The advantage of the Gaussian kernel estimator is that the probability density function (PDF) is independent of the discretisation of the probability domain (here the number of biomass categories), in contrast to a histogram or

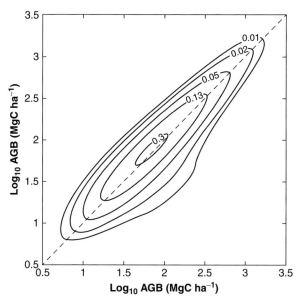

**Figure 14.3** Ensemble joint probability density function of biomass density over two successive census intervals, $t$ and $t + 1$, estimated from transitions for all 5-year census intervals between 1985 and 2010 using a Gaussian kernel estimator (see text), and using the raw census data without 'data cleaning' or correction for increasing heights of measurement. Correcting for increasing heights of measurement over time would increase biomass in later censuses relative to earlier ones, and thus alter transition probabilities.

box counting method. This allows us to use a large number of biomass categories without increasing errors in estimates of the transition probabilities. The use of a large number of categories improves estimates of dynamics (Zuidema *et al.* 2010). The PDF is dependent on the width of the Gaussian kernel estimator, which has a role similar to the bin size for box counting approaches. The width of the Gaussian kernel estimator is critical for estimating the PDF and is chosen as a best compromise between minimising the bias caused by smoothing (which increases for large width, causing excessive smoothing of the peaks of the distribution) and minimising the variance (which increases for small width in areas where little information is present, causing noise at the tails of the distribution) (Haan 1999). In our case, we use 100 classes (from 0 to 10 on a log scale of MgC ha$^{-1}$) and the width of the estimator was 0.25. All analyses were done in MATLAB (Version 7, The Mathworks Inc.).

We took advantage of the six censuses, and thus five census intervals, at BCI, which allowed us to increase the sample sizes used to estimate transition probabilities and also to investigate temporal variation in the transition

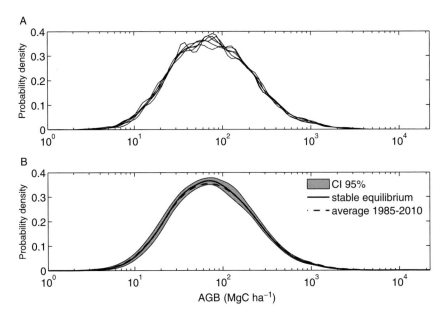

**Figure 14.4** (A) The probability density functions (PDFs) of biomass densities in 10 × 10 m subplots for the different census intervals on BCI. (B) The PDF for the projected stable equilibrium and its 95% confidence interval from stochastic simulations, compared with the average observed PDF. Biomass was calculated using the raw census data without data cleaning or correction for increasing heights of measurements.

matrix. We computed five separate 5-year transition probability matrices, and calculated a mean transition matrix by taking arithmetic means of joint and marginal probabilities for each element of the five matrices. The equilibrium mean biomass was computed from the equilibrium probability distribution of log biomass classes, $P^*$. The equilibrium mean biomass was 140 MgC ha$^{-1}$, which is slightly higher than the most recent census (137.5), and lower than other censuses (Figure 14.4). We also explored the influence of stochastic variation in transition probabilities by simulating biomass dynamics over time when one of the five transition matrices was randomly selected at each time step. We found that over 1000 iterations (equivalent to 5000 years given our 5-year time step), this led to biomass fluctuations over a range from 133 to 147, and a mean value of 140 MgC ha$^{-1}$ (Figure 14.5). The projected stable equilibrium from the mean transition matrix lies within the 95% confidence intervals of the PDF from the simulations (Figure 14.4B).

Analysis of the Markov chain model for biomass transitions on BCI, *when biomass is calculated without correcting for changing points of measurement* (see previous section), thus suggests that the plot is currently at its dynamic equilibrium in biomass given current environmental conditions, and is not undergoing directional change. It further suggests that variability among

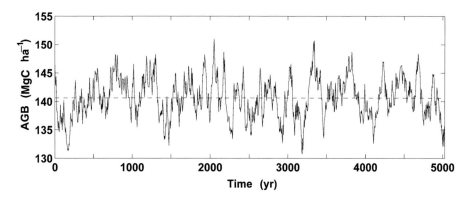

**Figure 14.5** Stochastic simulations of the Markov chain model of BCI, in which one of the five projection matrices (corresponding to one of the five 5-year census intervals) is randomly selected at each iteration. The dashed line indicates the deterministic equilibrium value. The projection matrices were based on biomass calculated using the raw census data without data cleaning or correction for increasing heights of measurements.

censuses may be explained by stochastic temporal environmental variation. This is consistent with the similarity in the biomass distribution across all six censuses evaluated here (Figure 14.4A), and with the lack of consistent directional change observed in the past 25 years (Chave *et al.* 2003, 2004). However, it is important to note that this approach has clear limitations, related to the limitations of the underlying data. The current analysis uses biomass estimated in the standard way – by using observed diameter at the maximum height of measurement in a given census, and plugging this directly into biomass equations without any adjustment for height of measurement. Monitoring is unlikely to capture rare, but potentially large, transitions such as major disturbances, and if these are missed in monitoring, their effects will also be absent from the resulting model. Further, as we showed above, estimates of biomass change can vary considerably and systematically with error correction routines, and with procedures for dealing with diameters measured at non-standard heights. Correcting for the increasing heights of measurement in later censuses would increase biomass in later censuses relative to early ones, thus leading to transition matrices with more weighting towards biomass increases, and thereby increased equilibrium biomass relative to current and past observed biomass. We are currently collecting field data on taper in order to develop accurate corrections for increasing heights of measurements, and will revisit this analysis once those data are in hand.

The Markov chain approach has some clear limitations, corresponding to the key assumptions stated above (Facelli & Pickett 1990). First, the first-order Markov chain models that we parameterised assume that transitions depend only on the current state of the system, and are invariant in space. Thus, for example, all areas of low biomass have the same transition probabilities to various higher (and lower) biomass states. In reality, some areas of low biomass may represent arrested gap succession owing to liana tangles (Schnitzer, Dalling & Carson 2000), or may be likely to stay in low biomass because of habitat effects such as location in a swampy area (Chave *et al.* 2003). Second, projections are made under the assumption that future transition probabilities are distributed in the same way as previously observed probabilities, in our case choosing randomly among the observed census intervals. Thus, this approach inherently cannot capture influences that are causing ongoing changes in transition probabilities – it only informs us about the logical endpoint of extrapolating current transition probabilities into the future. Increasing abundances of lianas, increasing atmospheric carbon dioxide and changing climates (Lewis *et al.* 2009a), among others, may be directionally changing transition probabilities over time, effects that are not reflected in projections of Markov chain models parameterised from past observed transitions. Third, the model assumes that biomass changes in adjacent subplots are independent. Our own analyses found no spatial autocorrelation in biomass change within the plot (Figure 14.2), suggesting that this assumption is appropriate for our site. The direct causal influence between patches is, in general, likely to be small most of the time; although gaps are commonly believed to be contagious and may be modelled as such (Sole & Manrubia 1995), a recent study found that areas next to existing canopy gaps have disturbance rates that are similar to those of areas far from existing gaps (Jansen, Van der Meer & Bongers 2008). On the other hand, large-scale disturbances, e.g. from hurricanes, blow-downs, fires and drought, are generally spatially structured with adjoining areas likely to transition to low-biomass states at the same time, whether or not they causally influence each other.

As we have shown here, parameterisation of Markov chain models for biomass transitions within subplots is potentially a useful way to capture gap dynamics and project future trajectories of biomass. This approach requires data for a large and fairly uniform area to obtain reliable transition matrices; large plots of 16–50 ha such as those in the CTFS/SIGEO (Center for Tropical Forest Science/Smithsonian Institution Global Earth Observatories) network are well suited to such analyses. Given that LiDAR-derived canopy height metrics are well correlated with biomass in tropical forests (Asner *et al.* 2011), landscape-scale LiDAR data are also well suited to such studies. Kellner *et al.* (2009) examined the canopy height distribution over 444 ha in a wet tropical forest in Costa Rica using LiDAR, and found that the observed distribution at 5 m grain is consistent with the stationary distribution of a Markov model parameterised using the transitions observed over an 8.5-year interval. Similar studies over larger areas would provide important information about whether and how tropical forest biomass is changing, and a first basis for projecting future changes. Future work should explore how statistical power is related to sample size (area and census interval) for this type of model. It is important to keep in mind that this phenomenological approach only projects forward based on currently observed dynamics, and that it cannot capture the effects of potential future changes in dynamics due to further changes in the environment.

## 14.4   Conclusions and recommendations

Forest biomass change in tropical forests is spatially variable, reflecting stochastic local variation as well as deterministic influences of topography, soil type, forest type, etc. Sampling uncertainty associated with stochastic local variation contributes random error in estimates of biomass change. The associated sampling errors can be quantified for individual sites by examining spatial autocorrelation patterns and then bootstrapping appropriately over subplots whose scale exceeds the local correlation length. When combining data from multiple sites differing in area and/or time interval, the appropriate weighting depends critically on the relative magnitude of within- and among-site variability, which in turn depends on landscape-level spatial patterns. Sampling errors for ensembles of sites can be assessed by bootstrapping over sites and subplots within sites (e.g. Chave *et al.* 2008). We recommend that all studies of biomass or biomass change examine autocorrelation patterns for the scales relevant to the study, and use this information to quantify sampling errors and determine appropriate weighting schemes, if necessary. Autocorrelation patterns are likely to differ among forests, and need to be considered carefully in any given application. Ideally, their assessment would be based on large-scale, fine-grained data such as that provided by airborne LiDAR, but in the absence of such information, plot data themselves can be used to assess this (e.g. through semivariograms).

Although sampling errors are inherently random, measurement errors and data cleaning routines can introduce systematic as well as random errors in estimates of forest biomass and biomass change. Even random ordinary diameter measurement errors on non-buttressed trees can introduce systematic errors in biomass because of the non-linear relationship of diameter to biomass. Further, common error detection and gap filling algorithms can actually introduce systematic errors in biomass change. On BCI, where measurement error frequencies are fairly low, these effects are currently small, but they have the potential to be larger depending on error rates and data cleaning practices (e.g. in earlier BCI censuses). It is important that all studies carefully document data cleaning practices, and describe these practices in publications in sufficient detail that they can be reproduced. We further recommend that studies quantify measurement errors, if at all possible; such information is extremely useful in quantifying any bias that may result from measurement errors, or changes in measurement error rates over time, and in enabling corrections for such biases. In general, data cleaning procedures should be carefully planned *a priori*; *post hoc* development or adjustment of such procedures is problematic as it raises the potential for conscious or unconscious biases towards expected results to influence outcomes. Research is needed to thoroughly evaluate alternative error detection and gap filling procedures for tropical forest biomass, and develop general recommendations for procedures that induce no systematic errors in key quantities of interest.

Trees whose diameter is measured above the standard height because of buttresses or other stem irregularities constitute a large proportion of biomass in tropical forests and create a very large potential for systematic errors in biomass and biomass change. Their potential to introduce bias follows from the interaction of current biomass allometry equations, which do not consider height of measurement, with variation among sites and over time in the heights of measurement. On BCI, different approaches to data analysis for buttressed trees produce very large differences in estimates of biomass change, including reversals in the sign of biomass change; at this time, it is not clear which approach and which estimate are best. It is critical that the methods for choosing measuring points and handling changes in measurement heights are clearly documented and reported. We strongly recommend that the height of diameter measurements always be measured, and that publications provide statistics on the distribution of measurement heights (and especially, any changes in this distribution over time, as seen on BCI). Ideally, the height of the top of the buttress would also be recorded, because existing biomass data often include only diameter measured immediately above buttresses. We further recommend the development and application of allometric equations that explicitly take the height of diameter measurement into consideration, and thus automatically correct for non-standard heights of measurement. Research that explicitly evaluates alternative approaches in simulated datasets could make clear the best approaches for obtaining unbiased estimates of biomass and biomass change for buttressed trees and stands that contain such trees.

A key challenge in predicting the future trajectory of forest biomass change is to control appropriately for the gap age distribution in the current dataset and/or landscape (the gap age distribution reflects the disturbance history of the site). Markov chain models for biomass offer a potentially useful means to do this. They require data for many transitions for reliable parameterisation, but this is within the realm of what is available for single large plots, such as BCI, or collections of small plots. In general, Markov models are a worthy area for future exploration, although it is important to keep in mind that these are purely phenomenological models, and only provide the ability to extrapolate current dynamics to their equilibrium. A critical question we did not address here concerns the confidence intervals on the probabilities and the projections of the Markov model; this is something that should be addressed in future work. The quantities estimated as part of parameterising Markov models are also themselves worthy of further examination – in particular, global change in forest dynamics would be expected to be evident in directional changes in transition probabilities over time.

This chapter has focused almost entirely on aboveground biomass data from field measurements, currently the main source of data on tropical forest carbon pools. This is likely to change in the future, as airborne LiDAR and other remote sensing tools become increasingly useful for quantifying biomass in tropical forests (Asner *et al.* 2011; Mascaro *et al.* 2011b), and as measurements of belowground pools become more common. LiDAR metrics such as mean canopy height correlate well with aboveground biomass in tropical forests (e.g. Mascaro *et al.* 2011a), and thus LiDAR is well placed to provide information on the spatial autocorrelation structure of biomass at landscape scales. Both LiDAR and other remote-sensing tools can provide landscape-scale data on canopy disturbance rates and the size distribution of disturbance events – critical quantities for determining the true power of a given plot sampling effort (Fisher *et al.* 2008; Gloor *et al.* 2009). However, most remote-sensing tools are likely to have limited if any ability to detect small increases in biomass in high-biomass forests (because most remotely sensed metrics saturate at high biomass), limiting their usefulness for quantifying potential subtle changes in old-growth forests. LiDAR, in contrast, can directly measure changes in canopy heights (e.g. Kellner *et al.* 2009) and in the density of vegetation beneath the canopy, both potential effects of global change that could affect biomass. Belowground stocks in soil and roots are also gaining attention, with standard methods increasingly applied across plot networks such as RAINFOR and SIGEO/CTFS. Future research should quantify random and systematic errors in associated estimates of carbon pools and fluxes.

Overall, ground plots remain an essential tool for quantifying impacts of global change on tropical forests, especially old-growth forests. Carbon stocks in these forests depend greatly on the diameters and heights of big trees, which are still poorly measured remotely. However, measurement methods and errors for ground plots can introduce random and systematic errors in estimates of biomass and biomass change. Methods should always be carefully documented and fully reported, and should include data cleaning procedures. Measurement errors should be quantified. It has generally been assumed that measurement errors and data correction routines have little or no effect. Here we show that although some effects are small, others are potentially large, and more worryingly, systematic. More investigation of the effects of these errors and procedures is warranted.

## Acknowledgements

We gratefully acknowledge the support of the HSBC Climate Partnership (H. C. M.) and the Smithsonian Institution Global Earth Observatories (SIGEO; M. D. and R. A. S.). We thank S. Joseph Wright for providing wood density data for central Panama. The BCI forest dynamics research project was made possible by National Science Foundation grants to Stephen P. Hubbell, by support from the Center for Tropical Forest Science, the Smithsonian Tropical Research Institute, the John D. and Catherine T. MacArthur Foundation, the Mellon Foundation, the Small World Institute Fund and numerous private individuals, and through the hard work of over 100 people from ten countries over the past three decades. The plot project is part of the Center for Tropical Forest Science, a global network of large-scale demographic tree plots.

## References

Anderson, T. W. & Goodman, L. A. (1957) Statistical inference about Markov chains. *Annals of Mathematical Statistics*, **28**, 89–110.

Asner, G. P., Mascaro, J., Muller-Landau, H. C. *et al.* (2011) A universal airborne LIDAR approach for tropical forest carbon mapping. *Oecologia*, **168**, 1147–1160.

Baker, T. R., Phillips, O. L., Malhi, Y. *et al.* (2004) Increasing biomass in Amazonian forest plots. *Philosophical Transactions of the Royal Society Series B*, **359**, 353–365.

Bormann, F. H. & Likens, G. E. (1979) *Pattern and Process in a Forested Ecosystem*. New York: Springer.

Chave, J. (1999) Study of structural, successional and spatial patterns in tropical rain forests using TROLL, a spatially explicit forest model. *Ecological Modelling*, **124**, 233–254.

Chave, J., Andalo, C., Brown, S. *et al.* (2005) Tree allometry and improved estimation of carbon stocks and balance in tropical forests. *Oecologia*, **145**, 87–99.

Chave, J., Condit, R., Aguilar, S. *et al.* (2004) Error propagation and scaling for tropical forest biomass estimates. *Philosophical Transactions of the Royal Society Series B*, **359**, 409–420.

Chave, J., Condit, R., Lao, S. *et al.* (2003) Spatial and temporal variation of biomass in a tropical forest: results from a large census plot in Panama. *Journal of Ecology*, **91**, 240–252.

Chave, J., Condit, R., Muller-Landau, H. C. *et al.* (2008) Assessing evidence for a pervasive alteration in tropical tree communities. *PLoS Biology*, **6**, 455–462.

Clark, D. A. (2002) Are tropical forests an important carbon sink? Reanalysis of the long-term plot data. *Ecological Applications*, **12**, 3–7.

Clark, D. A. (2004) Tropical forests and climate change. *Proceedings of the Royal Society Series B*, **359**, 477–491.

Clark, D. A. (2007) Detecting tropical forests' responses to global climatic and atmospheric change: current challenges and a way forward. *Biotropica*, **39**, 4–19.

Condit, R. (1998) *Tropical Forest Census Plots*. Berlin: Springer, and Georgetown, TX: R. G. Landes Company.

De Gruijter, J., Brus, D. J., Bierkens, M. F. P. & Knotters, M. (2006) *Sampling for Natural Resource Monitoring*. Berlin: Springer.

Facelli, J. M. & Pickett, S. T. A. (1990) Markovian chains and the role of history in succession. *Trends in Ecology & Evolution*, **5**, 27–30.

Fisher, J. I., Hurtt, G. C., Thomas, R. Q. & Chambers, J. Q. (2008) Clustered disturbances lead to bias in large-scale estimates based on forest sample plots. *Ecology Letters*, **11**, 554–563.

Friedlingstein, P., Bopp, L., Rayner, P. *et al.* (2006) Climate-carbon cycle feedback analysis, results from the C4MIP model intercomparison. *Journal of Climate*, **19**, 3337–3353.

Gloor, M., Phillips, O. L., Lloyd, J. J. *et al.* (2009) Does the disturbance hypothesis explain the biomass increase in basin-wide Amazon forest plot data? *Global Change Biology*, **15**, 2418–2430.

Haan, P. (1999) On the use of density kernels for concentration estimations within particle and puff dispersion models. *Atmospheric Environment*, **33**, 2007–2021.

Higuchi, N., Dos Santos, J. & Jardim, F. C. S. (1982) Tamanho de parcela amostral para invenários florestais. *Acta Amazonica*, **12**, 91–103.

Holtum, J. A. M. & Winter, K. (2010) Elevated [$CO_2$] and forest vegetation: more a water issue than a carbon issue? *Functional Plant Biology*, **37**, 694–702.

Horn, H. S. (1975) Markovian properties of forest succession. In *Ecology and Evolution of Communities* (eds. M. L. Cody & J. M. Diamond), pp. 196–211. Cambridge, MA: Belknap Press/Harvard University Press.

Jansen, P. A., Van Der Meer, P. J. & Bongers, F. (2008) Spatial contagiousness of canopy disturbance in tropical rain forest: an individual-tree-based test. *Ecology*, **89**, 3490–3502.

Keller, M., Palace, M. & Hurtt, G. (2001) Biomass estimation in the Tapajos National Forest, Brazil: Examination of sampling and allometric uncertainties. *Forest Ecology and Management*, **154**, 371–382.

Kellner, J. R., Clark, D. B. & Hubbell, S. P. (2009) Pervasive canopy dynamics produce short-term stability in a tropical rain forest landscape. *Ecology Letters*, **12**, 155–164.

Körner, C. (2003) Slow in, rapid out – carbon flux studies and Kyoto targets. *Science*, **300**, 1242–1243.

Körner, C. (2009) Responses of humid tropical trees to rising $CO_2$. *Annual Review of Ecology and Systematics*, **40**, 61–79.

Lewis, S. L., Lloyd, J., Sitch, S., Mitchard, E. T. A. & Laurance, W. F. (2009a) Changing ecology of tropical forests: evidence and drivers. *Annual Review of Ecology Evolution and Systematics*, 529–549.

Lewis, S. L., Lopez-Gonzalez, G., Sonke, B. *et al.* (2009b) Increasing carbon storage in intact African tropical forests. *Nature*, **457**, 1003–1006.

Lewis, S. L., Malhi, Y. & Phillips, O. L. (2004) Fingerprinting the impacts of global change on tropical forests. *Philosophical Transactions of the Royal Society Series B*, **359**, 437–462.

Lewis, S. L., Phillips, O. L., Baker, T. R. *et al.* (2004) Concerted changes in tropical forest structure and dynamics: evidence from 50 South American long-term plots. *Philosophical Transactions of the Royal Society Series B*, **359**, 421–436.

Luo, Y. Q. (2007) Terrestrial carbon-cycle feedback to climate warming. *Annual Review of Ecology Evolution and Systematics*, 683–712.

Macarthur, R. H. & Wilson, E. O. (1967) *The Theory of Island Biogeography*. Princeton, NJ: Princeton University Press.

Martin, A. R. & Thomas, S. C. (2011) A reassessment of carbon content in tropical trees. *PLoS One*, **6**, e23533.

Mascaro, J., Asner, G. P., Muller-Landau, H. C. *et al.* (2011a) Controls over aboveground forest carbon density on Barro Colorado Island, Panama. *Biogeosciences*, **8**, 1615–1629.

Mascaro, J., Detto, M., Asner, G. P. & Muller-Landau, H. C. (2011b) Evaluating uncertainty in mapping forest carbon with airborne LiDAR. *Remote Sensing of Environment*, **115**, 3770–3774.

Metcalf, C. J. E., Clark, J. S. & Clark, D. A. (2009) Tree growth inference and prediction when the point of measurement changes: modelling around buttresses in tropical forests. *Journal of Tropical Ecology*, **25**, 1–12.

Moffat, A. M., Papale, D., Reichstein, M. *et al.* (2007) Comprehensive comparison of gap-filling techniques for eddy covariance net carbon fluxes. *Agricultural and Forest Meteorology*, **147**, 209–232.

Myeni, R., Keeling, C., Tucker, C., Asrar, G. & Nemani, R. (1997) Increased plant growth in the northern high latitudes from 1981 to 1991. *Nature*, **386**, 698–702.

Odum, E. P. (1969) The strategy of ecosystem development. *Science*, **164**, 262–270.

Pacala, S. W., Canham, C. D., Saponara, J. *et al.* (1996) Forest models defined by field measurements: estimation, error analysis and dynamics. *Ecological Monographs*, **66**, 1–43.

Phillips, O. L. (1996) Long-term environmental change in tropical forests: Increasing tree turnover. *Environmental Conservation*, **23**, 235–248.

Phillips, O. L., Aragao, L., Lewis, S. L. *et al.* (2009) Drought sensitivity of the Amazon rainforest. *Science*, **323**, 1344–1347.

Phillips, O. L., Lewis, S. L., Baker, T. R., Chao, K. J. & Higuchi, N. (2008) The changing Amazon forest. *Philosophical Transactions of the Royal Society Series B*, **363**, 1819–1827.

Phillips, O. L., Malhi, Y., Higuchi, N. *et al.* (1998) Changes in the carbon balance of tropical forests: Evidence from long-term plots. *Science*, **282**, 439–442.

Phillips, O. L., Malhi, Y., Vinceti, B. *et al.* (2002) Changes in growth of tropical forests: Evaluating potential biases. *Ecological Applications*, **12**, 576–587.

Ricklefs, R. E. (2004) A comprehensive framework for global patterns in biodiversity. *Ecology Letters*, **7**, 1–15.

Rüger, N., Berger, U., Hubbell, S. P., Vieilledent, G. & Condit, R. (2011) Growth strategies of tropical tree species: Disentangling light and size effects. *PLoS One*, **6**, e25330.

Rustad, L. E., Campbell, J. L., Marion, G. M. *et al.* (2001) A meta-analysis of the response of soil respiration, net nitrogen mineralization, and aboveground plant growth to experimental ecosystem warming *Oecologia*, **126**, 543–562.

Saugier, B., Roy, J. & Mooney, H. A. (2001) *Terrestrial Global Productivity*. London: Academic Press.

Schimel, D. S. (1995) Terrestrial ecosystems and the carbon cycle. *Global Change Biology*, **1**, 77–91.

Schnitzer, S. A., Dalling, J. W. & Carson, W. P. (2000) The impact of lianas on tree regeneration in tropical forest canopy gaps: Evidence for an alternative pathway of gap-phase regeneration. *Journal of Ecology*, **88**, 655–666.

Scott, D. W. (1992) *Multivariate Density Estimation: Theory, Practice, and Visualisation*. New York: Wiley.

Sheil, D. (1995) A critique of permanent plot methods and analysis with examples from Budongo-forest, Uganda. *Forest Ecology and Management*, **77**, 11–34.

Shugart, H. H. (1984) *A Theory of Forest Dynamics*. New York: Springer.

Silverman, B. W. (1986) *Density Estimation for Statistics and Data Analysis*. London: Chapman and Hall.

Sironen, S., Kangas, A. & Maltamo, M. (2010) Comparison of different non-parametric growth imputation methods in the presence of correlated observations. *Forestry*, **83**, 39–51.

Sironen, S., Kangas, A., Maltamo, M. & Kalliovirta, J. (2008) Localization of growth estimates using non-parametric imputation methods. *Forest Ecology and Management*, **256**, 674–684.

Sole, R. V. & Manrubia, S. C. (1995) Are rainforests self-organized in a critical state? *Journal of Theoretical Biology*, **173**, 31–40.

Usher, M. B. (1979) Markovian approaches to ecological succession. *Journal of Animal Ecology*, **48**, 413–426.

Waggoner, P. E. & Stephens, G. R. (1970) Transition probabilities for a forest. *Nature*, **225**, 1160–1161.

Wagner, F., Rutishauser, E., Blanc, L. & Herault, B. (2010) Effects of plot size and census interval on descriptors of forest structure and dynamics. *Biotropica*, **42**, 664–671.

Wolf, A., Field, C. B. & Berry, J. A. (2011) Allometric growth and allocation in forests: a perspective from FLUXNET. *Ecological Applications*, **21**, 1546–1556.

Wright, S. J. (2005) Tropical forests in a changing environment. *Trends in Ecology & Evolution*, **20**, 553–560.

Wright, S. J. (2010) The future of tropical forests. *Annals of the New York Academy of Sciences*, **1195**, 1–27.

Wright, S. J., Kitajima, K., Kraft, N. J. B. *et al.* (2010) Functional traits and the growth-mortality tradeoff in tropical trees. *Ecology*, **91**, 3664–3674.

Yang, Y. H. & Luo, Y. Q. (2011) Isometric biomass partitioning pattern in forest ecosystems: evidence from temporal observations during stand development. *Journal of Ecology*, **99**, 431–437.

Yang, Y. H., Luo, Y. Q. & Finzi, A. C. (2011) Carbon and nitrogen dynamics during forest stand development: a global synthesis. *New Phytologist*, **190**, 977–989.

Zuidema, P. A., Jongejans, E., Chien, P. D., During, H. J. & Schieving, F. (2010) Integral Projection Models for trees: a new parameterization method and a validation of model output. *Journal of Ecology*, **98**, 345–355.

## Appendix 14.1  Details of methods for calculating AGB and AGB change for Barro Colorado Island

We calculated individual stem AGB (in kg dry biomass) using the moist forest equation based on wood specific gravity (wsg) and diameter (dbh, in cm) from Chave *et al.* (2005):

$$AGB = wsg \times \exp\left[-1.499 + 2.148(\ln dbh) + 0.207(\ln dbh)^2 - 0.0281(\ln dbh)^3\right]$$

We assumed dry biomass was 47% carbon (Martin & Thomas 2011), and we report AGB and AGB change in MgC.

We calculated AGB change per year in a quadrat as the sum of AGB changes per year for individual stems in that quadrat, thus taking into account differences in measurement intervals for different stems. Stems that were recruits in the final census were assigned an initial AGB of zero and an initial date corresponding to the date in which their quadrat was censused. Stems that were newly dead in the final census were assigned a final AGB of zero and a final date corresponding to the date in which their quadrat was censused.

We used species-level wood density values for 306 species, most obtained from field measurements in central Panama (Wright *et al.* 2010 and S. Joseph Wright, unpublished data), genus-level values for 12 species, and a plot-level basal-area-weighted mean of 0.521 for the remaining taxa and unidentified individuals (the later censuses have no unidentified individuals).

# CHAPTER FIFTEEN

# Analysis of anthropogenic impacts on forest biodiversity as a contribution to empirical theory

ADRIAN C. NEWTON

*Centre for Conservation Ecology and Environmental Science,*
*Bournemouth University*

and

CRISTIAN ECHEVERRÍA

*Facultad de Ciencias Forestales, Universidad de Concepción*

## 15.1 Introduction

The widespread loss and degradation of native forests is now recognised as a major environmental issue, even a crisis (Spilsbury 2010). During the first decade of the twenty-first century, global forest area declined by around 13 million ha yr$^{-1}$ (FAO 2010). However, such estimates based on national statistics are uncertain (Grainger 2008); Hansen *et al.* (2010) report a substantially higher annual forest loss of approximately 20 million ha yr$^{-1}$ for 2000–2005, based on analysis of satellite imagery.

The Food and Agriculture Organization (FAO 2010) also report that during the decade 2000–2010, the area of undisturbed primary forest declined by an estimated 4.2 million ha yr$^{-1}$ (or 0.4% annually), largely because of the introduction of selective logging and other forms of human disturbance. Accurate data on the extent of forest degradation at the global scale are difficult to obtain (Gibbs *et al.* 2007), but an indication of its impact is provided by a recent estimate of the amount of carbon stored in forest vegetation. Over the period 1990–2005, global forest carbon stocks declined, in percentage terms, by almost double the decline in forest area (UNEP 2007). Given the current emphasis of global forest policy initiatives on both deforestation and forest degradation, particularly in the context of the UN REDD+ programme, there is an urgent need not only for improved forest monitoring (Baker *et al.* 2010; Gibbs *et al.* 2007; Grainger 2008; Sasaki & Putz 2009), but for a deeper understanding of the processes responsible for forest degradation and their potential impacts on forest biodiversity.

Ideally, such an understanding would comprise a body of ecological theory, which would enable the impacts of human activities on forests to be predicted.

*Forests and Global Change*, ed. David A. Coomes, David F. R. P. Burslem and William D. Simonson.
Published by Cambridge University Press. © British Ecological Society 2014.

However, progress towards development of such a theory has been limited. It could be argued that this reflects a general lack of theory in ecological science as a whole; Peters (1991), for example, argued that ecology is a theoretically weak discipline. However, the impacts of disturbance on ecological communities have long been the focus of research interest. This is illustrated by the lengthy debate regarding the relationship between diversity and stability, which spans more than 40 years, during which time it has attracted substantial attention from theoreticians (Ives 2007). In the context of forests, increasing recognition of the role of natural disturbance in shaping community composition and structure contributed to a 'paradigm shift' in ecology (Pickett & White 1985), and the development of what has been termed 'disturbance theory' (Pickett *et al.* 2007). Although there has been progress in developing mathematically formalised theory relating to disturbance impacts on forests (see Clark 1989, 1991), development of disturbance theory has largely been conceptual, and is still at an early stage (Pickett, Kolasa & Jones 2007).

This raises the question of the nature of theory in ecological science, an issue that has been the subject of lively, even acrimonious debate (Keddy 1992). For Peters (1991), the key feature of theory is that it enables testable predictions to be made. On this basis, a regression equation would constitute an ecological theory (Peters 1991). For other authors, a theory should also include at least a measure of explanation, and ideally be expressed in mathematical terms (Hanski 2004; McLean & May 2007). In contrast, Pickett, Kolasa and Jones (2007) place less emphasis on the need for testable predictions and mathematical formalism; for these authors, a theory is 'a system of conceptual constructs that organises and explains . . . observable phenomena'. Following this definition a theory would comprise a number of components, which might include models and hypotheses, but would also incorporate empirical or factual information (Pickett, Kolasa & Jones 2007).

From the perspective of practical conservation management, tools are required that would enable the impacts of human disturbance on forest communities to be forecast (Newton *et al.* 2009). Such tools would enable appropriate management interventions to be identified, and inform the development of effective conservation plans. Ideally, such tools would be generally applicable, rather than specific to a given location. The identification of generalisations is a common element of ecological theory, regardless of how it is defined (Peters 1991; Pickett *et al.* 2007). However, at present there is a lack of either theory or generalisations that would enable the impact of anthropogenic disturbance on forest biodiversity to be predicted.

The objective of the research described here is to examine whether generalisations can be made regarding the impacts of human disturbance on forest biodiversity, to support the development of empirical theory. We use the phrase 'empirical theory' to differentiate the approach employed here, which focuses on integrated analysis of data obtained from a series of real-world case studies, from development of a purely mathematical or conceptual theory. In use of this term we follow Rigler (1982), who in common with Peters (1991) advocated the seeking of general relationships based on analysis of empirical information, to identify ecological properties and processes that were predictable (Pace 2001). Our goal is to identify insights that could inform the practical conservation and management of forest communities, and contribute to the reduction of further biodiversity loss.

This chapter presents results obtained from a series of research projects conducted in both moist and dry forests in Latin America, undertaken using a common set of approaches and analytical tools. Details of the research conducted in moist forests are summarised by Newton (2007b) and Newton et al. (2009), and in dry forests by Newton and Tejedor (2011) and Newton et al. (2012). Here, we integrate information obtained from both moist and dry forests to provide a basis for comparative analysis. Each of the study areas was selected on the basis of its importance for biodiversity conservation, while being characterised by intensifying anthropogenic disturbance. To place analyses of such disturbance in context, we first examine the pattern of deforestation that has occurred in recent decades. We then analyse the pattern of forest fragmentation, and its relationships with other forms of anthropogenic disturbance, together with their potential impacts on biodiversity. Impacts on forest biodiversity are primarily considered here in terms of forest structure and composition, with emphasis on tree species; information on additional components of biodiversity is provided by Newton (2007b) and Newton and Tejedor (2011). The principal objective of the analyses presented here is to identify any general patterns or responses, in study areas with contrasting socio-economic, biophysical and ecological characteristics. We also briefly examine whether any generalisations obtained in Latin America might be applicable to forests in other locations that are being subjected to human disturbance, with particular reference to a case study in the United Kingdom.

## 15.2   Study areas

The research was conducted in two phases, the first focusing on the temperate rain forests of southern Chile (two areas in Region X and one area in Region VII/VIII) and the montane rain forests of Mexico (Chiapas, Oaxaca and Veracruz) (Table 15.1a). The second phase focused on dry forests, including the Mediterranean forests and shrublands of Central Chile, the dry temperate forests of southern Argentina, the subtropical dry forests of northern Argentina and the tropical dry forests of Mexico (Chiapas, Oaxaca and Veracruz) (Table 15.1b). In both cases, the objective was to focus on forests of high conservation importance; for example, both the temperate rain forests

**Table 15.1** *Description of study areas in Latin America.*
(a) Moist forest areas

| Characteristics | Los Muermos, Region X, Chile | Chiloé Island, Region X, Chile | Región del Maule, Regions VII and VIII, Chile | Highlands of Chiapas, Mexico | El Rincón Alto, Sierra Norte, Oaxaca, Mexico | Xalapa, Veracruz, Mexico |
|---|---|---|---|---|---|---|
| | | | | *Study area* | | |
| Latitude | 41° 30'–42° 20' S | 41° 50' S | 35°–36° 30' S | 16° 15'–17° 10' N | 17° 18'–17° 23' N | 19° 13'–19° 41' N |
| Longitude | 73°–74° W | 73° 50' W | 72°–73° W | 91° 45'–92° 50' W | 96° 15'–96° 21' W | 96° 51'–97° 01' W |
| Elevation (m) | 0–250 | 50–100 | 0–350 | 1500–2840 | 1850 ± 150 | 1200–2000 |
| Mean annual temperature (°C) | 12 | 12 | 14 | 13–17 | 20–22 | 12–18 |
| Mean annual rainfall (mm yr$^{-1}$) | 2000 | 2090 | 700–800 | 1100–1600 | 1700 | 1300–2200 |
| Major vegetation types | Temperate rain forests | Temperate rain forests | Temperate rain forests | Tropical montane cloud forest, pine and pine–oak forests | Tropical montane cloud forest | Tropical montane cloud forest |
| Principal forms of human disturbance | Fire, plantation forestry, tree cutting (timber, fuelwood), livestock browsing | Fire, tree cutting (timber, fuelwood), livestock browsing | Fire, plantation forestry, tree cutting (timber, fuelwood) | Fire, shifting cultivation, tree cutting (timber, fuelwood) | Fire, shifting cultivation, tree cutting (timber, fuelwood) | Tree cutting (timber, fuelwood), livestock browsing |

**Table 15.1** (cont.)
(b) Dry forest areas

| | Southern Argentina | North West Argentina | Central Chile (Coastal Range and Central Valley) | Central Chiapas, Mexico | Upper Mixteca, Oaxaca, Mexico | Central Veracruz, Mexico |
|---|---|---|---|---|---|---|
| Latitude | 39° 30'–43° 35' S | 22° 00'–24° 00' S | 33° 30'–38° 00' S | 15° 50'–17° 00' N | 17° 00'–18° 00' N | 19° 17'–19° 25' N |
| Longitude | 71° 19'–72° 00' W | 63° 30'–65° 00' W | 71° 50'–72° 30' W | 92° 00'–93° 30' W | 97° 00'–98° 00' W | 96° 26'–96° 35' W |
| Elevation (m) | 800–1500 | 350–750 | 0–2260 | 500–1700 | 600–1500 | 40–1100 |
| Mean annual temperature (°C) | 12 | 21 | 13 | 19–26 | 16–18 | 24–26 |
| Mean annual rainfall (mm yr$^{-1}$) | 1500 | 900 | 100–500 | 800–1200 | 550–900 | 900 |
| Major vegetation types | Austral dry forest–steppe ecotone | Andean premontane forest, Chaco | Mediterranean sclerophyllous forest and shrubland | Tropical dry forest | Tropical dry forest | Tropical dry forest |
| Principal forms of human disturbance | Fire, tree plantations, tree cutting (timber), livestock browsing | Tree cutting (fuelwood and timber), livestock browsing | Fire, tree plantations, tree cutting (fuelwood), livestock browsing | Fire, shifting cultivation, tree cutting (fuelwood and timber), livestock browsing | Fire, tree cutting (fuelwood and timber), livestock browsing | Fire, tree cutting (fuelwood and timber), livestock browsing |

of southern Chile and Mexican montane forests are recognised as biodiversity 'hotspots' (Myers *et al.* 2000), and as priority ecoregions (Dinerstein *et al.* 1995; Olson *et al.* 2001). Similarly, each of the dry forest areas is recognised as a priority ecoregion (Dinerstein *et al.* 1995).

The research primarily focused on forest landscapes that are being subjected to human use, including areas lying both outside and within protected areas. Principal forms of anthropogenic disturbance include fire, impacts of browsing by livestock, and tree cutting for timber and fuelwood (Table 15.1a,b). Similar methods and research approaches were employed in both moist and dry forest areas, to facilitate comparative analysis. Five elements of the research are summarised here, namely analyses of deforestation, forest fragmentation, edge effects, seedling establishment and modelling of forest dynamics. Other aspects of the research, such as studies of genetic variation, are summarised by Newton (2007b), and Newton and Tejedor (2011).

## 15.3 Forest loss

The pattern of forest loss since the early 1970s was examined in four moist and six dry forest areas by analysis of satellite imagery (principally Landsat MSS, TM and ETM+). Forest maps were produced from these images using results from field surveys, and used to estimate annual deforestation rates (Cayuela, Golicher & Rey-Benayas 2006a; Cayuela, Rey Benayas & Echeverría 2006c; Echeverría *et al.* 2006, 2007a; Schulz *et al.* 2010). Results indicated that substantial net deforestation has occurred in each of the moist forest areas in recent decades, with the exception of Veracruz (Figure 15.1A). For example, in Chiapas, between 1975 and 1990 the forest loss rate was 1.5% $yr^{-1}$, increasing to 6.1% $yr^{-1}$ between 1990 and 2000. In Maule, Chile, 67% of the native forest existing in 1975 had disappeared by 2000, equivalent to an annual deforestation rate of 4.4% $yr^{-1}$. In Los Muermos, Chile, approximately 23% of native forest present in 1976 had disappeared by 1999, at an annual forest loss of 1.1% $yr^{-1}$. Although forest area increased in Veracruz, Mexico, this largely represented the expansion of disturbed secondary forest, for example on abandoned coffee plantations. In general, the decline in forest extent was less pronounced in the dry forest areas (Figure 15.1B). For example, in Central Chile, Schulz *et al.* (2010) found that 58% (113 605 ha) of the forest extent present in 1975 (195 773 ha) remained by 2008, representing a mean annual decline of 1.7%. This is the highest rate of forest loss recorded among the dryland study areas investigated, although all areas registered a decline in forest cover over the past three decades (Figure 15.2).

The factors responsible for forest loss were examined using statistical and rule-based modelling approaches, incorporating a variety of different socioeconomic and environmental variables (e.g. Echeverría *et al.* 2008). Overall,

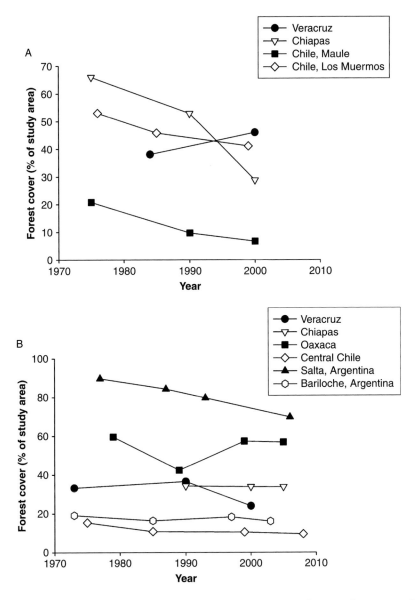

**Figure 15.1** Forest cover change over time in Latin American study areas, estimated from analysis of satellite remote sensing imagery. After Newton *et al.* (2009), and Newton and Tejedor (2011). (A) Moist forest; (B) dry forest.

the factors responsible for forest loss varied markedly between study areas (Table 15.2). The only result that was generally consistent was the finding that forest loss was more likely on slopes with a lower gradient, which was recorded in all areas except dryland Oaxaca. Other variables, such as distance to rivers, roads and human settlement, displayed contrasting results in

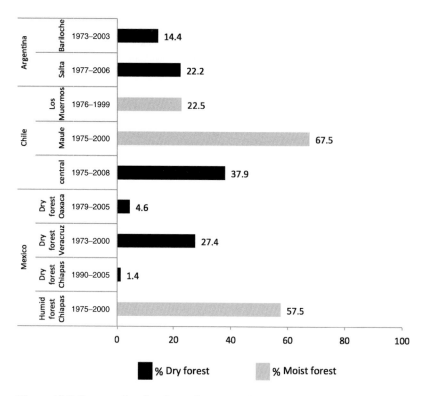

**Figure 15.2** Extent of native forest loss over the past three decades, estimated from analysis of satellite remote sensing imagery. After Newton *et al.* (2009), and Newton and Tejedor (2011). The date ranges reflect the availability of images when the analyses were conducted. The values presented indicate the loss of native forest area as a percentage of the earliest value with the date range.

different areas (Table 15.2). Neither were factors consistently related to forest type, although distance to patch edge was negatively related to forest loss in all of the moist forest areas, but was not significant in the dry forest areas. Such contrasting results highlight the difficulty of generalising about the factors responsible for forest loss.

## 15.4   Forest fragmentation

The dynamics of forest fragmentation were analysed by calculating a range of metrics for each of the forest cover maps generated from satellite imagery, using GIS and FRAGSTATS (version 3.3) (McGarigal *et al.* 2002). Analyses indicated that in each of the moist forest areas, deforestation was accompanied by substantial forest fragmentation (Cayuela, Golicher & Rey-Benayas 2006a; Cayuela, Rey Benayas & Echeverría 2006c; Echeverría *et al.* 2006, 2007a,b, 2012). The mean size of forest patches declined progressively, displaying most rapid decline in Chiapas (Figure 15.3A). This was accompanied by an

**Table 15.2** Drivers of forest cover change. Abbreviations: D, dry forest; M, moist forest. + indicates a statistically significant, positive relationship. – indicates a significant negative relationship. For example, in Central Chile, forest loss was more likely to occur with increasing distance from a road, whereas in Salta Argentina, the converse was true.

| Drivers of forest loss | Study area | | | | | | | | |
| --- | --- | --- | --- | --- | --- | --- | --- | --- | --- |
| | Salta Argentina | Central Chile | Maule Chile | Muermos Chile | Veracruz Mexico | Chiapas Mexico | Chiapas Mexico | Oaxaca Mexico | Veracruz Mexico |
| | D | D | M | M | M | M | D | D | D |
| Distance to rivers | – | | | | | | | | – |
| Distance to roads | – | + | | + | | | | | |
| Distance to agriculture | – | + | | | | | | + | – |
| Distance to towns or villages | – | | | | | | + | + | |
| Distance to forest | | + | | | | | | + | |
| Distance to patch edge | | | – | – | | | | | – |
| Distance to irrigation infrastructure | | | – | – | – | – | | | |
| Slope | – | – | – | – | – | – | – | | – |
| Annual precipitation | + | | | | | | – | | |
| Insolation/aspect | – | – | – | – | | | + | – | – |
| Forest patch size | | | – | | | + | | | |
| Soil fertility | | | | | + | | | | |
| Elevation | | | | | | – | – | + | |
| Density of non-forest areas | | | | | | + | | | |

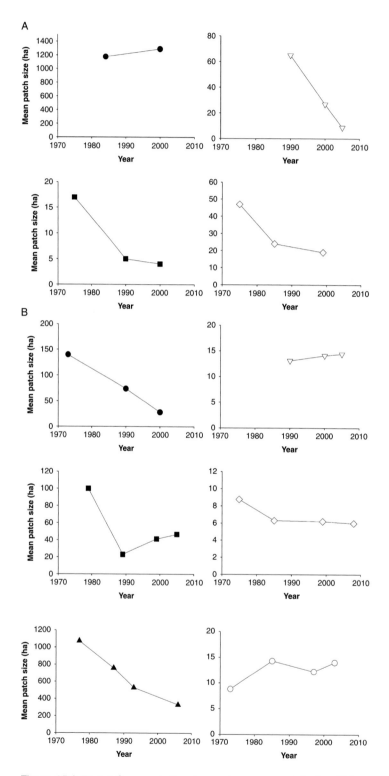

**Figure 15.3** Forest fragmentation dynamics: mean patch size. Values were obtained from analysis of maps of forest cover, derived from satellite remote sensing imagery.

increase in patch density, with highest rate of change again recorded in Chiapas (Figure 15.4A). In Maule, a decline in patch density was recorded during 1990–2000, reflecting the predominant loss of forest patches rather than their further subdivision. In all study areas, these changes were associated with a decrease in the percentage of area accounted for by the largest patch, a decrease in total interior area of forest patches and an increase in the isolation of forest patches.

Although some dryland forest areas similarly exhibited progressive fragmentation, others did not (Echeverría *et al.* 2011, 2012). Mean size of forest patches declined in four of the study areas, but values either remained stable or increased slightly over time in two others (Chiapas and Bariloche) (Figure 15.3B). Patch density similarly displayed contrasting results between study areas, with continuous increases recorded in two areas (northern Argentina and Veracruz) and declines recorded in two others (Chiapas and Central Chile) (Figure 15.4B). Overall, these results show that the spatial patterns of change of dryland forest were dynamic and did not necessarily represent a unidirectional process of forest fragmentation. The fact that contrasting results were obtained from different study areas is consistent with what has been described for some other landscapes, emphasising that spatial patterns of forest in human-modified landscapes can be highly individualistic (Lindenmayer & Fischer 2006).

## 15.5   Species richness

At the outset of the research, it was hypothesised that forest fragmentation would have a major influence on tree species richness and composition. Overall, however, the impacts of other forms of human disturbance were found to be more significant. Disturbances such as logging of timber, fuelwood cutting, browsing by livestock, fire and development of infrastructure (principally roads) were found to be chronic and widespread, both in moist and dry forest (Aravena *et al.* 2002; Galindo-Jaimes *et al.* 2002; Ramírez-Marcial, González-Espinosa & Williams-Linera 2001; Williams-Linera 2002; Williams-Linera & Lorea 2009). Substantial impacts of human disturbance on forest stand structure and composition were identified by analysis of field data derived from successional chronosequences (del Castillo & Blanco-Macías 2007) and

---

Caption for Figure 15.3 (cont.)

After Newton *et al.* (2009) and Newton and Tejedor (2011). (A) Moist forest. Filled circles, Veracruz; empty triangles, Chiapas; filled squares, Maule, Chile; empty diamonds, Los Muermos, Chile. (B) Dry forest. Filled circles, Veracruz; empty triangles, Chiapas; filled squares, Oaxaca; empty diamonds, Central Chile; filled triangles, northern Argentina; open circles, southern Argentina.

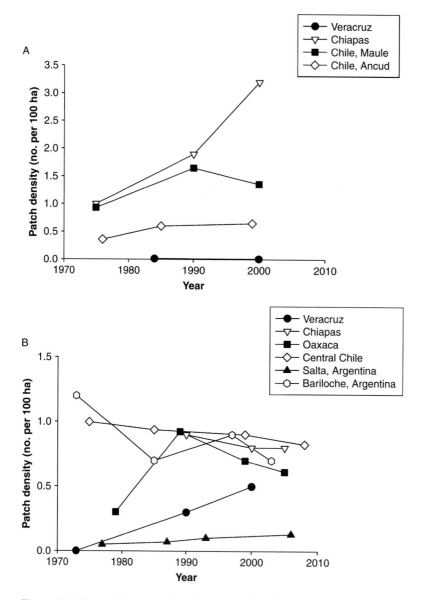

**Figure 15.4** Forest fragmentation dynamics: density of forest patches. Values were obtained from analysis of maps of forest cover, derived from satellite remote sensing imagery. After Newton *et al.* (2009) and Newton and Tejedor (2011). (A) Moist forest; (B) dry forest.

analysis of gradients of disturbance in four moist forest areas, although again contrasting results were obtained from different areas (Newton *et al.* 2007).

The impact of forest fragmentation on tree species richness was explored by relating the results of floristic surveys to different measures of forest

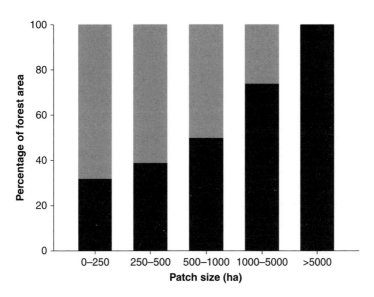

**Figure 15.5** Relationship of forest patch size to successional state, southern Chile (adapted from Echeverria *et al.* 2007b). Data were derived from analyses of satellite remote-sensing imagery, supported by field survey.

fragmentation. In southern Chile, the area, core area, edge length and proximity of forest fragments were each negatively associated with mean species richness of pioneer species, and positively associated with richness of forest interior species. Patch size was the most important attribute influencing different measures of species composition, being significantly related to the abundance of tree and shrub species associated with interior and with edge habitats (Echeverría *et al.* 2007b). These results also highlighted an interaction between forest fragmentation and anthropogenic disturbance within forest patches. Significant negative relationships were found between patch size and indicators of human disturbance such as the number of animal trails, counts of faeces produced by livestock and the number of cut tree stumps (Echeverría *et al.* 2007b). As a result of these processes, the smaller the forest patch, the greater the dominance of secondary forest; old-growth forest was largely restricted to larger forest patches (Figure 15.5). In the moist forests of Chiapas, diversity of tree species was found to be primarily related to climatic variables, particularly precipitation and temperature. Forest fragmentation was found to have relatively little impact on tree species richness; for example, variables such as patch size and connectivity were not found to be significant (Cayuela *et al.* 2006b). However, human disturbance was found to be associated with lower tree diversity at a local scale, particularly of late successional species (Cayuela *et al.* 2006b,d). In common with results obtained in Chile, research identified an effect of human disturbance on the successional status of forest patches.

Results obtained in dry forest similarly demonstrated little consistent effect of forest fragmentation, but significant impacts of human disturbance on tree species richness and composition. For example in Veracruz, Mexico, Williams-Linera and Lorea (2009) found that anthropogenic disturbances indicated by the presence of cattle and trails were associated with reduced species diversity, together with a marked influence of elevation, with sites at lower elevations being more disturbed and less diverse. Fragment area was related to species richness of adult trees only in Oaxaca, and to tree seedling abundance only in Chile (Smith-Ramírez *et al.* 2011). In Chiapas, no relationship was detected between forest patch area and adult tree species richness; however, a positive relationship was identified between tree species diversity and temperature and elevation (Rocha-Loredo *et al.* 2010).

## 15.6   Edge effects

The characteristics of the edges of forest fragments can have a major influence on the ecological processes influencing biodiversity, such as dispersal, establishment, survival and growth (Harper *et al.* 2005). A large number of studies have examined edge effects in different locations and have identified a wide variety of responses. These were reviewed by Ries *et al.* (2004) and Harper *et al.* (2005), who both present conceptual models of edge effects based on reviews of empirical evidence. However, progress towards developing quantitative predictive models for edge effects has been limited.

We undertook 22 field-based studies comparing forest edge and forest interior habitats, examining a range of different processes (López-Barrera *et al.* 2007a). These analyses were restricted to moist forests. Edge effects were detected on a wide variety of ecological patterns and processes (Figure 15.6), including seed rain, seed germination, seed removal and/or predation. Overall, more positive than negative edge effects were identified, a positive effect being defined here as an increase in the variables measured (Figure 15.6). From all of the response variables examined in three different study regions, only tree seedling growth and survival exhibited consistent responses in all regions, displaying higher values in edges.

As predicted by Harper *et al.* (2005), we found that the magnitude of edge effects was greater at edges with more pronounced contrasts across the edge. High- and low-contrast edges produced different responses in seed removal and seed dispersal across edges (López-Barrera, Newton & Manson 2005;

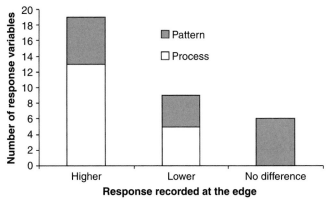

Figure 15.6 Summary of edge effects analysed in moist forest landscapes (adapted from López-Barrera *et al.* 2007a). The graph shows the number of response variables that showed higher, lower or no difference (no edge effect) in the values of a response variable that was compared at the edge and in the forest interior. The response variables were divided according to their type: 'pattern' refers to forest attributes such as plant species richness and tree seedling abundance; 'process' refers to ecological attributes and interactions, such as seed removal by animals, seed dispersal, seedling herbivory or fog capture.

López-Barrera *et al.* 2007b; Guzman-Guzman & Williams-Linera 2006), seedling herbivory (López-Barrera *et al.* 2006), seed germination (López-Barrera & Newton 2005), diversity and abundance of small mammals, and edge microclimate (López-Barrera *et al.* 2007a). Edge type affected animal movement, with low-contrast edges enhancing small mammal dispersal of seeds from the forest edge into adjacent old-fields, whereas high-contrast edges tended to concentrate seed dispersal along edges (López-Barrera *et al.* 2007a).

Another key finding was that edge effects were influenced by human disturbance within forest fragments, such as collection of firewood and livestock browsing. Most previous studies of edge effects have compared relatively well-preserved forest fragments with a highly disturbed surrounding matrix, ignoring the potential occurrence of human disturbance within forest fragments (Harper *et al.* 2005). Our results indicate that edge effects are more difficult to detect and are probably less ecologically important in forests subjected to such disturbance.

## 15.7    Seedling establishment

We conducted a series of experimental trials investigating the factors influencing tree establishment. A total of 33 experiments were established on 33 sites within six moist forest areas (Gonzalez-Espinosa *et al.* 2007). Most experiments focused on establishment of native tree species on former agricultural land, or floristic enrichment of impoverished secondary stands

(Alvarez-Aquino, Williams-Linera & Newton 2004). A range of factors were found to influence the growth and survival of established trees, including light availability, soil conditions and drainage, with results differing between species and sites. Most importantly, establishment of shade-tolerant tree species was often enhanced by presence of other plants, emphasising the importance of facilitation as an establishment mechanism.

An additional 20 experiments were established in the seven dry forest areas, again examining the ecological factors affecting the establishment and growth of native tree species (Newton & Tejedor 2011). In all of the study areas the main limiting factor for establishment was found to be drought. Restoration efforts in drylands have to confront a prolonged dry season, which affects seedling survival during early establishment. In some cases, supplemental irrigation was found to be effective in supporting tree establishment. Exclusion of herbivores was also often found to be essential for successful seedling establishment. Results from most field experiments suggested that despite the drought conditions in all study areas, natural regeneration can be obtained by protecting areas from herbivores, fire and selective cutting (Williams-Linera et al. 2011). In Oaxaca, restoration experiments showed a high dependence of the growth and survival of species on soil type; in addition, contrasting responses to soil type were demonstrated by different species. In common with the results from moist forest areas, facilitation was again often found to be important. For example, in a number of experiments the use of nurse species was found to be effective for protecting seedlings from desiccation, thus improving seedling survival and initial growth. In some areas (e.g. southern Argentina), tree establishment was found to be completely unsuccessful without such facilitation (Williams-Linera et al. 2011).

## 15.8    Modelling forest dynamics

Ecological models are particularly useful tools for forecasting the impacts of human disturbance on forest communities, enabling changes in forest structure and composition to be examined, potentially over very long time scales (Newton 2007a). Here, a variety of different modelling approaches were applied to different situations. The process-based forest model FORMIND was used to examine the potential impacts of different logging scenarios on tropical montane cloud forest (TMCF) in Veracruz, Mexico, and on temperate rain forest (TRF) in southern Chile. The TMCF was projected to regenerate rapidly after disturbance, supporting field observations, although the relatively slow-growing, shade-tolerant canopy tree species were not projected to achieve steady-state conditions until 300 years after a large-scale disturbance (Rüger et al. 2007a, 2008). In contrast, the dynamics of TRF were found to be slower, with some species reaching a steady state after approximately 1000 years following disturbance (Rüger *et al.* 2007a,b). In terms of impact on structure, the most notable effect of logging was the removal of large old trees from the forest, resulting in a simplified, more homogenous structure. The impacts of logging increased linearly with the amount of timber extracted.

In Chiapas, an individual tree-based gap model was parameterised using field data, and used to examine the process of forest recovery following different disturbance events, focusing on cutting of trees for timber and fuelwood (Golicher & Newton 2007). Results suggested that it may take several hundred years to re-establish a canopy dominated by shade-tolerant tree species. In forests subjected to recurrent disturbance, such tree species may become locally extinct. The relative dominance of different species under various disturbance regimes was also found to be related to their ability to resprout following cutting.

In four dry forest areas, the LANDIS-II model (Scheller *et al.* 2007) was used to explore forest dynamics under different disturbance regimes including fire, livestock browsing and tree cutting. LANDIS-II has the advantage of being spatially explicit, enabling the dynamics of forested landscapes to be explored. The model incorporated a range of ecological processes including succession, disturbance and seed dispersal (Scheller *et al.* 2007), and was parameterised using field data collected within each of the study areas. When applied to Mediterranean vegetation in Central Chile, model results indicated relatively little impact of disturbance on forest cover but substantial differences in forest structure, with relatively old-growth forest stands (>120 years old) being virtually eliminated from the landscape in scenarios with both browsing and cutting (Newton *et al.* 2011). Tree species richness tended to be lower in those scenarios without disturbance, providing evidence in support of the 'intermediate disturbance' hypothesis (Connell 1978). Interactive effects between different forms of disturbance were also recorded; for example, spread of the invasive exotic species *Acacia dealbata* was projected only to occur in the presence of fire when combined with browsing and/or cutting (Newton *et al.* 2011).

When LANDIS-II was applied to two dry forest areas in Mexico, modelling results indicated that dry forest can be relatively resilient to some forms of anthropogenic disturbance, primarily because of the high incidence of vegetative resprouting (Cantarello *et al.* 2011). Forest structure and composition differed markedly between the different disturbance scenarios. Projections indicated that over 400 years, under a regime of small, infrequent fires, the landscape becomes increasingly occupied by relatively shade-tolerant species, but only species with both relatively high shade tolerance and high fire tolerance can thrive under conditions with large, frequent fires. Interactive effects between livestock grazing and fire were also recorded. For example, in both study areas, grazing was found to reduce forest cover to a greater extent when combined with a frequent, high-intensity fire regime (Cantarello *et al.* 2011).

Together, these results highlight the importance of a small number of life-history traits in determining the impact of disturbance on the relative abundance of different tree species. This is consistent with the approach of Noble and Gitay (1996), who suggested a functional classification of species based on life-history attributes that can be used to predict the dynamics of plant communities subjected to recurrent disturbance. Key attributes include dispersal ability, resprouting ability, shade tolerance and the ability of individuals of different life cycle stages to survive the disturbance. These attributes are included as parameters in the LANDIS-II model employed here. Noble and Gitay (1996) also highlighted the possession of a long-lived pool of propagules that survive the disturbance (such as a seed bank); this is not explicitly included as a parameter in LANDIS-II, and its importance may therefore have been overlooked by our analyses. Despite this, our conclusions based both on modelling and field observations are broadly consistent with those of Noble and Gitay (1996), in that shade-tolerant species may be vulnerable to frequent disturbance, unless characterised by high dispersal ability. Conversely, shade-intolerant species may be vulnerable to infrequent disturbance, unless characterised by high dispersal or resprouting ability.

## 15.9   Some tentative generalisations

Based on the results obtained from this research, we propose the following generalisations regarding the impacts of human disturbance on forest biodiversity. It should be noted that these generalisations are highly tentative, but are offered to encourage further testing and refinement.

- In landscapes undergoing deforestation, forests will become increasingly fragmented. Relatively undisturbed, 'old-growth' forest will progressively disappear over time and become restricted to inaccessible areas (e.g. steep slopes).
- In landscapes where human disturbance is chronic and widespread, any negative effects of forest fragmentation on species richness are likely to be outweighed by the impacts of human disturbance occurring within forest patches. The process of forest fragmentation can interact positively with the incidence of human disturbance, as access to humans and their livestock is improved by fragmentation.
- Edge effects are common in fragmented forest landscapes and affect many ecological processes. However, such effects are more difficult to discern, and may be relatively less important, in forest fragments disturbed by human use.

- As a result of the combined effects of fragmentation, edge effects and disturbance within forest patches, remnant forest areas will become increasingly early successional in structure and composition.
- The impact of anthropogenic disturbance on the abundance of individual tree species can be predicted from knowledge of selected life-history traits, namely shade tolerance, dispersal ability, resprouting ability and disturbance tolerance (or the ability of different life cycle stages to survive the disturbance).
- Anthropogenic disturbance can maintain species with poor competitive ability in the landscape (consistent with the 'intermediate disturbance' hypothesis). However, disturbance can also lead to loss of tree species intolerant of disturbance, particularly shade-tolerant species with limited dispersal ability.
- Facilitation may be particularly important for enabling species to tolerate disturbance, particularly at forest edges.
- If land-use patterns permit localised forest recovery, successional mosaics can develop, which can be of high biodiversity value.

This final generalisation is best exemplified by areas that have been subjected to long traditions of human land-use, such as parts of highland Mexico. Here, traditional shifting agriculture has created vegetation that is spatially heterogeneous, consisting of mosaics of patches in different successional stages (Newton 2007b). Such landscapes indicate that maintenance of high species richness, and high biodiversity value, is not necessarily inconsistent with intensive patterns of human disturbance. This issue is explored further below, in relation to a specific example drawn from the United Kingdom.

## 15.10    Lessons from long-term disturbance: the case of the New Forest, UK

The New Forest is a National Park situated on the south coast of England, which was originally designated as a royal hunting reserve in 1079 (Tubbs 1968). Since that time, the New Forest has been continually subjected to intensive disturbance resulting from human activity. Uniquely, the area still maintains a traditional commoning system, which became formalised in late medieval times. This permits local people ('commoners') to use the Forest to support their livestock (cattle, ponies, pigs and donkeys). Although browsing and grazing by livestock is today the most significant form of disturbance, other traditional uses included collection of turf and peat for fuel, and harvesting of heathland plants (such as gorse, heather and bracken) for fodder, thatch and bedding. Burning of heathland was also carried out to provide fresh regrowth for livestock (Tubbs 2001).

**Table 15.3** *Importance of the New Forest for different groups of species. Based on information presented by Newton (2010). RDB, Red Data Book; NN, Nationally Notable.*

| Species group | No. species of conservation concern | Estimated total no. of species | Approx. percentage of total number of species in Britain |
|---|---|---|---|
| Birds | 37 | 302 | 17% |
| Mammals other than bats | 3 | 19 | 35% |
| Bats | 13 | 13 | 81% |
| Reptiles and amphibians | 12 | 12/13 | 92% |
| Fish | >2 | 22 | 88% |
| Invertebrates | 544 | 5000–10 000 | 17–33% |
| Dragonflies and damselflies | 9 | 31 | 69% |
| Saproxylic beetles | 53 | 326 | 55% |
| Butterflies and moths | 72 RDB, and 192 NN | 1488 (of which 33 are butterflies) | 66% |
| Other invertebrates | 403 including Coleoptera, Hymenoptera, Diptera, Orthoptera, Hemiptera, Crustacea | 1539 Coleoptera, 22 Orthoptera, 296 taxa of macro-invertebrate recorded from Forest streams | |
| Vascular plants | 72 RDB, 43 nationally rare or scarce | Approx. 540 | 36% |
| Lichens | 64 RDB, plus 78 other species of conservation interest | 421 | 18% |
| Fungi | 89 | 2600 | 22% |
| Bryophytes | 33 | 326 | 32% |

Today, the New Forest is of exceptional importance for biodiversity (Newton 2010). This is reflected in its many designations, with some 20 Sites of Special Scientific Interest, six Natura 2000 sites and two Ramsar Convention sites included at least partly within the National Park boundary (Chatters 2006). The Forest is described by Tubbs (2001) as the largest area of semi-natural vegetation in lowland Britain, and includes large tracts of heathland, valley mire and ancient pasture woodland, three habitats that are now fragmented and rare throughout lowland western Europe. The species richness of many groups is very high compared with the national situation. For example, more than two-thirds of the British species of reptiles and amphibians, butterflies and moths, fish, bats, dragonflies and damselflies are found in the area (Table 15.3). Even for those groups that are less well represented, at least one-sixth of all British species have been recorded. In every group considered, the New Forest is home to species of national conservation concern, and in some groups, the numbers of such species is very substantial: for example 115 vascular plant species, 264 butterflies and moths, and 142 lichens (Table 15.3).

The high biodiversity value of the New Forest can partly be attributed to its geographic location, with relatively mild winters and warm summers being conducive to relatively thermophilic species. The soils are generally nutrient-poor, and often poorly drained. However, the New Forest is not characterised by especially high endemicity (Newton 2010). Rather, the New Forest can perhaps best be viewed as a refuge for species that were formerly more widespread and abundant, but have declined elsewhere (Rand & Chatters 2010). This can largely be attributed to the maintenance of low-input pastoral patterns of land-use that have declined both in Britain and throughout much of mainland Europe. It is this pattern of land-use, relatively free from agricultural improvement and intensification, which accounts for the extensive areas of semi-natural habitats that characterise the New Forest today, on a scale that is now unique in lowland England. These characteristics can be attributed to the maintenance of traditional land-use practices over a period of centuries.

The vegetation of the New Forest is a complex mosaic of different habitats, including broadleaved woodland, heathland, acid grassland, scrub (or shrubland) and mire. Grazing (or browsing) pressure is the principal form of disturbance influencing vegetation composition and structure, although fire, wind, vegetation cutting and drainage are also influential. These forms of disturbance modify the transitions between vegetation types (Figure 15.7). In addition, the disturbance regime of the New Forest is highly dynamic over both time and space (Newton 2011). This is illustrated by the fluctuations in the numbers of grazing animals that have occurred over time. In the past, deer densities would have been much higher than currently; for example, around 8000 fallow and red deer were recorded in 1670 (Putman 1986). The number of fallow deer was reduced from around 6000 animals in 1800 to virtually zero, as a result of a major cull following 1851; since then, numbers have recovered to around 1700 today, a number that is regulated by culling. Numbers of ponies and cattle depastured on the Forest have also varied continuously; for example, the number of ponies has increased by more than threefold over the past 50 years. Over the past 200 years, there has been a general shift from deer to livestock, and from cattle to ponies (Newton 2010, 2011).

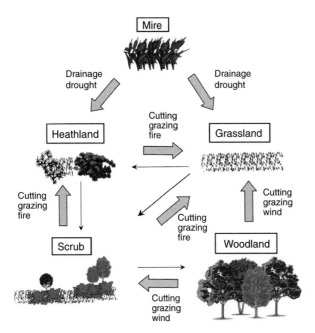

**Figure 15.7** Schematic diagram indicating the different ecosystem states and transitions in the New Forest, in relation to anthropogenic disturbance regime (after Newton 2011). Narrow arrows indicate successional changes, broad arrows indicate transitions induced by different forms of disturbance, which may be anthropogenic in origin. Some management interventions aimed at habitat restoration are not illustrated here; for example, mire communities can potentially be restored by reducing drainage, and heathland communities can be restored by removal of conifer plantations. See plate section for colour version.

The high biodiversity value of the New Forest can therefore be attributed to its high spatial heterogeneity, and to the intimate mosaic of different habitat types created by its distinctive disturbance regime. Many of the species that now characterise the area are clearly dependent on maintenance of this disturbance for their survival (Newton 2010). This case study therefore illustrates how an area subjected to intensive human disturbance can maintain high species richness over the long term. It also provides an insight into how biodiversity conservation can be achieved in forest landscapes subjected to human use. This is particularly dependent on the creation and maintenance of a successional mosaic through the localised recovery of vegetation following disturbance (Newton 2011). Some of the Latin American landscapes investigated here are also characterised by successional mosaics, such as the montane rain forests in southern Mexico.

A number of the generalisations listed above appear to apply to the New Forest. Although deforestation primarily occurred in antiquity, creating a fragmented forest landscape, the remaining native forest patches are largely restricted to relatively inaccessible areas such as slopes and poorly drained sites. The structure and composition of remaining forest fragments has been highly altered by human activity, and many are dominated by early successional species. The spatial dynamics of the vegetation are strongly dependent on the role of facilitation in protecting young trees from browsing, particularly at the edges of forest patches (Vera 2000). Many of the plant species that survive are characterised by poor competitive ability. However, some species have been lost over time. In particular, shade-tolerant species that are intolerant of browsing, such as lime (*Tilia cordata*), hazel (*Corylus avellana*) and elm (*Ulmus* spp.) have declined markedly, to local extinction in the case of the latter species.

## 15.11   Conclusions

The results of the research summarised here highlight the importance of local context, and the consequent difficulty of identifying generalisations. Each comparative analysis showed pronounced differences between study areas in terms of the factors responsible for forest loss and degradation, the factors influencing patterns of species richness and composition, the patterns of use of forest resources by local communities, and the patterns and rates of forest recovery. This highlights the difficulty of identifying generalisations in ecology, a problem that has been widely recognised (Cooper 1998), leading to doubts over whether applied ecology is ever likely to possess any general theories that can aid decision-making (Shrader-Frechette & McCoy 1994). However, although analysis of empirical patterns may not provide a firm basis for understanding, they can be effective in terms of supporting practical environmental management (Cooper 1998). As suggested by Shrader-Frechette and McCoy (1994), the solution for applied ecology may therefore reside in assembling empirical evidence through analysis of case studies, as presented here. The current research illustrates the advantage of investigating multiple case studies using common approaches, to help to identify generally applicable findings.

Despite the contrasting results obtained from different study areas, some tentative generalisations are presented here as a basis for future testing and refinement. In common with Noble and Gitay (1996), we propose that the impacts of anthropogenic disturbance on individual plant species can be understood with reference to a limited number of life-history attributes. This provides a basis for developing predictions of how forest structure, composition and species richness might vary in response to different anthropogenic disturbance regimes, as illustrated here through use of ecological models. There is clearly a need to test such predictions in order to evaluate this approach further. This highlights the need for increased monitoring of forest biodiversity, using statistically robust methods (Newton 2007a); such information is generally lacking for the study areas examined here. As a result, our current understanding of human impacts on forest biodiversity is characterised by a high degree of uncertainty.

The current research documented high rates of forest loss and fragmentation in a number of areas with high conservation value. According to empirical relationships such as species–area curves, the documented trends in forest cover are likely to be associated with declines in species richness, and potential loss of species. Although recent research has highlighted some potential limitations of species–area curves for estimating declines in species richness (Fangliang & Hubbell 2011), the potential conservation implications are profound (Newton *et al.* 2009). In addition to loss and fragmentation of forest, the results obtained have highlighted the intense, chronic disturbance resulting from human activities in remnant forest patches, and its impact on forest structure and composition. Action is urgently required in each of the study areas described here to strengthen forest conservation and restoration efforts, to address these causes of biodiversity loss.

The current results also demonstrate, however, that the impacts of human disturbance on biodiversity are not necessarily always negative. In particular, if localised forest recovery is permitted, successional mosaics can develop that can maintain high species richness over the long term, as illustrated here by the case of the New Forest. This is consistent with evidence indicating the positive contribution that secondary forests can make to biodiversity conservation (Dent & Wright 2009). It should be noted that successional landscapes are likely to differ markedly in terms of forest structure and composition from the situation prevailing prior to human intervention (Sodhi *et al.* 2009). One of the striking common features of the results described here was the progressive loss of 'old-growth' forest areas, and associated late successional tree species. These are now often very restricted, both in moist and dry forest study areas in Latin America. The introduction of human disturbance is therefore likely to result in loss of those species that are intolerant of such disturbance. In this way, disturbance can act as an extinction filter (Gardner *et al.* 2009). However, the species and communities that remain can be relatively resilient to human disturbance (Gardner *et al.* 2009; Newton 2011), such as the dry forest communities considered here, which were characterised by high incidence of vegetative resprouting. As noted by Lebrija-Trejos *et al.* (2008), the factors influencing forest resilience (or the speed of return to mature conditions after perturbation) also include the intensity of disturbance, the extent of degradation and the availability of propagules, which can be influenced by the degree of isolation of a forest patch.

Understanding the processes influencing forest resilience to human disturbance is clearly an urgent priority, if forest biodiversity is to be effectively conserved in an era of intensifying human impacts on forests (Chazdon *et al.* 2009). Given this, it is perhaps surprising that the development of disturbance theory has previously focused primarily on natural forms of disturbance (e.g. see Mori 2011; Uriarte *et al.* 2009). Anthropogenic disturbance has tended to be neglected by forest ecologists and conservation scientists (Fazey, Fischer & Lindenmayer 2005). There is a need for much greater research emphasis on human impacts on forest biodiversity, which should extend to other forest types of pre-eminent conservation importance. It is becoming increasingly clear that many lowland tropical rain forests have been significantly modified by human disturbance, even in areas as extensive as the Amazon (Peres *et al.* 2010), and these pressures are likely to intensify in future. Evidence from tropical rain forests has documented similar processes to those analysed here (Gardner *et al.* 2009, 2010), and as the types of human disturbance are common to many different forest types (Gardner *et al.* 2010; Newton 2007a), there is potential to develop a general synthesis or theory regarding their impacts on forest biodiversity.

As noted by Gardner *et al.* (2010), future research should examine disturbance impacts at the landscape scale, with respect to both the current composition of landscape mosaics and the legacy effects of past disturbances. As the impacts of forest loss, fragmentation and degradation may take many decades to emerge, there is an urgent need for improved monitoring data to quantify the impacts that are occurring, and to identify how these may best be addressed. Further information is also needed on the interactions between different causes of biodiversity loss and their impacts on ecosystem functioning and services, as well as their underlying socio-economic drivers (Sodhi *et al.* 2010). Such analyses could usefully inform the development and implementation of response strategies, including designation of protected areas and restoration of degraded forests (Birch *et al.* 2010; Newton *et al.* 2012). The widespread implementation of such approaches is paramount, if further major losses of forest biodiversity are to be averted.

## Acknowledgements

The research described here was undertaken by a large community of researchers drawn from a number of countries, including Mexico, Chile, Argentina, Germany, Italy, Spain and the UK. We gratefully acknowledge the dedicated research efforts made by this group over the past 16 years. We also thank the European Commission INCO Programme and the Darwin Initiative, UK, for financial support.

## References

Alvarez-Aquino, C., Williams-Linera, G. & Newton, A. C. (2004) Experimental native tree seedling establishment for the restoration of a Mexican cloud forest. *Restoration Ecology*, **12**, 412–418.

Aravena, J. C., Carmona, M. R., Perez, C. A. & Armesto, J. J. (2002) Changes in tree species richness, stand structure and soil properties in a successional chronosequence in northern Chiloe Island, Chile. *Revista Chilena de Historia Natural*, **75**, 339–360.

Baker, T. R., Jones, J. P. G., Rendón Thompson, O. R. *et al.* (2010) How can ecologists help realise the potential of payments for carbon in tropical forest countries? *Journal of Applied Ecology*, **47**, 1159–1165.

Birch, J., Newton, A. C., Alvarez Aquino, C. *et al.* (2010) Cost-effectiveness of dryland forest restoration evaluated by spatial analysis of ecosystem services. *Proceedings of the National Academy of Sciences USA*, **107**, 21925–21930.

Cantarello, E., Newton, A. C., Hill, R. A. *et al.* (2011) Simulating the potential for ecological restoration of dryland forests in Mexico under different disturbance regimes. *Ecological Modelling*, **222**, 1112–1128.

Cayuela, L., Golicher, D. J. & Rey-Benayas, J. M. (2006a) The extent, distribution and fragmentation of vanishing montane cloud forest in the Highlands of Chiapas, Mexico. *Biotropica*, **38**, 544–554.

Cayuela, L., Golicher, D. J., Rey-Benayas, J. M., González-Espinosa, M. & Ramírez-Marcial, N. (2006b) Fragmentation, disturbance and tree diversity conservation in tropical montane forests. *Journal of Applied Ecology*, **43**, 1172–1182.

Cayuela, L., Rey Benayas, J. M. & Echeverría, C. (2006c) Clearance and fragmentation of tropical montane forests in the Highlands of Chiapas, Mexico (1975–2000). *Forest Ecology and Management*, **226**, 208–218.

Cayuela, L., Rey Benayas, J. M., Justel, A. & Salas-Rey, J. (2006d) Modelling tree diversity in a highly fragmented tropical montane landscape. *Global Ecology and Biogeography*, **15**, 602–613.

Chatters, C. (2006) The New Forest – National Park status for a medieval survivor. *British Wildlife* (December), 110–119.

Chazdon, R. L., Harvey, C. A., Komar, O. *et al.* (2009) Beyond reserves: a research agenda for conserving biodiversity in human modified tropical landscapes. *Biotropica*, **41**, 142–153.

Clark, J. S. (1989) Ecological disturbance as a renewal process: theory and application to fire history. *Oikos*, **56**, 17–30.

Clark, J. S. (1991) Disturbance and tree life history on the shifting mosaic landscape. *Ecology*, **72**, 1102–1118.

Connell, J. H. (1978) Diversity in tropical rain forests and coral reefs. *Science*, **199**, 1302–1310.

Cooper, G. (1998) Generalizations in ecology: a philosophical taxonomy. *Biology and Philosophy*, **13**, 555–586.

Dent, D. H. & Wright, S. J. (2009) The future of tropical species in secondary forests: A quantitative review. *Biological Conservation*, **142**, 2833–2843.

Del Castillo, R. F. & Blanco-Macías, A. (2007) Secondary succession under a slash-and-burn regime in a tropical montane cloud forest: soil and vegetation characteristics. In *Biodiversity Loss and Conservation in Fragmented Forest Landscapes. The Forests of Montane Mexico and Temperate South America*. (ed. A. C. Newton), pp. 158–180. Wallingford: CABI.

Dinerstein, E., Olson, D., Graham, D. *et al.* (1995) *A Conservation Assessment of the Terrestrial Ecoregions of Latin America and the Caribbean*. Washington, DC: World Bank and WWF.

Echeverría, C., Cayuela, L., Manson, R. H. *et al.* (2007a) Spatial and temporal patterns of forest loss and fragmentation in Mexico and Chile. In *Biodiversity Loss and Conservation in Fragmented Forest Landscapes. The Forests of Montane Mexico and Temperate South America*. (ed. A. C. Newton), pp. 14–42. Wallingford: CABI.

Echeverría, C., Coomes, D., Hall, M. & Newton, A. C. (2008) Spatially explicit models to analyze forest loss and fragmentation between 1976 and 2020 in southern Chile. *Ecological Modelling*, **212**, 439–449.

Echeverría, C., Coomes, D., Salas, J. *et al.* (2006) Rapid fragmentation and deforestation of Chilean temperate forests. *Biological Conservation*, **130**, 481–494.

Echeverría, C., Kitzberger, T., Rivera, R. *et al.* (2011) Assessing fragmentation and degradation of dryland forest ecosystems. In *Principles and Practice of Forest Landscape Restoration: Case Studies from the Drylands of Latin America* (eds. A. C. Newton & N. Tejedor), pp. 65–101. Gland, Switzerland: IUCN.

Echeverría, C., Newton, A. C., Lara, A., Rey-Benayas, J. M. & Coomes, D. (2007b) Impacts of forest fragmentation on species composition and forest structure in the temperate landscape of southern Chile. *Global Ecology and Biogeography*, **16**, 426–439.

Echeverría, C., Newton, A., Nahuelhual, L., Coomes, D. & Rey-Benayas, J-M. (2012). How landscapes change: Integration of spatial patterns and human processes in temperate landscapes of southern Chile. *Applied Geography*, **32**, 822–831.

Fangliang, H. & Hubbell, S. P. (2011) Species–area relationships always overestimate extinction rates from habitat loss. *Nature*, **473**, 368–371.

FAO (2010) *Global Forest Resources Assessment.* Rome: FAO.

Fazey, I., Fischer, J. & Lindenmayer, D. B. (2005) What do conservation biologists publish? *Biological Conservation*, **124**, 63–73.

Galindo-Jaimes, L., González-Espinosa, M., Quintana-Ascencio, P. & García-Barrios, L. (2002) Tree composition and structure in disturbed stands with varying dominance by *Pinus* spp. in the highlands of Chiapas, México. *Plant Ecology*, **162**, 259–272.

Gardner, T. A., Barlow, J., Chazdon, R. *et al.* (2009) Prospects for tropical forest biodiversity in a human-modified world. *Ecology Letters*, **12**, 561–582.

Gardner, T. A., Barlow, J., Sodhi, N. S. & Peres, C. A. (2010) A multi-region assessment of tropical forest biodiversity in a human-modified world. *Biological Conservation*, **143**, 2293–2300.

Gibbs, H. K., Brown, S., Niles, J. O. & Foley, J. A. (2007) Monitoring and estimating tropical forest carbon stocks: making REDD a reality. *Environment Research Letters*, **2**, 045023.

Golicher, D. & Newton, A. C. (2007) Applying succession models to the conservation of tropical montane forest. In *Biodiversity Loss and Conservation in Fragmented Forest Landscapes. The Forests of Montane Mexico and Temperate South America.* (ed. A. C. Newton), pp. 200–222. Wallingford: CABI.

González-Espinosa, M., Ramírez-Marcial, N., Newton, A. C. *et al.* (2007) Restoration of forest ecosystems in fragmented landscapes

of temperate and montane tropical Latin America. In *Biodiversity Loss and Conservation in Fragmented Forest Landscapes. The Forests of Montane Mexico and Temperate South America.* (ed. A. C. Newton), pp. 335–369. Wallingford: CABI.

Grainger, A. (2008) Difficulties in tracking the long-term global trend in tropical forest area. *Proceedings of the National Academy of Sciences USA*, **105**, 818–823.

Guzmán-Guzmán, J. & Williams-Linera, G. (2006) Edge effect on acorn removal and oak seedling survival in Mexican lower montane forest fragments. *New Forests*, **31**, 487–495.

Hansen, M. C., Stehman, S. V. & Potapov, P. V. (2010) Quantification of global forest cover loss. *Proceedings of the National Academy of Sciences USA*, **107**, 8650–8655.

Hanski, I. (2004) Metapopulation theory, its use and misuse. *Basic and Applied Ecology*, **5**, 225–229.

Harper, K. A., MacDonald, E. S., Burton, P. J. *et al.* (2005) Edge influence on forest structure and composition in fragmented landscapes. *Conservation Biology*, **19**, 768–782.

Ives, A. R. (2007) Diversity and stability in ecological communities. In *Theoretical Ecology. Principles and Applications* (eds. R. M. May & A. R. McLean), pp. 98–110. Oxford: Oxford University Press.

Keddy, P. (1992) Thoughts on a review of a Critique for Ecology. *Bulletin of the Ecological Society of America*, **73**, 234–236.

Lebrija-Trejos, E., Bongers, F., Pérez-García, E. A. & Meave, J. A. (2008) Successional change and resilience of a very dry tropical deciduous forest following shifting agriculture. *Biotropica*, **40**, 422–431.

Lindenmayer, D. B. & Fischer, J. (2006) *Habitat Fragmentation and Landscape Change. An Ecological and Conservation Synthesis.* Washington: Island Press.

López-Barrera, F., Armesto, J. J., Williams-Linera, G., Smith-Ramírez, C. & Manson, R. H. (2007a) Fragmentation and edge effects on plant-animal interactions, ecological processes and biodiversity. In *Biodiversity Loss and Conservation in Fragmented Forest Landscapes. The Forests of Montane Mexico and Temperate South America*. (ed. A. C. Newton), pp. 69–101. Wallingford: CABI.

López-Barrera, F., Manson, R., González-Espinosa, M. & Newton, A. C. (2006) Effects of the type of montane forest edge on oak seedling establishment along forest-edge-exterior gradients. *Forest Ecology and Management*, **225**, 234–244.

López-Barrera, F., Manson, R., González-Espinosa, M. & Newton, A. C. (2007b) Effects of varying forest edge permeability on seed dispersal in a neotropical montane forest. *Landscape Ecology*, **22**, 189–203.

López-Barrera, F. & Newton, A. C. (2005) Edge type effect on germination of oak tree species in the Highlands of Chiapas, Mexico. *Forest Ecology and Management*, **217**, 67–79.

López-Barrera, F., Newton, A. C. & Manson, R. (2005) Edge effects in a tropical montane forest mosaic: experimental tests of post-dispersal acorn removal. *Ecological Research*, **20**, 31–40.

McGarigal, K., Cushman, S. A., Neel, M. C. & Ene, E. (2002) *FRAGSTATS: spatial pattern analysis program for categorical maps*. Retrieved January 20, 2009. Landscape Ecology Program web site: http://www.unmass.edu/landeco/research/fragstats/fragstat.html

McLean, A. R. & May, R. M. (2007) Introduction. In *Theoretical Ecology. Principles and Applications* (eds. R. M. May & A. R. McLean), pp. 1–6. Oxford: Oxford University Press.

Mori, A. S. (2011) Ecosystem management based on natural disturbances: hierarchical context and non-equilibrium paradigm. *Journal of Applied Ecology*, **48**, 280–292.

Myers, N., Mittermeier, R. A., Mittermeier, C. G., da Fonseca, G. A. B. & Kent, J. (2000) Biodiversity hotspots for conservation priorities. *Nature*, **403**, 853–858.

Newton, A. C. (2007a) *Forest Ecology and Conservation. A Handbook of Techniques*. Oxford: Oxford University Press.

Newton, A. C. (ed.) (2007b) *Biodiversity Loss and Conservation in Fragmented Forest Landscapes. The Forests of Montane Mexico and Temperate South America*. Wallingford: CABI.

Newton, A. C. (ed.) (2010) *Biodiversity in the New Forest*. Newbury: Pisces Publications.

Newton, A. C. (2011) Social-ecological resilience and biodiversity conservation in a 900-year-old protected area. *Ecology and Society*, **16**, 13. http://dx.doi.org/10.5751/ES-04308-160413

Newton, A. C., Cayuela, L., Echeverría, C. *et al.* (2009) Toward integrated analysis of human impacts on forest biodiversity: lessons from Latin America. *Ecology and Society*, **14**, 2. http://www.ecologyandsociety.org/vol14/iss2/art2/

Newton, A. C., del Castillo, R. F., Echeverría, C. *et al.* (2012) Forest landscape restoration in the drylands of Latin America. *Ecology and Society*, **17**, 21. http://www.ecologyandsociety.org/vol17/iss1/art21/

Newton, A. C., Echeverria, C., Cantarello, E. & Bolados, G. (2011) Impacts of human disturbances on the dynamics of a dryland forest landscape. *Biological Conservation*, **144**, 1949–1960.

Newton, A. C., Echeverría, C., González-Espinosa, M. *et al.* (2007) Testing forest biodiversity indicators by assessing anthropogenic impacts along disturbance gradients. In *Biodiversity Loss and Conservation in Fragmented Forest Landscapes. The Forests of Montane Mexico and Temperate South America* (ed. A. C. Newton), pp. 276–290. Wallingford: CABI.

Newton, A. C. & Tejedor, N. (eds.) (2011) *Principles and Practice of Forest Landscape Restoration: Case Studies from the Drylands of Latin America*. Gland, Switzerland: IUCN.

Noble, I. R. & Gitay, H. (1996) A functional classification for predicting the dynamics of landscapes. *Journal of Vegetation Science*, **7**, 329–336.

Olson, D. M., Dinerstein, E., Wikramanayake, E. D. *et al.* (2001) Terrestrial ecoregions of the world: A new map of life on Earth. *BioScience*, **51**, 933–938.

Pace, M. L. (2001) Prediction and the aquatic sciences. *Canadian Journal of Fisheries and Aquatic Sciences*, **58**, 63–72.

Peres, C. A., Gardner, T. A., Barlow, J. et al. (2010) Biodiversity conservation in human-modified Amazonian forest landscapes. *Biological Conservation*, **143**, 2314–2327.

Peters, R. H. (1991) *A Critique for Ecology*. Cambridge: Cambridge University Press.

Pickett, S. T. A., Kolasa, J. & Jones, C. G. (2007) *Ecological Understanding. The Nature of Theory and the Theory of Nature* 2nd edition. Burlington, MA: Academic Press.

Pickett, S. T. A. & White, P. S. (eds.) (1985) *The Ecology of Natural Disturbance and Patch Dynamics*. New York: Academic Press.

Putman, R. J. (1986) *Grazing in Temperate Ecosystems. Large Herbivores and the Ecology of the New Forest*. London and Sydney: Croom Helm.

Ramírez-Marcial, N., González-Espinosa, M. & Williams-Linera, G. (2001) Anthropogenic disturbance and tree diversity in Montane Rain Forests in Chiapas, Mexico. *Forest Ecology and Management*, **154**, 311–326.

Rand, M. & Chatters, C. (2010) Vascular plants. In *Biodiversity in the New Forest* (ed. A. C. Newton), pp. 84–111, Newbury: Pisces Publications.

Ries, L., Fletcher, R. J., Battin, J. & Sisk, T. D. (2004) Ecological responses to habitat edges: mechanisms, models, and variability explained. *Annual Review of Ecology, Evolution and Systematics*, **35**, 491–522.

Rigler, F. H. (1982) Recognition of the possible: an advantage of empiricism in ecology. *Canadian Journal of Fisheries and Aquatic Sciences*, **39**, 1323–1331.

Rocha-Loredo, A. G., Ramírez-Marcial, N. & González-Espinosa, M. (2010) Riqueza y diversidad de árboles del bosque estacional caducifolio en la Depresión Central de Chiapas. *Boletín de la Sociedad Botánica de México*, **87**, 89–103.

Rüger, N., Armesto, J. J., Gutiérrez, A. G., Williams-Linera, G. & Huth, A. (2007a) Process-based modelling of regeneration dynamics and sustainable use in species-rich rainforests. In *Biodiversity Loss and Conservation in Fragmented Forest Landscapes. The Forests of Montane Mexico and Temperate South America* (ed. A. C. Newton), pp. 244–275. Wallingford: CABI.

Rüger, N., Guitierrez, A. G., Kissling, W. D., Armesto, J. J. & Huth, A. (2007b) Ecological impacts of harvesting options for temperate evergreen rain forest in southern Chile – a simulation experiment. *Forest Ecology and Management*, **252**, 52–66.

Rüger, N., Williams-Linera, G., Kissling, W. D. & Huth, A. (2008) Long-term impacts of fuelwood extraction on a Mexican cloud forest. *Ecosystems*, **11**, 868–881.

Sasaki, N. & Putz, F. E. (2009) Critical need for new definitions of "forest" and "forest degradation" in global climate change agreements. *Conservation Letters*, **2**, 226–232.

Scheller, R. M., Domingo, J. B., Sturtevant, B. R. et al. (2007) Design, development, and application of LANDIS-II, a spatial landscape simulation model with flexible temporal and spatial resolution. *Ecological Modelling*, **201**, 409–419.

Schulz, J., Cayuela, L., Echeverria, C., Salas, J. & Rey Benayas, J. M. (2010) Land cover dynamics of the dryland forest landscape of Central Chile. *Applied Geography*, **30**, 436–447.

Shrader-Frechette, K. & McCoy, E. D. (1994) Applied ecology and the logic of case studies. *Philosophy of Science*, **61**, 228–249.

Smith-Ramírez, C., Williams-Linera, G., del Castillo, R. F. et al. (2011) Fragmentation and altitudinal effects on tree diversity in seasonally dry forests of Mexico and Chile. In *Principles and Practice of Forest Landscape Restoration: Case Studies from the Drylands of Latin America*. (eds. A. C. Newton & N. Tejedor), pp. 103–130. Gland, Switzerland: IUCN.

Sodhi, N. S., Koh, L. P., Clements, R. et al. (2010) Conserving Southeast Asian forest biodiversity in human-modified landscapes. *Biological Conservation*, **143**, 2375–2384.

Sodhi, N. S., Lee, T. M., Koh, L. P. & Brook, B. W. (2009) A meta-analysis of the impact of anthropogenic forest disturbance on Southeast Asia's biotas. *Biotropica*, **41**, 103–109.

Spilsbury, R. (2010) *Deforestation Crisis (Can the Earth Survive?)* New York: Rosen Publishing Group.

Tubbs, C. R. (1968) *The New Forest: An Ecological History*. Newton Abbot: David and Charles.

Tubbs, C. R. (2001) *The New Forest. History, Ecology and Conservation*. Lyndhurst: New Forest Ninth Centenary Trust.

UNEP (2007) *GEO4 Global Environment Outlook: Environment for Development*. Nairobi: UNEP.

Uriarte, M., Canham, C. D., Thompson, J. *et al.* (2009) Natural disturbance and human land use as determinants of tropical forest dynamics: results from a forest simulator. *Ecological Monographs*, **79**, 423–443.

Vera, F. W. M. (2000) *Grazing Ecology and Forest History*. Wallingford: CABI.

Williams-Linera, G. (2002) Tree species richness complementarity, disturbance and fragmentation in a Mexican tropical montane cloud forest. *Biodiversity and Conservation*, **11**, 1825–1843.

Williams-Linera, G. & Lorea, F. (2009) Tree species diversity driven by environmental and anthropogenic factors in tropical dry forest fragments of central Veracruz, Mexico. *Biodiversity and Conservation*, **18**, 3269–3293.

Williams-Linera, G., Alvarez-Aquino, C., Hernández-Ascención, E. & Toledo, M. (2011) Early successional sites and the recovery of vegetation structure and tree species of the tropical dry forest in Veracruz, Mexico. *New Forests*, **42**, 131–148.

# Index

*Abies* spp., 110, 312
abiotic stress
  asymmetric responses of species, 55–56
ABRACOS project, 27
acclimation of biological processes, 35–36
*Acer* spp., 255, 272
  effects of active fire suppression on, 115
*Acer platanoides* (Norway maple), 119
*Acer rubrum* (red maple), 116, 324, 325
*Acer saccharum* (sugar maple), 115, 119, 312,
    314, 320, 321, 331
acid rain, 119
*Adelges tsugae* (hemlock woolly adelgid), 118
aerial photography
  mapping vegetation, 344
aerodynamic roughness of vegetation, 25–26
aerosols emitted by forests, 39–40, 77
*African Tropical Rainforests Observation*
    *Network. See* AfriTRON
AfriTRON, xiii, 79
  dynamic changes, 88–91
  functional changes, 91–93
  observed increase in biomass, 82–88
  species composition changes, 91–93
  structural change, 82–88
  study methodology, 79–82
agent-based forest succession models,
    365–373
agriculture
  conversion of forests to, 21
  methane production, 39
  nitrous oxide ($N_2O$) emissions, 37, 39
  source of ammonium ($NH_4^+$), 309
  source of greenhouse gases, 39
*Agrilus planipennis* (emerald ash borer), 117,
    118
*Ailanthus altissima* (tree of heaven), 119
air pollution, 109
  effects on temperate forests of NE United
    States, 119–121
albedo of the land surface, 27
  effect of snow cover on different vegetation
    types, 22–23
  factors affecting, 22–23
  influence on energy balance, 22–23
  regional effects of deforestation, 30–31

*Alliaria petiolata* (garlic mustard), 118–119
aluminium (Al)
  concentrations in soil, 309
Amazon Basin
  mass balance of water, 30
  modelling, 32
Amazon dieback scenario, 13, 35, 131–132,
    144, 239
  support from DGVMs (dynamic global
    vegetation models), 132–133
Amazonia
  critical transition from forest to savanna,
    131–132
  drought impacts (2005), 93–95
Amazonian forests
  carbon sinks to carbon sources, 97–98
  drought tolerance of trees, 144–145
  evolution of, 133–136
  historical responses to climatic events,
    133–137
  history of resilience and stability, 133–137
  moisture stress effects, 98–99
  photosynthesis/respiration changes,
    99–100
  potential for adaptation to climate change,
    136–137
  potential future sensitivity to changes,
    97–101
  predicting the future of, 136–137
  range of modelling projections, 144
  resilience concept, 136–137
  species compositional changes,
    100–101
American beech (*Fagus grandifolia*), 118
American chestnut (*Castanea dentata*), 118
American elm (*Ulmus americana*), 118
ammonium ($NH_4^+$)
  from agricultural activity, 309
*Anacardium excelsum*, 214
Angiosperm Phylogeny Group III
    classification, 244
animals
  modelling plant-animal interactions,
    61–62
  plant-animal interactions, 60
  seed dispersal by, 60

*Anoplophora glabripennis* (Asian long-horned beetle), 118
Anthropocene, 77
anthropogenic disturbance in forests
    difficulty of identifying generalisations about impacts, 439
    edge effects, 430–431
    effects on seedling establishment, 431–432
    effects on species richness, 427–430
    factors influencing forest resilience, 440
    forest fragmentation dynamics, 426–427
    future research, 441
    importance of local context, 439
    long-term disturbance effects, 435–439
    modelling forest dynamics, 432–434
    New Forest, UK, case study, 435–439
    objectives of analysis, 419
    patterns of forest loss, 422–424
    positive effects, 440
    potential to develop a theory of impacts, 440–441
    rates of global forest loss, 417
    species–area curves, 439–440
    study areas, 419–422
    successional mosaics, 440
    tentative generalisations, 434–435
anthropogenic flux of $CO_2$, 30
anthropogenic impacts
    characterising, 110
    distinguishing climate change response, 121–124
    effects on the atmosphere–biosphere system, 77
    effects on resilience of ecosystems, 35–36
    on current and future temperate forests, 114–121
    range of, 109–110
    time scales of, 109–110
    uncertainty of effects, 13–14
arbuscular mycorrhizae, 316
ash. See *Fraxinus* spp.
Asia
    CTFS network, 79
Asian long-horned beetle (*Anoplophora glabripennis*), 118
associational resistance hypothesis, 210
associational susceptibility hypothesis, 210
atmosphere
    interactions with the land surface, 21
atmospheric global circulation models. *See* global circulation models (GCMs)
atmospheric pollution deposition
    effects of vegetation roughness, 26
*Avicennia marina*, 214

Barro Colorado Island, Panama, 101, 284, 289–292, 329, 349, 383
base cations in the soil, 119
    as limiting factor in tree performance, 330
    covariance with each other, 316
    covariance with N and P, 316

depletion through biomass harvesting, 311–312
    expected rates of change, 120
    importance for tree growth, 325–329
    loss through acidification and leaching, 309
    losses caused by soil weathering, 309–311
*Bauhinia rufa*, 139
beech, European (*Fagus sylvatica*), 48, 50, 119, 206
beech bark disease, 118
*Betula* spp., 255, 272
biodiversity
    assessment using trait-based remote sensing, 349–352
    evidence from Carnegie Airborne Observatory imagery, 349–352
    evolution of canopy chemical traits, 352–354
    factors influencing forest resilience, 440
    historical perspective, 196–200
    importance of tropical forests, 77–78
    influence of water availability, 294–297
    insurance value, 136
    link with spectral diversity, 349–352
    New Forest, UK, 435–439
    positive effects of anthropogenic disturbance, 440
    representation in models, 132–133
    taking account in models, 13
    unified neutral theory of biodiversity and biogeography, 201
    variety of plant responses to drought, 13
biodiversity and ecosystem functioning (BEF)
    analysis of forest inventory information, 216–220
    associational resistance hypothesis, 210
    associational susceptibility hypothesis, 210
    biodiversity gradients in natural forests, 216–224
    carbon sequestration function, 204–205
    comparative studies of natural forests, 221–224
    definition of biodiversity, 200
    diversity–productivity relationship, 202
    ecological insurance, 195–196
    ecosystem-scale diversity, 201
    forest biodiversity experiments, 209–216
    functional differences between tree species, 226
    functional diversity, 200–201
    future research directions, 227–228
    genetic diversity within tree species, 200
    landscape-scale diversity, 201
    modelling approaches, 224–225
    multidisciplinarity and multifunctionality approaches, 225–226
    niche complementarity, 195–196, 206
    observational studies comparing natural forests, 216–224
    plantation forestry studies, 205–209
    range of effects of changing tree diversity, 226–227
    review of studies, 200–205

role of N-fixing species, 205–206
sampling effect, 195–196
scientific study approaches, 205–226
silvicultural experiments on mixing trees,
205–209
species identity effects, 203–204, 226
species interactions, 227
studies on mixed forestry versus
monoculture, 200–205
synthetic community approach, 215–216
tree diversity effects, 201–205
biodiversity loss
effects on ecosystem functioning, 195–196
future research, 441
identifying impacts, 196
potential for a theory of anthropogenic
impacts, 440–441
species–area curves, 439–440
biodiversity mapping
monitoring effects of global change, 354
biofuel crops, 21
nitrous oxide ($N_2O$) emissions, 38–38
oil palm plantations, 36–37
biogeochemical cycles, 1
biogeography
unified neutral theory of biodiversity and
biogeography, 201
bioinformatics tools, xv
biomass
observed increase in tropical forests, 82–88
*See also* forest biomass
biotic interactions
Mediterranean Basin, 55–62
BIOTREE study, 215
black oak (*Quercus velutina*), 312, 320
Bray-Curtis distances, 244, 251
butterflies, 50

C3 photosynthetic pathway, 136
C4 grasses, 253
C4 photosynthesis evolution, 133
Caatinga Phytogeographic Domain, 240
caatinga vegetation, 240–242
Cactaceae, 240, 249
calcium (Ca)
concentration in soils, 119
covariance with other soil resources, 316
importance for tree growth, 325–329
losses caused by soil acidification, 309
losses caused by soil weathering, 309–311
California
fire regime, 54
*Calluna vulgaris*, 48
canopy
factors affecting albedo, 22–23
canopy biomass and productivity
traits related to, 113
canopy chemical traits
ecological causes, 352–354
evidence for evolution, 346–349
evolution of, 352–354
for light capture and growth, 345–346

for longevity and defence, 345–346
for maintenance and metabolism, 345–346
functional categories, 345–346
intraspecific variation, 347
link between spectral and biological
diversity, 349–352
mapping effects of global change, 354
mapping functional and compositional
change, 354
multi-trait correlation, 347–348
potential for chemical remote sensing,
345–346
taxonomic organisation, 348–349
use in biodiversity assessment, 352–354
canopy interactions
ecophysiological approaches, xiv–xv
canopy species distribution
trait-based remote sensing, 345
carbon cycle
implications of forest biomass change,
382–383
role of tropical forests, 77–78
terrestrial biosphere sink, 78
carbon dioxide ($CO_2$)
anthropogenic flux to the atmosphere, 30
fertilisation effect, 119–120
flux data, 34
sequestration from the atmosphere, 311
carbon dioxide ($CO_2$) concentration of the air
effects of deforestation, 30
carbon dioxide ($CO_2$) increase
influence on tropical forest biomass, 95–97
carbon emissions
due to land-use change, 131
reduction of, 359
carbon isotopic discrimination in leaves, 146
carbon sequestration, 1, 33–37, 311
influence of biodiversity, 204–205
carbon sinks
forests as, 33–35
influence of soil conditions, 311
tropical forests as, 97–98, 131
carbon sources
potential for tropical forests to become,
97–98
carbon stocks
effects of fast-growing tropical
plantations, 36
effects of oil palm plantations, 36–37
forest management to maintain, 36
in forests, 33–35
tropical forests, 77
carbon storage, 311
influence of forest biomass size, 381
carbon uptake rate
relationship to carbon loss rate, 99–100
Carnegie Airborne Observatory, 345
evidence for biodiversity, 349–352
*Carya* spp., 110
*Castanea dentata* (American chestnut), 118
*Cecropia* spp., 135
Center for Tropical Forest Science, xiii

*Ceratocystis ulmi. See* Dutch elm disease
*Cereus* spp., 249
*Cereus kroenleinii*, 249
Cerrado Phytogeographic Domain, 240
cerrado vegetation, 240–242
chaco vegetation, 240
chemical plant traits
    ecological causes, 352–354
    evolution of, 352–354
chemical remote sensing
    canopy chemical traits, 345–346
chemical signatures of taxa, 348–349
chestnut blight (*Endothia parasitica*), 118
*Choristoneura fumiferana* (spruce budworm),
    183
clearcutting, 116
climate gradients
    influence on species distribution and
        demography, 111
climate system
    impacts of deforestation, 21
    interactions with the land surface, 21
cloud condensation nuclei, 39, 40
cloud formation, 30, 31
coexistence of multiple species, 161–166
    challenge of explaining, 161
    forest ecology models, 163–166
    implications of Lotka-Volterra
        competition, 169–170
    influence of water availability, 294–297
    landscape-scale mechanisms, 187–190
    Lotka-Volterra competition response to
        environmental change, 169–170
    nature of potential mechanisms, 190
    negative feedback mechanisms,
        161–163
    perfect plasticity approximation (PPA)
        model, 171–174, 177–184
    predicting effects of environmental
        change, 190–191
    research studies, 164–166
    species-specific temporal variation,
        184–185
    stable coexistence, 169
    stand-scale mechanisms, 185–187
    temporal storage effect, 184–185
    TSR scheme in the Lotka-Volterra
        competition equations, 167–169
colonisation
    competition–colonisation trade-offs, 162
    impact of habitat fragmentation, 49–51
*Colutea hispanica*, 56
community phylogenetic analysis, xv,
    242–243, 249–251
community states. *See* state variables
competition–colonisation trade-offs, 162
competitive interactions
    differences across soil resource gradients,
        324–325
computer simulations, 365
conduction
    role in energy balance, 24

convection
    equation for, 24
    factors affecting heat transfer, 24
    role in energy balance, 24–25
convective boundary layer, 30
coppiced forests, 65
*Cordia* spp., 139
cork oak (*Quercus suber*), 47, 56
*Corylus avellana* (hazel), 439
Cotta, Heinrich, 198
Cretaceous, 133
CTFS network, 79
cuticular conductance for water
    influence on drought performance, 276

*Daphnia* spp., 162–163
Darwin, Charles, 198
data assimilation techniques, 362
data cleaning procedures, 389
    introduction of systematic errors,
        393–397
decadal-scale inventory data, xiv
deciduous and semideciduous site
    classification, 253–255
deciduousness
    influence on drought performance, 277
deforestation, 77
    carbon emissions related to, 131
    causes, 21
    difficulty of identifying generalisations
        about impacts, 439
    edge effects in forest fragments, 430–431
    effects on seedling establishment, 431–432
    effects on species richness, 427–430
    factors influencing forest resilience, 440
    forest fragmentation dynamics, 426–427
    future research on impacts, 441
    impacts on energy balance, 21
    impacts on the climate system, 21
    interaction with drought and fire, 36
    modelling forest dynamics, 432–434
    modelling large-scale effects, 30–33
    New Forest, UK, 435–439
    patterns of forest loss, 422–424
    potential to develop a theory of impacts,
        440–441
    rates of global forest loss, 21, 417
    species–area curves, 439–440
    tentative generalisations on anthropogenic
        disturbances, 434–435
demographic stochasticity
    representation in models, 132
denitrification process, 37
density-dependent seedling mortality, 163
*Didymopanax vinosum*, 139
disequilibrium in forest ecosystems, 109–110
disturbance theory, 418, 440
disturbances
    successional dynamics following, 113–114
drought
    desiccation avoidance mechanisms,
        273–279

desiccation tolerance mechanisms,
  273–279
ecosystem ability to withstand, 138
effects of local variation in soil moisture,
  289–292
effects on regeneration dynamics,
  262–263
experiments on seedling responses to, 264
impacts in Amazonia (2005), 93–95
interaction with fire and deforestation, 36
interannual variation in water availability,
  285–287
interspecific variation in seedling
  performance, 273
leaf tolerance to drought, 139–141
plant scale responses, 138
regional variation in rainfall, 292–293
seasonal variation in water availability,
  280–285
spatial variation in water availability,
  287–289
species variations in response to, 294–297
temporal variation in water availability,
  279–280
variety of plant responses to, 13
xylem failure caused by, 141–143
drought performance
  definition, 265
drought resistance
  definition, 265
  influence on regeneration dynamics, 297
  modelling, 146–147
drought stress research, 47
drought tolerance
  evolution of, 47
  in Amazon forest trees, 144–145
dry-adapted vegetation
  evolutionary significance, 239
  See also seasonally dry tropical forests and
  woodlands (SDTFs)
Dutch elm disease (Ophiostoma ulmi /
  Ceratocystis ulmi), 56, 118
dynamic changes
  tropical forests, 88–91
dynamic global vegetation models (DGVMs)
  accounting for whole-plant physiology,
  141–144
  development of, 369
  future developments, 145–147
  leaf functional traits, 137–138
  limitations, 132–133
  plant functional types (PFTs), 145–147
  support for the Amazon dieback scenario,
  132–133
dynamic models
  long-term forest dynamics, 361–363

Early Miocene, 133
Early Paleocene, 133
eastern hemlock (Tsuga canadensis), 110–111,
  116, 118
ecological insurance, 195–196

ecological science
  development of theory, 417–418
Ecological Society of America, 365
ecological strategies
  trade-off between, 137, 143
  whole-plant traits associated with, 143
ecological theory
  difficulty of identifying generalisations,
  439
  identification of generalisations, 418–419
  potential to develop a theory of
  anthropogenic impacts, 440–441
  tentative generalisations on anthropogenic
  disturbances, 434–435
ecophysiological approaches, xiv–xv
Ecosystem Demography model (ED model),
  132
ecosystem resilience, 35–36
ecosystem-scale diversity, 201
ecosystem services
  constraint by soil resources, 311
  effects of biodiversity loss, 195–196
ectomycorrhizae, 204, 316
  response to N deposition, 120
edge effects, 31, 430–431
El Niño events, 261–262, 279–280, 285–287
  drought in 1998, 98
El Niño Southern Oscillation, 131
elm. See Ulmus spp.
emerald ash borer (Agrilus planipennis), 117,
  118
emissivity (ε), 23
empirical models of forest responses,
  111–113
endomycorrhizae, 120
Endothia parasitica (chestnut blight), 118
energy balance, 22–29
  conduction, 24
  convection, 24–25
  differences between forests and grassland/
  crops, 40
  dry tropics, 29
  effects of forest-to-pasture conversion, 40
  evaporation, 24–25
  forest-to-pasture comparison, 26–29
  impacts of deforestation, 21
  influence of albedo, 22–23
  net radiation measurement, 23–24
  partitioning of absorbed energy, 24–25
  photosynthesis, 24
  role of photosynthesis, 24
  solar (short-wave) radiation, 23
  thermal (long-wave) radiation flux, 23–24
  tropical forest and tropical pasture
  comparison, 26–29
Ericales, 133
ethical issues
  tropical plantations, 36–37
EU Habitats Directive, 199
Eucalyptus grandis, 350
Eucalyptus spp., 205, 329
Euphorbiaceae, 143

evaporation
  from wet surfaces, 24
  Penman–Monteith equation, 25
  role in energy balance, 24–25
  through stomatal pores, 24, 25
evapotranspiration, 27, 30
  effects of deforestation, 30–31
evolution of C4 photosynthesis, 133
evolution of canopy chemical traits, 346–349
exotic plant species
  introduction into temperate forests of NE
    United States, 118–119
extreme climatic events
  recovery from, 50
extreme weather events, 261–262

*Fagus grandifolia* (American beech), 118
*Fagus* spp., 119
*Fagus sylvatica* (European beech), 48, 50, 119, 206
fast-growing ecological strategy, 137
feedback mechanisms, 78
fertilisers
  nitrous oxide ($N_2O$) emissions, 37
*Ficus* spp., 139
Filzbach software library, 175
fir. See *Abies* spp.
fire, 77
  and climate change, 52–53
  causes of wildfires, 51–52
  factors influencing post-fire regeneration,
    54–55
  historical impact of Native Americans, 111
  influence of land use, 53–55
  interaction with deforestation and
    drought, 36
  overall impact on Mediterranean
    ecosystems, 54–55
  post-fire regeneration strategies, 54–55
  results of active fire suppression in forests
    (NE United States), 115
  risk in caatinga vegetation, 240
  risk in cerrado vegetation, 240
  sustainable strategies for dealing with
    forest fire, 65
  temperate forests of NE United States, 110,
    111
  threat to biodiversity, 14
flood prevention, 1
floristic shifts
  responses to climate change, 136–137, 147
fog-preventing forests, 26
ForClim model, 369, 374, 375
FORENA model, 367–368
forest biodiversity
  historical debate between mixed and
    monoculture forests, 196–200
forest biomass change
  detecting change in old-growth forests,
    382–383
  implications for the carbon cycle, 382–383
  influence of atmospheric and climate
    change, 381

  influence on carbon storage, 381
  Markov chain models, 402–409
  old-growth forests, 381–382
  potential for positive or negative
    feedbacks, 381
  projecting biomass change, 402–409
  successional forests, 381–382
forest biomass change estimation
  belowground pools, 411
  data cleaning procedures, 393–397
  dealing with sources of error, 411
  influence of 'data cleaning' procedures,
    389, 393–397
  influence of measurement errors, 389,
    393–397
  Markov chain models, 410–411
  means of avoiding measurement error,
    409–410
  measuring buttressed trees, 397–402
  methodology for use of ground plots,
    411
  sampling errors in plot data, 383–384
  sampling uncertainty for ensembles of
    plots, 387–389
  spatial and temporal scaling of sampling
    uncertainty for single plots, 384–387
forest–canopy interactions
  ecophysiological approaches, xiv–xv
forest clearing and land abandonment,
    114–115
forest degradation
  factors influencing forest resilience, 440
  future research on impacts, 441
  modelling forest dynamics, 432–434
  patterns of forest loss, 422–424
  potential to develop a theory of impacts,
    440–441
  rates of global forest loss, 417
  tentative generalisations on anthropogenic
    disturbances, 434–435
forest dynamics
  addressing spatial and temporal
    challenges, 360–363
  and global change, 1–5
  importance of assessment of global change
    effects, 360
  measurement challenges, 359–360
  modelling, 432–434
  modelling forest community dynamics,
    109
forest ecologists, 163
forest ecosystem dynamics
  impacts of pests and pathogens, 118
  neighbourhood models, 113–114
forest ecosystems
  approaches to predicting climate change
    effects, 109
  goods and services of importance to
    humans, 359
  pressures and demands on, 359
  ranges of influences on, 109–110
  time scales of responses, 113–114

forest emissions
    aerosols, 39–40
forest fragmentation
    difficulty of identifying generalisations
        about impacts, 439
    edge effects, 430–431
    effects on seedling establishment, 431–432
    effects on species richness, 427–430
    factors influencing forest resilience, 440
    future research on impacts, 441
    New Forest, UK, 435–439
    potential to develop a theory of impacts,
        440–441
    species–area curves, 439–440
forest fragmentation dynamics, 426–427
forest gap models, 164, 365–373
forest inventories, 164, 216–220
    data at decadal-scale, xiv
Forest Inventory and Analysis (FIA) network
    (US Forest Service), 111
forest simulation models, xv
forest succession
    data assimilation techniques, 362
    experimental studies, 361
    observational studies, 360–361
forest succession modelling, 121–124
    agent-based models, 365–373
    approaches to, 361–363
    development of forest gap models, 365–373
    diversity of approaches, 373–375
    individual-based models, 360, 365–373
    reconsidering fundamental assumptions,
        373–375
    terminology related to, 363–365
    usefulness of current models, 375
forest understorey
    recovery after disturbance, 114
forests
    albedo, 22–23
    dependence of humanity upon, 1
    goods and services provided by, 1
    implications of different management
        scenarios, 36
    multidisciplinary approach to study, 1
    purpose of, 36
FORMIND model, 164, 369, 432
FORMIX model, 164
FORSKA model, 369
fossil fuel combustion
    source of nitrate ($NO_3^-$), 309
fragmentation of habitats
    detrimental effects on species, 49–51
    Mediterranean Basin, 49–51
FRAGSTATS, 424
*Fraxinus americana* (white ash), 312, 320, 331
*Fraxinus* spp., 118
functional categories of canopy chemical
    traits, 345–346
functional change in tropical forests, 91–93
functional differences between tree species,
    226
functional diversity, 200–201

Functional Ecology of Trees Database (FET),
    164
FunDivEUROPE project, 226

garlic mustard (*Alliaria petiolata*), 118–119
Gayer, Karl, 198
GEM network, xiii
General Circulation Models, 364
generalisations in ecological theory, 418–419
genetic diversity within tree species, 200
geographic distance decay patterns, 253–255
germination
    influence of water availability, 265–266
glaciation
    recolonisation following, 312
Global Biodiversity Assessment, 201
global change
    and forest dynamics, 1–5
    detecting, 10–13
    dynamic modelling, 10–13
    importance of measuring forest
        dynamics, 360
global change science
    terminology relating to uncertainty,
        363–365
global circulation models (GCMs), 31–33,
    99–100, 101, 132
    compared to small-scale models, 32–33
global integration of forest ecology research,
    xiii
global warming
    effects on photosynthesis, 35
    effects on respiration, 35
    predictions of effects on forests, 35–36
Global Warming Potential
    methane, 37
    nitrous oxide ($N_2O$), 37
GOTILWA+, 66
greenhouse effect, 35
greenhouse gases
    methane, 38–39
    nitrous oxide ($N_2O$), 37–38
    *See also* carbon dioxide ($CO_2$)
growth and survival
    effects of supplemental irrigation, 266–269
growth–survival trade-off
    influence of soil resources, 320–324

habitat fragmentation
    detrimental effects on species, 49–51
    Mediterranean Basin, 49–51
Hartig, Georg Ludwig, 197–198
harvesting
    depletion of soil resources, 311–312
Hawaii, 350
hazel (*Corylus avellana*), 439
heat sinks, 27
height-structured competition for light, 163
hemlock woolly adelgid (*Adelges tsugae*), 118
herbivores
    interaction with the growth–survival
        trade-off, 322

heteromyopia, 162
hickory. See *Carya* spp.
high-throughput sequencing, xv
Holdridge Life Zone model, 361
Holm oak (*Quercus ilex*), 47, 48, 56, 60
Holocene, 57
homeostatic properties of ecosystems, 35–36
Hubbell, Stephen P., 201
hunting, 77
HYBRID model, 374
hydrological cycle
    role of tropical forests, 77–78
*Hymenaea courbaril*, 147
hyperspectral imagery, xv
hyperspectral remote sensing
    link between spectral and biological diversity, 349–352
Hypoxilon canker (*Hypoxylon mediterraneum*), 56

identity effects, 203–204
individual-based forest succession models, 360, 365–373
infra-red thermometer, 23
insect pests
    factors affecting vulnerability to, 55–56
    shifts in distributional range, 55–56
Inter-Tropical Convergence Zone (ITCZ), 131, 134
interannual variation in water availability, 285–287
intraspecific variation in performance, 162
introduced pathogens
    temperate forests of NE United States, 118
introduced pests
    temperate forests of NE United States, 118
invasive species, 109, 118–119
    temperate forests of NE United States, 118–119
    tree species, 113
inventory data, 164, 216–220
    at decadal-scale, xiv
*Iolana iolas*, 56
iron (Fe)
    concentrations in soil, 309
irradiance interceptance
    influence of soil resource gradients, 318–320
isoprene
    emission by plants, 39, 40
    photo-oxidation products, 40

JABOWA-FORET model, 164
Janzen–Connell hypothesis, 113, 181
Japan
    fog-preventing forests, 26
Japanese stilt grass (*Microstegium vimineum*), 118–119
jay (*Garrulus glandarius*), 60

Kelty, Matthew J., 199

La Niña years, 280
*Lampides boeticus*, 56
land abandonment, 114–115
    influence on fire risk, 54–55
    Mediterranean Basin, 49
land surface
    interactions with the atmosphere, 21
land use
    influence on fire risk, 53–55
land-use change
    influence on species distributions, 343
land-use history
    legacy of, 114–115
LANDIS-II model, 433–434
LANDSAT-based measurements, 86
LANDSAT satellites, xv
landscape-scale coexistence mechanisms, 187–190
landscape-scale diversity, 201
last glacial maximum (LGM) event, 134–137
late-successional species, 162
leaf-based traits, 314–316
leaf chemical compounds
    functional categories, 345–346
leaf chemical traits
    intraspecific variation, 347
    multi-trait correlation, 347–348
    taxonomic organisation, 348–349
leaf economics spectrum, 138
leaf functional traits, 137–138
leaf-level photosynthesis module, 331–332
leaf-level view of plant physiology, 314–316
leaf mass per area (LMA), 138, 140–141
leaf mechanical properties, 138
leaf tolerance to drought, 138, 139–141
leaf turgor loss point, 139–141
leaf water potential at wilting or turgor loss point, 139–141
lianas, 91–92, 95, 101, 139–140
    contribution to carbon turnover (NPP), 143–144
    contribution to ecosystem transpiration, 143–144
LiDAR, xv, 360, 409, 411
light capture and growth
    compounds and elements required for, 345–346
lime (*Tilia cordata*), 439
logging practices
    effects on temperate forests (NE United States), 116–117
long-distance dispersal, 113
    as a process for colonisation, 113
long-term disturbance effects
    New Forest, UK, 435–439
long-term ecological monitoring sites,
long-term forest dynamics,
    addressing spatial and temporal challenges, 360–363
    measurement challenges, 359–360

modelling approaches, 361–363
reconsidering fundamental assumptions, 373–375
usefulness of current models, 375
long-wave (thermal) radiation flux, 68–70
longevity and defence
compounds and elements required for, 345–346
Lotka–Volterra competition
implications for empirical forest ecology, 170–171
response to environmental change, 169–170
Lotka–Volterra competition equations, 162, 167
predicting effects of environmental change, 190–191
TSR scheme, 167–169
lottery models, 162
LPJ-GUESS model, 369, 370, 373, 374
LTER, xiii
*Luehea seemannii*, 214

magnesium (Mg)
covariance with other soil resources, 316
losses caused by soil acidification, 309
losses caused by soil weathering, 309–311
maintenance and metabolism
compounds and elements required for, 345–346
Malpighiales, 133
Manaus equation, 80
Markov chain models, 383, 402–409, 410–411
*Mauritia flexuosa*, 350
*Mauritia* spp., 344
MCPFE, 199
Mediterranean Basin
asymmetric responses of species to abiotic stress, 55–56
biotic interactions, 55–62
changes in land management intensity, 49
disappearance of forests, 49
expansion of agricultural and urban areas, 49
fire and climate change, 52–53
fire risk and land use, 53–55
fire-risk predictions, 52–53
habitat fragmentation, 49–51
land abandonment, 49
land-use trends, 48–49
native habitat removal, 48–49
negative species interactions, 55–56
positive species interactions, 57
predicted effects of climate change, 47–48
shifts in distribution of pathogens and insect pests, 55–56
wildfires and their causes, 51–52
Mediterranean ecosystems
factors influencing post-fire regeneration, 54–55
overall impact of fire, 54–55
plant-animal interactions, 146–148
plant–plant interactions along stress gradients, 143–145
seed dispersal by animals, 60
Mediterranean forests
adaptive management approaches, 66
benefits of diverse stands, 65
benefits of mixed forests, 65
characteristics relevant to management approaches, 62–63
conservation of biological diversity, 65
extension of rotations, 64–65
modelling approaches, 66
principles for management under environmental change, 63–66
reducing intensity of management, 65
reduction of tree densities in previously coppiced forests, 65
regeneration strategies, 64–65
response to accelerated environmental change, 47–48
sustainable strategies for dealing with fire, 65
uncertainty of global change evolution, 66
use of flexible thinning schedules, 64
metacommunities, 163
methane, 39
Global Warming Potential, 37
methane production, 38–39
influence of soil conditions, 38–39
rice paddies, 38, 39
methanogenic bacteria, 38
microbial symbionts, 330–331
*Microstegium vimineum* (Japanese stilt grass), 118–119
Millennium Ecosystem Assessment, 195
modelling
accounting for biodiversity, 132–133
accounting for demographic stochasticity, 132
Amazon Basin, 32
approaches to forest community dynamics, 109
biodiversity and ecosystem functioning (BEF), 224–225
detecting and modelling global change, 10–13
distinction from simulation, 365
drought resistance, 146–147
dynamic global vegetation models (DGVMs), 132–133
empirical models of forest responses, 111–113
forest dynamics, 432–434
forest gap models, 164
forest simulation models, xv
forest succession modelling, 121–124, 361–363, 365–373
global circulation models (GCMs), 31–33, 99–100, 101, 132
individual-based forest succession models, 360
large-scale effects of deforestation, 30–33

modelling (cont.)
  leaf-based view of plant physiology,
    137–138
  Mediterranean forests, 66
  neighbourhood models of forest dynamics,
    113–114
  niche modelling techniques, 48
  nitrogen deposition and temperature,
    120–121
  over-simplification, 132–133
  plant–animal interactions, 148–150
  plant functional types (PFTs), 132–133, 137
  process models of forest responses, 111
  range of projection for Amazon forests, 144
  reconsidering fundamental assumptions,
    373–375
  small-scale and large-scale models
    compared, 32–33
  taking account of biodiversity, 13
  terminology related to, 363–365
  types of models of forest responses, 111–114
  usefulness of current models, 375
  See also perfect plasticity approximation
    (PPA) model
moisture stress
  effects in Amazonian forests, 98–99
molecular clock analyses, 241
molecular phylogenetic studies, 241
molecular phylogenies, xv
Möller, Alfred, 198
monoculture, 164, 195
  perfect plasticity approximation (PPA)
    model, 175–177
monodominance, 161
Monte Carlo approach, 397
moose
  herbivory and ecosystem diversity, 210
multidisciplinary approach
  forest studies, 1
  monitoring global change, 354
mycorrhizae, 119, 324, 330–331
  response to N deposition, 120

national forest inventories, xiii, 216–220
Native Americans
  historical impacts on the North American
    landscape, 111
necromass, 37
negative density dependence (NDD), 162
negative feedback mechanisms
  role in coexistence of multiple species,
    161–163
neighbourhood models of forest dynamics,
  113–114
Neolithic, 21
net competitive interactions
  differences across soil resource gradients,
    324–325
net primary production (NPP)
  increase in tropical forests, 95–97
neutral theory, 161
neutron probe, 29

New Forest, UK
  anthropogenic disturbance case study,
    435–439
niche complementarity, 195–196, 206
niche modelling techniques, 48
nitrate ($NO_3^-$)
  from fossil fuel combustion, 309
nitrification process, 37
nitrogen (N)
  covariance with other soil resources,
    316–318
  limitation in younger, temperate soils,
    309–311
  sources of atmospheric nitrogen, 309
nitrogen (N) deposition, 35
  and temperature, 120–121
  atmospheric deposition rates, 309
  effects of anthropogenic deposition,
    120–121
  mycorrhizal responses, 120
nitrogen-fixing species, 206, 208
  effects on productivity, 205–206
nitrous oxide ($N_2O$)
  Global Warming Potential, 37
  sources of, 37–38, 39
nitrous oxide ($N_2O$) production
  influence of soil conditions, 38–39
North Atlantic Oscillation, 131
northern mixed hardwood/conifer forests, 110
Norway maple (Acer platanoides), 119

oak. See Quercus spp.
oak/hickory forests, 110
oil palm plantations
  ethical issues, 36–37
old-growth forests
  detecting biomass change, 382–383
  effects of global change on biomass,
    381–382
  sampling error in plot data, 383–384
Ophiostoma ulmi. See Dutch elm disease
ozone pollution, 119

Pacific Decadal Oscillation, 131
pathogens, 162
  effects of biodiversity in ecosystems, 207
  effects on productivity, 207
  factors affecting vulnerability to, 55–56
  impacts on ecosystem dynamics, 118
  impacts on temperate forests of NE United
    States, 118
  shifts in distributional range, 55–56
Penman–Monteith equation, 25
perfect plasticity approximation (PPA) model,
  320
  baseline, 174–175
  coexistence of multiple species, 177–184
  for a monoculture, 175–177
  implications of two-species coexistence,
    180–181
  landscape-scale coexistence mechanisms,
    187–190

metrics, 173
predicting effects of environmental
    change, 190–191
rates, 172–173
species-specific temporal variation,
    184–185
stand-scale coexistence mechanisms,
    185–187
stand-scale coexistence via differential
    crown transparency, 177–180
stand-scale coexistence via species-specific
    density dependence, 181–184
states, 172
temporal storage effect, 184–185
traits, 173–174
traits-states-rates (TSR) scheme, 171–174
pests, 162
    build-up of species-specific pests, 181
    effects of biodiversity in ecosystems, 207
    effects on productivity, 207
    impacts on ecosystem dynamics, 118
    impacts on temperate forests of NE United
        States, 118
phenotypic plasticity in tree species, 47
phosphorus (P)
    covariance with other soil resources,
        316–318
    depletion through biomass harvesting,
        311–312
    leaching caused by acidification, 309
    limitation in older, tropical soils, 309–311
    loss by weathering over time, 309–311
photosynthesis, 33, 39, 40
    changes in tropical forests, 99–100
    evolution of C4 photosynthesis, 133
    leaf-level photosynthesis module, 146
    limiting factors as temperature increases,
        99–100
    rate in relation to respiration, 99–100
    rate of carbon uptake, 99–100
    response to global warming, 35
    role in energy balance, 24
Phylocom, 244
phylogenetic beta diversity, 242–243,
    249–251
Phylomatic, 244
physiological mechanisms of forest
    responses, xiv–xv
*Phytophthora cinnamomi*, 56
*Phytophthora ramorum*, 224
*Picea abies* (spruce), 206
*Picea rubens* (red spruce), 119
*Picea* spp., 110, 312
PICUS model, 369, 374
pine forests, 110
*Pinus banksiana*, 312
*Pinus contorta*, 312, 330
*Pinus nigra*, 55
*Pinus rigida*, 312
*Pinus* spp., 110
*Pinus strobus*, 312
*Pinus sylvestris*, 56

pioneer species, 162
*Pistacia lentiscus*, 59
planetary boundary layer, 30
plant–animal interactions, 146–148
    modelling, 61–62
plant emissions
    aerosols, 39–40
    isoprene, 39
    volatile organic compounds (VOCs), 39
plant functional types (PFTs)
    based on whole-plant physiology, 141–144
    classification, 137–138
    future developments in DGVMs, 145–147
    theory of, 137
    use in models, 132–133
plant–plant interactions along
    stress-gradients, 143–145
plantations, 21
    ethical issues, 36–37
plot data
    decadal-scale inventory data, xiv
    forest simulation models, xv
    sampling error, 383–384
pollen record, 367
*Populus* spp., 118
potassium (K)
    covariance with other soil resources, 316
    importance for tree growth, 325–329
    losses caused by soil acidification, 309
    losses caused by soil weathering, 309–311
precipitation patterns
    consequences of change for tropical
        forests, 261–262
    future effects on tropical forests, 297–299
    interannual variation in water availability,
        285–287
    local variation in soil moisture, 289–292
    rain recycling rates, 30
    regional variation in rainfall, 292–293
    seasonal variation, 280–285
    shifts caused by climate change, 261–262
    temporal variation in water availability,
        279–280
prediction
    terminology related to modelling, 363–365
Pretzsch, Hans, 196–197
primary productivity
    CO2 fertilisation effect, 119–120
*Prioria copaifera*, 286
probability
    terminology related to modelling,
        363–365
process models of forest responses, 111
processionary moth caterpillar, 56
productivity
    constraint by soil resources, 311
    effects of N-fixing species, 205–206
    influence of soil resource gradients,
        312–314
    relationship with diversity, 202
    responses to soil resource availability,
        325–329

*Prunus serotina*, 320, 321
*Psidium cattleianum*, 350
psychrometric constant (γ), 25

*Qualea grandiflora*, 249
*Qualea* spp., 249
Quaternary, 133
*Quercus alba* (white oak), 312, 325
*Quercus ilex* (holm oak), 47, 48, 56, 60
*Quercus rubra* (red oak), 320, 325
*Quercus* spp., 147, 255
    coppicing, 65
    effects of active fire suppression on, 115
*Quercus suber* (cork oak), 47, 56
*Quercus velutina* (black oak), 312, 320

R statistical program, 244
rain. *See* precipitation patterns
RAINFOR network, xiii, 79, 329, 411
    drought impacts (2005), 93–95
    dynamic changes, 88–91
    functional changes, 91–93
    observed increase in biomass, 82–88
    species composition changes, 91–93
    structural change, 82–88
    study methodology, 79–82
Ramsar Convention sites, 436
rate of change for state variables, 167
recovery aspect of resilience, 136–137
*Red Amazónica de Inventarios Forestales* network.
    *See* RAINFOR network
red maple (*Acer rubrum*), 116, 324, 325
red spruce (*Picea rubens*), 119
REDD (Reducing Emissions from
    Deforestation and Forest Degradation),
    131
REDD+, 417
regeneration dynamics
    effects of local variation in soil moisture,
        289–292
    effects of seasonal variation in water
        availability, 280–285
    factors affecting seedling establishment,
        431–432
    future effects of changing precipitation
        patterns, 297–299
    germination response to water availability,
        265–266
    growth and survival under variable water
        availability, 266–269
    influence of drought, 262–263
    influence of species drought resistance, 297
    influence of water availability, 297
    interannual variation in water availability,
        285–287
    interspecific variation in seedling response
        to drought, 273
    mechanisms of seedling responses to
        drought, 273–279
    regional variation in rainfall, 292–293
    responses to variable water availability,
        265–273

seedling size/age effects and water
    availability, 269–273
spatial variation in water availability,
    287–289
species variations in response to drought,
    294–297
temporal variation in water availability,
    279–280
regional variation in rainfall, 292–293
remote sensing, 360
    link between spectral and biological
        diversity, 349–352
    techniques, xv
    tools, 360
    *See also* trait-based remote sensing
resilience concept, 35–36
    recovery aspect, 136–137
    resistance aspect, 136–137
    tropical forests, 136–137
resistance analogues, 26
resistance aspect of resilience, 136–137
resource complementarity principle, 198
respiration
    changes in tropical forests, 99–100
    rate in relation to photosynthesis,
        99–100
    rate of carbon loss, 99–100
    response to global warming, 35
rice paddies
    methane production, 38, 39
Rondonia, Brazil, 27, 31
root depth and volume
    influence on drought performance, 275
roughness of vegetation
    and response to atmospheric conditions,
        25–26
    differences between forests and grassland/
        crops, 25–26

Saharan dust
    input to tropical forests, 96
sample-plot studies, 78
sampling effect, 195–196
sampling error in plot data, 383–384
satellite-based research, 343
savanna woodland
    conversion to pasture, 29
    energy balance, 29
*Sclerolobium paniculatum*, 142
SCOPE programme, 201
SDTFs. *See* seasonally dry tropical forests and
    woodlands
seasonal variation in water availability,
    280–285
seasonally dry tropical forests and woodlands
    (SDTFs)
    Caatinga Phytogeographic Domain, 240
    Cerrado Phytogeographic Domain, 240
    community phylogenetic analysis results,
        249–251
    community phylogenetic approach,
        242–243

comparison of caatinga and cerrado, 240–242
constraints on woody plant evolution, 240–242
deciduous and semi-deciduous site classification, 253–255
ecology of leaf deciduousness, 251–253
factors shaping woody plant biodiversity, 253–255
future prospects, 255–256
geographic distance decay patterns, 253–255
identification and conservation planning, 255–256
interaction of ecology and geographic distance, 253–255
model evaluation, 246–249
phylogenetic beta diversity, 242–243, 249–251
phylogenetic patterns of diversity, 240–242
problems with vegetation definitions, 240
selection pressures on woody plant evolution, 251–253
study explanatory variables, 244–245
study response variable, 243–244
seed dispersal by animals, 60
seedling establishment
    factors affecting, 431–432
seedling performance
    effects of interannual variation in water availability, 285–287
    effects of local variation in soil moisture, 289–292
    effects of regional variation in rainfall, 292–293
    effects of seasonal variation in water availability, 280–285
    influence of water availability, 297
    species variations in response to drought, 294–297
seedling responses to drought, 264
    interspecific variation, 273
    mechanisms of interspecific variation, 273–279
seedling size/age effects
    influence of water availability, 269–273
SEIB-DGVM, 132
short-term stressful events
    ecosystem ability to withstand, 138
short-wave (solar) radiation,
SIGEO/CTFS plot network, 411
silvicultural models, 163–164
silviculturalists, 163
simulation
    distinction from modelling, 365
    terminology related to, 363–365
site-centred study, 78
Sites of Special Scientific Interest, 436
size-structured populations, 163
slow-growing ecological strategy, 137
slow-in, rapid-out effect, 86, 87, 382, 383–384
small-scale models
    results compared to large-scale models, 32–33
snow cover
    albedo of different vegetation types, 22–23
soil acidification
    nitrogen deposition, 309
soil base cation status. See base cations in the soil
soil conditions
    influence on methane production, 38–39
    influence on nitrous oxide ($N_2O$) production, 38–39
soil moisture
    effects of deforestation, 30–31
    effects of local variation, 289–292
    spatial variation in, 287–289
soil pH
    effects of weathering over time, 309–311
soil resource gradients
    covariance among soil resources, 316–318
    effect on net competitive interactions, 324–325
    effects on interceptance of irradiance, 318–320
    influence on forest productivity, 312–314
    influence on forest species composition, 312–314
    spatial heterogeneity of resources, 314–316
    study areas, 312
    tree growth responses, 325–329
soil resources
    and the growth–survival trade-off, 320–324
    base cations as limiting factor, 330
    constraint on ecosystem services, 311
    constraint on productivity, 311
    depletion through biomass harvesting, 311–312
    effects of microbial symbionts, 330–331
    effects of mycorrhizae, 330–331
    heterogeneity at multiple spatial scales, 329–330
    importance of relationship with tree performance, 331–332
    influence on carbon sequestration and storage, 311
    losses caused by acidification, 309
    losses caused by nitrogen deposition, 309
    losses caused by weathering over time, 309–311
    particular nutrients limit different aspects of peformance, 330
    potential to mediate climate change effects, 312
    tree mechanisms to actively manage access, 330–331
solar (short-wave) radiation, 23
SORTIE model, 113, 164
SORTIE-ND model, 113, 121, 164

South America
  land cover map, 240
spatial storage effect, 162
Special Sensor Microwave Imager, 33
species-area curves, 439–440
species composition
  changes in tropical forests, 91–93, 100–101
  influence of soil resource gradients,
    312–314
species conservation
  forest management approach, 36
species distribution
  impact of habitat fragmentation, 49–51
  influence of water availability, 297
  link with drought resistance, 294–297
  mapping tools, 343–345
  pressures from environmental changes, 343
species diversity
  influence of water availability, 297
species identity effects, 203–204, 226
species interactions, 227
  along stress gradients, 58–59
  facilitative plant interactions, 57, 58–59
  negative interactions, 55–56
  positive interactions, 57, 58–59
species replacement
  and active fire suppression, 115
species richness
  effects of anthropogenic disturbances,
    427–430
species-specific density dependence,
species-specific negative density dependence,
  408–414
species-specific temporal variation, 414–417
species traits
  definition, 166–167
  responses to changing resource
    availability, 5–10
species variations
  response to drought, 294–297
spruce. See Picea spp.
spruce budworm (Choristoneura fumiferana), 183
spruce/fir forests, 110
state variables
  combination with traits, 167
  definition, 167
  rate of change, 167
states of a community See state variables
Stefan–Boltzmann constant, 23
Stefan's Law, 23
Stipa tenacissima, 59
stomata
  responses in drought conditions, 275–276
stomatal pores
  evaporation from (transpiration), 24, 25
stress-gradient hypothesis (SGH), 58–59
structural change
  tropical forests, 82–88
structural equation modelling (SEM), 219
successional coexistence, 162
successional dynamics
  factors affecting, 113–114

successional forests
  biomass change, 381–382
successional mosaics, 440
sugar maple (Acer saccharum), 115, 119, 312,
  314, 320, 321, 331
sulphur dioxide (SO$_2$)
  reduction in emissions, 120
sustainability concept, 197
sustainable forest management, 36
Sylvia spp., 60
synthetic community approach
  tree diversity studies, 215–216

Tabebuia rosea, 214
Tabebuia spp., 344
taxa
  evidence of chemical signatures, 348–349
technology
  multidisciplinary approach to monitoring
    global change, 354
tele-connections concept, 32–33, 40
temperate forests (NE United States)
  air pollution effects, 119–121
  anthropogenic impacts on current and
    future forests, 114–121
  conditions before European settlement,
    110–111
  differences in post-agricultural forests,
    114–115
  distinguishing climate change responses
    from other effects, 121–124
  ecoregions, 110
  effects of logging practices, 116–117
  evidence for long-term transient effects,
    110–111
  features of, 110–111
  forest clearing and land abandonment,
    114–115
  forest succession models, 121–124
  historical impact of Native Americans, 111
  impacts of pests and pathogens, 118
  introduction of exotic plant species,
    118–119
  legacy of land-use history, 114–115
  neighbourhood models of forest dynamics,
    113–114
  northern mixed hardwood/conifer forests,
    110
  oak/hickory forests, 110
  pine forests, 110
  results of active fire suppression, 115
  species demography along climate
    gradients, 111
  species distribution along climate
    gradients, 111
  spruce/fir forests, 110
  wildfires, 111
temperature increase
  effects on chemical and biological
    processes, 99
  inflection points for biological functions, 99
  limiting factors for photosynthesis, 99–100

temporal storage effect, 162
  coexistence of multiple species, 184–185
terminology used in global change science, 363–365
terpenes, 40
Tertiary, 57, 133
The Economics of Ecosystems and Biodiversity (TEEB) study, 195
theory in ecological science, 417–418
thermal (long-wave) radiation flux, 23–24
thrushes (*Turdus* spp.), 60
*Tilia americana*, 312, 314, 331
*Tilia cordata* (lime), 439
timber production
  effects of logging practices on temperate forests, 116–117
  fast-growing tropical plantations, 36
  historical debate between mixed and monoculture forests, 196–200
  implications of management approach, 36
time scales of anthropogenic impacts, 109–110
time scales of forest ecosystem responses, 113–114
trade-off between ecological strategies, 137, 143
trait-based remote sensing, 345
  canopy chemical traits, 345–346
  ecological basis, 352–354
  evolutionary basis, 346–349, 352–354
  link between spectral and biological diversity, 349–352
  multidisciplinary approach to monitoring global change, 354
traits of species
  changeable nature of, 167
  combination with states, 167
  definition, 166–167
traits–states–rates (TSR) scheme, 164–166, 190
  elements of the scheme, 166–167
  in the Lotka–Volterra competition equations, 167–169
  perfect plasticity approximation (PPA) model, 171–174
transient dynamics
  interactions in forest ecosystems, 110
  temperate forests (NE United States), 110–111
transpiration, 24, 25
  mechanisms to minimise water loss, 275–276
tree diversity
  effects on ecosystem functioning, 201–205
tree growth
  responses to soil resource availability, 325–329
tree harvesting
  depletion of soil resources, 311–312
tree of heaven (*Ailanthus altissima*), 119
tree performance
  effects of different nutrients, 330

  importance of relationship with soil resources, 331–332
  influence of soil resources, 312
  mechanisms to manage soil nutrient access, 330–331
TreeDivNet, 209, 227
TROLL model, 145–146
tropical broadleaf evergreen trees, 132
tropical broadleaf raingreen trees, 133
tropical forest biomass
  influence of carbon dioxide ($CO_2$) increase, 95–97
tropical forests
  as carbon sinks, 131
  biodiversity, 77–78
  carbon emissions related to deforestation, 131
  carbon sinks to carbon sources, 97–98
  carbon stocks, 77
  consequences of shifts in precipitation patterns, 261–262
  drivers of changes, 95–97
  drought impacts in Amazonia (2005), 93–95
  dynamic changes, 88–91
  functional changes, 91–93
  future effects of changing precipitation patterns, 297–299
  increase in net primary production (NPP), 95–97
  level of resilience to change, 131–132
  methods of measuring changes in, 78
  moisture stress effects, 98–99
  networked approach to study, 78–79
  networked study methodology, 79–82
  observed increase in biomass, 82–88
  photosynthesis/respiration changes, 99–100
  potential future sensitivity to changes, 97–101
  projected future precipitation changes, 261–262
  responses to variation in water availability, 262–263
  role in the carbon cycle, 77–78
  role in the hydrological cycle, 77–78
  site-centred study, 78
  species compositional changes, 91–93, 100–101
  species distributions and global change, 343
  structural change, 82–88
  study results and discussion, 82–93
  wide-ranging impacts of change, 77–78
  *see also* Amazon
tropical plantations
  ethical issues, 36–37
tropical rain forests
  evolution of, 133–136
tropical tree life stages
  responses to variable water availability, 265–273

tropical trees
  whole-plant physiology, 141–144
TRY database, 201
*Tsuga canadensis* (eastern hemlock), 116, 118
*Tsuga* spp., 110
turgor loss point, 139–141

*Ulmus americana* (American elm), 118
*Ulmus* spp., 439
UN Convention on Biological Diversity (CBD),
  199
UN-FCCC, 199
uncertainty
  terminology related to modelling, 363–365
unified neutral theory of biodiversity and
  biogeography, 201

vegetation
  factors affecting albedo, 22–23
vegetation roughness
  and response to atmospheric conditions,
  25–26
  differences between forests and grassland/
  crops, 25–26
  effects of deforestation, 30
*Vismia* spp., 135
Vochysiaceae, 249
volatile organic compounds (VOCs), 39
voles
  herbivory and ecosystem diversity, 210

water
  latent heat of vaporisation, 24
  mass balance for the Amazon Basin, 30
water availability
  future effects of changing precipitation
  patterns, 297–299
  influence on regeneration dynamics, 297

influence on species distribution, 294–297
influence on species diversity, 294–297
interannual variation, 285–287
local-scale variation in soil moisture,
  289–292
regional variation in rainfall, 292–293
seasonal variation, 280–285
spatial variation, 287–289
temporal variation, 279–280
water balance
  large-scale effects of deforestation, 30–33
water storage
  influence on drought performance, 275
  tropical forest and tropical pasture
  comparison, 27–29
water use
  tropical forest and tropical pasture
  comparison, 27–29
white ash (*Fraxinus americana*), 312, 320, 331
white oak (*Quercus alba*), 312, 325
white-tailed deer (*Odocoileus virginianus*),
  115
whole-plant traits
  and ecological strategies, 143
wildfires. *See* fire
wind speed
  effects of different types of vegetation, 26
  effects on convection, 24
windthrow
  temperate forests of NE United States, 110
'winner' species, 78
wood density, 141
wood production, 141

xylem
  factors affecting drought performance, 279
  failure caused by drought, 141–143
  vulnerability to cavitation, 141–143